Ralph Ellison

Ralph Ellison

— ◆ —

A BIOGRAPHY

ARNOLD RAMPERSAD

Alfred A. Knopf   New York   2007

THIS IS A BORZOI BOOK
PUBLISHED BY ALFRED A. KNOPF

Copyright © 2007 by Arnold Rampersad

All rights reserved. Published in the United States by Alfred A. Knopf, a division of Random House, Inc., New York, and in Canada by Random House of Canada Limited, Toronto.

www.aaknopf.com

All texts by Ralph Ellison are used with the permission of The Ralph and Fanny Ellison Charitable Trust. Some of the material in this book was originally published by Random House, Inc. in the following works: *The Collected Essays of Ralph Ellison, Flying Home and Other Stories, Going to the Territory, Invisible Man, Juneteenth,* and *Shadow and Act.* Owing to limitations of space, further acknowledgments to reprint previously published material may be found at the end of the volume.

Ralph Ellison, Central Park, 1950, reproduced facing title page, courtesy Library of Congress.

Knopf, Borzoi Books, and the colophon are registered trademarks of Random House, Inc.

Library of Congress Cataloging-in-Publication Data
Rampersad, Arnold.
    Ralph Ellison : a biography / Arnold Rampersad. — 1st ed.
        p.   cm.
    Includes bibliographical references and index.
    ISBN-13: 978-0-375-40827-4 (alk. paper)
    1. Ellison, Ralph.   2. Novelists, American—20th century—Biography.
3. African American novelists—Biography.   I. Title.
PS3555.L625Z8725 2007
818'.5409—dc22   2006026464
[B]

Manufactured in the United States of America
First Edition

CONTENTS

1 In the Territory 3

2 Leaving the Territory 37

3 In a Land Most Strange 52

4 A Shock of Transition 81

5 The Recognition of Necessity 114

6 The Numbed and the Seething 143

7 A Mighty Book, a Mighty Theme 170

8 The Agon of Writing 199

9 In the Home Stretch 224

10 Finish Line 247

11 *Annus Mirabilis* 268

12 Second Act 293

13 Adventure in Rome 316

14 The Pleasures of Home 347

15 Hanging Fire 381

16 Tell It Like It Is, Baby 412

17 A "Lone-Star" Negro 442

18 Professor in the Humanities 470

19 The Monkey on His Back 493

20 The Uncanny Penetration of the Past 520

21 Flying Home 546

Books by Ralph Ellison 567

Notes 569

Acknowledgments 625

Index 629

Ralph Ellison

1

In the Territory

1913–1931

There is no ancestor so powerful as one's earlier selves.
LEWIS MUMFORD (1929)

Decades after the blazing hot afternoon in June 1933 when Ralph Ellison, on his first and last outing as a hobo, climbed fearfully and yet eagerly aboard a smoky freight train leaving Oklahoma City on a dangerous journey that he hoped would take him to college in Tuskegee, Alabama, his memories of growing up in Oklahoma continued both to haunt and to inspire him. For a long time he had suppressed those memories; then the time came when he began to crave them.

The turning point had been his triumph in 1952 with his novel *Invisible Man.* That success had led to a cascading flow of honors such as no other African-American writer had ever enjoyed. In 1953, he won the National Book Award, besting *The Old Man and the Sea,* by Ernest Hemingway, one of his idols. Later, the American Academy of Arts and Letters elected him a member, one of the fifty distinguished American men and women who formed its inner core. At the White House, first Lyndon B. Johnson and then Ronald Reagan awarded him presidential medals. At the behest of the novelist and critic André Malraux, another of his idols, France made him a Chevalier de l'Ordre des Arts et des Lettres. The most venerable social club in America connected to the arts, the Century, in New York, elected him as its first black member. Harvard University, awarding him an honorary degree, offered him a professorship. Never out of print and translated into more than twenty languages, *Invisible Man* maintains its reputation as one of the jewels of twentieth-century American fiction.

Ellison's triumph in 1952 had also led to a tangled mess of fears and doubts about his ability to finish a second novel at least as fine as *Invisible*

Man. By the time of his death in 1994, his failure to produce that second novel had made Ellison, a proud man, the butt of surreptitious jokes and cruel remarks. The snickering and giggling behind his back often left him prickly and tart, if not downright hostile. Clinging fearlessly and stubbornly to the ideal of harmonious racial integration in America, he found it hard to negotiate the treacherous currents of American life in the volatile 1960s and 1970s. Although he always saw himself as above all an artist, and published a dazzling book of cultural commentary in 1964, his later successes were relatively modest. For some of his critics, his life was finally a cautionary tale to be told against the dangers of elitism and alienation, and especially alienation from other blacks. For his admirers, however, no one who had written *Invisible Man* and so skillfully explicated the matter of race and American culture in his essays could ever be accounted a failure. To some people—younger black writers mainly—who hoped and perhaps even expected him to help them, he frequently seemed cold and stingy. To others—whites especially—he was a man of grace, intelligence, wit, and courage who saw his nation with prophetic optimism and clarity.

Each of these conflicting views had, at the very least, an element of truth—and the roots of these conflicts may be traced, not surprisingly, to his upbringing in Oklahoma. Seeking artistic inspiration as the decades passed, he turned more and more to memories of his youth in what once had been the old Indian and Oklahoma territories. From this virgin land—as both whites and blacks saw it—the state of Oklahoma had been carved in 1907. Certainly he had no interest in living as a mature man in Oklahoma. It was more than enough for him to brood on the past, and to come back every seven years or so to visit the old neighborhoods, talk with old friends, bask in the glow of his celebrity, and revive his creativity at its ancestral source. On these visits, he looked sorrowfully on the banal evidence of "progress" and "urban renewal" that marred the city, and even more sadly on the spectral presence of those old friends now dead and gone. "When I get there I'm like a ghost," he declared once, "or a Rip Van Winkle who has slept for twenty years and awoke to discover that his world has changed—but how! . . . An obsessive refrain sounds in my mind: Where have they all *gone*? Where, oh where?"

Fascinated by the power of myth and legend, and alert to the ways in which geography often means fate, he saw Oklahoma as embodying some of the more mysterious forces in American culture. He believed that the region possessed or had possessed almost every element concerning power, race, and art that is essential to understanding the nation. It had Indians, whites, and blacks; treaties solemnly made and shamelessly broken; despair and hope, failure and shining success. Here was the legacy of the dispossession of the Five Civilized Tribes—Cherokee, Choctaw, Chickasaw, Creek, and Seminole—from their homelands in the South and their expulsion in the 1820s and 1830s, by way of the Trail of Tears, to Indian Territory. (Ralph cherished the fact that he was "a wee bit Creek!" on his mother's side, just as he was also proud of the white ancestry on both sides of his family and the black ancestry that was predominant in his physical features.) In 1879, whites had entered Indian Territory for the first time, with the avowed aim of seizing much of the land. Divided and united by history, Oklahoma was culturally the Wild West, the Southwest, and the Old South; it was ancient but also brazenly new. One day, Oklahoma City did not exist. The next day, April 22, 1889, after settlers had raced to stake their claims as part of the official Great Land Run, its population stood at ten thousand. The Oklahoma Territory was born. Ironically, helping to keep in line any indignant Indians were the famous black "Buffalo Soldiers" of the 10th Cavalry.

Ralph, born only six years after Oklahoma became a state, could put human faces—black, white, Indian, and mixed—on this past. For the freed slaves and their children and for free blacks in general, Indian Territory had meant at first an almost providential deliverance from Jim Crow. Many blacks rushed to claim the one-hundred-acre parcels of land allotted by the government to new settlers, so that by 1900 almost sixty thousand blacks lived in the Indian and Oklahoma territories. Many of them saw Oklahoma the way Mormons had seen the new territory that became Utah. Twenty-eight all-black towns sprang up. Edward P. McCabe, a passionate spokesman for black migration and the establishment of a black state, implored his fellow African-Americans to make history: "What will you be if you stay in the South? Slaves liable to be killed at any time, and never treated right; but if you come to Oklahoma you have equal chances with the white man, free and independent."

This was the promise that in 1910 lured a young, newly wed couple, Lewis and Ida Ellison, to Oklahoma City. Their first child, Alfred, died as an infant. Their second, Ralph Waldo Ellison, was born at 407 East First Street, in Oklahoma City, on March 1, 1913. For most of his life Ralph would offer 1914 as the correct year. Presented with a chance to do so, around 1940—and despite the fact that he was on the whole fastidiously honest—Ralph decided to shave a year from the record. The U.S. Census taker got it right in January 1920 when he listed Ralph Ellison as being six years old, born in 1913. A note in his mother's hand, written behind a photograph of Ralph as a toddler, sets his time and date of birth as 1:30 a.m. on Saturday, March 1, 1914. But March 1 fell on a Saturday in *1913,* not in 1914. Someone had changed 1913 to 1914 after an erasure. Moreover, Ralph always insisted he was three years old when the worst disaster of his life occurred: On July 19, 1916, his father died after an operation in the University Emergency Hospital in Oklahoma City.

Ralph was a healthy baby. A photograph of him at four months in a wash-tub shows him, as he later put it, as a "fat little blob of blubber." According to family lore, at six months he took his first steps. At thirteen months, he startled his father by seeming to crave steak and onions. At two, he began to talk. Blessed with a sharp memory, he recalled a doting father. "I rem[em]ber toys, toys, and still more toys," he wrote. He recalled his father allowing him one evening to splash in the bathtub while his mother went off with a friend to a concert. He also recalled his father reading incessantly but making time, too, for his young son ("my father had two passions, children and books"). Either his father or mother was responsible for "the first song taught me as a two-year-old" ("Dark Brown, Chocolate to the Bone"), as well as for his command of a wildly popular, risqué dance to go with it, the Eagle Rock. His father took him on his horse-drawn wagon through various neighborhoods as he delivered ice and coal to businesses and homes. Ralph never forgot his father's tenderness. "Mr. Bub," as some customers called Lewis Ellison, explained things "patiently, lovingly," as they ventured into "ice plants, ice cream plants, packing plants, shoe repair and blacksmith shops, bottling works and bakeries." Ralph also never forgot the day in Salter's grocery store when he watched his father climb some steps and attempt to hoist a hundred-pound block of ice into a cabinet. When a shard of ice pierced his stomach, Lewis Ellison staggered and collapsed.

Ralph remembered the lingering illness, the internal wound that would not heal, the decision to operate, and their last visit together in the hospital. As he prepared to leave with his mother, his father slipped a blue cornflower into Ralph's lapel and gave him pink and yellow wildflowers from a vase on a windowsill. Then his father was wheeled away and Ralph saw his father alive for the last time. *"I could see his long legs,"* Ralph would write (the emphasis his own), *"his knees propped up and his toes flexing as he rested there with his arms folded over his chest, looking at me quite calmly, like a kindly king in his bath. I had only a glimpse, then we were past."* The official death certificate identified the cause of death as "Ulcer of stomach followed by puncture of same." He was thirty-nine years old.

Ralph's life was changed forever. So, too, were the lives of his mother and his brother, Herbert Maurice Ellison, who was then only a few weeks old. The emotional cost was incalculable, and in all matters involving money the change was a disaster. Ahead lay years of shabby rented rooms, hand-me-down clothing, second-rate meals, sneers and slights from people better off, and a pinched, scuffling way of life. For the Ellisons, Oklahoma City took on a radically new character. Almost every aspect of Ralph's life became tougher, sadder. He would take many years to recover fully from the shock of his father's death, if he ever did. He inherited no money but rather a powerful physique; a nimble mind; a worn copy of a book of verse, which would perhaps compel Ralph to write his own book; and the name Ralph Waldo Ellison, in honor of Ralph Waldo Emerson, the famous American poet and essayist of the nineteenth century. He also inherited what his mother had "often warned us against," Ralph noted, "giving in to what she considered the Ellisons' sin of inordinate pride."

Ellison pride, which would both empower and hobble Ralph, could be traced back to the patriarch of the family, Alfred Ellison, and his wife, Harriet Walker Ellison, of the small town of Abbeville Court House, South Carolina. Harriet was long dead by 1916, but Alfred was still vigorous at seventy-one. He was the father of ten children, including Lewis and Lucretia Ellison Brown. Lucretia migrated to Oklahoma City in 1910 with Lewis and Ida, bringing with her Tom, Francis, and May Belle Brown, her three children by her divorced husband. The death of Lewis, Alfred's eldest son, hit him hard. At his request later that year, Tom and May Belle took their three-year-old cousin by train on an extended visit to Abbeville. Ralph found the visit both disturbing and a welcome diversion. Many decades later, he would recall "quite vividly" the train approaching Abbeville across a muddy river and Uncle Jim, one of his father's brothers, waiting in a horse-drawn carriage. He fondly remembered Alfred, who was a huge, muscular man, and other members of the Ellison clan.

The Ellisons lived in a large old house with fireplaces "into which I could walk around and see the light filtering down the chimneys." Ralph recalled an abundance of melons and vegetables heaped on the back porch. He walked in a grove of pecan trees that his father had planted as a boy (for many years afterward, at Christmas, a bag of pecan nuts from this grove reached the Ellisons in Oklahoma City). He slept in an enormous feather bed and was fascinated by a ruined church, its stained-glass windows intact, next door; now it served as a chicken house. He loved the profusion of luna moths and fireflies that glowed in the balmy South Carolina dark. "By way of entertaining a small sorrowful visitor from the west," a kindly local boy, Eddie Hugh Wilson, filled a glass jar with lightning bugs and presented them to the weepy child "as a glowing toy."

Ralph left Abbeville just before one of the more heinous crimes in its history. On October 21, a mob of whites dragged Anthony Crawford, one of the most prosperous black farmers in the region, from a local jail after the sheriff had arrested him for insulting a white man. The mob then lynched him. Ralph would not visit Abbeville again. Less than two years later, on May 23, 1918, Alfred died. Proud to be an Ellison, Ralph would learn about his paternal grandfather later in life. Alfred had been born a slave in South Carolina in 1845, had remained illiterate, but had also shown uncommon intelligence, integrity, and grit during the perilous Reconstruction. After the war he married Harriet, who was virtually white, and settled down with her in Abbeville. At first, they both worked in some form of domestic service. He also entered Republican Party politics during the brief postwar period when black voters outnumbered their white counterparts in the community. He was an important member of the black Union League, which aimed to preserve the advances made after Emancipation. He tried all his life to keep up with the flux of current events, and to recognize the maneuverings of power about him. His reward was first a post as constable, then as town marshal in Abbeville. Charged with preserving order among blacks and whites, he gained a reputation for being fair to all.

When Reconstruction ended with the Hayes-Tilden Compromise and the withdrawal of federal troops from the South in April 1877, Alfred's position became tenuous. Whites stepped up their efforts to recapture power and influence in the region. In elections held the previous year, violence had disrupted sleepy Abbeville. The white *Abbeville Medium* made it clear that "the Democratic party means to carry this state in the next election . . . by fair or foul means." Many blacks sank into a kind of neo-slavery, or headed north or west. Alfred Ellison was different. When whites killed one of his closest friends, he was defiant. On one occasion, he strode down the main street in Abbeville, trailed by unfriendly whites. "If you're going to kill me," he challenged them, "you'll have to kill me right here because I'm not leaving. This is where I have my family, my farm and my friends; and I don't plan to leave." Soon, whites stripped him and other blacks of power. In 1877, Lewis was born, after three daughters. Six other children came later. The family was never destitute; Alfred's prestige remained high in the black community, and not without substance in the white. Owning a valuable lot of land in town, he also maintained a horse-drawn dray that earned him money, especially during the cotton season. At times, he and his brothers built trestles for the Southern Railroad. In 1884, he made the local news briefly. "Big Alfred" Ellison, as a white newspaper reporter called him, got into a fistfight with "Beef Sam [Marshall], both tremendous specimens of physical manhood," when tempers flared as they were moving a piano to the train depot. Ellison was thrashing Beef Sam when Sam stuck a knife three inches into his stomach. Ellison recovered. After his wife and one of their children perished in a house fire, the family's standing was such that the white newspaper carried a notice of Harriet's death without reference to her race.

Unlike Alfred, young Lewis Ellison learned to read and write, although the extent of his formal education is unknown. Like his father, he was brave. On May 31, 1898, at the age of twenty-one, he responded to President William McKinley's national call to arms against Spain in Cuba and the Philippines by traveling to Atlanta, where he joined the U.S. Army as a volunteer. After basic training in Georgia, he was assigned to Company F of the 25th United States Colored Infantry. Although family lore placed Lewis with Company F and Teddy Roosevelt's Rough Riders at the battle of San Juan Heights, it's clear that he was not in Cuba at the time. He was sent to the Philippines, the other major theater of the Spanish-American War, in 1899. Showing courage under fire, he rose to the rank of lance corporal. Family lore also had him serving in the suppression of the Boxer Rebellion in China, but no evidence exists of that service either. However, two recorded episodes indicate that Lewis had become disillusioned with the Jim Crow army. First, he was demoted to the rank of private. Then, on April 9, 1901, he was court-martialed. He had refused to obey orders to drill in hot, humid weather as punishment for allegedly gambling (he was apparently sick with malaria). The court sentenced him to two years at hard labor. Released later that year, he was dishonorably discharged.

What might have spelled social disaster for a young white man was not as heavy a burden for a black man, whose opportunities were already constricted by Jim Crow. Returning to Abbeville around 1901, Lewis started an ice-cream parlor and candy store. The venture fizzled. Nevertheless, he had enough money in 1902 to finance a mortgage of $125 on his father's house and land. At some point, he took a job with a construction company in Chattanooga, Tennessee, that specialized in high-rise steel-and-concrete buildings. Soon, he found an enticing reason to stay at home in Abbeville. Among his friends was a handsome young couple—Maston Watkins, a fireman employed by the Southern Railroad, and his attractive wife, Ida Milsap "Brownie" Watkins, from the farming town of White Oak in southeastern Georgia, who had attended Ferguson-Williams Academy in Abbeville. One day, when Watkins was at his job on a train, a group of idle young whites placed a skiff on the tracks to see what would happen. The train derailed, and Watkins was killed. Lewis consoled Brownie, which turned into love and, eventually, marriage. Within a month of their marriage, the couple left Abbeville for a new life in the West.

In April 1910, they were living in Oklahoma City. Starting out as a common street laborer, Lewis soon returned to construction work. For a while, as a foreman, he hired and fired workers. Later, his son Ralph took pride in knowing that his father had helped to build some of the most impressive buildings in the city. Sprawling over the largest municipality in the United States, Oklahoma City should have provided ample opportunity for an experienced construction worker, but Jim Crow ruled even before the state was born in 1907, and Lewis could go only so far in any white-owned business there. In 1907, the populist Democratic politician William H. "Alfalfa Bill" Murray, then president of the Oklahoma Constitutional Convention (and much later a governor of the state), told whites that while "we must provide the means for the advancement of the negro race, and accept him as God gave him to us and use him for the good of society," the black man "must be taught in the line of his own sphere, as porters, boot-blacks and barbers, and many lines of agriculture. . . . It is an entirely false notion that the negro can rise to the level of a white man in the professions or become an equal citizen to grapple with public questions." Unless they worked for themselves, blacks got only menial jobs. By now most realized that emigration to Oklahoma probably had been a mistake, yet another black dream frustrated by whites. So Lewis believed. Late in April 1912, when he wrote to Ida from Texas, he mourned the fact that Oklahoma had brought him "much worry and much grief. I am sorry there ever was such a place." He hoped that his luck would change soon: "I don't want and don't intend to be there another winter."

As it turned out, he endured four more Oklahoma winters. Often he was away, working and saving money. At such times he was solicitous of his wife. "Your baby is sorry he cannot come to his baby when she wants him," he wrote once to her. "I know how you feel about that and I will pay you well when I get there." Back in Oklahoma City, he started his ice and coal business and planned to buy a house (though he now owned his father's old house in Abbeville). He and Ida were living in a rooming house when Dr. Wyatt H. Slaughter, the leading black physician in Oklahoma City, delivered Ralph. Needing more space, they rented a house not far away, and then another, on North Byers, surrounded by whites, as Lewis tried to make his family comfortable and give his son a secure start in the world.

When he died in 1916, Lewis left behind the well-thumbed "thick anthology of poetry" that became one of Ralph's dearest possessions. What did his father know of Emerson, really? Lewis's letters to Ida—the few that have survived—suggest a poor education, though it's possible that he had started life with certain interests and tastes only to have them, and his entire sensibility, coarsened by racism. This was, after all, the main purpose of Jim Crow laws and conventions, to reduce blacks to neo-slavery. It's also possible that his choice of Ralph's resounding full name was sparked by the fact that his boy was born in a house owned by a man named Jefferson Davis Randolph, who had named his eldest son Thomas Jefferson Randolph. Only late in life did Ralph assert that Emerson had meant much not only to his father but also to other blacks in Oklahoma. "I can't forget Emerson's powerful force in the life of my father," Ralph wrote then, "or the spiritual and intellectual support he provided several of my teachers and community leaders." According to Ralph, "Emerson's voice rang loud in Negro communities and influenced my own elders' decision to seek a broader freedom out in the Territory. . . . Emerson got to me in the classroom no less than at home; in drug store, barbershop, and dental chair, as well as on the playing field. He was also a spur to some of my father's white friends, and thus sponsored a community of hope."

The pretentious name would embarrass Ralph for much of his early life, when he sometimes used to claim that Ralph Waldo Ellison was a boy who lived next door. Then, as a teenager, he reconciled himself to, and even embraced, his full name. He didn't embrace the "hidden name and complex fate" because he came to believe in Emerson's transcendentalism. Instead, claiming the full American heritage, he began to treasure his nominal connection to the so-called American Renaissance, when Ralph Waldo Emerson, Herman Melville, Walt Whitman, and Henry David Thoreau, among others, penned some of the most influential works of American literature. Ralph would see this movement as a golden moment almost unparalleled in the evolution of the nation. In the Age of Emerson, abolitionist moral fervor had made the black man—the slave— the one true symbol of the American conscience. He also then came to appreciate, however faintly traced, his father's ambition for him. "After I began to write and work with words," he recalled, "I came to suspect that he was aware of the suggestive powers of names and of the magic involved in naming."

Thus the link between father and son continued long after Lewis's death. Ironically, the son probably wouldn't have become famous if his father had lived. Protected, perhaps even cosseted, by his father's love, he would probably have escaped the wounds of poverty, loneliness, and despair that came howling in the wake of Lewis's death. Later, he resented suggestions that his father's death had marred him. *"What quality of love sustains us in our orphan's loneliness,"* he asked, in words he himself stressed, *"and how much is thus required of fatherly love to give us strength for all our life thereafter?"* He protested—perhaps too much— against the idea that his father's death might have crippled him: *"What statistics, what lines on whose graphs can ever convince me that by his death I was fatally flawed and doomed—afraid of women, derelict of duty, sad in the sack, cold in the crotch, a rolling stone in social space, a spiritual delinquent, a hater of self—me in whose face his image shows?"* As Ralph told it, his mother's reverence of his father's memory had made all the difference: *"His strength became my mother's strength and my brother and I the confused, sometimes bitter, but most often proud, recipients of their values and their love."*

Nevertheless, as a youth he would be "bemused by a recurring fantasy in which, on my way to school of a late winter day I would emerge from a cold side street into the warm spring sun and there see my father, dead since I was three, rushing toward me with a smile of recognition and outstretched arms. And I would run proudly to greet him, his son grown tall." Astutely, Ralph would later define the blues, which may be at the core of modern African-American artistry, as "an impulse to keep the painful details and episodes of a brutal experience alive in one's aching consciousness, to finger its jagged grain, and to transcend it, not by the consolation of philosophy but by squeezing from it a near-tragic, near-comic lyricism." For him, the most dangerously "jagged grain," fingered in his youth and still wounding in his adult years, would be his father's untimely death. Only eventually would Ralph learn to make art out of this loss, and hope thus to transcend it.

The new life of poverty started almost at once. Finding money to bury Lewis was hard. His body had begun to rot and stink in the summer heat, as Ida told Ralph later, before she was able to bury him in Fairlawn Cemetery. Fortunately, she found a job quickly, as a nursemaid for a Jewish family. Lewis had counted several whites, including some members of the small Jewish community, among his friends. Now working in service for the first time, even as she cared for her own infant, Herbert, Ida would spend the rest of her life mainly as a hotel maid or a janitor. At first, people rushed to help her. Co-worshippers at Avery Chapel African Methodist Episcopal Church moved her into its vacant parsonage. She made friends easily. However, as Ralph grew toward adolescence and young manhood, he watched his mother slip down the social ladder until, in the end, she had lost whatever cachet she had brought with her to Oklahoma as a pretty young bride.

No one was more important to her and her little boys than the Randolphs, in whose rooming house Ralph had been born. Heading the family were Jefferson Davis (J.D.) Randolph and his wife, Uretta. Their eldest child, Edna Randolph Slaughter, was for some years Ida's closest friend; Edna was the wife of Dr. Wyatt Slaughter, the wealthy, property-acquiring physician who had delivered Ralph. After supper in the evenings, Ida, Ralph, and Herbert sometimes went window-shopping with Edna and her princely children, Wyatt Jr. and Saretta. Edna's two younger sisters, Camille and Iphigenia ("Cute"), were like older sisters to the Ellison boys. Edna's brothers—the dentist Dr. Thomas Jefferson "Bud" Randolph and the pharmacist Dr. James L. "Jim" Randolph—also took a lively interest in young Ralph. Separately, Tom and Jim would employ him even before he was a teenager.

The Randolphs and the Slaughters were a prominent part of the black leadership of Oklahoma City, which included men and women in business, religion, medicine, dentistry, education, and law. These people both tested segregation and sometimes grew rich from it. For many years, Jim Crow had caged the city's blacks into scattered pockets. After World War I, however, one area emerged to consolidate the power of the community. This neighborhood was near the thriving downtown district, as the city boomed as a result of the state's agriculture and abundance of oil wells. Its disadvantages included being close to the railroad tracks that served the bustling stockyards (soon to become the largest cattle market in the world). It was also close to the city's major red-light district, where prostitutes of all colors plied their trade in segregated whorehouses.

By the early 1920s, in Ralph's boyhood, the heart of black life in Oklahoma City would be the vibrant block on Second Street between Central
and Stiles that came to be known locally as "Deep Second" or "Deep
Deuce." This block housed the community's drugstores, doctors' offices,
funeral homes, hotels, haberdasheries, restaurants, pool halls, and repair
shops, as well as its crusading newspaper, the *Black Dispatch*. Here also
were the Aldridge Theatre (hailed as the finest theater for blacks south of
Chicago) and Slaughter's Dance Hall (taking up the third floor of Dr.
Slaughter's biggest building). Between visiting celebrities such as Duke
Ellington and Louis Armstrong, or hot local talent such as the Blue Devils Orchestra, Deep Second made Oklahoma City second only to Kansas
City among jazz centers west of Chicago. The major churches, too, were
there or nearby. On East California stood the main school for blacks, the
combined Douglass (Colored School) Elementary School and High
School. In 1919, Ralph would enter the first grade at Douglass; aside from
brief stints elsewhere, he studied there until finishing in 1932 (after completing work in one course) as a member of the class of 1931.

Before Ralph became thoroughly familiar with Deep Second, including its taverns and dancehalls, he led a sheltered life as Ida, his Aunt
Lucretia and her children, and the Randolph and Slaughter clans tried to
fill the terrible void caused by his father's death. Although Aunt Lucretia
was a formal woman, she dearly loved her brother's two boys; her children
also showered gifts and favors on their young cousins. Lucretia's irreverent son, Tom, was much older than Ralph but never played the serious adult with him. Instead, he treated him more like a pal. For fifty years
a brakeman on the Frisco Railroad, Tom loved whiskey, cigars, fishing,
tinkering with cars, and traveling. "He was also a ladies man," Ralph
noted, "whose attraction for good looking young women must surely have
influenced my own taste by the time I reached adolescence."

The Randolphs helped to provide a foundation for Ralph. They represented money, education, power, and love. Living mainly in a comfortable
brick house on East Third Street, near Deep Second, they also owned a
small farm within the city limits, on 23rd Street. Graciously, J.D. and
Uretta Randolph seemed to make little distinction between the Ellison
boys and their grandchildren. Their daughters often stopped by to fetch
Ralph and Herbert for weekends at the farm. Ralph would recall lush
grass and flowers cultivated and wild; he learned to care for chickens and
also to hunt. Some sixty years later, he would write to Camille Randolph,
now Camille Randolph Rhone, of how he and his brother still reminisced

about their happy days of youth with her family. They spoke of gala holiday dinners, especially at Christmas and Easter, when the boys helped to dye eggs for the Easter hunt. They remembered "the task we had of crawling beneath the quilting frame to retrieve needles and threads" dropped by Uretta ("Grandma" to Ralph) and her mother ("Grannie"), who sang or chatted as they quilted; "the fun we had licking the dasher after the delicious ice cream was frozen." Grandma and Grannie, "more Anglo-Saxon than Afro-American in appearance," disciplined Ralph and Herbert but did so gently. The boys never doubted that Grandma and Grannie, like J.D. and the others, cared for them. Ralph was thrilled when Grannie, an expert seamstress, tailored a plush black broadcloth coat for him. Once, she and Uretta may have saved them from freezing to death during a severe winter storm when their mother was away and young Ralph couldn't keep the fire going.

In the absence of his own father, the Randolph men loomed large above Ralph. All of them—J.D. and his sons Tom, Jim, Wade, and Taylor—loved to talk, to spin yarns, to crack jokes, to hoot and holler. But it was J.D., the patriarch and authentic Oklahoma pioneer, who stood out. He was probably the first person to compel in young Ralph a full admiration for language. Unlike almost every other grown-up he knew, "Grandpa" Randolph, as Ralph put it, "intimately loved books." He thus reinforced in Ralph what his father had started. Randolph also loved to talk. Ralph's most vivid memories of the good old days would be of "old J.D., with his legs [crossed] near the stove and with a pipe full of Granger's Rough Cut tobacco. *That's* when the good talk flowed—tall tales, jokes, history, personal confessions and maybe some outright lies. But lies told because in the strange, contradictory nature of experience, they got us closer to the truth. Perhaps that was my real college education because certainly I've done more with what I heard there than I'll ever do with my music." Here facts melded with myth and legend, truth morphed into the inspired lie, and the comic vied with the solemn and tragic to assert the vitality of life. Ralph would remain a lover of this dynamic American approach to language. In it, the black and white rhetorical traditions of the South blended with Southwestern humor to create an expressive style that was both unique and uniquely American.

J.D. Randolph's rich language expressed the dynamism that had made him a prime leader in black Oklahoma. Emigrating in 1887 with his wife and daughter (the first of ten children born to them) from Gallatin, Tennessee, to Purcell in Indian Territory (the end of the Santa Fe Railroad

line), Randolph fell in love with frontier life. With straight black hair and
what Ralph called "the highly-pitched, somewhat nasal timbre of an
Indian tribesman," he herded ponies with the Indians before joining the
ten thousand or more would-be homesteaders in the land rush that led to
the establishment of Oklahoma City. (His wife, Uretta, could easily pass
for white.) There he emerged quickly as someone to reckon with among
the city's blacks. For a while, he published a newspaper. He was a peti-
tioner on January 1, 1891, when the local board of education, dedicated to
Jim Crow, passed a motion to found a "colored school," designated Randolph as its principal, and authorized him to find a building to house it.
(Five years later, in 1896, the historic U.S. Supreme Court decision *Plessy
v. Ferguson* would only confirm the segregation that had been a fact of life
in Indian Territory and elsewhere in America.) Men like Randolph, who
knew how to blend foresight with caution and courage with shows of
humility, were crucial to the black community.

J.D. also helped to found the Colored Agricultural and Normal University a few miles north of the city. Established by the territory lawmakers in
1897, it was soon known popularly as Langston University. Later, after
Oklahoma became a state, the governor appointed him janitor of the law
library at the state capitol in Oklahoma City. He deserved much better,
but the government job was a plum for any black man and also placed
J.D. among law books and other records as well as the legislators who
used them. Instead of showing bitterness, he jauntily rode his stallion to
work, read in the tomes in his spare time, and watched his influence
quietly grow. As a regular visitor to the library to help Grandpa, Ralph
noticed with pride that some white legislators openly solicited Randolph's
opinion on legal matters.

His kindness, dashing style, and passion for storytelling made Randolph the central living male figure in Ralph's early life. However, in
Ralph's painful searching for his father, his disorientation as he tried to
set his own identity in the world led him to see a mystery in Grandpa
Randolph. "For you," Ralph would recall of himself in an unpublished
memoir, "he embodied the mysteries of place, change and identity. You
loved him like a grandfather, which he was not, so what was a family?" Why was Randolph considered black, or African-American, when he
seemed mainly Indian, or white and Indian? "What was his racial mixture?" And "what made him a Negro?" How had Randolph been able to
absorb the identity imposed on him? And how did these questions apply
to Ralph's own sense of family, ethnicity, identity? Randolph led Ralph

both to a fluid conception of American culture and to insecurity surrounding questions of skin color, ethnic origin, and power. Ralph's Aunt Lucretia was also something of a mystery to him. A laundress, she bristled with hauteur at the world, especially at the blacks she served. Remembering her imposing father and, perhaps, the virtual whiteness of her mother, she kept the flame of Ellison pride burning. Cool even to the Randolphs, she could be chilly with other prosperous blacks. If she detected any hint of condescension, she could be like ice. Lucretia drilled into Ralph the idea that he didn't need the largesse of such people. He was an Ellison. "Through her," he wrote about himself, "you received a sense of your father's background." Like her, Ralph would become notoriously hard at times not so much on the black masses as on the prosperous classes above them. Indeed, ruled in part by Ellison pride, later he would be hard on almost everyone until they measured up to his lofty standards.

Although as a child and a boy Ralph's world seemed secure, it was through these different relationships that he built his complicated sense of self. "You existed in the security of a love which you returned with an intensity which, perhaps, is experienced only by those upon whom fatherlessness has imposed a deep sense of loss," he wrote. Because of his "complex connection with genetic and elected families," he was spared the worst of "certain problems of class, color, and status." However, what was true of his boyhood began to change as he entered adolescence and young manhood, when he had to face the fact that the Randolphs and Slaughters were *not* his family, that he was a recipient of their charity, that his mother was a servant, and that he would be largely on his own in the world.

Even as a little boy, moreover, the "security of a love" could not restrain all the demons unleashed by his father's death. Ralph's early childhood showed signs of disturbance inspired perhaps by his choking grief and the rage that it fomented. Anger was a problem, as it would be for the rest of his life, although he learned to control it. In kindergarten one day, he shocked both himself and a teacher who tried to awaken him by slapping her hand, hard. At four, playing the role of the bridegroom in a Tom Thumb wedding at Avery Chapel, he threw a tantrum in the middle of the ceremony: "Rearing and pitching, you destroyed your high silk hat, tore off the tails of your wedding jacket! Ripped off your ascot tie, and rolled in the aisle! You screamed and howled like a banshee, scratched and bit like a wild-cat, snotted your nose, *and* pissed your britches. And all the while you were punching and kicking at anyone who came near you. . . .

But worst of all . . . you were utterly *un*-repentent! No one could explain it—nor can I, even unto this very day."

In elementary school, Ralph swung between shyness and aggression. "I was very quiet at first," he wrote, "and tried to leave other people alone"; then he learned "to 'dish it out.'" In the basic classes, which included English, history, arithmetic, and handwriting, he was only a decent student. Outside of class he played hard, spurred by an imagination so wild that he sometimes forgot himself. Playing Tarzan, King of the Apes, he badly sprained an arm. In another incident, he sustained a vicious cut near his right eye that left a permanent scar. Once he shocked his mother by taking some of her "prized baby chicks" (Ida sometimes raised chickens and guinea fowl), tying them to makeshift "parachutes" of rags and cord, then dropping them off the roof of a barn. The result was "my most impressive spanking." On another occasion, aiming at a fellow student, he instead punched his school principal. The two became tangled in a stage curtain before falling off the stage. Ralph landed on top of the man, who then chased him "straight up the aisle and out of the auditorium." Years later, Ralph looked with wonder back to the days when he "was constantly fighting until I reached the age when I realized that I was strong enough and violent enough to kill somebody in a fit of anger."

Filial tributes from Ralph to Ida are few and far between in his writings. "I loved her very much," he wrote once about his mother for publication, but he did so then to forestall any inference that he loved a certain woman (his main music teacher) more. In his unpublished memoir, Ralph paid tribute to Ida's keen, self-sacrificing sense of duty to him. "Your father's death," he conceded of himself, "had left you haunted by a sense of uncertainty but as a child you had been protected by one who understood your fears and gave comfort, even when she herself was suffering." Loving her boys, Ida was as responsible and as capable, within the limits of her education and opportunities, as she could be in rearing them. How well she was educated is not clear. Ralph would later claim that she taught him about socialism. "Ralph told me, two or three times," one of his closest friends said, "how terrifically proud of her he was, and especially by the way she went fearlessly, door to door, campaigning for the socialist Eugene Debs in 1920, while Debs was in federal prison." However, from her surviving letters one would infer that Ida knew nothing about politics, or about anything beyond the strictly domestic. Most of these letters were written, however, long after 1920. By that time, no doubt, years of poverty and humiliation had eroded her spirit and ruined the faith she probably once had in politics, ideas, books, music, and art.

Home for the Ellisons was invariably shabby. Money was always scarce. In Jim Crow Oklahoma City, Ida's only job other than as a maid or a janitor was, for about seven years, as a part-time unskilled helper in the medical arts laboratory at the hospital where Lewis Ellison had died. Not all her white employers were respectful. Ralph hated to hear some of them call her Brownie. Paying rent was often a problem, although the family lived mainly in properties owned by Dr. Slaughter, who seldom pressed Ida for arrears. They moved several times. Once, they lived among whites in an apartment house near Classen Boulevard where Ida worked as a janitor. Shabby or not, these boyhood homes left Ralph with some pleasant memories. As he wrote to Edna Slaughter in 1955 from Italy, "there is hardly a week that passes that I don't dream of home. Sometimes it's the little house in the Eight Hundred block on east Second, one of yours; or again it's 409 East Third, or, most frequently, the little house at 722 East Fourth Street."

Ida was kind to the point of softness. To Ralph's bemusement and sometimes anger, she fed the hoboes, most of them white, who came to their back door looking for a handout. Sincere in her faith, she took her boys to church on Sunday, taught them the value of politeness and good grammar and the importance of hard work, decency, and honor. Thus she tried to prepare them to exploit any chance the world gave them. "How often did I hear my mother insist," Ralph remembered, "that the future of Afro-Americans would depend upon our generation of young Negroes—and this at a time when things appeared (at least for me as an individual), most hopeless." If he seldom wrote glowingly about her, Ralph nevertheless recalled Ida as a nurturing figure, especially when he was a boy.

Ida was also brave. Once, she deliberately broke the Jim Crow rule at the city zoo. When a white guard rudely confronted her, Ralph, and Herbert, she defiantly pointed out that she was a taxpayer entitled to visit the zoo and needed no white folks' permission. "Well," the guard retorted, "*I'm* here to tell you that you're breaking the law! So now you'll have to leave. Both you and your children too. The rule says no niggers is allowed in the zoo. That's the law and I'm enforcing it." Ralph was proud of his mother's courage. The white man's ugly words became a family joke. Whenever something untoward happened, one of them was likely to tell the others, "You'll have to go now, you and your chillun too!" Then they would all burst into laughter, and the pain would pass.

She and Ralph had their differences. As an adolescent he was no longer religious, and her constant praying came to annoy him. He could see that she was devoted to him and his brother, but his recorded remarks suggest an uneasy mixture of love and disapproval. The latter was born, no doubt, of his understandable disappointment that she could do little for him in terms of money. Given his ambition, and the posh company that he wanted to keep, her menial jobs must have been galling to him. It must have been hard at times for Ralph to mourn his father (who, as a man, would probably have been a better provider) without blaming his mother, merely because she was alive and his father dead. To think or feel in this way is surely part of the ordeal that most children face when a parent dies, and poverty or abuse follows in the wake of this death.

Ralph probably never admitted to having such feelings, and eventually felt guilty about his resentment. There is no doubt he loved Ida. "Ralph also told me, with palpable sadness," a friend recalled, "that one of his principal regrets in life was that by the time he was in a position to do anything for his mother, she was gone." Part of his regret must have come from the fact that while she lived he was seldom tender with her, if we are to judge from many of his letters. In contrast, his brother, Herbert, a less complicated soul, adored Ida. "Mama was a wonderful woman," he wrote Ralph in 1942, "a brave, and wonderful woman. . . . You should try to put her life in a story. [I]t would make a very beautiful story some day." (If Ralph ever did so, the closest he came was the figure of the unhappy but purposeful mother traveling with her two young sons in "Boy on a Train," written around 1938 but published posthumously.)

In contrast to his knowledge of his father's people, he seemed ignorant about his family on Ida's side. He had little interest in where she came from or who her parents, Polk and Georgia Milsap, were. Similarly, although he would help his brother with money in later years and try to stay in touch with him regularly, Ralph was keenly aware of how different he was from Herbert. Genial but somewhat slow, Herbert never took to books, music, or any other kind of art. From his infancy, his pale skin, red hair, blue eyes, and freckles amused Ralph, who called him "Huck" for many years, no doubt because of his resemblance to some illustration of Mark Twain's hero. Undoubtedly, Ralph loved his brother, but "Huck" seemed to have little to offer him.

Anxious about her sons' future, Ida invested almost all of her hope in them, and especially in Ralph. In 1921, deciding that "my brother and I would have a better chance of reaching manhood if we grew up in the north," Ralph declared, she chose to move to the industrial town of Gary, Indiana, where one of her brothers worked. Ralph and Herbert returned home from school one day to find a white man and his two boys loading their furniture into a truck. Ida had sold even Herbert's beloved rocking horse and Ralph's prized rolltop desk, chair, and toy typewriter, a Christmas gift from her. Herbert burst into tears, and Ralph seethed with rage until the promise of a long train ride calmed them. A few days later, they left for Gary. They made only one major stop, in the prosperous black Greenwood section of Tulsa, where they stayed with their cousin Tom Brown and Othello, or Bert, his wife. The Browns owned a pleasant home with plush furniture and a baby grand piano.

They were not long in Gary. A sudden crisis in the steel industry cost Ida's brother his job, and Ida couldn't find work. The family was forced to subsist mainly on a diet of worm-infested beans and day-old milk and bread discarded by a dairy and a bakery nearby. When they faced eviction, Ida was reduced to pawning most of the jewelry Lewis had given her. She prayed for a return to Oklahoma despite an empty purse. Then one day, a chauffeured touring car arrived, looking every bit like a mirage—"a magnificent carriage with running boards and gleaming headlights, with spare tires on both sides and rear, a folding top and transparent side curtains against the rain." The owners were friends from Oklahoma City, the Cooks, a wealthy black couple who owned a movie house and other property. Every year they brought the carnival, with its rides and games and Ferris wheel, to Deep Second. Visiting relatives in Chicago, they had decided to drop in without notice on Ida and her boys in Gary. Of course they would take them home! Forty years later, Ralph thanked Hester Cook, now a widow, for rescuing them. "I realize now," he confessed, "that that was one of the most important trips of my life; because Lord knows what might have happened to us had we remained in Gary. Certainly I would not have grown up in quite the same way and so much of what I've become was formed in Okla[homa]."

At times the journey back was surreal. They passed over paved highways and dirt roads that took them deep into the countryside, where they crossed dangerously swollen rivers over rickety bridges or by horse-drawn ferries. "Descending the mountain to the plains," Ralph recalled, he saw "a dead white barkless tree which stood on what had been a river's bank which now writhed with snakes that climbed along its branches to escape the rising water. There was a smell of death in the air and buzzards circling in the sky." When they reached Tulsa, the smell of death became overpowering. The bustling black Greenwood section they had passed through a few weeks before was now destroyed. Tom Brown's home was a wreck, the elegant baby grand charred beyond repair. But this had nothing to do with the river.

On the morning of May 21, 1921, a young white woman named Sarah Page had been at her job, operating an elevator in the Drexel Building downtown, when a black shoeshine boy, Dick Rowland, entered her car. Apparently, the elevator lurched and he stumbled over her feet. She slapped him, he grabbed her arms, she screamed, and he fled in fear. At first, Page claimed that Rowland had assaulted her. After police arrested Rowland the next day, she recanted her story. Nevertheless, riled by rumors and crude reports in the white press, notably the *Tulsa Tribune,* vigilante forces (white and black) began to gather. Blacks aimed to prevent a lynching, while whites were bent on teaching the blacks a lesson. The police badly miscalculated the danger. In less than twenty-four hours, whites destroyed Greenwood. The official police report listed sixty-eight blacks killed, including men, women, and children. Nine whites died. Blacks lost over a thousand homes and businesses, leaving almost nine thousand persons destitute. Prosecutors indicted several local black leaders on charges of rioting. Yet, as one historian notes, "not a single white Tulsan was made to answer to the criminal justice system as a consequence."

Back in Oklahoma City, Ida and the boys resumed their old life. That year, Ralph entered the third grade. If anything, they were poorer now because of the failed gamble on Gary. Ralph had to wear young Wyatt Slaughter's hand-me-downs, and he hated it. Shuttling between the prosperous world of Randolphs and Slaughters and his own poverty disturbed him more and more. Later he would write respectfully about the fine community leaders who set its standards of generosity, self-respect, and hard work. However, "I remember the others too," he wrote sardonically in 1961, "the teachers who made you ashamed and the professionals who thought Herbert and I weren't good enough to play with their children." In one terrible episode at the funeral of two boys about his age, their grieving mothers—"rather cruel women"—had "cried out in public that they couldn't understand why the Lord hadn't taken Ida Ellison's boys instead. I remember and understand and forgive but I can't forgive the pain that some of this type of thing caused Brownie."

In her quest for a better life, Ida moved in 1925 to McAlester, Oklahoma, where Ralph attended the L'Ouverture School (for blacks) in the seventh grade. But the move proved futile, and she returned to Oklahoma City after a year.

Ida's two marriages after Lewis Ellison's death strained her relationship with Ralph. Little is known of either man, not least of all because Ralph stonily refused to write more than a few words about them. Only eleven and still malleable when Ida married her third husband, a laborer named James Ammons, on July 8, 1924, Ralph seems to have been on decent terms with this stepfather. Later, in one of his vicariously autobiographical early pieces of fiction (an unfinished novel called "Slick"), Ralph appears to credit Ammons with teaching him to hunt and shoot. (Ralph learned to shoot using Uretta Randolph's .22-caliber rifle.) Ammons apparently died within two years of marrying Ida. Her beauty and charm were such that in December 1929 she took a fourth husband, John Bell, a porter at J. W. Jenkins' Music Store, who at thirty was about a dozen years younger than Ida. Ralph, nearly seventeen, doubtless hated having to share his mother with yet another man, and especially one so young. To the end, John Bell remained "Mr. Bell" to him. Once, after a heated argument, Ralph stormed out of the house and walked north for fifteen miles or more. Finally, hungry and defeated, he hitched a ride back to the city.

To help Ida, Ralph started work before he was twelve. His first job was as a shoeshine boy. On Saturdays, he worked downtown from eight in the morning until nearly midnight, and on Sundays from eight until noon. Tips were excellent, but he gave up the job, he said, because he couldn't stand the arrogance of most of the white men and because other black workers resented him for being too proud to suck up to whites. Not long afterward, through an elder at Avery Chapel who was headwaiter at the fashionable Oklahoma Club, he became a bread-and-butter boy there. His pay was a free meal and tips, but later the club hired him as a waiter. As a senior in high school he earned a dollar an hour serving lunch at the Skirvin Hotel. He also picked up other part-time waiting jobs—once, for example, at the gala dinner that opened the Oklahoma City Golf and Country Club in Nichols Hills, the most prosperous residential area in the city. Now and then he washed cars at a filling station on Classen Boulevard, or helped in the kitchen as an assistant short-order cook in a local diner.

Perhaps his most stimulating job as a boy came around the age of twelve when he worked for Dr. T. J. "Bud" Randolph in his dental office in Deep Second. With a passion for technology that grew over the years, Ralph took to the job. He learned how to cast inlays, pour plaster-of-Paris

models, and make crowns and some of the simpler bridges. Randolph
thought that Ralph might make an excellent dentist. However, Ralph
detested working on patients with rotting teeth and stinking mouths. One
other aspect of this job made Ralph uneasy. To get to Dr. Randolph's
office he had to pass another, far more ominous office, that of the local
branch of the Ku Klux Klan. Following its revival with the popularity of
the 1915 film *The Birth of a Nation,* the Klan had come to Oklahoma in
1922, one year after the Tulsa Riot.

Ralph had more fun working for Bud's brother Jim, who had opened
the popular Randolph's Drug Store at 351 North East Second Street after
graduating from Fisk University and the Denver College of Pharmacy.
Although Ralph spent much of the time making ice-cream sodas and sun-
daes, his main task was to deliver medicine and other purchases to customers, and also to pick up supplies. Encouraged to use both the store's
motorcycle and its Model T Ford, he learned to drive when he was about
twelve. He found Jim Randolph a humane, trusting employer. One day,
he handed Ralph $1,000 to keep until he asked for it. Randolph, Ralph
recalled, was "a kind and tolerant boss who allowed his young employees
to stuff themselves on free ice cream and candy, taught us to deal
patiently and politely with a sometimes ornery public, and served me personally as an example of tolerant, responsible manhood." He made deliv-
eries all over the city, exchanging words with suppliers of all sorts, many
of them white. In this way, Randolph continued "the extra-curricular education which my father initiated as soon as I was able to sit erect on a
wagon seat." He helped to educate Ralph in "the processes of industry
and business—not to mention the ways of white folks!" It was rumored
that one of the Randolph brothers was his real father. Jim Randolph made
light of the rumor without actually contradicting it. On the surface, at
least, Ralph took the matter in stride.

Another job led him to learn much from a local leader almost without
peer because of his relentless crusading for the rights of blacks. As a barefoot boy, Ralph began delivering newspapers for Roscoe Dunjee, the
founder and editor of the community's only newspaper, the *Black Dispatch.* Born in Harpers Ferry, Virginia, Dunjee had left school after the
eighth grade. However, he grew into a shrewd, well-read, fiercely energetic enemy of Jim Crow. In 1915, he started the *Black Dispatch.* Four
years later, after whites invoked local ordinances to prevent a black man
from moving into property he had bought in the all-white 200 block of
North East Second, Dunjee financed the first legal challenges to Jim

Crow in the city. The result was a U.S. Supreme Court victory and the surging of black homeowners beyond Deep Second. He also helped with the protracted campaign to desegregate the state-owned University of Oklahoma. Over the years, white advertisers boycotted the paper, but Dunjee died a satisfied man. "My newspapers may be for sale," he always insisted, "but not my principles." Even when he was not peddling the *Black Dispatch,* Ralph would visit Dunjee at the newspaper offices in Deep Second, or chat with him in Randolph's Drug Store. "He was a great man and a great American," Ralph declared. According to him, Dunjee helped to shape his views about race in America because the editor always saw blacks in the largest possible context. Dunjee "did not approach events in some sort of stylized second-class citizen's way." (Ralph subscribed to the *Black Dispatch* until late in life.)

Later, as a celebrity in New York, Ralph would depend on his memory to return to his days as a poor black boy in the prison of Jim Crow. Then some of the slights didn't matter, and he saw himself as a child lucky to have faced certain challenges. Much of his Oklahoma life, good and bad, "*did* get into my imagination and it gets into the things I write. . . . All this is precious stuff for a child to have contact with and I know now that had I been white or rich or whatever, I couldn't have had a richer time of it."

Part of the richness was his friendship with a few particularly talented boys. Returning from Gary, Indiana, he moved in next door on East Fourth Street to Frank Mead—"the hero of my childhood"—whose gift as an artist inspired Ralph; also, Ralph received his first music lessons from the boy's father, which changed his life. Slightly older than Ralph, Frank was as kind as he was talented. As Ralph watched in wonder, he filled notebook after notebook with dramatic sketches of characters from the world of cartoons, popular novels, and movies. Because of him, Ralph declared, "our entire neighborhood took on a dimension of wonder." After Frank's father, Joe, a talented amateur musician who owned a barbershop, gave Ralph free lessons on the alto saxophone and the trumpet, Ralph took to the latter. He spent the next fifteen years or so trying to master the instrument. During his first years of practice, Ralph wrote, "I terrorized a good part of an entire city section." With a driving desire to succeed, "during summer vacation I blew sustained tones out of the windows for hours, usually starting—especially on Sunday mornings—before breakfast." He "sputtered whole days" struggling through various double and triple tonguing exercises, "with an effect like that of a jackass hiccupping off a big meal of briars." Some neighbors objected, but "there were more tolerant ones who were willing to pay in present pain for future pride."

However, the main musical influence on him was Mrs. Zelia N. Page Breaux, a teacher at the Douglass School and a key black leader as superintendent of music for the city's colored schools and as an arts promoter and entrepreneur. Inman E. Page, the principal of the Douglass School, was her father. Present at a second-grade class presentation one day, she noticed Ralph's intensity as he sang and danced to a nursery song: *"Oh busy squirrel with bushy tail and shiny eyes so round / Why do you gather all the nuts that fall upon the ground?"* Charmed, she sought him out, just as she sought out other boys and girls who showed artistic ability. Making music a major part of the curriculum, she had started boys' and girls' quartets, a boys' glee club, and a chorus. In 1923, she founded the Douglass High School Band. Tight and flashy, the band proudly entertained at parades, concerts, and sporting events, especially football games.

Breaux later invited Ralph to join this band, and eventually would appoint him student bandmaster. She taught him to think of himself as an artist. "It was Mrs. Breaux who introduced me to the basic discipline required of the artist," he claimed, "and it was she who made it possible for me to grasp the basic compatibility of the mixture of the classical and vernacular styles which were part of our musical culture." Her confidence and energy stamped Ralph; the fact that she drove a fine car with panache sealed her power over him. The musical world opened wider. The Aldridge Theatre, which she co-owned, showed movies but also staged concerts by classical, jazz, and blues performers such as Bessie Smith and Ma Rainey, whom Ralph met. It featured dancers and comedians, and staged plays by Shakespeare as well as by contemporary blacks. (Ira Aldridge, a gifted black American Shakespearean actor, had been a star in Europe.) Ralph became one of Breaux's darlings. Sometimes in concerts she accompanied him on the piano or lent him her own instruments, including her prized soprano saxophone.

Ralph began to think of a career in music and of Zelia Breaux as his main guide toward that end. "For more than ten years," he recalled, "Mrs. Breaux was a sort of second mother." Most likely she was the only woman in his pantheon of heroes in Oklahoma, and also the hero who moved him the most intimately in his adolescence. Each man in Ralph's life competed with his desire for his father. Without the tension that marked his relationships with men, Ralph opened himself to Breaux. In the process, he found the embryo of his life's work.

In marked contrast was the relationship between Ralph and her father. Born a slave, Inman Page had been the first black graduate of Brown University (in 1877) as well as the first president of nearby Langston University. In 1821 he became the principal of Douglass. (In fact, it was the venerable Dr. Page whom Ralph punched and toppled that day at a school assembly.) As a graduate of an Ivy League college, Page was to black Oklahomans a standard-bearer of the vaunted New England culture, with its history of abolitionist moral fervor—"and through him," Ralph would point out in paying tribute to both Page and New England, "its standards were imparted to many, many ex-slaves and their descendants." And yet although Page was "quite fatherly" to Ralph, "he possessed an aura of the untouchable" by virtue of his "quality of command." Almost all of Ralph's relationships with men like Page featured a tension between admiration and resentment, rebelliousness and a need to idealize male elders who possessed authority. When disenchantment came, as it did regularly, it usually hit Ralph hard. In time, he came to see how complex these early struggles with authority had been for a boy without a grounded sense of identity, a boy plagued by feelings of social inferiority, eager to learn but also envious, defensive, alienated, and angry. "He was a model, he was feared, and he was admired," he once reminisced about Page. "In other words, he inspired that ambivalence—love, hate, and envy—and that secret yearning to possess some of his authority, some of his power and some of his wisdom."

Encouraged by Breaux, Ralph found that his love of music flourished and with it a sense of the possibility of an honorable, perhaps even a lucrative career. He also became an insider both in the core artistic passion of black Oklahoma City—music—and in the roiling if often unspoken debates about three competing traditions: religious music, jazz and blues, and Western classical music. "I had been caught actively," he wrote later, between "Negro folk music, both sacred and profane, slave song and jazz, and that of Western classical music. It was most confusing." While one impulse "demanded that I play what I felt and heard around me," another "insisted that I play strictly according to the book and express that which I was *supposed* to feel." In addition, an entente cordiale existed between many church musicians and classical music, an alliance that began with their reverence for works such as Handel's *Messiah* but also embraced the strivers' hope that mastering classical music would elevate the race. "Jazz was regarded by most of the respectable Negroes," he wrote, "as a backward, low-class form of expression." Ralph also learned

early that many jazz musicians knew and respected classical music, and
were not inspired primitives from the American heart of darkness, as they
were often portrayed.

Although Breaux's classes emphasized the classics, few blacks could
escape the dominion of blues and jazz. Blues and jazz musicians, Ralph
wrote, "gave expression to attitudes which found no place" in the
churches and schools, "and helped to give our lives some semblance of
wholeness. Jazz and the public jazz dance was a third institution in our
lives, and a vital one." Growing up, he knew the two individuals who
would become the best known of Oklahoma City musicians, the instru-
mentalist Charlie Christian and the singer Jimmy Rushing. "With Christian," he observed in praise, "the guitar found its jazz voice." The Christian
family (including his blind father) lived in a slum but was famous locally
for its uncanny expertise in playing both popular and "light" classical fare.
Although Charlie and Herbert Ellison "were members of the same first-
grade class at Douglass," Charlie never played in Zelia Breaux's school
band. Leaving that well-worn path to his brother Edward, he went the
dangerous way of genius.

Jimmy Rushing, later acclaimed as the finest blues singer in America,
was to Ralph "a compact, debonair young man" with an astonishing voice
who was "official floor manager or leader-of-the-dance at Slaughter's Hall,
the leader of a public rite." In his youth, Ralph did not see the full implications of Rushing's art and life. Only later would he view the singer, a
businessman's son, as more than "simply a local entertainer." Rushing
"expressed a value, an attitude about the world for which our lives
afforded no other definition." Few people could resist Rushing's magnetism, and young Ralph didn't. Lying in bed at night four blocks from Dr.
Slaughter's music hall, he would listen to Rushing's voice and the band
behind it; or, too young to enter the dancehall, he and his pals would
gather on summer evenings under the corner streetlamp and "turn our
heads westward to hear Jimmy's voice soar up the hill and down, as pure
and as miraculously unhindered by distance and earthbound things as is
the body in youthful dreams of flying."

Eventually Ralph had to choose between jazz and classical music. One
side of him hankered for the race-rooted creativity of jazz, the free-floating
ambience of cool liquor, hot women, sticky close dancing, and panting
fans. For a while, Oran "Hot Lips" Page dominated the local scene, then
the saxophonist Lester Young showed up in 1929 with his battered horn
to "upset the entire Negro section of the town." The pianist William

"Count" Basie, whose orchestra had emerged from Benny Moten's group and the local Blue Devils, also came. Stars visited regularly. In 1930, Ralph attended concerts by Rex Stewart and Coleman Hawkins. He was also in the feverish crowds that welcomed the renowned orchestras led by Fletcher Henderson and Duke Ellington. He heard the big band singers Ivy Anderson and Ethel Waters. Twice he worshipped at the feet of Louis Armstrong. He did so at the Aldridge Theatre in 1929 and again in 1931, when Armstrong played at sold-out dances for blacks and whites—separately. These stars often exuded a sense of confidence that went well beyond art. In 1931, the *Black Dispatch* reported Armstrong's insouciant comment about his music, white folks, and Jim Crow. "Race prejudice is no trouble," he said. "When they find out that you have what they want and can't get it elsewhere, they admit you with a smile."

Music did not stop Ralph from reading books. The segregated Oklahoma City public library tried to do so when he was a boy, until an angry black Episcopalian priest, Father Frank N. Fitzpatrick, led the resistance to Jim Crow there. According to the *Black Dispatch,* blacks were banned after "several of the Colored boys from Douglass School were found flirting with white girls in the rooms of the library." Finally, in 1921, the city rented two rooms in the Slaughter Building in Deep Second and opened a "colored" branch. The white librarians "put in some shelves and dumped all kinds of books in there and appointed a lady as librarian and so we had a library." The Dunbar Branch, as it was called (named after the black poet Paul Laurence Dunbar), was a boon to Ralph: "I quickly began to read through those books along with a few of my friends." These included Frank Mead; Malcolm and Lloyd Whitby, sons of the prominent local physician and NAACP leader Dr. A. Baxter Whitby; Willard and Tracy McCleary, the latter a clarinetist and, later, a saxophonist; the top debater at Douglass, Hillard Bowen; and Harold Calicutt. In Dr. Whitby's own library Ralph first thrilled to the fiction of Maupassant and the plays and prefaces of George Bernard Shaw. He also craved the lavishly illustrated, upscale magazines, notably *Vanity Fair,* that his mother sometimes brought home from her jobs. Through *Vanity Fair,* above all, he became familiar with names such as Stravinsky, Nijinsky, Picasso, Steichen, Mencken, and Woollcott. The boys also established their own library in the garage of the McCleary home, "from which any of us were free to borrow anything that caught our attention."

Racing through "the so-called boys book[s], westerns and detective stories, in a rapid sweep," the youths soon moved on to adult fare. Ralph was taken by A. A. Brill's translation of Freud's *The Interpretation of Dreams*—"which I by no means understood." Eventually he began to get at something of its meaning. One day, he was shining the shoes of a white college student when he put this smattering of knowledge to use. After tossing around Freudian terms in bantering with a friend, the student bent over, rubbed Ralph's head, and asked, "Now isn't that right, George?" "Yes," Ralph replied, after thinking about punching the man (but "he was much too tall to topple"), "and if the super-ego doesn't get you the ego probably will." The student's jaw dropped, his friend roared with laughter, and Ralph lost any hope of a tip.

Novels fed his chronic daydreaming. After reading *Adventures of Huckleberry Finn,* he fantasized often about life on a raft floating down the Mississippi to New Orleans. He surely didn't see himself as the slave Jim. Perhaps he was *both* Huck and Jim, the Geminian embodiment of interracial democracy in America. Eventually, this fantasy died as he became more aware of the truth about slavery, about pestilential slave ships and hot cotton fields, baying bloodhounds and lynched black bodies. After meeting the pioneering black aviatrix Bessie Coleman, he daydreamed about flying away from Oklahoma. But the classic American romances bred his main fantasies. He loved *The Last of the Mohicans.* "Cooper was a great writer," he protested years later against people who dismissed the novelist as reactionary and unskilled (as Mark Twain had done, ironically); "I read *Last of the Mohicans* ten times." Later on, books began to sharpen his command of ideas. George Bernard Shaw's prefaces, which mocked religion and bourgeois morality, led him to inject what he hoped was an urbane, iconoclastic quality into his themes at school. However, "no one paid any attention to it." On one occasion, he set in verse a story by Albion Tourgée. His teacher was dumbfounded: "He looked at me as though I had gone out of my mind."

In school, his teacher Lamonia McFarland introduced Ralph and the other students to Dunbar and also to some of the main writers of the Harlem Renaissance, which was still going strong in New York in the work of poets such as Countee Cullen and Langston Hughes and novelists such as Claude McKay, Nella Larsen, and Wallace Thurman. Later, even before he became famous, Ralph would give little credit to such writing as exerting any influence on his own literary art. At Douglass, however, he was probably impressed by these black writers' skill in capturing in verse something of the pain of being black in America.

· · ·

For all of his reading, Ralph did not excel as a student. His self-education lacked system. Of his graduating class of about fifty pupils, at least four would go on to earn doctorates; he never earned a degree. Too many forces disrupted his life for him to take notes assiduously in class or accept the daily grind of homework. He got by in subjects such as mathematics, physics, and Latin, but "I was a very poor English student," he confessed just after *Invisible Man* appeared, "being too undisciplined and stubborn to learn the rules." This mulishness held him back as he grew older at Douglass, and intensified as his connections to the Randolphs and Slaughters and other upper-crust blacks weakened, as time laid bare the gap between their social station and his. The quarrel with his step-father that sent him walking miles out of town was no doubt only a token of his adolescent rebelliousness at home, at school, and against his life in general. Only his music training, into which he poured his rage and righteousness, kept him under control. In other ways, like many a sensitive adolescent, he saw his life on the edge of chaos.

No doubt seeking popularity, in 1929 and 1930 he went out for football at Douglass. Though blessed with a rugged physique, one that several observers would compare later to that of a prizefighter or a halfback, he often lost his concentration and at times even fumbled the ball without being tackled. One fumble led to a loss against a traditional rival. Ralph came to hate his head coach, who was as intemperate as he was unsuccessful (the *Black Dispatch* called for his removal). One day, after Ralph drew a penalty by striking back at an opponent who had been playing dirty, the coach kicked him. Outraged, Ralph would have jumped him except for the knowledge that he would be expelled. He forgave the other player but not the coach. "One day," he vowed to himself, he "would return and repay him in kind."

In another act of defiance, he stepped down the social ladder to befriend Virgil Dodge Branam. Neither bookish nor artistic, Branam was a newcomer to Oklahoma City who seemed to be all body except for a scandalous comic intelligence and a kind heart. Two years older than Ralph but still in high school, he stood close to six feet five inches. He was also fat and—as Ralph noted more than once—dark-skinned, in contrast to the color of many of Ralph's close friends to this point. Virgil read books mainly under duress, played no musical instrument, and didn't worry about his future, which would be as a cook and pastry chef on freighters and liners. Nevertheless, the two adolescents bonded. Over the decades none of Ralph's Oklahoma friends kept in steadier touch with him (although Branam did so for some years mainly by sending postcards from exotic lands).

Irresistibly, Virgil drew Ralph out of his brooding and dour self-doubt and into the world of fun and flesh. To Zelia Breaux they were like Laurel and Hardy (she knew hardly the half of it). Virgil also broke through Ralph's notions of sexual inhibition and propriety, his idealization of women based on beauty, class, and skin color, and his sense of shame about sex. One of Branam's stunts was to sidle up to sedate, middle-aged women and whisper a request: *"Hey, baby, step over here and let me see if your pussy's wet."* Stunned at first, Ralph was even more shocked to find out how many of the ladies enjoyed Virgil's antics. "Virgil always received the special privileges granted to those who have the nerve to *play* the fool (true fools being ignored as having no sense of right and wrong)." In his own crude fashion, Virgil schooled Ralph in essential knowledge. "Even today," Ralph wrote decades later, "I'm in his debt for teaching me so much about the difference between the public decorum of females and their private possibilities."

Ralph, Virgil, Harold Calicutt, and other Douglass boys were allowed to take off the last period before lunch to serve meals at the Skirvin Hotel. A letter from Calicutt written around 1940 gives a peek into the steamy side of Ralph's late adolescence, as he wrote giddily about pranks and girls and sex and "the hell we raised in school." Could Ralph remember "a certain lady having her daughter examine[d] to see if you *bad* boys had *stole* the cherry?" Did Ralph recall the Douglass principal, Inman Page, "kicking us off the Campus—Remember?" Douglass was near the red-light district, which the boys frequented not as paying customers but out of a disruptive curiosity, so that Calicutt also reminisced merrily about "those dames in the neighborhood chasing us back to school—because we interfered with their 'business.'" He fondly recalled, too, "the yearly proms—The fun at Virgil's home on First St.—Never looking at a book on weekends—The trips the school band made out of town—Remember? And the best memories are the ones we dare not tell."

Ralph struggled in those years against the handcuffs of respectability. He later wrote of himself and his close friends that "we held secret in our boyish hearts quite other ambitions: To be hard-walking, deep-throated drinkers of whiskey (then illegal), steel-nerved gamblers, experts and tire-less partners of the race horse-gaited girls at public dances; ruthless and skilled competitors in prize ring and on football field; and on the jumping bandstand, going for the [jugular] with trumpet or saxophone. We'd be men among men— And among women? Like studs among the mares." To get these women they would need fine clothes and cars, of course— especially the flashy cars. Ralph never lost his love of cars or forgot those of his youth in Oklahoma City, including "a beat-up yellow Stutz Bearcat once owned by a white playboy, a Duesenberg owned by a jazz musician from Kansas City, a beige Packard sports convertible driven by a slick-haired professional gambler from Dallas." But when he snapped awake from his daydreaming, he was still a repressed, confused brown boy living in near-poverty in a Jim Crow city with a hotel maid of a mother, a slow-witted brother, and few prospects in life.

As graduation approached in the spring of 1931, the pleasure in his fantasies, as well as in the oafish horseplay, began to lose its appeal. For those like Ralph who could not pay to escape to college, the deadly world of life as a black adult without means in Oklahoma City loomed. Picking up some spare change serving lunch while in high school was one thing, but waiting on tables for white folks for the rest of one's life was quite another. Much of the merriment began to die as Ralph and his friends prepared to face Jim Crow, and life in Oklahoma, as adults with adult needs and responsibilities.

How did one deal with whites, who held the power to make or break one's hopes? "Treat people as individuals," Ida always advised, as she warned Ralph and Herbert against what he called later "the distortions of perception imposed by pride." She wanted him to "develop a sense of self-worth" to support him as he confronted "the attitudes and opinions of others, whether they be black or white." His father, Ralph knew, would have preached the same message. "There was never a time when we didn't have white friends," Ralph declared. "There were friends of my father who would come by to see him, and he'd go by to see them." An amiable English couple owned and ran the Blue Front Grocery near his home. One of his pals for a while was a sickly but bright white boy, Henry Bowman Otto Davis, known to Ralph only as "Hoolie," the son of Rev. Franklin Davis, an Episcopal priest. Ralph clearly welcomed this casual but talismanic friendship and the chance to benefit from Hoolie's precocious knowledge of electronics, a field that would fascinate Ralph for the rest of his life. (Building crystal sets from a schematic he had found in a magazine, Ralph used doorbell wire as coil, which he wound on ice-cream cartons; his earpiece came from a discarded telephone. Eager to do more, he saved up to buy equipment he couldn't improvise—tubes and sockets, transformers, and variable condensers for more sophisticated equipment, which he also built.)

He found even friendly whites hard to read and capable of sudden, ugly change. The result was bigotry on both sides. "It was a nasty, depressing situation," he wrote, "because the denial of one's humanity on the basis of color led one to doubt—if not to deny outright—the humanity of others. And that, ironically, on the same shameful basis." The year before he died, Ralph looked back on the white folks of his youth and recalled their God-like power to make blacks feel, well, invisible. On the one hand, "I was all over Oklahoma City, and I don't recall ever having any serious trouble." Once in a while, an argument might flare up with a white kid, or even a quick fight. On the other hand, "they treated you or could treat you as though you had no personal identity," he told a reporter for the white-owned *Daily Oklahoman;* "you were part of a mass." In those days, blacks didn't have the power to talk back, much less react in kind, and still succeed. Instead, "you looked for nuances of voice or for nuances of conduct and interrelationships, and that's how one survived. And very often you wore a mask, very often pretending to be what you were not, just to survive or to keep out of trouble."

Ironically, among blacks he often also took on different identities. Among his bright friends he was easy and expansive, letting his intelligence and wit flash freely. With most other blacks he felt much less at ease, more defensive and more arrogant, especially facing those on whom he looked down. To them, he was quick to make his feelings known. "With you," Zelia Breaux scolded him, "the first thing up is the first thing out . . . and some day it will cause you serious trouble." Some of his supposed inferiors didn't wait that long. "For a lil' ole raggity-assed nigguh of yo' age and ugly," one of them warned him, "you got too dam much mouf!" Once, when Ralph insulted a dumb-looking kid in pig Latin ("Ogo ucky-fay ouya ammamay"), the boy got the message and punched him in the mouth. Worse, Ralph's hauteur, his notions of his superiority to most other blacks, actually undermined his self-confidence. More and more, Ralph saw himself as possessing at least two distinct selves. One self was a poor, brown-skinned Oklahoma City boy so at home in the vernacular language that he often descended into profanity and vulgarity. This self snagged Ralph without warning, "when your mouth was running; a self which [was] probably responsible for stirring up fights and charges that you were stuck up, nasty-tongued, ill-adjusted and, perhaps, a bit loony."

Although "for the most part hidden," this transgressive heat made him feel at times akin "to a circus sideshow freak whose act consisted of displaying a smaller fully-formed body which grew out of his enormous chest in such a manner as to appear to be hiding somewhere near its companion's heart."

The other self sprang mainly from his exposure to romantic fiction and Hollywood movies, both imported from the white world, which added to his own almost leprous insecurity about being poor, fatherless, and misunderstood. When this self spoke, it typically did so in a clipped, faux-Bostonian English marked by awkwardly formal diction and rhinestone words. As with his "low" self, Ralph could barely check this "high" self, which made him "vulnerable to unwelcome laughter" when ordinary blacks mocked his affectations without mercy. "It was as though a part of you," he recalled with some pain, "insisted upon dressing in a borrowed and ill-fitting morning coat, grey vest, striped trousers and grey spats while the rest of you was better suited for overalls or sports jackets and slacks." Of course, Ralph was hardly alone among blacks in this affliction. So much of African-American culture reflected this gear-grinding conflict as blacks strained to move onward and upward. Ralph would recall, for example, "the outrageous disparity" he stumbled upon one day when a finely tailored black man, after playing Chopin on a piano "with the technical skill and emotional sensitivity of a concert artist," showed by his ugly speech and foul manner that he was a dog.

The entire world, black or white, seemed to threaten Ralph. Despite his heady talk of being, along with his inner circle of friends, a Renaissance man, skilled in music, science, sport, and other forms of knowledge, he could depend on little. He fantasized about attending Harvard, especially after reading in a magazine an account of the eccentric teaching style of its famed Shakespearean scholar George Lyman Kittredge. He also dreamed of attending the Juilliard School of Music in New York City. But as graduation grew closer at Douglass High in his senior year, 1930–1931, reality bit. Because of failing grades in at least one subject (another indication of how unstable and rebellious his life had become), he did not earn his high school diploma with his class, although he was allowed to take part in the Douglass graduation ceremony. Several of his friends had been admitted to college. He hadn't even *sought* entry, since he had no way to pay for tuition, room, and board. Frank Mead was going to attend Langston University, Oklahoma's college for blacks. Poorly funded and without much of a history, Langston was low on Ralph's wish list but seemed his only realistic prospect, if he could save enough money in the coming months.

Two more years would pass before Ralph, fearful but with a determined heart, climbed aboard the smoking freight train that took him at last out of the territory of his youth and into the wider world.

2

Leaving the Territory

1931–1933

I've got to get out of this town or I'm lost forever . . .
RALPH ELLISON (n.d.)

Early in September 1931, after reading in Roscoe Dunjee's *Black Dispatch* that board had been reduced to $14 per month at Langston University, and that jobs were available to students, Ralph hitchhiked more than forty miles to Langston. There he hoped to meet with its new president, Dr. C. J. Young, secure one of the jobs, and sign up for classes. He reached Langston with some confidence. After all, Dr. Young was an old friend of the Ellison family. But his appointment by the recently elected, avowedly racist white governor of the state, Alfalfa Bill Murray, had enraged a number of black leaders, including Dunjee, who despised Murray and also Dr. Young for supporting him. Evidently, to Ralph's surprise, Young associated him and his mother with Dunjee's opposition. Refusing to acknowledge that he had known Ellison for years, Young crudely killed Ralph's hope of entering Langston. He returned home in a rage. Dr. Young's grotesque snub was a wound Ralph would pick at for years to come. The idealism still clouding his vision of powerful black men began to evaporate. Now he knew truly, as he wrote later, that he had to be "more wary of all contradictions between words and actions. And especially words that involved political motives that were modulated by racial realities."

Setting aside thoughts of college, Ralph looked for work. However, with the Depression deepening, no black man, with or without a high school diploma, could hope for much. By 1931, the dreams that had brought blacks to the Indian and Oklahoma territories, and then to the new state, were now mainly dust. Even the sprawling homesteads secured in the territorial past were slipping out of black hands. Jobs vanished because of the collapse of businesses and also because of competition from poor whites for even menial work, the few exceptions being mainly women like Ida who worked as maids and black men who toiled as laborers. Jim Crow ruled as never before. In 1933, Governor Murray used his executive power to impose racial segregation on the city. "I have no law for this," he admitted, "but I have the power and I'm going to use it."

Three generations later, schoolmates of Ralph testified to the pain that marred the lives of local blacks until the civil rights movement of the 1950s and 1960s forced Oklahoma City to change its ways. Zethel Chamberlain, the granddaughter of James H. A. Brazelton, one of the pioneers of black education in the city, recalled that "we were an isolated community. We tried not to be too concerned with what whites did, but we had to deal with them. Actually, lots of whites would help, but you never knew who they were until they stepped forward. And many were destructive. They helped as long as no white interest was threatened." In the stores, blacks could buy clothing and shoes but not try them on. Certain parks and schools were off-limits. Separate taxicab companies served blacks and whites. Blacks could not buy home insurance. Many whites pushed to the front of lines of blacks to be served first. Some white drivers even expected blacks to yield to them at intersections. "Jim Crow was very harsh," Ralph's boyhood friend Pauline Brown Vivette remembered ruefully. "Different people in the black community had different attitudes. A few would fight, kill even; most accepted it. But in truth it was almost futile to try to fight." A successful doctor recalled of Oklahoma City that "in those days, all blacks could do was preach, teach, or practice medicine." "During my Oklahoma boyhood," Ralph would write, "our aspirations were geared to the familiar, bound by the restricted range of possibility enforced by Southern tradition."

Ralph worked irregularly over the next two years as a substitute meal server at the University Club. Then, for $8 a week, he was hired as a janitor downtown at Lewisohns Clothing Store. Part of Ralph's duties was to man the elevator between the two floors of the store, but his main task was to keep the store clean. Glad to have the job, he also saw it as a daily humiliation. Actually, he was lucky to find work, and lucky in his employers. Three brothers had inherited the store from their father. As a black man, Ralph couldn't hope to become a salesman or handle credit accounts there, but the brothers treated him like a human being. When they saw him poring over a book of plays by George Bernard Shaw while sitting outside his elevator cab, they registered some surprise but no displeasure, as other whites might have done. Ralph's co-workers soon began to treat him with more respect. Eventually, assigned to help with window displays, he had a chance to dress the dummies in bespoke suits, crisp shirts, and elegant ties. When the Lewisohns learned that he could drive, they had him fetch their children from school and bring them to the store, where their mothers would come for them.

The Lewisohns were Jewish, and although Ralph had known some Jews almost his entire life, he had never been in such close contact with them. In segregated Oklahoma City, being truly white meant being Anglo-Saxon and of Southern ancestry. The resurgent Klan hated Jews and Catholics just as they hated blacks. This condition, Ralph knew, drove many Jews to prove their "true" whiteness at the expense of blacks and Indians. In his boyhood, Ralph had shared so easily in anti-Semitism that for some time he nicknamed his brother "Jewbaby," because of Herbert's nearly white skin, blue eyes, and only slightly kinky red hair. Even Roscoe Dunjee, crusading for justice at the *Black Dispatch,* promoted mixed messages. He attacked injustices to Jews but could also print "Here's a Jew Bet" as the title of a story about business corruption at Langston University. In 1931, Ralph was a maturing young man both careful about bigotry and more curious than in the past. Although he had no inkling of the extreme extent to which Jews, especially in New York City, would shape his future, he already saw that the Lewisohns, as Jews, embodied some key, complex features of American culture. Where, he wondered, did Jews like the Lewisohn brothers fit in that murky place in American life where religion met race, and both religion and race merged with class and culture? These brothers were unlike the Jewish pawnshop operators, who could be the bane of poor people. The Lewisohns possessed poise, education, intellectual intensity, and a distinct moral sense. Stylish dressers, their wives chatted happily about hit plays and musicals and jolly visits to Chicago and New York. Ralph must often have wondered if he would ever meet such people on equal terms.

The brothers challenged Ralph's immature anti-Semitism. Ralph saw himself as well read, but he was out of his depth with the youngest Lewisohn brother, who had been to college. And yet his intelligence seemed connected to something more than college, something racial or ethnic or religious. "He was Jewish," Ralph recalled, "which suggested, by definition alone, intellectual brilliance." Probably not for the last time in his life in facing Jews (and especially so after he moved to New York City), he felt himself "outclassed and vulnerable to ridicule, both racial and intellectual." The middle brother, Ralph recalled, seemed to be the one who disliked prejudice the most. Once, when a white customer genially rubbed Ralph's head for good luck, Ralph cursed the man. Enraged, he was seething in a corner, waiting to be fired, when this Lewisohn walked over, spoke quietly about the need to defer to customers, and sent Ralph home for the day.

Ralph saw that the employees in this little world—Jews, Gentiles, whites, blacks—formed both a cohesive working unit and one riven along lines marked by color, race, age, religion, education, and class. He rode the elevator, hauled away trash, swept or mopped the floors, and pondered the meaning of these differences. This was Oklahoma; this was America. Of his fellow employees he wondered about their signed and sealed contracts with life, their apparent embracing of their fate without a struggle. His brooding and idealism seemed to contrast with their practicality. He liked them, more or less, but also lived in fear that this job, or another like it, might be his fate for life.

Vivian Steveson was a star sophomore at Douglass, a princess, when she and Ralph began dating in his last year there. "She was my best friend," Pauline Brown Vivette recalled almost seventy years later. "She was very pretty and she had lots of nice clothes. She was also very fair-skinned." Vivian's father was a gambler, apparently, and a successful one, since his wife and daughter seemed to want for little.

Vivian's letters to Ralph suggest an affectionate, sensitive young woman who took her schoolwork seriously but who also loved genteel fun. That she was college-bound was taken for granted. Liking literature as Ralph did, in college Vivian would try writing short stories before subsiding into something more sensible. Loving her "Wallie" (he now claimed his full name), she wanted the best for him. The "best" definitely included going to college. "What are you doing about school?" she prodded him once, in a Valentine's Day card. "Stick with all your grit and *don't ever* give up. Be an Ellison!" In turn, Wallie was soon filling the pages of notebooks with bubbling assurances of love. Vivian, "the little girl" who inspired unselfishness in him, he said, was "the sweetest girl in the world."

When they were happy together, he was sure that she understood him better than almost anyone else did; certainly she seemed ready to accept the artistic quirkiness of his mind, the neurotic grasping of his ambitions. "If someone other than Vivian should read this book," Ralph declared about some unguarded jottings, "they would come quickly to the conclusion that I am a *nut*. I am but she knows that this is the only way I hav[e] to get things off my chest. It's better than having repressions by a long sight." Sometimes he gave her all the credit for inspiring him to heights of success. "Don't you sense Vivian underneath it all?" he asked himself. "Sweet baby," he promised, "if there's any success in this world for me she shall be the one to share it."

When Ralph dreamed now of "success in this world," most often he saw himself as a renowned black classical composer, writing symphonies based on the folk music of his people. Other blacks would then revere him as a credit to the race. Whites would respect him as a Negro genius transcending the limitations of his culture and creating a universal art. From Zelia Breaux he had heard about the late Samuel Coleridge-Taylor, born in 1875 in London of an English mother and an African father from Sierra Leone, a man whose compositions were jewels in the repertoire of black classical musicians. Louis Gottschalk, the white, New Orleans–born composer, had mined Negro and Creole folk songs and dances in creating symphonies, cantatas, and virtuoso compositions for the piano. In 1893, the Czech composer Antonín Dvořák had triumphed with *From the New World,* a symphony into which he had blended romantic orchestral strains with rhythms and melodies said to be common both to his native Bohemia and to black America. In young Ralph's time, a few black American classical composers had begun to make their mark. "Gee but I'd like some day," he scribbled about some of them, "to be numbered among such names as [William L.] Dawson, [Monroe] Work, [Nathaniel] Dett . . . [Clarence Cameron] White . . . etc. Not for just the fame of it but because I shall have given something to better Negro music, which is America's music."

Paradoxically, in those days black race pride could drive a black American to excel in classical European, or "white," music. People like Zelia Breaux hoped that blacks' success in classical music, painting, literature, and the other arts would offer final proof of their collective humanity. Unfortunately, that proof had substantive value only when tendered to whites, who were disposed to deny it. Left to their own devices, blacks would never have questioned their innate humanity.

"Success comes to th[ose] who wait," Ralph noted about this time, "but it's best to run and meet it." Wary of whites, he nevertheless turned now for help to a white man who was Breaux's counterpart on the white side of Oklahoma City. In 1928, the German-born musician Ludwig W.

Hebestreit had come to Oklahoma City to take charge of music instruc-
tion at Classen High School. Full of energy and imagination, he soon dazzled the city by putting together the award-winning Oklahoma City
Junior Symphony Orchestra. Although blacks were barred from attending
its performances, Ralph tried to meet the conductor. Hebestreit was soon
taken with this black youth's spunk and skill. "He offered to give me lessons," Ralph would write, "if I would cut his grass." In fact, he paid Hebestreit $2 a week for trumpet lessons, "but the contact," he noted shrewdly
at the time, "is worth ten times as much to me." He warmed to Hebestreit: "He's a regular fellow, and what a musician, what a teacher, he has
a knack of making things plain that others make difficult."

Hebestreit could certainly show Ralph the inner dynamics of a symphonic piece, and yet more was at stake for Ralph. Hebestreit stood for
the wider world beyond Oklahoma, which was also the whiter world that
Ralph was already eager to seduce, or conquer. His personal siege of
Hebestreit was only the first in the remarkable series of shrewd cultiva-
tions of whites on which Ralph, eager to succeed and optimistic about
human nature, would build much of his success. To such meetings across
the color line, as with Hebestreit, he would bring his intelligence, his
artistic skills, his winsome personality, his cunning, his magnetism, and
whatever else might secure for him an audience and an opportunity on
which to build. He also brought, it should be noted, a calm faith in his
own black humanity. Whites could then accept or reject him.

Probably on Hebestreit's advice, on April 22, 1932, he put down $21.50
on a new Conn Victor cornet at Jenkins' Music Store, where his stepfather worked. The instrument cost $157.50, a daunting sum for a person
of Ralph's means during the Depression. He promised to pay $2.50 every
week for just over a year. Between meeting Hebestreit's fee and paying off
his instrument, Ralph was now spending more than half of his salary on
music. On September 19 he showed off in public for the first time what
he had learned from Hebestreit when he performed at a concert in Oklahoma City, with Zelia Breaux at the piano. "Made it alright even go[t] an
encore," he confided to his notebook. "They seem to like it." That fall, he
also began taking piano lessons from Mrs. A. Elese Moore, a leading
black piano teacher in Oklahoma City. Undoubtedly this was part of his
preparation to be a conductor and a composer. Possibly at Hebestreit's
urging, he expanded his skills in order to communicate more effectively
with the musicians he expected to lead.

.   .   .

Ironically, it was precisely during this period of stepped-up musical training that Ralph stumbled into his first ventures in imaginative writing. In
the winter of 1932, after failing to shake off a racking cough, he took the
advice of a family friend, a nurse, and visited a clinic for a thorough physical examination. Above all, the attending doctor would look for signs of
tuberculosis, long a scourge in black communities. Arriving at St. Vincent's Hospital, he entered a waiting room full of people, almost all of
them white, whom he judged to be distinctly tubercular. "I was horrified,"
he recalled. Waiting for a chest examination, he found himself reaching
for a notebook and a pen: "I began to try to describe what was going on."
Almost instinctively Ralph adopted the hard-boiled style employed effectively by the journalist O. O. McIntyre, whose syndicated column "New
York Day by Day" appeared in an Oklahoma City newspaper. His writing
about the patients is lost, but not his response to the results of his own
tests: "Well, Hurr[a]h I didn't have T.B. after all!"

He began to write more. This literary turn in part reflected the near
obsession among Ralph and his most talented friends to be versatile in
their skills. His poverty couldn't elide the confident notion of personal
promise grafted onto him by Mrs. Breaux, J. D. Randolph, and Ida. Black
writers meant little to him then—or so he implied later, even before he
was famous. Nevertheless, around 1932 Langston Hughes seems to have
made some sort of impression on him. That year, Ralph copied into a
notebook the text of Hughes's brief, exhortatory "Youth" (first published
simply as "Poem"). Without direct reference to race, but addressed most
likely to younger blacks, the poem asserts an exuberant confidence ("We
have tomorrow / Bright before us / Like a flame") and even militancy ("We
march!"). Ralph probably noticed this poem around the time Hughes visited Oklahoma in March 1932 to read his poems at Langston University.
(The university was named after his great-uncle John Mercer Langston, a
black abolitionist, U.S. congressman, diplomat, and founder of the law
school at Howard University.)

By 1932 Hughes had published two notable books of verse, a novel,
and (in *The Nation*) a landmark essay, "The Negro Artist and the Racial
Mountain." Hailed as "one of the best poets of modern civilization" and
"the greatest living Negro poet," the thirty-year-old Hughes reached Oklahoma toward the end of an exhausting transcontinental tour. Reading his
poetry to mainly black audiences, he had begun the tour in New York City
the previous fall. With the onset of the Depression he had begun to veer
dramatically toward Communism. Handsome and apparently fearless, in

1932 he embodied for many blacks the image of the black proletarian poet defying capitalists, imperialists, Philistines black and white, bigots, and even the Ku Klux Klan. Of his reading at Langston, the *Black Dispatch* reported "a splendid recital" before a large and "deeply appreciative" audience.

Eventually Hughes and Ralph would become close friends. But at this time, Ralph hardly knew what he believed about Hughes's writing or anyone else's. Music was his future.

Late in 1932, urged by his friend Malcolm Whitby, Ralph wrote to Tuskegee Institute to inquire about admission there. He was five feet nine and a quarter inches and weighed 153 pounds. He identified his current job as "janitor." Whitby was certain that the Tuskegee band and orchestra, needing trumpeters as skilled as Ralph, would offer him all the financial aid he needed. With his hopes flaring, Ralph sent off his letter of application. "During the long silence which followed," he wrote, "I thought of suicide, of applying to the C.C.C. [the Civilian Conservation Corps, a Depression-era program], of joining a minstrel band." He lived now in "a manic-depressive state of hope and despair."

On December 27, the one-hundred-voice Tuskegee Institute Choir, conducted by Professor William Levi Dawson, took part in the gala formal opening concert of Radio City Music Hall at Rockefeller Center. This was the complex of skyscrapers and other buildings that John D. Rockefeller, Jr., was erecting, in defiance of the Depression, on eleven acres in the heart of Manhattan. The tightly disciplined, uncannily resonant voices of the black choir astonished and moved the audience and all of the critics and reporters present. Triumphantly the Tuskegee Choir then began an engagement of daily afternoon concerts at Radio City. On January 22, 1933, at the request of the newsreel company Pathé Films, the group sang a most fitting song, "Oh, What a Beautiful City," on the eighty-sixth floor of the Empire State Building, the tallest building in the world.

News of Tuskegee's singular triumph in the white world of money and power swept through black America. Soon Ralph was sitting in a darkened theater in Oklahoma City peering with pride and stomach-tingling anxiety at the flickering images of the event. The scrubbed young black men in their somber uniforms, the comely black women in their white blouses and dark skirts (at the gala opening, they were made to wear bandannas, to look like plantation darkies), touched him—but not nearly as much as did William Dawson, the man in command. "Oh what a beautiful city," Ralph exulted in his scrapbook. "How appropriate a song for Dawson to direct the Tuskegee [choir] in singing from the roof of the Empire State building, New York. The tallest piece of architecture known to man, God's children singing his praises from the heights." The appearance in New York in late January of the sixty-voice Fisk University choir only deepened his anxiety. "The Fisk choir appears at Carnegie Hall," he noted. "So much for me to do. I feel very small."

On February 15 at Carnegie Hall, the audience had responded emotionally to old slave spirituals. Whether the slaves themselves would have liked these Europeanized versions is another matter. To one black reporter, the choir "sang the songs of their slave forefathers in the idiom of the great classics—the form in which they should . . . undoubtedly be preserved." In early 1933 Ralph was less interested in this debate than in the prestige accruing to Tuskegee. The institute was a goal "always just beyond the horizon," he wrote to himself. "One phantom I intend to run to earth. To add my sour notes to that band."

Predictably, Ralph began to fixate on Dawson. His grip tightened with the news that Dawson had given Leopold Stokowski, the conductor of the Philadelphia Orchestra, the 537-page manuscript of Dawson's new, unperformed Symphony no. 1, or *Negro Folk Symphony*. In the *Black Dispatch*, Malcolm Whitby saluted "this quiet, unassuming musical genius." As a boy, Dawson had reached Tuskegee with $1.50 in his pocket. Joining the student band, he composed his first song at sixteen. Graduating in 1921, he was already successful when Tuskegee recalled him in 1931. He then formed the Tuskegee Choir, designed to rival that of Fisk University. Within two years it reached its present eminence.

Dawson was precisely the kind of man Ralph wanted to become. When Stokowski announced dramatically that the Philadelphia Orchestra would perform the *Negro Folk Symphony*, his enthusiasm reached its zenith. "William L. Dawson has me all excited again," he admitted. "Not satisfied to take the Choir to Radio City, he announced his 1st symphony to be introduced in its premiere by Leopold Stokowski." "Just think," he lamented, "a little money is holding me away from this Dawson man." He needed Tuskegee: "My desire to write music is darn near killing me, to have ideas to express and to be then unable to write it down is terrible." To do so, he needed Dawson. Wishing that he had been born a genius, he reminded himself that even geniuses "had to learn the principles. Dawson spent years in school. Beethoven was somewhat a dumbbell until forty so there's hope for me."

Tuskegee, however, had not responded. Now Ralph looked listlessly into the possibility of taking a job teaching music. He traveled to the State Training School for Negro Boys at Boley, Oklahoma—a reformatory—to interview for the directorship of the school's military band. The founder of the band, G. L. Buford, welcomed him; Ralph quickly concluded that he himself knew at least as much about music as Buford did. However, he didn't want to be stuck at Boley. The job, as he wrote Ida, was to "teach some of the dumb guys music." Boley itself was deathly dull. "I'm lonesome out here on this hill," he complained. He was hurrying home. "*Please* have me some clean shirts and underwear when I get home." He signed this letter, "Your son, Ralph W. Ellison."

He needed a clean shirt because that Sunday, March 26, he attended his first symphony concert. Quietly challenging Jim Crow, Ludwig Hebestreit had invited him to attend the final concert of the third season of the Junior Symphony Orchestra. That evening, a nervous but apparently self-possessed Ralph entered the lobby of the Classen High School auditorium. As Hebestreit's personal guest, he sat apart, in the conductor's box in the balcony and not next to white patrons, who might object vehemently to his presence. Painfully aware that white people were staring at him, he knew that his presence had startled many, outraged some, and pleased few. Feigning nonchalance but agitated inside, he scanned the program: Sibelius's *Finlandia*; a Slavic march by Tchaikovsky; Liszt's Piano Concerto no. 1. These were charming pieces, chosen mainly to please an unsophisticated audience.

Waiting, hoping, for the lights to go down, he drew a small notebook from his jacket pocket and scribbled a record of his feelings: "I'm here at Classen there are whites in the balcony with me some see me others don't. What they think I don't care. I won't give them a chance to insult me. 'Hebe' has me trapped for sure this time. By the way doing this [writing] gives [me] plenty [to] absorb my attention and thereby saves me from these stares. I hope to hold out until the concert [starts]. O what an excellent chance to develop poise. And how. There's a chap in the orch[estra] who is playing Carnival of Venice and he does a better job of it than I but I shall improve it will make me work all the harder. Time for the orch. to take their seats then these [whites] would forget me. There's an Indian here quite as dark as I and yet they discriminate between [us]. Next time I'll use make up it's very easy." After the final curtain, while he waited for the hall to clear, he made another note: "My first concert. I enjoyed it very much." Clearly, Ralph had already made the decision to live his life like a free man, and not according to white or black expectations. He would go where he wished to go and consort with whomever he wished, especially so in the world of art.

On May 14 it was his turn to perform, if at a much humbler concert, given by pupils of his piano teacher, Mrs. Moore, at the Tabernacle Baptist Church. Out of almost two dozen pupils, he was one of only two men to perform. Playing the cornet, he offered Wagner's "Evening Star" and a setting of Saint-Saëns's aria "My Heart at Thy Sweet Voice," from *Samson and Delilah*. Taking part in this musicale only intensified his urge to escape the soggy brown pool of Oklahoma mud in which he seemed stuck.

And then, late in May, the road to Tuskegee suddenly opened. With a mass of engagements at hand and regular students about to depart, its band and orchestra desperately needed a skilled first trumpeter. With Malcolm Whitby still pushing, an inquiring phone call from Tuskegee, then a letter, invited Ralph to apply for admission—again. However, there was a catch: He had to come at once. On June 10, Captain Alvin Neely, the registrar and dean of men, who would be a key player in Ralph's Tuskegee future, assured Ralph that Tuskegee had work for him "if you will get up as much money as you possibly can and will come at once."

"It was like a bad joke," Ralph remembered about the sudden need to hurry after Tuskegee's rude silence. The catalogue listed expenses, including uniforms and other clothing, that he could barely meet; "nor could my mother help here, for she herself was working part-time." By the time Ralph bought those of the items he could afford, his money was almost gone. And then it dawned on Ralph that he didn't have train fare. He didn't want to ask the Lewisohns, in part because of their farewell gifts (an overcoat and a felt hat), in part because he had "an almost instinctive reluctance to turn to white men when in trouble." However, no black man agreed to a loan. In vain he tried a bank. Then, suddenly, Edna Slaughter (J. D. Randolph's eldest child) came up with a plan for Ralph to drive her and her daughter Saretta to Nashville. From Nashville, Ralph would travel on to Tuskegee with a friend of Saretta and her friend's parents. Relieved, he was also moved by how fortuitously people had come to his aid.

The plan collapsed. Without explanation, Dr. Wyatt Slaughter refused to allow Ralph to drive to Nashville with his wife and daughter. Ralph was thunderstruck. Dr. Slaughter had always been sympathetic. Ralph tormented himself in search of a reason. Did Slaughter think that his light-skinned wife and daughter would be safer on the road without Ralph and his dark skin? Divisions based on shades of skin color were "a powerful and degrading motive from the past of slavery still all too active in shaping individual destinies." Dr. Slaughter liked to call local young blacks, most of whom he had delivered at birth, "my little niggers." "Are you one of my little niggers?" he would ask affectionately. One day, Ralph refused to answer him. Standing his ground, he stared at Dr. Slaughter. Now he wondered if Dr. Slaughter's jokes were innocent or revealed his contempt for his own people. Or was it class snobbery? Ida, once a bosom friend of Edna, was now seen as a servant; Ralph, as a chauffeur. Or was the doctor wary of the steamy intimacy of the car on a long journey? Years later, Ralph conjured up manic, comic fantasies. Pressed by Ralph to explain, the doctor explodes: "Because you, sir, are a randy little two-horned *billy-goat*! One horn you toot openly in the marching band and at football games, but in the shady privacy of house parties you thump the other against the heated bumps and grinds which you yourself stir into motion! And the same goes for public dances, where you have been observed indulging in such obscene couplings as the belly-rub, the hellish jelly-shake, the slow-drag, and the one butt shuffle! And I mean with strange black gals in countless numbers!"

This episode made it clear to Ralph that he would be able to call Oklahoma City home only in some highly selective, romanticized way.

Gloom and anger intensified when Ralph ran into former schoolmates back home from college for the summer: "They, as the old saying held, had rubbed their heads on college walls and were now diffcrent and of a different world. If you remained at home the gap between you would widen. They would become part of a different set while you would probably end up a waiter, or at best a jazz musician when you wished to become a classical composer. You would sink lower and lower, lost and hopeless." Every week, the "Social Whirl" section of the *Black Dispatch* carried gay notes about students home from Spelman and Clark in Atlanta, Fisk in Nashville, and even some white schools in the North or Midwest. As a hired entertainer, not a peer, Ralph performed in a duet at a garden party for two hundred guests at the home of the parents of daughters just home from the University of Kansas.

I've got to get out of this town, Ralph thought, *or I'm lost forever.* Standing in front of Jim Randolph's drugstore in Deep Second one day, he saw Charlie Miller, whose sister was Randolph's wife. The black sheep of a respectable family, Miller was a small man with blue eyes who could pass for white. He worked only when he felt like working, drank too much, and gambled heavily. To Ralph, none of that mattered as much as the fact that Miller was a notorious hobo, a skilled rider of the rails, a gutsy veteran of the kind of travel made mandatory by the Great Depression for otherwise respectable people. Charlie could help him get to Tuskegee.

At first, Charlie resisted Ralph. Hoboing was dangerous. Finally, however, he relented. Ida took the news hard, as if Ralph had just announced his "plans for committing suicide." The *Black Dispatch* and other newspapers were full of stories about the Scottsboro Boys, the nine black youths hauled off a train in Alabama on March 25, 1931, and indicted on March 31 on the charge of raping two white women who had also been hoboes on the train. Doctors found no evidence of rape, but eight of the "boys" were sentenced to die. In 1932, ruling that the defendants had received inadequate counsel, the U.S. Supreme Court overturned the sentences. Fresh trials began in 1933 in Decatur, Alabama, even though one of the two women recanted her accusation. On May 14, the local NAACP staged fund-raising rallies in almost every black church in Oklahoma City. Couldn't Ralph wait another year, Ida pleaded, before going off to school? Finally she left his fate in the hands of God.

On June 20, when a smoking freight train left Oklahoma City around three in the afternoon, Charlie and Ralph were on it. To Ralph's surprise, it headed north. Charlie explained that he couldn't risk being caught in Arkansas, where they might be thrown into a chain gang rather than driven off the tracks by the railroad police, or "bulls," as was the practice elsewhere. Almost every minute brought Ralph another bit of vital knowledge. His bones rattling from the rough ride, he learned to arch his body and suspend it between the palms of his hands and the soles of his feet, his chest thrust upward and his head thrown back. When the rhythm shifted abruptly, grit and splinters bit into his flesh.

In Kansas, Charlie shifted them onto a local train heading east to Missouri. At the end of its run the men entered a hobo jungle, a gathering of men and women huddled around fires cooking mulligan stew, strumming guitars, sipping cheap wine, singing ballads, and telling tall tales in the storied tradition of the American frontier. Charlie continued to school Ralph. When racing alongside a train, trying to hop aboard, Ralph learned to grab the front ladders of the boxcars and not the ladders in the back. If you missed up front and fell, the side of the car would knock you free. Miss the back ladder, and the next car could run over you. He learned to look for the documents stapled to the side of boxcars that revealed their schedules, routes, and destinations. "Keep away from thieves, drunks, crackers, and women—especially *white* women," Charlie warned. "If they get into a boxcar, you get out. If they follow you, go to another car. And don't flash your money or take any bull from anybody. Keep out of fights, but if someone forces you, win it. The main thing is to keep to yourself and remember that you're doing this for just one thing, that's to get to college."

Early one evening they reached the Missouri River at St. Louis. Leaving Ralph on the west bank, Charlie crossed to East St. Louis to scout the territory. He returned with word that guards on the other side were on the watch for hoboes heading to the World's Fair in Chicago. Charlie advised Ralph to cross just after he did, and to be honest with the guard about why he was traveling. "Look the bastard straight in the eye and tell it straight," Charlie advised, "but don't beg. Because if you do it'll give him a sense of power. The thing to do is make him believe you." Charlie crossed the mile or so between the banks. Then Ralph took a "lonely walk across the night-shrouded bridge." A guard stepped out of the shadows. Steeling himself, Ralph did as Charlie had told him. The man allowed him to go on.

At Evansville, Indiana, Charlie left Ralph to return home. From Evansville, Ralph sent his mother a brief letter. "If you would see me now," he assured Ida, "you wouldn't [know] me." Wary, he kept Charlie's lessons in mind. Some whites were hostile to him, others were indifferent. Some blacks were pleasant, others were not, especially after Ralph's Oklahoma twang told them that he was not of the South. The boxcars were hot and smelled of cottonseed meal (mixed with sorghum syrup as cattle feed). To escape the heat and the stench, Ralph sometimes climbed outside, locked his legs around the top of a ladder, and rode atop the cars. As the day grew warmer, more and more men surfaced atop the train, until "it looked like an excursion train, a Mardi Gras float. There were Negroes, whites, and Mexicans; old men, young men, amateurs and seasoned professionals. Only women were missing." Riding with whites in a boxcar had its tense moments. As the conversations rambled over topics he could have discussed with ease, Ralph remained silent. No topic was risk-free. In their prejudice and fears, whites needed to feel superior to blacks at every point. Off in a dark corner he kept to himself as much as he could. Drawn into talking, he watched his every word. When he feared that he might offend anyone, he shut his mouth.

With his head "full of readings of the *Rover Boys* and *Huckleberry Finn,*" he "converted hoboing into a lark" until he reached Decatur, Alabama, where he had his first, harrowing encounter with the feared railroad bulls. Waving their pistols, two of them ran Ralph and a gaggle of white hoboes off the train. At that moment, suddenly, "I saw with despair that some of those wearing pants were white women." In the panic, he apparently cracked his head against something hard, felt his blood gushing, but kept on running. "I had no idea of what the detectives intended to do with me," he wrote, "but given the atmosphere of the town, I feared that it would be unpleasant and brutal. I, too, might well be a sacrificial scapegoat simply because I was of the same race as the accused young men [the Scottsboro Boys] then being prepared for death." Terrorized, he "kept moving until I came to a shed with a railroad loading dock, under which I scooted; there I remained until dawn. . . . That scrape with the law—the fear, horror and sense of helplessness before legal injustice—was most vivid in my mind, and it has so remained."

In truth, Ralph was both elated and ravaged mentally by the entire week. He had discovered reserves of inner strength, and life as a hobo had its romantic side. But traveling in such a crude, dangerous, and criminal fashion was an insult to his self-esteem. In the end, he was glad he had made the journey. With Charlie Miller's help, and not unlike Huck Finn on the mighty river, he had taken his life in his hands and his troubles to the open road. In a few perilous days he had learned more about himself, humanity, and America, of action, independence, and manhood, than he had ever known before. No wonder, then, four years later, when he wrote his first short story, Ralph turned for his raw material to these few dangerous but exhilarating days riding the rails.

On June 24, 1933, near midnight, he reached Tuskegee. Never again would Oklahoma be central to his life. He would spend one more summer there, in 1935. Eighteen years would then pass before he returned again, and he would do so as a nationally acclaimed figure. Then he would look back with wonder and delight, as well as chagrin and pain, on the vanishing America of his youth.

3

In a Land Most Strange

1933–1936

You've felt hunger and embarrassment and debt and
Tuskegee.　　　　WALTER BOWIE WILLIAMS (1936)

On a rainy morning in June, Ralph awoke at last on the campus of the Tuskegee Normal and Industrial Institute, just outside the small town of Tuskegee in the rolling central plains of Alabama. After the frustrating months waiting for a reply to his application, this was the fulfillment of a dream. Tuskegee offered a vision of green hills, redbrick Georgian buildings, white columns, crisply tended grounds, and a clock tower that melodiously told the hours. "This is a beautiful place," Ralph wrote home. "It looks like a small town, the food is good enough and I'll like it here. I'm going to work hard to stay."

The institute, only fifty-one years old, was already rooted in African-American lore. The buildings named for Carnegie and Rockefeller testified to the benevolent power of white philanthropy, but nothing at Tuskegee was more evocative than a peaceful patch of earth overshadowed by the Washington Chapel A.M.E. Church. Between the church and a tiny cemetery stood the life-size statue of the school's founder, Booker T. Washington, in the bronzed act of lifting the veil of ignorance from the brow of a crouching, rudely clad black man. Eighteen years after his death, Washington's presence on the campus was almost as strong as when he was alive. His autobiography, *Up from Slavery,* a blending of slave narrative and American rags-to-riches saga, had become a classic text following its publication in 1901. Born a slave to a black plantation cook and a white man (probably their master), he had willed himself out of poverty after the Civil War, learned to read and write, and wheedled his way into Hampton Institute in his native Virginia. There, in a school for blacks staffed by Northern white men and women of abolitionist stock, he had honed the social and political skills that were to mark his life. After serving at Hampton following his graduation in 1881, he had accepted the mandate of the white state legislature to found and develop a school for blacks in rural, racist Alabama.

Washington was then only twenty-five years old. Starting out in a decrepit church and imposing his will on the world about him, he had drawn blacks and whites, poor and rich, into sharing his vision. In 1895, allowed to speak briefly to a gathering of leading Southern whites (and some blacks) at the Cotton States Exposition in Atlanta, he delivered an address almost as concise as Lincoln's at Gettysburg and as epochal in its impact on black America. According to him, American blacks should cease struggling for the right to vote and for social equality with whites. Instead, they should acquire those basic laboring skills that would give their people a foundation. "The wisest among my race," he declared, knew that insisting on equality "is the extremist folly"; segregation would lead both races to prosperity. "In all things that are purely social," he insisted, "we can be as separate as the fingers, yet one as the hand in all things essential to mutual progress."

Deliriously received by whites, his speech made Washington the most powerful black American even as critics such as the historian and sociologist W. E. B. Du Bois of Atlanta University argued vehemently that the vote, social equality, and a liberal education were essential to African-American success. By 1915, the year Washington died, Tuskegee had become the most renowned educational agency ever created by an American Negro and a model for vocational training around the world. Because of its emphasis on teaching trades, and because of Washington's subservience to the white South and white philanthropists, some blacks still sneered at Tuskegee. However, in the 1920s the institute had reorganized itself to include a "College" department and award bachelor of arts degrees. Moreover, in some ways Tuskegee seemed to embody race pride more aggressively than many of its rivals. Unlike Hampton, Fisk, and Lincoln in Pennsylvania, its faculty was black. The founder himself had insisted on this point. (In 1929, a survey at Lincoln had found that most students opposed diluting the faculty with black professors.)

In the summer of 1933 Ralph was proud to be a part of the racial achievement that was Tuskegee. He was eager to learn from a faculty that included eminent men such as William Levi Dawson in music and the scientist George Washington Carver, who had discovered more than three hundred uses for the humble peanut. He expected to work for pay as hard and as long as Tuskegee would allow him. In addition, he was depending on Ida, despite her own pressing needs, to help him. At first, the challenge seemed easy. The student manual bathed his need to earn money in a rosy glow: "It is an exhibition of noble purpose and determination on the part of a student to attempt to go through school on his own effort." At Tuskegee, to ask for financial aid was thought to be unseemly, almost like begging. Hard work for honest pay was the answer.

By that evening, Ralph had secured a room in a dormitory, Thrasher Hall, a job in the bakery at Tompkins Hall, and a blue meal ticket handed out by Captain Alvin Neely, a tall, commanding figure who welcomed Ralph as dean of students and the registrar of the institute. Neely also secured his promised place in the school band. The skeleton of his summer schedule was now set. Money, however, was an immediate problem. Board would cost him $20 a month and his job in the kitchen would probably pay less. Surely Dean Neely should have known, in writing to him, that working at Tuskegee that summer could not possibly "reduce your expenses for the fall term." Even if his hours of practice and public performances allowed time for another job, Tuskegee placed a strict limit on what any student could earn. Financially he would end the summer, at best, as he started it.

Ralph's direct supervisor, as head of the school band, was Captain Frank L. Drye. "Captain Drye was a true military type," Louis "Mike" Rabb (class of 1935) recalled. "He had been out west with the army. He was tall and light-skinned, and he was very much liked. He was tough and disciplined, but he had fun with us." Ralph could console himself that playing in the band would bring him campus recognition. The military aspect of the band aided its prestige, because in some respects Tuskegee was a military school. Every male student was a cadet, under an arrangement designed by the founder and legitimized by the Reserve Officer's Training Corps bill enacted by Congress and overseen by the U.S. Army. The current commandant of the institute—as distinct from its president—was an army veteran. The president, Robert Russa Moton, had been commandant at Hampton Institute when Tuskegee chose him as its leader.

Assigned to the bakery at Tompkins Hall (Tuskegee bought little that it could make), Ralph worked hard. He reported to the bakery at 5 a.m. and toiled there until 1 p.m. He cooked, cleaned, and served as a waiter. In the first few days he almost convinced himself that he was having fun. Working in a trough five feet by three feet—using "our hands, arms, and sometimes elbows (ha ha)"—he made flour bread for the students and corn bread for the teachers. He also helped churn as much as fifteen gallons of ice cream every day. After lunch, he practiced on his trumpet alone and then with the band. Following dinner, which was a dignified affair with tablecloths, napkins, and an adult host and hostess at every table, he practiced some more until bedtime.

Taking stock after four days, he itemized his needs to Ida. First, she should send him all of his money that he had left with her, as well as various items including books, sheets of music, and "some hair grease. (If you have it)." He reminded Ida that she had to keep up the weekly payments both on his cornet and at a clothing store. He asked her to "see just what you can do to help." He made her a promise: "You won't regret it the least bit."

Ralph had just begun to settle in when Vivian Steveson broke his heart. Writing from Oklahoma City, his stepfather, John Bell, informed him that Zelia Breaux had seen Vivian "going out with another boy." Ralph caught a bad cold and his stomach began to pain him—all his life he suffered intermittently from a delicate stomach. Angry and lonely, he felt his response to Tuskegee change. On July 23 he confessed to his mother: "I have wanted to come home pretty badly." Many of his co-workers and most of the students around the campus belonged to the institute's high school and summer school divisions, not to the regular student body. "I find them dull," he wrote. "They don't know what to talk about or how to talk."

In vain, Vivian kept writing to Ralph, protesting her love for him. "Vivian writes but I don't have time to think of her any more," he told Ida. "I don't have anything against her but now I can't afford to think of her." When Ida counseled forgiveness, Ralph said: "You must understand mama that I don't feel just as you do about things. That which bound me to V is gone and I don't have time to be sentimental about it." Within a few weeks he had moved on. "There are too many girls," he wrote Ida, "and strange to say they seem to like me." One of these girls was Julia "Chubby" Moore, who had just finished her junior year at Fisk. She was one of the friends of Saretta Slaughter with whom he had expected to ride from Nashville to Tuskegee. Her family lived in the prosperous Greenwood section of town. Julia's father, the chief medical officer at the U.S. Veterans Hospital, was almost as important as the head of the institute itself.

Handsome, intelligent, and polite, Ralph soon won over the Moores, and in particular Julia. She was "doing everything to make things pleasant for me," he assured Ida. "She is good looking, from one of the best famil[ie]s, and her father . . . has money." Fortune had been kind. "I was lucky enough to get in with the best here," he wrote, "and so you see I have plenty to do." He was also careful. "Though Chubb[y] and I like each other," he wrote, "we don't pretend we love. I respect her and she me, we don't kiss [and] we get along fine." On Sunday mornings after church, they often went hiking together.

In the late summer of 1933, he put on his best face and smartest clothes in meeting the Moores and their friends, who were members of the privileged younger set at Tuskegee. He was soon befriended by Booker T. Washington's family as well as by President Moton's. But as the school year drew closer his money problems worried him. With Captain Drye's help he earned a little cash playing in a band for private dances in some of the larger towns near Tuskegee. That wasn't enough. In just about every letter to Ida he begged her for money. She desperately wanted to help, but her hours as a hotel maid were long, and she earned only about $16 every two weeks. Her husband was in even worse shape. At Tuskegeee, Captain Neely, honey-sweet when he had asked Ralph to come quickly to the school, was now often tart: "He told me to tell you to start thinking about my uniform." Every male student wore a blue serge uniform at drill, supper, evening prayers, the mandatory Sunday chapel service, and other school exercises. Aware of Ralph's problem, Captain Drye offered practical advice: He should enroll now and "owe the school later on."

On August 24 Ralph sent his mother a strict accounting of his needs. Simply to cover his basic expenses, including books, library and other fees, cornet and piano lessons, and board, he needed $30 more, and then $26.25 every three months ("This *does not include the uniform*"). Valiantly Ida tried to help. On August 24, she sent $5 toward buying the uniform. Optimistically, Ralph signed up on September 4 for the School of Music, but he was out after a few days because he couldn't pay its bills. Disheartened, he enrolled in the cheaper, less desirable School of Education, then almost quit Tuskegee altogether. To stay, he would need about $15 a month from home. Challenged, Ida and John Bell redoubled their efforts. At the end of September, when Ralph opened a letter from "Mama," a money order fluttered out. "You could have pushed me over with a feather," he wrote. "I had no idea that you all could send me so much money and I don't know how to thank you and Mr. John."

Returning now to the School of Music, he resumed his study in subjects such as harmony (with William Dawson himself), the piano, and the trumpet. He also took courses in English composition and physical education. Ralph's favorite teacher was probably the gentle daughter of the president, Catherine Moton, who would be his piano instructor for several quarters to come. Captain Drye, who taught him the trumpet, was good to Ralph, helping him to adapt some of his old cornet favorites, such as the "Carnival of Venice" number, for the band. Enjoying his classes in music, he found those in English dreary, laden as they were with wooden exercises in composition, grammar, and vocabulary. He ignored physical education. Content with Bs or Cs, he worked accordingly.

In a major disappointment, he failed to win over Dawson. Smoothly handsome, with a neat mustache and a toothy smile, Dawson was sometimes affable but more often mercurial, driven, and blunt. Two years later, a profile in the *Tuskegee Messenger* declared that he had "a personality of steel." His students found Dawson a human dynamo: "His energy is prodigious. . . . His power of concentration is great; when he is thinking of one thing, everything else in the world is closed to him." But Ralph made only a tiny impression on his hero. In some respects, Dawson was a pure product of Tuskegee. Knowing the dangers that attended his rising fame, he was wary of crossing any of his superiors. He refused to bend any rules to help Ralph.

Traveling with the band in support of the Tuskegee Tigers football team provided Ralph some precious respites from the daily grind. Once, on a trip to Chicago, he sought out with some difficulty members of his mother's family who, like her, had abandoned Georgia in search of a better life. He found his Uncle Will, with whom Ida and her boys had lived during their ill-fated adventure in Gary, Indiana, in 1921. Will was now on welfare and hadn't worked in three years. He also drank a lot. Nevertheless, his nephew's enterprising visit so touched him that he made Ralph a present of a shirt and three ties. Ralph also visited for the first time Ida's sister Minnie, "a big yellow woman" with bobbed hair and a pleasant personality. Everyone seemed poor. "You might think you are having it hard," Ralph assured his mother, "but thank the Lord because of the three you are doing the best."

He, too, had it hard. Normally fastidious about his looks, he now did without regular haircuts. Two of his teeth had cavities. His three pairs of shoes—black, brown, and white—were quickly wearing out. He still had no uniform, he reminded Ida, "and now they are on me about it." His garments that required dry cleaning were a mess. One day, "my old suit was so dirty that one of [my] fellow students asked me what on earth was wrong." At a student recital in late October, when he played a cornet solo before a faculty jury, he was deathly ashamed of his outfit.

He did, however, enjoy the less expensive pleasures of school life. Near the end of October he watched Paul Robeson star in the movie version of Eugene O'Neill's turgid but memorable *The Emperor Jones,* which applied Freudian principles and faddish ideas about atavism to the race question. Robeson's virile presentation of black manhood, so unusual in the bigoted American motion picture industry, impressed him. On November 25, the original Broadway cast of Marc Connelly's Pulitzer Prize–winning musical of 1930, *The Green Pastures,* took the stage at Logan Hall. Based on sketches of Southern black religious life by a popular white writer, Roark Bradford, *The Green Pastures* was (according to the printed program) Connelly's attempt "to present certain aspects of a living religion in terms of its believers." The "believers" were the thousands of Southern blacks who, with "terrific spiritual hunger and the greatest humility," had adapted the Bible to their own needs. Ralph was overwhelmed. If *The Green Pastures* ever came to Oklahoma City, he wrote Ida, she *had* to see it.

Going to movies and plays was fun, but like many other students Ralph found Tuskegee's rules cramping. The student manual was candid: "Here, you will find every phase of your life systematically regulated and supervised for the purpose of aiding you in getting the most from your courses." Men could not escort women to and from the institute, the town of Tuskegee, or the Veterans Hospital, or sit beside them in church. They could not loaf on the White Hall lawn near the women's dormitories, much less ride in a car with a woman without a chaperone. Deportment was taken seriously. "Pick up your feet when you walk," the manual urged. "Never drag yourself along. Some people think that heavy feet indicate a light head." Students should never forget that "Tuskegee is a vast workshop," and "work is the chief element awaiting you at every turn."

"I don't fit in well just yet with these southern people," he wrote home. Far from being hostile to him, he noted, they were "too friendly" and often barged into his room without an invitation. He had only limited interest in pranks. His two years in limbo after high school, as well as his fierce ambition, made him impatient with such trifling behavior. Instead, he consciously sought as friends some of his most intelligent, cultivated classmates. These young people included Laly Charlton and Carolyn

Walcott, excellent students as well as campus beauties; Joe Lazenberry from St. Paul, Minnesota, a top debater; Carver Campbell, the scion of a leading institute family and a fine baritone; Robert Moton, Jr., the elder son of the president; Booker T. Washington III, grandson of the founder; and Mike Rabb.

The KiYi Club, supervised by Bess Bolden Walcott, Carolyn's mother, served the more cultivated student intellectuals and artists at Tuskegee, which forbade fraternities and sororities. She became one of Ralph's sturdier anchors at Tuskegee. "My mother was born in Ohio and went to Oberlin College," Carolyn Walcott recalled. "She met Booker T. Washington in 1907 and he invited her to come to Tuskegee to teach. She founded KiYi around 1926. It taught social skills—how to set a formal table, how to write to a girl a proper letter, that sort of thing. But my mother really loved reading, so books were very important. Not everyone here was a reader, but Ralph was, and Mother became very interested in him." According to Laly Charlton Washington, who had come from Beaumont, Texas, in 1932 at the age of fourteen, "scholastics were important in the club. We pinned tiny black and white ribbons on our shirts and blouses, and we stuck together as much as possible against the Ag boys— from the School of Agriculture." Mike Rabb arrived at Tuskegee in 1928 as a high school boarding student from a town in Mississippi where blacks could not go beyond the tenth grade. "I liked Ralph a lot," he recalled. "I liked his spirit. He was firm in his feelings about everything. He complained. He was one of the guys who felt rebellious about all the rules on the campus."

They often felt even more rebellious about the Jim Crow town of Tuskegee, up the road from the institute. "In the cinema there was a partition down the middle and up to the ceiling," Rabb said. "There were two screens. You had no contact with whites." Carolyn Walcott recalled that "my mother was always called Mrs. Walcott when she shopped in town." She was one of the few exceptions to the rule of disrespect for blacks. This was especially true of almost all of the rural whites, who couldn't imagine any reason to make allowance for the "niggers" out at the institute.

A rising star in music at Tuskegee, on December 17 Ralph took a leading role in the annual Christmas concert on the White Hall lawn. Still, he was sad. The keening harmonies of the carols and the mellow drifting of cool air down into central Alabama made him yearn to join the exodus of students heading home for the holidays. But he couldn't afford to return to Oklahoma. Invitations from the Moore and Drye families to their homes helped, but he remained lonely and soon felt that old gnawing in his stomach. As much as Ida wanted to see him, she did not press Ralph to return home. "I don't want you to think about coming back here Ralph," she advised. "I hope that you will make up your mind to stay there until you finish and then locate in another town."

The end of the year found him flat broke and dejected. "Things look bad for me just now," Ralph wrote home, "because the dean has ordered all who have not registered to leave the school Monday." Perhaps Tuskegee had hoodwinked him. "I really don't see how I am going to make it," he complained, "because I didn't understand it would cost that much when I started." Nevertheless, he planned to hang on to the bitter end. "My stomach still bothers me sometimes," he admitted in early January as he watched enrolled students going to classes from which his poverty barred him. "However I shall stay here until asked to leave." When he tried to sit in on certain music courses, Dawson looked out for himself and asked Ralph to desist "because it might get him into trouble." Paying Tuskegee what money he had—slightly less than $30—to meet his debts, he looked around for something else to do. Working in the bakery for 15 cents an hour had become insufferable. Instead, he looked for a job in the institute's new Hollis Burke Frissell Library. The finest library he had ever used, Frissell offered more than 20,000 circulating volumes, almost 2,000 reference books, a special Negro history collection, and more than 150 periodicals.

As a haven, the library provided Ralph both rest and intellectual stimulation. It became his favorite place on the campus. His frequent visits and his intense reading soon caught the attention of the head librarian, Walter Bowie Williams, in what would prove to be a major turning point in Ralph's life. For five years a Tuskegee employee, and only seven years older than Ralph, Williams was a graduate of the elite Williams College in western Massachusetts, with an additional degree in library science from the University of Illinois. Unabashedly in love with music, art, and literature, he had blundered badly in coming to Tuskegee. Born in Albany, New York, he had known little about the South except from reading books. The fine new library, which he had helped to stock, served a student body almost entirely indifferent to the pleasures of liberal reading. The historic ethos at Tuskegee was a constant worship of practicality that made the abundance of books and magazines at Frissell incongruous. The founder himself had jeered at poor Negroes who read too much. Such people needed to be "brought down to something practical and useful." Although Washington in fact knew the value of the liberal arts, his followers often took his words literally. Walter Williams, offended by the reigning Philistinism at the institute, embraced the few students who loved books and barely hid his distaste for the rest.

On February 1, Ralph made an important announcement to Ida: "I have found a new friend in the person of Walter Bowie Williams, the librarian." Although a distinguished man, his new friend loved "to curl up in his big chair and talk to me about the problems of the world, religion, art, music or anything else that might arise. Sometimes we talk and drink coffee until early morning." Carolyn Walcott remembered Williams as "a short man, sort of stocky, with light brown skin. He was lighthearted, not at all gloomy." He was one of a small circle of dedicated campus aesthetes that included Hazel Lucille Harrison in music, Morteza Drexel Sprague in English, and W. Henri Payne in Romance languages. Each would mean much to Ralph at Tuskegee. Fifty-two years old and a noted concert pianist on the faculty of music, Harrison accepted Ralph as a good friend. He, in turn, adored her. In the free air of Europe, she had studied with the bravura pianist Ferruccio Busoni and had also known Egon Petri, Percy Grainger, and Sergei Prokofiev. In her studio she proudly showed off sheets of music signed for her by Prokofiev. Morteza Drexel Sprague, who would teach Ralph the English novel during his junior year, in the single most significant course he took at Tuskegee, loved both British and American literature.

While these superiors seemed to take to Ralph mainly for the quality of his mind, other Tuskegee officials were much less idealistic. As early as the previous October, he understood that his handsome face and sturdy physique, in combination with his poverty, made him a sexual target for some men. "It's a hard go down here," he wrote frankly to Ida, "and when you don't have money you have to endure *too* much because the officials and department heads make you do just as they want you to." Ralph was referring both to routine humiliations and to homosexual demands. "You should know," he informed a close friend many years later, that "I was hounded out of college by a homosexual dean of men." Controlling most of the student jobs, the South Carolina–born Dean Alvin Neely (who had graduated from Tuskegee in 1908) was in a position to dominate the needy. With most, he no doubt wielded his power responsibly. However, his weakness for young men was known. "In the case of Cap'n Neely," the writer Albert Murray (Tuskegee '39) noted, recalling some of the oddities of speech among the faculty and staff, "the key word was 'boy' with the notorious Neely vibrato." (Murray later became one of Ralph's closest friends.)

Neely was hardly the only gay or bisexual adult at the institute. Later Ralph would recall an incident that tore at his emotions for a long time. One evening, he went to a teacher's apartment to pick up "certain books on the technique of poetry." Ralph's host, a former "honors student at Harvard" well known for his mordant wit, first talked of writing but soon turned their conversation in an odd direction. "I asked his opinion of *The Waste Land*," Ralph recalled, but his response was about Oscar Wilde's *The Picture of Dorian Gray.* "I asked about Conrad's *Nostromo,* he talked variations on Huysman's *Against the Grain;* I mentioned [Thomas Mann's] *The Magic Mountain,* he went into a . . . swoon over *Death in Venice. . . .* Then I was being asked about my sex life." Frustrated by Ralph's lack of interest in the last subject, his host suddenly pulled from a bookshelf an ornately bound volume of Shakespeare. "Life isn't like that," he insisted, rifling angrily through its pages. "You'll never get anywhere, because all this is meant to trap you and make you miserable. To defeat you." Then, feverishly, he began to tear the book apart. "Here," he told Ralph, "this is what I think of all this literature."

Appalled, Ralph knew that "in the destruction of that book all that I hoped for in this world had been attacked." Thirty years later, dedicating his book *Shadow and Act* to Morteza Drexel Sprague, he called Sprague "A Dedicated Dreamer in a Land Most Strange." These words clearly allude to Psalm 137 ("How shall we sing the Lord's song in a strange land?") in order to hint at the depth and the nature of his bitterness about Tuskegee. The embossed reference to Babylon in the psalm ("By the rivers of Babylon, There we sat down, yea, we wept") points to the gay "corruption" that Ralph long associated with his alma mater. It also served to remind him of his youthful poverty and vulnerability, the untimely loss of his father, and perhaps also of his hope, understandable under the circumstances, to be taken up or mentored by a man of substance who could comfort and protect him as his own father would have done. The face Ralph presented to the world was one that tolerated male homosexuality, but only barely. His fears did not lead to a compensatory womanizing. Rather, he would meet women with a kind of sexy swagger, even as he kept almost all of them at arm's length. Casanova he was not.

Ralph came to regard his contact with Dean Neely as one of the most degrading aspects of a young life already pockmarked by too many humiliations. And perhaps there is a concealed link between Ralph's loathing of Neely and his denunciation of William Dawson. Although Dawson offered Ralph a few small tokens of friendship—a compliment here, an inscribed concert program there—he denied him anything more valuable. After various rebuffs and an incident in class when Dawson threw a piece of chalk at him, Ralph knew that he couldn't charm his way into this professor's heart. Ralph's response was to hate him. He had gone to Dawson as a son to a father. Instead of acknowledging his filial need, if not his talent, and embracing him, Dawson had done nothing for him. This remoteness tore at Ralph. "My trip to Tuskegee," he would write later, "was my journey into the 'heart of darkness.' My Kurtz was W. L. Dawson: the artist corrupted by his environment."

Ralph's blossoming friendship with Williams calmed him during his quarter out of school but also began to mark him. "I spend my time reading," he told Ida. "I shall start collecting books for my personal library as soon as I finish school," he went on, "because books are far better friends than most people." This remark mirrored the sense of ennui that seems to have infected Williams's view of life. The quality of despair in Williams would eventually kill their friendship. For the moment, however, it probably seemed to his young friend like the height of sophistication.

In February, free of classes, Ralph made his debut as an actor. For its eighth annual celebration of Negro History Week, Tuskegee offered special programs about black race pride. In a staging of Willis Richardson's "folk drama" *The Compromise,* he appeared in the major role of Alec, a sensitive young man who is disgusted by the timidity of his family and friends living with him in the South. When his sister becomes pregnant by a white youth, Alec thrashes the young man and flees town. Praising the production, the *Campus Report* did not mention Ralph.

The winter quarter examinations came and went. On March 1, he quietly celebrated his twenty-first birthday (as he was then counting his birthdays). As her main birthday present Ida sent him a quilt, which Ralph pronounced "really too nice for the room in which I live." However, now he no longer needed to cover himself with his overcoat during the cold nights.

On March 5, also with Ida's help, he was back in school as the spring quarter began. "Don't get discourage[d]," she had urged him. "Every thing will come out so you can stay there." She would try to send him "about $50.00 and it may be that I can get the other for the rest of the year."

Philosophical up to a point—"I have stopped worrying"—Ralph remained as needy as ever. "My black shoes have worn out on the tops as well as the bottom," he complained. "I work in the gray ones and the brown ones need half soleing." Although he loved his mother, many of his letters to her seem insensitive to her plight. In March, after receiving a package of shirts and socks, he asked for more. "I have been admitted to the College dept.," he wrote, "but I am $10.00 short on my music fees. Won't you please send this by return mail[?] I am [losing] valuable time on my instruments especially the piano." In May, he was again impatient with her. "I have no razor, no blades, no soap, no hair cut[,] no toothpaste, no anything," he wrote. "I wish you would send as many of these . . . as soon as possible. You could send a box, and you could cook a cake? And send a few sardines etc. The food here isn't the best in the world and the chance to eat anything else is welcomed." He signed this soliciting, if not importuning, letter to Ida "Love, Ralph." Until then, he had signed almost every letter to her "Ralph Ellison" or "Ralph W. Ellison."

By this point, despite his dire needs, he no longer worked in the bakery but had settled into a quite different job at the library. Mainly he patrolled the front desk, accepting returned books and fetching volumes from the stacks. With few customers he was able to read much of the time. He also had the run of the library, including the volumes on Tuskegee's own *Index Expurgatorius,* such as Radclyffe Hall's lesbian classic *The Well of Loneliness* and James Joyce's "obscene" *Ulysses.* Under lock and key, they were stowed far from the few undergraduates who knew these texts existed, or cared at all that they did.

For Ralph, this was the refined side of institute life. However, another, much raunchier side involved bouts of boozing and fervent hunting for sex, furtive trips to bootleggers, homemade alcohol, cynical seductions, near-rapes, and other examples of the more aggressive male student culture. Three years after leaving school, Ralph would write a steamy letter to Harry Brooks, a former co-worker in the bakery who still lived at the institute, in which he painted Tuskegee life mainly in scarlet. "Say, do they still sell liquor at Red Gap," he asked, "and do the boys still slip out to Eli Crossing? Remember the time Parker and I went out to Seelie Williams' place and screwed her? What happened to the slut, the big yellow one who worked in the dining hall, who left Tom Campbell for me, and where is Mabel Patton? Remember the time we made the liquor behind the oven and got the old lesbian gal drunk who was working out on the food slide and how she served everybody everything and how she didn't ever beg us for whisky after that. Those were the days and I shall never forget them."

With the coming of spring to central Alabama in 1934, the grounds of the institute burst into flower. The scent of wisteria floated sweetly in the air, the twisting vines sprouted blue, purple, and white, and at night the mockingbirds sang. Ralph was touched but not overwhelmed. "Things are dull here," he wrote. "The Campus is pretty but that's about all." The most anticipated campus event, at least for the administration, was the annual spring visit of the institute trustees, most of whom were white and from the North. From one point of view these men embodied the noble spirit of philanthropy; from another, they stood mainly for money and power. These people had made Tuskegee possible. They were also feared. No one dared to question their right to oversee a black school. Especially during the Depression, they were essential to its survival. However, the trustees' visit was only one burden or distraction, as a succession of tiring, often tiresome springtime events taxed the powers of the young musicians. "School has been like a nightmare," Ralph wrote home. Then, after the last notes of the recessional sounded at graduation, he again watched with chagrin as most of his fellow students decamped. "I wanted to come home very badly the other night," he admitted to Ida, "after seeing all of the students leaving for home." However, he faced unfinished business at Tuskegee. After a maddening squabble with the accounting office over bogus charges for the winter quarter, when he was not enrolled, he still owed the institute $72. Only a generous gift from Walter Williams prevented Ralph from being booted out.

They then took a holiday together. Accompanied by two friends, former Tuskegee students who taught school in Atlanta, they headed south in Walter's car to Pensacola, on the Gulf of Mexico. There they spent three days on the humid, briny Florida coast at the home of a former Tuskegee student who had just graduated. "We spent each day in the Gulf swimming and laying in the sun," Ralph wrote to Ida. "You should see me now. I am so black you wouldn't know me." Setting out, Ralph had noted privately, momentously, of Walter and himself, "At last I think I am about to discover the meaning of true friendship. That happy condition of like tastes and understanding with just enough mystery to make it perfect." He believed that a reserve of personal mystery was important: "A condition of complete confidence is not to be desired." He also knew that he and Walter were already closer than some observers thought appropriate, given their different stations in life. What would people think now? "Hereabouts, when men become friend[s], either one or the other is accused of being homosexual." Nevertheless, Williams was the center of his life, "my dear ego."

This closeness made Ralph more imperious than ever with his mother, who had just moved into a new apartment but then lost her job at the Biltmore Hotel. He seemed almost unconcerned by her predicament. After a perfunctory expression of sympathy in one letter, he launched a litany of his needs. "I am getting ragged," he wrote. "My grey suit is worn out and the pants of my brown one are very thin in the seat." He was down to one pair of shoes. Also, "it's so hot here that I do need a white suit of some kind but I could make it with a couple of good linen pants and a sweater." For Ralph, helping him achieve his goals now seemed to be Ida's main purpose in life. "You know I travel with the rich gang here," he reminded her, "and this clothes problem is a pain."

In the summer of 1934 he didn't return home, even after he learned of the death of his aunt Lucretia Ellison Brown in Oklahoma City. Instead, he spent much of the time with Williams and Julia Moore, who had just graduated from Fisk. They went dancing and hiking, and shared books. Ralph also began to think about moving to New York. "I intend to study there as soon as I get a chance," he wrote. "I want to attend the Juilliard School of Music in N.Y."

He and Walter then decided to return to Pensacola. This decision led to perhaps the worst crisis of Ralph's Tuskegee years. In order to leave the campus and travel so far, Ralph needed the permission of both Dean Neely and Ida. Alerted by Ralph, Ida wrote to Neely that her son suffered from persistent stomach problems and must have a vacation. Perhaps jealous of Williams, Neely killed the holiday by sitting on Ida's letter until August 18, when the two men were scheduled to leave Tuskegee. He then summoned Ralph and curtly denied him permission. He had almost blocked Ralph from making his previous visit to Pensacola, but had finally allowed him to go. Ralph noted about that trip that "the boss" had exacted a price: "I paid for the trip in advance but that['s] one of life's little jokes. What is e[c]stasy to one man is the essence of disgust to another."

Neely's refusal enraged Ralph. Furiously he complained to Ida that the dean had threatened "that if I left he wouldn't give me work when school starts. He also said that if I was sick I should be in the hospital." Ralph was under no illusions: "I know the cause of his acting in this manner. This is just some more of the mess I've mentioned before. I see nothing I can do about it. He is the biggest man here as far as the student is concerned and if I kick up a racket now I would never get a job when I graduated, this dump is too powerful." Ralph was bitter. "You must understand," he told Ida, "that the reputation that this place has and what it really is, are two different things." He had made "one big mistake" in coming here. First, a music student should be exposed to "good music," but "I've heard no worthwhile music since I've been here." Worse, "no person trying to study should be worried and nagged at because he does not consent to prostitute himself. . . . Nor should one have to listen to the ravings of a bunch of small minded niggers who won't be satisfied unless they show how important they are." His poverty was demoralizing: "On top of it all I have to go without haircuts & shaves without shoes and with holes in my pants and constantly worrying if I will have money to get in school or if I will have enough to stay." His patience was at an end. "If some change doesn't take place I shall have to leave—in fact I want to leave. I feel I am wasting my time staying here. . . . If I get away from here I am through with negro schools."

In the following weeks Ralph simmered in anger. His money would pay for one more quarter, "providing that this negro who has caused me all the trouble will leave me alone." He hated Tuskegee. Although most of its officials wanted him to bow down to them, "I know they are dumb and shallow and think that money is all there is in the world, never realizing that the finer things can't be bought, and that a few people in the world, yes even negroes, love books, music, art, beauty, nature and the other things that are good and great." Alienated, he kept mainly to himself, reading or listening to music when he was not at work. Also, "I talk to Walter and discuss the different aspects of art." He made a vow: "I doubt Mama, if I'll ever be rich but I will be as big a man as possible and if I don't become a great composer I hope that I will be respected because of the way I shall try to live. I'll try to do what's right. . . . Like you I have learned not to allow talk [to] keep me from it and I shall try to understand people and forgive them their faults even though they condemn me . . . because of mine." Some people at Tuskegee even thought he was gay. "I got in an argument with a girl I sent from the Library for talking," he wrote Ida, "and she said she doubted that I was a man (ha! ha!). I don't know whether that is the general opinion but it's funny."

The turmoil gripping Ralph, however, was about more than Tuskegee and Neely. A musical performer to this point, he was also going through a change in some ways almost as radical as birth itself. He was beginning to see the world as a writer. The impact of Williams's ideas and attitudes was remaking Ralph's life. At first inducing Ralph to imitate his style and tastes, Walter was also drawing out of him a latent, original quality. This quality grew with Ralph's increasing engagement with multiple questions and examples of art and culture. It also proposed an aesthetic career that would find its most appropriate form not in music but in words. Ralph was not a blank slate on which Walter inscribed completely new ideas. Even before Ralph began to work for him, Williams had been impressed both by the degree of his familiarity with modern writers such as Eugene O'Neill and Gertrude Stein and by his quality of mind. "Your breadth of interests and the liberal attitudes you express," he told Ralph, "have impressed me, and I feel that you will be able to build up a splendid liberal background if you continue to exercise them." The genuinely cultured man was tolerant and generous. Ralph could become such a man. "I don't know whether you have genius or not," Walter conceded, "but I believe you have capacity. If you use it to seek to evaluate the phenomena of this life and express the result of your examination of them as your philosophy, you will be an artist—and the great artist, you will remember, seeks to express his philosophy in universals, whatever medium he chooses as a physical means for rendering tangible his ideas. Nothing would please me more than to see you progress in that direction."

These were flattering words for a freshman to read—even if Walter's taste in books, music, and art was in some ways a barrier for the freshman to overcome. His ideas were elegantly expressed but often somewhat trite. Taking too solemnly the letters written by his beloved Keats, he was eager to expound ideas about Truth and Beauty that were much more satin than silk. Like the lyric poet A. E. Housman, another of his favorites, he saw male friendship in an angled Neoplatonic light that left the forms mainly in shadows. His literary vision verged on the precious. Art effaced or transcended the vexing issues of race and nationalism. Apparently he had little to say about African-American writers. The poet Countee Cullen, who also worshipped Keats and wrote self-pityingly about Negroes being forced to wear "the shroud of color," probably appealed most to Walter. Perhaps this is why, about this time, Ralph scribbled four lines from the ending of Cullen's signature poem, "Heritage," in one of his notebooks. "Heritage" explores the two warring aspects of the poet's dramatized being. He is pagan and Christian, primitive and modern, African and Western, sexual and chaste, and—covertly—gay and straight. Later, Ralph would recall thinking of Cullen's work as "artificial and alien"; but he did not think so at this time.

In writing his own verse, Walter routinely employed archaic, not modernist, literary forms. At first, Ralph aped him. One early effort, dated August 26, 1934 (the month of his clash with Dean Neely), reflects Walter's evident belief that good poetry affects stylized rhymes, rhythms, and syntax, and enacts emotion mainly in heroic terms ("You are so far, and sorrow stands so near, / I wonder if you hear my silent eloquence . . ."). Another poem is almost saved by a flash of wit. It ends:

> *We danced and played at Cupid's game,*
> *Old Bacchus was the spirit of the hour.*
> *But now these change, washed by Fancie's shower,*
> *And now as trace a card alone remains.*
> *Legend on its paper reads, "Miss Julia Moore,"*
> *And, "Please Present This At The Door."*

"Warning!!" Ralph scribbled below the text, probably to Walter. "Laugh and Distroy!!"

These few pieces from 1934 and 1935, academic and Anglophilic, suggest that if Ralph was to find himself as a writer, he would have to challenge Williams and his ideas. It seems that he understood so. Walter later recalled him as typically "half asleep or growling or dispensing your summations of things and even now and then being half-way agreeable." To Ralph, Williams was too soft and despairing. Walter believed that he had squandered his chances in life. "I have tasted ecstasy, both of grief and joy," he wrote. "Illusions have come and gone. Shame, remorse, humiliation" were now his lot in life. Such despair was not for Ralph. Even as a young man he was eager to do battle with the circumstances of life.

When the 1934–1935 academic year began, Ralph, a sophomore, was now the band's student leader. In an operetta, *Ask the Professor,* designed to present various instruments, he showed off on the trumpet. At a Sunday concert near the end of September, he conducted half of the program. His knowledge of the other arts also expanded. Traveling with the band to Chicago for a football game, he attended his first opera while many of his friends looked for sex. In November, probably with Williams, he went to Montgomery to view "An Exhibition of Italian Paintings" at the Houghton Memorial Library of the Women's College of Alabama. This was perhaps his first viewing of such renowned painters as Veronese, Tintoretto, and Canaletto. "I had a wonderful time of it," he informed Ida, "and came back feeling a lot better afterward."

The main arts event of the fall for Ralph occurred in Philadelphia on

November 16, when Leopold Stokowski led the Philadelphia Orchestra in the premiere of Dawson's *Negro Folk Symphony*. Although the concert also included works by Maurice Ravel and Manuel Ponce, for most black Americans the first performance of a symphony by an African-American composer to be played by a major orchestra was its sensational core. The rousing ovation that followed confirmed their belief that with this "first" the race had taken another major step forward. (In the *New York Times*, Olin Downes heard in Dawson's symphony "dramatic feeling, a racial sensuousness and directness of melodic speech, and a barbaric turbulence.") Returning in triumph to Tuskegee, Dawson accepted a loving cup on behalf of the faculty from Portia Washington Pittman, the founder's daughter and a piano teacher in the music school.

Ralph's personal disappointment in Dawson didn't eclipse his sense of wonder at the event. With a black artist from lowly Tuskegee succeeding on the national stage, Ralph hoped to do the same. In more specific ways Dawson probably also influenced him. Thirty-seven years later, as a famous writer, he would assess his former teacher far more charitably and subtly than he had done while at Tuskegee. When Dawson conducted, "you had the sense that you were dealing with realities beyond yourself— that you were being asked to give yourself to meanings which were undefinable except in terms of music and musical style." His "elegance and severity," the precision and subtlety with which he taught his students, "all this gave you a sense that through this activity and dedication to the arts, you were going beyond and were getting insight into your other activities."

As before, Ralph faced the Christmas season with sadness and self-pity as he watched other students pack up and eagerly head home for the holidays. Even Walter had left for New York, "making this a lonesome place for me. There will be a few dances but I can't make them. . . . I will be glad when school starts. . . . I am getting so that the only time I feel safe is when I am with my music." He wrote home less frequently now. The well was almost bone-dry in Oklahoma City. Ida had only a half-day job. In mid-December, John Bell lost his job when his employer's business failed. Loathing school, Herbert had dropped out, but had no job.

Nineteen thirty-five thus began on a somber note. In Oklahoma, dust storms were sweeping the plains and farm folk were uprooting their families and heading west in a ragged exodus toward California. To help with the rent, Ida opened her home to some friends. On December 19 she turned fifty. To Ralph she was as optimistic as ever in her letters. "Every one that say anything about me," she assured him, "say that I look like I am 35 or 40." Miraculously, her once stark gray hair was darkening again. In fact, Ida was getting desperate. Probably going through menopause, she fell into sudden crying spells that exasperated her husband. "I think both of us would be better off apart," she decided. "He don't understand why I am like I am." She was thinking seriously about leaving Oklahoma for good. "I don't like [it] out here," she confessed, "and never have."

It hardly helped that Ralph had forgotten her birthday. Embarrassed, he responded with expressions of tenderness. The sublet of her room was "a gift from God"; and he insisted on having a new photograph of Ida. "I would like to see your hair," he explained. "What do you think has caused it to change?" Pleased, Ida sent him a pair of shoes, a pair of trousers, five pairs of socks, and a sweater—although within days she was out of a job.

At Tuskegee, Ralph suffered from his usual stomach trouble, with Walter Williams his main source of comfort. "He is the only person I spend any time with other than Hazel Harrison," Ralph wrote. "These are the two most interesting people down here, and both mean a lot to my development. They both want to know you." Williams "usually invites me up to drink milk or chocolate and to eat a snack after work. Friendship between members of the faculty and students are frowned upon here, but we don't let that stop us. I am able to learn a lot from him that I won't get in the class room, and beside we like the same things, books, music, poetry, pictures etc."

Ralph's friendship with Harrison, then in her early fifties, also bridged differences in age and station. The cascading notes of her piano as she practiced almost every day in the music studios charmed and inspired him. Despite a fairly busy concert schedule, at home she was almost always available. More than once Ralph went with her on meandering car rides into the countryside. Later he would write to her about "that beautiful and memorable Sunday spell when we . . . picked up the echo that had been wandering down the ages for you to transmute through the Intermezzo."

One day, probably at the time of the annual music school recital in the spring of 1934, when Ralph had worn his first tuxedo as he performed a cornet solo, Harrison gave him advice that he would value for the rest of his life. As he recalled, "I had outraged the faculty members . . . by substituting a certain skill of lips and fingers for the intelligent and artistic structuring of emotion that was demanded in performing the music assigned to me." Chastised by them, he had "sought solace" in Harrison's basement studio. She had not rushed to console him. "You must *always* play your best," she admonished him, "even if it's only in the waiting room at Chehaw Station [the little station that linked Tuskegee to the main railroad line], because in this country there'll always be a little man hidden behind the stove . . . whom you don't expect, and he'll know the *music,* and the *tradition,* and the standards of *musicianship* required for whatever you set out to perform!" At first her folksy dressing-down only irritated him. Then, as she launched possessively into a rhapsody by Liszt, "the little man of Chehaw Station fixed himself in my memory. And so vividly that today he not only continues to engage my mind, but often materializes when I least expect him."

His playing and overall musicianship steadily improved. By the spring of 1935, as a model student, he played various cornet solos and led the brass quartet. He was more confident, too. On April 16, when Duke Ellington and his renowned orchestra stormed the campus, Ralph pushed his way forward and chatted with Ellington. Almost all of his grades were better now. In an education course he earned the top mark among students in three sections. Excelling in the practical art course offered by another one of the select circle of campus aesthetes, Eva Hamlin, a graduate of Pratt Institute in New York City, he developed an interest in sculpture. He did less well in English 103, a composition course. "I am convinced you can write," his professor noted on one paper, which he awarded a C+, "but you do not work at the fundamentals of composition." Nevertheless, he deemed the essay "a *good* theme." When Ralph wrote his mother late in April, his happiness showed. "The spring is beautiful here as always," he observed lyrically, "and the air is filled with the scent of honey suckle while the nights are filled with singing voices of mocking birds."

Still, Ida missed her boy: "I want to see you so much I feel like getting on the Highway some time." Instead, he went to her. What he found when he returned to Oklahoma City near the end of June 1935 mainly depressed him. Tuskegee had its elegant fringes and corners; his home had none. Ida now worked as a maid for Dr. Slaughter and his wife, who hadn't been in touch with Ralph since the debacle of 1933. Ida, John, and Herbert were living in a previously white area, but only at the cost of tangling with the police and even going to jail once or twice—a fact she had kept from Ralph. One day, Herbert had angrily shoved an annoying white man off their porch. The man no doubt deserved to be shoved, but on the whole Herbert was hard to handle. Earlier in the year, after a spotty attendance record, "Huck" had rebelled when his school asked him to repeat the eighth grade. He was now nineteen. Dr. Gravelly Finley, the physician from Meharry who that year married Saretta Slaughter, remembered Herbert as mentally handicapped but at heart a good young man who was more popular than Ralph. "Saretta liked him more than she liked Ralph," Dr. Finley said. "She looked out for Herbert. Saretta used to give Ralph a hard time about not paying more attention to Herbert."

Ralph had little interest in helping Herbert; he had his own problems. He felt much the same way about his mother's struggles with the police. To him, nothing had changed in Oklahoma City. At the Oklahoma Club, where he found a job, sleek white men still ate heartily and licked their lips while humble, humiliated black men waited on them. The hours were long, the pay poor. Gripped by the Depression, the city was even more segregated than when he had left.

He reunited with Zelia Breaux and with Ludwig Hebestreit. He visited the Lewisohns at their clothing store. He also tried to rekindle his relationship with various boyhood friends, but some had moved away and others seemed to be stagnating or worse. Malcolm Whitby, the doctor's son who was now a veteran of both Langston University and Tuskegee but still had no degree, worked at the Capitol Theatre. Ida had spotted him in a uniform, sweeping the sidewalk. When Ralph ran into his old love, Vivian Steveson, he was polite but indifferent to her. Indeed, he seemed cynical about women. To his schoolmate Joe Lazenberry he wrote that he now had two girlfriends in Oklahoma City to serve his needs. "Though they have the brain power of a monkey," he reported with pleasure, "they also possess the morals of that animal." The summer was helping to round out "my personality" and to give him "a better conception of my physical being." Ralph likely had a love interest at Tuskegee around this time as well. The following summer she would write to ask why she hadn't heard from him: "When I asked you if there was anyone else (darling) I had no particular person in mind." In another affectionate letter, in which she mentioned his sculpture ("I haven't forgotten your promise about 'Shoe Shine Boy'—will you do a small figure for me sometime?"), she ended on what seems like a risqué note: "Don't forget to wear your rubbers when it rains—(smile)."

When he left Oklahoma City at the end of the summer of 1935, he did so gladly. If he had his way, he would never return.

Two sweet notes that summer from Captain Drye to "My dear friend Ellison" urged Ralph to return to Tuskegee. Perhaps Drye was aware of cer-

tain tensions that might keep Ralph away. However, a terse message to
Ralph from Alvin Neely confirmed that he was expected back at the institute
in the fall.

Ralph came back to find two major changes. Frederick Douglass Patterson, a veterinarian and bacteriologist, had succeeded Moton as president. Facing a financial crisis, he announced that Tuskegee would hew
once again in its course offerings "to the Tuskegee pattern of practical
application" from which it had strayed in recent years. The School of
Music was doomed. And Walter Williams had fled Tuskegee for good. By
August 20, when he wrote Ralph for the first time that summer, he was in
despair. He hoped never to return and face its "hypocrisy, meanness, pet-
tiness and ugly situations or to be under arrogant ignorance." Perhaps his
close friendship with Ralph had something to do with his decision. He
suggested that Ralph should spend two more years there and finish his
degree: "That will give us a couple years to get ourselves together and get
the ducks lined up." In the meantime, he would help by sending Ralph
money. Walter signed this letter, "Votre père devoué."

Bereft of his "devoted father," Ralph stoically returned to his job at the
library and his place in the band. An upperclassman, he moved now with
an air of authority that awed some of the younger students. Albert Murray, a freshman from Mobile, Alabama, would remember him as a glittering campus leader. A greedy reader, Murray was at home in the library,
where each book included a slip of paper bearing the names of previous
borrowers. Quickly he realized that Ralph "was reading the books I was
going to read." In the library Ralph was a sort of Argus-figure, "a loner-
type guy, watchful-eyed, so I didn't venture to introduce myself to him."
Murray, after reading in André Maurois's popular biography of Shelley
that the Romantic poet at one point liked to fold books and carry them
around in his pocket, began to affect this habit. One day, approaching the
library desk, he pulled out a folded copy of Sinclair Lewis's novel *Arrowsmith*. Staring at the disfigured book, then at the freshman, Ralph pinned
him with a question: "What do you think this is, a pocket edition?" Murray apologized, and they became friends. (Murray once found a brief poem
by Ralph tucked among the pages of a library book: "Death is nothing. /
Life is nothing. / How beautiful these two nothings!")

He also recalled Ralph as a dashing dresser: "He was straight out of
Esquire magazine." His blue serge uniform was crisply tailored, his slacks
contrasted smartly with his coats, and his hand-tied bow ties and two-
toned shoes were beyond the sartorial range of most of the other stu-

dents. While this description is at odds with the contents of Ralph's letters to Ida, it is possible that Ralph had come back from Oklahoma City with a replenished store of finery and, as a result, an almost empty pocket. Once more unable to pay for the music school, he settled unhappily for the college. "It was a bitter pill to take at first," he wrote to Herbert. This pill soon proved a tonic. With the winter quarter of 1936 came the start of what turned out to be Ralph's most important courses at Tuskegee: two two-quarter sequences in sociology and in English.

Morteza Drexel Sprague, a graduate of Hamilton College and Howard University (he would also earn a Ph.D. from Columbia in 1955), taught the two courses on the English novel. An aesthete like Williams and Harrison, he didn't struggle much against the institute yoke. He endured Tuskegee's backward ways when many kindred souls fled the school in varying degrees of disgust. Not much older than his students, he had arrived with ideas new to Tuskegee. "Teachers of English," he declared in 1934, "must get away from so much emphasis on plot retaining; they must stress interpretation, criticism, and analysis." They should teach new writing, not harp forever on the old. He had in mind as new Sinclair Lewis, Theodore Dreiser, and Edgar Lee Masters. He read current literary magazines—some academic, others such as the eclectic upstart *Esquire*—which he then passed along to his favorite students. (While at Tuskegee, Ralph eagerly read in *Esquire* stories and other pieces by Hemingway and Langston Hughes.) Dressed in tweedy Ivy League fashion, Sprague seldom walked the campus paths without a load of books in his arms. Early in December he offered a formal public critique of the Dramatic Circle and its presentation of Shaw's *Candida*. He also helped to organize, or perhaps revive, the Athenaeum Club, which featured lectures on literary topics.

"I loved Mr. Sprague," Laly Charlton Washington recalled. "I dearly loved him. We all did. He was a wonderful teacher, handsome, brown skinned, very quiet, dignified, calm and cool." "He was an honest teacher," Ralph would tell an interviewer. Unusual for a school that stressed blind obedience, Sprague freely admitted his ignorance when he knew little or nothing about a topic. He also made many of his students thirsty for knowledge by treating them as potentially his peers. At Tuskegee, Ralph said later, "most of the teachers would not speak to a student outside the classroom. The students resented it, *I* resented it, and I could never take them very seriously as teachers." Teaching English composition, Sprague lauded the virtues of spontaneity. Murray recalled him reading aloud from

William Saroyan's "The Daring Young Man on the Flying Trapeze" in order "to illustrate how free and natural and expressive of your own personality, your own sense of individuality he wanted everybody's informal theme to be." He also respected the canon. His reading list for English 409 included *Jane Eyre, Wuthering Heights, The Mill on the Floss, The Egoist, The Return of the Native, The Portrait of a Lady,* and *The Way of All Flesh.* In addition, he asked students to give reports from a list of more than twenty texts, including *Jude the Obscure, Lord Jim, Middlemarch,* and *Kim.*

Three novels above all gripped Ralph: Fyodor Dostoyevsky's *Crime and Punishment,* Emily Brontë's *Wuthering Heights,* and Thomas Hardy's *Jude the Obscure.* Each has at its center a misunderstood young man, ambitious, tormented, transgressive; each thus held up a mirror to his nature. Decades later Ralph could still recall "the wrenching that I went through" reading Hardy's novel: "Oh, Lord, I suffered." "While I was reading these works," he said elsewhere, "I felt such a compelling identification with their respective heroes that I literally suffered through their every trial and exalted in their every triumph." If he missed some of the structural subtleties of these works, "I missed none of the action and there are memory traces still in my throat which were put there by the poignant and tragic developments of these fictions."

Ralph pushed deeper into literature. In a real sense, he no longer needed Walter Williams. Mort Sprague, far less melodramatic, much more disciplined, now became the focus of his intellectual life. Sprague, in turn, thought highly of Ralph, who earned an A in both quarters. His surviving course papers do not suggest an astute critical mind. On *Wuthering Heights,* for example: "This work, a first novel, has many of the faults of such work, but is one of the most powerful in English literature." Clearly, though, Ralph's life had reached a turning point. Outside of class, he read *The Waste Land,* T. S. Eliot's book-length poem of 1922 that so radically exemplified the spirit and practice of artistic modernism with its myriad literary allusions, rhythms, and tones, its terse footnotes, its complex syntax, and its mysterious, montage-like structure. *The Waste Land* offered, as Eliot wanted it to offer, a severe intellectual and aesthetic challenge; the poem was not for lazy, conventional readers. Ralph accepted its challenge. His encounter with the poem and his diligent exploration of its footnotes, "although I was then unaware of it, was the real transition to writing." Understanding this notoriously difficult poem was a task that possessed him, especially because he saw a link between it and his own life. "Somehow its rhythms were often closer to jazz than were those of the Negro poets, and even though I could not understand then, its range of allusion was as mixed and as varied as that of Louis Armstrong. Yet there were its discontinuities, its changes of pace and its hidden system of organization which escaped me."

The link between *The Waste Land* and jazz improvisation is obvious. Both were responses to the deforming cultural pressures during and after the disaster that was World War I. Nevertheless, the idea proposed by Ralph—that he made genuine progress on his own trying to decipher the poem, and that it led him, about this time, consciously or unconsciously, toward becoming a writer—is debatable. Later, as he cultivated his own organic myth of origins as an artist, he repeatedly gave the magisterial Eliot, and his own capacity for self-education, a huge share of the credit. Publicly (and privately, as far as we know) he would give none whatsoever to Walter Williams, who undoubtedly helped him to negotiate its territory. His homage to Eliot also plays down the specific role of Mort Sprague in guiding him through the classics of the English novel when his knowledge of English literature was still meager. *The Waste Land,* however, was indeed crucial to Ralph's turn away from music and toward writing.

Although his sociology grades were not nearly as good as those in English, Ralph was much more impressive in that subject. His instructor, Howard M. Nash, elicited some heated responses from Ralph in examining Negro culture. Here was born his lifelong distaste for sociology. Their sharpest disagreement came, as Ralph recalled, when "I had been made furious" not simply by an assertion in one textbook about the essence of black character but by Nash's reluctance to challenge it. The offensive passage was from Robert E. Park and Ernest W. Burgess's *Introduction to the Science of Sociology,* where the authors assert that while the Jew stands for idealism, the East Indian for introspection, and the Anglo-Saxon for adventure, the Negro "is primarily an artist, loving life for its own sake. His métier is expression rather than action. He is, so to speak, the lady among the races."

Several of Ralph's sociology essays at Tuskegee bristle about the assumptions underlying this remark, which reflected views commonly held at that time. Even black sociologists, including W. E. B. Du Bois, once shared these beliefs, however differently they might have expressed them. The previous spring, Ralph had probably squirmed through an oration by the revered, seventy-two-year-old Dean Kelly Miller of Howard University, in which Miller defined the Negro by qualities such as humility, submission, and forgiveness, which are "inalienable coefficients of his blood." Ralph couldn't abide such thinking. His views in 1936, expressed in his course essays, are surprisingly, even astonishingly, consistent with the core views on culture he would expound in his maturity. Even in 1936, he disliked the idea that separate races existed with distinctly separate endowments, but believed instead in the fertility of culture and the dynamic of cross-cultural change. He decried thinking that could lead an allegedly educated person to employ the disastrous metaphor of "lady-hood" to describe any culture. Seeing fluidity of culture everywhere, he already resented sociological definitions of black Americans. He found sociology dogmatic and arrogant, a discipline reluctant to accept its limitations and quick to flaunt its vaunted empiricism as Truth. In America, he believed, sociology had become a fearsome academic engine that used statistics as a kind of ethanol, supposedly free of harmful emissions, in segregating and demonizing African-Americans.

By this time, Ralph also already matched his dislike of sociology with an equal dislike for black racial propaganda. In May 1936 he anticipated aspects of his fight with Black Power separatists some thirty years later when he began an essay thus: "There is a school of thought that would have the American Negro a race culturally apart from the rest of America. A group with its own art, ideals, economy, traditions, attitudes and other cultural factors. This same attitude is found among those critics of Negro literature who urge the Negro writer to keep to Negro themes and ideals. Negro music must, for them, remain in a static state having reached its highest development in the simplicity of the spirituals. The exponents of this type of race development argue that this will bring about a condition of race consciousness and pride not possessed by the Negro today." He did not share such thinking: "To look at the position of the Negro in American life and take into consideration the sociological factors involved, is to doubt the possibilities of such a program." Whatever the source of his intellectual debt, he already believed in race pride but not racial separation. Already he refused, in trying to study the problems of black America, to see graphs and statistics as dogma. Already he sought to bridge the divide that appeared to separate, on the one hand, the European cultural tradition at the core of his formal education and, on the other, the black vernacular culture in speech, music, and dance that pulsed like warm blood in his veins.

When another shortage of cash almost prevented Ralph from registering for the 1935 winter quarter, the new president himself, perhaps at the urging of his wife (Ralph's piano teacher Catherine Moton), ordered him admitted to courses. President Patterson was also trying to get him a school loan, Ralph wrote Ida ("My shoes are all worn out," he complained for the umpteenth time). The music school was still too expensive for him. However, as Ralph read more and more novels, and his interest in sculpture grew, he began to miss his music courses less. Still admired by Captain Drye, he continued to lead the band and the brass quartet. He enjoyed the concerts by distinguished visiting artists and the chance to meet them. Between such events and stimulating courses on the novel and on sculpture, Ralph found the winter quarter the most satisfying he had spent at Tuskegee. For the first time, he made the dean's list.

On Founder's Day 1936, in Washington Chapel, Ralph heard one of the most memorable addresses of his college years (an experience he stored away in his memory for future use in his fiction). The speaker was Dr. Emmett Jay Scott of Howard University, who had been second in command to Booker T. Washington for many years at Tuskegee. In the flower-scented chapel, an organ prelude by Brahms preceded a reading from Scripture, the recitation of a prayer, and the singing of a Negro spiritual. Then, as Ralph listened intently, Scott's rippling arpeggios of rhetoric and his tremulous remembrances of time past and of the ways of the founder during the institute's golden age filled the old church, and an almost mesmerizing spiritual aura seemed to envelop the Tuskegee community. But Scott's oratorical skill, or his tricks, could not overwhelm Ralph's belief that his three-year sojourn there had been an experience both sublime and tawdry. The contrast between Scott's spinning evocation of the founder's genius, on the one hand, and Ralph's experience of the Tuskegee dream as a metastasizing cancer, on the other, was stark.

Perhaps it was then, or soon after, that he decided to leave Tuskegee and head for New York. Other events that month also pushed him in this direction. One was his meeting with one of the major leaders in the interpretation of African-American literature and culture, Dr. Alain Locke of the Department of Philosophy at Howard University. In 1925, Locke had edited a special number of the national magazine of social service, *Survey Graphic,* which he revised and published later that year as *The New Negro.* The volume of essays, poems, stories, and other material became a sort of bible of the Harlem Renaissance. Locke, a Rhodes Scholar educated at Harvard and Oxford, was a fastidious cosmopolitan who knew personally almost everyone of any consequence in the black world of education, art, and culture. He had strolled the boulevards of Paris with Countee Cullen and scattered the pigeons in the Piazza San Marco in Venice with Langston Hughes. Now he had come to Tuskegee to visit his close friend Hazel Harrison. A connoisseur of gifted young men, he took some interest in Harrison's protégés, including Ralph. And it was probably about this time that Hazel broke the news to Ralph that, recruited by Locke, she was moving to Howard in Washington, D.C. She was well aware that Dr. Patterson was about to padlock the doors of the music school at Tuskegee.

On May 18, referring no doubt to the popular summer vacation ships on the Hudson River, Ralph wrote Ida that "I want to go to New York and work on the boats." Returning for another summer in Oklahoma "would kill me." He was working with Mike Rabb in the records and research department at the institute, interviewing families about the dire effects of the Depression. However, the pay was trifling and Ralph wanted to move on. New York, he mused, "offers so much I need to help my education."

Meanwhile, Ida herself was packing up and preparing to leave Oklahoma for good, taking Herbert with her. John Bell would stay behind, uncertain when or if he would rejoin them. "Oh Ralph," Ida had written stoutheartedly, "I a[l]ways thank God for his goodness to us. I do know that is why it is as well with us as it is, and I believe it will be better if I leave this wicke[d] place." Like the destitute white Okies heading valiantly westward to California, munching on dust and the grapes of wrath, she and Herbert were on the move, if in the opposite direction. Without a firm plan, they headed by train to Ohio on the Fourth of July. They visited Ida's sister Annie Hill in Cincinnati before spending several days with a friend in Cleveland. Finally, Ida chose to settle in Dayton, which she found less smoky than Cleveland and also possessing "a better class of people." Among these people were more than thirty relatives on her mother's side.

Now Ralph's main lifelines to Oklahoma were cut. Ida expected him to join her in Dayton, but when Ralph was done with Tuskegee, he would be done with living in the provinces. The chance to leave for New York came suddenly. In June, the state of Oklahoma belatedly made good on the payment of a scholarship awarded to him for the academic year just ending, 1935–1936. On June 22, a check for $119.02 reached him in Tuskegee. After settling his debts, Ralph had about $100 left. This sum would go a long way toward paying for his senior year at the institute. He easily convinced himself that he needed more. Once in New York City, he would look for work. Perhaps he would return to Tuskegee at the end of the summer. Perhaps he would not.

4

A Shock of Transition
1936–1938

Workers of the World Must Write!!!!
RALPH ELLISON (1937)

Neither the heat nor the humiliations of Jim Crow on the long ride from Tuskegee detracted much from Ralph Ellison's exhilaration, mingled with fear, at reaching New York on July 5, 1936. "I confronted the city," he would recall, "with all the excitement and dread of a pioneer facing the wilderness." In Manhattan, he entered a steamy subway car that rattled and rolled its way north until it disgorged him, amid a roiling sea of mainly black humanity, in Harlem. Like many a black migrant before him, in coming from the South he had moved in an instant from a relatively sleepy world to one entirely different: "The change of pace between New York and Tuskegee was so sudden that I suffered a shock of transition. My responses seemed retarded, I felt a puzzling disjuncture between myself and the scene." And yet so many black Americans had described this journey that the chaos seemed oddly familiar. "I felt beneath the teeter-totter dizziness a strange sense of being at home," he would assert, "and even in a way I'd never felt in Oklahoma."

"Home" was, for the time being, a dowdy room at the YMCA on West 135th Street, the hotel of choice for many black visitors to New York since the dawn of the century. Ralph set down his bags and breathed the air of what he hoped was freedom and opportunity. He had a sense of a fresh beginning, so much so that on his first evening in Manhattan, "moving like one hypnotized," he took a decisive step. He opened sealed letters of introduction written on his behalf by various members of the Tuskegee community to their friends in New York. One of them, from a Dr. Curtis to an artist, Robert Savion Pious, shocked and dismayed him by its negative tone. He shrugged it off. The other letters were encouraging, but he decided to destroy all but one, from his Tuskegee art instructor, Eva Hamlin. He would find out for himself if his own efforts, plus good luck, would see him through.

The next morning, good luck showed up in the lobby of the YMCA in the persons of Alain Locke and Langston Hughes. The men, who had known each other since 1923, were chatting when Ralph walked resolutely over. Ralph's reunion with Locke would matter little. Meeting Langston Hughes would change his life forever. Hughes liked Ralph at once. A generous man, he might have seen in Ralph something of himself in 1921, when, at the age of nineteen, he had reached New York City for the first time. Ostensibly he had come to enroll at Columbia University and study mining (his father, an ambitious Philistine, owned some abandoned silver mines in Mexico). In reality, Hughes wanted to live in Harlem, which James Weldon Johnson had recently predicted was bound to become "the greatest Negro city in the world." By dint of his writing, he had conquered Harlem, if not New York. A year after one of his plays, *Mulatto*, opened in 1935, it was still running on Broadway. *Mulatto* had helped Hughes solidify his reputation, earned during the Harlem Renaissance of the 1920s, as perhaps the most brilliant young writer in black America.

Since then, the renaissance had collapsed, its energy drained by the Depression. On March 19, 1935, Harlem had erupted in an explosion of violence set off by poverty and Jim Crow. That year, Hughes wrote his stirring anthem for the Depression, "Let America Be America Again." Once a romantic socialist, he had hardened his tone with the onset of the Depression. He had spent a year in the Soviet Union. Instead of blues and jazz, his poems now stressed radicalism, as in "Good Morning Revolution" and "Goodbye Christ." Nevertheless, he remained a friendly, generous man. Still boyishly handsome, he faced the world with a broad smile. Hughes seemed to be in love both with his own people—black Americans of all classes and colors—and with the wider world. He was poor, despite his apparent success on Broadway (where a hostile white producer was making most of the money) and as a populist writer. Currently on a Guggenheim Foundation fellowship, he was living off and on with his ailing mother in Cleveland. Since mid-June he had been staying at the YMCA and attending to various pieces of business.

For Ralph, this proved to be an extraordinary piece of good luck. Until Hughes left New York to return to Cleveland, where the Gilpin Players of Karamu House had been staging some of his plays, he saw a fair amount of Ellison. Recognizing that Ralph knew little about leftist politics and literature, he lent him a volume by the radical British poet Cecil Day Lewis, as well as two books by André Malraux, *Man's Fate* and *Days of Wrath*. Both novels would be crucial guides as Ralph began his own turn toward the left.

Before leaving New York, Hughes also volunteered some personal advice to Ralph. "Be nice to people," he urged, "and let them pay for meals." Ralph took the suggestions literally. A few days later he earnestly informed Hughes that "it helps so very much. Thus far I've paid for but two dinners." He had enjoyed reading Cecil Day Lewis's stirring if somewhat equivocal treatise *A Hope for Poetry*. "Don't be surprised," he alerted Hughes, "if you see me on a soap box next time you're here." Ralph soon picked up a job serving breakfast and lunch for $2 a day in the YMCA cafeteria. This would be his safety net as he tried to climb the Harlem social ladder. Using his letter of introduction from Eva Hamlin, he met the accomplished sculptor Augusta Savage at her studio on West 143rd Street. However, Savage declined to accept him as a pupil. Ralph could make use of her studio, but she was too busy as an art supervisor for the Works Progress Administration to take on anyone new. Savage tempered her refusal with an invitation to lunch that Ralph never forgot. Taking the elevated train rolling south from Harlem past the massive, neo-Gothic Cathedral of St. John the Divine and the penthouses on Central Park West, they ventured to mid-Manhattan and the dining room of Kress Fifth Avenue, the flagship store of Samuel Kress's five-and-ten retail empire. Probably for the first time in his life, Ralph sat down to eat with whites in a public dining room. This was his first, tentative nibble at "the bread of freedom" for which he had been hungering all his life.

Ralph's disappointment with Savage's rejection was such that later reports that she had taught him sculpture riled him. *"I was never her student,"* he insisted. When Robert Savion Pious—Ralph looked him up despite Dr. Curtis's treacherous letter of introduction—mentioned another young African-American sculptor, Richmond Barthé, Ralph recalled that at Tuskegee he had exchanged letters with Barthé after seeing one of his masks. "I fell in love with clay myself last year," Ralph had assured Barthé, "but with no satisfaction to myself, and still less am I satisfied after seeing this wonderful work of yours." Helped by Pious ("one of the most sincere people I've ever met"), Ralph visited Barthé at his studio in Greenwich Village. There he found someone not unlike Hughes—handsome, brown-skinned, and affable. Born in Bay St. Louis, Mississippi, near New

Orleans, the thirty-five-year-old Barthé had left the South and enrolled in 1924 at the Art Institute of Chicago before moving on to New York. Reaching Harlem just as its renaissance was dying, he nevertheless saw his work win quick acceptance by some prominent galleries and the Whitney Museum of American Art. His sculpture of a lithe, sinuous black male figure, *Feral Benga,* was now considered one of the defining works of contemporary Negro art.

After several lively hours of conversation Barthé agreed—"to my surprise and joy," Ralph wrote—to accept him as his first pupil in drawing and sculpture. Soon Ralph was able to quit his cafeteria job, which had become "too nasty and took up too much time," when Barthé found him work elsewhere. On August 17, filling in for an employee on extended leave, Ralph began work as a receptionist and clerk for one of the most renowned psychiatrists in America, Dr. Harry Stack Sullivan, at Sullivan's exquisite townhouse at 158 East 64th Street. The hours were convenient— five days a week, from 8:30 a.m. until 1 p.m.—and the pay $12.50 a week. "It is a very pleasant job," Ralph assured his mother, "and my boss is very nice." In addition, Ralph moved out of the YMCA and into Barthé's apartment at 236 West 14th Street in Greenwich Village. They shared the basic living expenses, but Barthé, a former butler in New Orleans, did the cooking—"and let me add that he does a good job of it," Ralph assured Ida. "So you can see that things aren't as bad with me as they might be."

For an eminent white professional to hire a black receptionist, even temporarily, was almost unthinkable. Moreover, Dr. Sullivan treated Ralph with courtesy and even deference. "When he asked me to read excerpts from a book he was writing," Ralph wrote, "I was both flattered and impressed by his humility." (Sullivan wanted Ralph to vouch for the clarity of his prose.) He also made it his habit to take his simple lunch, usually milk and crackers, sitting with Ralph. "I was encouraged to talk about myself," Ralph said, "and under his quiet questioning I learned to relax and talk quite freely." He would remember the psychiatrist's pale blue eyes, delicate white skin, and gentle but disturbing remoteness. "I suspected," he wrote, "that my real function at lunchtime was to break some of his loneliness." Whatever his functions, he did them well. The following year, Sullivan would declare in a letter of recommendation that Ralph Ellison "impressed me as intelligent, neat and tidy, courteous, and punctual."

Ralph decided not to return to Tuskegee in the fall. His office job had come too late for him to save much money; besides, he was enjoying the pleasures of life in New York as the summer heat and humidity gave way to cooler weather and the city returned to more invigorating rhythms. Buoyed by a sense of success and by Barthé's cooking, his weight rose to 170 pounds. His daily routine was simple. After work, he returned home to begin his own aesthetic wrestling with clay. (In October, Ralph sent Hazel Harrison a snapshot of a little head he had done with Barthé. "My, how you have improved," she wrote back. "Oh I am sure you are going to make us very very proud. Keep on, go on. You will.") In the evening the two men attended movies, plays, and lectures or visited Barthé's many friends. Meeting whites socially on an equal footing was new to Ralph, but he relished the change. Slowly building his own library, he liked to browse among the used-book sellers on 59th Street. In August he bought a copy of T. S. Eliot's *Complete Poems* ("I feel I knew his best work before I bought this collection," he told Hughes) and also sought to buy a second-hand copy of every text cited in Eliot's often arcane footnotes to *The Waste Land*. Still interested in music, he picked up a biography of the composer Hector Berlioz. Ralph was now also exploring a different kind of reading matter. As he wrote to Hughes, "I don't wish to be ignorant of Leftist Literature any longer."

A curious aspect about Ralph's life that vital fall, given his critical although tolerant attitude to male homosexuality, was that he was working for a gay or bisexual man and living with one who was openly gay. In fact, Ralph's job had probably come about because of a circle of gay acquaintances, male and female, of which Barthé was a part. Although Ralph's relationship with Dr. Sullivan was almost certainly circumspect, his ties to Barthé might have been more complicated. This was another of Ralph's early friendships about which he later spoke or wrote virtually nothing. Perhaps in Barthé's case he had something sexual to hide; perhaps not, because even before he became famous, Ralph was not inclined to admit any personal debts. The same was true of his friendship with Langston Hughes, about whom it was whispered even in the 1930s that he was gay. Later, Ralph would brush off such talk. "During the long extent of our friendship," he wrote privately about Hughes's sexuality, "he never once revealed it to me. Indeed, he always struck me as asexual. . . . Thank God that even friendship has its boundaries and levels of mystery!"

Soon after Ralph's arrival, Walter Williams came from Albany to see him. Having abandoned his job at Tuskegee, Williams was now unemployed, broke, and depressed. Despite his elite education, he was having a hard time finding a decent job. With mixed feelings he noted Ralph's initial social success in Manhattan with people like Hughes, Savage,

Barthé, and Sullivan. "What I prophesied is coming to pass," he wrote Ralph, in the serpentine language of envy; "you are finding people who can open up to you infinitely vaster resources than I could." An October trip by Ralph to Albany to see Williams did not close the gap. Ralph and Barthé were optimists, Williams mourned, but he was doomed to fail. Ambitious, Ralph disliked hearing such plaintive notes. At Tuskegee, while Williams had the power to help him, his wailing had a certain charm. Now, with Ralph eager for success, Williams's moping was unseemly. Ralph decided to drop him.

He had no wish to drop his mother and brother, but he found it harder now to be much concerned with their comings and goings, although Ida and Herbert were struggling in Dayton. Pleased to be near her sister Annie in Cincinnati, Ida found her Dayton relatives disappointing, and Herbert despised them. When, as in Oklahoma City, she found work as a maid, at the local Biltmore Hotel, the hours were brutal and the pay low. When she found a place to live, it was "nasty." (Her husband, John Bell, was hanging on in Oklahoma City.) Ida didn't like Dayton: "There is as much Jim Crow here as there is in G[eorgia] as far as I can see." Jobless, Herbert was hard to handle ("he get[s] mad when I say anything to him and walk[s] out").

Although Herbert angrily asked why Ralph was not with them or helping out, Ralph had no intention either to go to Dayton or, apparently, to send money. No longer needing Ida's help, he now wrote to her infrequently. He loved her, but his mind was elsewhere. At Christmas, a telegram from him to Dayton, signed "Ralph Ellison," was more formulaic than sincere: "THOUGH FAR AWAY OUR THOUGHTS ARE CONSTANTLY WITH YOU THIS CHRISTMAS SEASON." When Ida tried to offer some personal advice, Ralph was icy. "I must settle my own affairs," he insisted, "and alone." In May, for the first time in many years, he failed to send her a Mother's Day card. "I must admit I was a little disappointed," Ida wrote. As Ralph trained his eyes on his distant goals, he seemed not to notice her pain.

Although he lived among whites downtown in Greenwich Village, he began to explore Harlem from his first days in the city. Since the heyday of its renaissance, Harlem had expanded as blacks moved into other once white adjoining sections that then became popularly known also as Harlem. Now it began at 110th Street, or Central Park North, and spread uptown—irregularly, to be sure—as far as 160th Street. It grew close to Columbia University on the west, without claiming Riverside Drive on the

Hudson, which was resolutely white. The hilltop City College of New York, located around 138th Street and Convent Avenue, was almost all white.

Restless and expanding, in other ways Harlem had regressed. A challenge to Ralph's imagination, Harlem was, as he would write, "the scene of the folk-Negro's death agony," on the one hand, and "the setting of his transcendence," on the other. Among white people downtown, life was also intense—but nicely patterned and predictable. A busy Harlem street, such as 125th Street near Fifth Avenue, or Lenox Avenue near 135th, was neither. In Harlem, the urbane came along with the volatile, the inspired with the certifiably lunatic. To the sympathetic watcher the black and brown faces on the streets exhibited all too often symptoms and signs of psychological disorder, the result of the denial, pain, and humiliation that made up life for most blacks in the industrial North. A walker in the city, relentlessly curious, Ralph did not fail to note the complexity of Harlem life, its incongruities and paradoxes. He saw its restrained majority, law-abiding, often devout, but dogged by the racism and poverty on which irrationality fed. He could hardly miss the popularity of its soapbox orators and especially the colorful black nationalist agitators, among them the Garveyites of the Universal Negro Improvement Association, or fiery members of the African Patriotic League, whose members ascribed almost all black misery to the iniquitous white man.

On Edgecombe Avenue on "Sugar Hill," the toniest address in Harlem, he saw the privileged few at play when he attended a party at Duke Ellington's home at the invitation of Langston Hughes. Elsewhere, Ralph noted the power and variety of the black church, the vigor of its responses to the unique challenges of Harlem—from the stiff Episcopalian propriety of wealthy St. Philip's to the Pentecostal exuberance of the storefront chapels of the poor. As in Oklahoma City, he acknowledged the rival authority of the dancehalls and cabarets, from the Savoy, Renaissance, Alhambra, and Rockland Palace to shabby joints where one sometimes heard even more amazing music. At the Apollo Theater on 125th Street he saw celebrated jazz bands, dancers, and comedians; in nightclubs, often alone, he nursed a glass of beer and took in the unpredictable human scene. "I used to stand on Sunday nights at the bar at Small's Paradise," he later recalled about one of the fabled nightspots of the 1920s and 1930s in Harlem; or, tired of cigar smoke and booze, he strolled in Harlem's several green spaces, such as Mount Morris Park, where he watched with a sense of love and acute personal distance people playing baseball, football, tennis.

However, black Manhattan was never enough for Ralph. "I did *not* come to New York to live in Harlem," he later stressed; "I was not exchanging Southern segregation for Northern segregation." Although Harlem was a "very romantic" place to him, too many blacks seemed to be intimidated by Jim Crow or shackled by provincialism. To them the artistic treasures of the city simply didn't exist. The symphony orchestras, the ballet companies, the galleries, and other centers of culture such as the Metropolitan Museum of Art, the Whitney, and the Museum of Modern Art were white possessions, off-limits to blacks. A few patronized the branch library on 135th Street, which housed the Schomburg Collection of African-American materials; for most, however, the marble lions guarding the New York Public Library on 42nd Street were too fierce ever to be crossed. On September 13 he accompanied the composer David Guion to Carnegie Hall, where the General Motors Symphony Orchestra performed a medley of movements from popular symphonic works. Guion, yet another friend of Barthé, was a Texan who had trained at the Royal Conservatory of Music in Vienna but was devoted to Southwestern American themes (he wrote "Home on the Range"). Such friendships, as Ralph saw them, boosted one's confidence, improved one's knowledge of the world, and opened professional doors to those blacks who wanted to advance.

Some encounters with whites ended poorly, with insults routine. Trying to deliver a manuscript in person to Jacques Gordon of the famed Gordon String Quartet (he had heard it play at Tuskegee), Ralph was rebuffed by a doorman "with a European accent who was so rude that you were tempted to break his nose." After Ralph refused to use the service elevator, Gordon himself had to come down to escort him up to his apartment. Some social disasters could not be blamed on whites. Taken by Hughes to see his first Broadway play, *Tobacco Road*—the stage version of Erskine Caldwell's best-selling novel of 1932 about poor whites in the South—Ralph simply lost control as he followed the hilarious sexual carryings-on of Caldwell's Ellie May and Lov. "I laughed and laughed," he wrote, "bending and straightening in a virtual uncontrollable cloud-and-dam-burst of laughter, a self-immolation of laughter over which I had no control. And yet I was hypersensitive to what was happening around me, a fact which left me all the more embarrassed."

Far too many blacks, in Ralph's opinion, were deaf to the deep historical resonance of the city, blind to the architectural and cultural treasures of old districts such as Washington Square and Gramercy Park. Embracing New York would take courage, he knew, and a thick skin. Even in artsy Greenwich Village, restaurants often refused to serve blacks, or laced their food with salt, or smashed their dishes at the end of their meals in full view of everyone, as if blacks routinely spread disease. Nevertheless, to hang back was to fear life itself. Thus he pushed forward bravely and with stern self-control. "I was testing myself against being turned away," he wrote later, "entering with the conscious control of an actor, while plotting a dignified retreat if service was refused; determined, for all the damage to my digestion, to act the New Yorker, twenty-two, black and fresh out of Alabama." Like his hero Hemingway, he saw himself as a prizefighter: "Never dodge until a punch is thrown your way; then slug with the boxers and outbox the sluggers."

As Ralph "moved inevitably toward the most tabooed area of all: the white woman," he refused to glorify her. He remembered how, in 1934, when the Tuskegee band had visited Chicago, several of his friends had rushed in search of white prostitutes. Ralph, however, had "a bottomless disdain" for the idea that any white woman—"the ugliest, baggiest, most phlegmatic, hag-ridden"—was irresistible to him because of her white skin. Nevertheless, he believed that black men shouldn't shun the company of white women. At Carnegie Hall one evening, "in a cold sweat of anticipation," he arrived to meet a young woman who had offered him a free ticket to a concert. "I feared," he recalled, "the racial embarrassment of being separated from my friend at the door, the insult to my masculinity of being separated from a woman." No one separated them at the door, but the ordeal was not over: "Then the endless walk down the endless aisle of the orchestra. I moved, composed of face and steady, even relaxed, of stride . . . as I forced my legs in their measured labor through the gauntlet of turning heads and rising eyebrows."

On December 31, after almost five months, his job with Dr. Sullivan came to an end. However, the father of one of the doctor's patients hired Ralph the following month as a laboratory assistant for $1,900 a year at the A. C. Horn Paint Company, which operated a factory across the East River, on Long Island. The job had at least two drawbacks. He was indoors the entire working day. Worse, he was (as far as he knew) the only black employee and most of the whites resented him.

By this time he and Richmond Barthé had parted company. "The roommate situation had been volatile," a Barthé scholar said. "According to a close friend of Barthé, Ellison was nosy and messy. Barthé tended

towards obsessive-compulsive behavior. He was also very, very careful
about who had access to his private life. Ellison had come too close to
him." About this time Ralph practically gouged Barthé's name out of his
address book. He returned to Harlem, at 530 Manhattan Avenue, to live
in a house owned by the mother of a college friend of Langston Hughes.
Langston's longtime friend Louise Thompson also lived at this address. In
October, Hughes had mailed Ralph two books, one of which was *Literature and Dialectical Materialism* by the leftist British literary critic John
Strachey, which Ralph was to read and then return to Louise.

Pretty, bright, and a Communist, Louise Thompson had survived a
lonely childhood in the West with her mother, then graduated in 1923
from the University of California, Berkeley. As an idealistic young teacher
at Hampton Institute in Virginia, she had been forced out because of her
criticism of the reactionary, white-dominated administration. Moving to
New York, she found herself caught around 1930 in a war of wills among
three notable parties—Langston Hughes, Zora Neale Hurston (with whom
Hughes had been collaborating on a play about Negro folklife called *Mule
Bone*), and Mrs. Charlotte Osgood Mason, their elderly, imperious white
patron, who had hired Thompson to work for them. Fired rudely by
Mason because Hurston had become jealous of her friendship with
Hughes, an affronted Thompson began marching to the left. In 1932, as
secretary of the Harlem chapter of the Friends of the Soviet Union, she
led a band of young black Americans, including Hughes, to the USSR to
make a motion picture about race in the United States. Returning home
after the project flopped, she joined the Communist Party and became a
prominent figure in the International Workers Order, its giant fraternal
organization, as well as one of its top recruiters among Harlem artists and
intellectuals.

The influence of Hughes and Thompson, in the context of the Depression and his raw ambition, virtually ensured Ralph's radicalization. On
Hughes's next trip to New York, he encouraged Ralph at every turn. When
he bought a new typewriter, he lent Ralph his old one indefinitely. Ralph
watched with fascination as Langston winnowed his radical verse for *A
New Song,* published by the International Workers Order after Hughes's
longtime publisher, Alfred A. Knopf, refused to print such stuff. On
March 7, when Ralph joined Langston and the progressive white poet
Genevieve Taggard in a taxi ride across the Brooklyn Bridge for their joint
reading at the Brooklyn Institute of Arts and Sciences, Taggard's glowing
silk gown, the scent of her perfume, Langston's air of dash and daring, the

electric response of the audience—all exhilarated Ralph: "For the first time I felt a certain sense of possibility about a life in the arts."

When Hughes left town, Ralph missed him—especially after a brace of Thomas Mann volumes, including first editions, arrived as a gift from Hughes. As Langston had suspected he would, Ralph saw himself in the troubled young hero—a writer—of Mann's story "Tonio Kröger." "It has a value to me all its own," he wrote Hughes. "It made clear many of the things we talked about and despite myself I found it impossible not to identify myself with the character." In New York, the movies and dance-halls still pleased him, but "they don't seem quite the same after you and your conversation." Intimates now, Ralph and Langston talked tenderly about Ralph's chronic feelings of hurt and confusion. "He tells me there is no use," Ralph wrote Ida. Peace, according to Langston, "isn't even to be desired. He said he had the same trouble and was surprised to discover I was going through the same experiences. I suppose this has made us friends, all for which I am very glad."

For Ralph, this was a part of his gestation as a writer. He no longer wanted to be a sculptor. ("Patience is not your forte is it?" Hazel Harrison chided him from Howard University.) In April, he took a few lessons from Wallingford Riegger, the white, Georgia-born modernist musician whose compositions often fused avant-garde atonality with classical structures. Ralph also took some trumpet lessons from a member of the New York Philharmonic. But words were displacing sculpture and music at the core of Ralph's being. He was still writing poor verse; as yet, he had no skill to blend his feelings of loneliness and vulnerability with his outrage at America's cruelty to blacks. Unlike Langston, who bridged this divide almost instinctively, Ralph trailed off into incoherence when he tried to capture such ideas. Instead, he fondled his pain. "Sometimes I wish I had the nerve to go on and take a boat and go until I grow tired," he wrote Ida. "Nor is it only in the Spring I feel these impulses, but in the dead of winter, at parties, when walking along the streets, early in the morning and in the dead of night. Especially in the night. Nights on which the skies remind me of southern moons which used to turn me soft inside. Sometimes I wonder if I shall ever grow out of this way of feeling about things. For so far there seems to be no hope."

If such emoting stood at odds with radicalism, Ralph's job in the A. C. Horn paint factory, the racism he faced daily, and the tough working conditions for everyone brought him down to earth. The paint factory became a vivid symbol of the evils of capitalism. After only a few months there, his job became untenable. He resigned in June 1937. Jobless and bitter, he was now ripe for radical politics.

Harlem in 1937 was a battleground of conflicting ideologies and politics. Unemployment was the most egregious problem facing the community, specifically the refusal of most white-owned businesses to hire blacks. Of 25,000 persons employed by the Bell Telephone Company, only three were black. The struggle for jobs had led to habitual conflicts and unholy alliances. Leading the struggle was, at first, the charismatic figure of Sufi Abdul Hamid, the founder of the Negro Industrial Clerical Alliance in Chicago. Wary of charges of gangsterism and anti-Semitism aimed at the Sufi, a coalition of Harlem ministers and other middle-class leaders had organized a rival labor movement, the Harlem Citizens League, out of which the Harlem Labor Union evolved. White merchants founded their own, exclusively white Harlem Merchants Association, while the socialist Negro Labor Committee sought to unify and shelter the various smaller groups fighting for jobs. As if the situation were not complicated enough, in 1936 the crusading Committee for Industrial Organization (CIO) entered the struggle in Harlem as part of its project to organize vast sectors of the American workplace against the bigotry and elitism of the established American Federation of Labor (AFL).

None of these groups was as tenacious or as rigidly organized in its will to shape Harlem's future as the Communist Party. Since 1933, when the Party designated Harlem "a national concentration point" for Communism, radical activity had spread into a wide range of the community's institutions and activities, including the churches, the schools, and even sports. Leading ministers such as Adam Clayton Powell, Jr., the pastor of Abyssinian Baptist Church, and William Lloyd Imes, of St. James Presbyterian, looked past Communist atheism to find common cause with the Party. Above all, the Communists reached out to Harlem's artists and intellectuals. According to a former Communist leader, some 75 percent of such persons, including Langston Hughes, Augusta Savage, the painter Aaron Douglas, and Paul Robeson, "had Party membership or maintained regular meaningful contact with the Party."

Although artists rarely criticized the Party, Claude McKay, whose poetry and best-selling novel *Home to Harlem* (1928) had helped to define the Harlem Renaissance, had strong reservations about Communism. In 1922, as a radical socialist, McKay had addressed the Fourth Congress of the Communist International in the Kremlin. Under the aegis of the Popular Front, promulgated in 1935 by the Seventh Congress of the Communist

International, the Communists encouraged all organizations of goodwill to work together against the threat of Fascism. To McKay, the Communists in Harlem nevertheless willfully undermined and sabotaged rival organizations for their own purposes, not for the welfare of blacks. He attacked leading black Communists such as James W. Ford (the vice presidential candidate of the Party in 1936), Ben Davis, Jr. (the Harvard-educated lawyer who headed the Harlem bureau of the *Daily Worker*), and Louise Thompson as willing to sell out blacks for the greater glory of Communism. The Negro intellectual should know that the Party wished to make him "an appendage of his race—a red Uncle Tom of Communism. They are striving for control of the political mind of the Negro so that they may do his thinking for him."

Such were the choices facing Ralph as he found himself fallen among radicals in New York. He probably became, at least for a while, a dues-paying Party member. Herbert Aptheker, a scholar and Communist who knew Ralph from these years and believed that he was a fellow member, recalled that "it was really easy to join the Party. You simply signed up. Ralph would not have had to submit to tests or special study or anything like that. He would have been welcomed right away." Later, Ralph only hinted at close ties to the Party during these years. "I was in some of the first sit-ins which involved WPA," he offered, in referring to protests against the dismantling of Franklin Roosevelt's Works Progress Administration. He admitted to taking part in agitation that led to the creation of the National Maritime Union, and also in "a traffic stopping riot protesting the Axis involvement in the war between Loyalists and Fascists" in Spain. Here he was probably referring to the picketing on July 1, 1937, of the Italian consulate, at Rockefeller Center in Manhattan, by over a thousand leftists. They were determined, according to the *Daily Worker*, "to raise their voices in protest against Mussolini's barbaric invasion of Spain."

In the spring of 1937, the civil war in Spain was the most vivid—and glamorous—focus of radical energy in New York. The Loyalist defense of their elected government against Franco and his German and Italian allies had already inspired almost three thousand young leftist volunteers to join the Abraham Lincoln Brigade in Spain. Blacks, too, rallied to the Loyalist side both as soldiers and as artists, as in Hughes's fiery poem "Song of Spain" ("I must drive the bombers out of Spain! / I must drive the bombers out of the world!"). Hughes and Louise Thompson both supported the Communist-led North American Committee to Aid Spanish Democracy, with its several chapters across the nation. Ralph knew Langston was going to Spain soon; Louise also had firm plans to visit the front. Ralph decided he, too, would go, as a volunteer in the Lincoln Brigade. Before he could act on his decision an attack of tonsillitis laid him low. He then decided he could be more useful to Spain in some other way.

On June 30, Ralph was at the West 50th Street pier in Manhattan, along with Thompson and other friends, to bid farewell to Langston as he embarked on the liner *Aquitania*. Bound for Paris, where he would attend the Second International Writers Congress, and thence to Spain, Hughes would report on the war for the *Baltimore Afro-American* and other black newspapers. The next day, Ralph applied for a passport. The application form required him to provide a specific date for his departure, his exact destination, and the extent of his financial support. Although this seemed harmless, the passport office was on the alert for radical young Americans traveling to Spain. Joining Great Britain and France, the United States had imposed an embargo on aid to either side. Ralph was willing to lie about his goals, but was nevertheless caught in the net. "The bastards waited until the morning I was to have sailed," he wrote two years later, "to investigate." For about two hours agents of the State Department grilled him about his plans. He lied resolutely, but in vain.

Ralph did not give up his plans, even after news came of the battlefield death of Oliver Law, the black machine gunner who commanded American volunteers in the International Brigade. In the *Daily Worker* Ralph read stories every day about bloody offensives and counteroffensives, aerial bombardments, and Americans killed in action. In July, he met Sterling Rochester, a black American wounded on the Jarama front who had come home both to convalesce and to rally support for the anti-Fascists. What he read and heard made Ralph more eager to serve. At the office of the Friends of the Lincoln Brigade in mid-Manhattan, he secured a note of introduction to its Medical Bureau. The unsigned note announced simply that the bearer was "one of us & was all fixed to go to Spain but was prevented through some technical difficulty. He can drive a car and I thought maybe the Med Buro could send him as an ambulance driver."

As Ralph waited to be summoned by the Medical Bureau and sent to Spain, he spent the rest of his money. On July 21 he withdrew his last $1.12 from the New York Savings Bank. Quitting his rented room, he camped out at the one-bedroom apartment of Toy and Emerson Harper, Langston's adoptive "aunt" and "uncle," at 634 St. Nicholas Avenue in

Harlem. His determination to travel only increased on August 11 when Louise Thompson sailed for Paris on the *Queen Mary* to attend the International Congress on Races and Anti-Semitism and to visit Spain. With no news from the Medical Bureau, on September 1 he made a sworn application to the Bureau of Marine Inspection and Navigation for a certificate of service as a mess man. His plan was to work on a ship going to Europe, then to jump ship and head for Spain—just as Langston had done in heading for Paris in 1923, a young poet eager to see more of the world.

Finding a ship was hard. As he waited, his situation became embarrassing. Toy Harper was a seamstress and the apartment was often busy with her clients. "People come in at all hours," Ralph noted unhappily. "I can't impose on them much longer." In fact, Ralph had a choice—perhaps even a rival obligation. He could keep waiting for a ship to Spain, or he could go to his mother's aid in Ohio. Ida was ill. Early in August she had slipped and fallen on some steps. When the pain in her left hip persisted, she went to see a doctor, who diagnosed arthritis without ordering an X-ray. Ida stopped working. Hearing about Ralph's crisis she sent him a dollar that she could hardly spare. He tried to release her from any sense of obligation to him: "You must not try to send me anything as long as you yourself are unable to work." But he declined to go to Ohio, even though he knew that Herbert could not help Ida and that John Bell wasn't leaving Oklahoma to join her. "I told him to stay," Ida had written in May, "because I am not going to come back there no never." By August she was even more blunt: "I don't want to see him again."

Ralph should go ahead, she wrote him plaintively, "and try and get yourself straight and don't worry about us," although "I am cripple." Clearly Ida wanted Ralph to come to her. For Ralph, Dayton with his ailing mother and indigent brother meant political and aesthetic death. Life in New York was rich in promise. For example, at a book party to mark the publication of *The Road to Liberation for the Negro People*, a pamphlet putatively composed by a committee of top Communists, from James W. Ford to Louise Thompson, he mingled freely with radical stars. His copy of the pamphlet was autographed by perhaps the most influential Communist writer in the United States—"Your comrade, Mike Gold." Gold, the author of the autobiographical novel *Jews Without Money* (1930) and the former editor of *New Masses*, now wrote a pugnacious column for the *Daily Worker* called "Change the World!"

. . .

Ralph never got to Spain that summer or fall. He also remained unemployed. "I often wonder," he admitted, "if the winter will catch me still looking for a job." Instead, he had become a frequent visitor to the offices of the Harlem bureau of the *Daily Worker* at 200 West 135th Street. He had a new friend there—Richard Wright, a handsome and young black writer lately come from Chicago, where he had been on the Illinois Writers' Project and a former leader in the local John Reed Club and other Communist Party literary ventures. The Party had founded the club to attract younger writers and artists. After clashing with Party officials largely over his wish for artistic independence, Wright had come to New York. While he waited to satisfy residency requirements for the New York Writers' Project, he worked in Harlem as chief reporter on black affairs for the *Daily Worker*. Wright's early life had been harder than Ralph's, and his response even more remarkable. Born in Mississippi in 1908, he had endured his father's desertion, his mother's partial paralysis from a stroke, the hostility of his extended family, and the raw racism of the Deep South without being broken. Schooled only as far as the tenth grade, he had read so widely in literature, history, philosophy, and sociology that he had become a bona fide intellectual who could hold his own with the best of the Party thinkers. He was a Communist, but his liberal reading and writing were his life. Already he had finished one novel, several short stories, and many poems, several of which had appeared in *Left Front, Anvil, Partisan Review, International Literature, New Masses,* and other respected magazines.

Knowing that Ralph admired Wright's poems, and that Wright was moving to New York, Langston Hughes had written to alert his friend in Chicago about Ralph's interest in him. Wright had then sent Ralph a postcard ("Langston Hughes tells me that you're interested in meeting me"). The day after he reached New York, the two met. In the next few days, they sat together like chums through various sessions of the Second American Writers' Congress, which started on June 4. For both men, the highlight of the congress was the aggressive plenary address at Carnegie Hall delivered by Ernest Hemingway. Ralph also recalled a heated session downtown at the New School for Social Research, when the maverick philosopher and literary critic Kenneth Burke—who would exert a pivotal influence on Ralph as a writer—delivered an unusually controversial lecture, "The Rhetoric of Hitler's Battle." Burke's lucid fusion of Marxist and Freudian analysis, applied to the structure of Hitler's autobiography, *Mein Kampf* (a text most leftists deemed unspeakable), intrigued Ralph even as it infuriated many in the audience. At the end of the session, Ralph pressed his way through the crowd to shake Burke's hand.

Of reading T. S. Eliot and Ezra Pound on his own at Tuskegee, Ralph later wrote, "I'd become fascinated by the exciting developments that were taking place in modern literature." One day, a poem by Wright in *New Masses* suddenly revealed "traces of the modern poetic sensibility and technique that I had been seeking." Ralph could find these "traces" in poems such as "I Have Seen Black Hands," "Between the World and Me," and "Transcontinental." Although these pieces do not reflect the practices of "high" modernism typical of Eliot and Pound, Wright was indeed committed to modernism. His novel "Cesspool" (first published after his death as *Lawd Today!*), is modernist in its bleak, despairing tone, and bristles with devices lifted from contemporary writers such as James Joyce, Gertrude Stein, Theodore Dreiser, and James T. Farrell.

Charming but shy, Wright was also a driven man, determined to succeed as a writer, suspicious of rivals and potential rivals. Seeing Ralph at first as neither, he welcomed him as a new friend. The two men, nevertheless, already shared certain binding attitudes and beliefs. Both had grown up as essentially fatherless boys nurtured by poor, suffering mothers whom they both loved and resented (like Ida, Wright's mother was still alive). Hating racism, both men were also haunted by what would soon be called a sense of existential chaos in life. Both were hungry for fame, in love with art and ideas, and adoring of Western learned culture. Both Wright and Ellison admired and yet had also grown more and more critical of black culture. They had become especially disdainful of its political and religious leaders.

This disdain was probably essential to the success of the two men. It helped to detach them from what they saw as the dead weight of black racial chauvinism. In 1941, Wright would publish a commissioned paean to black culture, *12 Million Black Voices*. Ralph, too, would later sponsor the idea of the redemptive, transcendent power of blues and jazz in American culture. But aside from Wright's anomalous tribute and Ralph's wordy theorizing, both men would live out their lives as if black American culture, and especially its educated classes, had done little that the two writers needed to respect. In his autobiography, *Black Boy* (1945), Wright would make explicit his thoughts on this score when he wrote about how, "after the habit of reflection had been born in me, I used to mull over the strange absence of real kindness in Negroes, how unstable was our tenderness, how lacking in genuine passion we were, how void of great hope, how timid our joy, how bare our traditions, how hollow our memories, how lacking we were in those intangible sentiments that bind man to man, and how shallow was even our despair."

Ralph's difficulties with black American culture would never be as intense as Wright's. "For me," he wrote in response to this passage, "keeping faith would never allow me to even raise such a question about any segment of humanity." Spotting the textual source of Wright's eruption— Henry James's famous catalogue in his biography of Hawthorne of what American culture lacked in Hawthorne's day—he put some distance between himself and Wright. "Thank God," Ralph would declare, "I have never been quite that literary." Nevertheless, his own view of many if not most African-American educators, scholars, preachers, political leaders, and artists would often be intensely critical. That critical instinct freed him to ascend, without inhibition, the heights of the Euro-American artistic and intellectual tradition (but it also may well have been a decisive factor in his eventual decline as an artist, because it took a toll on his imagination and morale). In any event, these similarities help to explain why Wright succeeded (where Langston Hughes, for one, had failed) in serving as the catalyst that converted young Ralph, between 1937 and 1938, from a near-dilettante into a disciple committed to becoming a writer.

Never had Ralph found someone black who was also so versed in modern trends in literature and politics; never had he lived so close to a working writer. Fascinated, he watched as Wright pounded out articles about black life as propaganda for the *Daily Worker*. Wright's intensity, his willingness to write and revise and then revise again, made an indelible mark on Ralph's understanding at last of how a serious writer works. Wright sealed his role as guide by allowing Ralph to read freely in the thick folders of his fiction and poetry that he kept in an open desk drawer. By the middle of September, rather than return to the Harpers' apartment, Ralph often slept at the *Daily Worker* bureau. He was thus on hand when Wright began—on orders from the Party—a major effort to breathe radical life into the moribund black magazine *Challenge*.

Dorothy West, one of the youngest members of the Harlem Renaissance, had founded and edited *Challenge* through half a dozen humdrum numbers. Now, *New Challenge* would proclaim radical ideas and standards. Unofficially, Ralph joined Wright, West, and Marian Minus, a former member of Wright's South Side writing group in Chicago, to help launch the project. At first he assisted mainly by collecting subscriptions from blacks and progressive whites. However, the process of putting together the first issue fascinated him much more. He also gained valuable experience by serving on the editorial board of Lewis Allan's *The Champion* magazine, "re-writing but also reporting."

One day, pressed for copy, Wright asked Ralph to write a review for the first issue of *New Challenge*. Ralph was taken aback: "To one who had never attempted to write anything, this was the wildest of ideas." Nevertheless, he agreed to try. Wright had already composed for the first issue a revolutionary literary manifesto, "Blueprint for Negro Writing," in which he scornfully dismissed most earlier black authors as "prim and decorous ambassadors" of the Negro race "who entered the Court of American Public Opinion dressed in the knee-pants of servility," and who whites received "as though they were French poodles who do clever tricks." Henceforth, black writing must be bold, aware of black cultural nationalism but inspired by Marxism, and always conscious of daring modern writers such as Joyce and Stein.

With these marching orders, Ralph quickly finished a stern review of *These Low Grounds,* the first novel by Waters Turpin. Although the book was "the first attempt by an American Negro to essay a saga," Turpin's literary skills were obsolete. The black writer's responsibility is "to utilize yet transcend his immediate environment and grasp the historic process as a whole." No writer could get far with "dull sensibilities, or by lagging in the cultural, technical or political sense." Ralph's phrase "utilize yet transcend" loudly echoes Wright's demand in his "Blueprint" that black writers recognize the power of black nationalism "in order to transcend it." Black writers must learn from modern literary masters. Turpin, Ralph concluded, "might profit by a closer acquaintance with the techniques of his contemporaries."

Not surprisingly, Wright liked the review. To Ralph's astonishment, he then asked him to try his hand at a short story. At first Ralph demurred, but then he accepted the challenge. His primary model now was Hemingway. The narrator of Ralph's story, "Hymie's Bull," is a young black hobo, riding the rails in the middle of the Depression, who witnesses the brutality of the railroad bulls but escapes their attempts at revenge after a white hobo kills one of them. Although Hemingway's shadow is all too visible, "Hymie's Bull" is compelling. The first-person narrative is always under control, and the symbolism fairly well camouflaged. The incident is not strictly autobiographical. Nowhere in his various accounts of his train rides as a hobo in 1933 does Ralph ever mention anything like it. Is Hymie

Jewish? If so, why? ("Hymie" had become a common term for a Jew among blacks in New York.) Is he a figure of redemption? In killing his bull, Hymie appears to avenge the injustices visited on blacks, who seem powerless and timid. Is Hymie's bull in some respects akin to Hemingway's celebrated sacrificial bulls, as in *The Sun Also Rises*? None of these questions is answered, as Ralph spins a tale about racism, the black and white poor, the sadism of the railroad owners' police, and an act of violent resistance by one of the oppressed masses.

Over coffee in a café, Ralph turned over the story to Wright. According to Constance Webb, Wright's friend and biographer, he could see that Ralph "was between anguish and joy—a state where he could as easily tear the story to shreds or exult that it was approved." Wright "put the story away in his briefcase to read later and he kept it for two months" before sending it to the printer. Given the closeness of the two men, and Ralph's excitement, such a cool response must have disturbed Ralph. Then Wright said that he was saving the story for the second issue. As it turned out, *New Challenge* had no second issue. "Hymie's Bull" would be published posthumously.

Wright's competitiveness did not stop Ralph from writing. Two other stories, also published after Ralph's death, were probably written in the weeks following "Hymie's Bull." One of them, "I Did Not Learn Their Names," also draws on his adventure as a hobo. Written in a style again resembling Hemingway's (Wright's influence is nowhere evident in these three stories), it tells of a touching encounter between a young black man riding the rails and a tender, elderly white couple on their way to see their son, who is in prison. "Boy on a Train," also autobiographical, draws on the tense train ride taken by Ida and her two sons in 1925 from Oklahoma City to McAlester, Oklahoma, when Ida made an ill-fated attempt to settle there.

Ralph's days spent at the *Daily Worker* office incensed him more than ever about the evils of capitalism. "I am very disgusted with things as they are and the whole system in which we live," he wrote Ida in August 1937. "This system which offer[s] a poor person practically nothing but work for a low wage from birth to death; and thousands of us are hungry half of our lives. I find myself wishing that the whole thing would explode so the world could start again from scratch." He saw Ida's hard life as a sad example of the basic injustice of America. The citizens of Soviet Russia were building "a new system. I wish we could live there." Here, the rich cared more about their dogs than about the poor. He noted the often bizarre medley, fair and foul, that was the New York street scene: "All the fruit and fruit smells and fruit colors become all mixed with smells of washed and unwashed bodies and perfume and hair grease and liquor, and the bright and drab colors of dresses and overalls, and that which the dogs leave on the side-walk. I like to walk on such streets. Life on them is right out in the open and they make no pretence of being what they are not."

Ralph's long letter to Ida alarmed her. She begged him not to write "such a sad letter. Try to forget the pas[t], look for the sunshine in the future." Ida also sent bad news. "I can't walk yet," she informed him. "I got up on crutches yesterday, and fell back in a chair on the same hip." She did not hide her sense of foreboding: "I know that my hard working days is over, because I will be 53 on the 19th of Dec[ember] if I live to see it." Ralph responded by pawning his cornet in order to keep up the payments on her life insurance policy.

Early in October an urgent message from Cincinnati, where Ida was staying with her sister, summoned Ralph to her bedside in a local hospital. When he reached the city on October 15, she was so racked with pain that she could not recognize him. Her doctor—a black man, Ralph would note—offered no hope or, indeed, explanation. In a silent rage, Ralph listened to the doctor's fumbling talk. Clearly he had misdiagnosed her illness. The next day, Ralph arrived at the hospital early. Keeping vigil at his mother's side, at some point he stepped outside. When he returned, Ida was dead. Two nurses—black women—glanced at him furtively and hurried out. Then it occurred to him to feel under her top sheet for the watch she had been wearing. It was gone. The cause of death, according to her death certificate, was "Tuberculosis of left hip joint."

"This is the end of childhood for us," he wrote later that month about Herbert and himself. "This is real, and the most final thing I've ever encountered." The funeral, at Hillcrest Cemetery in Dayton, was modest. In his mother's papers he discovered three insurance policies. Two were quite small and the companies paid at once. The third proved more difficult. It required detailed information about Ida's illness, but her doctor was as poor at keeping records as he was at diagnosis. For the rest of his life, Ralph would see this man as the embodiment of black bourgeois incompetence. The incident would also underwrite his skepticism about black professionals who were quick to use racism as an excuse for their shortcomings. The physician who wants Negroes to patronize him because he is black, he told a white *Daily Oklahoman* reporter decades later, "and then has not mastered his craft . . . then he is immoral and he leads to the destruction of life—like the man who caused my mother's death."

While the insurance case was being resolved, Ralph stayed with Herbert for what he hoped would be a brief spell in the cramped little home of Ida's surviving maternal aunt in Dayton. His great-aunt, nearly a hundred years old, told him graphic stories about slavery and about Ida's father, Polk Milsap. Although she was entertaining, his other relatives were dull. Worse, he and Herbert grated on each other. Ralph pitied but had little respect for Herbert, and "Huck" resented Ralph's air of superiority and his coldness. "I feel very sorry for my brother," Ralph wrote to Wright. "We avoid talking of certain things," he admitted, even as he marveled at Herbert's raw grieving for his lost mother. "I see that he spends much time away from me so as not to mention these painful things. It is terrible."

By the end of October, low on cash, Ralph and Herbert had left their relatives' home—after a series of nasty arguments—and moved into the nearby home of John Strange, his pregnant wife, Ollie (who was in the hospital), and their three young children. An unpretentious man, Strange was a jobless laborer barely holding on. Most likely, he took in Ralph and Herbert partly out of compassion, partly to help meet his expenses. Meanwhile, Ralph pretended to friends in New York that his sojourn in Dayton was a bit of a lark. "Gee but it's swell to be the man of the world in a small town," he informed Wright, "and quite, quite amusing." Discovering the public library downtown, he borrowed several books, including Thomas Mann's *Freud, Goethe, Wagner,* and read copies of the *New York Times.* Splurging, Ralph also bought a copy of Hemingway's new novel, *To Have and Have Not.* "I have Hem's new book," he wrote Wright, "which I read the first day and regretted it wasn't longer."

Ralph and Strange enjoyed roaming the woods about Dayton. At first they hunted rabbits in the cold, bright fall weather with Strange's hound and a .22-caliber rifle. Then, after the season opened in November, they used shotguns and went after quail. Initially, Ralph was a poor hunter. "I walk along thinking, rifle ready, eyes supposedly looking for the cotton tailed gents but lost in the color of leaves," he confessed, "then suddenly the sound of fast falling feet and mister rabbit is laying tracks up the hill to beat hell and the bullets which usually I'm unable to send into him." The two men ate some of the rabbits but sold most of their kill to neighborhood groceries and cafés. A dozen quail might fetch as much as $9, so the hunters were willing to risk the stiff fine for shooting them even after the season had ended. The hunting also stirred Ralph's imagination to think of himself out on the trail as a young Hemingway. At Tuskegee, Ralph had read in *Esquire* Hemingway's "Remembering Shooting-Flying," a dazzling memoir about learning to shoot snipe with his father. Looking up the piece in the Dayton library, Ralph later gave Hemingway credit for teaching him that winter how to shoot birds on the wing.

Ralph did not spend all day reading and hunting. As a young radical, he had his political obligations. However, when he wrote to New York asking about Party activities in the area, his contacts there told him that he was on his own. He knew that for a fact when some workers insisted that the CIO was a railroad. The local struggle for civil rights was lame and radicalism almost unthinkable. The *Daily Worker* and *New Masses* were unavailable for purchase. "Where in hell," he sputtered, "is the revolution?" Luckily, Marian Minus, a native of Dayton, had given him a letter of introduction to her old friend Marie Stokes. Marie's father, W. O. Stokes, a prominent lawyer and Republican Party committee-man, took an immediate liking to young Ralph. Stokes invited him to use a corner of his office, a spare typewriter, and—as paper—the blank sides of an abundant supply of obsolete letterhead stationery. No Communist himself, Stokes enjoyed jousting with Ralph about politics. "He was a man of great curiosity," Ralph would recall, "who put much effort into learning just what made me tick, enjoyed arguing with me, and appeared not to mind when someone the age of his youngest son scored telling points."

Through Stokes, Ralph met other black leaders in Dayton, including Frank Sutton, an architect who also opened his office to Ralph; Charles T. Isom, the pastor of Bethel Baptist Church; and Dayton's bravest activists, the funeral home director Clarence Josef McLin and his son, Clarence Jr. As a leader of the local Democratic Voters League and president of the local NAACP, the elder McLin struggled to register voters and to press reluctant white merchants with businesses in the black community to hire at least some blacks. With the McLins' encouragement, Ralph helped to found the Dayton Youth Movement, a civil rights organization. This was a serious step, because Dayton had its Klan affiliations. Early in June (after Ralph left), dynamite blew up part of McLin's funeral home in the second bombing of a black-owned business. The struggle continued. In July, Herbert would write to Ralph in New York about "the Dayton Youth

Movement, the shit you helped start, they are picketing the stores, and have been somewhat successful in hiring colored clerks."

Ralph's stay in Dayton was no longer a lark. With Ida gone, Christmas was bleak. On December 31, the hunting season ended. Then John Strange's wife, Ollie, returning from several weeks in the hospital, lashed out at the brothers after she discovered that she was probably going to lose the child she was carrying. Although they had given John almost all their money to pay her doctor, she ordered them out of the house.

With this eviction began the most humiliating period of Ralph's life to this point. Marked by hunger, cold, and homelessness, this ordeal pushed him close to despair. At first, he and Herbert spent their waking days wandering about, before returning near midnight to sleep inside John Strange's decrepit Ford sedan parked in his frigid, open-sided garage. For food, they made do mainly with milk and doughnuts charged at a local store. After Herbert secured the key to a tailor shop where he had worked for a while, the brothers were able to quit the icy garage and sleep inside the shop on a makeshift bed of clothing. Luckily, one of the owners of a café, a man known as "Big Stuff" Crawford who had played basketball for Tuskegee, offered Ralph credit on food in exchange for help in preparing Social Security statements for his employees. Also, the lawyer W. O. Stokes stepped in once again and allowed them to sleep and wash up in his office. "I shall never forget his kindness during what seemed like a period of hopelessness," Ralph wrote privately many years later. "During my hour of despair he was, in a sense, a figure of hope who appeared out of nothing more substantial than a letter. Here too, as with so many things, in the beginning was the word."

The word was growing in power in another way. Even as he suffered, Ralph was writing fiction. The harsh living conditions, his incoherent processing of his grief for his mother, his passion to rise above the shabby in life—all drove him onward. When, near the end of February, the insurance company finally settled Ida's account and he prepared to leave town, Ralph's dossier of creative writing had made all of Dayton's humiliations worthwhile.

On March 2, Ralph left by train for New York. Herbert remained in Dayton. The brothers would exchange a few letters over the years, but decades would pass before they met again.

"WORKERS OF THE WORLD MUST WRITE!!!!" Ralph had joked to Wright the previous November from Dayton. It was in Dayton, he would recall, "that I turned my full attention to the task of learning to write fiction." This body of work includes the unfinished draft of a novel, "Slick"; a novella, "Tillman and Tackhead"; at least four short stories; and miscellaneous scraps. Wright had urged him to read works about the art of fiction, including Henry James's celebrated prefaces (to the 1907 New York edition of his novels) edited by R. P. Blackmur; Joseph Warren Beach's survey *The Twentieth Century Novel;* and some of Joseph Conrad's essays. In Wright's eyes, James and Conrad (different writers, to be sure) stood for certain qualities sadly lacking in proletarian fiction, as well as in fiction by black American writers in general. James and Conrad sought psychological depth; they took a subtly oblique approach to the issue of narration; they sought precision of language even as the density of their texts challenged the reader. As expressed famously by Conrad in his preface to *The Nigger of the Narcissus,* the goal was "that the light of magic suggestiveness may be brought to play for an evanescent instant over the commonplace surface of words: of the old, old words, worn thin, defaced by ages of careless usage."

The major influences on Ralph were still Hemingway and Wright. Hemingway is visible in virtually every costive line of the short story "Last Day," in which two hunters are out on the last day of the hunting season. Another of the four Dayton short stories, "Goodnight Irene," is the polar opposite in some ways. Trying to render the consciousness of a drunken, ineffectual black man whose wife has taken up with a white man, Ralph descends into a coarseness remarkably like Wright's: "Funny she had to go do me this way. . . . Usta put her arms around me, the bitch, the white livered bitch! Maybe ah ought to beat her more. Ah always hated to beat her. So sweet. So gawddam yella' and sweet. Oh that slut, doing me this a-way." The popular song "Goodnight Irene" offers a leitmotif to a story that peters out: "Then something in him was falling down, crumbling down like a toppling wall, down to meet the inner darkness. . . . 'Ahrene,' he breathed, 'Goodnight, Ahrene.' "

In "The Black Ball," a black father (the narrator) is tested by the sudden appearance of a white union organizer whose hands had been burned badly one day in Alabama when he had tried to defend a black friend falsely accused of raping a white woman. The narrator must overcome his suspicion of whites and must also risk losing his job by joining the union. The ending is inconclusive, but the narrator is on the verge of joining. Tempered in this way, the doctrinaire aspect of the story is muted. The intelligence at the core of the story is balanced and literate. Although the narrator is reading Malraux's *Man's Fate,* Ralph undercuts the literariness of this reference: "I had to give that up also. Those hands were on my brain, and I couldn't forget that fellow."

The last of the four stories, "A Hard Time Keeping Up," is much less solemn. Narrated by a black train worker, it leads the reader off a train and into the Negro section of a town. In a bar, the narrator is pure Hemingway: "The girl was very lovely as I looked back from the door. All in blue-and-white and the smile still nice in spite of her being high. And when the fellow stood up they made a fine sight." The story ends in deliberate burlesque, but on the whole, it works. Little observed incidents, darting flashbacks, and amusing observations make it pleasant to read. The injustice of racism, offered only as a subtext, adds a measure of gravity to the burlesque.

Ralph's most ambitious pieces of fiction emerged directly from Wright's commanding effect on him at this time. The novella "Tillman and Tackhead" (sporting an epigraph from T. S. Eliot) mimics Wright's naturalistic fictional world of gritty living, raw dialect, and violence. Set in a club not unlike the white Oklahoma Club where Ralph had worked, the tale is of a waiter, Tillman, who thinks of himself as different from his fellow black workers and as potentially an artist. Winslow Homer's *The Gulf Stream,* a painting that depicts a black man adrift on a raft, menaced by sharks, hangs in a room at the club. Enraged by it, Tillman hates the white artist who has depicted a black man in such a helpless situation. He mutilates the painting with a knife. Before he is discovered he stabs a white man who has assaulted him, eludes his hunters, reunites with his mother, then heads for the train yard, where he hopes to ride the rails north to Chicago. Although the story draws in part on Ralph's early life (Tillman's mother is long-suffering and devout; her fatherless son, who loses himself in books, feels near-hatred for her; he discovers, to his dismay, that "the books proved false" and that "reality began with Jim Crow signs"), the link between Tillman and Ralph ends soon enough. Tillman's consciousness and intelligence are limited. His alienation leads not to insight but to incoherence.

Ralph's unfinished novel "Slick," begun in Dayton and developed in New York, also shows Wright's keen influence. An uneducated but brave man, Slick Williams is out of work because of the Depression. When his pregnant wife, Callie, needs a doctor, Slick tries to get the money by gambling, but loses what little he has. Through a series of misadventures with a white policeman, he barely escapes death. While running from the police, he encounters Booker Small, a black man who resembles Ralph, and whose name suggests Tuskegee and perhaps Ralph's criticism of the man (and perhaps of himself) for being to this point only an intellectual. Unlike Slick, who speaks in dialect, Booker uses only standard English. Agreeing to hunt with Slick, he reminisces about his boyhood in Oklahoma, where he learned to shoot rabbits and snipe with his stepfather during one tough season around 1926 (about the time Ralph's stepfather James Ammons taught him to hunt). Booker bemoans the fact that despite his years of education, he again survives by hunting rabbits. He had tried to go to Spain to fight the Fascists. To a befuddled Slick, Booker speaks about Karl Marx and Marx's musings on the ironies of history. But Booker knows that he is not as brave a man as Slick, who was wounded in "the war." Perhaps he isn't brave at all. Nevertheless, he lectures Slick, in a paraphrase of Karl Marx, about the "great things done by common people." "You know," Slick responds, "yuh bout the talkinest son-of-a-bitch what's not a preacher that I ever heard."

"Slick" documents Ralph's ambition in the winter of 1938 to build on "Hymie's Bull" and become a serious writer. Inspired by proletarian fiction, Ralph shows here that he could develop a character in that limited context. Maintaining a fairly consistent point of view, able to construct simple scenes, he creates plausible if rude dialogue and shows a sense of proportion in working on the large canvas of a novel. Honoring modernism, he also shows some restraint in stealing from its bag of technical tricks. Nevertheless, as a novel "Slick" is stillborn. Ironically, its main weaknesses are personified in the patronizing, didactic, self-absorbed, and timid Booker Small. If, in the winter of 1938, Ralph was aware of this irony, he did not yet possess the vision and the courage to resolve it. (A year later, *Direction* magazine of the League of American Writers accepted an excerpt from "Slick." It would be Ralph's first appearance in print as a fiction writer.)

With a feeling of pride and a fresh sense of possibility, Ralph returned to Manhattan early in 1938. "I came back to the city," he would write the following year, "with a sort of strength, a feeling of lyrical self confidence, not a feeling that this was the best of all possible worlds, but that as long as there was a world and under any circumstances I could *make my way*, could survive and grow from whatever soil I found myself in."

Ida's death and his ordeal in Dayton had freed him in certain ways. Now he had no obligation to family beyond the tenuous link to his brother. Liberated, he could now try to refashion his identity as he saw fit. In a phenomenon usually associated with men and the death of their fathers, Ida's passing had triggered in him a pungent release of creativity. The circumstances of his mother's death and the ensuing humiliations had made him more cynical about the world. His main concern now was to make sure that he would never again be so vulnerable and abused as in Dayton. If it was at all within his power, he would take his life into his own hands and live it exactly as he wanted.

In Manhattan, Ralph set down his bags at the home of two white comrades, Jack and Nina Naguid, with whom he had been in touch while in Dayton. The Naguids lived with their Scottish terrier, Kiltie, at 20 West 69th Street, opposite Central Park. Here Ralph scrubbed away the grime of Dayton, soothed his skin with soft sheets and thick towels, and ate heartily. Although not much is known about this friendship, clearly the Party had brought the Naguids and Ralph together. Nina, who took her recruiting duties seriously, seemed much closer than her husband to Ralph. Their few surviving letters to each other reveal sharp if good-natured teasing and genial insults back and forth—not least of all about Ralph's sexist assumption of superiority to Nina, his arrogance in debate, and his sloppy spelling and punctuation. "You have absolutely no sense of humor," Nina scolded him once. He was genuinely fond of the couple—although they soon vanished from his life. The Naguids, Ralph wrote the following year, had been crucial after Dayton in his "regaining faith in human nature."

Seeking out Richard Wright, Louise Thompson, and Langston Hughes, he found all three flourishing. Louise was now national English secretary of the International Workers Order. Langston was back from several months in Spain and living in a studio apartment on St. Nicholas Place in Harlem. Aided by Louise and the IWO, and fired with a renewed radical zeal, he had founded the Harlem Suitcase Theater. Its first production, an agitprop drama with music (*Don't You Want to Be Free?*), was in rehearsal. Wright was doing best of all by far. Living with fellow Communists Herbert and Jane Newton (she was white, he was black) and their children in Brooklyn, he was rising fast. In December, he had joined the federally funded New York Writers' Project. That month, in a national competition organized by *Story* magazine, Wright's short story "Fire and Cloud" had won him the $500 first prize and a book contract from Harper & Brothers. Within days of Ralph's return, Wright's *Uncle Tom's Children: Four Novellas* appeared to fine reviews, including one prediction of a Pulitzer Prize for its author. Modestly, Wright gave all praise to the Party. "The Communist Party," he declared, "will always be a guide and inspiration to my work."

Wright, too, welcomed Ralph back. Hefting his young friend's dossier of fiction, he urged him to revive his application for a place on the Writers' Project—but eventually took exception to the Dayton work. "This is my story, my style," he complained vehemently. "You have copied my ideas, my words and my structure! You must find your own symbols—you must tap the content of your own unconscious and use it!" As Ralph later told it, he had shown Wright a story about a fight between a chef and a "hallboy" in a club (probably a piece of his "Slick" novel). Wright "kept it and kept it without saying anything. I let a few weeks go by and then I finally said, 'Well, what *about* it? What *about* it?' And he said, 'This is *my* stuff.' And I said, 'O.K., but what do you expect? I thought I was taking your advice.'" Wright's response disturbed Ralph: "After that I never showed him another piece of fiction."

Trained as a musician to respect imitation as a necessary step toward mastery, Ralph had not hesitated to tread in Wright's footsteps. He had made a habit (one he continued) of diligently typing or copying out by hand extended passages from writers such as Joyce, Stein, Hemingway, Malraux, and Faulkner, the better to grasp their genius. At this point he had few illusions about the quality of his work. He was certain only that he needed to read, observe, write, and revise if he was ever to develop as a writer.

Done with sculpture, he marked a belated finis to his career as a musician. In March 1938, when Alex North, another of his young Jewish friends and later a major Hollywood composer, put together a little orchestra to perform his ballet music for the dancer Anna Sokolow, Ralph played the trumpet. Never again would he play in public.

As one way closed, another opened. That month, a visitor to the Naguids (who were perhaps matchmaking) snagged Ralph's attention. Vivacious and brown-skinned, Rose Poindexter was a popular entertainer. Born Rosa Araminta Poindexter in 1911 in Harlem to Clarence Poindexter, a messenger, and his wife, Anna, Rose had gone to Europe as a teenage singer and dancer in the *Blackbirds* review of 1929. Quitting the company in Berlin, she spent the next few years performing in Europe, including several small roles in German movies, before returning home in 1935. Since then, in addition to nightclub and radio work, she had been on Broadway in the *New Faces* review of 1936 and in a one-act Eugene O'Neill drama. Petite at slightly over a hundred pounds, Rose was both a bohemian and a radi-

cal. For her, the turning point had been witnessing the July 1934 putsch
by Austrian Nazis, orchestrated by Hitler, that led to the assassination of
the Austrian chancellor.

At this point in his life, Ralph was looking for a woman physically
attractive and smart who would love, honor, and obey him—but not challenge his intellect. Rose was "not an intellectual by any means," he told a
friend the following year, "but possesses a sensitive intelligence, is beautiful, cooks well, and is skillful at all those other things a man is interested
in finding in a woman he marries." She was also "politically alive" and had
"a good supply of what is called 'guts.' " Adding to her appeal, no doubt,
was the fact that she had a fairly steady income and her own apartment.
Within weeks, if not days, of meeting Rose, Ralph moved in with her at
312 West 122nd Street in Harlem.

Ralph and Rose made an attractive couple as they stepped out to
events such as the book party to launch Hughes's pamphlet of radical
verse *A New Song* or the premiere in April of Hughes's *Don't You Want
to Be Free?* The fact that Rose was brown-skinned was not insignificant.
Virtually all the leading black Communist men, from James W. Ford to
the relatively unimportant Herbert Newton, had white wives. Indeed, as
one black woman Communist complained (and Claude McKay gleefully
reported), "all the bright Negro men and all the leaders were connected
legitimately or otherwise with white women, while the Negro women
remained wallflowers." Many black men thought intermarriage asserted
the ideals of radicalism; to many black women, it was usually a gross
betrayal. Ralph was not against mixed marriages, but believed it was
not for him. He knew how fond Wright, for one, was of white women,
despite his insistence that he would never marry one. In May, Wright
would suddenly announce plans to marry a black woman. When she failed
the mandatory Wassermann test for syphilis, he dumped her. He would
soon marry a white woman, and then, when that union quickly failed, as
quickly marry another.

Wright's sexual preferences were of little concern to Ralph. What mattered was Wright as a literary model, their friendship (despite Wright's
displeasure at Ralph's use of his technique), and Wright's growing power.
In April, that power paid off for Ralph when it helped to get him a job at
the New York Writers' Project. The job paid about $25 a week, offering
security of a sort. Since its start in July 1935, the Project had been beset
by tensions, controversies, and strikes. Stalinists and Trotskyites clashed
regularly over such inflammatory issues as the war in Spain and the terri-

fying show trials taking place in the Soviet Union. The Communist dominance of the Project in New York made it a target of the conservative
congressman Martin Dies of Texas and his new House Committee on
Un-American Activities. From 1936, when it supported some seven thousand writers across the country, the Project had declined dramatically as
part of the assault by the political right on the WPA. A broad coalition
of groups, notably the Communist Workers Alliance, had fought against
the cuts—with Ralph's zealous backing. "These rich bastards here," he
protested, "are trying to take the W.P.A. away from us. They would deny a
poor man the right to live in this country for which we have fought and
died."

In the spring of 1938 he was elated to have a Project job when he joined
a group of about thirty researchers and writers led by the veteran black
journalist Roi Ottley. Their task was to develop material about African-
Americans in New York. Blacks had barely been mentioned in the first
of the highly praised, Baedeker-like guides to the various states produced
by regional Project offices. In 1936, the published poet and critic Sterling Brown of Howard University (Ralph had met him at Tuskegee) was
appointed national editor of Negro affairs. Brown then made plans not
only to integrate black history and culture into the state guides but also to
make major independent studies of African-American life. The goals of
Ottley's group were to provide material about blacks for various publications of the New York office, especially the highly anticipated guide to
New York City, and also to produce a separate, comprehensive study
called "The Negro in New York." In addition to Wright (who would soon
be gone) and Ralph, the Project members included such diverse figures
as Claude McKay; Waring Cuney and Richard Bruce Nugent, who had
been minor figures in the Harlem Renaissance; the journalist Ted Poston,
who had traveled to Moscow with Hughes and Thompson in 1932; J. A.
Rogers, the Jamaican-born popular historian whose books about famous
blacks from antiquity to the present inspired many black cultural nationalists; and Ellen Tarry, who wrote books for children.

As Ralph soon discovered, the black corner of the Writers' Project had
its share of conflicts over politics and personalities. For example, although
he had met McKay in 1937, when Langston, who admired McKay, had
introduced them to each other (McKay had just published his fascinating
autobiography, *A Long Way from Home*), Ralph kept his distance because
he knew that Wright dismissed McKay as an obsolete literary force. So
McKay believed, and not only from reading Wright's scornful "Blueprint

for Negro Writing." "All I remember about him," McKay recalled of Wright, "was that he was very rude, when he was an active Communist." He added: "He knew from which side his bread was buttered." Like McKay, Ellen Tarry abhorred Communism; she would help convert him to Roman Catholicism. Openly gay, the flamboyant Richard Bruce Nugent certainly had his detractors. Ralph tried to keep to himself; he knew who was buttering *his* bread. Some writers whispered that Ottley, an imperious figure, was much more interested in sex and power than in serving the Project, so Ralph made sure not to cross him. With only one published piece— a meager book review—to his name, he did not join those writers who resented curbs on their genius. Unlike several, he was not lazy or a drunk. In October, after six months on the job, he would be promoted to "Senior Newspaperman."

Ralph now launched a new, mature phase of his life. He was more confident when he attended an event such as the gala reception in honor of Wright at the Harlem International Workers Order center, or mingled with guests at a private fund-raiser for the Spanish cause at which André Malraux spoke. He found his job stimulating. It led him to records and archives in different parts of the city, notably the New York Public Library on 42nd Street and the Schomburg Collection in Harlem. At the Schomburg he soon knew all the leading librarians and archivists, including the historian Dr. L. D. Reddick; Regina Anderson, a friend to writers in the Harlem Renaissance; Jean Blackwell, a Barnard graduate who would guide the library for many years; and Arturo Schomburg himself, the Puerto Rican–born bibliophile whose private collection had formed the heart of the library's archives. To Ralph, this saturation in black American historical material was a revelation. Some of the work was dull, but "the drudgery was good for me," he insisted. "When you start researching the history of Negroes you plunge into European history and that goes in all directions."

Occupied with his Project tasks, Ralph had little time to write fiction. Perhaps he worked on his "Slick" novel; if so, at some point in midstream he let it go. Instead, he changed focus and took aim at the most influential of the national radical journals—the weekly *New Masses*, where his sponsor, Richard Wright, had just joined its editorial board. On August 16, 1938, Ralph made his debut there with a review of *Sojourner Truth: God's Faithful Pilgrim*, a biography of the African-American mystic and abolitionist by the black writer Arthur Huff Fauset. Ralph's essay was doctrinaire, as he knew it had to be in order to please the editors of *New Masses*.

Ponderously he both gave and took away. Although Fauset's biography was useful, he wrote, its style was dated and "its analysis of religious and mystical experience" wanting. In analyzing Sojourner Truth, who had humbly followed a mystical leader before giving herself to abolitionism, Fauset showed "a confused historical approach and a static philosophy." The correct approach, Ralph made clear, would emphasize the dynamic possibilities of black consciousness, especially if granted an outlet superior to the "very inadequate church."

In *New Masses,* Ralph's review was a small thing. Nevertheless, the sight of his name in print among a list of contributors that included W. H. Auden, Christopher Isherwood, Granville Hicks, and William Carlos Williams might well have stopped his heart for one delirious moment. Only two years before, he had arrived in New York a bookish bumpkin out of Oklahoma by way of rural Alabama. Now, at the very least, he found himself among the crowd of anxious petitioners milling about outside the house of fame.

On September 16, to seal his sense of arrival, Ralph took another step that would have been unthinkable a year before. In New Haven, Connecticut, slightly more than an hour by train from New York, he married Rose Poindexter. Of his friends, only Wright was certainly present, to serve as one of two witnesses. With this consummate act, Ralph closed the door irrevocably not only on his humiliating ordeal in Dayton the previous winter but also on the bitter years in Oklahoma City and at Tuskegee.

5

The Recognition of Necessity
1938–1941

For the Marxist, freedom is the recognition of necessity.
RALPH ELLISON (1940)

Newly wed, with a comfortable apartment in Harlem, a steady if small salary from the Writers' Project, and his debut in *New Masses,* Ralph had good reason in the fall of 1938 to be pleased with the way his life had changed since the previous winter. Satisfied he was not. Ambitious, he knew that stern challenges lay ahead. He had to consolidate his position with the Federal Writers' Project. He had to read even more widely in European and American literature, including philosophy and literary criticism. And he had to set the foundation of a healthy marriage that might lead to children and the kind of stable family life he had never had but always craved.

Ralph had plunged into marriage almost recklessly. "It took nerve," he conceded, "for a broke guy to go after my wife in the manner in which I did." To the marriage he had brought no money, no college degrees, and no reliable professional contacts. Sooner or later, money was going to be a problem. Moreover, Ralph's basic view of women at this time, conditioned by the habitual sexism of men in Oklahoma City and at Tuskegee, was hardly expansive. When he looked toward his mentor, Richard Wright, for guidance, he found little to lead him to egalitarianism. Wright's love life was marked by affairs with white women, dwindling interest in black women, and little gallantry. This approach perhaps influenced Ralph. In a letter to Wright in 1940 about the reception of Wright's best-selling *Native Son* (a novel that breathes a degree of contempt for women, especially black women), he used the kind of coarse language he thought Wright would like. A gathering of radical white women in a Greenwich

Village apartment was made up of "nice, if insipid bitches" who needed to be told "just why Bigger felt like laying Mary [the young white woman he kills] when he had a hand full of breast." Elsewhere, a black woman activist who argued publicly with Ralph became "she of the big ass, gargantuan breasts and bad breath." Responding to Wright's desire (in planning his next novel) to discover the "image of woman's thought process," Ralph offered his own view. That image would "come from Biology." In women, the intellectual process is inherently limp, he believed. On the whole, they "never seem to stray . . . far from biological reality—even when they cloak themselves with intellectual sheep's clothing." Women "waver between their biological craving for security, which manifests itself as fear and inaction, and the emancipation, both sexual and spiritual, that is there to be achieved. In many instances they don't give a dam[n] about revolution at all; only to throw off their girdles and let their behinds expand. Dam[n] man's inhumanity to man—and woman!"

Such ideas probably didn't make for happiness in a marriage with a woman who was sophisticated, a Communist, and also "full of piss and vinegar," as Ralph put it. Eruptions of her temper were met not by violence—he found violence against women unspeakable—but typically by a cool withholding of affection. It did not help that Rose's middle-class parents, who still lived in Harlem, didn't care for Ralph. "They thought I should go out and get a steady job," Ralph's friend John F. Callahan remembered him saying. "They didn't think much of a career in writing, and they didn't care whether I knew it or not! They would have much preferred if I had a position in the post office, for example. To them, Rose had married down." Still, Ralph savored the pleasures of his own neat home. Slowly but surely, he was liquidating the past. When an old box left behind at Tuskegee finally reached him in Harlem early in 1939, he seized the chance to enact this new mastery. "To open the old box after almost three years," he noted, "was like opening a t[omb]." Inside he discovered, among other things, precious boyhood pictures of his dead mother, his brother, and himself, as well as sundry files and folders. Sitting by the fireplace in his cozy apartment, Ralph was hardly sentimental: "I'll be burning old papers for weeks to come."

At the Writers' Project, Ralph obeyed his superiors' instructions and worked hard. Throughout his four years there, his main task was to read and to submit memoranda to his editor that might be included in some larger historical portrait of the black presence in New York State. He sought out signs of radicalism on the part of the black masses. A notable insurrection of 1741 and a conspiracy of 1744 excited him, and he was dismayed to discover leaders such as the poet Jupiter Hammon intimidated by Jim Crow. Indeed, now and then he had to be restrained by his editor in venting his radical zeal. He was fascinated by the Draft Riot of 1863, when Irish mobs turned on blacks in revenge for the conscription of whites into the Civil War. Investigating "Famous New York Trials," he read avidly in the Court of General Sessions archives, including those in the sensational Rhinelander case of 1924, in which the scion of a rich white family, Leonard "Kip" Rhinelander, married and then repudiated a young woman, Alice Jones, who turned out to be black.

The "Living Lore" unit of the Writers' Project, headed by Nicholas Wirth, emphasized New York life through the spoken word. Ralph staked out areas in Harlem and recorded the ditties, songs, and improvised street games of children. He enjoyed tracing the language back to its Southern roots, and compared the lore of New York children with what he remembered of his youth in Oklahoma City. His interest in folklore would become almost scholarly in the coming years—with major effects on his fiction—as he probed the links between folklore, myth, ritual, drama, and history. Ironically, explaining New York street life had taken him back into the arcane world he had entered in exploring the footnotes of T. S. Eliot's *The Waste Land,* and especially the indebtedness of Eliot to Jessie Weston and other British scholars in the so-called Cambridge School of myth and ritual studies. Very little that Ralph composed for the Project rose to the level of literature. What mattered far more was his exposure to a vast store of information and theorizing that, over the years, drastically altered his sense of the past and of human nature and culture itself.

Despite his radical bent and expanding knowledge, Ralph went largely unnoticed—which was what he wanted. He was polite and friendly to blacks and whites alike, to radical leftists and black cultural nationalists, to the domineering men and the few women who also served at the Writers' Project. He escaped an anti-Communist purge there, forced by Martin Dies, that drove out Roi Ottley. Ottley responded by spiriting away thirty-five boxes of manuscript material, which he drew on liberally—but without acknowledging its origins—for his 1943 book *New World A-Coming.* (He then turned the material over to the Schomburg Collection.)

When control of the project passed from the federal government to New York City, Ralph was one of the survivors. In October he was appointed a senior newspaperman, the narrow basis of his campaign to become a successful writer. In this campaign, Wright's "Blueprint for Negro Writing" remained crucial. The manifesto saluted those thinkers who demanded liberal reading and writing, on the one hand, and those who hewed to the cast-iron Communist line, on the other. Like Wright, Ralph aimed to steer between these extremes—as long as it did not jeopardize his new place among the Communists. Of the major institutions in American life, only the Communist Party officially defined blacks as socially and intellectually equal to whites. "I was a Communist because I was a Negro," Wright later pointed out. "Indeed the Communist Party had been the only road out of the Black Belt for me." Both men of course knew that this equality was only token. The white ex-Communist Ben Burns, later the first editor of John H. Johnson's *Ebony* magazine, recalled that most white Communists remained "ignorant of black institutions and society, of black businesses and churches, of black universities and fraternal groups." Instead, there was "the contrived, fawning, tiptoe behavior of Party people in relationship to Negroes."

Nevertheless, this sense of equality was essential to black progress. In "Blueprint," Wright had insisted that black writers must aim for a complexity that they would acquire mainly by learning from major white writers. "His vision need not be simple or rendered in primer-like terms," Wright had written of the Negro artist (in words lifted from Joseph Conrad): "All the complexity, the strangeness, the magic wonder of life that plays like a bright sheen over the most sordid existence, should be there." Wright went on: "To borrow a phrase from the Russians, it should have a complex simplicity. Eliot, Stein, Joyce, Proust, Hemingway, and [Sherwood] Anderson; Gorky . . . and Jack London no less than the folklore of the Negro himself should form the heritage of the Negro writer."

In the fall of 1938, Ralph cared little about what most people, black or white, thought of his cosmopolitanism. He was immersed in studying such matters as the relationship of bourgeois writing to radicalism and the political implications of the avant-garde. In John Strachey's *Literature and Dialectical Materialism* he found support for his own position. To call a writer bourgeois was not to dismiss that writer out of hand. Proust and Joyce, for example, exposed the ills of modern capitalist culture better than almost all radical writers did. Nevertheless, bourgeois writers formed a threat because their regressive ideas often wore gossamer literary garments. Hemingway, for all his gifts, possessed a "ferocious despair" that made him (in 1934) an outstanding nihilist in an epoch "of great Nihilist writers." Quoting a term invented by the radical Mike Gold, Strachey also pointed to the "Fascist Unconscious" lurking behind recent work by the popular American poet Archibald MacLeish, one of the many men "who feel the necessity for some revolt against the existing situation, but who also feel that it is quite impossible to identify themselves with the only people who can, in fact, undertake that revolt, with the working masses."

Although Hemingway's work mesmerized him, Ralph was anxious to avoid its ideological pitfalls; so, too, with T. S. Eliot, whose elitist, religious sympathies should have made him anathema to radicals. Ralph saw evidence of the sometimes acidic debate over liberal versus Communist writing even in the pages of *New Masses*. With the arrival in 1934 of the academically grounded Granville Hicks as literary editor, the journal had returned to its earlier policy of maintaining some distance between art and politics. Hicks defined Communism in such an exalted way that it appeared to subsume all knowledge and experience. "The philosophy of Communism, Marxism," he declared, "is broader than any philosophy the bourgeoisie had evolved. The sympathies of the Communist are more inclusive than the sympathies of even the liberal bourgeois. And the idea of Communism can broaden and grow, whereas the ideas and attitudes of liberalism are bound to shrivel in the violent heat of capitalism's last struggle." Critical of much writing by radicals, Hicks praised Proust and Eliot: "For more than one radical, indeed, Eliot is almost the only modern poet who will bear re-reading."

Wright was now showing the way by example. Surprisingly open, he allowed Ralph and a few other close friends to share in the rapture of creativity from which *Native Son* was emerging. For Wright, this new novel would vindicate all the prescriptions of "Blueprint for Negro Writing." However, neither "Blueprint" nor Wright's short-story collection of 1938, *Uncle Tom's Children,* prepared Ralph for *Native Son.* Aiming to press on his readers a novel "so hard and deep that they would have to face it without the consolation of tears," Wright had succeeded in his task. He had written the story of a poor, ignorant, rebellious young black man from Chicago, Bigger Thomas, and of Bigger's blighted circle, his ill-fated encounter with hypocritical white liberals, feckless radicals, virulent racists, and, finally, of his dawning sense of his humanity just before his execution. For Ralph, reading the story was an astonishing, baffling experience. "I read most of *Native Son* as it came off the typewriter," he recalled, "and I didn't know what to think of it except that it was wonderful."

No writer had ever applied the abrasive of naturalism so ruthlessly to black life, or used Marxism to cut so deeply into its core. No other book matched the inhuman essence of Bigger's life in a rat-infested slum with his mother, sister, and younger brother. Dreiser, Sinclair Lewis, Dos Passos, and others had exposed the corruption of capitalism and liberalism, but no one had linked this corruption so pervasively to racism. Wright also explored some terrifying ideas. *Native Son* suggested the inevitability of black hatred of whites; the desire of blacks for violent revenge; and, most appalling, the idea that violent revenge might be essential therapy for the black mind. He had created a demonic hero, a doomed angel of retribution. The novel left Ralph at once aghast and exultant. After *Native Son* appeared, Ralph would be called upon again and again to explain and defend its meaning. He did so eagerly. Nevertheless, he knew that his own vision was different from Wright's, and also that Wright's triumph was not a solution to his own writing problems.

André Malraux's novel *Man's Hope* came out at roughly the same time. It completed a trilogy of dramatically influential novels begun with *Days of Wrath* and his masterpiece, *Man's Fate (La Condition Humaine)*. These books now placed the French novelist at the center of Ralph's pantheon of writers —a group that would comprise Eliot, Hemingway, Dostoyevsky, and, later, Faulkner and Kenneth Burke. Ralph was hardly alone in revering Malraux. In November, *Time* magazine hailed him as "the world's foremost novelist of revolution and one of the most exciting and provocative of living writers." Wright, too, admired Malraux—and was working on a novel he called "Black Hope." A versatile intellectual (Ralph had read his cerebral articles in *Verve* magazine that would be published as *The Psychology of Art*), Malraux was also a fearless revolutionary and a writer who, believing in the basic loneliness of the human heart, had both the insight and the command of literary form that such fusions demanded. "Malraux's real theme," as Malcolm Cowley told readers of *The New Republic,* "is a feeling that most men nurse, secretly, their sense of absolute loneliness and uniqueness, their acknowledgement to themselves of inadequacy in the face of life and helplessness against death— that is what he means by *la condition humaine;* this is man's lot, his destiny, his servitude. And he has chosen to depict this emotion during a revolutionary period because it is then carried, like everything else that is human, to its pitch of highest intensity."

While Wright was pushing Ralph toward a grotesque view of America, Malraux was challenging him in other ways. How, Malraux asked, can one make the best of one's life? As Ralph explained to a friend, Malraux answered: "By converting as wide a range of experience as possible into conscious thought." As a young Frenchman, Malraux had challenged French colonialism in Asia and (or so it was then believed) had joined the revolutionary movement involving Communists, nationalists, and the foreign powers occupying Shanghai. Out of this material had come *Man's Fate*. But could there be any genuine link between such epic action in China and black American life, in which political resistance typically assumed petty, token, or criminal forms? Ralph was sure it existed, because black people were an essential part of humanity.

Malraux provided Ralph with an entrée into contemporary Continental European thought, which would prove decisive in shaping his future as a writer. Through reading *Man's Hope* both he and Wright became interested in the Spanish philosopher of Basque descent Miguel de Unamuno, who is a figure in the novel. Early in life Unamuno had undergone a crisis of religious faith that had led him to confront core ideas about death and immortality, pessimism and happiness, the banal and the tragic, in his murky treatise of 1913, *Del sentimiento trágico de la vida* (translated and published in 1921 as *The Tragic Sense of Life in Men and Nations*). He proposed that our physiological construction, mediated by a perhaps innate pathology, determines our ideas, including our pessimistic or optimistic vision of life. To Ralph, hunting for links between blacks and the wider world, Unamuno's ideas about the human condition seemed to harmonize with the bedeviling qualities of fatalism and passivity with which African-American culture had long been identified. In *The Souls of Black Folk,* Du Bois had written about "the tragic soul-life of the slave," who expressed it "under the stress of law and whip" in the songs called the spirituals or "sorrow songs." Black religion, responding to slavery and Jim Crow, had stressed the need for humility and the endurance of suffering. Neither Ralph nor anyone else (including Langston Hughes and Zora Neale Hurston, the main champions of the blues among black writers) had begun to theorize the blues as the secular articulation of a philosophy of life that blended tragedy, comedy, joy, and art in a form peculiar to black American culture although accessible to other people. To Ralph, it seemed appropriate to apply Unamuno's sense of the tragic to a culture usually denied a tragic dimension—indeed, to a people deemed to be outside history.

Such ideas were important to Ralph as he searched with the zeal of an autodidact for bits and pieces of knowledge that bolstered his sense of himself as an intellectual on a quest to parse African-American reality in his fiction. Traces of Unamuno's language in *The Tragic Sense of Life* would surface stealthily in *Invisible Man,* as the scholar William E. Cain has noted privately. For example, Ellison's narrator identifies himself in the opening of the prologue as "a man of substance, of flesh and bone"—an echo of Unamuno's first chapter, "The Man of Flesh and Bone." Other writers associated with gloom helped to sharpen Ralph's vision. As Cain has also noted, at least two striking allusions to Edgar Allan Poe's short story "The Landscape Garden" exist in Ellison's novel. According to Poe's narrator, "no more remarkable man ever lived than my friend, the young Ellison." The narrator goes on to say: "There *might* be a class of beings, human once, but now to humanity invisible, for whose scrutiny and for whose refined appreciation of the beautiful, more especially than for our own, had been set in order by God the great landscape-garden of the *whole earth.*" But neither Unamuno nor Poe would be as essential to Ralph as the tragic sense of life expressed in Dostoyevsky. It was important to Ralph to point out that he had read Dostoyevsky before meeting Wright: "He assumed that I hadn't read any of . . . Dostoyevsky. . . . I was somewhat chagrined by his apparent condescension." Yet Wright probably pressed on Ralph, to excellent effect, the potential of Dostoyevsky's novels as a guide to the black writer. These novels illuminated some of the complex ethical questions facing black Americans in their hunger for social justice, their relationship to the committing of crime in a nation that criminally abused them, and the diabolical prospect that crime might be essential psychotherapy for black people.

Dostoyevsky understood the ordeal of searching for a sense of dignity and identity in a hostile world; his works explore the threat of chaos underlying the human condition. Ralph would argue later that America in the twentieth century resembled Russia in Dostoyevsky's day in that both societies were "plunging headlong into chaos" because of the disruption of old hierarchies and the formation of new alliances. Black Americans had lived with this perception of social, psychological, and ethical chaos both during and after slavery. Eventually, Dostoyevsky's *Notes from Underground* and *Crime and Punishment,* in particular, would be crucial to Ralph's writing, as they were to Wright's.

Looking back on this period, Ralph would make an odd admission and an odd distinction. He said he was eating the Communists' bread but nurturing opposite ambitions as a cultural worker. "I never wrote the official type of fiction," he later insisted. "I wrote what might be called propaganda—having to do with the Negro struggle—but my fiction was always trying to do something else. . . . I never accepted the ideology which the *New Masses* attempted to impose on writers. They hated Dostoyevsky, but I was studying Dostoyevsky. They felt that Henry James was a decadent, some sort of snob who had nothing to teach a writer from the lower classes—I was studying James. I was also reading Marx, Gorki, Sholokhov, and Isaac Babel. I was reading everything, including the Bible. Most of all, I was reading Malraux."

In other words, Ralph should have been aspiring not to *New Masses* but to *Partisan Review*. Originally the organ of the John Reed Club of New York, a Communist outlet, *Partisan Review* had resumed publication in 1937 (after a one-year lapse) as a journal explicitly opposed to Communist totalitarianism and suppression. Although still devoted to radicalism, its editors (Philip Rahv and William Phillips) wrote now about the "forms of literary editorship, at once exacting and adventurous, which characterized the magazines of aesthetic revolt." Nevertheless, it was the far less tolerant *New Masses* that had welcomed Ralph in 1938, in part because of the influence of Wright and Langston Hughes, but ultimately because of Communist egalitarianism. He faced the dilemma of making the most of this chance even as he nurtured dreams of literary glory beyond anything the Communists had to offer.

Living this double life wasn't easy. In November, for example, when he and Rose, along with a wide swath of the left with ties to the black community, attended the second-season opening of Langston Hughes's Suitcase Theater, he was of mixed mind about what Hughes was contributing to the cause. Ralph was friendly and even deferential to Hughes, who was presenting a less racially chauvinistic version of *Don't You Want to Be Free?* as well as some satirical skits. Enjoying Hughes's work did not mean that Ralph still admired Hughes's propaganda-driven art. The more Ralph read Malraux and Dostoyevsky, the more he found it hard to praise Hughes (and every other black writer save Wright) as an artist. He also found it hard to respect fully anyone who, like Hughes, appeared to set relatively low standards for himself as an artist. Ralph knew firsthand how well read, cosmopolitan, and sophisticated Hughes was. Why weren't these qualities better represented in his art?

Ralph still liked Langston. In June, he and Rose had joined Toy and Emerson Harper, Louise Thompson, and other friends of Langston for the funeral of his mother, Carrie Langston Clark. Langston and Ralph even worked together, as part of Hughes's ongoing collaboration with the black composer James P. Johnson, on a one-act, radical blues "opera" about trade unionism called *The Organizer*. The song "Got to Do It"— music by Jimmy [James P.] Johnson, lyrics by Langston Hughes and Ralph Ellison—was copyrighted in 1939. And Ralph still tagged along at Langston's major readings in the metropolitan area. In November, when Hughes and Muriel Rukeyser read their work at the New York Public Library, Ralph went backstage as Langston's main guest. Nevertheless, Ralph was also drawing away from Langston. Bedeviled by serious money problems, Hughes had been backsliding even more into political and artistic compromise. "The only thing I can do," he confessed to an anti-Communist friend, "is string along with the Left until maybe someday all of us poor folk will get enough to eat." Desperate, he went out to Hollywood to work on a film with Clarence Muse, a veteran black actor and musician well connected to the Hollywood studios. The movie, set in the Old South, was riddled with Hollywood stereotypes of black life. Released in June 1939, *Way Down South* would be lambasted and Hughes condemned in the radical press.

Ralph was severe with Hughes, although he knew that he and Wright were themselves by no means always consistent in ideological terms. He and Wright were ready to consort quietly with certain anti-Communists. Early in December, they visited the progressive writer Waldo Frank at his Manhattan home. Frank had fallen out of favor with the Communists after calling for a formal investigation of the soon infamous Moscow show trials of 1936–1938 that led to the execution of many alleged enemies of Stalin and the Soviet state. In July, at the Second American Writers' Congress, organized by the League of American Writers, of which Frank was nominally chairman, Earl Browder denounced him. (Since 1935 Browder had led the U.S. Communist Party.) In fact, Frank deserved Ellison's and Wright's respect. An innovative writer of fiction and a provocative essayist and editor, he had also championed the black writers Jean Toomer and Claude McKay early in their careers. When Browder launched his attack on Frank, McKay stalked off the stage.

Ralph would remain something of a Stalinist for years to come. The Moscow show trials, he said, were a legitimate response by the government to "widespread sabotage and wrecking," as he wrote in April 1939 to his Tuskegee schoolmate Joe Lazenberry. He also accepted the Party's proposal to create, if blacks so desired, an autonomous black state to be carved out of the South's Black Belt. This hallucinatory idea, which the executive committee of the Comintern (the worldwide organization of

Communist parties) first outlined in 1928, had been adopted as policy by
the Party in the United States. Much as he disliked black nationalism,
Ralph hewed even here to the Party line. "If we are ever to attain independence in the Black Belt," he wrote solemnly to Lazenberry about a
possible alliance between radical blacks and their Mexican counterparts,
"or rather, if that independence comes to depend upon armed uprising,
then these people [Mexicans] will be our logical allies; their history is
such that they could not help but offering some help. They are fighting
now for their independence from American capitalist[s] and in time they
will become an important factor for democracy in the Americas."

In two years, so much had changed in his life. To Lazenberry, Ralph
boasted about the differences in him since Tuskegee. There, he had been
a romantic, charmed by "the moonlight and mockingbirds; now it is the
other experience which has become the more meaningful. Conscious
thought has converted it into an impulse to creation; in these times it is
the positive reality. One sucks experience through the body into the mind
and there makes something of it to change, improve the realities from
which the experience came." Too many younger blacks were interested
only in security; the more worthy goal was "to influence the consciousness of the entire next generation of Negroes." Not merely a member of
the black vanguard, he was now one of a trio of artists who would inspire
revolutionary change. Wright, of course, was another. The third was the
playwright Ted Ward, a close friend of Wright from Chicago, where he
had worked on the Federal Theatre Project. Just after Christmas, Ward
arrived in New York and was soon at work on a stage adaptation of
Wright's short story "Bright and Morning Star," as he tinkered with his
major play, *Big White Fog* (the title taken from a Wright story). Although
Ralph knew that his own credentials were skimpy compared with those of
Wright and Ward, he nevertheless proposed himself as their peer. Wright,
he noted, had his first book and the manuscript of a new novel, and Ward
his play. "I am mapping a novel of the Negro college," he confided.
"Frankly, we are angry; but not so much that we can't see." With Wright
now openly discussed (by at least one reviewer) in the same breath with
Hemingway, "we have overcome the cultural and intellectual isolation
which has been characteristic of Negro writers."

All the same, he admitted that he was having a hard time with this
novel. Early in 1939, the editor of *Story* magazine, Whit Burnett, rejected
a section. An article on blacks and Jews commissioned by the leftist *Jewish People's Voice* did appear the following spring. Moved by the plight of
European Jews, he was also aware of the extent to which Jews were shap-

ing the radical milieu around him. To Ralph, this was a plus. Although Jews sometimes discriminated against blacks, on the whole they opened doors for them. The ideal New York Jewish spirit was personified for him in the "enthusiastic, bright-eyed little old Jewish lady, fresh from an art exhibition with color catalogue in hand," who engaged him in talk one day on a Madison Avenue bus shortly after his arrival from Tuskegee. Brushing aside his mumbling shyness, she insisted that he must visit the famed museums in the city. "This is one of the world's great centers of art," she admonished him, "so learn about them! Why are you waiting?"

The Writers' Project, the League of American Writers, and other centers of intellectual activity threw him into regular contact with bright, energetic, welcoming Jews. For many Harlem blacks, the black-Jewish relationship was fraught with problems. In his essay, Ralph tried to arbitrate between the two groups. Although most black newspapers denounced the oppression of Jews, some journals, including the influential *Pittsburgh Courier* and the *New York Amsterdam News,* resented those American Jews who detached the matter of Nazi oppression from that of Jim Crow. The fact that some Jewish businesses refused to hire blacks and that some Jewish landlords exploited them was also part of the volatile issue. Ralph's approach followed the Party line. Although some complaints by blacks about Jews had merit, Fascists were behind much of the trouble. Black anti-Semitism must not be tolerated, Ralph said, because no racial discrimination should be tolerated. "Life in the United States," he insisted, "has taught Negroes that Democracies are democratic only when they are mobile. They feel that closer functioning between the Jewish and Negro people will furnish a great impulse toward that mobility."

Many blacks wanted a more aggressive voicing of their grievances, but more important to Ralph (in addition to preserving his personal contacts and friendships) was the welfare of the Party and the anti-Fascist cause, which suffered badly in the late winter and spring of 1939. In March, the Spanish republic fell to the rebel general Francisco Franco's forces and Germany invaded Czechoslovakia. In April, Italy entered Albania. In May, Adolf Hitler and Benito Mussolini formally signed a pact. These disasters overwhelmed the grumbling of black nationalists. Ralph was far more attentive to the eloquence of younger white writers on the left such as W. H. Auden, Christopher Isherwood, and Louis MacNeice when he heard them speak in April during a public discussion about the danger to poetry and art in a world under the threat of global war.

At this time of foundering confidence in anti-Fascism, the Third American Writers' Congress opened in New York. Thrilled by a plenary address by Thomas Mann, Ralph was also stirred by the presence on the conference program of Negro writers, including his friends Wright, Hughes, Ward, Alain Locke, and Sterling Brown. On the first day, Langston addressed a special plenary session at Carnegie Hall. On the last day, in what the *New York Times* called "one of the most dramatic incidents" of the gathering, he read aloud the names of forty-five writers from nine countries who had been killed by Fascists. In between, Ralph attended a variety of lectures and sessions. He was frequently in the company of Wright, who was greeted almost everywhere as a risen star. Offered a coveted Guggenheim Foundation fellowship, Wright had just resigned from the Federal Writers' Project. This was precisely the kind of freedom of which Ralph dreamed.

In another show of freedom, Wright chose that summer between the two leading candidates—both white—for his hand in marriage. He picked Dhimah Rose Meadman, a tall, commanding dancer of Russian Jewish ancestry who sometimes passed herself off as Egyptian. In doing so, he rejected Ellen Poplowitz, a pretty, quiet, but intelligent young Communist from New York to whom he had proposed marriage but who had shyly put him off. Ralph knew both women. He had acted at times as a go-between on Wright's behalf—just as at the writers' conference in June he had served, at Wright's request, as an escort for the young black Chicago poet Margaret Walker, who seemed to be infatuated, if not obsessed, with Wright. (By now, as his biographer Michel Fabre would note, Wright was probably incapable of marrying a black woman.) Admiring Dhimah, Ralph thought her far too cultivated for Wright, whose tastes and manners—his choice of clothing, his behavior as a host—he found plebeian, and sometimes crude. Ralph recalled thinking about Wright, "Man, you have to fall out of love with this woman." Nevertheless, on August 12, Dhimah and Richard were married in the sacristy of the Episcopal church on Convent Avenue, near the brownstone home of Meadman's mother on historic Hamilton Terrace. Ralph and Rose served as their witnesses.

As Wright flourished, life coincidentally became harder for the Ellisons. After Ralph missed several days at the Writers' Project with a foot infection, he was denied immediate reinstatement because of strict regulations governing leaves of absence. Fortunately, Rose landed a role in a play. Rehearsals and performances took her to Stamford, Connecticut, where she spent most of the summer. Later, she worked as an entertainer at the Communist-sponsored Camp Unity in Wingdale, New York. When Ralph visited her, they traveled to the Mohegan Colony, up the Hudson River near the town of Peekskill, to visit Richard and Dhimah, who had moved there shortly after their wedding.

Keeping up his writing, Ralph had two successes that summer. Fiction-like at first, then coolly reporting the facts, his article "Judge Lynch in New York" tells the story of three young black men, just up from the South, who live on West 150th Street (as Ralph did). Innocently wandering westward to the almost exclusively white Riverside Drive, they are insulted and abused by white police and a gang of white toughs. Indignantly, Ralph's article tells of similar incidents in New York City and the brave efforts of progressive groups to curb them. It ends with a warning: "Every effort is being made to curb these incidents which, if allowed to continue, are sure to precipitate the sort of emotional reaction that made for the riots of 1935." With this piece in *New Masses* Ralph added an edge of radical militancy to his reputation. Employees at the *New Masses* office sat up nervously when police arrived to inquire about Ralph's notes and sources. A police captain questioned Ralph at his home. The mayor, Fiorello La Guardia, announced steps to stop similar acts of violence against blacks.

The commotion pleased Ralph but was overwhelmed on August 22 by the astounding news that, after months of secret negotiation, the German foreign minister, Joachim von Ribbentrop, was flying to Moscow at that moment, on Hitler's orders, to sign a nonaggression pact with his counterpart in the Soviet Union, Vyacheslav Molotov. The news utterly confounded most American radicals. Alfred Kazin, a young Jewish intellectual and writer from New York, hard at work that morning on an ambitious study of American literature, remembered his reaction: " 'No!' I shouted at the radio. 'It's not true!' " Granville Hicks, no longer literary editor of *New Masses* but still a Communist, was also stunned. "Jesus Christ," he blurted out. "That knocks the bottom out of everything." Sustaining organized anti-Fascism was the certainty that the Soviet Union was the mortal enemy of Nazi Germany and a guaranteed deterrent to Hitler's expansionist goals in the east. "That morning," Kazin went on, "the Second World War had begun. Stalin had opened the door to war, Stalin had lighted the fuse in Hitler's hand."

While many radicals left the Party, Ralph stood fast. He believed, as the black Communist Harry Haywood would put it, that the pact was "a brilliant and necessary diplomatic move" to save the USSR. The pact was needed, obviously, after Britain, France, and other nations rebuffed Soviet attempts to organize against Hitler. Ralph stood fast even when virtually every one of his leftist literary heroes, including Mann, Hemingway, and Malraux (but not Wright), recoiled from the Soviet Union in varying degrees of horror. A week after the signing of the pact he was unmoved when German armies overwhelmed Poland, just as he would be unmoved in November when Soviet armies entered Finland. "None of the people who are so hot about Finland," he noted even as he questioned fund-raising for the Finns, "are saying a word about the 3,000,000 homeless, foodless, sharecroppers we have in this country, let alone the millions of us who don't have decent jobs."

He inched upward as a writer in September when *Direction*, edited by Marguerite Tjader Harris, published his story "Slick Gonna Learn," an excerpt from his stillborn Dayton novel "Slick." The story ends with Slick trying to understand the meaning of both his ordeal at the hands of brutal white law officers and one white man's gesture of kindness toward him. With this taut piece of fiction, Ralph had reached another milestone—his first publication as a fiction writer. As a display of literary skill, "Slick Gonna Learn" is no advance on "Hymie's Bull." Nevertheless, with the story in *Direction* his identity as a professional writer was starting to take hold.

On September 1, Ralph and Rose left nondescript West 150th Street for an apartment with a small rose garden at 25 Hamilton Terrace, near the landmark former home of Alexander Hamilton. Next door lived the swing pianist Teddy Wilson, celebrated as a member of the racially integrated—unprecedented in the annals of jazz until then—Benny Goodman Quartet, along with the clarinetist Goodman and the drummer Gene Krupa (both white) and the black vibraphonist Lionel Hampton. The alto saxophonist Benny Carter also lived nearby.

Ralph lived among the stars but he was not yet one of them. The rent ($38.50 a month) was not exorbitant, but he and Rose were on shaky financial ground, especially after Rose fell ill early in the fall. Not so Richard and Dhimah Wright. In August, with the publication of *Native Son* only weeks away, the influential Book-of-the-Month Club began negotiations with his publisher, Harper & Brothers, about making the novel one of the club's main monthly offerings—provided that Wright agreed to tone down some risqué passages. (He quickly agreed.)

Nothing so wonderful was in sight for Ralph. Acting perhaps under

Party orders, he worked as a publicist for the predominantly black Greater New York Committee for Employment. Formed the previous year, 1938, with Communist support, its leadership comprised Adam Clayton Powell, Jr., his fellow Harlem minister William Lloyd Imes, and A. Philip Randolph of the Brotherhood of Sleeping Car Porters, a veteran socialist whose dogged leadership of the railroad porters in the face of strenuous opposition by the AFL had ended in full union recognition for the brotherhood. The most charismatic was Powell, pastor of the powerful Abyssinian Baptist Church. Tall and handsome, with light skin, notably thick, wavy black hair, and an ebullient personality, he was a pragmatist. "To help my people," he declared, "I used everyone that had any strength whatsoever, including the Communists." The committee faced a defining task. Most businesses and public utilities refused to hire blacks, especially for white-collar jobs. Only after rallies, picketing, and other forms of agitation did a few stores on 125th Street, in the heart of Harlem, hire a few blacks as cashiers and salespeople. Bell Telephone took on four black women as operators. The World's Fair, scheduled for New York City, promised to hire some Negroes.

Although Ralph found working for the committee stimulating, he was relieved when the Writers' Project, revived by the City of New York, rehired him. He also reached an informal agreement with Samuel Sillen, one of the two editors of *New Masses,* to publish more often in the magazine. In December, Ralph placed two brief reviews of novels there. One was of Louis Cochran's *Boss Man;* the other examined Gene Fowler's *Illusion in Java.* He summarily dismissed both books—the first for not stressing the social and economic forces that cause feelings of isolation, the second as "a subtle piece of escapist fiction." With these two reviews, he began a notable run in *New Masses.* In the following three years, or until he ceased writing for the journal late in 1942, he would publish thirteen more literary essays and reviews, three essays of political reportage, and two short stories. Faced with the problem of Wright's growing eminence—and remoteness—the Communists were betting on Ralph Ellison as his successor.

This was also true of the League of American Writers. For example, early in 1940, Ralph received a request from the league, through the young short-story writer Len Zinberg, for an antiwar pamphlet. As a result of the pact, the Party was more opposed than ever to American involvement in the war. Now Zinberg wanted a piece "stressing the jim-crow and shovel work that the Negro troops experienced in the last war," which

Ralph could do anonymously. Ralph promptly submitted a draft in which he lashed out at W. E. B. Du Bois for having published during World War I (in his magazine, *Crisis*) "some of the most disgusting war propaganda . . . couched in sentimental, pseudo-religious imagery." (In particular, his editorial "Close Ranks," which urged support for the Allies and a temporary halt to civil rights agitation, angered some readers.) Ralph believed in the Party's antiwar position. When he wrote his brother in February (after some prompting from Rose), he begged Herbert, "Let no one fool you into the army, or navy."

In February 1940, his importance to *New Masses* was again evident. The February 6 number carried his name on its cover. His essay "Camp Lost Colony" opens with an extended reference to John Steinbeck's landmark novel *The Grapes of Wrath*, then goes on to report on a defiant group of black and white sharecroppers living in Missouri. Ralph calls for federal intervention to alleviate the plight of farmworkers, and underscores the antiwar, pro-Soviet message now central to *New Masses*. He ends by expressing the hope that President Franklin Roosevelt would "turn his attention from" Finland and its apparently unimportant (to Ralph) invasion by the Soviet Union long enough to deal with this matter.

Later in February came "The Good Life," a stinging review of the British writer J. B. Priestley's sentimental, insufficiently radical novel *Let the People Sing*, and "TAC Negro Show," in which Ralph reviewed a left-inspired variety show, *Saturday Night in Harlem*. Not only was it "notable for its avoidance of comic Negro stereotypes" but the performers were "excellent"—including the first one he mentions by name, Rose Poindexter. The "pièce de résistance," in which Rose also starred, satirized the hit movie *Gone With the Wind*. "Comedy of this quality," Ralph wrote somewhat ludicrously, "is achieved only when there is as much understanding and emotion as is required of tragedy." However, nothing he published in the winter of 1940 meant much compared with the thunder of Wright's novel *Native Son* when it appeared on March 1 from the Book-of-the-Month Club. Later, the socialist cultural critic and editor of *Dissent* magazine Irving Howe would assert that when *Native Son* appeared "American culture was changed forever." Reviewers responded with striking comparisons of Wright to Harriet Beecher Stowe, Dostoyevsky, Steinbeck, and Dreiser, as well as with predictions of a Pulitzer Prize. Within three weeks, about 215,000 copies were sold—"more copies than any novel Harper had published in the previous twenty years."

With this book, Wright had backed up his cruel words about black literature in "Blueprint for Negro Writing." He had blasted all sales records for black writers even as he earned praise from whites that no black writer had ever received. Wright was soon on the move. Early in March, he, Dhimah, her young son (from a previous marriage), and her mother sailed for Cuernavaca, Mexico, where Wright was expected to stay for several months as he worked on his new novel, "Black Hope." In his absence, Ralph became his eyes, ears, and voice in New York. "I have talked about the book," he eagerly assured Wright, "trying to answer attacks against it until I am weary." Praising Wright for making "a terrific indictment of capitalist America," his good friend and Party superior in Harlem Ben Davis complained in the *Daily Worker* that blacks in the novel were mainly victims, not revolutionaries. But in his "Change the World" column in the *Sunday Worker,* Mike Gold defended Wright. "It is no exaggeration to say," Gold declared, "that at one stroke he has become a national figure." The debate picked up momentum. Was *Native Son* compatible with Communist thought, or was it a renegade act? Was its depiction of black life accurate or slanderous? Was it likely to help or to hurt the cause of civil rights?

Many blacks, in part spurred by envy, attacked the book. Some leading black Communists detested Wright—James W. Ford apparently hated him—because of his alleged arrogance. Ralph spent several hours one evening arguing with Abner Berry, the former head of the League of Struggle for Negro Rights, and Theodore Bassett, whom the Party had appointed director of education for its Harlem operation. They seemed obtusely unable to distinguish between propaganda and good fiction. Approving of Wright's prescriptions in "Blueprint," they loathed their application in *Native Son.* In a letter to Richard, Ralph also took on Ben Burns, perhaps the leading Communist reviewer of race literature. Although Burns, who was Jewish, "sounded like a broad scholar of deep perception" after the Philistine mouthings of Berry and Bassett, he remained critical of the novel's ideological integrity. Even after V. J. Jerome, editor of the journal *The Communist* and the Party's foremost authority on matters of culture, endorsed the book, the noisy, sometimes nasty argument went on.

For Ralph, the controversy raised some disturbing questions. "How far can the Marxist writer go," he asked Wright, "in presenting a personalized, humanist version of his ideology?" Preoccupied with economics, Marx and Lenin had written little about the human personality. Now *Native Son* had brought Ralph face-to-face with the central ethical question on which his ambitious way of being in the world turned. His answer was righteous but odd. Touting the idea of "the revolutionary significance of Bigger," he attacked readers who saw the murderer Bigger as a bad man. "They fail to see," he argued, "that what's *bad* in Bigger from the point of view of bourgeois society is *good* from our point of view." For Marxists, *"freedom* is the recognition of necessity." Bigger became free when he violently acted to resolve his problem of oppression by both whites and blacks. Quoting Hegel about "indignant consciousness" (Bigger's state of mind at the start of the novel), which gave way to the superior "theoretical consciousness" (his state of mind at the end), Ralph saw sharp implications for Negroes: "Would that *all* Negroes were as psychologically free as Bigger and as capable of positive action!" Too many people, black and white, clung too rigidly to bourgeois notions of right and wrong: "Hence a [Granville] Hicks . . . jumps off the train when the USSR signs a pact with Germany. No doubt there will be similar sharp turns in the course of history relative to the Negro questions, and these people will be caught short." About blacks who hated *Native Son* he was finally scornful: "These bastards here are hollering their heads off because Bigger became a man rather than a political puppet! To hell with them."

Thus aroused into a tumescent sense of possibility, he headed to Washington, D.C., on April 26 for the third convention of the National Negro Congress. The convention would have a startling effect on him. For the first time, he (with his chronic distrust of black groups and institutions) attended a predominantly black gathering of the left. The NNC was the latest of various Communist-backed efforts, notably the League of Struggle for Negro Rights (of which Langston Hughes had been the figurehead president), to gather key black organizations under its radical umbrella as the Party regrouped in the wake of the pact.

Some black delegates were city people, confident and stylish; others, country folk, looked ill at ease but not timid. The mood darkened following the presentation of a plaque by John P. Davis, executive secretary of the NNC, to John L. Lewis, the white leader of the CIO, to honor what Davis called his distinguished service to black Americans. Then came the most dramatic episode of the convention. Facing growing antagonism to the Communist Party both from the right and from the non-Communist left, especially because the Communists opposed American aid to the Allies in Europe, the NNC had been careful in its pre-convention literature to avoid endorsing Soviet or Communist Party USA policies. But the theatrical attempt by Davis to flatter the CIO showed that part of the NNC leadership was bent on taking the organization far to the left. So it appeared to the nominal president of the NNC, A. Philip Randolph, a leading member now of the American Federation of Labor, opposed to the CIO. With his powerful union ties and his national reputation for probity and courage, Randolph had seemed poised to help the NNC achieve its goals of unity, civil rights, and economic prosperity for blacks. Now he did the opposite. Following Lewis at the podium, he denounced the Communist tendencies implicit in the new NNC strategy.

Counterattacking the next morning, Davis endorsed the antiwar position of the Communists and lauded the Soviet Union as the true bastion of democracy. The delegates—and Ralph—wildly endorsed this speech. (Randolph resigned from the presidency of the NNC, to be replaced by a rising black Communist, Max Yergan, well known among blacks as a professor at the then mainly white City College in New York.) That afternoon, at panel discussions on topics including economic security, unemployment, and the black woman, Ralph saw that Randolph had lost the support of the delegates.

Most important to Ralph, as he reported in *New Masses*, were the rank-and-file delegates, especially those from the South, "whose very presence here means a danger faced and a fear conquered, and danger to be faced again." When he pressed a tall black woman from Arkansas about religion as a source of her strength, she replied calmly, "Well, son. We used to go to the graveyard and preach to folks 'bout heaven. But I done found that the way to serve Christ is by helping folks here on earth." Despite the folksy aspect of his account, Ralph was genuinely moved by the congress, which he reported to Wright as "the most exciting thing to happen to me." It had changed his life: "I found in it the first real basis for *faith* in our revolutionary potentialities." The source of his faith was not black Communist leaders (he wrote Wright about "the stupidities of black CP leaders") but the people themselves. As if for the first time, Ralph was now seeing the Negro in an epic light. Once, following a boxing victory by Joe Louis, Wright had raved in print about "the wild river" of "pent-up folk consciousness" that he had seen in celebrating blacks—a river "that's got to be harnessed." At last, Ralph now believed, "the 'river' is harnessing *itself*! For me, this is the soundest basis for emotional and intellectual optimism. You told me I would begin to write when I matured emotionally, when I began to *feel* what I understood. I am beginning to understand what you meant. I suppose that's why the experience of the congress was almost mystical in its intensity. When will the Marxist psychologists explain the material-dialectical meaning of the mystical experience?"

This impact showed in almost every line of his *New Masses* report, "A Congress Jim Crow Didn't Attend." Brilliant as propaganda, the essay combined Hemingway's terse lyricism with a deadly serious bias. "We drove all night to beat the crowd," Ralph began. "Outside of Baltimore we began passing troops of cavalry. They were stretched along the highway for a mile. Young fellows in khaki with campaign hats strapped beneath their chins, jogging stiffly in their saddles." The reporter feels the delegates' sorrows, fears, and joys. Of the episode involving A. Philip Randolph, he writes: "The auditorium had that overwhelming air usually associated with huge churches, and I remember what André Malraux once said about the factory becoming for the workers what the cathedral was, and that they must come to see in it not ideal gods, but human power struggling against the earth." Rhetorically, Ralph assassinates Randolph. When the latter speaks, "his voice droned out abstract phrases; statistics rolled forth." The delegates become restless. Some walk out. "I did not realize it," Ralph laments, "but I had witnessed a leader in the act of killing his leadership." Roaming the convention, he finds among the delegates (slyly echoing Hegel) "a temper of militant indignation." He ends with hosannas: "And there in the faces of my people I saw strength. There with the whites in the audience I saw the positive forces of civilization and the best guarantee of America's future."

New Masses loved the essay. Ecstatic at having the services of such a skilled, loyal black reporter, the editors sought more material from Ralph. In fact, nothing he could write would be of much help to the magazine— and the Party—in its goal of radicalizing the black masses. The rupture with Randolph, celebrated by Ralph, proved a disaster for both the National Negro Congress and the Party. "Not only did Randolph leave the congress," one historian has noted, "but he used his action as the occasion to call for the destruction of Communist influence in Afro-American life." Nevertheless, Ralph was locked in so securely at *New Masses* that he spoke about it in the first person. "We are running three pages of Letters to the Editor," he wrote to Wright about *Native Son*. He was eager to seize this chance both for himself and, he said, for his race. "I think there will be more coverage on Negro problems," he alerted Wright, "and that here is the chance to evaluate Negro life."

Very little came of this scheme. Once Nazi Germany invaded the Soviet Union, the Communist Party backed what Harry Haywood would later call "a people's war aimed at the defeat of fascism." It demoted black rights as an issue.

Ralph's grander scheme for himself at *New Masses* failing, he made sure that his more routine role survived. Routine it was. In his reviews he was more a sort of schoolteacher than a subtle literary judge; he rapped knuckles when authors made ideological errors. With the fall of Paris, however, Ralph's antiwar messages were at odds with the rising sense among many Americans, encouraged by a popular president, that their entry into the war was only a matter of time. With Hitler in control of France, Belgium, the Netherlands, Denmark, and Norway, his conquest of Great Britain seemed imminent. Even as the United States maintained diplomatic relations with Germany, the nation organized for war. Congress passed legislation for the draft to begin that fall. Many black leaders stepped up their demand for a more honorable role for African-Americans in the services. Until recently, the entire U.S. Army boasted about half a dozen black officers, most of them chaplains. Black units provided mainly support services. The navy accepted blacks only as mess men; the all-volunteer marines remained lily-white.

Ralph staunchly kept up his support of the Soviet Union. In a letter to Wright, he stuck by the Communist position that the war was a conflict of imperialist powers with imperialist designs: "As for Hitler, I'm hoping he'll be able to invade England and break up the Empire. For in the same stroke he'll dig his own grave." This tough stance seemed to soften in August of that year, 1940, with the murder of Leon Trotsky in Mexico. Among other errors, Trotsky had defended the independence of the artist from interference by the state. He had many admirers in the United States, including C. L. R. James, the Trinidadian-born author of the novel *Minty Alley* and a study of the Haitian revolution, *The Black Jacobins,* who had become an intimate member of Wright's circle. James's Trotskyite arguments did not convince Ralph, and even the sensational murder of Trotsky disturbed him only up to a point. "This Trotsky business seems phony to me," he ventured. But he clearly began to reexamine his priorities in light of the killing. "I've never before realized how necessary it is that I write," he assured his mentor, "and I assure you that I *intend* to write rather than fight."

In June, Ralph and Rose welcomed home from Mexico Dhimah, her son, and her mother. Wright had come back to the United States separately, via the South, where he visited some of the people, including his father, who had shaped his unusual sensibility. Except for the necessary legal steps, the Wrights' marriage was over. Ralph and Rose helped Dhimah settle into an apartment two doors away. Soon, Dhimah invited them to save money by sharing the apartment, in which a kitchen and bath separated two bedrooms. In July, Ralph and Rose moved in, paying half the rent, $28 a month.

When Wright reached New York in August, *Native Son* was still in the news, mainly because a stage version was in preparation. He now saw much less of Ralph. Aside from one frosty visit to see Dhimah, he kept away from Hamilton Terrace. Within months, he would be divorced and ready to marry again. This time, he returned to Ellen Poplowitz. Ralph liked Ellen. In fact, she would tell one of Wright's biographers (about sixty years later) that Ralph had "played his own cards first" and " 'made a pass' at her. . . . 'But Ellison never appealed to me.' " In March 1941 Richard and Ellen married. Ralph found out about the nuptials afterward.

In July *New Masses* brought out Ralph's second published short story, "The Birthmark." This tale was probably inspired by the National Negro Congress convention in Washington and Ralph's conversation there with a lynching survivor, James McMillan, whose neck still bore the mark of the rope. In a gesture at Hawthorne and his tale of the same name, "The Birthmark" tells of two blacks who have come to identify the mutilated body of their brother. His wounds show that he has been lynched, although the hostile police claim he died in a car accident. In place of his genitalia is "only a bloody mound of torn flesh and hair." In America, the birthmark of the black man is castration.

Another story, "Afternoon," possibly also inspired by Ralph's surging faith in the black masses, would appear later that year in the anthology *American Writing*, published by the League of American Writers. For the first time, Ralph drew clearly on memories of his boyhood in Oklahoma. "Afternoon" is the first of an informal series of stories involving two black boys, Buster and Riley (one of them resembling young Ralph), in a town not unlike Oklahoma City (oil wells thump, thump in the background). The story is fresh and convincing, if modest in skill. Oddly for a story written at this time in Ralph's life, "Afternoon" expresses only a flicker of political consciousness. The narrator stays within the limited intellectual range of the two boys. Through his most astute use of symbolism to this point, Ralph conveys the sense of emptiness in most black lives. He makes real the dearth of genuine love, the familiarity with decay and violence. Buster fears his mother ("Her voice had been like a slap in the face"). Riley threatens to retaliate one day against his brutish father for whipping him with a piece of electric wire: "I'm gonna beat the hell outa my ole man. I'm gonna learn to box like Jack Johnson, just so I can beat his ass." Finally, Ralph was starting to explore an internal territory that previously he had been unable to engage, and in language almost as natural as his breathing. Nevertheless, even as he inched away from dogma, he was still an ideologue, still a polemicist unable to free himself from dogmatism.

Ralph scarcely had time to enjoy the appearance of "The Birthmark" in *New Masses* on July 2 before he fell seriously ill with wrenching attacks of nausea and stomach pain. A doctor diagnosed "an acute attack of Hepatitis." Ralph stayed at Mount Sinai Hospital in Manhattan for three weeks while he underwent a battery of liver tests. This illness came just as Rose landed a role in a play at the Community Playhouse in Stamford, Connecticut. Rose had no choice during rehearsals but to leave Ralph to fend for himself. However, a few friends from work trooped to his bedside. Passing the hat, they also gave him $6 to help pay his bills.

His illness made Ralph appreciate Rose's finer qualities. "You've been a grand wife," he wrote her, "despite all the trouble we've had these two years, and I love you for it." What he meant by "all the trouble" is unknown. But his phrasing suggests that he saw himself more as an offender in their marriage than as the person offended; it also suggests that he typically found it hard to apologize to Rose for his mistakes. This would have been in keeping with his fierce, self-serving drive to succeed, his aversion to feelings of obligation or gratitude.

As an entertainer, Rose provided him an entrée into the world of nightclubs and jazz in New York City—but he, too, knew some musicians, including Charlie Christian of Oklahoma City, then at the height of his fame in a sextet led by Benny Goodman. He and Rose were among the first patrons at Minton's Playhouse, the nightclub in the Hotel Cecil on 118th Street that would become a historic jazz site. Within two years of its opening in 1940, under the popular bandleader Teddy Hill, it would help to popularize, in after-hours sessions that attracted the cream of jazz musicians, the amazing, controversial music known as bebop. Almost twenty years after the club opened, Ralph would salute its memory in an evocative essay called "The Golden Age, Time Past." In it he would write about the club and its gifted musicians, and about strangers black and white drawn together by the inventive beauty of black music at a time when the future seemed uniquely perilous. All were "caught up in events which made that time exceptionally and uniquely *then,* and which brought, among the other changes which have reshaped the world, a momentous modulation into a new key of musical sensibility; in brief, a revolution in culture."

But books remained at the center of his life. Without becoming a systematic collector, he kept an eye open for the rare find. One day, in Harlem, he made what he would consider his most stunning buy. For $1.25, he bought the 347th copy of James Joyce's *Anna Livia Plurabelle,* a section of *Finnegans Wake* published in 1928 in an edition of 800 signed copies.

The taint that attached itself to a Communist who liked to read bourgeois literature apparently did not apply to that Communist when he listened to the classical music of bourgeois composers. Even Wagner, exploited by the Nazis, remained one of his favorites.

Ralph was fully recovered in September when he and Rose attended a fund-raising gala in Harlem hosted by Richard Wright and Paul Robeson for the newly formed Negro Playwrights Company, which Ralph saw as another major step in the radicalization of black American creative life being led by Wright, Ted Ward—and himself. Intended as the radical black counterpart to the mainstream Dramatists Guild, the company would promote African-American interests on the stage. "Only through portrayal of the deepest tragedy of the Negro people," its organizers argued, "their oppression at the hands of American rulers, their struggle for equality and recognition, can a Negro culture be truthful and strong."

Ralph listened as Wright read—and read and read, to the annoyance of the crowd—from an essay about *Native Son.* Sultry Hazel Scott of Trinidad (who would marry Adam Clayton Powell, Jr.) sang and played the piano, and Robeson's bass voice rumbled through a radicalized version of his signature hit, "Ol' Man River," from *Show Boat.* The gala was a success, with five thousand persons attending despite the $25 ticket price. The fact that almost all were white should have given Ralph pause. More likely, he saw instead further proof that the radical ideas he shared with Wright were taking root. Indeed, Ralph was so confident of the correctness of his radical position that he took the decisive step that month of publicly rebuking someone who had served him for years as a friend and mentor—Langston Hughes, on the appearance of Hughes's autobiography, *The Big Sea.* Ironically, Hughes had been a founding member of the Negro Playwrights Company, a tangible response to the challenge he set down the previous March in *Crisis* in his popular poem "Note on

Commercial Theater" ("You've taken my blues and gone—"). For generations, whites had hijacked black cultural forms for their own gain. He
wanted blacks to take command of the way they were seen on the stage
and screen and the way their music reached the world. Nevertheless,
Hughes also knew well how little the black masses cared for radical propaganda, which often struck them as phony, or for "high" culture, especially classical music. As he had joked wearily that summer, after his best
efforts in Chicago to stage a black historical pageant flopped: "Just how
much culture can the masses take, unless Little Egypt is around to
shake?"

Now, invoking his new faith in the Hegelian "indignant consciousness"
of the black masses, Ralph rebuked Langston for lacking radical seriousness in *The Big Sea*. Deploring what he saw as the author's languid pad-
dling on the surface of his life story, he lamented Hughes's refusal of
didacticism. "In the style of *The Big Sea*," Ralph wrote, "too much attention is apt to be given to the esthetic aspects of experience at the expense
of its deeper meanings." Hughes's restraint was a disservice to people who
might learn from it. "To be effective," Ralph lectured, "the Negro writer
must be explicit; thus realistic; thus dramatic." Instead, Hughes had
denied something important to "younger writers and intellectuals," who
"should be allowed to receive the profound benefits of his experiences,
and this on the plane of conscious thought." Ralph's rebuke startled and
hurt Hughes, although he responded mildly. Wright shared Ralph's sense
of the book, but he was more diplomatic in reviewing it in *The New
Republic*. In dubbing Hughes an "ambassador" of black culture, he nevertheless invited readers to recall that in "Blueprint for Negro Writing" he
had denounced almost all older black writers as "prim and decorous
ambassadors" to the white world.

Ralph's public commitment to radical ideology surfaced again when he
reviewed the first production by the Negro Playwrights Company, Ted
Ward's *Big White Fog*, at the Lincoln Theater in Harlem. In the play, an
older man with a passion for the politics of Marcus Garvey's back-to-
Africa movement pursues "the dead-end utopia of Africa" until his radical
son teaches him about interracial Communism and "the techniques of
realistic political struggle." With the help of men like Wright and Robeson (Ralph did not mention the prolific Hughes) "a group of young playwrights has launched in Harlem the most advanced attempt yet made to
establish a Negro theater." Although the play was "not without weaknesses," Ward "reveals greater social insight than has been shown by any

previous Negro dramatist." Ralph closed by quoting grossly inflated praise of Ward's work by V. J. Jerome of *The Communist*: "Seldom in literature or on the stage has the inner dignity of an oppressed people struggling to affirm its nationhood risen so indestructibly, so magnificently, as in the Negro family portrayed in *Big White Fog*."

Reporting in November in *New Masses* on a regional conference of the National Negro Congress, he continued to write mainly as a hack. Not surprisingly, by the end of the year his critical writing, too, seemed in the doldrums. Although he published three more reviews in *New Masses* late in 1940, all followed Party dogma. In his favorable review of his friend Len Zinberg's novel *Walk Hard—Talk Loud,* he enthusiastically explains how far a writer "is able to go with a Marxist understanding of the economic basis of Negro personality. That, plus a Marxist sense of humanity, carries the writer a long way in a task considered extremely difficult: for a white writer successfully to depict Negro character."

Early in 1941 the Selective Service administration declared Ellison 1A— the group most likely to be summoned into service. The notice alarmed Ralph. Not so his brother, Herbert. Despite Ralph's lurid warnings, Herbert had volunteered for service and was now a private in the virtually all-black 368th Infantry Division, stationed at Fort Huachuca in Arizona.

When Germany invaded the Soviet Union, the Party's main goal became getting the United States into the war. Ralph persisted in refusing any role for himself as a combatant. In July, he helped organize a mock trial in Harlem sponsored by pacifist groups. He was still opposed the following month when, in a *New Masses* number that also carried an essay by him, the seven-hundred-member League of American Writers fell into line with the Party. The league had supported "every genuine anti-fascist struggle—whether it be that of the Spanish people, the Chinese people, or the people of Germany." Now, with the alliance between Russia and Great Britain, the chance to destroy Fascism was at hand. Near its end, this statement insisted that the new policy "cannot and must not be conducted at the expense of civil liberties, trade union rights," and similar freedoms. The league remained "unalterably opposed to anti-Semitism and discrimination against Negroes and the foreign born." But the Party's about-face affected its view of the claims of Negroes as a group. With the future of the USSR at stake, the struggle for civil rights in the South became less pressing than the need for the Party to win over the white masses there. Responding to a call in January by A. Philip Randolph for a massive "March on Washington" to "demand jobs in national defense and placement as soldiers and officers" for blacks, the Party had discouraged him at first. When it tried belatedly to join the march (which was abandoned after Roosevelt made a major concession to Randolph's group), it lost even more credibility. Overnight at *New Masses,* Ralph's stock as an expert on black culture plummeted. Had he joined the pro-war chorus, he might have saved himself. Unwilling to do so, he became expendable.

This was the beginning of the end of Communist influence on him. It was the beginning of the end, too, for several organizations. The League of American Writers was doomed—although, ironically, that June it elevated Ralph into its leadership. The National Negro Congress faded into oblivion. The Negro Playwrights Company disappeared. Nevertheless, Ralph still had some way to travel before he could free himself entirely of the radical institutions that had empowered him in his search for success and fame. He still needed them to publish his work even as the sudden shifts in Party policy pushed him steadily back toward liberal cosmopolitanism. Like Wright (but much more quietly, because he was no prosperous celebrity), he was in the process of repudiating the Party line on literature. Also like Wright, what separated him from most black intellectuals and artists turning away from the Party was his refusal to make a blanket indictment of whites and their intellectual and aesthetic values and traditions. If the Party had betrayed blacks, it had also betrayed the historic legacy of Western liberal humanism. Resisting the Party, he would stand by both his faith in the integrity of black folk culture and his faith in Western art and learning.

This process of repudiation and reappraisal between 1940 and 1942 was the single most trying passage in his evolution as an artist and intellectual. In the summer of 1941, drawing on Wright's "Blueprint for Negro Writing," he offered a muted manifesto of his own in a *New Masses* essay, "Recent Negro Fiction." (*Direction* published an abridged version as "Richard Wright and Negro Fiction.") Earlier black writers had "ignored the existence of Negro folklore," its symbols and images. "Oblivious of psychology" and "unconscious of politics," these authors had evaded the "deeper problems" of black culture. Their "narrowly nationalistic" arts had failed. However, they had also ignored "the technical experimentation and direction being taken by American writing." Although the Depression had bred "a new proletarian consciousness among black people," the "crude mechanism" of the black writer's prose could not capture it effectively. During the Depression, novelists such as Arna Bontemps, Zora Neale Hurston, and William Attaway had struggled, with only mixed success, to voice the new idiom: "The general effect of these novels is one of incompleteness; something is not fully formed in them."

This inadequacy came from racial chauvinism. Black writers needed now to engage their counterparts in the white world. Because of Wright's role as secretary of the mainly white John Reed Club in Chicago, and his saturation as a Communist in all aspects of the writer's life, he had flourished as an artist. "It is no accident," Ralph argued, "that the two most advanced American Negro writers"—Wright and Hughes—"have *experienced freedom of* association with advanced white writers." At stake was the prize of acquiring Western culture, and "in the United States even the possession of Western culture is controlled on the basis of color." It was no accident "that Hughes and Wright have had, as writers of fiction, the greatest effect upon Negro life."

With this essay, which praises Joyce, Gertrude Stein, Sherwood Anderson, and Hemingway, Ralph summed up the core ideas that had shaped his rise as a writer from Tuskegee to the present moment. Prominent among these was the habit of friendship with white people. Now he argued for the absolute necessity of such friendships for the black writer, even as that writer also respected black racial feeling. Questions about black dialect, or folk consciousness, or racial difference could be truly answered only by intellectuals who dared to cross the color line. For Ralph, "Recent Negro Fiction" was a declaration of dependence, interdependence, and independence. The relative success of his story "Afternoon" had not been an accident. What remained now for him was to find a way out of his commitment to Communism, which had made possible but also had clouded the vision of liberal cosmopolitanism to which he would commit himself once again.

6

The Numbed and the Seething

1941–1943

We are not the numbed, but the seething. God! It makes
you want to write and write and write, or murder.

RALPH ELLISON (1941)

On August 31, after a year sharing Dhimah Meadman's apartment, Ralph and Rose moved to a ground-floor apartment at 453 West 140th Street in Harlem, an address in no way as pleasant and distinguished as Hamilton Terrace. He slid down the social scale in another way. The rent was $50 a month, from which $12 would be deducted as payment for Ralph's part-time responsibilities as superintendent of the building. This job took a toll on his time and morale just as he was engaged in a major revaluation of his role as a writer. The job of janitor (at which his mother had worked) grated on Ralph's pride. Solidarity with the masses was one thing. Being a janitor and belonging to the masses was quite another.

He and the other tenants soon clashed. "May I again suggest," he wrote to them sarcastically at one point, "that in such instances wherein liquids, or garbage with high liquid contents, is left, that such be placed in a *leakless* container? And again (and this is not meant to be as peevish as this 'catalogue' might sound), can not all disposable tissues, Cleanex, etc., be placed in a bag or wrapped in a newspapers? Perhaps yours are only facial tissues, but I can't be too sure."

Rose was working less frequently now. Her loss of income did not help the marriage, with Ralph and Rose often tense and defensive in their dealings with each other. Ralph's fear of being drafted also put him under some stress. With a massive increase in military spending under way, the Writers' Project and almost all other Depression-era relief organizations had been curtailed. The army offered not only the humiliations of Jim Crow but a daily regimen that would leave little time for writing and for professional ties that meant everything to Ralph as he struggled to build his literary career. The combination of pressures toward the end of 1941 made Ralph literally sick to his stomach, in his chronic response to psychological burdens. Once again, Wright helped to relieve those burdens.

In October, just when Ralph was sure that he had taken the measure of his mentor, Wright published *12 Million Black Voices*. A marriage of black-and-white pictures taken by various photographers collected by the WPA artist Edwin Rosskam and a romantic text by Wright, the book is a bittersweet paean to black America. The text, unstinting in describing the squalor of black life, is also an epic celebration of humanity—it presents itself as nothing less than the autobiography of a race. (It begins: "Each day when you see us black folk upon the dusty land of the farms or upon the hard pavement of the city streets, you usually take us for granted and think you know us, but our history is far stranger than you suspect, and we are not what we seem.") Wright's text moved virtually all reviewers, but especially blacks. In the *Pittsburgh Courier,* Horace Cayton saluted it as "magnificent in its simplicity, directness and force." The book amounted to "a philosophy of the history of the Negro in America and a frame of reference for the study of Negro-white relations in this country."

Catching Ralph at a particularly vulnerable time, *12 Million Black Voices* hit him harder than any book he had read in years. It forced him to confront his conflicted feelings about black America, which repelled him at least as much as it compelled his admiration. Wright's account of black life, melodramatic as it sometimes is, struck Ralph with the urgency of breaking news. It pressed him to link his muddled sense of kinship with black America to certain elements in his own life—his unassuaged bitterness about his early life; his ongoing rage at the world, in which so often he felt alone and embattled; his conflicted feelings about his brother, Herbert, who did not share his interests and ambitions; and his unresolved guilt about the mixture of love and shame that he had felt so often for his mother.

Ralph broke down. His life, he confessed now to Wright, had been in large part "a lacerating experience." Hounded by feelings of "bitterness" and by urges toward the "criminal," he had barely held them at bay. "I know those emotions," he admitted, "which tear the insides to be free and memories which must be kept underground, caged by rigid discipline lest they destroy, but which yet are precious to me because they are mine and

I am proud of that which is myself." He was unused to sharing such thoughts—"the fact that I mention them now is an indication of the effect which your book has had upon me." Wright had written of the "numbness" induced in blacks by the trauma of their history. In response, Ralph conceded his own sometimes arctic numbness, and his often painful episodes of defrosting as he faced the world in general and blacks in particular. "I have had to rigidly control my thawing," he confessed, "allowing the liquid emotion to escape drop by drop through the trap doors of the things I write, lest I lose control; lest I be rendered incapable of warming our frozen brothers." Reading Wright's book, "I felt the solder of my discipline melt and found myself opened up and crying over the painful pattern of remembered things." Forced to recall "the bitter searching journeys of my mother and my own early childhood, jerking from Georgia, to Oklahoma, to Indiana, back to Oklahoma and finally to Ohio," he had wept. But his tears generated only more rage: "They were tears of impatience and anger."

Having read 12 *Million Black Voices,* he revealed, "I am sure now more than ever: that you and I are brothers." In addition to their common suffering at the hands of blacks, whites, family members, and strangers, they were as one in their refusal to forget, much less forgive. "We are the ones who had no comforting amnesia of childhood," he wrote, "and for whom the trauma of passing from the country to the city of destruction brought no anesthesia of unconsciousness, but left our nerves peeled and quivering. We are not the numbed, but the seething. God! It makes you want to write and write and write, or murder." Of his real brother, he had nothing to say. About his mother, whose presence is almost palpable in his letter, he made one revealing gesture. Alluding to the plot of Wright's story "Bright and Morning Star," Ralph unwittingly exposed his unresolved anxiety about his behavior as a son and the extent to which his "numbness" had stood in the way of filial love. "As between Sue and Johnny-Boy," Ralph wrote his "brother" Richard, "as was between my mother and I, speech is not necessary. We are immersed in the same flow of reality."

Wright's vision of the black world was a medley of fact and fiction, sincerity and poetic license, but it combined with other disturbing elements in Ralph's life at this time to set him to thinking in new ways about the future. The book encouraged in him both racial militancy and a reverence for heroic individualism. It unsettled everything, even as it readied him for a major change in his life as a writer and an intellectual.

·   ·   ·

Change came slowly. That month, November 1941, when *New Masses* published Ralph's short story "Mister Toussan," he was still in his ideological briar patch. As with "Afternoon" the previous year, Ralph mined his childhood for another story about the two black boys Buster and Riley. Racism and capitalism are personified in the white man who zealously guards his fruit trees and hates blacks. With folklore pressed—mechanically—into service, the story is framed by rhymes traditionally used (as a note tells the reader) as a prologue and epilogue "to Negro slave stories." Black narrative art is historically a radical act. So is the lyric language of a spiritual that Riley's mother sings. The song promotes the idea of resistance despite its otherworldly theme, and the genius of black singing furthers this disruption by its power to compel praise. History, folklore, and narrative artistry come together as a stealthy opposition to capitalism and racism. The blacks in Ralph's story are poised between folk consciousness and industrial modernism—which is precisely where Ralph located the masses of black Americans in 1941. In an April letter to Wright about race trouble in Detroit, he had declared: "There is the drama, the tragedy of this period: Negroes acting as the tools of fascism and the Negro middle class utterly helpless."

Despite its awkward elements, "Mister Toussan" attracted more mail than any other story published recently in *New Masses*. A Tennessee reader hailed it "as the best piece of brief fiction published thus far in 1941." According to this reader, "not only is the dialogue real . . . it has a sort of rhythmic quality, like something that might be given by a chorus." In the past, such praise might have satisfied Ralph. Now it wasn't enough. He wanted fame. He also wanted and needed the money that usually came with fame. But he got only a token sum from *New Masses* for "Mister Toussan." Marguerite Tjader Harris paid $25 for two pieces appearing in the leftist *Direction* magazine (a version of his *New Masses* essay on recent black fiction and his report on Philippine leftist writers). When Sam Sillen at *New Masses* asked for a contribution by Ralph to a new anthology of proletarian fiction, Sillen did not mention money at all. Something more dramatic would have to happen if Ralph was ever to break through as a professional writer.

The League of American Writers now seemed to Ralph to offer him the best promise of a breakthrough; *Direction* saluted him as "an outstanding Negro League member." Although the league was beset by accusations of radicalism, it still boasted some of the finest American writers, including Hemingway, Dreiser, Steinbeck, Erskine Caldwell, Lillian Hellman, and Wright. If the best known were outside his circle, Ralph prized his friendships with the poet and academic Genevieve Taggard, the novelist Alvah Bessie (whose book *Bread and Stone* he would review later in the year under a pseudonym), and the poet and playwright Alfred Kreymborg, the author of the radical study *Our Singing Strength: An Outline of American Poetry (1620–1930)*. Other blacks often avoided the company of such whites out of either a sense of intellectual intimidation or racial distrust, but Ralph sought them out, the better to educate himself and extend his influence, despite the inevitable psychological strain of being one of the few blacks around. He felt welcomed. The black writer Frank Marshall Davis declared of the league: "Never before had I worked closely and voluntarily in equality with a number of whites."

In the middle of 1941, Ralph began to take a special interest in a league project to study the feasibility of creating a journal (based on *The Clipper: A Monthly Literary Magazine,* published by the Hollywood branch of the league). This journal would be far more literary than *New Masses,* reach for a much larger audience, and espouse a less radical aesthetic. That fall, Ralph was on a committee that explored various questions of organization, scope, and focus. On virtually all questions Ralph had opinions—but he did not often share them. His shyness, his discomfort with white people, intervened. When he spoke, he often stammered a little.

Then, on December 7, the bombing of Pearl Harbor by the Japanese changed everything. Soon after Roosevelt's declaration of war, the War Writers' Board, headquartered in Washington and led by a former league member, Rex Stout, assumed control of the contribution of American writers to the national defense. The league, hamstrung by its reputation as a redoubt for radicals (despite the fact that the Soviet Union and the United States were now allies), was left behind. The case for a national journal vanished. Slightly more than a year after Pearl Harbor, the league dissolved. This loss made Ralph even riper for change in 1942.

In November, he had had a brief but turbulent affair—they were together hardly more than a week—with a white woman, Sanora Babb, the vivacious secretary-treasurer of *The Clipper.* Like Ralph, who was seven years younger, Sanora Babb was a struggling fiction writer. Unlike him, she had come tantalizingly close to a major success. At Random House, Bennett Cerf had all but bought her first novel, about desperate migrant camps in the Midwest during the Depression, when the sensational arrival of Steinbeck's *The Grapes of Wrath* in 1939 made him drop the book. "What rotten luck," he had said to console her; "obviously, another book at this time about exactly the same subject would be a sad anticlimax!" Also like Ralph, Sanora Babb was Oklahoma-born, although she had grown up in rural Colorado before moving to Los Angeles. Beautiful enough to have attracted the attention of Hollywood, she was determined to be a writer. In addition to working as a reporter, she had published several stories in little magazines, including *New Masses*. In Los Angeles, she had lived daringly for the past eight years with the Chinese-born cinematographer James Wong Howe (later her husband) at a time when laws existed against interracial marriage. She also socialized with several members of the radical black leftist community, including its leading member, the lawyer and civil rights activist Loren Miller, who had once traveled to Russia with Langston Hughes.

At a league meeting in Manhattan, Ralph caught Sanora's eye. Taking the initiative, she quietly made it clear that she wanted to see him in private. In a note on the stationery of the St. Moritz Hotel on Central Park South, she defended her forwardness. "I am filled with doubts, and embarrassment," Sanora admitted; "but my desire . . . toward you has overcome the cool caution of my mind." Although she felt "like a 'brazen hussy,' " she declined to apologize for wanting him. "Desire, I think, is an unashamed and beautiful urge," she wrote, "and nothing to do with appetite, with which I wouldn't insult you or myself." Ralph was obviously reluctant to become sexually involved with Sanora. In part, perhaps, he held back because of his marriage vows, although he informed her that his marriage was virtually over ("you consider your marriage gone," she reminded him in January). In part, his rigid sense of pride, personal and racial, forbade easy sexual relations with white women. Scrupulous about not wanting to give in to those seeking clandestine thrills, he was suspicious of Sanora's motives. She, in turn, refused to see herself in this role. "I am not a Negrophile, or any other–phile," she insisted, "and I won't ever permit myself to fall into that narrow and rather sterile position."

Nevertheless, despite his reluctance, he and Sanora enjoyed being together and went to bed at least once in New York. Walking under autumn skies in Central Park, or strolling on the crowded streets of Manhattan, or sitting in little cafés, they talked a great deal—not so much about themselves as lovers as about being leftists and writers who burned to succeed. Ralph both encouraged and put off Sanora. Weeks later, when their affair was dead, she would recall tenderly "the way you smiled down at me when we were walking, the ways you looked across the room from me in the meeting, the way you withdrew from me there the first night, the terrible and heavy detachment in you one moody evening, the foolish, sentimental songs we heard in cafes . . . the scar by your eye, the sudden sweetness of the way you smile which is so different from the sober expression of your serious face, the lazy way you move."

Ralph gave Sanora no reason to be sure that he was falling in love with her. As prickly a man as he was polite, the night before she left New York he hurt her by implying that she, as a prosperous white woman, was slumming in consorting with him. "I did not get into racial problems," Sanora admonished him, "as an exercise in socialism but because of a natural a-racial humanity." She had just about given up on Ralph when, overcome by a dramatic rush of passion, he turned her world upside down. Arriving at her hotel too late to see her off, he caught up with her at Grand Central Station. There, in the privacy of her cramped quarters, he unleashed hot kisses—and promises—that thrilled Sanora to the bone. For the first two hours of the train ride, she declared in a daze, "I kept remembering all the things you had said, and the ways you looked, and the crazy half hour before the train left." Now she asked urgently, "Ralph, Ralph, Ralph, how will it be not to see you?"

In a telephone call to Sanora during her layover in Chicago, Ralph talked boldly about leaving Rose and starting a new life with her. "You said to me," she would remind him, that "when the time came you'd do it." Unfortunately for Sanora, his passion soon ebbed. She became frantic: "Darling, why don't you write to me? There isn't anything you can't say to me, surely. Anything would be better than not hearing at all." In Los Angeles, when letters trickled in from him, none comforted her. In each of her replies, she complained about Ralph's needless cruelty, as when he criticized Sanora for her supposedly luxurious Hollywood life, for owning a car and wearing fur coats. Self-pityingly, he sketched painful pictures of how her partner, Howe, and their white friends would respond to the news that she had taken a black lover. Ralph also questioned her commitment to writing. "You may tell me," she protested, "whether or not I am a writer, but don't now heckle the little confidence I have. This is a tender and delicate feeling in everyone of us, and it is not good to hurt it."

Both Rose Ellison and James Wong Howe quickly found out about the affair. Howe "accidentally" discovered Ralph's letters in Sanora's purse, but Ralph broke the news to Rose. Wounded, Howe nevertheless offered to pay for Ralph to come to Los Angeles to be with Sanora, if that was what she wanted. He and their friends were ready to accept them. "Your nationality was mentioned," she wrote, "precisely because J. did not think it any humiliation, nor did my friends think it anything strange." In New York, in contrast, the news devastated Rose. As with his caustic remarks to Sanora, he had confessed his infidelity out of a sense, no doubt, that he needed to be honest. In both cases, he clumsily inflicted pain. Then Rose became furious. Money alone kept her at home, she assured him. She was about to audition for a role in a play. If she got the part, she would move out. Her blazing anger brought Ralph a new perspective. Despite their difficulties, he explained now to Sanora, as a black woman and a radical Rose was essential to his writing. Deep down inside, he really loved her. He couldn't leave her. "Did you know these things," Sanora asked him bluntly, "only when you thought you might lose her?"

Race was the major reason Ralph offered in explanation, but he perhaps had other, related reasons. Timidity cannot be discounted. Tough with words and capable of an adventure now and then, he was already a cautious man. Although aligned with radicals, his instinct was to avoid risk. In writing to Sanora he did not mention the risks facing a black man who dared to marry a white woman. Instead, he explained his choice of Rose in a remarkably bloodless way. He must live with his symbols, Ralph wrote about his marriage. What other people thought about him was important. Sanora was stunned that he might be rejecting her because of symbolism: "I think I will always hear in my dreams, 'I must live with my symbols.' " She seemed both sad and relieved that "faced with a kind of inner choice between us, you want R., not more or most, but want her definitely instead of."

Ralph's marriage to Rose would never recover. Perhaps his coldness and cruelty—the result of his own lifetime of suffering—had already worn her down. He could be funny, charming, even loving, but he also could not help inflicting pain. After Sanora finally knew his decision, she mourned his inability to distinguish honesty from a grating self-righteousness. "After all these things," Sanora wrote, "which I found hard to understand, you write, 'I want to quit writing like this *for awhile,* before I say something you'll find hard to understand.' You will hurt me some more? And all this was nothing? Ralph, what is wrong between us, that we could on such little acquaintance be so many things to each other in just these ways, and now, you hurt me in these same ways with so little thoughtfulness for any sensitivity?"

She tried to bring a cordial end to the episode. When Ralph fell ill that winter, she fussed over him from across the continent, dispatched a supply of vitamins, and mailed him a sweater. Ralph welcomed this cordiality but put the affair behind him. In the years to come, he and Sanora exchanged letters and notes infrequently. More than a year passed between the end of the affair and Ralph's next letter to Sanora—and another year passed between that letter and her reply. By that time, his marriage to Rose was over. If Rose had been to Ralph a symbol of racial and ideological solidarity, then his respect for what she symbolized was now also in question, as his politics continued to shift from the far left toward the center.

Even as he began to feel an inexorable pull in the opposite direction, Ralph clung to the values of black cultural nationalism and Marxist radicalism, embodied, or symbolized, by Rose. He demonstrated his loyalty, just about the time he met Sanora Babb, when he took part in a panel discussion of the black writer William Attaway's second novel, *Blood on the Forge,* with Attaway, Sam Sillen of New York University, and Roy Wilkins, the editor of the NAACP magazine *Crisis.* Ralph was primed to the point of agitation for the debate. How had Attaway succeeded when he had so far failed? Less than a week later, when *New Masses* published his review of the book, an editor there assured him that it was "one of the best critical pieces we have ever run."

Blood on the Forge tells the story of three brothers who, fleeing a lynch mob in Kentucky, head for the steel mills of the Allegheny Valley. Worn down by the pressures of modern industrial life, they are stripped of their defenses and soon begin to fail. The novel stirred Ralph by its degree of artistry and because it reinforced his idea of black Americans as a people caught between a dying folk consciousness and a looming industrial reality. For Ralph, however, modernizing was inevitable and not to be feared. The fatal fault of the novel, he argued, was that it nowhere asserts the ability of human beings, especially Negroes, to understand and thus control the factors that make for progress. Instead of offering a glimpse of historical truth, *Blood on the Forge* disintegrates finally "into a catalogue of meaningless casualties and despairs." Echoing an idea that also anchors much of Wright's fiction, he declared: "The true adversary of the Negro and all democrats is Nature." One conquers nature, he wrote, by "acquiring the techniques through which Western Civilization reached its highest development." Nature dominates the folk spirit, which must give way to a (Marxist) understanding of capitalism and industrialism. Although Attaway was "one of the most gifted Negro writers," he had fallen short of greatness in this novel.

To men such as Sillen and Joseph North at *New Masses,* Ralph was now writing with almost singular authority about the tricky business of the war, race, and radicalism. Because the Party wanted blacks to see not betrayal but farsighted wisdom in its new position, Ralph and black intellectuals like him were more important than ever. The following January, when the editorial board held a meeting to discuss the future of *New Masses*, Ralph was invited to attend, and did so. But he was already deeply disturbed by the turn of world events and on his way to a reassessment of radicalism and the kind of literature championed by *New Masses*.

Publicity for the *Blood on the Forge* panel discussion led to a significant invitation. He received a note (addressed to "Dear Ellerson") asking him to contribute an essay to a new journal of African-American affairs, to be sponsored by the recently formed Negro Publication Society. The society, tightly linked to the radical left, included the young Communist historian Herbert Aptheker, the black intellectuals Arthur Huff Fauset and Alain Locke, the dramatist Marc Blitzstein, the novelist Theodore Dreiser, the artist Rockwell Kent, and Henrietta Buckmaster, also white, who that year published *Let My People Go,* an animated account of the Underground Railroad and the abolitionist movement. The most celebrated person involved was the proposed editor of the journal, Angelo Herndon. Herndon's fame was almost on par with that of the Scottsboro Boys of Alabama. In 1932, when he was nineteen and already a Communist, Herndon had helped to organize an interracial hunger march in Atlanta. Prosecuted by Georgia authorities under old slave insurrection laws, he was sentenced to twenty years on a chain gang by a hostile white judge. A massive campaign by the Communists was stymied in 1935, when the U.S. Supreme Court refused to hear Herndon's appeal. However, in 1937 the same court struck down Georgia's insurrection laws and freed Herndon, who arrived in New York a hero of the left. That year, Random House published his autobiography, *Let Me Live.* The heroic death of his brother, Milton Herndon, as a soldier in the International Brigade in Spain, added luster to his name.

Now, in 1941, as secretary of the Negro Publication Society, he was the editor of *The Negro Quarterly: A Review of Negro Life and Culture.* The relationship of the Communist Party to the project is not clear. While some people assumed that the Party supported it, Ralph would insist later that Herndon published the magazine in defiance of the Party, which presumably saw it as a diversion from its goal of uniting blacks and whites in the war effort. Herndon was much more of a "race man" than the cosmopolitan intellectual Ralph wished to be. When he asked Ralph for an essay on the Negro and the war, Ralph submitted an updated version of his *Blood on the Forge* review. Herndon accepted it. As the chance for a League of American Writers journal faded, Ralph became even more interested in the fate of *The Negro Quarterly*. He applauded the society's aim "to treat critically all aspects" of recent changes affecting black Americans "and to aid in furthering the literary, social, and cultural advancement of the Negro people."

In March 1942, when Herndon launched the journal with a party at the fashionable Gramercy Park home of one of its supporters, Harry Levine, he invited Ralph. Severe teeth problems—Ralph had some pulled just before the party—could not keep him away. He liked the look of the first number. Dominated by a long, heavily footnoted article on slavery by Aptheker, it projected an image of seriousness, if not severity. Either at this party or shortly afterward, Ralph agreed to join the staff as managing editor at a salary of $35 a week. Herndon, a dashing figure with a gift for glittering talk—he was fond of quoting Aristotle—was better suited to his preferred role as the journal's chief fund-raiser. Ready to contribute a piece of writing now and then, he was out of his depth trying to run a magazine of ideas. Ralph, who had picked up some expertise hanging around the *New Masses* office, nicely filled the void. "I was a functioning editor," he declared later, "and did the actual writing of most, though not all, of the editorials."

In March, Ralph was shocked by the death in New York of young Charlie Christian. Redefining the role of the jazz guitar, Christian of Oklahoma City had exploded into national stardom. Less than four years later he was dead of tuberculosis. In 1943, grieving for Christian, Ralph struggled to understand the meaning of his death and its relationship to his own rage for fame. Ralph believed, as he would later state, that jazz, as much as any disease, had killed Christian. "Jazz, like the country that gave it birth," he said, "is fecund in its inventiveness, swift and traumatic in its developments and terribly wasteful of its resources. . . . Many of its most talented creators die young." Ralph had chosen a safer path. As a musician he had turned away early from the "fecund" chaos of jazz to the sublime orthodoxies of classical music, which tended to conserve and sustain where jazz, in negotiating excess, rushed both to create and to exhaust. Then he had turned to the life of the writer. Here, too, he had depended on safety nets—the certitudes of radical ideology and the defensive interests that patrolled it. Christian's death both confirmed the wisdom of Ralph's choice and challenged it. In one way, Christian's death was a caution against plunging fully into art, into the vortex of black culture. In another, it challenged Ralph to make a similar sacrifice, to step away from the safety net of radical ideology and the largely white left toward the chaos and creativity of black art and black people. Moving to join Herndon in *The Negro Quarterly* was a giant step in that direction.

On April 30, 1942, Ralph finally severed his ties to the Federal Writers' Project. Resigning graciously, he thanked the Project director, Frederick Clayton, for "a most fruitful relationship; having not only allowed me to live, but, more importantly, made it possible for me to continue my personal writing. It would be impossible to calculate the value of this to me (it has made possible the beginnings of a writer's reputation for me)." It had also given him an extended link to a community of black writers, as well as the friendship of many white writers also excited by politics and culture. When Ralph resigned, only a few isolated parts of the FWP remained. "The biggest literary project in history," as the FWP was called, had spent just over $27 million and produced "enough material to fill seven twelve-foot shelves in the library of the Department of the Interior" in Washington. It had also made possible a literary career for Ralph Ellison.

Although *The Negro Quarterly* was clearly aimed over the heads of the black masses, Ralph felt surges of satisfaction as he surveyed the passing scene through the plate glass window of his office at One West 125th Street, where Harlem's busiest thoroughfare crossed teeming Lenox Avenue. In tandem with Herndon, he was determined to lift the magazine to intellectual heights never before scaled by an African-American periodical. Despite the limitations of blacks as intellectuals (as Ralph saw them), the *Quarterly* hoped to surpass in quality magazines such as the *Crisis* and *Phylon: A Journal of Race,* launched in 1940 by sociologists at Atlanta University. Although the *Quarterly* would publish sociology, it would also delve into literary and cultural questions; its radical socialism and racial militancy would further set it apart from its competition.

Ralph's ambition led some people, black and white, to think of him as habitually overreaching. The snubs came, but so did the rewards. In late March, when he took part in a panel discussion about European writers and the war sponsored by the League of American Writers, Ralph might very well have been the only black person in the room. The other speakers were all white: Klaus Mann of Germany (the son of Thomas Mann); the exiled Czechoslovakian novelist Franz Carl Weiskopf; and the German refugee Harry Slochower, a psychologist who also taught German and comparative literature at Brooklyn College. Slochower lectured first, on the effects of Fascist violence on the many European writers expelled from their countries. He had invited Ralph to join the responding panel because his speech touched on Wright's *Native Son* in the context of a dilemma he saw plaguing European writers such as Erich Maria Remarque, Peter Mendelssohn, Stefan Zweig, and Ernst Toller, who faced a unique threat. Such writers, "deprived of their distinctive roles" as artists because of an oppressive barbarism, met unprecedented barriers in creating new art. Art requires the enemy to have a human face, but the Nazi horror made it impossible to see such a face on the enemy. In addition, mass exile tended to deprive each writer of his individual identity, conferring instead a form of identity based in a collective sense of victimhood. Thus Fascism doomed the writers to a bleak form of art, or to silence, or to worse—Zweig and Toller had committed suicide. In *Native Son*, Slochower argued, Wright had found a way, in his creation of Bigger Thomas, to face the same dilemma (that of the writer exiled from home and deprived of his individuality) but to triumph technically and philosophically over it.

Slochower's argument fascinated Ralph both by its emphasis on psychology and by its stress on individual identity in creating art; it linked Fascism, American racism, and, perhaps, Communism as factors inimical to art. He had settled almost comfortably into the debate when the snub came. After Klaus Mann expressed pessimism about the ability of Germans ever to recover from the Nazis, Ralph disagreed. If African tribesmen could survive the horrors of the slave trade and build a viable culture in America, then Germans certainly could survive Hitler. The comparison of Germans to blacks seemed to offend Mann, who turned cold and dismissive. Mann seemed to assume that Ralph had no understanding—and *could* have no understanding—of German culture. Ralph thought differently. "I viewed German culture as tough, vital, and creative," he recalled. "As a lover of music and literature, art and architecture, how could I have felt otherwise? Therefore I believed that Germany could, and would, survive the madness of Hitler and resuscitate its dedication to humanist values."

Mann's contempt stung Ralph, but he was tough and stubborn about his right to take part in such a conversation. Ignoring Mann's rudeness, he secured Slochower's text (part of a forthcoming book) for the *Quarterly*. Thus began a crucial friendship with the author. Slochower's arguments would provide a set of keys as Ralph opened a succession of doors on his way out of radical socialism. In addition, this friendship would lead to others even more crucial to his future. When Ralph and Rose attended Slochower's wedding in December that year, Ralph would meet a brilliant young critic, Stanley Edgar Hyman, with whom he would forge one of the most significant relationships of his life. Through Hyman, Ralph would become a friend of Hyman's mentor, Kenneth Burke, whose ideas about literary form would dominate Ralph's writing over the following ten years. Slochower's approach to literature, which attempted to fuse Marx and Freud (Burke had been doing this, too, as in his 1941 book *The Philosophy of Literary Form*), thus opened up for Ralph in 1942 a new vista on literary and cultural criticism. To converse with Burke and young disciples of Burke gave a fresh, human dimension to his reading. Now he was ready to embrace ideas that would supplant the influence of pure Communism, weaken the persisting distractions of black nationalism in his thinking, and give order to the impulses toward liberal humanism that he had suppressed in his radical writing.

As managing editor of the *Quarterly*, he reached out boldly across the racial divide. Aware that *Trend* magazine, tied to the University of Chicago, had published work by two young black writers, he wrote to encourage its editor. "This is as it should be," Ralph declared, "a really Democratic assumption which cuts across the usual lines of demarcation." Seeking "critical articles which see American reality wholly enough to see the Negro in his many sided relationship thereto," he was curious to find out what a distinguished British critic (David Daiches), "with his European conditioning, would have to say along these lines." Ralph even tried to inveigle Malcolm Cowley (a close friend of Burke) of *The New Republic* into writing an essay for the *Quarterly*.

He continued to write as a leftist ideologue—but only surreptitiously. In March, when he published an essay in the *Daily Worker*, he used a pseudonym, David Wilson. Reviewing an anthology of black literature, "Wilson" declares clumsily: "Negro writing awaited the emergence of writers from the class-conscious proletariat, commanding the instrumentalities of Marxist thought, to make lucid the mystery of the Negro experience." Similarly, when Joseph North and Sam Sillen tried to keep Ralph in the fold at *New Masses* by naming him a contributing editor in September, they included a deft piece of propaganda by Ralph (in a special issue dedicated to "The Negro and Victory") that seemed to underscore his commitment to *New Masses* and its principles. "The Way It Is" tells of a visit paid by a nameless reporter to the Harlem apartment of a Mrs. Jackson and her two young children. Her son Wilbur is in the army. Life is tough for her. Mrs. Jackson frets about the injustices blacks face—especially the denial of jobs—despite the war propaganda. Nevertheless, she says, quoting trade unionists, "we got to fight the big Hitler over yonder even with all the little Hitlers over here."

Ralph had risen far in the literary world. Later in the fall, he was prominent when more than six hundred guests gathered at a gala banquet at the Murray Hill Hotel on Park Avenue in honor of *New Masses*. Seriously conflicted about the entire radical left, but cagey as always, he hid his true feelings. "The Way It Is" was his last piece to appear in *New Masses*. Never again would his byline appear in any radical leftist journal. Without breaking openly with Sillen and North, Ralph simply eased himself out of the *New Masses* offices and vanished as mysteriously, in some respects, as he had first appeared among the radicals in 1937. Later, he would never be frank in public about his former links to the Communists. Perhaps only once, in a private letter, did he ever acknowledge that early in the 1940s he had drastically altered his way of thinking about art and politics. Five years after the Murray Hill banquet, Ralph would deny permission to the Communist intellectual A. B. Magil of *New Masses* to reprint his short story "Mister Toussan." Perhaps a twinge of conscience led him to confess to Magil that "during 1942 I found it necessary (at the expense of a great deal of psychological and emotional wrenching) to change the direction of my literary efforts."

Although he had little respect for most black academics and intellectuals, he was determined to publish the best of them. In April he traveled to Washington to visit the so-called Capstone of Negro Education, Howard University. There, a number of professors, including the sociologist E. Franklin Frazier, promised to send him articles. (Very few kept their promises.) Eventually he published work by Frazier and by Eugene Holmes, a Communist member of the Department of Philosophy with an interest in the humanities in general. Ralph shared with Holmes his ultimate goal for the *Quarterly*: "It is our purpose to make the most advanced concepts and ideas [an] active part of Negro thought processes."

The second number of the *Quarterly* was richer in content than the first. It began with a lengthy editorial by Ralph. Two essays commented on the troubled relationship between Jews and blacks. Following an excerpt from *12 Million Black Voices* came essays on India and the war, civic corruption and trade unionism in Detroit, and racism in Cuba. A satirical short story (by Langston Hughes) was balanced by another story more tragic in tone. There were poems, a brief sketch of slavery, two book reviews, and, finally, "Publishers Are Awful," a trenchant attack by L. D. Reddick, curator of the Schomburg Collection, provoked in part by the insensitive dust jackets of two recent books. Langston Hughes's *Shakespeare in Harlem* featured a banjo and dice; the jacket of Arna Bontemps's *Golden Slippers* (an anthology of poetry for youths) lauded "the genius of the Negro spirit—gay, childlike, with its note of smiling melancholy." An "Editorial Comment" about the war insisted that the global conflict was a new stage in the liberation of the darker nations of the world. While the Allies persisted in maintaining their old colonialist and imperialist ways, *"this is a peoples' war for national liberation,"* the editorial stressed, *"and it must be fought and won by the people."* A drastic expansion of black power was needed at home, with "Negro members of the House of Representatives, the Senate, the Supreme Court, the President's Cabinet, and all other powerful governmental committees." While this call for a say in national affairs and for black advancement most likely came from Herndon, Ralph was certainly in full support of its demand for black power.

Mixed reviews greeted this number of the *Quarterly*. In the *Daily Worker,* Abner Berry called it vigorous and filling "a great gap on the Negro cultural front" (without mentioning Ralph). In Oklahoma City, both Roscoe Dunjee's *Black Dispatch* and the white *Daily Oklahoman* acknowledged Ralph's prominent new role. Some black nationalists disliked its interracial approach. Hard-line Communists sniffed at its eclectic version of Marxism. Within the office itself, tension between Herndon and Ralph was inevitable. From the start Ralph had difficulty collecting his full pay on schedule from Herndon, who was usually full of odd reasons why the journal could not meet its financial obligations. The *Quarterly* quickly slid into debt. About a year later, Ralph bitterly summed up both his high hopes for the *Quarterly* and the problems that would eventually kill it. "I went into it," he said privately, "feeling that it was badly needed, since so little is understood about Negroes even by themselves or by those dedicated, supposedly, to leading us. I tried to translate Negro life in terms of Marxist terminology, hoping that by so doing to offer cues and insights to those whose field is that of action." However, blacks as well as whites resisted his best efforts: "I didn't get very far with those I thought I was working with. The usual distrust of a Negro who dares to attempt to think. I was accused of everything from going over to the talented tenth [black elitism] to being a Trotskyite!"

On the domestic front, by the summer of 1942, as his one-year lease approached its end, his fellow tenants had revolted against him. They accused him of allowing garbage to remain uncollected and letting his dog repeatedly foul the basement. Angrily, he denied these charges. When Herndon's salary checks to him bounced, his own checks did, too. The telephone company cut off his service. In late August, he and Rose moved to a smaller apartment nearby, at 306 West 141st Street, in a building owned by the Macedonian Baptist Church. His days as a janitor were over.

In the middle of this turmoil, Ralph brought out the third (Fall 1942) number of the *Quarterly*. Its main feature was Slochower's essay "In the Fascist Styx," about Fascism, European writers, and Richard Wright. At least three other pieces are of special interest. One is "Rosalie," a selection from an autobiographical narrative, *No Day of Triumph,* by J. Saunders Redding, perhaps the most talented young African-American literary scholar. The second, "The American Negro: Three Views," by Eugene Holmes of Howard University, was a review of three new books. The third was Stanley Edgar Hyman's review of *Tap Roots,* a novel of the South by a white writer. Hyman's style was in dramatic contrast to Ralph's. Where Ralph tended to be self-conscious, solemn, ideological, and ponderous, Hyman was direct, engaging, and smart. ("The thing to do with a book like *Tap Roots,*" he began, "is to get the worst things said first. In many respects it is a bad book and a cheap book.") From such vigorous writing, and from the witty Hyman when they became fast friends, Ralph learned much about confident self-expression. In fact, Hyman (with Kenneth Burke hovering above him) would soon succeed Richard Wright as the major intellectual and professional influence on Ralph.

In June, Hyman had mailed Ralph a postcard offering to write for the *Quarterly*. "I have known of your work for quite some time," Ralph responded enthusiastically. "If you still find it possible to do reviews, articles or anything else for a magazine which does not pay, I will be only too glad to get any books from the publishers that you might suggest." Six years younger than Ralph, Hyman had grown up in New York City. In 1940, after graduating from Syracuse University, he had married a fellow student, Shirley Jackson, who had already begun to write fiction. The couple settled in New York City, where Hyman worked as a staff writer at William Shawn's *New Yorker* magazine. Between the sophisticated *New Yorker* and the deadly earnest *Quarterly* there should have been a chasm.

In fact, Hyman's writing for *The New Yorker* gave only glimpses of his various intellectual passions. Reared as an Orthodox Jew before losing his faith, in college he had read widely in numismatics (he collected ancient coins), anthropology, psychology, mythology, religion, and British and American literature. Hyman loved books. By the time he died, his library numbered over thirty thousand volumes. A Marxist, he nevertheless took an eclectic approach to criticism. In this respect, as in other ways, he showed the influence of Burke, who had taught him at Syracuse. He also supported the struggle for civil rights for blacks. In college he had taken to jazz and the blues—even as he freely confessed that he was a "musical illiterate." A Jew married to a Gentile, Hyman saw himself as a cosmopolitan intellectual—just as Ralph, labeled a Negro, saw himself as a citizen of the world.

On July 15, after reading an essay on Steinbeck by Hyman in the *Antioch Review,* Ralph sent him some new books, but also an open invitation: "Feel free to send us anything of a critical nature concerning American experience—let it deal with the novel, folk lore, swing, folk music, or what have you. As we visualize the *Quarterly* it is elastic enough to allow for the only real democracy now possible in America, an intellectual democracy." Discovering Hyman's interest in the blues, Ralph suggested that "a piece on the social background and content of the blues lyric would make an excellent essay." When Hyman, in responding, offered a theory of the blues that Ralph found provocative but flawed (it denied the unusual class fluidity of black culture, Ralph argued), their debates began. This relationship was strengthened in August when Hyman revealed that he was a disciple of Burke. Was Ralph surprised, since Burke had a reputation for obscurity and needless difficulty as a writer? "No, I am not at all surprised," Ralph responded, "having noticed similarities in your approaches to art. But, perhaps, most of all because he is also a hero of my own . . . and I'm never able to understand critics who don't admire him." In a telling comment, Ralph then contrasted Burke and Slochower, on the one hand, to "my friend Sam Sillen" of *New Masses,* on the other. Unlike Sillen, Burke and Slochower possessed "a *personal* vision which gives their theories of personality and society a feeling of urgency and which fires within them that emotion which gives rise to critical insight and synthesis of concepts and ideas. It is true that their 'aliveness' sometimes leads them out on futile paths; but true criticism, it seems to me, disdains being 'safe.' " After years of denying the personal in favor of the Marxist collective, Ralph had begun to embrace it.

On December 19, when the men finally met at Slochower's wedding in New York, they found each other charming. Lean, bearded, and irascible in his discussion of books and ideas, Hyman cut a distinctive figure. Fearless and frank in debate, but with conventional career goals, Hyman was also openly respectful of Ralph. That winter, he introduced Ralph to Kenneth Burke. They, too, hit it off. When Burke learned that Ralph had been unable to find certain books of his, he sent him copies of *Counter-Statement* and other titles. Ralph had made a solid impression on the sage.

As important as men like Slochower, Hyman, and Burke were to Ralph's seismic shift in 1942, none as yet was more indispensable than Richard Wright. The two were still good friends. The year had been a turning point as well for Wright, who was now living with his wife Ellen and their young daughter, Julia, in Brooklyn. In the fall, he completed "The Man Who Lived Underground," a novella that marked a major departure in his writing. "It is the first time," he wrote to his agent, "I've really tried to step beyond the straight black-white stuff." Echoing Dostoyevsky's *Notes from Underground* and Victor Hugo's *Les Misérables*, Wright's story to some extent anticipated Albert Camus (as Wright's biographer Michel Fabre would point out). A black man falsely accused of a crime is savagely beaten by the police, "confesses," and then escapes down a manhole into the bowels of the city. There he sees "not reality in reverse," as Fabre writes, "but the reverse of reality; he is still within the world, but because he is a spectator freed from himself and invisible, he is now omnipotent." Suddenly the novella becomes "a surprising existentialist metaphor of human and divine existence."

Wright's new breakthrough in fiction accompanied an ideological rupture. After Pearl Harbor, when his close friend Horace Cayton informed him that the Party would not support legal action against the government over Jim Crow, he broke quietly with the Communist Party. Asked to contribute to the special "Negro and Victory" number of *New Masses* in which Ralph's "The Way It Is" appeared, Wright refused. Later, Wright would declare that his resignation caused him no crisis of conscience—"indeed, I felt a kind of grim exhilaration in facing a world in which nothing could be taken for granted." The fact that he had earned almost $30,000 in 1940 probably facilitated, perhaps inspired, this "exhilaration."

Poor and unprotected, Ralph could afford fewer scruples. But perhaps something else, neither expediency nor opportunism, helps to explain how he could publish ultra-Marxist criticism under a pseudonym even as he was abandoning the radical left in and around 1942. Honest on the whole, Ralph struggled, as he stated in praising *12 Million Black Voices,* with the "criminal" tendencies fostered in him by American racism. Along with a rigid, self-righteous desire for order, he also harbored a temptation toward violence, subversion, and dissimulation, which his fierce pride and force of will held in check. "Chaos," the antithesis of moral rectitude and civilization, would become perhaps the single most compelling term for him in the following years; he was fascinated by characters who create and exploit chaos. These characters slip in and out of disguises, wear masks, ventriloquize conflicting messages, sow confusion, and appear invincible until the very end. This was the criminal-artist (the confidence man) demanded by the endlessly compromised American reality, and Ralph was probably both honest artist and devious "criminal" as he tried to function within, and to master, that reality.

About this time, he finished perhaps his last effort in proletarian fiction. On April 2, 1943, the editor of the centrist *Common Ground,* M. Margaret Anderson, wrote to ask him about a short story he had read recently to Langston Hughes (fleeing the far left, Hughes published more pieces in *Common Ground* during the 1940s than in any other journal). Reworked after Anderson's friendly criticism, "That I Had the Wings" (the last of the four "Buster and Riley" stories to be printed) appeared that summer. It was Ralph's most densely structured text to date—a cornucopia of symbols, myths, and rituals involving oppositions of flight and fall, sexuality and repression, male and female, faith and atheism, freedom and bondage, life and death. As a parable it reflects both on black American history and on the human drama of maturation. While the story endorses progressive politics, it also marks a step away from a radical aesthetic.

Ralph's signaling of his withdrawal from a commitment to the Communist Party (if he had ever been a member) would be like Wright's in one way. The following year, when Thyra Edwards at the Communist *People's Voice* asked for a short story for a special May Day issue on the Negro and labor struggles, he either refused or never answered her letter. But where Wright surrendered his Party membership while remaining a Marxist and a radical at heart, Ralph was on his way toward the political center.

In the winter of 1943, Ralph and Herndon were struggling to keep the *Quarterly* from sinking. The magazine owed its printer, the Dryden Press, several hundred dollars. In April, the Harlem Check Cashing Company threatened to take Ralph to court after yet another check from Herndon (for $20) was returned because of insufficient funds. That month, Herndon wrote Ralph from Philadelphia ("Guess you have been wondering what the hell happened to me") with stories of money-raising schemes, as well as a check for $55 "to make up for the recent jam you were left in." (In 1954, the black gossip magazine *Jet* would report that Herndon, operating under the name Gene Braxton, was arrested and charged with swindling. He had allegedly accepted $25,000 from five different prospective buyers of the same six-apartment rental building.) Herndon's slipperiness dismayed Ralph but did not drive him to abandon the *Negro Quarterly*. With the war raging, its demise would put him at the mercy of his local draft board, which had recently reclassified him. On March 3, he wrote to the board arguing that "my job as managing editor of a magazine of general information is one of a category listed as essential to the war effort."

Unable to bring out a Winter number in 1943, he and Herndon decided to publish a combined Winter–Spring issue. This number would mark the end of the *Quarterly*—but the real beginning, in some respects, of Ralph's new intellectual life. The most important essay was his unsigned "Editorial Comment," which confirmed the crucial impact that Slochower, Hyman, and Burke, among others, were having on him. Without abandoning Marx, Ralph had begun to move away from Marx and the logic of realism, naturalism, and dialectical materialism toward the subtleties and mysteries of myth and symbol, Freudian psychology, and surrealism. The essay begins with a scathing assessment of black responses to the war. Many blacks, placidly accepting Jim Crow, show "a fear and uncertainty that is almost psychopathic. It results in the most disgusting forms of self-abasement." Other blacks, rejecting the war out of excessive black nationalism, engage in "a political form of self-pity, and an attitude of political children." What is needed instead is a policy of "critical participation, based upon a sharp sense of the Negro people's group personality." Black intellectuals must turn to psychology in order to understand the full range of black cultural expression, and must become skilled readers of "the myths and symbols which abound among the Negro masses, but are not transparent. Much in Negro life remains a mystery; perhaps the zoot suit conceals profound political meaning; perhaps the symmetrical frenzy of the Lindy-hop conceals clues to great potential power—if only Negro leaders would solve this riddle. For without this knowledge, leadership, no matter how correct its program, will fail."

Ralph's invocation of the phrase "myths and symbols" indicates the extent to which (encouraged by Hyman and Burke, but also by his earlier interest in Eliot's *The Waste Land*) he had begun serious reading in the mythology critics connected to the so-called Cambridge Group. He had been studying Jessie Weston's *From Ritual to Romance,* which Eliot praises in a footnote to *The Waste Land,* and such related texts as Jane Harrison's *Themis,* Gilbert Murray's *Greek Tragedy,* Lord Raglan's *The Hero,* and J. G. Frazer's *The Golden Bough,* the fountainhead of myth criticism of this era. The core idea here for Ralph (although Frazer later repudiated it) was that myth is not corrupted history but the narrative that derives from ritual. Ritual, in its original forms, is the dramatic enactment of impulses and urges, fears and desires, primary to the human condition. This concept allowed into humanistic critical thinking a respect for mysticism and irrationality. Under Communism, "mystery" and "magic" were virtually forbidden terms—unless used scornfully. Now Ralph had decided to enter this forbidden world and the literary styles, including surrealism, that it inspired. He was coming close to acquiring a literary language appropriate to his vision of chaos.

Late in May, seeking a quiet place to write after correcting proofs of the Winter–Spring number, Ralph left Rose behind in New York while he traveled to Waitsfield, Vermont, for the first of several visits to the farm of John and Amelie Bates (he was black, she white). John was the brother of Add Bates, a skilled cabinetmaker and a radical from Harlem who was a close friend of Richard Wright. If John was notoriously argumentative, he was also a considerate host. The direct descendant of a Civil War general, Amelie was as loving and generous as she was politically progressive. They had a baby daughter, a quiet, smiling child to whom Ralph liked feeding cereal in the morning.

The Bates house was old, with parts dating back to the late eighteenth century. Together, Ralph and John devoted a part of each day to its renovation. They jacked up the house in some places, knocked out ancient plaster, replaced it with fiberboard, and set down new planks for the floor. Ralph welcomed this physical labor. After the dinginess of New York, he found Vermont and New England in the spring beautiful beyond belief. The nights were cold and the mornings foggy, but then the sun came out even as the surrounding mountains and the secluded gorges were still white with snow. Spring had come late that year, but now the brooks and streams rushed and burbled with clear, clean water. Lilacs and apple blossoms flowered, robins and swallows flitted and twittered, the chickadees sounded their shrill call, rabbits and squirrels ran freely. For the first time in his life Ralph went trout fishing. Savoring the feeling of being "alone with the noise of the stream and the flies," he both enjoyed the solitude and found it a little painful—deeply content, and yet "feeling sad that I was alone and had no one to share it with."

At first he wrote little. "Wonderful country this," he wrote Stanley Hyman on June 2, "but not inspiring of fiction." The Hemingway-like tone of this remark was not accidental. As an exercise, he had typed out "The Short Happy Life of Francis Macomber." Too many personal pressures weighing on him blocked his own creativity. The heaviest came from his marriage. If Rose, as he had implied to Sanora Babb, symbolized for him a commitment to radical Marxism and black nationalism, then his political and artistic realignment was bound to strip her of much of her allure. Rose was not unaware of the seriousness of his changing. While Ralph was in Vermont, she missed him more than he missed her. "Why the 'hell' don't you write?" she finally snapped. It was probably about this time that, lonely and too often put down by her husband, she began an affair with a police officer.

In Vermont, Ralph turned out some reviews. Katherine Woods at *Tomorrow: The Magazine of the Future* paid him $10 for a review of Roi Ottley's *New World A-Coming*, a book about blacks in America. Pleased by Ralph's work, Woods paid him another $10 for a review of the white writer Bucklin Moon's *The Darker Brother*, again about African-American culture. In the next two years, Ralph wrote seven reviews for *Tomorrow*, which displaced *New Masses* in his life. But fiction mattered far more to him, and fiction was not coming. He returned to Harlem in a bleak mood. When, late in June, he received a letter from Sanora, her first to him in more than a year, he opened himself to her in a way that was closed to Rose. "You were always easy to talk with," he wrote Sanora. Perhaps by now he knew about Rose's affair. "You've caught me at a moment when I'm giving up things," he admitted, "being so full of disgust, and sickness and despair." Bemoaning the dying of the *Quarterly* ("there was never anything like it before in Negro journalism"), he also explained his break with *New Masses*: "I can't write for NM nowadays because they say few things about my people that I can agree with." He was a changed man: "I'll never waste time with organizations again, but will write of the things I believe in and of what my people believe in, hope for and feel. If organizations like it, wonderful; if not, I'll try to write with such honesty that rejecting it they will be forced to recognize the point of view." And he was done with dogma. He was heading now in a new direction: "I'm trying to map a new course for my writing, based upon those things that are abiding in Negro experience in the U.S. It will be much harder than before, there'll be no token fame to go with it nor pictures in NM, but I'll learn to write so that it will be read because it is true and perhaps now and then with a streak of beauty, but like some of the passages out of letters I wrote when homeless in Dayton it will have a feeling of having been lived."

Ralph's friendship with Stanley Hyman and his wife steadily flowered. On August 1, after a long, wonderful afternoon and evening of food, wine, and stimulating talk at their home in Woodside, Queens, he was preparing to stay for the night when he suddenly decided to go home to Harlem. Emerging from the subway at 137th Street, he found a riot in progress—the first major civil insurrection in Harlem since 1935, and the worst by far. A black woman, improbably named Polite, had provoked a loud dispute with a white policeman in the lobby of a Harlem hotel. When a black soldier intervened, perhaps violently, the policeman shot and wounded him. He later recovered, but Margie Polite ran into the street screaming that a white cop had killed a black man. Harlem exploded. Windows were smashed and stores looted. Five people died, about four hundred were injured, and $5 million in property was reported lost. Thousands of volunteers, policemen, and troops from the New York State Guard finally restored peace—but not before five hundred were arrested.

That night, and the next morning, Ralph roamed the streets. The underlying reason for the riot was clear, he would write in the *New York Post*. It was "the poorer element's way of blowing off steam," of showing their resentment at police brutality and attacks by whites on black women and children. But he was stunned by the bizarre, even surrealistic juxtaposition of behaviors among the rioters. A crowd of looters paused long enough from their stealing to buy bottles of milk from a passing truck. One man disavowed being a member of the mob. He hadn't stolen anything, he pointed out: "I just broke windows." A woman declared the event "a colored man's New Year." A group of black boys put on blond wigs, silk hats, and other formal wear "and danced in the streets." Toting stolen boxes of soap powder, a man explained truculently, "I gotta keep clean, aint I?" When one woman tried to force a boy to give her a stolen table, "he laughed in her face and cursed a passing policeman." Residents of one building asked police for help in clearing it of people, then torched it with their belongings inside. Ralph passed a woman loaded down with stolen goods. "Forgive me, Jesus," she muttered. "Have mercy, Lord." He saw other signs of "shame and self-disgust . . . among the more stable people," especially as the disorder subsided. He witnessed attempts by law-abiding folks to console shop owners. Mainly, however, the dominant vision was of chaos.

On Monday, when the *Post* called to ask him to report on the uprising, he agreed at once—and made $50 for two days' work. After Ralph's column appeared, Mike Gold noticed it in the *Daily Worker:* "Ralph Ellison paints the picture of something pathetic and naïve . . . a spontaneous, unorganized revolt of dumb masses against economic conditions." Gold was not unfair to Ralph, who had first praised the police for restoring order, then described "the pathetic and naïve nature of the riot." Ralph's report ended as a jeremiad. The rioters' rejection of appeals for calm by the mayor and various leading Negro organizations was ominous: "It was as though they spoke different languages." If more significant change did not come, "new riots can be soon expected."

From the day he arrived in Harlem in 1936 to this episode seven years later, the neighborhood had been a spectacle unto itself for Ralph. Now, even as he embraced the notion that psychology was the key to understanding black culture, Harlem projected images of psychological devastation, of comedy mixed with tragic despair, sufficient to challenge any systematic attempt at analysis or definition. Soon, Langston Hughes would write about the Harlem community as the living embodiment of "a dream deferred." Ralph was groping now toward some more complicated rendering of the mythic and symbolic dimensions of a community that epitomized joy and sorrow, hope and despair, poise and social dereliction.

With the *Quarterly* now dead, Ralph had no legitimate excuse left for staying out of the war. Still adamant about not serving in the Jim Crow army, he opted instead for the merchant marine. In February, his friend Add Bates, now in the merchant marine, helped to find him a job as a third cook. The merchant marine was hardly the timid man's way out. If anything, it was more dangerous than the regular army. A friend of Ralph, a young white poet, had died at sea on his first voyage.

No one could get into the merchant marine without proof of his date of birth—which Ralph could not provide (in 1913, Oklahoma did not require birth certificates). Ralph appealed for help to his old employer in Oklahoma City, the pharmacist James L. Randolph, who organized six persons to provide affidavits that they had known Ralph Waldo Ellison since he was a child. Only Randolph swore that Ralph "was born in Oklahoma City, Okla., on March 1, 1914." (The others cited no year.) Ralph was thirty, but Randolph made him twenty-nine. Ralph made no effort to correct the mistake. According to his National Maritime Union certificate, he now weighed 180 pounds. His hairline was slightly receding on his left side, as he noted wistfully in a letter to Sanora Babb.

More dramatic change came later in December as Ralph's marriage to Rose Poindexter came to an abrupt end. According to legal papers filed in 1945, on September 30, 1943, Ralph committed an act of adultery in their apartment. Because Ralph was eager in 1945 to have the divorce, it is possible that such an act never took place but was invented to speed the process and leave Rose's reputation unblemished. Later on, Ralph would say even less about his first marriage and its end than about his break with the Communists. The only surviving reference to the breakup in his correspondence is in a letter to Sanora: "In September Rose left me." It is indeed possible that Rose had been the adulterer. In October, the police officer with whom she had an affair, Charles Wilson, wrote her a letter that came into Ralph's possession. Wilson spoke ruefully of Rose having ended their affair and taken up with another, more reliable man. Rose's side of the story is unknown. She and Ralph remained cordial to each other whenever their paths crossed, but their break was complete. Eventually they would live in the same apartment house on Riverside Drive, but not together.

Late in September, Ralph officially joined the U.S. Merchant Marine. For about three months thereafter he found himself assigned to one ship or another but not at sea. His new freedom and responsibilities—and his loneliness—spurred his creative energies. In October, *Harper's Bazaar* politely sent back a story. "I like what your story says," an editor informed Ralph, "but the treatment isn't altogether successful." At *The New Yorker*, William Shawn also returned a story. But interest in Ralph as a writer was growing. That month, the Book Find Club asked him for a review of a new biography of George Washington Carver, and a publisher asked him to read the galleys of a novel about a black woman in the South. (Writing to Hyman, Ralph despaired about being tied forever by editors to books about race.) Henrietta Buckmaster begged him to read the manuscript of her latest book, "because I am a profound admirer of your critical faculties."

On November 18, perhaps for the first time, Ralph appeared on a radio program (at the New York City educational radio station WEVD), for a discussion of Roi Ottley's *New World A-Coming* and Bucklin Moon's *The Darker Brother*. Ottley and the poet Countee Cullen were also present. Ralph was fearless. Comparing Ottley's book to Wright's *12 Million Black Voices,* he found it sneering and apologetic about blacks; also, as he wrote in his review, "being neither scholarly nor responsible journalism, much of its value as information is distorted." (As in the review for *Tomorrow* magazine, Ralph refrained from pointing out that Ottley's book was based on material gathered and written up by members of the Negro unit of the Federal Writers' Project, including himself.) One result of this stern but informed criticism, expertly phrased, was a flurry of inquiries in December from publishers and literary agents alike. Henry Volkening, a prominent agent, had already approached Ralph, on the advice of Bucklin Moon, about representing him. (Ralph's favorable review of Moon's first novel, *The Darker Brother,* appeared that month in *Tomorrow.*) A publisher asked Ralph if he indeed was at work on a novel, as Langston Hughes had told him. The William Morris Agency wrote to say that it was "particularly interested" in the development of "unknown writers." The Writers' Literary Agency also wrote Ralph to ask about representing him. Two days before Christmas, Edwin Seaver's publisher, L. B. Fischer, informed Ralph that Seaver had chosen his recent story "Flying Home" for inclusion in Seaver's forthcoming book *Cross Section: A Collection of New American Writing*. Enclosed with Fischer's letter was a check for $25, as an advance against royalties.

Gratifying as was all this attention, Ralph had little time to digest its meaning. Even as he seemed to be poised on the brink of a breakthrough as an artist, he was about to risk everything in compelled service to his country. On December 27, after taking the oath of loyalty, he was certified for duty as a second cook and baker. The next day, he joined the crew of the Liberty Ship SS *Sun Yat-Sen* as it steamed out of New York Harbor.

7

A Mighty Book, a Mighty Theme
1943–1945

To produce a mighty book, you must choose a mighty theme. HERMAN MELVILLE (1851)

Crossing the Atlantic Ocean in a merchant ship was dangerous business in the winter of 1943, when German U-boats, operating solo or in wolf packs, had made the merchant marine the most vulnerable branch of the Allied effort. In 1942, the worst year of the war for the seamen, German submarines sank 1,200 Allied ships. Nevertheless, men like Ralph had to live with the irony that many people saw service in the merchant marine as a likely sign of cowardice. But he knew exactly why he had chosen it. "It is the most democratic of all the services," Ralph declared, "and though some sneer at it I am able to maintain some sense of dignity—a thing which for me would be impossible had I been taken into the army."

A novice at sea, he watched and waited nervously for signals of trouble. The crossing was uneventful. He had been kept ignorant of his destination (for security reasons), and discovered only on docking that he was now in Swansea, Wales, the most southwesterly of all the United Kingdom ports and a hub of naval traffic to and from North America. Despite the hardships of wartime, and the behavior of white Americans, who struck him as boorish, arrogant, and bigoted against blacks and against the native white populations, Ralph's first visit outside the United States turned out to be surprisingly pleasant. The Welsh, proud of their distinct cultural values, had a passion for music, dance, and talk that seemed to unite them and their black American visitors; unlike white Americans, the locals also seemed unconcerned by interracial dating. Later that year, Ralph would declare privately of the Welsh, "I love them like my own people." He was happy "that hundreds of Negro boys are acquiring their first notions of real democracy among these people who, strangely, are culturally so similar."

One evening he went to a Red Cross social club outside Swansea directed by a black American, George Hayes. As Ralph entered, a new recording by Count Basie's orchestra blared over the loudspeakers; on the dance floor was "some of the most expert, international, interracial Lindy-hopping I'd ever seen." Black and white soldiers seemed relaxed, and the Welsh girls seemed at ease with the black men. "These here is some good white people," a black corporal informed him. "All in all they are about the best all-around white folks I ever seen." Like music and dance, good manners were important in this culture. Talking to locals, Ralph discovered the strength of Welsh nationalism and their interest in socialism. "They, like the Russians," he decided, "are a mature people while we Americans are yet in painful adolescence."

At least two short stories would come out of this visit. One, "In a Strange Country," was about a black American roughed up by white soldiers outside a Welsh pub. Entering in a state of rage and despair, the black man is slowly made to feel his own humanity again because of the way the local people receive him. In "A Storm of Blizzard Proportions," a black American visitor to Wales must part from a blue-eyed local woman who wants to marry him. She has no inkling, he believes, of the ordeal they would face in the United States. Brooding on the figure of Jack Johnson, the black boxer who twice had defiantly married white women, the man must concede that he lacks Johnson's fighting spirit, as well as Johnson's capacity for joy.

Proceeding uncertainly here, Ralph leaned on certain elements from his own past, including his sojourn in Dayton, the death of his mother there, and hunting for snipe. In places, the influence of Hemingway and of Joyce—especially the memorable last paragraph of "The Dead"—is obtrusive. Perhaps Ralph also drew on his tangled emotions and ideas involving Sanora Babb, one white woman he might have married. If so, he could not get past the same chilly emotional blockage that had brought their relationship to an awkward close. Eventually he would give up this story and move on—and never again try to tell the story of a man and a woman in love.

After a brief stay in bombed-out London, the *Sun Yat-Sen* headed back out into the Atlantic for the voyage home. This trip was an ordeal. His appetite gone and his stomach on fire, Ralph lost ten pounds. When his stomach ailments persisted in New York, the local draft board was skeptical but classified him 2A. He was now temporarily ineligible for the draft.

Back in his apartment at 306 West 141st Street, he rested and nursed himself as best he could. The most important woman in his life now was old enough, at seventy-eight, to be his grandmother—Ida Espen Guggenheimer. At times impulsive and eccentric, but intelligent and warmhearted, Guggenheimer befriended Ralph in 1943, although she might have met him earlier, perhaps through Harry Slochower. The main link between this hungry young black writer and this aged Jewish woman activist was a twin love of literature and the left. The rich widow of a conservative lawyer from Richmond, Virginia, Ida was a member of the American Labor Party and a Communist Party supporter, if not an actual member. Her involvement in civil rights was only part of her activism. Born in 1866 into a wealthy Philadelphia family and educated there and in Europe, she eventually embraced a number of social and political causes, including Hadassah, the premier Zionist women's organization, which she supported from its infancy. In the 1930s, she had helped to bring a stream of German refugees to the United States. She championed the lot of women workers through the Women's Trade Union League and the League of Women Voters. She also backed the American Civil Liberties Union. A lover of literature—she knew scads of Milton by heart—she read incessantly. Beset by various infirmities, she nevertheless attended lectures, plays, movies, and political events. She also welcomed guests, including Ralph and other blacks, to her home in the Ansonia Hotel (admired for its over-the-top Beaux Arts design) at Broadway and 74th Street in Manhattan.

By the winter of 1944 Ralph was a frequent visitor at Ida's apartment, where he met her daughter, Clara Binswanger, Clara's husband, Isadore, and Clara's best friend, Beatrice Stein Steegmuller, a painter married to the writer Francis Steegmuller. Ida came to love Ralph. To her, he embodied intellectual vitality and shrewdness, a commitment to socialism, and the promise of literary greatness. (That he was black was also essential to his appeal.) Quick to burst out with an opinion, she was also quick to admit when Ralph was right and she was wrong. With her he was as unsentimental as he had been with his mother. He loved Ida as he had loved his mother—his mother had been useful to him, and he hoped Guggenheimer would be, too. On several occasions Ralph asked Ida for financial help, which she gave readily—not least of all because he never sought money unless he needed it, and never asked for more than he needed. He also repaid loans.

With Ida's comforting, Ralph nursed himself back to health. In the meantime, "In a Strange Country" made its way awkwardly among the magazine editors. With an agent now—Russell & Volkening, on Fifth Avenue—Ralph hoped to break through into the more lucrative magazines. But after four of them (including *The New Yorker* and *Harper's*) turned down the story, Henry Volkening placed it in familiar territory, *Tomorrow*, for $100. Then, on April 19, after reading Ralph's pieces in *Tomorrow*, Frank Taylor, a senior editor at the young but respected publishing house of Reynal & Hitchcock, proposed to pay him $100 a month for twelve months to work on a novel.

Ralph did not leap at the offer, or at the prospect of a rival offer from the more established Harcourt Brace. Unsure of his ability to write a novel, he did not want to commit himself to such a project. He was still sharply aware that he was an apprentice writer of fiction who had to labor over his stories. Judiciously, and ethically (he would not have to return the money if Taylor rejected his manuscript), he decided to wait. In late May he savored the appearance of his first work in a clothbound volume when "Flying Home" was published in Seaver's anthology of new writing, *Cross Section*. Ralph presented an autographed copy to a doting Ida Guggenheimer, for whom the offer to him of a contract for a novel was "an augury of wider recognition of one who is outstanding among men."

"Flying Home" is a heavily symbolic story—weaving realist narrative with parody and stream of consciousness—of a young black man's painful lessons about individual and racial identity. Todd, a young Negro army pilot, flying too high and too fast, crashes in an Alabama field owned by a vicious white man. He is found by an old Negro, Jefferson, whom he instinctively disdains. Jefferson then tells him about his own flying: "Well, I went to heaven and right away started to sproutin' me some wings. Six-foot ones, they was. Just like them the white angels had." He had flown fast and high despite St. Peter's warnings about speeding: " 'Jeff, you and that speedin' is a danger to the heavenly community. If I was to let you keep on flyin', heaven wouldn't be nothin' but uproar. Jeff, you got to go!' Son, I argued and pleaded with that old white man, but it didn't do a bit of good. They rushed me straight to them pearly gates and gimme a parachute and a map of the state of Alabama." As Jefferson laughs crazily, Todd believes that the old man is mocking him for thinking himself equal to white men. Todd wants him to keep quiet. But the end of the story, as Todd lies near death, offers him a moment of truth. As the white men come not to help but to evict the "nigguh" pilot, Todd centers his sight on Jefferson's face, "as though somehow he had become his sole salvation in an insane world of outrage and humiliation." As Jefferson and his son carry him gently away, Todd feels lifted out of his isolation "back into the world of men. A new current of communication flowed between the man and boy and himself." The story ends in filtered light: "Then like a song within his head he heard the boy's soft humming and saw the dark bird glide into the sun and glow like a bird of flaming gold."

Like a warning flare, this story illuminates two of the main sources of conflict in Ralph's personal and professional life: his punitive reserve with most blacks (whom he associated with poverty and ignorance) and his ambition to scale cultural heights attained thus far, in his opinion, only by whites. Although the discovery of an elemental kinship with an old, "backward" black man that is Todd's salvation ironically still eluded Ralph, this story documents nevertheless his unsparing knowledge of himself as a young man, including his awareness that his own conflicted state mirrored the shared conflict of identity faced by all blacks in a country dominated by Jim Crow.

"Flying Home" attracted readers. In the *Chicago Tribune,* Paul Engle pointed approvingly to "a very remarkable story" by Ralph: "I think it's the finest thing in the book." (Engle's opinion was "very nice to me," Ralph cracked modestly, "but makes an awful fool of him.") This was a coup, because the volume featured six novelettes, one each by Richard Wright, Jane Bowles, and Norman Mailer (an excerpt from *The Naked and the Dead*); seventeen short stories, including work by Shirley Jackson and Brendan Gill; two plays, one by Arthur Miller; and verse by fifteen poets, including Langston Hughes. No other important critic put Ralph first in quality (the *New York Times Book Review* failed to mention him in its disdainful glance at the "Negro" stories), but several others praised him. The *New York Herald Tribune* described his "white-hot protesting story" as excellent. On the far left, key reviewers frowned on his modernistic style. *New Masses* reported on "the Joycean interior monologue which has caused more than one young writer to come a ridiculous cropper."

The reception of "Flying Home" was gratifying but also soon overwhelmed by the invasion of Normandy on June 6, 1944, by Allied forces led by General Dwight D. Eisenhower. In this momentous operation some 2,700 merchant vessels took part in the first wave of beach landings.

Merchant mariners scuttled ships and performed other perilous operations to aid the invasion, on which the success of the entire war depended. The merchant marine needed manpower desperately, but Ralph stayed on the sidelines with his chronic stomach condition.

A week after the landings, on June 13, in Manhattan, Ralph met Fanny McConnell Buford. Ralph and Fanny had a friend in common, the veteran sculptor, painter, and printmaker Charles "Spinky" Alston, who was convinced that Ralph and Fanny, with their love of books, their seriousness, and their glowing ambition, should meet. When Alston failed twice to set up a meeting as promised, Fanny called Ralph on her own. She selected the restaurant—Frank's, one of the best known in Harlem but with relatively modest prices—out of regard for Ralph's status as an unemployed writer. She ordered the cheapest dish on the menu— chicken à la king—but barely touched it because she found Ralph so attractive. He, too, was mesmerized. They "just sat there looking at one another," she recalled fifteen years later.

Fanny Buford, like Ralph, was married; but her marriage to Ligon Buford was, like Ralph's to Rose Poindexter, dead. Five feet five inches tall, slender, and with light brown skin and a freckled face, she was a striking woman. Older than Ralph, she was born on November 27, 1910—although she later claimed 1911 and then settled on 1914. Her poise belied the struggles of her life. She was born Fannie Mae McConnell in Louisville, Kentucky, to a hapless, unprepared couple from Tennessee. Her mother, Willie Mae McConnell, was nineteen at Fannie's birth; her father, Ulysses McConnell, was twenty-two. Fannie wasn't a year old when the marriage folded. She and her mother then moved to Pueblo, Colorado, to live with Willie's father (her parents were divorced). Fannie next saw her father when she was seventeen.

In Colorado, her loving grandfather urged her to compete hard at school and always to aim high. Then, in 1917, when Fannie was about six, Willie married again. Three years later, because of "her husband's cruelty and extravagance," the marriage ended. According to notes made by Fanny later in life, her stepfather abused her sexually and left her guilty and ashamed. ("What has bothered me all these years," she wrote Ralph in 1958, "was that I ran and told. After having encouraged him, I ran and told.") Mother and daughter moved to Denver, where Willie found work as a pantry girl in a cafeteria. After two grinding years of poverty and insult, they migrated to Chicago to live with Willie's mother and her son by a separate marriage. Following several hurtful clashes, they moved in with another, unrelated family. Fannie did well at school until 1927, when her mother fell seriously ill. She then quit school and found work as an assistant to two doctors and a dentist, educated black men who would have "a revolutionary effect upon my character and mind." She also fell in love with Louis Hickman, a nephew of one of the doctors and a student at Columbia University in New York. Louis, who loved poetry, bred "ambition in me." Fannie began to read with "a more discriminating taste." She also changed the spelling of her name from Fannie to Fanny, to underscore her break with the past.

The following year, still working as a secretary, she returned to school. Two years later she enrolled at Fisk University in Nashville. She arrived there a determined young woman. "Between you and me," she wrote her mother (who had just married again), "I think I am the best looking girl in the freshman class. I am going to make it my business to be one of the smartest too." Pledging the elite Alpha Kappa Alpha sorority, she was a mainstay in chapel life, published fiction in the *Fisk Herald,* and acted in theater productions. Like Ralph at Tuskegee, she was plagued by a lack of money. Falling back on her experience as a skilled secretary, Fanny worked for the dean of women, then for the university president, the sociologist Charles S. Johnson, and finally in the office of James Weldon Johnson, the poet, novelist, diplomat, and NAACP leader lured to Fisk near the end of his career. Nevertheless, in the spring of 1934, Fanny was forced to leave Fisk because she couldn't pay her bills.

That fall, backed by a state scholarship, she enrolled as a junior majoring in drama at the University of Iowa, in Iowa City. Her two years at the almost exclusively white school were tough. Allowed to direct some plays and to act in at least one radio production, Fanny was barred from the stage by Jim Crow. After graduating in 1936, she had little to do with Iowa. Later, in 1959, she would write with bitterness to a friend about "my old Alma Mater, about which I've never given a damn. . . . The school was full of prejudice and things were awkward for all Negro students. Now, I understand, all that's changed. One just has to live long enough."

Graduating with a bachelor of arts in 1936, she sought but failed to find a teaching job in Chicago. For some months Fanny worked for the local Republican Party, helping to register black voters in a presidential election year. On November 27, 1936, in Crown Point, Indiana, she married Rodney G. Higgins of St. Louis, a graduate student at Iowa. According to divorce papers, Fanny left Higgins the next day. On August 26, 1937, the court granted her a divorce. Writing to Fanny, Higgins conceded that he was immature but complained that Fanny hadn't given him a proper chance. Because of her upbringing, she had become "self-confident so much that you are even afraid to look to someone else as a provider." To Higgins, she was also "ambitious, courageous, capable and aggressive."

Fanny became a belle of black Chicago. "How is the pretty, Venus shaped, exotic Fanny?" someone asked one of her friends about this time. For a while she worked with the Play Readers' Bureau of the WPA, but resigned in June 1937. She dreamed of a career in Hollywood and came close to moving to California that year. She then worked as an assistant to handlers of Joe Louis, as a researcher for the sociologist Horace Cayton, and as a drama instructor at a YMCA. She also earned a few graduate credits at Northwestern University. She took a major step in the theater in 1938 when, after directing an anti-lynching sketch by Ted Ward, *Even the Dead Arise,* she founded the Negro People's Theatre in Chicago. In November, she directed its production of *Don't You Want to Be Free?* Langston Hughes, who visited the company more than once, liked Fanny. Hardly a radical, Fanny decried the idea of a propaganda outfit in a letter to members. "It is no such thing that we want," she insisted. The Negro People's Theatre must show blacks as human beings.

By mid-1938 Fanny was in love with Ligon Buford, a cultivated, stylish man from Washington, D.C., who had worked as a publicist with the WPA Federal Theatre and had acted in the Ward play. On September 26, 1939, he and Fanny were married in Waukegan, Illinois. Not long afterward, Fanny resigned from the faltering Negro People's Theatre to begin work as an assistant to John Sengstacke, general manager of the influential weekly *Chicago Defender.* As Fanny Buford she also wrote a column, "Along the Political Front," for the *Defender,* as well as reviews and other essays. In 1941, she was suddenly dismissed. Angry, she left Chicago.

For a while, she lived in Groton, Massachusetts. Sometimes she was with Buford, sometimes not. Buford had joined the black 366th Infantry as a supplies manager and evidently enjoyed his life away from Fanny. She moved on. Just after Pearl Harbor, in part because of patriotism, she arrived in Washington to work first as a typist for the navy and then in a more technical capacity with the War Production Board. In July 1943, fed up with the nastiness of life in Jim Crow Washington, she moved to New York. There she quickly found work at the National Urban League as an assistant to its director, Lester Granger. Now her marriage to Buford, who was managing a Red Cross club in Manchester, England, existed in name only. A certain letter from him, Fanny noted dryly, "marks the first time you have indicated that you needed me as a wife for more than a year." On June 1, two weeks before Fanny met Ralph, Ligon was ready to "accept our friendship as another casualty of the war."

Reminiscing about her first meeting with Ralph, Fanny would write about "the lonely young man I found one sunny afternoon in June." She liked almost everything about him—his shyness, his acute intelligence, his cool wit, his brazen ambition. Ralph loved Fanny's beauty, but also her passion for literature, drama, and the arts, and her respect for his goals. With a college degree and secretarial skills, she was also better placed than Rose had been to support him. Moreover, Fanny was of the political center, with middle-class tastes that Ralph was appreciating more and more (although by July he had her reading Malraux). Rose was bohemian and headstrong. Fanny was equally willful, but she was ready to submit to a man she saw as her intellectual and artistic superior.

Lunching one day with two *New Masses* employees, radical literary companions from the old days, Ralph let them know that he was a different man from the fledgling who had sought refuge at *New Masses*. Now his mission was distinct from theirs: "There was a time when I was willing to die in the interest of their ideas, my ideas, but now things are different. In the meantime there is work to do, the kind of work that I've been preparing myself to do."

Ralph's confidence about his new path increased when he read the bound galleys of Wright's autobiography, which Harper's was set to publish later that year, 1944. Struck by its power, he quickly wrote a long review (for *Tomorrow*) in which he concentrated on the last third of the book, Wright's account of his life among the Communists in Chicago. As with *Native Son,* the Book-of-the-Month Club stepped in to acquire *Black Boy* but decided that the book should end with Wright's flight from the South, before his involvement with Communism. The book was postponed until March 1945. Ralph's review was shelved. Early in July *Tomorrow* published "In a Strange Country." Ralph got a ripple of praise from his friends, including his first letter from Sanora Babb in more than a year, and two important inquiries. Both Atlantic Monthly Press and Little, Brown indicated that they might offer him a contract for a novel. This was encouraging news, especially since he had developed, as he put it with some excitement to Ida Guggenheimer, "the most ambitious and conceptually mature fiction idea that I have ever attempted."

Exactly what this idea was is not known. His poor health was preventing him from concentrating on his work. His stomach remained chronically upset, and one day his systolic blood pressure dropped to an alarming 106. He wrote hard or took notes in the mornings, but by the early afternoon he was exhausted. He needed to get away from hot, humid Harlem, where the summer had brought with it startling waves of crime, including gang activity. On the Fourth of July, Ralph managed to get to Sag Harbor, Long Island. Among black professionals in New York, Sag Harbor was the most prestigious vacation spot within a reasonable distance of the city. Several doctors, lawyers, and businessmen owned homes there—"a typical Babbitt watering place," Ralph reported disapprovingly. He enjoyed talking politics with some of the money-obsessed black Philistines there just the same. The prominent black political leaders in New York, Ralph believed, were a scandal. Perhaps the gang members would "turn against some of our Negro politicians and hang them from the highest steeple in Harlem." As for the black Communist leaders: "I am beginning to believe that nothing comes closer to justifying the fallacious theory of Negro inferiority than some Negro Communists. Which is a mean thing to say and I blame my saying it partly upon the heat."

Kept close to the city both by poverty and by merchant marine regulations, Ralph fell into a prolonged depression. He longed to escape to the Bateses' farm in Vermont again—or even to Canada, where Wright and his family had taken a place, and where Ida Guggenheimer had a country home in Westport, Ontario. A letter to Ida in mid-July started with an urgent request: "I am flat broke and I need to borrow some money (1) for my rent—which can wait a while longer—(2) for my dental work—which has stopped altogether—(3) for my doctor,. to whom I went yesterday." His blood pressure was down a few more points, probably because he couldn't afford the prescribed drugs. His life would be "extremely disgusting," he believed, were he not so accustomed to misfortune. The city was "very unpleasant." August came without a respite. Near the end of the month, his agent pressed him gently to make up his mind between rival offers by Harcourt Brace and by Reynal & Hitchcock for his first novel. Moved as much by his dire need for money as by confidence that he could finish a novel soon, Ralph signed in September with the latter firm and received the first payment on his advance. (Reynal & Hitchcock would pay Ralph $1,500 spread over a year.) He was to deliver the manuscript by September 1, 1945.

The literary sensation of the hour was the appearance in *The Atlantic*

Monthly in August and September of Wright's defiant "I Tried to Be a Communist"—a two-part essay drawn from the section of *Black Boy* cut by the Book-of-the-Month Club. In it, Wright angrily described his troubles with the Party in Chicago. To these charges, the Party, and its top blacks, reacted harshly. As usual, Ralph felt obliged to report to Wright even the most personal and private of attacks on him. "I did hear the rumor that you were neurotic again; first it was Bigger, and now you." Ralph had then silenced Wright's critics—or so he said—by pointing out that "everyone of us in the room *did* show some form of neurosis." At the same time, Ralph sent the "latest ravings" of Ben Davis, Wright's old friend and still a die-hard Communist, who had called him "ridiculously uninformed" about the Party and civil rights. The writer Shirley Graham (later Mrs. W. E. B. Du Bois) had denounced him—so Ralph had heard—as a "sadist." William Attaway had endorsed his public censure as an anti-Semite by the cartoonist and Party leader Robert Minor, because of Wright's cruel description of a Jewish comrade. James Ford, in his *Daily Worker* screed "The Case of Richard Wright: A Disservice to the Negro People," criticized his "shameful manner" in writing about the black masses, which, according to Ford, "is disgusting and damaging to their dignity."

Constantly reminding Wright that he had enemies came in part from Ralph's habit of frankness, but perhaps also from a growing sense of competition as he felt his own momentum growing. He was not yet so confident that he could begin to match Wright as an outspoken political critic. Vitriolic about Communists and Communism in private, he would never publish his own counterpart to Wright's "I Tried to Be a Communist." Even as they bonded on questions of art and politics, Wright and Ralph were beginning to separate as friends. Near the end of August, looking ahead, Ralph sent away for application forms for a fellowship in creative writing from the Julius Rosenwald Fund, the premier source of fellowships for black writers and artists. He also applied, with less hope of success, for a fellowship from the more prestigious John Simon Guggenheim Memorial Foundation. For the Guggenheim he marshaled an impressive array of referees, including Wright and Kenneth Burke.

Ralph now had a plan for a novel to be set in a Nazi prison camp. Its central character would be a captured black airman whose challenge is to overcome the "deep feelings of humiliation" instilled in him by his experience in the United States and create a democracy in the camp despite the fact that many prisoners will resent and attack him. Eventually he will succeed. But because democracy in the camp is "a forced regression and a form of death, thus he *must* be killed off. The novel, in effect, will be an ironic comment upon the ideal and realistic images of democracy."

This plot invited trouble. Ralph knew next to nothing about the military, or about prison camps. As he had seen Wright do with *Native Son,* he carefully gathered newspaper accounts about repatriated American prisoners that seemed relevant ("Interned Fliers Got Set to Battle Nazis—Rescue Gamble Told"). While he made notes, he completed the first of four book reviews for *Tomorrow,* which appeared in the fall and winter. Three were of novels by white writers; the last was of *Modern Negro Art* by the Howard University art professor James A. Porter. All suggest a new level of confidence on Ralph's part. His former reflex of shaking down each book for its radical political meaning is almost entirely gone. For example, he flays Porter for allowing racial romanticism to shape his thinking, and offers a tough assessment of both Porter's volume and African-American art in general.

Other, more highbrow magazines noted Ralph's rise as a critic. Near the end of September, Paul Bixler of the monthly *Antioch Review* asked him to assess perhaps the most highly acclaimed study of race relations published to that point in America, Gunnar Myrdal's *An American Dilemma: The Negro Problem and Modern Democracy.* Produced by the Swedish sociologist for the Carnegie Corporation, the study had been hailed as the mightiest blow against segregation since the end of the Civil War. Brought to America in 1937, Myrdal had assembled a team of experts, including African-American scholars such as Ralph Bunche. He had then shaped the sections into a narrative hailed for its unprecedented rigor and brilliance. If Bixler expected Ralph to join the chorus merrily, he was disappointed. Ralph had some compliments for Myrdal, but assailed the condescension of sociologists, especially whites, concerning blacks and race. Myrdal's study was no product of pure science; his vision of black culture was pathological. Although many elements of Negro culture might be negative, Ralph emphasized, it also possessed much that was rich and valuable.

In submitting his review, Ralph called it "a mess of loose ends and shallow thinking." Agreeing, Bixler rejected it. Ralph knew that he had barely touched the text, but instead had taken too broad and unsupported (though not insupportable) a view of its subject. "This rather brash review," as he called it, remained unpublished for twenty years, until it appeared in his collection *Shadow and Act.* Nevertheless, the essay was another step forward for Ralph. It marked for him "a break with sociology as a guide to understanding my own life and background of experience."

On September 26, 1944, about three months after meeting Ralph, Fanny moved in with him at 306 West 141st Street. If her employer, the National Urban League, found out that she was living with a man not her husband, it might fire her. "What a kick in the teeth it would give to our economics," Ralph explained about his secrecy concerning his telephone number. They wanted to marry. Two or three days after moving in, she left for Chicago to set her divorce in motion.

Fanny's absence threw Ralph into a bizarre panic. The evening she was due in Chicago he sent her an imperious yet pathetic telegram: "YOUR SILENCE PREVENTING WORK. WIRE ME EVEN IF MIND CHANGED." A few minutes later Fanny, who had barely set down her bags, replied: "NOTHING HAS CHANGED I AM THE SAME AND LOVE YOU." In what was probably his first letter to her, Ralph poured out his anguish or hysteria. "Like a lovesick fool I've been unable to sleep since you've been gone," he wrote. "Food is uninteresting to the point of nausea. . . . Darling, I *resent* the way I feel. I don't want to be this way. It is a dependence I've never known before, and it's not at all pleasant. Even my imagination, which has been my friend always when I've been unhappy, now has turned against me. Instead of consolation it gives me fears. . . . I feel murderous and suicidal, the latter which I haven't known for years. . . . I started to fly out to Chicago this afternoon, but that would have been foolishly impulsive, and my health is not too good." Then Ralph struck an odd, more manipulative note: "There is enough suspense and tension in my life without your becoming the main center of it."

With the news of his Reynal & Hitchcock contract, Ralph was increasingly in demand professionally as well as socially. On October 24, he was one of two main speakers at a gathering sponsored by the National Urban League at the prestigious East and West Association in Manhattan. Here Ralph met the Nobel Prize–winner Pearl Buck. In his lecture Ralph explored the depiction of blacks in recent novels by white Southerners, with an emphasis on Lillian Smith (*Strange Fruit*), Bucklin Moon, and Lonnie Coleman. These novels seemed to him to portend a new maturity in American writing on race. This lecture led to an invitation in November to speak twice on black writers in a class at New York University.

The appearance that month in *Tomorrow* magazine of his latest short story, "King of the Bingo Game," would be his last to appear before a section of *Invisible Man* came out three years later, in October 1947. It marked a major turning point in his fiction. Eventually Ralph would reveal that "it was while writing the short story that he found the 'touch' he was searching for: 'It had the realism that goes beyond and becomes surrealism.' " A black man, living up north but still a country boy, goes to the movies for the bingo game that follows. He needs money for his sick wife. When his numbers come up, his win entitles him to press a button at the end of a long black cord that spins a wheel. If the wheel stops on the right number—double zero—he wins the night's jackpot, $36.90. Overcome by the moment, the man seeks to control his fate by keeping the button depressed. Pandemonium breaks out in the crowded hall. Two uniformed men come for him. In the struggle that ensues, he loses control of the button—then sees the wheel settle serenely at double zero. The prize is his, he thinks. One man seems to assure him of that fact. But another, behind him, smashes down on his head viciously. "He only felt the dull pain exploding in his skull, and he knew even as it slipped out of him that his luck had run out on the stage." (As Ralph made clear elsewhere, the man is shitting as he falls.)

"King of the Bingo Game" brought nothing utterly new to African-American fiction. (In the 1920s, a decade of black writing largely dismissed by Ralph and Wright, Jean Toomer had explored the surreal and absurd in urban black life to more brilliant effect.) Nevertheless, the story marked an advance for Ralph as an artist. If the task of integrating his ideas about what ideally should animate his fiction—black folklore, political protest, humor, interior monologue, the use of myths and symbols—still remained a challenge for him, "King of the Bingo Game" was also the least mechanical of his stories to date. Dwelling on the chronically absurd, sometimes lunatic, features of black urban life (something that had struck him from his first day in Harlem), Ralph allowed this fantastic element its freedom. The result was a fiction about mental derangement shaped largely by comic constructions that helped along Ralph's determination to use symbols. It also embraced, in its exploration of delusions of power, crucial mythological references (to Midas, Tantalus, Sisyphus, Jesus, King of the Jews, and other timeless "heroes" caught in dilemmas of desire and frustration). From this fusion Ralph hoped would emerge historical and universal resonance. The story is certainly complex. The king is up against white and black people—in the theater, both revile him. Ralph had moved beyond blunt radical propaganda to explore and depict the psychological results of social injustice.

The year 1944 closed nicely. Maxwell Geismar, a respected critic, interviewed Ralph on WHN in New York. *Tricolor: A New American Newsfront* sought him out to commission an article on Harlem and the war. In the mainstream *Chicago Sun Book Week,* Langston Hughes surveyed black American writing and concluded: "The most promising of the younger Negro writers of prose is Ralph Ellison of Oklahoma. His recent stories in *Common Ground* and *Tomorrow* capture nuances and flavors of Negro life that had hitherto not been put down on paper." When Hughes repeated his praise in his weekly column in the *Chicago Defender,* the message reached even deeper into the black world—helped additionally by a reprint of "In a Strange Country" in *Negro Digest.* Through ambition, hard work, and shrewdness, Ralph was still on the rise.

Genuinely ill at times, and other times not so ill, by October 1944 he was declared fit for sea duty. He didn't want to return to sea. On the day of his pre-induction physical in January 1945 he went to Brooklyn to seek advice from Wright. According to Wright's journal, Ralph arrived a badly frightened man. Wright suggested that Ralph consult a psychiatrist friend, Dr. Frederic Wertham, who offered to see Ralph on condition that Ralph first cancel the appointment he had made with another psychiatrist. Although Ralph said he would do so, Wright went to bed "wondering if Ralph would keep his word; for the first time in my seven years association with him I detected a willingness to gyp, to doublecross." Wright's entry points to the corrosion of trust between the men. Describing Ralph as "scared" is in keeping with Wright's dogmatic belief around 1945 (as he delved into psychiatry) that the dominant emotion of black Americans was fear. "To think that even Ralph had been touched that deeply," Wright marveled. Then, echoing a white psychiatrist (not Wertham) who once enraged Ralph by suggesting that he, as a Negro, was thinking too much, Wright added, "Perhaps it is well that Negroes try to be as unintellectual as possible." He was not far off in noting the mixture of fear, confusion, anger, and despair in Ralph's agonizing over military service. "What a horrible life," Ralph grumbled to Fanny as he tried to justify his artful dodging. "I believe I would have more self-respect these days if I were in jail, but even that is a pitiful choice. I am more than ever convinced that as a people our horizon is narrow less because we are intellectually inferior, than because we need to protect ourselves from the chaos and indignities of our condition. And people like us are caught in the trap; somehow we opened our eyes for a second and the horror has kept them wide to ever more terrible and pitiful horrors."

Just after the middle of February 1945, assigned to the *Sea Nymph* but kept ignorant of its destination, Ralph shipped out into the Atlantic. Bristling with guns and traveling in a convoy under heavy escort, the *Sea Nymph* crossed the Atlantic in fine weather but in a state of highest alert. Although the threat from submarines had dwindled, the ship's hold and decks groaned with crates of ammunition and other explosives needed by Allied forces following the Battle of the Bulge. Launched by Hitler on December 16, the surprise attack had been repulsed by the Allies only after massive losses on both sides. Now the Allies were headed for a climactic struggle with the Nazis on German soil.

For the first two days Ralph's stomach tormented him; then he slipped into the regimen of a cook. The daily routine on the *Sea Nymph* turned out to be typical of merchant marine life—"work and petty quarrels under the tension and of course petty politics and racial strife." He found himself brooding on the magnificent monotony of the sea, on the ship as "the symbol and the fact of man's consciousness, intellect and courage." The patterns traced on the immense ocean canvas by the convoy, each ship in its assigned lane, fascinated him. Time seemed suspended, as he wrote to Fanny—"the same sun rising from the same green sea, the same sea birds flighting through the sun into and through a foamy wave tip, like a small white and silver butterfly. And out toward the far reaches of the convoy, the same destroyers, small dogs of war, armed to the teeth, that appear like bell buoys gently rocking on the horizon." One looked to him like "a whale, a Moby Dick . . . its white sides flashing in the sunlight." Ralph drafted these lyrical letters to Fanny, sometimes in multiple versions on a typewriter, as if writing for posterity. As for his reading, he had with him a book of Greek tragedies, and was also making his way through Joyce's *Stephen Hero*.

On March 4, after sailing up the Seine, the *Sea Nymph* docked in Rouen, renowned for its medieval cathedral and as the place where Joan of Arc was burned to death in 1431. Ralph was pleased to find himself in France—"the country where I've always desired to go." On a swift ride by jeep through the city, he saw near the bomb-shattered walls of the cathedral the burned-out hulks of German Tiger tanks and scout cars, wrecked artillery guns, and piles of unused ammunition. American soldiers with rifles and submachine guns marched lines of Germans prisoners to and from their pens. "And you see many of our Negro boys all over the place—but mostly doing the heavy, dirty, unrecognized work," he reported home. As for the French, he said, "I like the people." France affected him in ways England had not. (Except for regretting the dead and wounded in London, he asked later that year, "what are the symbols and monuments of Britain to me that I should feel a sense of loss?") France was different. "Even the negative symbols," he wrote, "contain enough of their lost vitality to make one regret he failed to get there sooner." Thrilled by "the fields of Normandy such as Van Gogh painted," he loved, too, "the beautiful, well tilled hills where Flaubert saw the rains and mists come down when he wrote Madame Bovary."

As during his visit to Wales, Ralph was struck again by "the stupidity and chauvinism of white Americans" in dealing with foreigners even on the foreigners' soil. "They are about just as contemptible toward these people as toward the English or Welsh. And the extent of their psychological disintegration as revealed in their sexual preoccupations is amazing. I don't mean the usual obsessions of men kept away from women for long periods of time, but of the specific forms of aggression as revealed in their sex attitudes." These attitudes would affect postwar America. "Look for very chronic post-war conditions at home when these return; political unrest, new forms of gangsterism, etc. It is exhausting to even think about it."

Trouble with his kidneys kept him from sleeping. At the army hospital a doctor gave him a sulfa drug and recommended that he undergo "a minor operation, though I must admit in a very major spot," when he returned home. He would bring home the hospital statement "so the skeptic there won't think I'm faking." The statement attested to a mucoid urethral discharge, for which he was treated with sulfathiazole, the drug of choice for such infections before penicillin.

Put ashore in Boston, Ralph returned home to a passionate welcome from Fanny, who was now divorced and so ecstatic about it that "when I came home I took an enema and threw out old clothes." Ralph had pledged himself to her. "I love you enough to do something very wonderful or very foolish," he wrote in one draft, and then, "I love you enough to spend my life with you." He was happy to be home again with Fanny and with Bobbins, a purebred Scottish terrier puppy he had bought at a Long Island kennel just before leaving. They adored their dog. "Bobbins told me to tell you that she grows more beautiful everyday," Fanny cooed in one letter, with Ralph responding in kind.

He also reunited with Ida Guggenheimer, one of the few persons to whom he had written while abroad. Ralph did not rush to let his editor, Frank Taylor, know he was back. Having done very little work on his novel, he was talking now about writing a book of essays on black American culture. Thanks to Fanny, his mass of drafts and records was in excellent order. (His multiple drafts of even brief essays surprised her: "Truly you bear out the theory that genius is 90% work and 10% talent.") Reading his mail, he learned that the Guggenheim Foundation had denied him a fellowship; two more publishers had belatedly inquired about his interest in writing a novel. Also, Paul Bixler at *Antioch Review,* which had rejected his essay on *An American Dilemma* as well as a piece on three recent novels of black life by white Southerners, now wanted a long review of the literary sensation of the moment, *Black Boy.*

Bixler's previous rejections did not faze Ralph. A thick file of articles about the book clipped by Fanny showed him how controversial *Black Boy* had become. W. E. B. Du Bois, writing in the *New York Herald Tribune,* but moving closer than ever to Communism, questioned Wright's honesty in writing such a stark history of injustices wrought on him. Other blacks wondered even more about the bleak portrait of black culture sketched by Wright. A two-paragraph aside early in the second chapter was like a satanic catalogue of his people's sins.

On April 12, Wright telephoned Ralph with the news that President Roosevelt was dead. The same day, Rose's attorney served him with divorce papers. Amicably, Ralph paid most of Rose's attorney fees. Later that month, she sent him a postcard from Los Angeles signed simply, "Love, Rose." The draft board extended Ralph's shore leave—past the end of the war, as it turned out. He also learned that the Julius Rosenwald Fund had awarded him a fellowship in creative writing. The terms were better than Ralph's book contract: $1,800 to be paid over twelve months. Now Ralph was set for a major effort on his novel—but which novel was he working on? In a letter to the fund in July, begging for an early start to payments, he mentioned that "I have been at work on my project since last May." In May he should have been at work on his Reynal & Hitchcock novel. Had he abandoned that one, then started work in May on his Nazi prison camp novel, the basis of his fellowship applications? Or was Ralph working on a new idea altogether?

On May 14, when Ralph mailed his review of *Black Boy,* he told Paul Bixler that the essay was longer and "much different from what I had anticipated." In some respects, "Richard Wright's Blues" (published later that year) is a pretentious piece of writing. The essay is studded with showy references to an array of literary luminaries, including Aeschylus, Dostoyevsky, Joyce, George Moore, Valéry, Hemingway, Yeats, Malraux, and William Empson. Nevertheless, it is a brave, brainy attempt by Ralph to explore *Black Boy* by defending Wright, expanding on his definition of Southern black culture, and moving toward psychoanalyzing the "typical" Negro. Ralph's identification of the blues as the form central both to black culture and to Wright's autobiography counterbalances his pedantic allusions. For Ralph, the blues expresses the essential modern African-American temper. "The blues is an impulse," he explains memorably, "to keep the painful details and episodes of a brutal experience alive in one's aching consciousness, to finger its jagged grain, and to transcend it, not by the consolation of philosophy but by squeezing from it a near-tragic, near-comic lyricism. As a form, the blues is an autobiographical chronicle of personal catastrophe expressed lyrically." In embodying the blues, Wright had been able to endure and resist oppression, escape the trap of ideology and Communism although lured by it, and finally mature as an artist and a man.

Far more so than *Black Boy* itself, this essay asserts the humanity of blacks. For Ralph, white American intellectuals had so excluded blacks from consideration that many people "forget that human life possesses an innate dignity and mankind an innate sense of nobility; that all men possess the tendency to dream and the compulsion to make their dreams reality; that the need to be ever dissatisfied and the urge ever to seek satisfaction is implicit in the human organism; and that all men are the victims and the beneficiaries of the goading, tormenting, commanding and informing activity of that imperious process known as the Mind—the Mind, as Valery describes it, 'armed with its inexhaustible questions.'" The myth that Negroes are inherently at one with nature serves mainly to exempt whites from guilt about their oppressive ways. So, too, the common white "misjudgment" of black passion leads to an idealization of the black as "a symbol of sensation, of unhampered social and sexual freedom." Like Wright, Ralph denounced any evaluation of black culture that sees it as being in any way ideal. The Negro in America is "a Western type" (not some exotic being) "whose social condition creates a state which is almost the reverse of the cataleptic trance." Instead of being mentally hyperactive but physically inert, the Negro is all body in response to the cruel world around him. Even his apparent hypersexuality comes from this frustration of "the transforming, concept-creating activity of the brain." He is like a man who resorts to "violent gesturing" in his effort to express "a complicated concept with a limited vocabulary; thwarted ideational energy is converted into unsatisfactory pantomime, and his words are burdened with meanings they cannot convey."

Ralph's reverence for the blues was not entirely new in African-American literary culture. In the work of Hughes and Hurston, the power of the blues is felt everywhere. The difference is that they seldom undertook, as Ralph did, to locate the meaning of the blues in the context of Western (white) learned culture. He offered the blues as a kind of quasi-philosophical entity akin to existentialism, which was then emerging as an intellectual force in liberated France. Perhaps he went too far. Certainly Wright himself (who even wrote a few blues pieces) believed that Ralph "overrated" the blues in his review. And Kenneth Burke, whose writings inspired many of the insights of the essay, would be skeptical about Ralph's conclusions concerning Wright. How could one become more universal, Burke wondered, by becoming more insular? Ralph should lay off race: "If he never yields more than half to his temptation to be an intellectual Garveyite, he'll go on getting better and better. And he's damned good already."

"Richard Wright's Blues," like *Black Boy* itself, aims to rebuke Marxist orthodoxy about a heroic, idealistic black America. Wright's major point about the deficiencies of black culture, Ralph pointed out caustically, "should be obvious (especially to his Marxist critics)." To him, the Communists had now lost their way completely. The major change for Ralph, one directed by Earl Browder (who had deployed the Popular Front in the 1930s), was the sudden ending of the struggle for black civil rights. On international affairs, he also found Browder bewildering when Browder hailed the meeting of Roosevelt, Stalin, and Churchill in Tehran as the emergence of a new world order, anti-Fascist but also inclusive of an enlightened capitalism. (In 1944, the Party dissolved itself. In the spring of 1945, soon after Ralph's return from Europe, the French Communist leader Jacques Duclos released a letter attacking Browder's vision of the Tehran conference. Browder was dismissed and the Party restored.)

For Ida Guggenheimer it was a trying time. "I am so ashamed of them," she wrote to Ralph, "yes and humiliated." For Ralph, this was sweet vindication. "We have become the fathers of our elders," he wrote to Wright about Ida and other confused figures. "The unquestionable authority of the left-wing politicians is tottering like a punch drunk prize fighter; now people are looking for someone who can answer questions and they are looking in our direction. Your prestige should rise by leaps and bounds now. And the wonderful thing is, I feel, that this will be because you dared to be simply what you are, an artist." At Ida's behest, he visited the American Labor Party headquarters to discuss the state of black workers. There he learned things that only reinforced his contempt for black political leaders such as Ben Davis and Adam Clayton Powell, Jr. Elected to Congress, Powell was already compiling a sorry record of absenteeism and other abuses. Ralph was incensed: "All in all, it seems that the coalitions are breaking up and the white folks find themselves with a couple of black frankensteins—or black elephants—on their hands. They aren't sure if they have leaders with followers behind them, or simply inflated symbols incapable of functioning in the real world. So now they come to folks like us asking if these obscene monsters they have created are real or imaginary."

Who exactly were "folks like us" to Ralph? Attending a convention of black journalists in Manhattan with Fanny, he found their discussions pitiably shallow. He seemed to identify with blacks when he saw the future of America riding on the recognition of hard, cold realism—because only blacks seemed to possess such realism. He faced what he called "the greatest joke, the most absurd paradox, in American history: that simply by striving consciously to become Negroes we are becoming and are destined to become Americans, and the first truly mature Americans at that." But Ralph's true crusade was toward individualism, not group identity. He rejoiced in a terse encounter in July with Eugene Holmes, the Howard University professor whose work he had once gladly published in *The Negro Quarterly*. Had Ralph read a certain review of *Black Boy* by a well-known leftist? No, Ralph replied, he did not read such stuff anymore. "So you and Wright are together?" "No, Wright is by himself and I am by myself. We are individuals."

In the summer of 1945, Ralph found added inspiration in the intellectual life of postwar France—at least as he knew it through magazine articles about writers such as Jean-Paul Sartre, Simone de Beauvoir, and Albert Camus. "France is in ferment," he informed Wright. "Their discussions of the artist's responsibility surpass anything I've ever seen; out of France, the Soviet Union or anywhere else. They view the role of the individual in relation to society so sharply that the leftwing boys, with the possible exception of Malraux, seemed to have looked at it through the reverse end of a telescope." Sartre so impressed him that he copied a long passage from an essay (the gist of which he had already absorbed and rendered as his own wisdom earlier in his letter to Wright). Sartre had written: "By becoming a part of the uniqueness of our time, we finally merge with the eternal, and it is our task as writers to cast light on the eternal values which are involved in these social and political disputes." Resolving the tension between the eternal and the political is the central challenge facing the writer.

Such questions took on new meaning on August 6, when the United States dropped an atomic bomb on Hiroshima, destroying almost 90 percent of the buildings and killing over 100,000 persons. On August 9, a second bomb fell, on Nagasaki. The surrender of Japan followed. World War II was over. Harlem and New York City celebrated wildly, but for Ralph the bombs marked not so much victory as a deepening of the age's spiritual and intellectual malaise—and especially that of American culture.

On Tuesday, August 10, just as the *Antioch Review* published Ralph's *Black Boy* essay, he and Fanny left hot, sticky New York and headed north to the Bateses' farm in Vermont. Ralph had last visited in the late spring of 1943 but had almost ruined his chances of another invitation by exploding in anger after John or Amelie Bates had given out his telephone number without his permission. (Neurotically, he also wrote several scathing drafts of a letter to Stanley Hyman over the same issue.) Since then, he and John had patched up their differences. Bates had insisted that Ralph and Fanny spend as much of August as they wanted at the farm, where his wife and their three children lived while John remained in the city.

Once again, in contrast to seedy, noisy Harlem, the serene beauty of the Vermont farm in summertime moved him. The bright green fields, woods, and mountains, the soothing sounds of brooks, calmed his frayed nerves. The first two days he and Fanny slept long and late. Finding food and beverages in short supply, he sent Ida Guggenheimer a check and an urgent request for a shipment of sharp American cheese and four pounds of Maxwell House coffee. In 1943, he had been acutely lonely and uncertain of his prospects on the farm. Now Ralph had Fanny with him on a sort of honeymoon—their first vacation together, even if they were not yet married. He had a yearlong fellowship to support him, as well as a sense of standing on the brink of the literary success to which he had aspired since starting to write seriously in 1937. Fanny's presence was crucial, because Ralph was a man in love. They shared magical moments together. Strolling hand in hand to the brook to wash, they came upon two white-tailed deer, which stared at them with plashy eyes before slipping silently into the woods. They loved the smell of hay in the barn where Ralph worked, the genial cows lumbering into the yard despite Bobbins's frantic yelping, the murmurous haunt of bees, grasshoppers, and doodlebugs. Food remained scarce, but they made do with lots of cucumbers, potatoes, and raw milk, and an occasional orange.

His makeshift writing studio was just inside the doorway of a barn, from which he looked across a field ripe with hay and goldenrod and fringed with sugar trees. Behind the trees, the land rose above four thousand feet as part of the Green Mountains that form the sturdy backbone of Vermont. "Beyond the mountains," he wrote Ida Guggenheimer in a kind of ecstasy, "the clouds form ever-changing in huge, cottony amorphous masses, set in a pure blue sky; and when the clouds shift in the wind they make dark shadows against the mountain and shade the farms that rest serene against its rolling, day-dreaming slopes." As in his 1943 visit, he read the landscape as moral history—with special implications for the Negro. Banning slavery in 1777, Vermont became the first state in the Union to give all men the right to vote. In 1850, it nullified the U.S. Fugitive Slave Law, and it sent almost 35,000 volunteers to the Civil War. In Ralph's mind, these actions epitomized the historic spirit of New England. This was the landscape of Emerson, Thoreau, Hawthorne, Melville—and of Mark Twain, who had transplanted himself to Connecticut from Missouri. (In his reverie, Ralph ignored the tragic fate of the Algonquin and Iroquois nations.) "It is truly no land for the near-sighted or the narrowly self-centered," Ralph judged now as he sought to enter this history psychologically and spiritually, "and the rise of the mountains reminds us of the depths to be inwardly plumbed in man to reach that inner balance from which springs the humanism so indispensable when man goes forth to wrestle Nature."

Oklahoma, Alabama, New York—none of these places resonated with what he wished to see now as the most profound source of American moral and intellectual power. This complex power, although neither infallible nor unstoppable, had been the main legacy of the Founding Fathers. Ralph's reading of national origins was distinctly patriarchal. "This country was hewn out of the wilderness," and then the axe-wielders, having triumphed over nature, had gone westward to help achieve the nation's destiny. Nature, as Ralph saw it, was feminine—not to be violated (as many axe-wielders had done) but to be seduced. "Everywhere one looks," he wrote to Ida about Vermont, "it is possible to imagine huge maternal women . . . reclining languidly, with their smooth mountainous breasts, nipples erect, to the hungry lips of the clouds." The ravagers had moved on, but nature and its challenges remained, to be faced by a new generation of men. Ralph Waldo Ellison would be a leader of these men, and thus would take his place alongside his namesake, Ralph Waldo Emerson, and other princes of the New England past. "We are not the same Americans now," he declared, "and much that was won by these men must be rewon by us in our time; only now the battle is much more difficult. It's not so hard to win and become aware of one's dignity when one's strength is pitted against a mountain. In the city it is to be won against an opponent as elusive as charged electrons."

Seeking out some of the local people, he was determined to see himself as strong but to see as weak the descendants of the "Golden Day," as the critic of industrialism Lewis Mumford (himself a biographer of Herman Melville) had designated the culture of Emerson and his contemporaries in his 1926 book of the same name, which Ralph had read along with Mumford's *The Condition of Man,* about the development of Western personality and the need for a renewed emphasis on religion and morality. Ralph looked for, and found, evidence of social decay around him. "I'm told that there is quite a lot of incest in these mountains," he informed Ida, "the sign of a region gone to seed, a frontier exhausted and abandoned." A farmer took him and Fanny to see a summer theater production of *Arsenic and Old Lace,* which they rather liked; but a dance afterward depressed him. The dancing and the music were dreadful—the latter "an anemic fox-trot that demanded a stethoscope to find its pulse." The square-dancing was even worse. Ralph had square-danced in his youth and seen excellent white square-dancers out west, but these folk were hopeless in expressing their sense of life—"for the most part they hopped about uncouthly." Not even winning a raffle for a handsome handmade quilt lifted his spirits.

This deep social decay in Vermont matched the social decay of America as a whole. Americans no longer understood their own culture, its historic purpose and achievement. Blacks, denied access to the most vibrant aspects of civilization, could contribute little to the rebirth of the nation without a dramatic development of fresh ideas in their own lives.

.   .   .

During this brief sojourn in Vermont, *Invisible Man* was born. "In the summer of 1945," Ralph would claim in 1954 and reaffirm in *Shadow and Act,* "on a farm in Vermont, where I was reading *The Hero* by Lord Raglan and speculating on the nature of Negro leadership in the United States, I wrote the first paragraph of *Invisible Man,* and was soon involved in the struggle of creating the novel."

Ralph indeed had read, or read in, Raglan's *The Hero*—"a cheeky, snobbish, and frequently irritating book," as Stanley Hyman called it even as he praised its brilliance. *The Hero* is a prized book for many admirers of the myth-and-symbol school, as Ralph had become. In it, as Hyman pointed out, Raglan tries to trace the origins of celebrated heroes, both secular and religious, emerging from different cultures at different times, to "one archetypal hero." Heroes from Moses to Robin Hood are never historical, as usually reported, but are "always derived through a myth from a ritual drama."

Perhaps Ralph wrote the first paragraph of what became *Invisible Man* during this Vermont holiday; perhaps not. In the years 1944 and 1945 he seems to have been involved in writing three novels. One was his Nazi prison camp project (of which fewer than a dozen pages survive). The second, set in a Southern college, has as its principal character a black man named Bard. Then there was a third novel about an invisible man, started at least by the previous winter. On March 14, 1945, writing to Ralph in Europe about the huge impact of Wright's *Black Boy* on incredulous blacks, Fanny had asked with glee, "What will they think when the invisible one drops on them?" But the start of *Invisible Man* as we know the novel likely came in or around July 1945, when Ralph wrote to Ida that he was trying to get "down upon paper the most ambitious and conceptually mature fiction idea that I have ever attempted. I work on it during the morning, reading and making notes, feeding my imagination." If *Invisible Man* indeed started in 1944, then the Bard novel is probably the interim novel to which Ralph alludes in *Shadow and Act*—although in the thirtieth-anniversary edition of *Invisible Man* and elsewhere, he would identify the aborted Nazi prison camp novel as the interim novel. Perhaps Ralph then returned to his invisible man in August 1945. Most likely, that moment was when the sentence "I am an invisible man" sprang into his head, bringing with it certain basic guides to the new form, tone, and texture of the story. As for placing the start of *Invisible Man* precisely at that time and in that place, Ralph was hardly the first artist, or creator, to develop a myth of origin peculiarly suited to his most intimate sense of himself, his goals, and his achievement. Whether or not it was so, he relished the idea of *Invisible Man* being born in New England and in the atomic summer of 1945.

Ralph faced candidly the evidence that he was not a "natural" novelist. As he admitted to Wright, who read "Richard Wright's Blues" and wondered whether Ralph's métier was nonfiction prose, not fiction, "I have considered the possibility that I might not be a novelist myself." However, more than anything else he wanted to be a novelist. Just as Wright had persisted through early rejections, he would keep going "even if the work in progress fails." He could now write dialogue and build a scene, but his goals were larger: "It's the form, the learning how to organize my material in order to take the maximum advantage of those psychological and emotional currents within myself and in the reader which endow prose with meaning. It's an uncertain battle on a dark terrain, but as you know, brother, the victory is the best, most satisfying thing a writer could achieve."

In Vermont that summer a shaft of light broke through the darkness. Starting several pages inside a small, fragile, undated notebook is a long entry in Ralph's handwriting—a narrative followed by notes—entitled "The invisible Man." With slight variations, it begins as *Invisible Man* begins: "I am an invisible man. No, I don't mean a spook nor one of these Hollywood movie ectoplasms. I am a man of substance[,] of mass bulk and liquids. I'm invisible simply because people refuse to see me. I'm not complaining. It's sometimes an advantage to be unseen." In significant other details, this embryo deviates from the plot and character of *Invisible Man*. The notes (as opposed to the narrative) also predict but sometimes differ from the letter and spirit of *Invisible Man*. The embryonic hero's brutishness, for example, is unlike the hero of *Invisible Man*, who is a less potent and a more mocking observer of women. However, the remaining notes anticipate some memorable elements in the published novel. An old black woman sings a spiritual. Invisible hears a slave on an auction block pleading with a "voice like his sister's," begging the buyer not to disrobe her. A preacher intones: "Brothers and sisters my text this morning is the blackness of blackness."

This last detail, lifted almost directly from *Moby-Dick* (when Ishmael stumbles into a black church as he looks for a place to spend his last night ashore), indicates that Melville was on Ralph's mind from the very start of *Invisible Man*. So, too, perhaps, was Ishmael's defense of the Big Book, as

Ralph began what would turn out to be a multi-year effort to write his own epic. "One often hears of writers," Ishmael confides, "that rise and swell with their subject, though it may seem but an ordinary one. . . . Such, and so magnifying, is the virtue of a large and liberal theme! We expand to its bulk. To produce a mighty book, you must choose a mighty theme."

Invisible Man is not Ralph's autobiography, but he clearly drew on distinct elements of his past even in this embryo. The most obvious link perhaps is the hero's involvement with, and later rejection of, the Communists. At this time, his main concern, apparently, was the extent to which his years among the Communists had impaired his creative powers, which were now in their ascendancy. "There was a time when—and recently too," he wrote to Wright, "I hung back because of my poor education and clumsy writing; but no more. I'm stubborn enough to overcome some of this, and I find that when I have the broadest range for my passion it improves my writing, although that is still sadly lacking. . . . The break with the c.p. has allowed me to come alive."

Others factors were also at work. His recent appearances in mainstream journals counted heavily. Money also counted—winning a book contract, then a fellowship; his divorce from Rose Poindexter; his blossoming love affair with Fanny McConnell; his stirring visit to Wales and France; the ending of World War II; the awe and horror of Hiroshima and Nagasaki; and the coincidence of finding himself, at this moment, deep in rural New England, where he saw around him the beauty of the American landscape and the ruins of its Golden Day culture. In August 1945 the world was new again—*he* was new again—and the time had come for a rebirth of American culture, which he, as an artist and an intellectual who had known poverty, despair, radicalism, and now a transcendent wisdom, would endeavor to shape. "I think our destiny," he ventured (echoing James Joyce on Ireland), "is to become the conscience of the United States." He had been just as certain that he and Fanny, the only blacks in the dancehall, were going to win the raffled quilt: "It was a minor symbolic moment for me, aware as I was of the cultural decay of what had once been the most vital part of America." Out of the ruins of the war, and the ruined greatness that was America, a "new humanism" was being born, "the need of which is stated most dramatically in the destructive-creative potential of atomic power."

As for the form of *Invisible Man,* the two most decisive elements were, first, Ralph's decision to entrust his story to the first-person narrative; and second, to suffuse it in surrealism. Although Henry James had warned about its limitations, the first-person narrator had served American literature well. In America, identity is less a fixed entity than a license to improvise. The first-person narrator had shone not only in epochal novels such as *Moby-Dick, Adventures of Huckleberry Finn, The Great Gatsby,* and *The Sun Also Rises,* but also in the poetry of the most original of American poets, Walt Whitman. The landmark essayists of the Golden Day, Emerson and Thoreau (whose "intuition" to reject New England society "was correct," according to Ralph), also believed in the first-person voice and subject; their best work amounted to a meditation on the self in the face of a desperate society and the exhilarating divine. Black writing, too (as Ralph knew), had been founded on the first-person accounts of the slave narratives, another product of the Golden Day and white abolitionism. If any one work inspired Ralph's decision in this respect it was probably *Moby-Dick.* "I am an invisible man," the story begins, as "Call me Ishmael" begins Melville's novel.

Surrealism, already rehearsed by Ralph in "King of the Bingo Game," would be subtly modulated throughout *Invisible Man* and as crucial as any other aspect of form to its success. Full-blown surrealism would flitter only occasionally, mainly in the prologue, but a measure of surrealism suffuses all of *Invisible Man.* Absolutes, even those of time and place, are constantly in flux, agitated by the consciousness of the novel's naive, increasingly neurotic, and to some extent unhinged if not deranged narrator. Where did Ralph find the confidence in 1945 to invest so heavily in the surreal? Part of it came from his attraction to certain European writers. "Fanny is reading Kafka," he wrote on August 21. Another part, however, came from his absorption in jazz and the blues. Jazz (and especially the bebop jazz that exploded in New York during the war) was inspirational because of its devious challenges to the conventions that had come to dominate popular music; blues also mattered in its equally determined refusal of an orderly separation of the comic and the tragic, laughter and tears. Both forms combine to orchestrate the sometimes surreal nature of much of what makes up modern African-American urban consciousness. The figure of Louis Armstrong, singing an unnamed song in the embryo text, then singing Fats Waller and Andy Razaf's "(What Did I Do to Be So) Black and Blue" in *Invisible Man,* embodies both jazz and the blues. "Perhaps I like Louis Armstrong because he's made poetry out of being invisible," the narrator of the novel tells us. "I think it must be because he's unaware that he is invisible."

"This section of the novel is going very well," Ralph wrote to Stanley Hyman from Vermont, "—though God only knows what the hell it's all about. Of one thing I'm sure, any close symbolic analysis of it will reveal how completely crazy I am. Anyway, it's fun."

8

The Agon of Writing

1945–1948

*I'm sure I have one thing straight: PURPOSE, PAS-
SION, PERCEPTION.*   RALPH ELLISON (1947)

Anxious to avoid the ebb tide of summer vacationers flowing back to
New York City after Labor Day, Ralph and Fanny cut short their stay
in Vermont. The ride south was pleasant, but once home they faced a
nasty problem. The Macedonian Baptist Church (their landlord) wanted
them out of their apartment at once, needing the space urgently. Ralph
and Fanny decided to resist. The last thing they needed, he complained
angrily, was to "enter the hell of finding a place to live" in a city desperately short on housing following the war.

Ralph was also disappointed to find a letter from William Shawn at *The
New Yorker* rejecting two stories (they would remain unpublished). On
the other hand, Ralph's essay on *Black Boy* in *Antioch Review* was creating a stir. The journal had sold out its reprints (Ida Guggenheimer had
additional copies printed). Its authority, its lyricism about the blues, its
daring application of psychology to race—all compelled attention. The
English Journal hailed it as "an eminently distinguished piece of literary
criticism." Ralph asserted that no one could grasp the full meaning of his
article in a single reading, although in the same breath he mocked himself
for saying so: "I don't expect Dick [Wright] himself to grasp it all without
study—even when I consider that most of it might simply be tommy rot
and speculation." Influential people were now appreciating the power of
Ralph's mind and his skill with a pen. *The New Republic* asked Ralph to
review some books—"Negro books, of course," he complained, even as he
quickly agreed to do so. Pascal Covici of the Viking Press inquired about
Ralph's "literary program."

His first review for *The New Republic,* "Beating That Boy," appeared in October. The "Negro" book was Bucklin Moon's *Primer for White Folks,* an anthology of short stories, essays, and other material on race written by black and white Americans. Perhaps Ralph should have recused himself from writing a review. He and Moon had the same agent and Moon had been one of Ralph's recommenders for the Rosenwald fellowship. Not surprisingly, perhaps, he lauded Moon's skill as an editor as he also underscored key ideas about race and writing, one of which, consistent with the genesis of *Invisible Man,* insisted on the psychologically distorted, even grotesque, nature of the racial problem—its sheer irrationality, its status as "a nightmarishly 'absurd' situation." Another idea (one of the pillars of Ralph's view of American history) was that from the Declaration of Independence in 1776 to the end of Reconstruction in 1876 "there was a conception of democracy current in this country that allowed the writer to identify himself with the Negro." As Ralph saw it, Whitman, Emerson, Thoreau, Hawthorne, Melville, and Mark Twain were in this heroic camp: "For slavery (it was not termed a 'Negro problem' then) was a vital issue in the American consciousness, symbolic of the condition of Man, and a valid aspect of the writer's reality." Only with the resurgence of the racist white South during Reconstruction was "the Negro issue pushed into the underground of the American conscience and ignored."

Most of Ralph's essay tries to illuminate this "underground of the American conscience," in which white guilt is assuaged by "the anesthesia of legend, myth, hypnotic ritual and narcotic modes of thinking," which had crippled "even our social sciences and serious literature." "Beating That Boy" resembles Ralph's rejected review of Gunnar Myrdal's *An American Dilemma* in its blending of astute insight with loose writing. The racial situation was like an X-ray machine concealed in a radio. While the listening white writer enjoys hearing black jazz or the jokes of a black comedian, "he is unaware of his exposure to a force that shrivels his vital sperm. Not that it has rendered him completely sterile, but that it has caused him to produce deformed progeny: literary offspring without hearts, without brains, viscera or vision, and some even without genitalia." Despite such weak writing, Ralph had ventured where few American intellectuals had ever gone in applying psychology. So it seemed to Thomas Sancton of *The New Republic,* who thought the second half of the essay "profound." It helped explain to Sancton why even as gifted a writer as Hemingway was finally so unsatisfying. Stanley Hyman, on the other hand, considered the piece "too superficial, too vague and unspecific, and entirely too flattering to that amiable idiot Moon."

Aside from another review for *The New Republic,* Ralph saved his time and energy that fall for his novel. He took only one significant break, to deliver his first lecture to a college assembly. Arranged by Hyman as one of his first public acts at Bennington College, in Bennington, Vermont, it offered Ralph an opportunity to see New England in the fall and earn an honorarium of $25. Bennington was a young, pioneering, and expensive women's college designed to break down the walls between faculty and students and also between the curriculum and the world beyond it. That year, its faculty included such stars as Kenneth Burke, the poets Stanley Kunitz and Theodore Roethke, and the German émigré psychologist Erich Fromm, whose 1941 study *Escape from Freedom,* about the crisis of identity caused by industrialization, had impressed Ralph. In a note to his sponsors, he confessed that "the broader conceptional framework" of his lecture would draw on Burke and Fromm.

Early on November 1, 1945, Stanley Hyman met Ralph and Fanny at the North Bennington railroad station. They were soon reunited with Stanley's wife, Shirley Jackson (now pregnant with her second child), and their little son, Laurence, in their fourteen-room, book-filled home on a leafy street in North Bennington. That evening, Ralph nervously addressed a packed hall on "American Negro Writing—A Problem of Identity." As he would do for virtually the rest of his life, he spoke from notes only. To forestall his slight stammer he spoke slowly, dryly, in an accent free of almost all traces of Oklahoma. If his audience expected him to protest against racism, it was disappointed. The aim of the writer should be to contribute to a whole view of human nature and the finest national ideals. Tracing the history of black American writing, Ralph noted the steady decline in poise from the era before Jim Crow, when—according to him—Negro writers identified their lot with the nation's, to the crises and confusions of the present day: "Today, most Negro writing is devoted either to a violent rejection of American values or to a questioning of them." (He had no inkling of how violent the rejection would become later.) The challenge now was to protest while "setting forth the forms and values under which man must live." Led by Wright, "the Negro writers of today are beginning to examine reality, to try to bridge the vast psychological distance existing between the two races in this country."

The next day, in Hyman's class, Ralph led a discussion on *"Black Boy* and *Portrait of the Artist as a Young Man*—Two Studies in Cultural Alienation." Offering Joyce as both a guide and a caution, Ralph saw Wright and the Irish writer as linked in their mutual alienation from their native cultures and also in their desire to create something new and profound out of that alienation. For Ralph, as for many writers invested in transcending racism or colonialism, nothing so epitomized his burning sense of destiny as the words of Stephen Dedalus that close *A Portrait of the Artist as a Young Man:* "Welcome, O life! I go to encounter for the millionth time the reality of experience and to forge in the smithy of my soul the uncreated conscience of my race." Finding Ireland intolerable, Joyce had refused to cherish Gaelic over English, to endorse a blind Irish nationalism, or to abase himself before the Catholic Church. In his most radical act of alienation, he had, in a sense, created a new language in the almost impenetrable *Finnegans Wake.* Black Americans, Ralph argued, must be wary of such an extreme. "The Negro writers must know," he insisted, "that there is no escaping of language and of his national identity. His job is discovering just what his relationship is to the whole national aspect of America. If he attempts to escape language, he must escape politics and then he is abstract and therefore lost. He must find some way of speaking to Negroes in order to clarify the relationship of America with the Western civilization generally."

Later, the students would vote Ralph's visit among the top three events at Bennington that year. Much of the appeal of his visit was undoubtedly its liberal daring—a black speaker was highly unusual at any white American college. "Negro Writer Gives Lecture," the local *Evening Banner* marveled. The Associated Negro Press, a national news service, offered a report of the event. Despite the strain of being always on point before liberal whites, always responsive to their cooing and their compliments, Ralph and Fanny enjoyed their visit. He soon let it be known that they "fell completely in love with Bennington and would hurry back at the drop of a hat." Probably he was fishing for a chance to teach at Bennington. But in 1945 the appointment of a black professor at a white college, especially a man at a women's college, was virtually out of the question.

Back in Manhattan, he and Fanny had missed Doubleday, Doran's party for Chester Himes's first novel, *If He Hollers Let Him Go.* Ralph knew Himes, who had recently moved to New York from Los Angeles—to which he had fled from Ohio, where he had served seven years in the state penitentiary for armed robbery. They found him at times charming, at times enraging. (Later, the poet Michael S. Harper remembered that Fanny once told him about Himes "teasing and provoking Ralph by putting his head in her lap.") While in prison, he had begun writing. Soon after his arrival in New York, at a party given by Langston Hughes, he had met Wright. Himes, who had published fiction (mainly in *Negro Story* magazine), revered Wright's work, especially *Native Son*. Wright had accepted him as a gifted disciple. Eager to launch *If He Hollers Let Him Go*, Wright alerted readers to the existence of "a sea of prose so blindingly intense that it all but hurts your eyes to read it." To Ralph, Himes's story seemed crude and uneven, and its author as hungry and neurotic as its hero. Ralph was not happy to be lumped in reviews with Himes as fellow pupils of "the school perhaps founded by Richard Wright when he created Bigger Thomas in his 'Native Son.'" But he had to face the fact that yet another young black writer had published a novel while he still struggled at the task.

At about this time, Fanny's professional situation improved, bringing greater stability to Ralph's. In December, she began work as director of publicity for the New York City Housing Authority. The position gave her authority over whites, who openly resented her. Moving on, she found a job in April in which her color was deemed unimportant and her skills and efficiency recognized. She became private secretary to the executive director of the International Rescue Committee. Dedicated to the relief and resettlement of refugees since 1933 (Albert Einstein inspired its founding to help Germans fleeing Hitler), the IRC was resolutely anti-Communist in its politics. Fanny would serve there for several years as an executive secretary, office manager, and fund-raiser. This job became the rock of economic stability that sustained Ralph as he labored on his novel.

The other dramatic event early in December 1946 was their eviction and subsequent move to a smaller, two-room apartment at 749 St. Nicholas Avenue in Harlem. The change—and the humiliation—heightened what Ralph described to Maxwell Geismar as "the *agon* of writing what I like to think of as a novel." While he fussed and fumed over packing, unpacking, and storing his stuff, Ralph finished his second review for *The New Republic*. John Beecher's book *All Brave Sailors: The Story of the S.S. Booker T. Washington* is an account of life on the first U.S. Merchant Marine vessel to sail with a racially integrated crew led by a black captain, the West Indian–born Hugh Mulzac. This captaincy had caused a sensation in the black world. John Beecher, a white man and a Southerner, was descended from an American family celebrated for its abolitionists, notably Harriet Beecher Stowe and Henry Ward Beecher. In his review, Ralph's focus is not on the ship's captain or its racial integration but on John Beecher himself. Once again, he harped on the theme of America's lost moral,

intellectual, and artistic heritage. Beecher's father, "the heir of Abolitionists and theologians," had become a businessman in Alabama, where,
ironically, "his son was to absorb the mores and attitudes which it had
been his forefathers' most intense passion to destroy." By confronting his
role in the drama of American history, John Beecher had "rediscovered
the fighting tradition of his fathers." America must do the same.

Unlike his first review in *The New Republic*, this one went generally
unnoticed—except by Ralph's agent and his publisher. Early in March,
Henry Volkening pressed Ralph somewhat archly. Reynal & Hitchcock
("the nice patient guys") had not been in touch about the book but "would
you like to take me into your confidence?" In truth, Ralph had been avoiding his agent and his publisher because his Nazi prison camp novel was
now dead. Although he dreaded breaking this news to Reynal & Hitchcock, he came clean with his agent. He sent Volkening manuscript pages
from the new novel, along with an apology. "I have great misgivings over
having to present these fragments for your inspection," he wrote, "and my
only reason is to let you know that despite all instability I have been at
work on an idea." These "fragments" established the fact that the "invisible" man was now his main character.

Uncertain as to the body of the book, Ralph was clear about its spine.
"I myself know only this," he revealed. "The invisible man will move
upward through Negro life, coming into contact with its various forms
and personality types; will operate in the Negro middle class, in the left-
wing movement and descend again into the disorganized atmosphere of
the Harlem underworld. He will move upward in society through opportunism and submissiveness. Psychologically he is a traitor, to himself, to
his people and to democracy and his treachery lies in his submissiveness
and opportunism." Betraying even the women who love him, he is also
keenly aware of his weaknesses. "He is something very rare," Ralph
noted, "a true Negro individualist. . . . He is also to be a depiction of a certain type of Negro humanity that operates in the vacuum created by white
America in its failure to see Negroes as human. You might call him the
repressed American moral sense which causes so much confusion: he is
unseen and ignored, yet he is a human fact and he creates conflicts which
are always detected too late."

Ralph's difficulty in delivering the novel could not have been a shock to
his agent or his publisher, who were accustomed to such delays. And yet
neither one could know the extent to which Ralph was hamstrung in writing a novel under a tight contract, or the depth of his commitment now to

write a truly major work of fiction. Since the summer of 1945, when he had experienced his Joycean "epiphany" in Vermont, he had dedicated himself to creating a novel so rich in its symbolic, allegorical, psychological, social, and historical insight that it would be acclaimed as a masterpiece. He was committed now to writing the Great American Novel. In paying homage to Melville and *Moby-Dick* in the embryo of the manuscript, he had also already taken to heart Ishmael's justification for the oceanic vastness of his story. Having at last found his mighty theme, he must now write a mighty book.

Ralph's ambition, greater perhaps than that of all black writers of fiction before him (because few were as concerned with mastering experimental techniques as he was), could easily have led him into paralysis. Fortunately, he also knew his limitations. He knew how late he had come to writing fiction, how much he had to labor to create stories, and how weak had been his grasp of literary technique. He had been patient and diligent, with a degree of self-discipline grounded in his early training as a musician. In hindsight, Ralph would recall "playing a game with myself, the game of discovering whether I could write a novel." Play and patience, wit and diligence, combined both to make *Invisible Man* possible and to shape its meanings. "The play becomes a function," Ralph revealed, "of the patience required of one who writes with the barest shreds of techniques and with only the vaguest notion of where he is headed. It protects us from the terror of failure and from the awareness of the deadly seriousness of those forces which are the deep motives behind fiction."

Kenneth Burke's *A Grammar of Motives*, which Ralph read in galleys in 1945 courtesy of Burke himself, was vital to the creation of *Invisible Man*, as was the sprawling corpus of Burke's writings, including *Counter-Statement* (1931) and *The Philosophy of Literary Form* (1941). After hearing Burke read "The Rhetoric of Hitler's Battle" in New York in 1937 (as Ralph wrote to Burke), he "was moved to adopt you as my guide through the world of ideas." Ralph had chosen one of the most intimidating of literary guides. Compared to the essays on the art of fiction by Henry James, for example, Burke's writings are not simply more difficult to understand; on the whole, they appear much more related to criticizing fiction than creating it. Burke was not only a literary critic, as Stanley Hyman pointed out. He was also a semanticist, a social psychologist, and a philosopher. As a critic, his aim was a synthesis of disciplines and ideas, "the unification of every discipline and body of knowledge that could throw light on literature into one consistent critical frame." Although Burke's precise

influence on the manuscript of *Invisible Man* is impossible to track,
Ralph scribbled throughout his manuscript drafts, as a kind of inspirational mantra, the Burkean formula: "Purpose to Passion to Perception."
This phrase was itself a compression of Burke's notion of "the process
embodied in tragedy." Proposing "to consider poetry as a kind of *action*
rather than a kind of *knowledge*," he described its structure (act, scene,
agent, agency, purpose) as essential to understanding the human motives
and relations behind a rhetorical message.

With this "dramatistic" approach to poetry, as opposed to the "episte-
mological" approach, and with the idea of language as symbolic action—
speaking definitively against positivism, scientific absolutism, and ideological
orthodoxy—Burke helped Ralph make, around 1943, his seismic shift away
from a literature of socialist propaganda. Burke led Ralph toward the
embracing of a formalist literary logic, in which the science of Communism was supplanted by an emphasis on the complex meanings of every
aspect of the linguistic world constituted by and within a work of literary
art. Psychology became a pervasive instrument for understanding literature; symbols and mythic references constitute meanings that ideology
can barely begin to plumb. By defining the nature and scope of literature in this encyclopedic and heterogeneous way, Burke gave Ralph the
license to mark the entire realm of knowledge as his proper territory. "One
of the most important things I learned," Ralph later told "K.B. the liberator!" with gratitude, "was the possibility of creating depth and resonance
in my fiction by taking the gambler's chance of alluding to things I'd read
in the Bible, in literary classics, scientific works, folklore, or to anything
else that might be conveyed through the written word—And you made
me feel that this was possible even when it seemed unlikely that the
reader would suspect the presence of such allusions in the work of an
Afro-American writer." If "social integration" was extremely difficult, Ralph
could expedite it "through the manipulation of symbolic forms, and in a
process which vastly increased such social freedom as I [possessed]."

Ralph was on his way at last as a fiction writer. Now he was unwilling
even to think of taking a regular job (in the fall he had refused an offer to
serve as steward on a ship). In April, painting a gloomy picture of his
recent past and a roseate prospect for his novel-in-progress, he applied to
the Julius Rosenwald Fund for an extension of his fellowship. He was
"about two-thirds" done with the novel, "plus several scenes, sketches
and developments belonging to later sections of the narrative," which had

all been "accepted" by Reynal & Hitchcock. Believing that his theme needed "a more extended treatment than I had anticipated," he wanted six more months of support. He spread the word about his ordeal and its likely triumphant result. On April 27, a gossip columnist in the *New York Amsterdam News* reported that Ralph's first novel wouldn't be ready "for another 12 months." However, "it's a killer Mr. Miller."

Intensifying his efforts, that month Ralph packed his suitcase and his typewriter and took a train to the quaint but upper-crust village of Quogue, Long Island. There, in a shack rented for $11 a week from a black couple, he settled down to work for as long as he could afford to stay there. "Harlem is killing me, I know that now," he had complained in Vermont the previous summer. "There my emotions are pulled in a thousand directions before I can have coffee in the morning." Here, in Quogue, his only distraction was the lure of the sunny shore, the rolling blue ocean, and the moon and stars. Fanny visited on weekends, but Ralph avoided coming into New York except for special events. On May 1, they were at the dock to wave goodbye to Richard, Ellen, and Julia Wright, who sailed on the SS *Brazil* to France on a visit of several months as official guests of the government. It was no secret among friends that the Wrights were thinking of settling there. Fanny began to take French lessons, but immigrating to Europe was never a serious consideration for Ralph. Being black was a battle best fought on native ground.

On May 17, as the guest of Langston Hughes, he attended the annual joint ceremony of the American Academy and the National Institute of Arts and Letters. As Ralph watched, Hughes received a medal of merit and a grant of $1,000; Kenneth Burke also received a grant. In America, this was Parnassus itself. The institute comprised 250 elected members—all distinguished writers, musicians, or artists. The academy, or golden inner circle, consisted of fifty men and women chosen from the institute. That afternoon, the institute formally inducted Wallace Stevens, Lillian Hellman, and Charles Ives. Robinson Jeffers entered the academy.

Ralph returned to Manhattan again in mid-June to attend a party for friends of the Lafargue Psychiatric Clinic. Founded by Wright's German-born friend Dr. Frederic Wertham, and assisted by a few farsighted blacks and whites, including Earl Brown of *Life* magazine and Dorothy Norman—the gathering was at her home—a wealthy socialist who wrote a column in the *New York Post,* Lafargue was Harlem's first psychiatric clinic. It operated out of two rooms in the basement of St. Philip's Church with a volunteer staff of blacks and whites. Wertham charged a fee of 25 cents per visit to encourage "a feeling of responsibility for oneself" and a sense of dignity in the patients (for which he became known in Harlem as "Doctor Quarter"). Resisted by the city government and many blacks when first proposed, the clinic was a hit with the people. "Not only is it the sole mental clinic in the section," Ralph noted, "it is the only center in the city wherein both Negroes and whites may receive extended psychiatric care. Thus . . . it represents an underground extension of democracy."

Ralph's dedication to working on his novel was both tested and reinforced when he had to deal in Quogue and its environs with middle-class blacks who showed no interest in art, much less his writing. One weekend, at the vacation home of a black psychiatrist, Ralph decided that life for them consisted of "money, the table, the stool, and for those still young enough, the bed. Being among them is like discovering oneself in the midst of an obscene nightmare." When they fished, their aim was to load the boat with kill; as an angler, Ralph saw himself as a kind of Hemingway, trying "to pit skill and artifice against the instinct of the animal." He was no less critical of black artists whose work he disdained. In 1941, the playwright Ted Ward had seemed to be one of the leaders of an imminent black literary and cultural revolution. In May 1946 Ralph, running into him, found Ward clinging to the shibboleths of Communism, arrogant, and something of a lush. "He has aged visibly," Ralph reported to Wright, "and the membrane of his lower lip is now a bright red; as I watched him, little old man that he is, I wondered if it came from too much whiskey or, on the morbid side of my mind, if it was evidence of a suicide attempt." Ward was out. Wright and Ralph were in: "Our names continue to crop up in circles far outside the sway of the Left."

In June 1946, Ralph published "Stepchild Fantasy," a crisp review of Era Bell Thompson's autobiography, *American Daughter,* in the *Saturday Review of Literature,* a popular magazine with no leftist connection. As a responsible black intellectual, Ralph was impatient with privileged African-Americans who evaded what he saw as the darker truths of life. Thompson, a prominent black journalist and an executive at the *Chicago Defender,* had grown up mainly among whites in the Midwest. As a youngster, she had experienced neither poverty nor (so she claimed) overt racism. Only later was she hurt by the power of Jim Crow. In contrast to Wright's *Black Boy,* Thompson's book bubbled with optimism but was also superficial and emotionally flat. It was not "a serious contribution either to American biography or to the rising discussion over the damaging effect of our system of race relations upon Negro personality or our democratic health."

At the end of June, buoyed by the news that the Rosenwald Fund would give him another $500 (spread over five months), Ralph quit his shack near the ocean. He found Harlem noisy, obnoxious, and barely tolerable in the summer, when virtually all windows remained open to catch any hint of a breeze. Renting the cottage in Quogue had cut so deeply into his funds that a true vacation was out of the question. Ralph and Fanny's main excursion that summer was probably to Andover, New Jersey, to visit Kenneth Burke and his wife, Libby, at their regressive home in the country, where they lived without electricity and indoor plumbing. Burke surprised Ralph by handing him a letter he had written to him but decided not to mail. It addressed a question of central importance to Ralph: how to create a Negro hero who embodies the contradictions forced on blacks by white racism but remains appealing to white readers. Burke's solution was out of Dostoyevsky's *The Idiot*—like Prince Myshkin, the Negro hero would cling to his spiritual beliefs (through Negro spirituals). This approach intrigued Ralph, but he had already launched his "invisible" hero in the far more secular and atomistic direction influenced by *Notes from Underground*. Nevertheless, Ralph enjoyed the conversation with Burke and his other guests, the Oklahoma-born poet John Berryman and the Princeton University critic R. P. Blackmur and his wife, Helen.

Ralph and Fanny now took a decisive step. On August 28, 1946, they were married quietly, with only the bones of a ceremony. They broke the news by telephone to Ida Guggenheimer, who sent a check the next day. "You must know," she wrote, "that long ago I took you Ralph to my heart and now I am happy in the knowledge that you Fannie have also found a place there all on your own." Methodically they shared the news. "We promised you that we would let you know when we legalized our name," they wrote to Ellen Wright in late September. "So now you know. We finally got around to doing it. Can't say that it feels so differently but Bobbins says it is much nicer to be legal."

Early in the fall, attracted by the fee of $100, Ralph agreed to contribute an essay to a special issue of Paul Kellogg's *Survey Graphic* magazine devoted to racial segregation and its effects. The issue editor, Thomas Sancton (who had praised Ralph in *The New Republic*), was a white Southerner who admired William Faulkner and was a friend of Eudora Welty. He asked Ralph for a piece about such matters as the conflicted treatment of racism in Faulkner and the virtual exclusion of blacks in Welty's fiction.

Ralph plunged into this topic but also veered off in a new direction. His essay, "Imprisoned in Words," again set the problem of race and writing in a historical context. Ignoring Welty (whose finest book of fiction, *The Golden Apples,* appeared three years later), he concentrated on Mark Twain, Faulkner—and Hemingway. "How is it," Ralph asked, "that our naturalistic prose—one of the most vital bodies of twentieth century fiction . . . becomes suddenly dull when confronting the Negro?" In recent fiction written by whites, most Negroes were "counterfeit." It was not always so. In *Adventures of Huckleberry Finn,* Mark Twain solved Huck's moral crisis of conscience over Jim in the black man's favor. Central to this American classic is the "conception of the Negro as a symbol of Man," an idea that empowered the literature of Emerson, Thoreau, Whitman, and Melville. In contrast, Hemingway had liked Mark Twain for the "technical aspects" of *Huckleberry Finn* but was blind "to the moral values" of the story. This evasion of responsibility concerning race had gutted most American fiction: "It is not accidental that the disappearance of the human Negro from our fiction coincides with the disappearance of deep-probing doubt and a sense of evil." For the first time, Ralph acknowledged publicly a major failing in Hemingway. Turning to Faulkner, he was much less critical. His writing about race might be confused, but Faulkner purposefully "fights out the moral which was repressed after the nineteenth century." Although clearly aligned with the white South, he was always "actually seeking out the nature of man."

Sancton startled Ralph by deeming his essay unsuitable for the special issue, although it might appear, if revised, in a later issue. Ralph calmly accepted the decision. But a day or two after Christmas, when Sancton's suggested changes reached him, he became livid. Cutting Ralph's text, Sancton had then patched it with words Ralph had published elsewhere. Indignantly returning the magazine's check for $100 to Paul Kellogg (who had telephoned Ralph with news of the rejection), he refused to revise the essay. "For one thing, I can take no more time from my book to rewrite it; for another, after experiencing Sancton's editing, if I took the time the only such article of which I am capable would be one titled 'Paternalism at the Editorial Desk.'" (When he dispatched the essay to his agent to place elsewhere, Volkening found it somewhat muddled and advised Ralph to let it marinate awhile. Eventually, it would appear in 1953 as "Twentieth-Century Fiction and the Black Mask of Humanity," and later still in his 1964 collection *Shadow and Act.*)

Ralph continued to work hard on his novel. Orchestrating the developing lines of plot and subplot was more difficult than he had imagined. He needed time to think and revise. As the finish line seemed to recede into the distance, toward the end of winter a rumble from Reynal & Hitchcock reached Ralph in Harlem. Curtice Hitchcock's widow, Margaret Unwin Hitchcock, had taken over as leader after Hitchcock's death the previous year, but the transition was not going well. In March, Ralph's editor, Frank Taylor, went to Random House along with another gifted editor, Albert Erskine, who believed as strongly as Taylor did in Ralph and his novel. (Within a year or two, Taylor went to Los Angeles and Erskine became Ralph's editor.) Their departure left him vulnerable. The following month, when Hitchcock's widow wrote Ralph asking for a meeting to "hear something of your novel," Ralph stalled for time. He knew that Taylor was trying to convince the top Random House executives, including its president, Bennett Cerf, to buy out his contract.

Ralph was eager to move to Random House with his two supporters, not least of all because a new contract would give him more time to finish and perhaps an additional advance. With the Rosenwald extension exhausted now, he depended almost entirely on Fanny for money. To satisfy Cerf and other executives, Taylor needed a clear outline of the novel from start to finish. Seeking a quiet place to develop the outline, Ralph rode a train north to Bennington to visit Stanley Hyman and Shirley Jackson, discuss with Hyman the shape of his novel, and tie up its plot once and for all. With Stanley's help, he hammered out a coherent statement about the novel he was now calling "The Invisible Man."

The new outline was a success. As Cerf now moved aggressively to acquire "The Invisible Man," the residue of bitterness between Reynal & Hitchcock and its former employees was set aside. Later that year, after Random House repaid his advance of $1,500, Ralph's old contract was declared null and void. At first, Random House offered him $500 to provide the three additional chapters that would close the novel according to Ralph's new outline. His agent negotiated it up to $2,000. Ralph received a substantial part of this sum when he signed the agreement on July 17, 1947. The rest would be paid on November 30, when, everyone assumed, the manuscript would be ready to go to press. The end was so clearly in sight that Frank Taylor, without going through Ralph's agent, offered the first chapter to the English magazine *Horizon* for a special number on art in America. Its editor, Cyril Connolly, accepted the chapter at once.

Now an even sharper sense of urgency gripped Ralph as he hurried to make the November 30 deadline. The new money added to his sense of obligation. Then came the bittersweet day in July when Richard, Ellen, and Julia Wright sailed away on the SS *America* into voluntary exile in France. Ralph sympathized with Wright's unhappiness with life in America, where neither critical nor financial success had guaranteed a sense of belonging. He knew that Wright's marriage to a white woman brought them humiliations and insults almost without respite. Nevertheless, most of his friends had tried to persuade Wright that emigration was a mistake from which his career, and perhaps his personal life, would never recover. "I can only be useful here as a writer," he had replied, according to Anaïs Nin, "and here as a writer I am strangled by petty humiliations and daily insults. I am obsessed with only one theme. I need perspective. . . . I need to live free if I am to expand."

Ralph did not believe that emigration to Europe would bring a reliable "perspective," but he also knew better than to challenge Wright's sense of his own needs. All of his life Wright had made fools of people who underestimated him. In France, welcomed as a literary lion, he would have social freedom unimaginable in the United States. He counted Jean-Paul Sartre and Simone de Beauvoir as friends; Gertrude Stein would meet his train in Paris. Still, Ralph saw the Wrights off with regret. No one had been more important to his growth as an intellectual and a writer than Wright. No one had given him a clearer sense of the possibilities of the literary life for a black American. No one had been a more sympathetic companion as Ralph had matured into a man.

The summer reached its scorching midpoint before Ralph finally got away from New York. He now loathed Harlem. "Harlem is a ruin," he would write shortly for publication, "—many of its ordinary aspects (its crimes, its casual violence, its crumbling buildings with littered areaways, ill-smelling halls and vermin-invaded rooms) . . . quiver in the waking mind with hidden and threatening significance." Some of his neighbors were uncontrollably loud; their music reverberated at almost all hours, their visitors—and casual passersby—added to the cacophony. Not surprisingly, then, after an inconvenient visit to the tiny apartment by Fanny's mother and her husband from Chicago, Ralph snatched at a sudden invitation for him and Fanny to spend two weeks in August in the mountains of Vermont.

This time, they went as guests of Beatrice Stein and her husband, Francis Steegmuller, to Winhall in Bennington County in southern Vermont. Beatrice was an accomplished painter despite being severely handicapped physically. Steegmuller's writing career had blossomed in 1939 with the publication of *Flaubert and Madame Bovary: A Double Portrait*.

Devoted to French culture, he was finishing a biography of Guy de Maupassant. The cottage, which Bea and Francis had renovated, was on a large estate owned by Bea's brother, Edward Stein, and his wife, Gretchen, of Park Avenue in Manhattan. While Bea and Francis were away, Ralph and Fanny could stay there.

At Brattleboro, Vermont, when Ralph and Fanny, and their dogs—they now had two—left the train, Gretchen Stein was waiting to drive them thirty-five miles to the estate. Soon she seemed to Ralph "one of the kindest, most considerate people ever." Moreover, the Steegmullers' cottage, although only two rooms and a bath, was "much larger than our apartment and a million times quieter." The land was beautiful. The cottage rested on a sloping hill above the confluence of two streams. The contrast to raucous Harlem was striking, Ralph told Langston: "There are no cats—either colored or feline—to howl in the dubious ecstacies of fornication at midnight (is they ferking or is they fighting?); no sad voiced homeboys to stand outside the window at 4 a.m. and holler to someone above you: 'Hey Joe! Hey, Joe!' " As a result, "I've been getting more work done than in the city." When he was not at his typewriter, he and Fanny took strolls in the fragrant meadows and woods, or down to the streams with their gamboling dogs. They offered carrots and apples to the horses grazing in the nearby fields. The Steins, knowing why Ralph had come, allowed them their privacy.

Although the visit went well, Ralph's novel nevertheless was still unfinished when he and Fanny returned to New York after two weeks. Waiting in the pile of mail, too late for Ralph to make changes, were the galleys of the excerpt from his novel in *Horizon* magazine. Back in the cramped, seedy Harlem apartment, impatient at the distractions, he despaired of meeting the November 30 deadline. He then decided, with Fanny's support, to return alone to Vermont after Labor Day for one galvanic effort to complete the book. Both he and Fanny knew the sacrifice involved. Fanny would not be able to hop aboard a commuter train and visit on weekends, as she had when he was in Quogue. Most likely, this would be their longest time apart since their meeting in June 1944.

On September 15, nervous with a twin sense of adventure and anxiety, and with his dogs Bobbins and Red (another Scottish terrier), Ralph again took the train to Brattleboro. This time, he and the dogs caught the daily bus and headed toward the mountains around South Londonderry. A frightening thunderstorm made Ralph glad to leave the bus when it reached South Londonderry. At the little station, Arthur Amsden—he and his wife, Mabel, were employed by the Steins—was waiting to drive him to the cottage. Alone at last, Ralph savored the moment, his sense of climactic purpose. He also felt with more than a mere twinge the loneliness of the cottage without Fanny. That evening, subdued, he dined with the Amsdens and another couple, who had brought Ralph some ears of fresh corn. After dinner he walked home alone. The night was cold, the temperature hovering around forty degrees. The sky blazed with stars that Harlem couldn't see.

At five the next morning, the thunder of pounding hooves awakened him as a herd of horses, released from their warm stalls, ran by on their way to the dewy meadows. Sniffling with a slight cold, and somewhat disoriented, he waited for the sun to rise. When it was warm enough, he sat outdoors with the dogs and read. When he came in to begin work, he found it hard to get started. In the next few days he tried to ease into a schedule of writing, especially after some cash and supplies—including dog food, a carton of cigarettes, cold medicine, writing paper, and Bengay ointment—arrived from Fanny.

Ralph edged toward despondency, especially after Bobbins had a horrible run-in with a porcupine, then limped home with a leg and shoulder studded with quills that sank deeper into her flesh as she moved. At the Amsdens', Ralph had to muzzle her, kneel on her, and pull out the quills one by one with a pair of pliers. Blood spurted at each extraction— "and there she lay looking so reproachfully out of her eyes." Some barbs, too deeply embedded, had to be left to work themselves out of her flesh. "I felt like hell," Ralph wrote Fanny. "If I had had a car here I would have packed and come home last night. I felt bad about Bobbins, then sorry for myself; and when I went down to the garden and found many of the string beans and tomatoes frostbitten and going to waste, I actually felt like crying." His head cold kept his spirits down, as did the frosty weather. Morning was Ralph's crucial time to write, but he first had to get the fireplace going. Arthur Amsden had found him an oil stove, but its fumes had made Ralph so sick he had to give it up. He decided to shorten his stay—"I see no point in staying here if it doesn't increase my output."

Then, just as he was about to give up, an Indian summer set in, and he saw for the first time the famed shimmering russet, gold, and brown colors of New England in the fall sunshine. "Down in Bennington and Manchester," he wrote Ida, "it is so beautiful that it makes you wish to get out of the car and simply stare." Ralph took many photographs. He hunted a bit. Taking long walks, he occasionally stopped by the houses of locals he knew through the Steins and Steegmullers as well as artists from New York in their country retreats. But he feared the return of wintry weather. "I have known it, known it all," he mocked himself as J. Alfred Prufrock, "the mid-noon sunshine, the morning fogs, I've measured out my days in fireplace logs." And every day he missed Fanny—her help, her spirit, her body. "To paraphrase myself," he went on, "I love you, write me, I'm lonely; and envious of your old lovers, who for whatever pretext, have simply to walk up the street to see you."

"My dear, all my former lovers are dead," Fanny replied soothingly. "I don't even remember who they were." On October 3, she drove up for the weekend with the Steegmullers. Otherwise, they were apart for two months. Their separation pained Fanny so deeply that, early on, Ralph had to insist that she suppress her anguish and steel herself as he did. "It's lonely here, and cold, and the beds are hard," he told her; "but my reason for being here is neither warmth seeking nor comfort—except for my work—and since our mutual solitude is the sacrifice we make in the interest of a far more important thing, let's not either of us make a mockery of that sacrifice with our letters." Fanny nevertheless couldn't hide her pain: "It's as if my breath were abated while waiting to be with you." She was sprucing up the apartment for Ralph's return, as she told him in words that also hinted surely at chronic domestic tensions and explosions sparked mainly by his edgy temper: "Preparing for you is important—not carpet and flowers and grapes but a semblance of comfort to make 749 a little improved, to make for better tempers, better digestion and more leisure in the evenings to come."

Encouraged by Ralph to return to writing, Fanny started a story but found it hard going. "I'm very excited about your story," Ralph responded; "by all means let me see it. You mustn't assume that aesthetic expression is the prime motive for writing, it is really only a means to the more profound end." Patiently, he tried to show her how Faulkner achieved some of his effects in his story "Old Man." Meanwhile, he counted on her to preserve, in his absence, his special ties to Ida and her family. Polished and assured, Fanny interacted with whites about as confidently as any black American could. She knew when to flatter people, when to be frank, and when to be quiet; when to be warm and when, mainly with certain blacks, to be icy. Fanny and Ralph knew the importance of having wealthy white friends who admitted them as social equals and offered opportunities, such as Ralph's sojourn in Vermont, which they could not have afforded otherwise. More than once, Ida took Fanny to dinner at the elite St. Regis Hotel in mid-Manhattan, an event that thrilled Fanny as much as it must have startled the other diners, unaccustomed to seeing a brown face in the dining room. Nevertheless, she also saw some patronizing in this patronage. She once observed that "we now have the Steins, the Steegmullers, the Guggenheimers and the Binswangers taking care of our interests in every way they possibly can. Well, anything for the book." Dealing with Ida's frailties and eccentricities, her impulsive telephone calls, even her voluble praise, was sometimes trying. But she and Ralph had set out on a grand venture, and Fanny would do almost anything in her power to assure its success.

October brought a sparkling foretaste of that success. Ralph was still in Vermont when copies of the new issue of *Horizon* reached him from London. In it was "Invisible Man," the first chapter of his novel, and Ralph awaited its reception nervously. When Ida had read a copy of the galleys in late August, she was astonished by the definitive power of Ralph's story of race in America. When she received an inscribed copy of the magazine, her praise overflowed: "I glory in knowing you and being aware that here is a man who has enormous understanding and penetration and universal compassion. . . . You have written something stupendous and I am humbly proud to call you friend." To Ralph's relief and delight, other readers shared Ida's enthusiasm. Stanley Hyman reported quickly that the excerpt was causing a sensation at Bennington. At *Harper's Bazaar,* Pearl Kazin, an associate editor and Alfred Kazin's sister, assured Ralph that "Invisible Man" was "the most extraordinary and moving work I've read in a very long time." In the *Irish Times,* Donat O'Donnell called it "by far the most remarkable piece of writing in the collection"; if the whole novel was of the same quality, "it will be one of the most important pieces of fiction for years."

This was amazing praise indeed, because the *Horizon* number included work by W. H. Auden, Christopher Isherwood, Wallace Stevens, Marianne Moore, e. e. cummings, and John Berryman. In New York, at *'47: The Magazine of the Year,* John Hersey rushed to buy the excerpt. ("Hooray! Hooray!" Frank Taylor exulted at Random House.) Since '47 paid 10 cents a word and the excerpt ran to about 5,600 words, Ralph would make the most money he had ever received for a story. When '47 wanted some cuts, he gave in without a fight. Because the tattoo of the American flag above the white woman's crotch seemed excessive, Ralph removed it. Also cut was "the erection which projected from" the biggest of the black boys in response to her. (The tattoo and the erection would return in *Invisible Man*.)

Appearing as "Battle Royal" in the January issue of '48: *The Magazine of the Year* ('47 renamed), the excerpt was again a hit, but this time with a far bigger American readership than the British *Horizon*. In the magazine, "Battle Royal" appeared to overshadow an essay by Albert Einstein and poems by Stephen Spender. The editors were so happy with the "exceptionally fine" response to it that they begged Random House (in vain) for a second slice. "All in all," Ralph informed Wright the following February, "the reaction[s] to both publications of the piece were pleasing and I would be extremely gratified if only the dam[n] thing was finally out of my hands!"

"Battle Royal," or "Invisible Man," brilliantly incorporated the range of fictional techniques, and the ideas about ideal fiction, with which Ralph had wrestled over the previous few years. Founded on the genre of autobiography, with distinct overtones of the classic slave narrative and the rags-to-riches saga so dear to Americans, the chapter sits on the bedrock of literary realism. Many people assumed—incorrectly—that Ralph was telling his life story. Almost seamlessly, he builds on this foundation by introducing elements of myth and ritual that render the basic story more complex but in covert ways. The three major rituals are the "Battle Royal" episode in which young black men fight one another to amuse whites; "The Speech," delivered before the audience of drunken whites; and the parading of the naked blond woman before the black young men. Parodying the Virgin Mary, this American Venus is not a heroine of epic lore as, for example, in Virgil, but venereal and tawdry, sexually charged but forbidden to the black men, beautiful and yet grotesque and obscene, her eyes smeared blue like "the color of a baboon's butt."

Ralph's blending of comedy and violence, earnestness and profligacy, maintains its momentum from beginning to end. The narrator's intelligence is curtailed by his fumbling naïveté, yet is resilient in its possibilities. Although he is hardly erudite, he possesses a measure of wit and a flaring eloquence. The prominent rituals speak to both the African-American present, with its daunting predicaments, and its long, historic past. The grandfather's birth in slavery, his preservation of slave values, allows the text to resound with mythic power deep into the nineteenth century. His cruelty to Invisible reflects the dynamics of black life, old and new, as deformed by oppression; it also puns on the historic cruelty of the infamous Grandfather Clause, introduced by many Southern states to block blacks from gaining power through the ballot. Ralph was delighted when Kenneth Burke caught this sly if mordant allusion, as he caught several others that lesser minds missed: "Would that all of my readers were so skilled in Burking around!"

After years of labor he had achieved a piece of fiction startling in its suggestiveness. Certainly he had struck notes not heard before in African-American fiction. The psychiatrist Karl Menninger, who distributed the piece to a hundred young psychiatrists at his training hospital in Topeka, Kansas, was intrigued. Was the story based on facts? To which Ralph replied coolly that his story was "to be read as a near-allegory or an extended metaphor. Indeed, its 'truth' lies precisely in its 'allegory' rather than in its 'facts.' The facts in themselves are of no moment, are, for me, even amusing. And for all the detailed description of the prose, the aim is not naturalism but realism—a realism dilated to deal with the almost surreal state of our everyday American life." For example, the blond dancer "is at once a woman; a symbol of a debased 'white' democracy; an object of fascination comb[in]ing a threat of death with overtones of possible beauty; and, to make the list brief, the embodiment of a most potent sex taboo."

As eager as he was to finish the novel, Ralph also wanted as fine a book as possible. Certain object lessons were at hand. One was the fabulous success in 1946 of *The Foxes of Harrow,* a novel of the antebellum South by the young black writer Frank Yerby, who would sell tens of millions of similar romances of the Old South. Far outstripping even Richard Wright in sales, Yerby had started out as a writer invested in race as a topic, then discovered the rich rewards of novels appealing to white fantasies of the kind exploited in *Gone With the Wind* by Margaret Mitchell. *The Foxes of Harrow* was a book about whites written for whites, with blacks in the deep background. Ralph was offered another temptation that fall in the success of Willard Motley's novel *Knock on Any Door,* about an Italian boy growing up in a slum. It became a best seller (and, subsequently, a popular movie). But Ralph wanted no part of a novel by a black writer that skirted the issue of race.

More germane to his concerns was the arrival in September of *Lonely Crusade,* the second novel by Chester Himes. Not unlike Ralph's work-in-progress, at its center was a black hero, Lee Gordon, who one reviewer described not altogether inaccurately as psychopathic, just as Ralph's Invisible hovers at times on the brink of paranoia. Both novels traverse a political world in which Communists, black and white, feature prominently. There the similarity ends. "Personally I was disappointed with the book," Ralph wrote the following year, after *Lonely Crusade* had flopped. "I found it dishonest in its pseudo-intellectuality." Himes's creation, Ralph believed, had deteriorated into sensationalism and fetid ideas about politics and human relations. He had not done his homework. "After all," Ralph concluded (pointing implicitly to his own heroic effort since 1936 to educate himself), "if a man is serious about his politics and its relationship to man, then he should at least attempt to master the ideas (artistic, technical, philosophical, metaphysical, etc.) which that political position embodies explicitly." Moreover, the novelist's main task—"of giving shape to the *implicit* [ideas] which radiate about any philosophical position . . . like the invisible rays projected by a radioactive substance"—only began at this point.

Sensitive to and competitive about how Wright saw him, Ralph could not resist telling him that Himes was now representing "your recent work . . . as simple opportunism—missing completely the self-struggle with which you earned the right to publish those pieces." Finally, Himes had included Ralph in the book as a minor character called Ellsworth. Himes had not defamed him, Ralph conceded, but had simply used a conversation he had had with him as fodder in his fiction. Nevertheless, Ralph felt abused. Lately, he and Fanny had not seen Himes. "Could he fear that I might put him in *my* book? If so, he should forget it; *you* put him in a book [*Native Son,* as Bigger Thomas] seven years ago."

About the middle of November, after two months in Vermont, Ralph returned to New York. Threats of forest fires following an arid summer and fall, and the frigid approach of winter, had sent him home. Exactly how much progress he had made on his book is unclear. It is certain, however, that he worked on an essay on the Lafargue Clinic in Harlem for '48 magazine. No single task honed more sharply Ralph's ability to depict Invisible's experience in Harlem and New York City. Avoiding the mundane, he aimed to capture the elusive. "I am working on a piece," he informed Richard Wright, "describing the social conditions of Harlem which make the clinic a necessity." Throughout the winter of 1948, he labored to expand on this précis and to extend it to the psychological state of black America in general. If Harlem is nowhere, as the title of the piece proclaims, then Harlem is everywhere. Ralph's ultimate hope was that Harlem might be seen as the world. Its protocols against chaos having been smashed, the world itself had become a madhouse.

"Harlem Is Nowhere" should be seen as a kind of apologia for both the substance and the style of *Invisible Man,* especially when its hero moves to the North (though the essay illuminates the first section as well). Ralph's basic questions about the clinic might have come directly from *Invisible Man.* "Who is this total Negro," he asked, "whom the clinic seeks to know; what is the psychological character of the scene in which he dwells; how describe the past which he drags into this scene; and what is the future toward which he stumbles and becomes confused?" Although some blacks up north had made money, and even found a degree of spiritual peace, Harlem was now mainly decay and disease, a macabre setting out of Kafka, Munch, Dostoyevsky, or Dante. "To live in Harlem," Ralph ventured, "is to dwell in the very bowels of the city; it is to pass a labyrinthine existence among streets that explode monotonously skyward with the spires and crosses of churches and clutter underfoot with garbage and decay." The district was nothing less than "the scene and symbol of the Negro's perpetual alienation in the land of his birth." The hallucinatory was almost routine. It was "a world so fluid and shifting that often within the mind the real and the unreal merge, and the marvelous beckons from behind the same sordid reality that denies its existence."

The signs of Harlem's suffusion in insanity are everywhere. One familiar character throws imaginary hand grenades at passing traffic. A boy takes part in the rape and robbery of his mother. A man thrashes his wife in a public park even as, fastidiously, he observes the Marquis of Queensbury's rules of boxing. While two men pin a third man in place, a lesbian slashes him to death with a razor. These were "normal" acts (according to Ralph) in a community that could no longer live within the bounds of reason. Deformed by extreme mental pressures that come with relentless injustice, "life becomes a masquerade" in Harlem. "Exotic costumes are worn every day," Ralph noted. Unable to afford a horse, one man struts about dressed in a flashy riding habit; another, unable to hunt or buy a gun, brandishes a shooting stick. In the South, blacks had created certain bulwarks against chaos, including religion, folklore, stable families, and a canny knowledge of Jim Crow. In Harlem, defeated blacks fall easy prey to "the irrational, incalculable forces that hover about the edges of human life like cosmic destruction lurking within an atomic stockpile." Instead of cherishing "a semblance of metaphysical wholeness," they worship glittering fantasies of celebrity success that fly apart in "the slum scenes of filth, disorder and crumbling masonry."

For ten years, Dr. Wertham had tried to convince civic and philanthropic interests that Harlem needed a psychiatric clinic. Skeptical of his motives, whites persisted in denying both the humanity of Negroes and the fact that white racism had sponsored Harlem's breakdown. As Ralph saw it, "a thousand Lafargue clinics could not dispel the sense of unreality that haunts Harlem." Nevertheless, the clinic, which opened with meager resources but soon included a volunteer staff of fourteen psychiatrists and a dozen social workers, aimed "to give each bewildered patient an insight into the relation between his problems and his environment, and out of this understanding to reforge the will to endure in a hostile world." As he wrote his essay, Ralph also worked on the story of the bewildered Invisible, who would have to do without the benefit of psychiatry in his effort to gain at last a sense of psychological and moral equilibrium.

To do justice to its subject, Ralph believed, his essay had to be accompanied by photographs. He worked closely with Gordon Parks, a friend about his own age who would soon become one of the most honored of black American photographers. Ralph brought Parks into his "Harlem Is Nowhere" project because he believed that pictures, carefully chosen, were essential to the success of his essay. "I've worked out a scheme to do it with photographs," he informed Wright, "which should make for something new in photojournalism—if Gordon Parks is able to capture those aspects of Harlem reality which are so clear to me." Born in Kansas in 1912, Parks had developed his skills as a WPA employee in Washington, D.C. He captured one of the enduring images of Jim Crow when he photographed a dour black woman janitor holding up a mop in front of a large American flag, in a parody of Grant Wood's celebrated 1930 painting *American Gothic*. In 1941, Parks won the first fellowship awarded to a photographer by the Rosenwald Fund. The same year (1948) he worked with Ralph on "Harlem Is Nowhere," he became one of *Life* magazine's staff photographers, a major appointment at that time for a black man.

Brother artists, Ralph and Parks roamed Harlem together, seeking stark images of the psychological chaos that, in Ralph's mind, was now its essence. "The article developed into quite a time-consuming assignment," he recalled late in 1948. Shooting took several months "due to weather conditions and the nature of the material." Both Ralph and Wertham hoped that "Harlem Is Nowhere" would provoke controversy and thus boost support for Lafargue. Unfortunately, the essay never appeared anywhere. In May, citing financial troubles, the board of directors of '48 voted to suspend publication. When Ralph asked the board to release his essay at once, its lawyers refused. The magazine had declared bankruptcy, so its assets were frozen.

Joining a queue of unhappy creditors, Ralph filed a legal claim for

$306.40 against the magazine. He never saw any of this money, but regained control of his essay. After it was rejected by *Harper's*, which thought it too impressionistic, Ralph retired "Harlem Is Nowhere" to his files. Sixteen years later, without photographs, it would appear at last in *Shadow and Act*.

In New York Ralph had befriended Albert Murray, who would become almost as close to him as Wright once was. Murray (Tuskegee '39, a freshman in Ralph's third and last year) was now a professor of English there but had come to New York on leave with his wife, Mozelle, and their daughter, Michele, to study English for a year at Columbia.

With Wright's defection, Murray's arrival in New York was timely for Ellison. Well read in contemporary literature, especially fiction, Murray possessed a dazzling mind—one perhaps faster than Ralph's—with a prodigious gift of recall. Energetic and fun-loving, he was a much needed black companion for Ralph in his uneasy ascent of the predominantly white literary world. Increasingly some blacks were finding him aloof and critical, so that five years later Fanny would recall "the days when Ralph and I were an isolated two . . . peering through the keyhole at each knock to see if it were friend or enemy." Murray was now one of the few black people with whom he could converse as an intellectual equal, and who found his ideas about race, art, and politics persuasive and far-sighted. Murray also possessed a convivial, jiving effervescence to match his sharp intellect. His love of jazz and the blues ran at least as deeply as Ralph's, even if Ralph wrote more eloquently than Murray about these forms.

Born in Tuskegee, the light-skinned Mozelle Murray was beautiful and capable. Fanny liked her at once, so that the two families became close. Between himself and almost all other blacks Ralph now saw a widening divide. Langston Hughes was still as helpful as ever, but Ralph had lost almost all of the respect he once had for him. Hughes had read the excerpt from his novel in *Horizon,* Ralph complained to Wright, "but has studiedly refused to discuss it with me—which would be O.K. with me, if he hadn't, while knowing how busy I am, called up to ask me to edit a pot-boiler he's getting together from his *Chicago Defender* columns (!), offering, of course, to pay me. What does one do with people like that?"

Ralph was as unsentimental with his other former leftist colleagues. When A. B. Magil asked him for permission to reprint his story "Mister Toussan" in a *New Masses* anthology, Ralph's response was clipped: "My permission is hereby denied." Charles Humboldt, a former friend who was now literary editor of *New Masses,* lamented the fact that Ralph "would want to disdain your own past work"; but Ralph was unmoved. Mount Parnassus was at last in sight. "I'm getting some of the same reactions produced by *Native Son,*" he confided with pride to Richard Wright. "People look at me a bit differently now, and [an] undertone of reservation comes into their voices. God, but how they fear one who can name a situation, who attempts to capture significance!"

9

In the Home Stretch
1948–1949

He is a man born into a tragic . . . situation who attempts
to respond to it as though it were completely logical.

RALPH ELLISON (C. 1950)

Ralph's triumphs in *Horizon* and *'48* raised his literary standing as no other piece had ever done. But as much as he wanted to finish it quickly, *Invisible Man* resisted all efforts to hustle it into life. In October 1948, about a year past its due date, Frank Taylor was sure that the moment was at hand: "You must be in the home-stretch." He wasn't.

Lured to a Tuskegee alumni gathering at St. Mark's Methodist Church in Harlem in April 1948, where he listened to pieties about the value of education and the hallowed history of Tuskegee delivered by his former tormentor there, Dean Alvin Neely, Ralph was probably inspired to revisit and revise the first major section of *Invisible Man,* which is set partly in the South. Following the first, or "Battle Royal," chapter, the plot resumes with Invisible at the State College for Negroes. Invisible is a reliable young Negro who wants little more from life than to teach at the school. One spring afternoon, its president, Dr. A. Hebert Bledsoe, entrusts him with the care of a rich Bostonian, Mr. Norton, one of the institute's white trustees. On a drive into the countryside, they stop at the cabin of Jim Trueblood, a notorious local farmer. Trueblood's wife and daughter are pregnant, and he is the father of both children. After listening in horror and fascination to Trueblood's account of his first act of incest with his daughter, Norton needs a drink. Invisible takes him to the Golden Day, a local bar and whorehouse, where Norton is abused by mental patients from the nearby Veterans Hospital. Bledsoe is furious. Blaming Invisible for endangering the white trustee and thus the future of the college, the president sends him away with letters of introduction so that he might find a job in New York. As this first major section ends, Invisible arrives in New York.

When Ralph began writing his novel, he had no precise idea where it would go. Unlike the literary masters he admired, he did not work out the details of his plot from start to finish before sending Invisible on his way. This organic method had its advantages, but it would demand much time and many revisions before it generated a coherent story. However, as he moved outward from the central insight that in 1945 had sparked the idea of writing about an "invisible" man, he probably had two overlying schemes in mind, each complicated by his commitment to employing symbolism, folklore, and camouflaged literary allusions and references to leaven the basic text and embed it in the continuum of world literature. In one sense, Ralph believed in the serious writer's commitment to the past as outlined in T. S. Eliot's celebrated essay "Tradition and the Individual Talent," which he revered. (To Ralph, the fact that Eliot, a political reactionary, hardly had black writers in mind when he formed his thesis was beside the point.) In another sense, he wanted genuine world fame— not the kind of condescending, provisional compliments that major critics had accorded even the best of African-American writers, including Wright.

One plan was based on the facts of Ralph's life. In his search for inspiration, he wanted to build on what he knew firsthand, in the manner of Hemingway. Here he would succeed only too well. After *Invisible Man* appeared, he would be taxed for the rest of his life by false assumptions that the novel was his autobiography. However, his life provided its foundation. The other major plan, parallel to his life story, was to follow the general history of blacks in America, which took them from slavery and abolitionism through the Civil War and Reconstruction and its collapse; then to the rise of Jim Crow laws in the 1890s; and later to the mass migration of blacks to Northern cities and the ensuing failure of that movement. At the same time, it took them from domination by a folk consciousness to one shaped by industrialism. Ralph did not seek to align his plot according to the facts of history. Dating the events in the novel precisely is impossible. Invisible states that his grandparents had been freed "about eighty-five years ago." If they were emancipated in 1863, when Lincoln freed most of the slaves, then Invisible starts writing around 1948. However, his grandparents were perhaps freed before Emancipation (as was an old man in the text). Major events and eras are ignored in *Invisible*

Man. The Depression is not identified. Allusions are made to World War I, but not to World War II. These omissions deliberately boost the allegorical element so important to Ralph's aims.

While not Ralph's autobiography, as his artistic creation *Invisible Man* nevertheless offers some telling clues to the nature of his life. Like Invisible, Ralph could look back, through his mother and the elders of his Oklahoma youth, to slavery, Reconstruction, and the rise of Jim Crow laws. Within his novel he inserted teasing references to his own past. Greenwood refers both to an actual area of Tuskegee and to the black Tulsa section of the same name destroyed in the 1921 riots. Mr. Colcord is a reference to the owner of the (then) tallest office building in Oklahoma City, on which Ralph's father had worked. The State College for Negroes is based on Tuskegee Institute, down to the presence of Rabb Hall, Ralph's sly joke about his schoolmate Louis "Mike" Rabb, who now worked there. The two schools share wisteria and mockingbirds, a statue of the founder with a crouching slave; they have quasi-military traditions, a regimented chapel life, and a colored Veterans Hospital peopled by disturbed patients and seductive nurses. Rich white trustees descend annually from the North on the trembling campus. Like Ralph, Invisible flees to New York at the end of his junior year.

Often the evidence points, however tentatively, to Ralph's desires and anxieties otherwise concealed or understated. In this first major section, he develops the basic character of his young hero—innocent, ignorant, repressed, timid, gullible, and yet ambitious. But if Ralph's assessment of himself as a young man at Tuskegee obliquely inspired him here, he looked beyond himself to make Invisible an Everyman in whose face the whole world might see its own. As the novel unfolds, some of his symbols are yeasty—for example, white paint, pork chops, and hot yams—but others become stale, or even start off trite. So does his use of numbers. Ralph exploits their symbolic value both in Western literature (for example, *The Divine Comedy* has three books and is written in terza rima) and in the numbers racket, which Ralph had known since childhood. Three (as in the Trinity or the Fates), seven (as in the Seven Seals of the book of Revelation), and nine (as in the Muses) are probably the most important symbolic numbers in Western lore—and in *Invisible Man.* Trios of men appear ominously; a trio of women claims a dead body after the man is shot three times; Invisible muses on the identities of three young black men on a subway. Invisible heads north with seven sealed letters, and thus with seven seals; when the seventh is broken, it sheds an almost unbearable light on his life.

Although *Invisible Man* is in many ways an epic, Ralph adopted the form mainly to improvise on it like a disciplined jazzman. An epic is a story told by a reliable narrator about the journey of a young man through ordeals on the resolution of which the future of his people depends. Ralph's core subject, the fate of black Americans, would not allow for an orthodox epic. In white-dominated America, no black American could possibly secure definitively the welfare of his race or his racial "nation." Thus *Invisible Man* is at various times an epic, a mock-epic, and an anti-epic, as in the picaresque mode—the adventures of a rogue, which Invisible becomes. As Ralph knew, an example of *Bellerophontes litteras* (or *Bellerophontis litterae*) sets this epic in motion. In Greek mythology, the King of Argos, determined to kill Bellerophon but reluctant to slay a guest under his roof, asks him to deliver to Iobates a sealed letter ordering his death. Sent on various life-threatening missions by Iobates, Bellerophon prevails and eventually inherits Iobates' kingdom. As a Negro in America, Invisible could never be so successful and remain plausible; neither could any modern human being, black or white, achieve the assurance of identity that is Bellerophon's. Thus the epic form must always be distended and distorted in the modern world.

The myth of Bellerophon, in which the specter of evil haunts human innocence and makes us all suspicious and fatalistic, fuses in Ralph's artistry with Bledsoe's nasty trick with his letters to give a universal and also a local ring (as Ralph hoped it would) to this episode involving two Negroes of apparently no significance whatsoever. So, too, with incest. Ralph introduces this theme early and urgently. First one sees it dimly in the repressed Mr. Norton as he fondles a picture of his dead daughter. Then it surfaces raw in Jim Trueblood, a little black man who has sex with his daughter during one night of confusion (or so he says; we don't know the facts). Despised by the haughty blacks at the college, Trueblood nevertheless achieves in Ralph's skilled hands a measure of moral eminence. Said to be a fine singer, he is also a dazzling raconteur who spins a marvelous web of words around the self-deceiving Mr. Norton. As funny as it is appalling, his tale is adorned with dreams and reveries, hilariously comic flashes and tragically arresting details about the violation of his daughter Mattie. However, despite his artifice as a narrator, Trueblood accepts responsibility for his act. He even invites his marauding wife's vengeance. His terrible scar, the result of an axe she wields, is the badge (once blood red) of his humanity. Thus Trueblood is both an abominable sinner and a delivered saint. He is resolutely of this earth and also beyond it. To the learned reader he is, in lightning flashes of illumination, pagan

Oedipus, the biblical Lot who slept with his daughters, and divine Christ; but then again he is only a little Negro man who did a nasty thing, knows it, and sings the blues. To Invisible, Trueblood is only a yokel. He does not know that this man is a sacred text, the answer to the riddle of identity that will baffle him for years to come.

Norton has a separate, though related, symbolic function. He embodies Ralph's crucial belief in the decline of white American moral power as epitomized in New England abolitionism in the era when the Negro had been the preeminent symbol of the dignity of man. Representing the atrophy of the abolitionist spirit—his name suggests Charles Eliot Norton, a famous Harvard educator—Norton has let his moral conscience decline into mere philanthropy. He gets roughed up and denounced at the Golden Day, a speakeasy bearing the same name that Lewis Mumford had given to the heyday of New England's cultural and moral excellence. (To Ralph's chagrin, Mumford had left blacks out of his account of the era.)

In the action at the Golden Day, Ralph constructs a kind of opéra bouffe surrounding Invisible and Mr. Norton. If much of the episode is farce, the comedy is haunted by the mental diseases spawned in part by war (as in shell shock) but more so by white racism. Injustice has ruined the minds of some of the most brilliant patients, especially the former physician who denounces Norton and Invisible. Virtuosity flares again when, as Invisible awaits Dr. Bledsoe's punishment, Ralph offers an astonishing intermezzo in the form of an elegiac oration about the founder by a visiting preacher, Barbee, who is blind. Like its literary antecedents (including Father Mapple's sermon in *Moby-Dick* and also the retreat sermon preached in *A Portrait of the Artist as a Young Man*), Barbee's speech subdues the turbulence of the narrative and readies the reader for what is to come—Bledsoe's rape of Invisible's innocence. For all its baroque beauty and its core of facts, Barbee's eulogy for the founder is a fake, as part of the confabulation of lies that is the college.

Nevertheless, although Bledsoe seems to be a monster as he crushes Invisible, from another angle (one that Ralph would stress later in life) he is an entirely justifiable specimen of Southern black manhood. Bledsoe is as unconquerable as Trueblood. Who is to say which "sin"—incest, or a black man's lust for power in a Jim Crow world—is the more grievous? Insofar as he identified with his characters, Ralph was Invisible, Trueblood, and Bledsoe. He was part Bledsoe even though, in creating the character, he drew on individuals at Tuskegee whom he hated while he was there, including Neely and William Dawson. Bledsoe coldly sends Invisible north with his Bellerophonic letters of doom. Each letter elegantly rephrases the message that Invisible had dreamed was inscribed in a sealed envelope in his shiny new briefcase: "Keep This Nigger-Boy Running."

Ralph was keenly aware of mental illness in Harlem, and his main bulwarks against it were his novel-in-progress and Fanny. Although their life together was not nearly as magical as in its early days, and was often roiled by his bad temper and moods, Ralph recognized that he had in her an excellent breadwinner, an efficient housekeeper, and a companion who loved him. Nevertheless, he did not have something that he believed he wanted badly—a child. Al Murray had a child, Richard Wright and Stanley Hyman had children; his brother, Herbert, had a stepchild. "It's time we here were doing something along that line," he wrote to Hyman after the birth of Wright's second daughter, Rachel.

Whatever the practicality of Fanny becoming a mother when she was the main breadwinner (with Ralph as needy at times as an infant), he convinced himself that he wanted a child. With growing intensity, Fanny felt the pressure to produce one. Both believed she was the problem. According to the Margaret Sanger Research Bureau in Manhattan, his semen was "normal in every respect." Fanny threw herself into the campaign with her usual efficiency. Noting the days of her ovulation by monitoring her temperature, she did her best to conceive. Her failure began to corrode their relationship. In 1957, Ralph would tell Fanny that, virtually from its start, their marriage had been a disappointment to him. Although he might have had other complaints, the core of his disappointment (if in fact he was truly disappointed and not simply lashing out at Fanny) was her infertility. This was also perhaps his main weapon as he dominated his wife and kept her focused on his needs.

In the fall of 1949 Fanny was still working with the infertility service at the Sanger Bureau, without success. Now thirty-eight, she despaired of conceiving at this point. She was willing to adopt a child—if that was what Ralph wanted—but here Ralph was at best equivocal. Some years later, according to Charlotte Wilbur (she and her husband, the poet Richard Wilbur, were for many years close to Ralph and Fanny), Ralph explained his odd position on adoption. "Ralph told me one day that he would never be able to adopt a child," she recalled, "unless the poor kid was exactly the same in its genetic makeup as he was. In other words, a child acceptable to Ralph would have to be part Indian, and part white, and part black, and part this, and part that. I was absolutely flabbergasted, and I told him so. It was a strange kind of thinking, really. He was quite serious about it."

Obsessed by his writing, Ralph certainly thought of his long-gestating novel, conceived only after long frustration, as his most precious offspring. It had no serious rival for his affections. This did not make Ralph a monster, only a necessarily self-absorbed master artist who would rather lose a wife or lover than surrender his identity as an artist. A child's demands would have placed a notably severe burden on Ralph as he worked in his cramped apartment. However much he enjoyed the idea of being Daddy, he cherished far more the actual life of the artist, the agony of composition, the promise of eternal fame from the progeny of his craft. Fanny must have feared that, in his zeal for a child, Ralph might turn to a younger woman. Fortunately for her, he seemed to have little interest in having sex with other women, although he also seemed ready to frighten and worry Fanny with the prospect of his infidelity. In the spring of 1948, she felt threatened when the vivacious Sanora Babb, who herself was still trying to publish her first book, came from California to New York to speak to editors at Random House. At her invitation, Ralph called on her. After some initial awkwardness, they were soon talking pleasantly about their works. He brought along parts of his manuscript, and Sanora remembered them lying fully clothed on a made-up bed, reading each other's writing in respectful silence.

She believed that Ralph was waiting to see if she was ready for something more intimate. "I had moved on with my life," Babb recalled. "By that time I was more in love than ever with Jimmie [the cinematographer James Wong Howe, whom she would marry the following year, when California finally lifted its ban on marriage between whites and Chinese persons]. I wanted to be friends with Ralph. After all, we were two writers each working on a novel." After a couple of hours, Ralph said goodbye and left the apartment. Sanora assumed she would not see him again, certainly not on this visit. The next day he showed up unannounced at the apartment. "The first thing he told me," according to Babb, "was that he had gone home and told Fanny all about us. I was shocked. All that business was long over, as far as I was concerned. It seemed such a needlessly cruel thing for him to do, especially when he also let her know that he intended to see me again. He told me that she was very upset, but he didn't seem to care. I don't know what good he thought would come of it."

Ralph seemed to her oddly "grounded in the past. He thought I would be jealous of Fanny, when that was the last thing I would ever be. And I certainly did not want to revive our intimacy, which maybe he thought was the case." On the train heading west toward California, she closed a letter—and, to a large extent, their friendship—with a valediction that stressed their separate identities as artists: "Dear Ralph, I have learned something out of my own pain and varied troubles: many interruptions may occur, but nothing finally prevents us from writing. You are a writer. You know that now. I know it of myself, but the assurance was a long time maturing within. I want you to write; that is a part of my love for you. And you must let me say love; there is no good friendship without it."

With every passing season, as he worked to finish his novel, Ralph withdrew more and more from the life he led when he was green and eager to sample the pleasures of New York's nightclubs and dancehalls. He now favored more cerebral adventures. In their ambition, he and Fanny were hypersensitive about their social standing. As much as they wanted to like people for themselves, they needed to believe that they were moving upward in the world. Race, class, and money all played major roles in their decisions about who should be welcomed, encouraged, solicited—and who should not. Their friendships with fellow blacks such as Gordon Parks or Albert and Mozelle Murray were vital to Ralph and Fanny. That was also true of Ralph's boyhood friend Virgil Branam, who was living in New York. As fat and as irrepressible as ever, Branam was a veteran ship's cook who served up an abundance of anecdotes and tales about exotic ports the world over. Ralph loved to visit with the exuberant Virgil, who evoked precious memories of their youthful days in Oklahoma.

Given the warped dynamics of American racism, the Ellisons' friendship with whites was crucial to their sense of success and that of the national ideals in which they believed. Unlike many other blacks, who refused to pay the psychological toll of trying to be friends with whites, they sought to cement their place in the tiny part of white society that would receive them. In New York, most of these people were leftist Jews. At a time when anti-Semitism was still a routine feature of most clubs, colleges, and other social institutions, Jews had an incentive to identify at least sometimes with the lot of African-Americans, even if the "Battle Royal" of American ethnicity led many, perhaps even most, to define their "whiteness" by shunning blacks. Ralph and Fanny made the most of this incentive. According to one of his neighbors (herself Jewish) during the years when he and Fanny owned a vacation home in New England, Ralph could speak Yiddish fairly fluently. "He told me that he had picked up a lot of it when he was young, in Oklahoma City," Harriet Davidson, a friend, said years later, "and his mother had worked for Jews. Maybe he learned more after he moved to New York, because he and my husband would sit on the porch and converse very easily in Yiddish. Ralph had no trouble speaking or understanding it. It brought him even closer to us."

Ida Guggenheimer remained the Ellisons' main link to white society. Although Ralph no longer depended on her for money, he was still a beneficiary of her charitable nature and made several useful friends among her wide circle of admirers. Ralph also gained from knowing Ida's daughter, Clara Binswanger, and, to a lesser extent, Clara's daughter, Martha Bernard, whose marriage in 1946 Ralph and Fanny attended. Certainly Ralph cultivated his relationship to Francis and Beatrice Steegmuller (Francis was not Jewish). The Ellisons' few surviving daybooks of this period indicate lots of dinner dates and other invitations to visit Ida at the Ansonia on Broadway, or the Binswangers on West 88th Street, or the Steegmullers on East 66th Street, or—less frequently—Bea's brother Ed Stein and his wife, Gretchen, on Park Avenue. Visiting these homes lifted Ralph and Fanny temporarily out of the grimy world of Harlem into a setting of cultivated privilege. Such people were a godsend in an emergency, as in 1950, when the Ellisons borrowed $300 from the Steegmullers in part to pay for medical treatment for Fanny. (They repaid the money within a year or two.)

Ralph was on particularly relaxed terms with Clara Binswanger. "One of my sisters always believed that our mother was in *Invisible Man*," Martha Bernard remarked decades later, referring to one or another of the three white women who either flirt with Invisible or have sexual relations with him. "Ralph spent an important amount of time with my mother. She was a bit older than Ralph [fifteen years]. She wasn't as much on the left as Ida was, but she had her causes. She and my father were divorced by this time, and she never remarried. Ralph would come over, usually by himself, and drink Scotch, and he would argue with my mother about politics and all sorts of things. Later, after his book came out, he began to drink more, and then he would often berate her, and she would get quite upset. He was drinking her liquor but at the same time he was berating her. She didn't like it at all."

Among Ralph's white friends, only Ida was more important to him than Stanley Hyman as he labored to finish *Invisible Man*. The link here wasn't money. In fact, Hyman, a spendthrift, would borrow money from Ralph, at least until Shirley Jackson's career rocketed. When the Hymans left North Bennington briefly in 1949 to live in Westport, Connecticut, much closer to Manhattan, Ralph saw even more of them. In a world in which Jews lacked absolute social prestige, Ralph and Fanny also sought to make friends among white Anglo-Saxon Protestants. Frank and Nan Taylor and the well-connected Albert Erskine proved to be invaluable contacts. Whether hosted by Jews or Gentiles, Ralph and Fanny craved what superior whites had to offer them in the way of stylish cocktail or dinner parties, fine wines, urbane conversation, and social éclat. At the Steegmullers', Ralph first gazed on the elfin Truman Capote. At Dorothy and Edward Norman's home on East 70th Street they could chat with celebrities such as the anti-Communist journalist Arthur Koestler (who in 1933 had roamed Soviet Asia with Langston Hughes) or Stephen Spender. They also met Lewis Mumford and his wife. Mumford was Jewish but a champion of white New England culture. Alfred Kazin also championed that culture but was more relaxed about his working-class Jewish background.

Resolutely, Ralph knocked on closed doors. Sometimes he was admitted, sometimes not. His presence at a meeting of the James Joyce Society at the National Arts Club created ripples of curiosity and perhaps even concern. Because of his love of Joyce, he ignored the snickers at his back. Joining the Steegmullers, he and Fanny went to Philadelphia for the opening of a Matisse exhibition. On occasion, whites gallantly opened doors before he knocked, as when William Van O'Connor of the University of Minnesota, planning the scholarly magazine *American Quarterly,* asked him for a contribution. Many doors, though, were bolted shut. Ralph and Fanny were also troubled because they could not reciprocate the hospitality of their white friends except in token ways. "Our quarters are very small and cramped, badly ventilated and lighted," she complained in April 1948 in seeking access to a nicer place. "Since my husband is a writer and works at home the situation is continuously grievous for him."

Even if they had the money to entertain stylishly, Ralph and Fanny understood the delicate rules of racial etiquette for liberal whites. Almost always, Negroes formed only a token presence at social gatherings hosted by whites. Adding even one other black couple might compromise the tone of the gathering. Whites rarely played a token role in a social gathering dominated by blacks. To place white friends in such a situation was to risk their friendship. In addition, one couldn't always count on other blacks to behave "properly"—that is, docilely—in the company of whites. Far too often, somebody acted up. Ralph and Fanny learned therefore to live divided social lives. One life was black and homey, comfortable but also almost always second-rate in amenities and intellectual weight, while the other life was white and almost always somewhat alien if also stimulating. Moving between the two worlds helped Ralph to understand better the matter of race in America. However, he was also participating, albeit with little choice if he wished to succeed, in a version of Jim Crow, in that he was moving in white circles that allowed only a token, minuscule black presence. This dilemma would bedevil his sense of place within the black world and perhaps, ultimately, his ability to function as an artist.

Ralph wrote brilliantly about Negro "educators" like Bledsoe in part because he had come to have a low opinion of many Negro leaders, organizations, and institutions. Now and then he asserted that he cared more about black opinion of his work than about white. "I get the feeling that most times the stuff is seen mainly by whites," he wrote Al Murray, "and that, I'm afraid, doesn't mean much in the long run." But the opinions of informed, influential whites—the people who bought and read books in quantity—were at least equally important to him. Even in editing the *Negro Quarterly* in the early 1940s he had placed a premium on reaching whites. He made few concessions to the black audience. When the Chicago publisher John H. Johnson sought to reprint "Battle Royal" in his *Negro Digest,* Ralph watched impassively as the request failed. After Wright passed on Ralph's name to Alioune Diop, a founding editor of the Paris-based journal *Présence Africaine,* as a potential contributor, Ralph never replied to Diop's letters.

His lack of interest in this kind of relationship would only grow. Learning that some Harlem leftists had organized a writers' workshop and planned a new magazine, *Harlem Quarterly,* he was skeptical. "I talked with one of the editors the other day," he wrote Wright, "and was depressed. Already it's torn with those who want to learn to write and those who want to use the group for political ends. And there is the same old mammy-made provincialism, envy, and ignorance. Those sonsabitches can't change the world, but they certainly know how to make time stand still!" When John Henrik Clarke, a largely self-educated black nationalist intellectual, asked Ralph to contribute to *Harlem Quarterly,* he replied stiffly that because of "previous editorial commitments," he couldn't help "at this time."

Although he wrote *Invisible Man* in an era of major changes in the colonial world, such events have no place in the novel. When he noted these changes, he was unsentimental. In October 1949, when Ralph attended a reception at the Normans' for Jawaharlal Nehru, the prime minister of India, which had achieved independence in 1947, this sense dominated. "I was amused," he wrote Hyman, "to watch some of our touted intellectuals perform like school children, throwing Nehru the old 'moral leader' unworldly, isn't-he-wonderful line—only to have him suggest that since it was supposed to be a meeting of intellectuals, that they forget the crap and get down to intellectual matters. Very politely, of course, but he'd have none of the sentimental foolishness." Ralph had no romantic confidence in the ability of India to function well without the sahibs. The expectations in many quarters for the entire anti-colonial movement seemed excessive to him.

At some level, Ralph was living a life that was not unlike that of the hero of his novel. In his search for identity, Invisible learns to shun most of the blacks about him. Hating the black nationalist leader who confronts him, he flings a spear through his jaw. But Invisible also rejects those who touch his heart, such as Mary Rambo, a black woman in Harlem who offers him motherly love. To some extent, Invisible's isolation at the end of the novel mimics Ralph's growing distance from the blacks about him. His sense of difference and superiority expanded even as he continued to want to live among blacks and as he sought to interpret their culture through the lens of fiction.

If the first section of *Invisible Man* is its finest, the second main section, which comprises the six chapters starting with Invisible's early days in New York, is scarcely less brilliant. Ralph's style here, especially in the science fiction surrounding Invisible's electroshock therapy (which may be only a trauma-inspired dream following the explosion), is distorted and expressionistic rather than surrealistic, impressionistic, naturalistic, or simply realistic, as it is earlier in the novel. The marvel is that these diverse styles combine as smoothly as they do for most readers. Ralph's parade of carnivalesque yet shadowy figures, of the real yet mythical, is both vividly human and hauntingly allegorical. In earlier versions of the manuscript, Mary Rambo's home becomes the setting for a return to realism and naturalism, as Invisible interacts with other blacks under her roof. However, Ralph then decided to tell a more expressly political story. Favoring the political, mythical, and allegorical, he suppressed domestic realism. Invisible evades Mary Rambo and her tender black womanly graces as he plunges toward his rendezvous with the radical politics of the Brotherhood, the black nationalism of Ras the Destroyer, and his life in a hole.

As in the first section, a skeleton of biographical facts supports at least a part of this narrative. Like Invisible, Ralph worked in a paint factory (A. C. Horn, in 1937), where he faced trade union agitation. Just as young Emerson, the patient of a psychiatrist, gets Invisible this job, so probably did a patient or a friend of Dr. Sullivan secure him a job at the factory. (The high-quality paint in Sullivan's townhouse, according to one of Sullivan's biographers, came specially made by A. C. Horn.) Emerson's invitation to gay life may have something to do with the fact that Sullivan was gay or bisexual. The sculptor Richmond Barthé, with whom Ralph had lived for a while, was both gay and a friend of Sullivan. Here in this second section Ralph signals his resistance to the homosexual chances offered to him at Tuskegee and then early in New York. A less defensive image of Invisible's sexuality is postponed until late in the novel. As for Mary Rambo, Harlem was undoubtedly full of women like Mary, who offers Invisible a bluesy, homespun therapy in his painful search to find himself.

With Invisible's entry into the Brotherhood, the link between fiction and biography becomes more tenuous. Ralph's passage into Communist circles was much more mundane than Invisible's into the Brotherhood. Ralph was no gifted orator. Certainly Invisible does not stammer, as Ralph did under pressure. He was never the spellbinder that Invisible becomes after his electroshock therapy. Curiously, Ralph had created a hero limited physically and also sensitive about those limits—a token of his own personal insecurities. Invisible once calls himself "a little black man" and wishes he were taller. His skin is "ginger" colored, or light brown; he wishes that it were ebony. He believes that other blacks resent him because of his color. Sexually, Invisible has had some experience with women (whores at the Golden Day), but he lacks confidence. His libido is restrained. It is aroused mainly by a mixture of rage and desire for the forbidden when he encounters white women, and then only episodically. Invisible seldom notes the sexual attractions of black women, and never up north.

Starting in late June 1948, while Francis and Bea Steegmuller spent almost a year in Paris, Ralph enjoyed some welcome relief from his hot apartment. Generously, Steegmuller had invited him to use his writing sanctuary in an office building at 608 Fifth Avenue in the heart of Manhattan's Diamond District, where skilled dealers and merchants sold precious stones, jewelry, and watches. Steegmuller's office was in a suite belonging to two jewelers, Samuel and Augusta Mann.

Few blacks worked in this business, except perhaps as janitors; most of the owners were Jews, as were the Manns. If Ralph had serious fears about his reception, the Manns quickly dispelled them. Respecting Ralph's needs as a writer, they guarded his privacy, fussed over him, and encouraged him to write—and also to take breaks for lunch, for which they sometimes paid. They made the Fifth Avenue office a true refuge. "Interestingly enough," Ralph wrote later, "it was only the elevator operators who questioned my presence in such an affluent building." To catch the sunlight, Steegmuller had set up his typewriter next to a window that looked across to the roof of Radio City Music Hall. When white people there saw a black man sitting at a typewriter, they sometimes could not hide their curiosity or their alarm. "With some," Ralph wrote Hyman, "it's as though they had looked across to see me doing number 2 out of the window—and I'll let *you* worry about the metaphor, chum." Unperturbed, he pressed on with his epic. In roughly seven weeks he wrote more than 150 pages and revised several sections. "It has helped me a lot to be able to work away from home," he admitted, "though I don't know what I'll do when Steegmuller returns."

This Fifth Avenue setting, Ralph later remarked, might have been a serious handicap to his work "had I not been consciously concerned with a fictional character who was bent upon finding his way in areas of society whose manners, motives and rituals were baffling." Meanwhile, people in his Harlem neighborhood speculated, as he knew, about his occupation. Why was his woman content to have him lounge at home all day? According to Ralph, "a wino lady" once drunkenly exclaimed, "Now that nigger *there* must be some kinda sweetback, 'cause while his wife has got her some kinda little 'slave,' all I ever see *him* do is walk them damn dogs and shoot some damn pictures!" With the cool office available, Ralph stayed in Manhattan all through the summer of 1948. Not until the end of the year did he and Fanny get away briefly. The day after Christmas, with Bobbins and Red—now known as Rudy—they took the train to wintry Vermont to visit the Hymans. Shirley had catapulted to fame, or notoriety, following the sensational appearance in the June 26 *New Yorker* of her short story "The Lottery." (In a small New England town, the good citizens run a lottery each year in which the "winner" is stoned to death.) A few weeks later, quietly but to respectful reviews, Stanley had brought out *The Armed Vision: A Study in the Methods of Modern Literary Criticism,* a huge book of essays about modern literary criticism.

Ralph seemed to have mixed feelings about the Hymans' success. In "The Lottery," Jackson had dipped into the well of myth and ritual from which he had been hauling water. "If Shirley does anything else in this vein," Ralph alerted Stanley, "let me know, we're beginning to work in the same vein." In Stanley's case, Ralph's response was even more ambivalent. Like his mentor, Kenneth Burke, Hyman aimed in *The Armed Vision* to probe the work of acclaimed modern critics such as R. P. Blackmur, I. A. Richards, Maud Bodkin, Yvor Winters, and William Empson in order to see "the ancestry of their techniques and procedures." He wanted to suggest a way toward "an integrated and practical methodology that would combine and consolidate the best procedures of modern criticism." A would-be novelist, Ralph also craved the authority of the learned critic. He hefted Hyman's fat book, flipped through its pages replete with scholarly references, and imagined himself in Hyman's place, as an authority on literature and culture. He enjoyed sparring with Hyman about the nature of tragedy, the functions of folklore, the politics of the blues. Both men were confident and often overbearing about what they knew; both could be abrasive and even cruel in debate. Ralph might as well have been talking about himself when he teased Hyman that "I know that it is fast becoming part of your myth to be annoyed as hell by ignorance and incompetence."

In high spirits, Ralph and Fanny rang in 1949 with much drinking and carousing with Hyman's family and friends in the big old house on Prospect Street in North Bennington. On this trip, as during others, they met the poet and critic Howard Nemerov, who would become a luminary at Bennington. The Ellisons particularly liked a young instructor, R. W. B. "Dick" Lewis, who, with his wife, Nancy, a recent Bennington graduate, would become one of their closest friends. Dick would later teach at Princeton and Yale but was then near the start of a brilliant academic career based on the success of the book he was finishing, *The American Adam.* It was a foundational text in the postwar growth of American Studies; its meditation on the themes of innocence and identity in the nation's literature, and on American moral "exceptionalism" or uniqueness among world cultures, held Ralph's attention. Dick Lewis also appealed to Ralph as a fun-loving, hard-drinking, generous man. "Ralph and I, and later Fanny and Nancy, we all hit it off right away," Lewis would recall. "In 1947, I had read the 'Battle Royal' chapter in *Horizon* and was excited to meet Ralph. In person, he didn't disappoint me. He knew a great deal about nineteenth-century American literature but more importantly he loved it, passionately, as I did. He believed in its greatness, its moral power but also its complexity. And he and Fanny were also fun to be around."

At the Hymans' in North Bennington, Ralph had a comfortable room to himself when he visited, and also the run of Stanley's massive library, rich blues collection, and loaded liquor cabinet. At sundown, especially on weekends, Hyman began his own heavy drinking, in which Ralph and other friends joined with gusto. "You missed a fine party Friday night," Hyman wrote Ralph once. "It broke up at six, consumed fifteen bottles of whisky, and is still being talked about. Next time you and Fanny come up we will have a *real* big one." The arguments, many of them rowdy, were usually as free-flowing and stimulating as the liquor.

Ralph could imagine himself as a thriving Bennington professor, even if he had no degree. As a black man he stuck out in North Bennington but acted as if he didn't. At Percey's Newsroom he could buy New York newspapers and browse magazines. Strolling with his camera about North Bennington, or on the campus grounds, he was a figure few could miss. To many of the townsfolk, clannish and wary of the liberal college ever since it opened in 1931, the fact that he stayed with the Hymans made him almost as sinister as the fact that he was black. One of the Hyman children would recall how North Bennington viewed Ralph and the Hyman family: "It was, 'That Shirley Jackson's a witch, married that Jew from New York. That nigger comes visit them once in a while, he teaches at the Commie place up the hill, where the girls are.' "

On January 11, 1949, Ralph and Fanny were back in Manhattan when, for a fee of $50, he took part in the program *Books on Trial* on radio station WMGM. The book that week was *Black Odyssey* by Roi Ottley, Ralph's superior a decade before at the Federal Writers' Project of New York. With a judge, jury, prosecutor, defender, and co-defendant—the author himself—*Books on Trial* mimicked a courtroom in action. Ralph had emerged as prosecutor with a stern review of *Black Odyssey* in the *New York Star*. His opponent was Professor Monroe Berger of Columbia University, who had praised Ottley's book in the *New York Times Book Review*. Although respectful, Ralph was not intimidated by Berger's credentials. Ottley had emphasized the struggle for civil rights rather than the more profound ways in which blacks assert their humanity. "One misses any conception," he had argued in the *Star,* "that Negro Americans constitute a specific cultural grouping of Americans which, forged in the experience of slavery, has evolved, from disparate influences, a folk culture embodying among other things a conception of human life, a 'style,' a musical culture, a somewhat crude psychology, and a very advanced philosophy of human freedom; a culture which is now undergoing transformation under the pressures of industrialization."

The phrases "a somewhat crude psychology" and "a very advanced philosophy of human freedom" asserted acute angles of vision on black life almost entirely beyond the ken of Ottley or any other commentator on black culture, black or white, writing at the time. It took courage to assert both ideas. Blacks hardly wanted to hear their psychology called "crude." And few blacks believed they had much freedom or any philosophy, much less an advanced philosophy, given what little freedom they possessed. In any event, Ralph's dazzling radio performance led to fresh queries from editors and publishers. M. Margaret Anderson of the moderate *Common Ground* magazine, in which he had already published, begged him for something new. Nevertheless, he resisted all invitations that threatened to take him away from his novel. He spoke publicly on February 25 at an afternoon tea given by the Women's Conference of the Society for Ethical Culture at West 64th Street mainly to please Ida Guggenheimer and Gerda Stein (Bea's mother), who were stalwarts of the organization (and to pick up the fee of $25). Saying nothing new, Ralph instead recycled his unpublished essay of the previous year on Melville, Mark Twain, Faulkner, and Hemingway. The real challenge was to keep his remarks relatively simple. "I do get myself into the damndest situations!" he complained to Hyman. "I'll have to boil everything I have to say to the point where I won't know whether I'm saying anything or not."

With Francis Steegmuller back from Europe, Ralph lost the comfortable office on Fifth Avenue, but he kept at his novel. The third major section of *Invisible Man* comprises chapters 14 to 20—from Invisible's entry into the Brotherhood to the death of his tragic beau ideal, Tod Clifton (Ralph knew, of course, that the German word *Tod* means "death"). A tall, black-skinned, handsome, and popular young veteran of the political wars in Harlem, Clifton is the most compelling Brotherhood official. Months before he is shot dead by a white policeman, he abruptly quits the Brotherhood. The ragtag group led by Ras the Destroyer, a Marcus Garvey–like black nationalist who despises the white-dominated Brotherhood, cannot hold him. Heartsick and dazed, Invisible ponders the mystery of Clifton's last months: "Why should a man deliberately plunge outside of history? . . . Why should he choose to disarm himself, give up his voice and leave the only organization offering him a chance to 'define' himself? . . . Why did he choose to plunge into nothingness, into the void of faceless faces, of soundless voices, lying outside history?" The last pages of chapter 20 are crucial to Ralph's goal of presenting the true face of black America as he saw it. Central to this project is his near despair, echoed by Invisible, about black Americans and history. Trapped in a white culture that denies their humanity, many blacks choose, like Clifton, to disdain a place in history and the challenge of making history constructively. Like Ralph, Invisible is horrified at the obscene Sambo doll that Clifton peddles on the streets of New York after he has quit the Brotherhood (symbolizing perhaps the fate of blacks always to dance attendance on whites or to live as puppets).

This is perhaps Ralph's saddest lament, because his main purpose in writing *Invisible Man* was to inscribe blacks into history through surpassingly fine literary art. He deliberately echoed at one point early in the novel those rousing words of Stephen Dedalus, about "the uncreated conscience of my race." Ralph feared that blacks may have already opted to slide outside history into an expressionist demi-life of sometimes morbid, sometimes ecstatic signs, symbols, and gestures that signal their abandonment of, and by, civilization. As this third section ends, the challenge before Ralph is both to place his "epic" hero Invisible squarely in the midst of this philosophical chaos and to find a way out for him that is consistent with human dignity, yet honest about the realities of American life.

As Ralph labored down the home stretch, his growing love of photography provided some welcome relief. Under Gordon Parks's informal tutoring in the field and the darkroom, Ralph began to work more expertly, with an emphasis on portraiture. Not long after spending $80 on a used Rolleicord twin-lens reflex camera, he ordered letterhead stationery announcing himself as "Ralph Ellison: Photographer." Later that year, he bought an even costlier used Rolleiflex TLR. Having an excellent eye and the patience to achieve his desired effects, inspired mainly by images in *Vogue,* he startled his friends with prints that were sometimes slick but were also sometimes stunning. He pleased Albert and Mozelle Murray, Ida Guggenheimer, Francis Steegmuller, Stanley Hyman, and Shirley Jackson with handsome portraits of themselves. Fanny, too, was a frequent subject—and at least once he photographed her in the nude.

When Howard Nemerov thanked him for "the splendid photographs you took, enlarged and sent to us," he also mused about having Ralph's work appear on his next dust jacket. Random House had already hired him to prepare a portrait of Steegmuller for the jacket of his book on Maupassant. Ralph photographed Mary McCarthy in her apartment for the jacket of her 1949 novel, *The Oasis.* That year, the *Nashville Tennessean* (unaccustomed, probably, to using work by blacks) used his portrait of Albert Erskine to accompany a story about the native Tennessean. For the Boston Institute of Contemporary Arts, Ralph copied two paintings by Jacques Villon (Bea Stein's teacher in Paris) owned by Ida Guggenheimer. Pleased, the institute had him copy other works. Ralph was not above more mundane tasks. "I did some ambulance chasing doing accidents," he would recall. In November 1948, an insurance company paid him $18 to shoot pictures of an accident on 145th Street between St. Nicholas and Edgecombe avenues. Without success, he submitted some nature studies, shot mainly in Central Park, to *Collier's* magazine.

On his tax return for 1949 Ralph reported $191 in income from photography and $270 in writing fees. His total income was thus $461, as against $1,434 in expenses (including $660 for the office rental). Fortunately, Fanny earned $2,687, on which they could live decently. Whatever their financial constraints, they were not threatening enough for Ralph to think seriously of taking a salaried job.

Early in 1949 Ralph wrote to Stanley Hyman that his novel was just about done. Impatient, he wanted "to get the dam[n] thing ready for Fall publication." He was sure about meeting the deadline. "Things go on fairly well," he wrote. "I'm now fighting out the political and final section of my book." Nevertheless, he was "all full of doubts and stubbornness, like a man juggling boulders into a pile which he hopes will be a house. I haven't lost sight of my form, but I must admit that I am somewhat swamped by the proportions of the thing—and by the many possibilities of which I cannot possibly take advantage."

In fact, he was not nearly done. No factor kept him stumbling in the home stretch more than the political maelstrom then sweeping across America and the fact that he had once been a Communist sympathizer or an actual Communist. Viewed in the pages of newspapers and magazines, on radio and television, the Cold War pitted the Soviet Union and the international left against the United States and its anti-Communist nationalism. How should these factors affect the composition of his novel? How might they affect its reception? What did he actually now believe about the right, the left, America, the Negro, and politics in general?

Ralph could not miss the positive signs that the nation was beginning to abandon its Jim Crow past, but he did not believe that a new day had come for Negroes in America. Still, in July 1948, President Harry Truman had signed Executive Order 9981 barring segregation in the armed forces. In its election platform that year, the Democratic Party (following a walkout by Southern delegates to form the Dixiecrat Party led by Strom Thurmond) had stressed the civil rights of all racial and religious minorities. The Republican Party had come out against lynching and in favor of civil rights for blacks. The federal government had joined various antidiscrimination lawsuits. Ironically, some of the crucial advances were taking place in Oklahoma. In *Sipuel v. Board of Regents*, the U.S. Supreme Court ruled in favor of Ada Lois Sipuel, a black woman who had applied without success for admission to the University of Oklahoma Law School. Since Oklahoma did not have a separate law school for blacks, the Court ruled, Ada Sipuel was entitled to admission. Not long afterward, the Supreme Court barred the same university from segregating a black student in its library, classrooms, and cafeteria. Some colleges and universities had taken the initiative to desegregate. The University of Arkansas allowed blacks into their professional schools. The U.S. Naval Academy graduated its first African-American midshipman. One of the most heartening signs had come on the playing field when, in 1947, amid intense controversy, Jackie Robinson of the Brooklyn Dodgers had integrated major league baseball. In 1949 he was named the Most Valuable Player in the National League.

But in 1949, segregation was still the law throughout the South. Ralph understood that much of the reactionary spirit behind anti-Communism was also against freedom for the Negro. "I have become so disgusted with politics that I hardly read the newspapers," he had declared in 1948, as the momentum began to build for the presidential race in which Henry Wallace's Progressive Party would be routed and Truman would upset Thomas Dewey. In 1948 Ralph had not written off the Communists, not when the economy was on the downswing and goods were scarce. "They stand a good chance to survive and become a force again if the present trend of events continues long enough," he had asserted. "Reality is becoming stern enough to make people reject anti-Communist propaganda." Nevertheless, he absolutely disdained the black Communists. With satisfaction he watched the nasty infighting among some of them, as when Doxey Wilkerson of Howard University attacked the *People's Voice* under the control of Max Yergan, even as both leaders became the target of the FBI and HUAC.

   With so much at stake with his novel, Ralph tried to keep his views to himself. He kept his head low in January 1949 when twelve Communists, including Ben Davis, who had been chief of the Harlem bureau of the *Daily Worker,* went on trial in New York on the charge of conspiring to overthrow the U.S. government. In the *Chicago Defender* Langston Hughes called the trial "the most important thing happening in America today. . . . All poor people, Negroes, Jews, un-white Americans, un-rich Americans, are on trial." Ralph knew how much Hughes was risking in supporting the far left. His public readings were drying up. His publishers, too, had become wary of his work. *Reader's Digest* and *Life* vilified him. In April 1949, for example, Hughes was among those attacked by name in *Life* in reporting on an international conference organized by the leftist National Council of the Arts, Sciences, and Professions that met at the Waldorf-Astoria in Manhattan. According to a headline in *Life,* "Red Visitors Cause Rumpus: Dupes and Fellow Travelers Dress Up Communist Front."

   Ralph clearly could see other blacks were also paying for their radical associations past and present. Paul Robeson now saw his American career facing extinction. That summer, opponents violently disrupted his appearance before a leftist gathering at Peekskill, New York. Allegedly (Robeson denied it), he had insulted his country by telling a peace conference in Paris earlier that year that black Americans would never take up arms against the Soviet Union, where racial discrimination was illegal. A few months later, Jackie Robinson testified before Congress against Jim Crow but made headlines above all by briefly criticizing Robeson for his alleged statement. One of the first black officers commissioned in the middle of World War II (after much agitation), Robinson was sure that blacks would fight against the USSR if ordered to do so by their government.

   Years later, Ralph insisted that in 1949 he had seen no wisdom in Robeson's alleged position. "It got my back up," he would declare. "That's nonsense! Since slavery we've been fighting to get *in* the Army and then fighting in the Army for absolute freedom." Thus he glossed over, to some extent, the fact that during the war he had tacitly refused to serve in the Jim Crow army. In 1949, although he knew that he would never fight against the Soviet Union (just as he had not fought against Germany and Japan), he was also sure the mass of blacks would do so. And yet he was also now profoundly anti-Communist. The challenge for most readers of *Invisible Man* on this score is the extent to which they see the Brotherhood as the same as the Communist Party, despite the fact that Ralph would point out repeatedly that the Brotherhood is an invention. It is, indeed, no more the Communist Party than Invisible's college is Tuskegee Institute. Even so, it is the key metaphor Ellison uses to assail the totalitarian left in its dealings with blacks. The Brotherhood, which enters the text ominously, is never defended, much less rehabilitated. Ralph's animus as author against the group even led him to make one technical mistake: He does not give the Brotherhood a clear reason for deserting the black cause in Harlem.

Some friends, among them Ida Guggenheimer, would see the Brotherhood as virtually the same as the Communists and resent the narrative—and Ralph personally—as a result. ("My grandmother not only stuck by Communism," Martha Bernard remembered, "she stuck by Stalin! Even after he died and certain revelations came out about his crimes, she didn't run away from him. So she and Ralph had lots of things to argue about.") They would wonder why Ralph as author pressed his case against the Brotherhood so hard. Did Ralph intensify his denunciation of the Brotherhood out of fear of the political right, which had already begun to destroy careers in the name of freedom? The answer is almost certainly no. Ralph was not a coward. He created out of his core beliefs, and he did so with a personal integrity of which he was proud.

In other ways Ralph was still a political moderate. Only later would he openly and repeatedly laud the Constitution or speak of "sacred" American documents that form an ironclad contract between blacks and the nation as a whole. His commitment to making his epic novel out of a gossamer philosophy of indeterminacy and irresolution was more active in its effect on his patriotism in *Invisible Man* than was any residual leftist or black nationalist bias. This commitment to forms of existentialism prevented any but the most modest expression of optimism. Ralph's commitment came from two sources. First, he understood existentialism to be the core of modernity in his narrative (although he also knew that existentialism has an ancient pedigree). Second, he saw existentialism, properly identified in its Negro strain, to be uniquely authentic to the story of Invisible and the Negro. Unlike Kafka's or Sartre's existentialism, this Negro existentialism often flourished in the world attended by properties such as lyricism, folkloric grace, exuberance, and sensuality. Trueblood is the ideal here. Ralph alluded to these qualities in his review of Ottley's *Black Odyssey* when he spoke of black culture as stylish and musical, embodying the power of "a very advanced philosophy of human freedom."

And yet this Negro existentialism had a worrisome relationship to chaos. It did not lend itself easily to building social institutions that could form a reliable bulwark against chaos. Indeed, this form of existentialism, under the pressure exerted on the black mind by industrialism, the urban experience, and continuing injustice (as in Harlem), was a major purveyor of chaos. Here Ralph in his evolving *Invisible Man* and Richard Wright in *Black Boy* had much in common as they meditated on the place of blacks in the modern world. No wonder both men constructed allegorical stories (as Wright did in "The Man Who Lived Underground") that permitted no wholesome resolution of their heroes' dilemmas of identity and consciousness. Instead, they left these heroes isolated in a hole or a room, bound for an early death in Wright's case, in a limbo of uncertainty about the future in Ellison's. Near the end of his book, Invisible will speak with elation about life's infinite possibilities. However, by this time the reader is not sure whether this is a considered judgment or a manic episode.

In the fall of 1949 Ralph was still far from his conclusion, still writing and revising, cutting and pasting. He kept revising even as Fanny typed diligently in the evenings and on weekends to prepare a pristine version of what he was sure was the final draft for submission to Random House. To the very end, he searched for allusions and inferences that would make his novel resound with greatness. One plan called for the development of an *Othello*-like plotline, in which, presumably, a jealous black man assaults or kills his white lover or wife. Most likely Invisible would have been Ralph's Othello, although little in his character as it had emerged so far suggests anything approaching the nobility (despite his fatal flaw of jealousy) of the Moor of Venice. In fact, jealousy seems almost entirely inappropriate to a character as repressed as Invisible. Evidently Ralph saw the weakness of this plan and gave it up. "I have made further cuts," Ralph wrote Hyman in October, even as he described "the old monotony" of his work on the novel and its effect on his life, "and have decided to leave out the 'Othello' theme, which I'm now convinced would complicate thing[s] too much."

10

Finish Line

1950–1952

The end is where we start from.
T. S. ELIOT (1942)

While he drove himself to finish his novel, Ralph stuck as resolutely as he could to his determination not to turn away to other writing, not to short stories or reviews or essays that might bring in a few desirable dollars but also lead him astray. When he worked at his typewriter on something other than his novel, he mainly addressed some of its same urgent themes and questions. Late in 1949, for example, he explored certain intriguing new aspects of the race question in America when he published a brief but probing essay in a new magazine, *The Reporter.* In the long aftermath of World War II, the nation, or some significant part of it, seemed genuinely serious about abandoning Jim Crow. In "The Shadow and the Act" (the title comes from T. S. Eliot's long poem *Four Quartets*), Ralph scrutinized several startling recent Hollywood films about race. Three were *Pinky,* about a light-skinned black woman passing for white; *Home of the Brave,* about black soldiers and cowardice under fire, an association that had dogged them during both world wars; and *Intruder in the Dust,* a dramatization of Faulkner's novel in which a black man in the racist South refuses to conform to stereotypes. Like Jackie Robinson's breakthrough and the desegregation of the armed forces, this brace of movies strongly suggested that, at long last, white America had reached a moment of true enlightenment in its understanding of blacks and race relations in general.

Was this change genuine or a chimera? Ralph harbored no illusions about Hollywood's past treatment of blacks. In 1915, as he pointed out, D. W. Griffith's *The Birth of a Nation* had inspired the revival of the

Knights of the Ku Klux Klan and, in the process, also "forged the twin screen image of the Negro as bestial rapist and grinning, eye-rolling clown." The tradition of racial stereotyping of Negroes in Hollywood was born. For more than thirty years the Negro on the screen was mainly either criminal or clown. These new films promised a new day, but as Ralph pointed out, this progress was as yet only provisional. Exciting as they might be to some viewers, these movies were "not about Negroes at all; they are about what whites think and feel about Negroes." Only Faulkner's black hero Lucas Beauchamp corresponds to reality as folks in Harlem recognized reality. Apart from *Intruder in the Dust,* the only one of these films that could be shown in Harlem "without arousing unintended laughter," each movie showed black life drawn according to white fantasies—albeit liberal white fantasies—about race. When pale Pinky renounces her love for a white man who wants to marry her and settles instead among blacks in order to avoid "violating the race," the film thus asserts that in an interracial marriage both partners violate their integrity. To Ralph, their defiant marriage is in fact "the concrete expression of their integrity." Even in the film version of *Intruder in the Dust* (as opposed to the novel) Lucas Beauchamp functions mainly as the conscience-keeper of the whites around him. In the novel, in contrast, Lucas's emphasis is on saving his own life. No solution to the racial problem can come until white Americans keep their own conscience, take responsibility for their own actions, and accept the Negro not as a symbol of evil or a token of false redemption but as an essential part of humanity.

Despite his criticism of Hollywood's incoherence, the sudden appearance of this cluster of movies reassured Ralph that the novel on which he had been laboring so long was urgently needed. Paranoid or sane, its hero sought to delve as deeply as possible into the murky mysteries of race and identity in America. No aspect of the American dilemma seemed more important and challenging to Ralph than that involving the need for individuals to accept personal responsibility for their conscience and their actions. Certainly none seemed more germane to the resolution of his plot. In this situation, a compelling grasp of truth and responsibility sometimes eluded even great artists. Ralph's response in April to a Princeton undergraduate who asked for his opinion of Faulkner's racial attitudes suggests the complexity of the matter. As a Negro, Ralph replied, "I reject Faulkner, I distrust him." Nevertheless, in Faulkner's work as a whole "I catch glimpses of a rich and very warm human being and a very great literary artist." Faulkner "starts like all of us as the victim of his culture" but finally achieves a matchless level of literary artistry by rejecting cultural stereotypes and then smashing his way "through the illusion to the reality of life."

In the years immediately following World War II, Ralph was hardly alone in trying to take fiction written by blacks to new heights of excellence. Determined to write the Great Modern American Novel about race, which he may have believed only a black man could compose, he was constantly aware of his black rivals. In January 1949, when he evaluated J. Saunders Redding's novel *Stranger and Alone* for the *New York Times Book Review,* he outlined a plot that probably had startled him at first reading. Both Redding's novel and Ralph's were about a young man from the provinces (Lionel Trilling's formulation for key heroes of the nineteenth-century English novel). Like Invisible, Redding's hero is enrolled at an all-black college. He then teaches at a black college over which presides a black president who, remarkably like Ralph's Dr. Bledsoe, hoards power "through playing the obscene game of the collaborator." At this point, to Ralph's relief, the similarities begin to fade away. So did his fear that Redding's book might upstage his own as a work of art. *Stranger and Alone* has its moments of excellence. "For the first time in fiction," Ralph notes, it offers certain intimate details of middle-class black life, including details about its sexuality. Nevertheless, as an artist Redding had aimed too low. Creating a hero "too limited in personal appeal," he also wrote in a manner inadequate to his goals. He had relied on stale narrative devices and done little to explore the possible relationship between modern fiction, on the one hand, and myth and symbol, allegory and folklore, on the other. He seemed ignorant of thinkers such as Freud, Jung, Marx, and Thorstein Veblen. Somewhere along the way he had settled, said Ralph, like so many provincial Negro intellectuals, for mediocrity.

About this time, adding to the pressure on him, another black writer won an unparalleled honor. In the spring of 1950, Gwendolyn Brooks of Chicago captured that year's Pulitzer Prize for poetry with her collection *Annie Allen*. Like Ralph, Brooks had schooled herself as a modernist, one bent on fusing the ideas and aesthetic practices of white writers such as Eliot and Pound with the colorful reality of black America. White America had responded by awarding her its finest literary honor. The world was changing. Black Americans were on the move. Ralph needed to be part of it with *Invisible Man*.

. . .

With the steadily improving racial climate, Ralph and Fanny enjoyed Manhattan more than ever in the winter of 1950. Increasingly their acquaintances crossed the color line, cosmopolitan Jews making up most of their circle of white friends. For example, early in January they dined with Alfred Kazin and some members of his family. Two days later they spent Sunday with the Hymans at their new home in Westport, Connecticut. On January 16 they attended a formal dinner hosted by Ida Guggenheimer, then later that week dined casually with her at her apartment in the Ansonia. Ida remained central in Ralph's life. Although her physical state was deteriorating with age, Ida's bubbling, maternal affection for him, as well as her effervescence about books, music, art, and ideas, still made her dear to him. Three days later, in Harlem, they attended a rousing party at the home of Add Bates. At the home of the black psychologists Dr. Kenneth Clark and his wife, Dr. Mamie Clark, they met Lillian Smith, whose novel about lynching, *Strange Fruit,* was becoming a classic. Closing out the month, they joined a Saturday-evening dinner party hosted by Francis and Bea Steegmuller.

On February 4, the high-spirited Virgil Branam stopped by their apartment on West 149th Street after another one of his ocean voyages, bearing gifts from Formosa. A week later he came over to dine with them and tell ribald stories about his adventures in the East. At the armory on the East Side they took in the major annual dog show, always a favorite item on Ralph and Fanny's calendar. When the Steegmullers sailed off on yet another long visit to Europe, the Ellisons attended their farewell party. Drinking too much, Ralph suffered often from hangovers ("Ralph in Bed All Day—As Usual," Fanny noted once). He also succumbed to serious colds. After dining with Albert and Marisa Erskine later in the month, and visiting with Ida at least twice, he took to his bed again. Not until March 6 did he resume work on his novel. Three days later, with particularly keen interest, he and Fanny watched the hit movie version of Robert Penn Warren's Pulitzer Prize–winning novel of 1946, *All the King's Men.* Ralph applauded Warren's attempt in this novel to compose an epic, first-person narrative about politics, philosophy, love, slavery, corruption, the South, and America—all inspired in large part, according to Warren himself, by his meditations on Dante's *Inferno,* Machiavelli's *The Prince,* and the life of the assassinated Louisiana populist demagogue Huey Long. Thus Warren had tried to link the humdrum reality of the South to the grand tradition of Western writing. Ralph saw similarities between Warren's novelistic ambitions and his own. Although the narrator in *All the King's Men* is a well-connected young white Southerner, he and Invisible are alike in their almost overwhelming sense of disillusionment and despair.

As Ralph struggled with his novel, he remained alive to new hobbies and interests. Still in love with photography, around 1950 he developed another expensive passion that combined art and technology. "Just all of a sudden one day," Fanny recalled two years later, he decided to build a deluxe amplifier. Poring over diagrams and instructions in a magazine, Ralph painstakingly put together the machine. When it failed to work, he boldly telephoned the author of the article, whom he had never met. About eight years younger than Ralph, David Sarser was then living with his mother at 548 Riverside Drive, on the edge of Harlem. "I asked him at once," Sarser said about that first call, "did you test the amplifier on your bench before hooking it up? He told me he didn't have a bench. He'd built it more or less in his living room, which was remarkable. I asked him where he lived. It wasn't far away, so I suggested that he should come over. A while later, this colored boy shows up at the front door loaded down with pieces of equipment. We hit it off right away. Ralph was smart and determined and enthusiastic. My mother loved him, he had such fine manners."

David Sarser would remain a dear friend, just as Ralph's passion for excellent sound equipment lasted for the rest of his life. Growing up in Kansas City, Missouri, Sarser had come to New York at sixteen in 1937 to study the violin at the Juilliard School of Music. After the war, he joined the NBC Symphony Orchestra while also working as a sound engineer. His reputation among technicians began to soar. "It was while I was there at NBC," Sarser said, "that I developed the amplifier Ralph tried to build. I called it the Musician's Amplifier, and it became pretty popular." Fascinated by the technology, Ralph became for a while Sarser's unofficial assistant. Together they installed a complex sound system in the Riverdale, New York, home of Arturo Toscanini, the conductor of the NBC Symphony Orchestra. On his own, Ralph then began to build and repair systems for other people. "He was a good engineer," Sarser recalled. "He had an instinct for the work." Ralph also saw in these skills, as with his interest in photography, a possible source of income while he tried to establish himself as a successful writer.

Sarser would be behind landmark discoveries in the world of sound reproduction. Working for the Philips Electronics Company, he developed reliable techniques for the mass-scale duplication of tape recordings. He was also a sweet-natured friend to whom Ralph would turn for help with the various gadgets and machines that so fascinated him. Sarser would be his main guide through the unfolding and compelling world of modern electronics, including—in the distant future—the personal computer, which Ralph began to use almost as soon as it reached the market. "He was always for anything new," Sarser said, "and he loved gadgets and devices and machines. He would stop his writing in a second if there was something fresh to explore in science or technology." Ralph's love of technological precision would extend even to brewing coffee, in which he would be schooled by a friend on the Tuskegee faculty. Saul Bellow remembered that "he had been taught by a chemist to do it with ordinary laboratory paper filters and water at room temperature. The coffee then was heated in a bain-marie—a pot within a pot. Never allowed to boil." Using a thermometer at every brewing, he precisely kept the water between 195 and 200 degrees Fahrenheit.

Soon Ralph and Fanny had a sound system that was the envy and perhaps also the bane of many of their neighbors. He and Fanny liked to play their music very loudly (although the time would come when they complained bitterly about the assaulting noise of the boom box in their neighborhood). "When the radio isn't playing loud I feel compelled to go and turn it up," she confessed. Nearing home after work, she could "hear it on the outside sidewalk." According to her, no one complained. "Our neighbors are extraordinary. I can only assume that they must like the music as much as we do." The music was more often classical than jazz, the equipment as refined as it was powerful. "When over a set like this," Fanny trilled (she was writing to a European friend), "we hear the pure, sweet voice of [Lily] Pons or the rich warm and exciting voice of Jennie Tourel, the beauty shakes your soul."

As much as Ralph wanted to finish his novel, he felt compelled at times to try his hand at other writing. In May, after one of these deviations, he submitted a short story to *Charm: The Magazine for the Business Girl*. Its editor, June Merkin, had been a close friend of Stanley Hyman and Shirley Jackson since their student days at Syracuse University. Ralph knew that the women's magazines paid handsomely (Shirley had just signed a deal to write stories for *Good Housekeeping* on a retainer of $6,000 a year). Merkin rejected the story. After he failed to interest *The New Yorker* in it, he concluded that the short-story form was not for him. Unlike most of the major writers whom he admired, including Hemingway and Faulkner, Ralph would do little in this genre. His sole collection, *Flying Home,* would be published after his death.

In July, finally, he was sure that he was ready to submit his manuscript, admittedly with its final chapter still unwritten, to Random House. Fanny prepared the dense pile of typewritten pages for delivery to Albert Erskine. On August 1, 1950, she wrote to Bea Steegmuller that the novel, minus the missing chapter, had gone off—"and all week Ralph has been walking the floor. He's in an absolute state of suspension and I do hope that Albert completes the reading before both Ralph and I have breakdowns."

Whatever Ralph had meant a year earlier in writing to Stanley Hyman about working on the "political and final" section of his book, by July 1950 that last section, which begins just after Tod Clifton's tragic killing, clearly comprised what would become chapters 21 to 24. After arranging Clifton's funeral, Invisible delivers a eulogy that, not unlike Mark Antony's over the body of Julius Caesar, is an explosive mixture of grief, irony, and vengeance. "Forget him," Invisible advises the mourners about Clifton, invoking his name repeatedly. "When he was alive he was our hope, but why worry over a hope that's dead?" Rejecting the Brotherhood, Invisible now dissolves his identity, such as it was. Donning dark glasses and a rakish ghetto chapeau, he becomes a sinister but popular Harlem hustler named Rinehart, a pimpish ladies' man, a briber of police, a numbers runner, a dope dealer, and also the Reverend Bliss P. Rinehart, a "Spiritual Technologist." In short, Invisible is now chaos incarnate, a con man extraordinaire. Ralph's main debt here is probably to Melville and the eponymous hero of his bitter novel of 1857, *The Confidence-Man.* Although he found this work clearly inferior to *Moby-Dick,* he regarded it as "quite exciting. I'm sorry that I didn't read it before I started my book, for there are certain similarities between the main characters. . . . Melville's imagination was so rich that his character speaks even for that type of man of whom I write."

Invisible's entire moral and psychological being is now in danger of imploding. In a world irremediably corrupt and unjust to blacks, he is reduced to despair. "Outside the Brotherhood we were outside history," he muses, "but inside of it they didn't see us." Seeking inside information, Invisible now has his second sexual encounter with a white woman. The ditzy wife of a Brotherhood leader, she begs him to rape her, just as a black brute had ravished one of her friends. This woman, Sybil, confirms his worst fears about how even Brotherhood whites see black men. Amused but also appalled, Invisible only mocks her. Next, when a frenzy of looting breaks out in Harlem, he rushes uptown.

At this near-climactic point, Ralph's novel-in-progress stalled once again. Searching for inspiration—and still awaiting Erskine's response to the manuscript—he meditated upon the range of political, philosophical, and aesthetic options open to him. Little of this meditation could ignore the fact that he was a black man about to publish a political novel at a pivotal moment for politics, ideology, and race in America. Adding to his anxiety in the summer of 1950, the sudden outbreak of the Korean "conflict" shattered the brittle postwar peace. America was now at war with a Communist state. Communists and former Communists in America, already under intense scrutiny and suspicion, faced threatening questions about their loyalty.

Early in August, Erskine relieved the main tension of Ralph's life by stamping his imprimatur on "The Invisible Man," as the novel was then called. All his critical objections were minor. Ecstatically Ralph moved to close out the project. On August 16 he rented a hot, cramped basement room (not unlike Invisible's last known place of abode) from his landlord at 749 St. Nicholas Avenue and set to work. Four furious weeks later he was sure he was done. On September 25, Fanny wrote to a German friend, Elsa Brandel, that on the previous night she had read the last pages of the novel. "It is such a good book right to the very end," she marveled. "The long years of doing have been well spent and all the pain that went into it well compensated." (In fact, Ralph was still to write the epilogue.)

In the final chapter, Invisible comes face-to-face during the riot with the deranged black cultural nationalist Ras the Destroyer—Jamaican in his speech, like Marcus Garvey—who flings a spear at him. Flinging it back, he sees it rip through Ras's cheeks, locking his jaws shut. Invisible flees. Hoping to find sanctuary at Mary Rambo's house, he instead tumbles down an open manhole. Between dreaming and waking, while "great invisible waves of time flowed over me," he has a vision in which he is a prisoner of Brother Jack, Bledsoe, Norton, Ras, and other exploiters "who had run me." On the bank of a river near an iron bridge, cutting off his testicles, they toss them into the high arch of the bridge. Three times, a butterfly circles the two bloody blobs. Inexorably the bridge then moves off while Invisible cries out in a vain attempt to stop it. Awaking from this vision, Invisible knows now that he has no one, not even Mary Rambo, to whom he can turn for relief, much less redemption. He had been invisible to everyone, black or white. Pondering the meaning of it all, he decides to remain where he is: "Here, at least, I could try to think things out in peace, or, if not in peace, in quiet. I would take up residence underground." The last line of the novel, as Ralph conceived it before writing his epilogue, is: "The end was in the beginning." It paraphrases one that opens the "East Coker" section of Eliot's *Four Quartets*: "In my beginning is my end."

For the scenes of looting, Ralph drew on his memories of the Harlem riot of 1943, about which he had written for the *New York Post*. Although the section certainly does not surpass the tragiccomic brilliance of earlier scenes of social disorder, it vividly captures the collapse of Invisible's insupportable political world. A more serious deficiency may be the relatively vague reasons offered for Invisible's break with the Brotherhood. The Communist Party decided in the early 1940s to play down the racial question because it believed that the Nazi threat to destroy the Soviet Union called for a pragmatic approach to American race relations. Ralph had rejected this reasoning in part because he was a race man, but perhaps also because it threatened his future as a writer by making expendable his writing about race for radical publications. In *Invisible Man,* he gives the Brotherhood no plausible reason for deserting the cause of black rights in order to promote issues more national and international in nature. This failure leaves behind something of a dramatic gap. Brother Jack and his comrades are diminished, but so, to some extent, are Invisible and his story.

A crisis of spirit and technique haunts this last section. White members of the Brotherhood are cynical and racist. Loyal blacks are Uncle Toms. Black nationalists are grotesque. Many Harlem blacks are sociopaths. Technically, too, the novel falters. Most of the old symbols, such as Invisible's briefcase and its contents, have grown weaker by this point. The new ones, such as the iron bridge and the butterfly, are uninspired, as Invisible rants about himself and his fate. Ralph's recourse to italics, in the manner of Faulkner, seems rhetorical. Eventually it dawned on Ralph or Erskine, or both, that the book was not finished. Ralph needed to add something in order to reassert a final measure of control over his epic.

Most of 1951 passed uneventfully for Ralph and Fanny, except for the chronic gnawing at his stomach because of his fear of his book's possible failure. But starting in September, excitement about the novel began to build at Random House, where the decision was made to call the book

"Invisible Man" and not "The Invisible Man." An encouraging sign that month came when the English publisher Hamish Hamilton cabled Henry Volkening, inquiring about the English rights. When the agent wrote to Ralph about the matter early in October, Ralph seized the chance to break his ties to Volkening. Writing later to Ellen Wright, he told her about his calculated response: "After failing to hear from my former agent for about three years (doubtlessly he thought I'd never finish my book) I waited until I had turned in my ms. and then proceeded to free myself of Russell and Volkening. It was done painlessly and we parted pleasantly."

Though over the years Ralph had given Volkening very little to sell, Ralph clearly believed that his agent didn't deserve a cut of his royalties. For some reason he was unhappy about the way Volkening had treated him during his years in the wilderness. Volkening, unwilling to mud-wrestle over what might prove to be a pittance, settled with Random House, although he knew he could have prevailed over Ralph in almost any court of law. After a pleasant lunch with Albert Erskine, he let Ralph know that "we hereby relinquish all rights and interests" in the novel. It was "an amicable release."

Meanwhile, Ralph had finished his all-important epilogue. Promising to be "honest" with the reader, Invisible insists that he has learned to speak positively, optimistically, even when his guts tell him differently. He had suppressed those deeper feelings, although he knows (here Ralph drew on Spinoza) that sometimes "a man's feelings are more rational than his mind." Mired in psychological conflict, he found his hole a valuable mental asylum. He ponders the meaning of it all. Had he acted correctly in his recent dealing with the world? He recalls his grandfather's deathbed advice about whites. "I want you to overcome 'em with yeses," the old man tells Invisible's father, "undermine 'em with grins, agree 'em to death and destruction, let 'em swaller you till they vomit or bust wide open." Gamely, Invisible tries to puzzle out the key mysteries inherent in the conflict between the noble founding principles of the nation and the putrid practices of racism. What had his grandfather seen as the proper way to arbitrate between these extremes? "Did he mean 'yes' because he knew that the principle was greater than the men?" But weren't blacks a part of white culture as well as apart from it? And vice versa?

In an act of will and faith, Invisible asserts in the end his umbilical connection to the world about him. At long last, "my world has become one of infinite possibilities." These possibilities are structured by social reality, not by chaos or excesses of the imagination. Chaos is the abomination of the idea of freedom. "That too I've learned in the cellar," he says, "and not by deadening my sense of perception; I'm invisible, not blind." Echoing Ralph Waldo Emerson, and perhaps Melville, Invisible argues for seeing the social world (America) in natural divisions to be honored and embraced. "Whence all this passion toward conformity anyway?" Invisible asks rhetorically. "Diversity is the word. Let man keep his many parts and you'll have no tyrant states. . . . America is woven of many strands; I would recognize them and let it so remain. . . . Our fate is to become one, and yet many—This is not prophecy, but description." Invisible's overwhelming desire is to see America, history, and himself honestly and whole, not through political slogans and fantasies. The horrors of slavery and Jim Crow ("Bad Air"), like the human condition itself, had produced both suffering and the magical art of jazz as embodied in Louis Armstrong. "Old Bad Air is still around with his music and his dancing and his diversity, and I'll be up and around with mine."

To forgive, Invisible learns, may be divine; but it is also necessary. He recalls a chance encounter in New York with Mr. Norton, the trustee who had precipitated Invisible's disaster early in the novel. Now Norton doesn't even recognize him. Although Norton had set in motion Invisible's quest, he is unaware of it. The lesson here is about time as opiate, alembic, therapy, absolution. Accepting this lesson, Invisible is now ready to return to the world. He also knows now the absolute value of love and also of a belief in his own black humanity. His humble grandfather, he now sees, never doubted his own humanity. About to leave his hole ("I'm coming out, no less invisible without it, but coming out nevertheless"), he has one last thought about himself, his somewhat manic philosophizing (his "buggy jiving") in the epilogue, and the reader. The thought that "frightens" him is this one: "Who knows but that, on the lower frequencies, I speak for you?" Who knows for a fact that all people aren't invisible to one another, plagued by conflict between head and heart, mind and body, and incapable of seeing the humanity in others? Who knows but that each and every one of us needs a spell of solitary confinement to make us understand ourselves and other human beings?

With Invisible's question, the novel ends. (Kenneth Burke cleverly pointed out, to Ralph's surprise, that the first word of his novel is "I" and the last is "you.") The ending rests on a fusion of aesthetic and ethical commitments: aesthetic, in that Ralph understood the value of the optimistic if also ominous ending over the arid and despairing; ethical, because although spirituality as a topic is alien to *Invisible Man*, he finally could not ignore or resist the moral imperatives of the secular American literary tradition descended, ironically, from the Golden Day of New England transcendentalism. For all its shaggy questioning, the epilogue seals the identity of *Invisible Man* by at last grounding Ralph, after his years of dialectical wandering, in this noble lineage.

He waited impatiently for his galleys to arrive. At some point early in November, anxious and restless, he drove to Westport, Connecticut, at Stanley's request, to stay at the Hymans', where Shirley Jackson was massively pregnant with her fourth child. With Stanley unable to drive, Ralph arrived in an aged station wagon he had recently bought, ready when the time came to ferry Shirley to the hospital. After some days, tired of waiting, the Hymans and Ralph drove into New York to attend a party. Speaking to Judy Oppenheimer, Jackson's biographer, Ralph recalled that afterward "we all had enough to drink, but only I was capable of driving home." Miles from home, he ran out of gas. Ralph was sitting helplessly in the dark when deliverance came in an almost surreal fashion. A car filled with Hispanics pulled up. None could speak English, and Ralph spoke no Spanish. Nevertheless, they "got out, siphoned a couple of gallons from their car into mine, without exchanging a word, got back into their car, and shot off."

Another week, then another, passed. "The damn baby wouldn't show up," Ralph recalled to Oppenheimer. Finally, after a huge dose of castor oil prescribed by her doctor failed to move Shirley, she decided to go to the hospital anyway. While she awaited contractions, Stanley and Ralph camped out in her room, drinking whiskey and munching from a big box of maple cream candy. The next morning, November 21, 1951, Barry Edgar Hyman was born. When the Hymans asked Ralph and Fanny to be his godparents, they agreed at once. On the same blessed day, the galleys of *Invisible Man* arrived.

With the official publication date set for April 14, 1952, the first copy of *Invisible Man* appeared around the middle of March. Ralph had dedicated the book to Ida Guggenheimer, passing over both his wife and the memory of his dead mother. Fanny had been present at the conception of the novel. Her fresh presence in Ralph's life, their blossoming love for each other, had helped to inspire it. Her sacrifices over the years had been much greater than Ida's. One can only speculate why he ignored her. Whatever Fanny's feelings about it, she buried them.

Ironically, far from consolidating his relationship with Ida, *Invisible*

Man drove her away. Most likely the anti-Communism of the book appalled her. By the end of the year, Ralph could not count on her for money. "I no longer receive that nice bit of patronage that buoyed us up for so long," he informed Hyman the following January.

Following custom, Random House sent off copies not only to the various reviewing journals but also to a long list of persons chosen by Ralph as he acknowledged debts, precious connections, and perhaps now and then special rivalries. Books went to his brother, Herbert, as well as to Richard Wright and Langston Hughes; to the Steegmullers, the Murrays, Chester Himes, and Horace Cayton; to the former Tuskegee librarian Walter B. Williams, now estranged from Ralph; and to Ralph's most important professor of English at Tuskegee, Morteza Drexel Sprague.

The initial responses, published and private, to *Invisible Man* were like the first tremors of a major earthquake. This was especially true once *Partisan Review* published the prologue (as "Invisible Man: Prologue to a Novel") in its January–February issue. In February, the important previewing journal *Virginia Kirkus Bulletin* reported "an extremely powerful story" that had "implications far beyond the obvious racial parallel." "You've created a work of such stature," one man (a friend of Frank Taylor) wrote from Los Angeles, "that I sincerely doubt whether its height and value and genius will be either understood or appreciated in our generation." From Tuskegee, Mort Sprague sent simpler but no less welcome words of blessing about the book: "I think it beautifully conceived and presented." Now Ralph and Fanny had reason to believe that *Invisible Man* might realize a success grander than almost anything that they had imagined.

"We feel these days," Fanny wrote portentously to Langston on April 2, "as if we are about to be catapulted into something unknown—of which we are both hopeful and afraid." Praising him for his generosity over "the six agonizing and beautiful years" of labor, she ended by betraying her fear that success might open a divide between the Ellisons and some of their friends. "Now on the threshold of this new and looming thing which awaits," she ventured, "(whether only in our minds or really outside our closed door) we want and beg you to share with us the good parts of it and to never forget that your friendship has, does, and will in the future always mean much and be necessary to us." Fanny signed the letter firmly and clearly. Much less sentimental, Ralph added his name but in an almost illegible scrawl. "You must gonna be great," Hughes teased Ralph, "because I cannot read your name."

The first review in print, by Harvey Curtiss Webster in the *Saturday Review of Literature,* swept them away. From the start of *Invisible Man,* Webster wrote, "you are carried forward by an intensity rare in the fiction of any time or place." The reader becomes "Mr. Ellison's protagonist, a dark Gulliver" whose progress is as unreal "as a surrealistic painting, as believable as Raskolnikov's through crime and punishment." With pride and joy, Fanny hurried to show the piece to her colleagues at work, who, like many other people, had only a vague sense of what use her husband had been making of his freedom. On April 13, Random House launched *Invisible Man* with a party at the Four Seasons Bookshop in Manhattan. A large, buzzing crowd turned up following an almost full-page story in *Time* magazine hailing this "remarkable first novel" by a Negro who was "an unusual writer by any standard." At least two writers there would become among Ralph's closest friends—Robert Penn Warren, already famous, and the young Canadian-born Jewish writer Saul Bellow, who had published two respected novels, *Dangling Man* and *The Victim.*

Soon praise rained down on Ralph almost every day from newspapers and magazines. To his disappointment, a few reviewers tried to keep *Invisible Man* shackled to the term "Negro literature." In the daily *New York Times,* for example, Orville Prescott called *Invisible Man* "a sensational and feverishly emotional book," one that would "shock and sicken" some readers, but also "the most impressive work of fiction by an American Negro which I have ever read." Lewis Gannett in the *New York Herald Tribune* found the opening and closing chapters (probably the prologue and epilogue) "rather murky"; nevertheless, he called *Invisible Man* "perhaps the most distinguished Negro novel to appear since Richard Wright's 'Native Son.' " But many notices judged the novel against all comers. The *Herald Tribune Book Review* dubbed Invisible "the young dark Ulysses" in reporting that "intimations of the sculptural and musical artist are prevalent in the symmetrical and symphonic prose." Perhaps the single most glorious salvo establishing the novel as an event transcending black writing came in the *New York Times Book Review.* "The geography of hell is still in the process of being mapped," Wright Morris wrote, and now *Invisible Man* "belongs on the shelf with the classical efforts man has made to chart the river Lethe from its mouth to its source."

Although they expressed some canny reservations, a number of other brilliant young writers applauded the novel—R. W. B. Lewis in the *Hudson Review;* the poet Delmore Schwartz in *Partisan Review;* Bellow in *Commentary;* the cultural critic Irving Howe in *The Nation.* Lewis declared

Invisible Man the most impressive work of fiction since Faulkner's *Light in August* in 1932. To Bellow, who saw Ralph's wish to transcend his Negro identity as akin to his own urge to surpass the fact of his Jewish upbringing, the book had faults, "but it is an immensely moving novel," one marked by "greatness." A dedicated socialist, Howe found the entire Brotherhood element unconvincing. He also aggressively defended the idea of bracketing the book racially: "Of course 'Invisible Man' is a Negro novel—what white man could ever have written it?" All the same, this fact didn't limit Ellison's achievement. He possessed "an abundance of that primary talent without which neither craft nor intelligence can save a novelist; he is richly, wildly inventive; his scenes rise and dip with tension; his people bleed, his language stings. No other writer has captured so much of the confusion and agony, the hidden gloom and surface gaiety of Negro life."

Only one New York daily newspaper loathed and also grossly misrepresented the novel. "For the most part brilliantly written and deeply sincere," the *World-Telegram* judged, "it is, at the same time, bitter, violent, and unbalanced." In *Invisible Man,* "savage joy" is expressed "in scene after scene when a white man 'gets his' with knife, fist or bullet." Ellison's work was "virtually a battle-call to civil war." And in Boston, the strictures of piety compelled the *Christian Science Monitor* to take no notice of the book, in the belief (as it stated later when it won an important prize) that it was obscene. (The Republic of Ireland added *Invisible Man* to its long list of books banned for indecency or obscenity.)

Delighted by the vast majority of the responses, Ralph tried to strike a modest pose. "I am stewing in the reviews," he wrote to his boyhood friend Harold Calicutt; "some, incidentally, are pretty good." Pleasantly surprising the Ellisons, the Southern press, white and black alike, was fair and respectful. It was "a new and startling revelation for us," Fanny wrote to a friend. The *Washington Post,* noting "the scornful power" of prose that was written "at a white heat" but which the author manipulates "like a veteran," saluted "a memorable performance. Mark the name well: you will hear of Ralph Ellison again." The *Nashville Tennessean* deemed *Invisible Man* "a very formidable" first novel. Facing up to the issue of white racism, the *Charleston* (South Carolina) *Gazette* noted that the book made "extremely unpleasant reading" but that it "should arouse a strong feeling of guilt in the hearts of those who are responsible for the conditions he describes, if they can only be persuaded to read it."

If most white reviewers liked the book, most black reviewers did not. (Fortunately for Ralph, virtually every major newspaper and journal used white reviewers only.) Twice chastised publicly by Ralph for the quality of his writing, J. Saunders Redding now exacted his revenge. "The book's fault is that a writer of power has put all his power into describing the diurnal life of gnats," he said of *Invisible Man*. "It is as if a steam shovel were used to dig a compost heap for a kitchen garden." The gossipy *Jet* magazine hailed the arrival of "a bright and shining new Negro literary star" but also saw Ralph falling into "every possible stereotype in terms of story and characters." In the radical *Masses & Mainstream* (where the dying *New Masses* had been interred), Lloyd Brown saw Ralph "conforming exactly to the formula for literary success in today's market . . . despite the murkiness of his avant-garde symbolism." This formula called for sadism, sex, and shock in support of "the central design" of modern American literature, "anti-communism." Ridiculing Ralph for worshipping T. S. Eliot and other "wailing eunuchs of decay," Brown mourned that "the first-born of a talented young Negro writer" should enter the world "with no more life than its maggots." In the *Daily Worker,* under the headline "Ralph Ellison Shows Snobbery, Contempt for Negro People," his old friend Abner Berry assured readers that "Ellison's work manipulates his nameless hero for 439 pages through a maze of corruption, brutality, anti-communism slanders, sex perversion and the sundry inhumanities upon which a dying system feeds." Elsewhere the novelist John Oliver Killens was equally blunt: "The Negro people need Ellison's *Invisible Man* like we need a hole in the head or a stab in the back. It is a vicious distortion of Negro life."

Writing the following year to Richard Wright, Ralph said that such attacks by the Party had "only made members desire to read the book." He also knew that these attacks made him exempt from being called a Communist sympathizer, much less a Communist. Nevertheless, the attacks stung him. His indignation showed to some extent in his response to his main defender in print among black writers, Langston Hughes. From the start, Ralph acknowledged, Hughes publicized the novel in his weekly column in the *Chicago Defender* "and has used every opportunity to advance it." But Ralph now had no use for Langston's adoptive "aunt" Toy Harper, who had fed and sheltered Ralph at times during his early years in New York. She had invited him over, he claimed, "so that she can fight with me about the book but I have so little patience with that type of foolishness that I dare not go. I would crush her." In some respects, his attitude to Toy was a token of his increasingly hostile attitude to blacks who, questioning the quality of his art, seemed bent on sabotaging his hard-won success. Many of them seemed to him ill-equipped by education, and perhaps intelligence and sensitivity, to appreciate the complex brilliance of his book. Perhaps he also saw sheer envy in some of the attacks on him.

By April 30, Random House had sold just over six thousand copies. On May 11 *Invisible Man* appeared in tenth place on the *New York Times Book Review* best-seller list. The following week it rose to number nine, before dropping steadily over the next few weeks. On June 22, it rallied to number eight but soon fell off the charts for good. The novel was only a modest best seller. Only about eight thousand copies were sold in the six-month period starting on June 1. (After its publication the Book-of-the-Month Club offered Ralph's novel to its subscribers as one among many choices.) The year's best-selling novel, Thomas Costain's religious epic *The Silver Chalice,* sold about 250,000 copies. In May 1952, after deducting its advance payments, Random House sent Ralph a check for $1,537, which included a Signet paperback reprint advance payment of $1,500. In November, his Random House check came to $4,557.

Invisible Man remained a critical success. Admiring letters arrived from fellow writers Maxwell Geismar and Kenneth Rexroth. A Hebrew chaplain at a state prison in Comstock wrote Ralph that his office "has literally been stormed" by men begging him to acquire a copy of the book. (Ralph mailed the rabbi a copy.) In the early fall, young James Baldwin, as yet without a published novel, stopped by to pay his respects, and also to take Ralph's measure. However, one response to *Invisible Man* especially disappointed Ralph. On May 27, soon after receiving the book, Wright wrote to thank Ralph for the gift. Not until September or October, though, did he "finally get around to reading your powerful novel." (He had been toiling on *The Outsider,* which was due out the following year as his first published novel since *Native Son* in 1940.) Wright "liked" *Invisible Man,* he assured Ralph; it was "by far the best prose you've done." Only toward the end of his letter did he offer a sterling compliment: "You've entered the ranks of literature with your book, and there is no doubt about it." Ralph allowed almost three months to drift by before he answered Wright.

Interviews on two nationally broadcast radio shows drew letters from friends and admirers far away. The first, on *The Readers' Almanac* on WNYC, came near the end of April; the other, *The World in Books* on WEVD, was heard in early May. In response he was modest yet assertive,

humble yet urbane, as if the hubbub was pleasant but really a distraction. Early in May the *New York Times* sent a man to interview him for a
story. "His face is firm and sensitive and remarkably handsome," Harvey
Breit reported. "He's a standout in any company. The name is Ralph Ellison, heard here and there and one hopes everywhere these days." According to a gossip column, Ralph was one of the celebrities expected at a
cocktail party on May 23 at the Hotel Theresa in Harlem to promote a
play sponsored by Philip Morris, the tobacco company. The American
Library Association invited him to be a panelist on book censorship and
race relations at its annual convention at the Waldorf-Astoria. Late in
August, *Life* published "A Man Become Invisible," a story about Ralph
and his novel, with photographs by his friend Gordon Parks. (As a *Life*
staff member, Parks probably arranged this coup.)

Ralph cherished the feeling of vindication. "It has been very amusing,"
he wrote to Wright, "to watch the reactions of some of the people who
assumed I was just kidding about writing. Some can't quite forgive me for
having done a good book and others feel that I have perpetrated a hoax."
At Random House, Bennett Cerf and other top officials treated him like a
star, because few of its books had ever earned finer reviews. Someone at
the *Saturday Review of Literature* offered him the use of her apartment to
write while she went off to Europe. A white woman Ralph and Fanny
barely knew shocked them with a large check to help them enjoy Ralph's
"very real success with less harassment for a few days anyway." The
upsurge in celebrity had indeed opened holes in their pockets as they
tried to dress and act the glamorous parts that fate had suddenly assigned
them.

Except for a few days on the Long Island shore at a cottage co-rented
with some of Fanny's colleagues, the summer passed without a vacation.
They were saving money to make a down payment on a townhouse, a
major goal after six uncomfortable years at 749 St. Nicholas Avenue.
Finally, seizing a rare opportunity, they signed a contract to rent a small
apartment at 730 Riverside Drive in Manhattan, at the corner of West
150th Street. This was a giant step up. For one thing, although they would
move only a few blocks, they would no longer be in Harlem. In this
respect they were like Invisible at the end of the novel. Although countless critics have placed his room or hole in Harlem, he lives on the white
side of its border. "The joke, of course," he writes about his theft of electricity from Monopolated Light & Power, for which he knows black
Harlem will be blamed, "is that I don't live in Harlem but in a border
area."

Ralph and Fanny were lucky to find this vacancy. Apartments on Riverside Drive facing the long, green ribbon of Riverside Park and the waters of the Hudson River were highly desirable. From West 72nd Street all the way north past 157th Street, middle-class whites had resolutely kept blacks out of virtually every apartment on the river. However, with the colored population of uptown Manhattan swollen by migration from the Spanish-speaking Caribbean in particular, "apartment houses on Riverside Drive are fast clearing now," Fanny wrote to a friend abroad about the phenomenon that would be known as "white flight." Rents shot up and services slumped when whites fled—"but we've always wanted to live on the Drive; in fact, it's the only New York location which would half-way compensate having to live in New York proper."

Ralph and Fanny were the first blacks to move into any one of the sixty-three units at the Beaumont, an eleven-story apartment house designed in 1912 by the prominent architectural firm Blum & Blum. They were the first beneficiaries of the purchase of the building by Eugene Ramsey, a black West Indian who had used white lawyers to slip past the informal exclusionary racial covenants that guarded such buildings. Ralph and Fanny moved into a three-room apartment (7B) on the seventh floor, cozy but without a river view. In fact, they looked out on a brick wall. Perhaps they had no choice among the available apartments; perhaps they were being frugal. (Although they hoped to switch soon to a river-view unit, for many years Ramsey would refuse to allow tenants to change apartments.) Some of their white neighbors were frosty, but Jim and Frances Curry next door welcomed them warmly. Writing from Vermont, Stanley Edgar Hyman mocked Ralph. "I always thought of Riverside Drive as strictly Jewish middle-class," he teased, "but I suppose that's what you are, really." (Hyman was glad to see his friend flourishing at last. In November he accepted a sheepskin coat cast off by Ralph. The next month, after alerting Ralph that "Brother Wolf is at the door," he secured from his friend a loan of $300.)

With cash in the bank, Ralph and Fanny picked up various items they had long needed or coveted. Ralph paid $257 for a new electric typewriter; $250 for new bookshelves to accommodate his growing library; $1,400 for a new eight-cylinder Chrysler sedan. They donated small amounts of money to various charities, as they would do faithfully for the rest of their lives. They gave $25 to the NAACP Legal Defense Fund (the spearhead of the attack on Jim Crow through the courts); $10 to the American Red Cross; $5 to the National Kids Day Foundation; and half of that amount to an organization for disabled veterans.

.   .   .

Slowly the balloon of publicity deflated. By Thanksgiving, the formal honoring of *Invisible Man* and its author was virtually over except for small gestures that Ralph nevertheless appreciated. The *Chicago Defender* named him to its honor roll of outstanding blacks of 1952. Invited to join the governing board of the newly formed Institute for Jazz Studies, led by Marshall Stearns, a jazz expert and professor of medieval literature at Hunter College in Manhattan, he quickly agreed to do so. Where he had once been mainly a curiosity, an implausibly brown face amid a sea of whites, he was an honored guest at the Institute for Advanced Study in Princeton, New Jersey, after the director of the Christian Gauss Seminars in Criticism personally invited him to hear Edmund Wilson deliver a series of talks on the literature of the Civil War. (This material would form the core of Wilson's acclaimed collection *Patriotic Gore.*)

The honors were dwindling in number, but Ralph had reason to believe that he had arrived. Because of the quality of his book and the admiring response to it, he was now a respected presence on the New York literary scene. He understood and appreciated the significance of his rise. Sixteen years after arriving in New York as a disillusioned, humiliated, and fairly ignorant youth from Oklahoma City and Tuskegee, Alabama, he was now respected by some of the finest writers in America. The foundation of his career was set, and on the granite bedrock of Manhattan. He had bested all of his black rivals, even Richard Wright. In the course of reviewing *Invisible Man,* learned experts had linked his name affirmatively to Defoe, Molière, Dostoyevsky, Gogol, T. S. Eliot, Faulkner, Céline, and Thomas Wolfe.

And yet Ralph was in no sense complacent about his success. In fact, his honors both relieved and exacerbated certain tensions with which he had lived for much of his adult life. This nagging discomfort was in part a function of the high psychological price he had paid for his success, especially the distance he had put between himself and his brother and between himself and his memory of his father and mother (the dedication of his novel was a token of that distance). The challenge of appeasing or evading those ghosts would haunt him for the rest of his life.

Almost certainly he knew that. Already he had started work on "a novel which demands that I go West," as he informed Richard Wright early in the following year. Moreover, he was well aware of the perils he faced in reentering "the Territory." Writing to Ellen Wright just before *Invisible Man* appeared, he had mentioned almost whimsically a sudden feeling of wanderlust. Perhaps he and Fanny would sail away to Europe. Perhaps they would visit Paris. Now, however, a force began to draw him somewhere else. He wanted, or needed, to head west. "Now my instincts tell me to go in the other direction," he said, "toward Oklahoma, where lies my destructive element, that substance I'm told the artist must dunk himself in. Don't know, but I plan to give it a try."

11

Annus Mirabilis

1953

Lightning struck me, leaving me standing amazed.
RALPH ELLISON (1953)

One cold morning early in January 1953, Ralph was at home, alone. Taking a break from writing, a pair of pliers in his hand, he was tinkering with the thicket of wires leading to and from his tuner, amplifier, turntable, speakers, and assorted other high-fidelity sound equipment when the telephone rang. After he spoke, a woman's voice responded. "Congratulations," she said. Then the line went dead.

Puzzled, Ralph replaced the handset. Instinctively he knew the call had something to do with *Invisible Man.* In London the previous week, Victor Gollancz had launched the British edition with an advertisement that cited Stephen Spender's opinion that the novel was "a work of near-genius." The book was slowly making its mark in Europe—the Norwegian rights sold that summer. On January 2, the American branch of the professional organization PEN (Poets, Essayists, and Novelists) had invited him to become a member. Was the woman a crank? "I spent the next 24 hours wondering, congratulations for what?" he wrote.

The next morning brought the answer, this time in a telephone call from his editor, Albert Erskine. "This is absolutely on the q.t.," he said to Ralph. "You mustn't tell a soul 'til it's announced, but you've won the National Book Award." Five judges had just decided—four votes to one—that *Invisible Man* was the outstanding American novel of 1952. Competing against the veterans Hemingway (*The Old Man and the Sea*) and Steinbeck (*East of Eden*), he had beaten them. "I thought something was wrong," he admitted later. "Hemingway, Steinbeck—they were the real writers. I was just an upstart."

In 1953, the National Book Award possessed an unmatched aura of youthful vitality and prestige among American literary prizes. As Bennett Cerf put it, with the exception of the Nobel Prize and "possibly the languishing Pulitzer nominations," the National Book Award was more noteworthy than "all the other literary contests and medal bestowals put together." In 1950, when Eleanor Roosevelt had presided at the Waldorf-Astoria over about a hundred authors and a thousand other guests at the first awards ceremony, a Nashville newspaper had called it "just about the biggest literary event since Dickens visited America." In Ralph's case, a poll of four thousand librarians, editors, and booksellers resulted in the nomination of fifty-nine candidates in the field of fiction, from which the selection committee had chosen the winner. The committee comprised one university professor, Howard Mumford Jones of Harvard; one editor, Martha Foley of Houghton Mifflin; and three young writers—Alfred Kazin, Saul Bellow, and Irving Howe. The one dissenting vote was Jones's for *The Old Man and the Sea*.

Ralph was lucky in having three young, progressive Jewish writers as a majority on the panel. Their presence spoke to the emergence of a dynamic Jewish-American school of literature after World War II, a school that also included Bernard Malamud, Norman Mailer, Delmore Schwartz, Allen Ginsberg, and Karl Shapiro. Moreover, Ralph counted Kazin and Bellow among his friends; at least once he and Fanny had dined with the Kazins and with the Bellows. As Bellow shed the dour style of his early work, which emphasized the Jew as a suffering human being, and embraced a more exuberant definition of American ethnicity, Ralph raved about him as a writer. "Watch out for Bellow's novel," he advised Wright about *The Adventures of Augie March*, which appeared later that year—and also won the National Book Award for fiction; "it is the first real novel by an American Jew, full of variety, sharp characterization and sheer magical prose." He and Bellow met regularly after the Christian Gauss Seminars delivered by Edmund Wilson in Princeton, where Bellow was living while he taught for a short while at the university. Ralph admired Kazin's gift of eloquence as a literary and social critic whose book *On Native Grounds* had reassessed American literature in vigorous fashion. As an ethnic artist himself, but one also cosmopolitan and patriotic, Ralph had made it easy for Bellow, Howe, and Kazin to vote for him and *Invisible Man* in 1953 because of their common interests and values. "With a positive exuberance of narrative gifts," the committee said of Ralph, "he has broken away from the conventions and the patterns of the tight, 'well made' novel. Mr. Ellison has had the courage to take many literary risks, and he has succeeded with them. His book is a humane work of imaginative power and originality of scene."

In something of a daze, Ralph and Fanny prepared as best they could for the ceremony only a few days away, as well as for the deluge of publicity predicted by Random House. Fanny needed a chic new outfit, Ralph his sharpest suit and, most important of all, a five-minute acceptance speech. After several drafts—"it took me five days to write it"—he was finished, if not entirely satisfied. On Monday, January 26, escorted by an official of the NBA, Ralph visited radio station WOR to make a sound recording of his speech. The next day, his ordeal began shortly after noon when he posed for photographs and then filmed an interview for use the following morning on the *Today* show on NBC. Just after three o'clock he and Fanny entered the Century Room at the Commodore Hotel. Again he posed for photographs and answered questions from critics and reporters. At last, shortly after five o'clock, the fourth annual National Book Awards ceremony began when Frederick Lewis Allen, the editor of *Harper's Magazine,* stepped to the microphone as master of ceremonies.

Although three Fifth Avenue bookstores had broken the news embargo earlier that day by displaying the winning books in their windows, a murmur of surprise rippled through the room when Allen announced that the gold plaque in fiction would go to Ralph Ellison. The two other winners spoke before Ralph. The poet Archibald MacLeish, who had flown in from the West Indies, reflected informally on the relationship between books and civilization. The historian Bernard DeVoto, the winner in nonfiction, spoke almost as casually about modesty and the writer's art. When Ralph's turn came, it was clear at once that he—one of only two or three blacks in the room—took the occasion far more seriously than did either MacLeish or DeVoto. As the columnist Mary McGrory noted in the *Washington Star,* his speech (almost as long as the previous two combined) was easily "the most literary."

Striving to avoid his tendency to stammer under pressure, Ralph stuck to his prepared text. To him, "the chief significance of *Invisible Man*" as fiction was "its experimental attitude and its attempt to return to the mood of personal moral responsibility for democracy which typified the best of our nineteenth-century fiction." The American novel was in a state of crisis. Our novelists—he was no outsider—having lost their bearings, he had won the award "by default, as it were." On the one hand, American reality was too volatile for the gleaming polish of a typical Henry

James novel. "Hardboiled" fiction, on the other hand, which had been all the rage in the 1930s, was dedicated to "physical violence, social cynicism, and understatement," and its language was "embarrassingly austere." The American novelist needed "to burst such neatly understated, dead-certain, and to an extent now defeated forms of the novel, asunder." The American novelist had "to conceive of a novel unburdened by the narrow naturalism" that had led to "the final and unrelieved despair" which marked so much contemporary fiction, and also to forge a uniquely American prose that, "leaving sociology and case histories to the scientists, can arrive at the truth about the human condition, here and now, with all the bright magic of the fairy tale."

The finest writers of the nineteenth century, Ralph argued, had produced works that were "imaginative projections of the conflicts within the human heart which arose when the sacred principles of the Constitution and the Bill of Rights clashed with the practical exigencies of human greed and fear, hate, and love." The will "to dominate reality as well as the laws of artistic form" had been missing from recent fiction. Invoking the classical figure of Proteus, Ralph proposed that the god stood for America and for "our sins against those principles we all hold sacred. The way home we seek is that condition of man's being at home in the world, which is called love, and which we term democracy." For all of America's variety, "we are yet one." By writing novels worthy of that truth, he said, we achieve our potential and also "anticipate the resolution of those world problems of humanity which for a moment seem to those who are in awe of statistics, completely insoluble."

Ralph's lofty tone, his references to the "sacred" in American culture, probably caught much of the audience off-guard. Next came an odd oration by the somewhat eccentric U.S. Supreme Court Justice William O. Douglas that cleared the air of any residue of solemnity before Ralph and the other winners plunged into the reception. Pushing his way slowly toward the bar, Ralph shook hands with such prominent figures as William Carlos Williams, Eudora Welty, Langston Hughes, Brendan Gill, Elizabeth Bowen, and Rachel Carson. Undoubtedly, Ralph was most impressed when he faced a handsome little man in a tattersall vest who spoke with a Mississippi drawl when he spoke at all. "A small graying man, quietly courteous but stubbornly unaddicted to small talk" (as Mary McGrory described him), William Faulkner, the Nobel Prize–winner for literature in 1949 and a fellow Random House author edited by Albert Erskine, fielded a compliment from Ralph about seeing lots of Faulkner's children roaming the ballroom. Faulkner murmured an inaudible reply, then turned blankly to endure yet another question.

Eventually Ralph and Fanny slipped away to a celebratory dinner in their honor at the Fifth Avenue home of Donald Klopfer, the co-founder with Bennett Cerf of Random House. It was almost midnight when they finally made their way uptown to their apartment, tired but happy and proud following the most glamorous day of their lives.

The next day was almost as busy. At 9:30 a.m. he was at the NBC studios at 30 Rockefeller Plaza for a live radio interview. At one o'clock he appeared on Mary Margaret McBride's nationally syndicated interview radio show on WJZ, and at 5:30 p.m. Bill Leonard interviewed him on CBS. Following the program, Ralph and Fanny were the center of attention at cocktails and another dinner party, given by Nan and Frank Taylor, who toasted Ralph and his signal triumph over all doubters. Among the other guests was Robert Penn Warren, yet another major author edited by Albert Erskine. Warren, who would play a major role in Ralph's future, invited him on the spot to join him as a scriptwriter on a proposed television project on American history. Although Ralph did not commit himself to the project, he was probably moved that the Kentucky-born Warren, once a member of the reactionary Fugitive movement of intellectuals and artists defending the South, should have greeted him so warmly. Still a lover of the South but now a dedicated liberal, "Red" Warren, for his part, was pleased by the prospect of getting to know a black writer of Ralph's rare caliber. "I look back frequently on our meeting," he wrote Ralph some time later. He hoped for other meetings soon.

A week later, in a letter to Warren, Ralph regretted "this hell of a schedule which they set up for me in relation to the Book Award. I haven't had a single day and few evenings to myself. And the merry-go-round still turns." His voice on the radio reached many people, including Kenneth Burke in Los Altos, California, near Stanford University, which he was visiting. So much lionization did not sit well with Burke, who chose to stay out of the corrupting public eye as much as possible. Ralph seemed "to be faring quite well," he noted; nevertheless, Burke saw a danger in his sudden popularity. "In his joyous world of T. S. Eliots and Harvey Brights and Irving And Hows," Burke punned to Stanley Hyman, "he doesn't need the like of me to bid him yea. (Incidentally, the situation being what it is today, I think he has a good chance of being 'groomed' for a role of considerable politico-cultural importance. I say this in all seriousness.)"

In fact, Ralph's reception as winner of the National Book Award in fiction was mixed in the extreme. Some whites, ashamed of racism, approached him as near-penitents. When one white woman from Maryland asked him timidly to tell her "how you want me to behave," he was unassuming; "be yourself," he advised her. Many acclaimed writers were happy for him. "Usually such awards give me no pleasure at all," the poet Theodore Roethke wrote Ralph, but "this one really did." Other admirers did not go quite as far. In *The Atlantic Monthly,* Edward Weeks called *Invisible Man* powerful, if overwritten and confused in places, but regretted that again Hemingway was passed over for a major prize. (Hemingway had also never won a Pulitzer Prize.) *Invisible Man* "was not, I believe, the finest novel published in 1952," one newspaper critic wrote, even as he conceded that it "ran a close second" to *The Old Man and the Sea.* To the *Cleveland News,* Ralph's novel was "a worthy prize winner as a first novel, but it is an absurd pretense to say it was the most distinguished American novel" of 1952.

Openly hostile responses were few but memorable. The *Christian Science Monitor* of Boston finally revealed why it had ignored not only *Invisible Man* in 1952 but also Ralph's acceptance address in 1953 even as it carefully reported the other, less serious speeches. "While applauding Mr. Ellison's sincerity and effort," the *Monitor* explained, the newspaper boycotted the author and his novel because of "the morbidity and violence of its approach and its quite unnecessary disregard of the decencies." At least two black critics were not so restrained. The *New York Amsterdam News* columnist Margaret Cartwright mockingly announced her new organization of the "Society for the Prevention of the Defilement of Negro Males"; in addition to the usual stereotypes of blacks in white fiction, "now another ubiquitous Negro has appeared on the scene. I call him the neurotic Negro." *Native Son* had started the vicious trend of self-hating black heroes, and *Invisible Man* now capitalized on it. Appropriately, its hero ends up in a sewer; the novel itself is an "undisciplined diarrhea of words." In the *Pittsburgh Courier* another columnist announced that he had banned *Invisible Man* from his home because "I did not want my wife to read it. My wife does not talk sex nor tell vulgar stories. Abnormal sexual behavior is not a subject which interests her. She does not appreciate profane and filthy language."

Winning the National Book Award—not the publication of *Invisible Man* itself—was transforming Ralph's life even as he looked on with fascination. "For the first time I've seen an American publicity machine in action and it is truly something to observe," he wrote. "I'm developing a television tick and microphone stammer! I watch me with a cold eye as I penetrate new areas, yes, and I can't help but feel that some mistake was made somewhere." Needing a new agent now since his parting with Russell & Volkening, he signed with the top-notch William Morris Agency. Helen Strauss, who also represented Robert Penn Warren, assumed control of his contracts. (The first request was from *Holiday* magazine, which begged for an essay on jazz that Ralph agreed to write but never delivered.) Fanny would manage his invitations to read his work or to lecture. Since he was now a celebrity, he adjusted his basic fee accordingly, as he did when he appeared February 1 on ABC's *Time Capsule* radio program. By the summer he had raised it from $150 to $175; it became $200 in the fall. Some heavy doors opened before he touched them. On February 5, the board of trustees of the MacDowell Colony for writers and artists, waiving its usual requirements, invited him to spend a month or two on its six-hundred-acre estate in Peterborough, New Hampshire. Later that year, unsolicited, the John Simon Guggenheim Memorial Foundation assured Ralph that "any application [for a fellowship] you may present will be carefully considered."

Sunday-morning listeners to CBS radio heard him on the program *Invitation to Learning* discussing Faulkner's novella "The Bear" (a text he had chosen) with Irving Howe and the host, Lyman Bryson. Praising Faulkner, Ralph also signaled the guiding themes and aesthetic of his own next novel. "The Bear," he noted, has "an almost direct link with our classical nineteenth-century fiction." In Faulkner's story one found everything crucial to American literature—"you have all the experimentation; you have the frontier humor; you have the wilderness theme; you have the Indian theme; you have the encroachment of modern civilization; and you have this moral problem involving Negroes, Indians, and whites, which through extension now has become the problem of the West." Specifically, these elements were missing in the work of all writers, white and black, who had taken on the Negro subject: "No one in American fiction has done so much to explore the types of Negro personality as has Faulkner." Ralph's next novel would follow Faulkner's lead, including his profound respect for folklore. "Folklore is concerned only with abiding experience—it is equipment for living," Ralph told a reporter. "I have drawn upon that element rather than the sophisticated patterns of many American and European writers. Folklore is an accumulation of universal wisdom."

Ralph was now speaking with unprecedented authority for a black American. Wright had sold far more books, and in 1950 Gwendolyn Brooks had won the Pulitzer Prize for poetry. However, critics had harped on the crudeness of Wright's art in praising its power, and poets had lost much of their influence. Ralph's supremacy was uncannily confirmed in 1953 with the appearance of Wright's prophetic but awkward second novel, *The Outsider*. Ralph did not crow about this reversal of fortunes. Declining a call from *Partisan Review* to write about *The Outsider,* which denounces capitalism, Communism, and America itself, he could only have agreed with assessments such as that in the *Herald Tribune Book Review* about Wright's "sometimes strained and fumbling" prose and the "fatal weakness" of his book. He and Wright had gone their separate ways as artists and Americans, and he had emerged, by almost all accounts, the finer thinker and writer. Magnanimously, and aware of the tricky ways of racism, he tried to avoid being drawn into a literary battle royal with his former mentor. When *Time* magazine lauded *Invisible Man* in dismissing *The Outsider,* Ralph complained privately that what the powerful magazine had done to Wright "was quite unfair"; he regretted "especially their using me to beat him over his head for rejecting both Russia and America." Nevertheless, he concluded, "I suppose it was inevitable, since our positions on these matters are very much in opposition."

Only a couple of weeks earlier, in late January, he had finally finished a letter to Wright that broke a long silence. "I have lost the delight of corresponding," he explained. Modestly he reported the success of *Invisible Man.* He also urged Wright to revisit America: "Despite all, you are recognized as a leading American writer." His name had come up several times in Princeton at recent lectures in the Christian Gauss Seminars in Criticism. America had changed: "Negroes are now attending Princeton as a matter of course." If for no other reason, Wright should return because Ralph had no black writer with whom he could speak as equals: "One thing that I am a little sorry about is that right now I know of no young Negro writers here in the States"—except Albert Murray of Tuskegee— "with whom I can talk over the problems of craft and technique. . . . This is frustrating to me because I feel the responsibility of passing along some of the stuff which I learned from you and which I had to dig out for myself."

In fact, Ralph's sympathy for Wright was limited. Breaking with the Communists, Wright had also lost an enlightened sense of American reality. For this loss he had paid a steep price. Ralph had a similar view of C. L. R. James, who on April 15 delivered the first of three lectures on

American culture in Hamilton Hall at Columbia University. Once, like Ralph, a radical and an admirer of Wright (his wife, Constance Webb, would be Wright's first biographer), James was now fighting to stay in the United States. Eager to deport him, the U.S. attorney general had cited James's publication in 1937 of *World Revolution,* a Trotskyite treatise. He had never been a Communist (a fact uncontested by the U.S. government) and he had broken with the Trotskyites. Nevertheless, the U.S. immigration service had interned him on Ellis Island for several months. While there, James had found inspiration, as Ralph himself had done, in Melville's writings, especially *Moby-Dick.* He had written *Mariners, Renegades and Castaways,* a study of that novel as a jeremiad about the modern industrial and political world. After reading *Invisible Man,* he had written Ralph to praise it as "a splendid piece of work"; it was "in many ways, the finest novel I have read for years." Ralph liked the compliment but probably also saw James's story as, like Wright's, a cautionary tale. Not long after his lectures, James was deported.

The hubbub started by the news of the award continued. "For several weeks," Fanny wrote, "we rarely had time to have dinner at home." Requests for Ralph to appear on various programs continued to pour in. On February 19, for example, he took part in the television network program *The Author Meets the Critics,* from the stage of the Ambassador Theater in Manhattan. Speaking in praise of *Invisible Man* was Lillian Smith, the author of *Strange Fruit* and *Killers of the Dream,* while an Associated Press journalist spoke (following the format of the show) "against" the novel. Academics wanted Ralph in their classrooms. On the morning of March 4, at the behest of his friend the psychologist Dr. Kenneth Clark, he discussed his novel in two psychology classes at City College in Harlem, where almost all the students were white. "Man must discard what is illusionary in the process of achieving humanity," he told the students. Each individual must "plunge himself into life" and thus "learn from experience." Two weeks later, on March 18, he returned for an appearance in one of Clark's seminars. He was fascinated by, but also ambivalent about, Clark's work as the main expert witness when the U.S. Supreme Court finally ruled the following year, 1954, on school segregation. Despite his work years before with Dr. Wertham's psychiatric clinic in Harlem, Ralph distanced himself from psychology. "I am not trying to run a case history in sociology or psychology," he insisted to a college reporter about his approach to fiction as a writer. "I want to investigate the nature of leadership through a literary technique: purpose to passion to perception, the basic pattern of prose fiction."

At a gathering of editors at the Advertising Club on Park Avenue near 35th Street, he joined the arch-conservative but usually entertaining black journalist George Schuyler of the *Pittsburgh Courier,* as well as his former colleague on the Federal Writers' Project Ellen Tarry, to answer the question "Is There a Renaissance in Negro Writing?" The discussion was later broadcast on WNYC radio. Then, on March 14, to close off his furious winter schedule, Ralph flew down south to Winston-Salem, North Carolina, where he spent most of the next day at Bennett College in Greensboro. To this point, almost all of his post-award appearances had been before whites. Now he faced blacks. Donning a black robe, he heard himself introduced by President David D. Jones before he delivered an oration at Vespers in the college chapel—not unlike the many orations he had heard at Tuskegee or the one delivered by the blind Homer Barbee in *Invisible Man.* Inspired, Ralph offered complex advice—not banalities—about the peculiar challenges facing black youth, who must have "courage, a cold, hard eye toward reality and the ability to meet all situations." Self-knowledge was crucial: "We must all discover who we are, what we are and why we are, so that we can face reality creatively." To many listeners he seemed masterful, as when a reporter for the local *Twin City Sentinel* compared him to Thoreau: "No man for literary finery or show, Ellison . . . talks from a tower of serenity, and with a grave and becoming humility." As for his sudden fame, "I'm amazed, and I'm puzzled by it," Ralph admitted. "But I am awfully pleased. I hope my future work justifies it."

Almost providentially, given his belief that his next novel would take him deep into his past, this visit offered an unexpected connection to his father's family still living in the South. Greeting him at the airport were a cousin, Alexander Morrisey, and his wife, Juanita, with whom he stayed while in Winston-Salem. Roughly Ralph's age, and the only black reporter on the local *Twin City Sentinel* (another sign of racial change), Morrisey had contacted him after the success of *Invisible Man* and then had visited him in New York. In Greensboro, North Carolina, he met Alex's mother and stayed with other cousins. The Piedmont region seemed full of relatives. The most moving event was his encounter with his father's sister Mamie, who seemed so much like her sister Lucretia Ellison Brown of Oklahoma City "that I found myself carried back many years." Ralph vowed to come back, because "I enjoyed talking with her very much." His aunt and cousins, he wrote soon after, had "opened up vistas of the past which I thought forever closed." He decided that he had to go back to Oklahoma City. Unwilling to return as a nobody to a place he associated with his mother's poverty and his own often unhappy youthful striving, he was ready now that he had become "Ralph Ellison, the young Negro author who skyrocketed to literary fame with his first novel," as the *Greensboro Daily News* wrote. Alerting May Belle DeWitt Johnston (Lucretia's daughter) of his plans, he begged for secrecy, "as I would like to sneak in and look around for a few days as part of the book I am planning and I wouldn't want people putting on their Sunday manners before I look into a few things."

Returning to New York, Ralph had much to say to friends about his venture into the South. About the signs of improvement in race relations he was optimistic. He was dismayed that many blacks sneered at his rosy view. "They're calling me Rinehart" (the embodiment of deception in *Invisible Man*), he jested, but with genuine concern. "What an emotional stake some of them have in the old, harsh, bitter conditions of Negroes!" When he suggested that some whites were ready "to move faster than we are pushing them, I am felt to be not only lying but mad. I suppose the possibility of a real change in race relations frightens them."

His intense schedule so drained him that shortly after his return Ralph came crashing down with a severe cold. His doctor gave him penicillin shots and insisted on several days in bed. Unable to resist the whirl of public appearances, he roused himself on March 25 to join other notables, including Eleanor Roosevelt, Norman Cousins of *Saturday Review,* and the playwright Marc Connelly, at a tea party at the Columbia University faculty club for the Japanese artist and novelist Yoshiro Nagayo. A few days later he and Fanny visited Dorothy Norman at her home on East 70th Street for a party in honor of the Indian ambassador, G. L. Mehta. Pressed by organizers of the New York City Festival of Books, Ralph recorded a program for WNYC radio on their behalf.

Soon Ralph was back in the South, driving with an apprehensive Fanny to Fisk University in Nashville. Twenty years before, she had arrived as a pretty, talented, and ambitious freshman from Chicago; then, humiliatingly, she had been forced to quit school because she could not pay its fees. Now, thanks to Ralph, she returned in style, if not triumph. Also helping her to relax was the fact that she knew the president—the sociologist Charles S. Johnson (the founding editor of *Opportunity* magazine during the Harlem Renaissance), for whom she had worked part-time as a student. Proudly she sat next to Johnson as Ralph lectured to a packed hall on the challenging subject of "Minority Provincialism as a Problem for the Creative Writer." The head librarian, Arna Bontemps, a prolific writer since the Harlem Renaissance, chaired the event, with the outstanding poet Robert Hayden and the noted literary scholar Philip Butcher serving as respondents. Aaron Douglas, also on the faculty, and perhaps the defining painter of the renaissance, was also present. So, too, were several black professors of literature from around the country who were in town for the annual convention of the College Language Association (the black counterpart to the Modern Language Association). Ralph was forthright in playing down the notion of race as an empowering category in art. "There is no racial novel," he insisted, in words that disputed the wisdom of prominent writers of the Harlem Renaissance, including W. E. B. Du Bois and Langston Hughes; there is "no racial art. . . . All literature marks the road through which we (civilization) have come and points the way we are to go."

Ralph emphasized what he saw as the New South—not sordid Jim Crow laws and customs but the auguries of black racial advancement that validated American ideals. Looking around him, he saw many prosperous, well-dressed blacks and a university seeking to expand its horizons. More people, especially blacks up north, should see for themselves how the country was changing. "I think the great problem of Americans is a failure to really know the country," he told the *Nashville Banner.*

Ralph's next trip to lecture once again took him back to his painful past—on April 30 to Antioch College near Dayton. There he finally met Paul Bixler of the *Antioch Review,* who had both rejected and embraced his work in the 1940s. The visit to Antioch went so well that the school invited him to return for a brief stint in the near future as a Centennial Visiting Professor. Far more vividly, however, the journey to Antioch allowed Ralph to visit Dayton and rekindle memories of his terrible ordeal with his brother as they endured poverty, hunger, winter cold, and homelessness after they had buried his mother and awaited the payment of her life insurance policy. His mother's many relatives were still subsisting almost as dismally as they had in the Depression, when they had possessed little to offer the Ellison boys. With a sense both of sadness and relief, as well as a quiet pride about how he had survived those months and then put them behind him as he moved into the future, he returned to New York. He made no promise that he would return.

Two days later he lectured at Princeton University. In McCosh Hall, the home of the English Department, he looked out on a warm circle of white friends and admirers, including Saul Bellow, R. W. B. Lewis, R. P. Blackmur, and John William Ward of the Program in American Civilization. Next came an invitation from Dexter Perkins of the University of Rochester, the president of the Salzburg Seminar in American Studies, who asked him to go to Austria to teach in one of its sessions. Against the backdrop of the Cold War, the Salzburg Seminar aimed to attract bright young Europeans eager to learn about American culture from American professors. Ralph—and Fanny—hardly hesitated before accepting the offer. Although they would receive only $600 toward travel expenses, plus free room and board, they seized on this chance to live for a few weeks in the heart of Old Europe. Here was more evidence of how the Negro world was changing for the better, a message that Ralph was eager to take to Europe in part to counter Soviet-inspired anti-American propaganda. Quoted in a special report on black Americans in the May 11, 1953, issue of *Time,* he brushed off talk about the irremediably harsh effects of racism in a nation obviously rising to the challenge of defeating racial injustice. Modestly he hinted that he was proof of the nation's will to eradicate Jim Crow. "After a man makes $10,000 or $20,000 a year," he told a *Time* reporter, "the magic fades. He is just another man with his problems."

In the middle of May he and Fanny visited in triumph yet another setting that Fanny associated with past humiliations. In Chicago, Ralph's host was the *Defender* newspaper, where Fanny once had her own column. The *Defender* had summarily fired her, for reasons unknown. Appointed again to the annual *Defender* "Honor Roll," Ralph accepted one of the Robert S. Abbott Memorial Awards at a luncheon at the Parkway Ballroom. He was the only artist on the list of honorees, which included Mary McLeod Bethune, some white judges who had made unpopular liberal decisions, and the FBI for its anti-Klan work. Ralph was pleased to know that blacks saw his book and the National Book Award as milestones in the evolution of American justice and black progress. "I addressed my book to Negroes," he wrote to John Sengstacke of the *Defender,* "and now, at last, through you my own people have answered." At the same time he also won the Russwurm Award (ten awards were given annually) from the black National Newspaper Publishers Association, based in Chicago, for "upholding those highest traditions considered as the American Way of Life." Again, recognition by the black world genuinely moved him. "Few things during this most eventful period of my life," he said, had given him

Ralph Ellison, c. 1914 LIBRARY OF CONGRESS

Ralph and his younger brother, Herbert, 1916
LIBRARY OF CONGRESS

Ralph's father, Lewis Ellison, c. 1910
LIBRARY OF CONGRESS

Zelia N. Breaux, with whom Ralph studied as an emerging musician in Oklahoma City RESEARCH DIVISION, OKLAHOMA HISTORICAL SOCIETY

Ralph's mother, Ida Ellison, Oklahoma, 1919 LIBRARY OF CONGRESS

1931-1932 CLASS REUNION
JUNE 20-22, 1975
Oklahoma City, Oklahoma

DOUGLASS HIGH SCHOOL

Inman Page, principal of the Douglass School, which Ralph attended in Oklahoma City LIBRARY OF CONGRESS

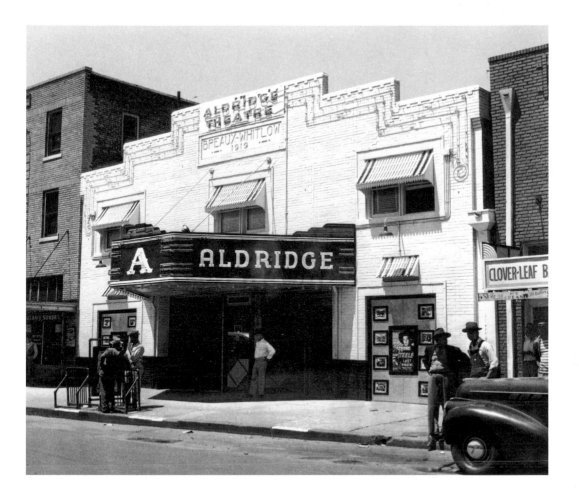

The Aldridge Theatre, 303 N.E. Second Street. Ralph carried with him for a lifetime the memories of music he heard here and elsewhere in Oklahoma City. RESEARCH DIVISION, OKLAHOMA HISTORICAL SOCIETY

Renowned jazz guitarist Charlie Christian, a product of Oklahoma City in Ralph's youth, and Harlan Leonard's band, c. 1940 NEW IMAGES, INC.

Ida [Ellison] Bell, Oklahoma City, 1934
SEVEDRA BARNUM / LIBRARY OF CONGRESS

Ralph Ellison, c. 1931
SEVEDRA BARNUM / LIBRARY OF CONGRESS

TUSKEGEE NORMAL AND INDUSTRIAL INSTITUTE

DATE FIRST ENTERED **June 25, 1933** CLASS **Freshman** HOW { ENTERED OR TRANSCRIPT }

BIRTH MONTH **March** DATE **1** YEAR **1913** PLACE **Okla. City** AGE **20** HEIGHT **5' 9¼"** WEIGHT **153**

FORMER OCCUPATION

THE LAST SCHOOL ATTENDED BEFORE ENTERING TUSKEGEE INSTITUTE **Douglass High School** **Oklahoma City, Oklahoma**

RESPONSIBLE GUARDIAN'S FULL NAME **Ida Ellison Bell** RELATION **Mother**

GUARDIAN'S ADDRESS **710 East Second Street** PHONE NUMBER

GUARDIAN'S TELEGRAPH STATION **Oklahoma City, Oklahoma**

FATHER'S FULL NAME **Dead** OCCUPATION

FATHER'S ADDRESS PHONE NUMBER

FATHER'S TELEGRAPH STATION

MOTHER'S FULL NAME **Ida Ellison Bell** OCCUPATION **Maid**

MOTHER'S ADDRESS **710 East Second Street Oklahoma City, Oklahoma**

MOTHER'S TELEGRAPH STATION

RE-ENTERED				WITHDRAWAL		
DATE	CLASS	DATE	CLASS	DATE		REASON
-10-'34	*Freshman*					
-7-'35	*Junior*					

PHOTO ON ENTERING	DAY OR NIGHT	1. DEPARTMENT *College*	3. DEPARTMENT		PHOTO ON LEAVING
	1.	2. DEPARTMENT	4. DEPARTMENT		
	2.				
	3.	1. DIVISION *Music*	DAY	6. DIVISION	DAY
	4.	2. DIVISION		7. DIVISION	
	5.				
	ACADEMIC DAY	3 DIVISION		8. DIVISION	
		4. DIVISION		9. DIVISION	
		5. DIVISION		10 DIVISION	

Registration record, Tuskegee Institute, 1933–1936 TUSKEGEE UNIVERSITY ARCHIVES

The Tuskegee Institute drama group; Ralph, at left, stands out with his cap and sweater. At center, Robert Russa Moton, president of Tuskegee LIBRARY OF CONGRESS

"Remember that a good book is brother to a good dinner." — Walter B. Williams, Tuskegee Institute, c. 1935 Williams helped to shape Ralph's love of literature. LIBRARY OF CONGRESS

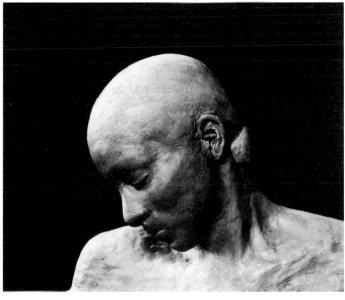

Bust of Marie Howard of Tuskegee Institute, sculpted by Ellison around 1936 LIBRARY OF CONGRESS

"To Langston [Hughes], the Dream keeper, in sincerity and admiration." April 23, 1937 LANGSTON HUGHES PAPERS, BEINECKE RARE BOOK AND MANUSCRIPT LIBRARY, YALE UNIVERSITY

Ralph's passport photograph for his planned voyage to Spain, 1937 LIBRARY OF CONGRESS

With his first wife, Rose Poindexter, c. 1939 LIBRARY OF CONGRESS

Richard Wright, who urged Ralph to become a writer © BETTMAN / CORBIS

Ellison's intimate friend, the writer Sanora Babb, c. 1941 LIBRARY OF CONGRESS

Ida Espen Guggenheimer, Ellison's longtime friend and sponsor, c. 1950. He dedicated *Invisible Man* to her ("To Ida"). LIBRARY OF CONGRESS

Ellison's editor, Albert Erskine, of Random House LIBRARY OF CONGRESS

With Ida Guggenheimer in her Manhattan apartment, c. 1950 LIBRARY OF CONGRESS

Fanny McConnell Ellison
and "Bobbins," c. 1946
LIBRARY OF CONGRESS

Ralph and Fanny, c. 1948
LIBRARY OF CONGRESS

The writer Albert Murray—one of Ellison's
most valued friends—his wife, Mozelle, and
their daughter, Michele, c. 1950 RALPH ELLI-
SON / LIBRARY OF CONGRESS

Kenneth Burke, a writer and intellectual who
greatly influenced Ellison, 1969
© OSCAR WHITE / CORBIS

Photographing Langston Hughes, near Hughes's home in Harlem, c. 1949
LIBRARY OF CONGRESS

Signing books in Greenwich Village, 1952 LAYNE'S STUDIO, HARLEM / LIBRARY OF CONGRESS

Stanley Edgar Hyman, reading from the manuscript of *Invisible Man* in Francis Steegmuller's New York City office, c. 1950. Hyman played a significant role in the evolution of the novel. RALPH ELLISON / LIBRARY OF CONGRESS

Ellison at the National Book Awards ceremony, New York, 1953, with (from left) Frederick Lewis Allen, Archibald MacLeish, and Bernard DeVoto AP IMAGES

Fanny Ellison, Munich, 1954 RALPH ELLISON / LIBRARY OF CONGRESS

With friends from the American Academy in Rome, c. 1955 LIBRARY OF CONGRESS

Robert Penn Warren, Eleanor Clark Warren, and their children, Rosanna and Gabriel, in Italy, c. 1956
R. P. WARREN COLLECTION, UNIVERSITY OF WESTERN KENTUCKY

"so much pleasure." And indeed, for the rest of his life he listed the Russ-wurm Award as one of his major honors.

Another sign of his eminence was a burst of requests for him to endorse, or "blurb," forthcoming books, but Ralph noted disapprovingly that most requests were for books written by or about blacks. On the one hand, critics had praised his book for its universal power; on the other, most white editors and publishers obviously still saw him as a Negro, lim-ited in his authority. Standing on principle, he declined almost all of these requests. As a result, he refused to write in praise of Gwendolyn Brooks's autobiographical novel, *Maud Martha,* although he would claim later to have "always admired" Brooks's work. Asked for a blurb to help launch the American edition of the West Indian writer George Lamming's first novel, *In the Castle of My Skin,* he declined. He chose not to endorse the paper-back release of Chester Himes's novel *The Third Generation.* When the *New York Times Book Review* asked him to review *The Narrows* by Ann Petry, whose naturalist novel *The Street,* published in 1946, had been a best seller, he also refused. Making exceptions, Ralph provided pithy comments for James Baldwin's first novel, *Go Tell It on the Mountain,* and for Richard Wright's book about West Africa, *Black Power.*

To some people, his refusals seemed to reflect selfishness or snobbish-ness, when the truth was far more complicated. His relationship to some of these writers was strained because critics almost invariably and invidi-ously compared new "black" novels to *Invisible Man.* When *The New Yorker* put Ellison's and Baldwin's first novels side by side, "the deficiency immediately declares itself," the reviewer judged; *Invisible Man* was "extremely serious" but also "rich in comic invention," while *Go Tell It on the Mountain* was "without vitality" and Baldwin was "humorless." Ralph was happier when a publisher asked him for a blurb for a translation of one of Ignazio Silone's novels, or when the National Book Award asked him to be one of five jurors in fiction for 1954. (Probably to conserve his time, he declined the latter invitation.)

Wishing to keep a sense of proportion, he did not always insist on a fee for public speaking. On May 27, he talked gratis in a class taught at Hunter College in Manhattan by his friend Marshall Stearns. Ralph liked to chat about his novel with young people. In Stearns's class he gamely answered questions from the students, almost all of them white. *"Is Mr. Norton* [the white philanthropist] *all bad?"* No, he makes "a mistake of pride. His interest in the black campus is not in human beings but in building up his own esteem." *"What can the I.M. do? What contributions can he make?"* "When he accepts himself," Ralph responded, "he is ready to function as a human being."

Invisible Man was taking root. In June, the New American Library launched a Signet paperback edition at 50 cents a copy. The paperback version ensured that the novel would reach a much larger audience. In fact, *Invisible Man* would never go out of print during Ralph's lifetime.

On June 22 Ralph took another momentous step into his past when he returned, for the first time since 1936, to what he had once called his "heart of darkness," Tuskegee Institute in Alabama. He was now arguably its most famous living former student. Though he had modeled his dreadful black Southern college in *Invisible Man* on Tuskegee, the institute was ready to receive him on his terms. For the faculty and administrators, his celebrity trumped his implicit characterization of Tuskegee as a historic fraud. It helped that Ralph had friends at the institute who either sympathized with his portrayal or respected his freedom as an artist. Morteza Drexel Sprague was now the institute librarian; Albert Murray was a professor of English; Mike Rabb, a student with Ralph, had become one of its key administrators.

Staying with Al and Mozelle Murray and their young daughter, Michele, Ralph walked the green grounds of the campus past buildings that brought back a rush of memories pleasant and painful. He cruised the region in Al's car, visited his old haunts, and checked any urge that he felt to crow over his old enemies. On the steamy morning of June 24 Ralph addressed an assembly of summer school students, and four days later he also delivered the main oration during the still mandatory weekly chapel service. The new president of the institute, Luther Foster, held a dinner in his honor. The rebellious son had come home to a hero's welcome. From Mort Sprague, Ralph learned that "I am to be asked formally to return there in the fall for lectures or a series of seminars, to be decided later, and there was talk of a visiting professorship."

From some points of view, Tuskegee had regressed. The arts and humanities had not recovered from the Depression, when President Patterson had been forced to shut down the School of Music and returned to the founder's emphasis on agriculture and other practical skills. That emphasis had not produced a more curious or accomplished student body. Taking Ralph into the library stacks, Sprague pulled books from the shelves to show (from the record slip pasted in each book) that in almost every case the last person to borrow them had been Ralph or Albert Murray. He made up with the now much more mellow Bill Dawson, whose unwillingness to take any risks to help Ralph had been a source of deep disappointment. Dawson was unabashedly thrilled by Ralph's success. This reconciliation lifted Ralph's spirits. Inscribing Dawson's copy of *Invisible Man,* Ralph honored him as one "who, before I knew him, inspired me, and who after I came to Tuskegee taught me by example the discipline of the artist." With the former dean of students, Captain Alvin Neely, his main foe as a student, there was no reconciliation.

The single most important trip into the dark landscape of his past still remained. Since 1936, Ralph's memories of Oklahoma City had nourished, haunted, inspired, saddened, and enraged him even as he tried to contain their power over him. "There is so much about those days that I remember," he wrote his cousin May Belle, "that I am sure you would be surprised." The decision to return home now, without waiting for an invitation, sprang from his hope that going back to the scenes of his boyhood, adolescence, and young manhood would inspire the core of his next novel. Swearing May Belle to secrecy, on June 29 he left Tuskegee with a one-way ticket by air from Atlanta to Oklahoma City. The past seemed to know he was coming. When he stepped out of the airport taxi near the city depot, he saw his old friend Frank Mead puffing nonchalantly on a cigar. Returning in 1921 from their failed adventure in Gary, Indiana, Ida, Ralph, and Herbert had settled into a house next door to the Meads, "where I spent some of the happiest years of my childhood," wrote Ralph. Frank had stunned Ralph with his brilliant sketches and illustrations. His father, Joe Mead, now dead, had given Ralph his first music lessons. Frank had stayed behind in Oklahoma, while Ralph had ridden the rails out of town. The two men talked happily for almost an hour before Ralph recalled that his cousin and her husband were waiting for him at their home, where he would live while he remained in Oklahoma City.

Staying with May Belle and DeWitt Johnston at their home on Northeast 10th Street was soul nourishment for a man starved of family love, hungry for some of the familiar ways of his youth. Avid hunters and fishers, May Belle's brother Tom Brown and his wife, Othello, or "Bert," took him to their favorite lake. Ralph found the experience so satisfying that when he got back to New York he bought a shotgun and hunting gear. "Did very well too," he reported back to Oklahoma, "quail, grouse, squirrels and ducks— quite a few ducks." Ralph fondly remembered reading children's books to May Belle in her mother's home, and now in her presence he recalled the past vividly. Staying indoors most mornings to work on a new short story, later in the day he strolled the streets with his camera and visited friends. His rambling conversations with May Belle, his chance encounters with figures from his deep past, the sight of downtown buildings on which he knew his father had worked, the evidence of renovation and progress, the wrinkled signs of the city's aging, all made Ralph glad that he had come home. "The city has changed, grown," he wrote Fanny, "but not so much that my dreams of it are invalid; for I can see the stages of metamorphosis undergone by many of the buildings and sections, and even some of the people."

This visit made Ralph think sadly about his mother, about the days when her love and devotion swaddled him; but he also remembered his shame about their poverty and her lowly jobs, and also the yawning distance between himself and his brother, whom he had not seen since 1938. "As far as he will let me know," Ralph wrote to May Belle, "he seems to be all right." Inspired by this visit, Ralph wrote to Herbert to share news about Oklahoma City. Gone was the porch at the back of the house on Byers Street where Herbert was born, but the little house on East Fourth Street where "we ha[d] such wonderful times" was still there. "All changes are not for the better," he complained. "The tall apricot tree we used to steal stuff from, cut down and now [there's] an oil well above the Mead house." He had gone by the house on Stonewall Street, a white neighborhood when Ida had moved in with Herbert, who once threw a troublesome white man off the porch. "Mama certainly had courage," Ralph wrote in tribute to Ida, "moving in there and going to jail in defiance of that restrictive zoning ordinance." In Deep Second, most of the wooden buildings, including the Slaughter Building, were gone, replaced by banal brick units. "I feel a little sad when I look at these scenes, they're all so familiar and memory filled and yet so small and distant. That's what happens when you grow up and go away, even the streets shrink and ghosts range in the mind."

At the *Black Dispatch*, the old crusader Roscoe Dunjee had trumpeted the success of the barefoot boy who used to deliver his newspapers. Even the white *Daily Oklahoman*, which had mentioned his National Book Award (although it called his book "Invisible men"), published what May Belle called "a wonderful write up." Freely, Ralph admitted to the man from the *Daily Oklahoman* that he had returned in part "because I thought if I came back home and looked around, the ideas for my next book would take a more definite form." A Sunday-evening lecture and reception on

July 12 drew over a hundred enthusiastic guests to the black Dunbar Branch Library, where the head librarian lauded him for his literary success. At a supper hosted by one of Ralph's classmates, Ralph mingled with other figures from his past, including teachers and fellow students proud of him and happy he had returned for a visit. He came face-to-face with his most important teacher and champion at Douglass, the music instructor Zelia Breaux—but sadly she could no longer remember him.

Through all of this lionizing, he remained humble. According to May Belle, "everyone who saw Ralph when he was here" talked about how his success "had not [a]ffected him." He did not gloat or strut, but observed poignantly how the whirligig of time had brought in its revenges on many of the figures of his youth. "Already I can see," he wrote to Fanny early in his visit, "the effects of sloth and ambition, indulgence and discipline, illusion and reality, and age and desire, sickness and health, defeat and triumph; the decline and fall of old stars, the rise and shine of new." Here, as at Tuskegee Institute, "I can see the harsh reversal in the lives of certain people who affected my own destiny in terms of such tragedy that I feel pity in my heart." Sympathetic to the fallen, he was happy for "those who have remained young and alive despite change of fortune and the ravages of time—and that too is part of the story."

The searing Oklahoma summer sun only added to his sense of hovering between present and past. "My skin has burned black again," he noted. Deliberately he refused to change the time on his watch, "because it is a steady, concrete, audible, link-and-reminder that I am living twenty years in the past when I'm here." He oscillated now between two senses of home—one present and yet also vanished; another hundreds of miles away but real and awaiting him. Disturbed by this venture into the world that had made him, he also felt acutely the power of the world in New York that he had made for himself. "Last night I grew lonely and thought of coming home," he wrote to Fanny, "but that would turn the trip into an indulgence."

Suddenly, as so often happened in this bewildering year, a telegram from Fanny swung his gaze from the past to the present, from blacks to whites, and from the provinces to the seats of power. Fanny had opened a letter to him from the assistant director of the Harvard University summer school, inviting him to take part in its annual conference on the American novel. The compulsively prolific French novelist Georges Simenon, Stanley Hyman, and Katherine Anne Porter would also speak. Without consulting Ralph, because she had no doubt what he would want to do, Fanny canceled a prior commitment and wired an acceptance to Harvard.

At about two o'clock on the morning of July 21, after more than a month away, Ralph set down his bags in his Manhattan apartment. To a joyful Fanny, he arrived "looking younger and very handsome." Ralph was eager to tell her everything about Oklahoma City, his family and old friends there. Popping open a celebratory bottle of champagne, they talked and talked—"and we will be talking about the trip, I think, for a long time to come," she assured May Belle Johnston. "Most people run like fire away from their past," she said of Ralph, "but he is always trying to recapture his."

Harvard loomed. To Ralph, there seemed no end to the glory wrought by winning the National Book Award. A Tuskegee Institute dropout, he would be lecturing at the oldest and most illustrious university in America (if only at a summer program). On August 2, after a drive of some five hours, he and Fanny saw for the first time, across the scudding Charles River, the domes of the grand Harvard houses gleaming in the summer sunshine. Soon they were meeting with other eminences drawn to the conference, including the Southern, former Fugitive literary leader Andrew Lytle and the poet Anthony West. At the faculty club they relaxed over supper with Stanley Hyman and Shirley Jackson, whose *Life Among the Savages*—an amusing account of life in the tumultuous Hyman household—had just appeared.

To Ralph, Harvard was awe-inspiring. "If we ever have a boy," he wrote privately, "Harvard will be his college." In a sense this was part of his "ancestry" by virtue of its associations with his namesake, Ralph Waldo Emerson, and the moral and intellectual tradition epitomized by Emerson. If others saw him as merely a Negro author, Ralph possessed a far more acute sense of association. This sense only intensified when he took part in a session after dinner on August 3 in Sanders Theatre in Memorial Hall, an exquisite building erected in tribute to the young men of Harvard killed in the Civil War. Inscribed in marble on an interior wall was the long list of names. Twenty-one years later, Ralph would tell another gathering at Harvard of the epiphany that overwhelmed him in that place on that evening in 1953. Ironically, it came shortly after a well-dressed white woman stopped him outside Sanders Theatre to praise his talk and then to assure him that she was in constant contact with beings from outer space. Fleeing this lunacy, Ralph found himself suddenly alone, elated by his success and yet flustered by the woman's blathering.

"And it was then that it happened," he told the Harvard class of '49 in 1974. "As I stumbled along, my attention was drawn upward and I was aware of the marble walls, somber and carved with names." Out of mere curiosity he paused to read them, but "then came a moment in which perception leaped dizzily ahead of the processes of normal thought." Until then, no account of the Civil War had overwhelmed him personally, capturing his conscience and psychology by linking him to the battlefield dead now represented by the reliquary list set in marble. Suddenly, what had been almost a tourist's curiosity flamed into something harrowing. "I knew its significance almost without knowing," he said, "and the shock of recognition filled me with a kind of anguish. Something within me cried out 'No!' against that painful knowledge, for I knew that I stood within the presence of Harvard men who had given their young lives to set me free." Those young men had not freed him personally, but they had freed his people and had thus made him what he had become. In the process of freeing him, they "had paid what Abraham Lincoln termed 'the last full measure of devotion,' for an ideal of freedom." Filling him with "anguish," Ralph declared, was the fact "that I had been ignorant of their sacrifice, had been unaware of my indebtedness. Standing there I was ashamed of my ignorance."

Instead of eternal gratitude, he (like most Americans) had responded to their sacrifice with ignorance and indifference: "Upon them a discontinuity had been imposed by the living, and their heroic gestures had been repressed along with the details of the shameful abandonment of those goals for which they had given up their lives. Without question, the consequences of that imposed discontinuity, that betrayal of ideal and memory, are still with us today." These elegiac words of honey and rue, echoing the majesty of Lincoln's Gettysburg oration, were not cooked up to please members of the class of '49. In 1953, the time and place were exactly right for an epiphany that would last with Ralph. The wheel of destiny had brought him from poverty, obscurity, and shame in Oklahoma City to an honored position in this New England place made sacred by the sacrifice of its youth for the ideal of freedom, and by the poetical, prophetic glory of Ralph Waldo Emerson. In a real sense, insofar as he was the would-be hero in an epic of history and language, Ralph Waldo Ellison was home at last. From this moment on, he would see himself as a commissioned American.

Before the conference was over he had tested out his new authority and confidence. Tense at first, "once we began the discussions I found myself on familiar, if not safe, ground and everything went well enough."

At one point, when the Irish writer Frank O'Connor made facetious remarks about the function of literature, Ralph startled the slumbering audience with a somewhat harsh censuring of O'Connor. The sight of a black man rebuking a prominent white writer must have seemed to at least one or two of those present an almost criminal act. One audience member would write to Ralph about "your violent reaction" to O'Connor's suggestion that writing be viewed with "more humor and less serious-ness." Ralph did not apologize. O'Connor had been "making a mockery of everything for which the conference was supposed to stand," and "it was this that gave me the courage 'to go for him.' " He was afraid of no one, intimidated by no setting.

Ralph's performance made a strong, positive impression on Dr. Henry Kissinger, a young émigré professor of government at Harvard and the editor of *Confluence: An International Forum.* "I am most eager to have a piece from you," Kissinger wrote a few days later; he was "particularly interested in the impact of the race problem on literary consciousness and artistic creativity." Other magazines, including *The Atlantic Monthly,* also asked Ralph to submit material. For Kissinger, Ralph rifled through his files and blew dust off an essay written and rejected in 1946. Thanking Kissinger for his role in "one of the high points" of what was certainly "one of our most remarkable years," he sent him a copy of "20th Century Liter-ature and the Dark Face of Humanity." Renamed "20th Century Fiction and the Black Mask of Humanity," the essay would appear in *Confluence* in December of that year, 1953.

Restlessness became almost the hallmark of this magical year. Ralph had been home from Harvard for only a week when he set off impulsively with Fanny on another journey into New England. After stopping briefly in Bennington, where the Hymans were living once again after a failed attempt to relocate nearer to New York, the Ellisons plunged on to Williamstown, Massachusetts, the seat of Williams College. There they stayed with Richard Weaver, a well-known scholar of American literature, and his wife, Edith. Then restlessness deteriorated into disorder, into what Fanny wearily denounced as "one of the most mixed, crazy and dis-organized sojourns we've ever spent in our lives." While Ralph sped madly about New England with vague destinations in mind, she tried to navi-gate. Between the summer heat, the mocking "rotary circles," or round-abouts, the deceitful road signs, her innate insecurity as a navigator, and Ralph's testiness and obstinacy, their holiday fell apart. "All I needed to do," Fanny wrote about one of the low points of the journey, "was wet my pants in order to regress completely."

Eventually they reached Gloucester, Massachusetts, where they joined the mob of fellow tourists swarming the fishing town. As seagulls wheeled and cried overhead, they strolled about the docks and inhaled the briny smell of salt and tar. Fanny wanted to stay, but Ralph decided to push on to Cape Cod. To get there they had to pass through Boston, where despite her pleas and his ignorance of the city, Ralph doggedly refused to ask anyone for directions. "I began to think I was married to some sort of fiend," Fanny wrote, only half in jest; Ralph kept saying, "Why in the hell don't you read the map, and, what in the hell is wrong with you. . . . Shit!"

Exhausted, they pulled into East Orleans around eleven at night, had coffee and sandwiches at a Howard Johnson's, and then set off again, this time for the beach. Once there, Ralph switched off the engine and tumbled into a deep sleep as Fanny tried to settle herself into the backseat under a makeshift blanket of beach towels. The next morning, near dawn, glad to be on the shore, they watched a man pull in a thirty-pound striped bass. They had no such luck when they cast their own lines—only sea robins and rays, which they considered vermin. Ralph then decided to head for Provincetown, about thirty miles away. Strolling down busy Commercial Street they ran into the well-known photographer Arnold Newman, a jolly cigar-puffing friend whose portraits of famous people often appeared in *Life*. This was a lucky accident. The local hotels, he warned them, routinely refused to admit blacks. Newman found Ralph and Fanny a room in a creaky old house run by two creaky old New England ladies. The bathroom was downstairs, so every visit there meant dressing completely. "It was not until the morning that we got ready to leave," Fanny recalled to Edith Weaver, "that we found the thunder-mug tucked away in a cupboard."

Early on August 20, after a few days of surf fishing and lively parties (with the Newmans guiding them), they headed home. Again Ralph seemed to be feeling unusual pressures. Restless and irritable, he had been home only one day when he decided that they should go to Montauk, 120 miles away, at the eastern tip of Long Island. Again, the result was elements of horror for Fanny. "You know how he can't bear to have any cars, not even three, within 100 yards of him on the highway," she complained to the Weavers. Adamant about knowing a shortcut through Queens, Ralph was soon lost. As usual, he blamed everything on Fanny: "Ralph was disgusted all over again and my personality had really begun to crack." Their aim was to visit the summer home of an executive at New American Library, the paperback publisher of *Invisible Man,* but they never got there. Looking for a winding, bumpy cow path, they found instead two diverging cow paths, neither of which led them to the house. Defeated, they parked at a local beach, fished awhile, slept overnight, and then headed back to the city.

To Fanny, Ralph's ill temper and obstinacy were painful. Intimidated at times, she tried to laugh away her sense of injury and hurt and explain it as one of the unhappy dividends of genius. "The whole experience has become funny to me as of about 48 hours ago," she wrote to Richard and Edith Weaver, "but I'm not quite sure how Ralph is working out of it. I probably won't really know until I hear him talk about it politely among a couple of friends with whom we'll have dinner on Friday."

In Manhattan that fall, invitations arrived at a brisk pace as hosts and hostesses found the Ellisons an engaging, unusual couple with their prestige, poise, intelligence, good looks, and freshly fashionable (in some white circles) brown skins. At Dorothy Norman's home in particular they met other people of influence and made prosperous or accomplished new contacts. On September 21, for example, G. L. Mehta, whom they had met at Norman's, welcomed them to the gala opening of an arts and crafts of India show at the American Museum of Natural History. At parties attended by editors, publishers, agents, and writers, Ralph was now a sleek young literary lion, as when in early October he and Fanny attended a lively New American Library book party in honor of Saul Bellow's best-selling *The Adventures of Augie March,* now in paperback. A few days later, at the Town Hall on West 43rd Street, Ralph lectured under the auspices of the PEN American Center. Invited to join PEN in January 1953, he was elected to the executive board of PEN America before the year was out.

Most of these events took them to mid-Manhattan, or further south, away from the Beaumont, where whites were steadily quitting their apartments and blacks taking their place. The same was true up and down Riverside Drive north of Columbia University. They watched with curiosity as Spanish became the lingua franca on Broadway around 145th Street, and exuberant Caribbean migrants took over the neighborhood. "We live in Puerto Rico sometimes I think," Fanny wrote to a white friend, "and the women are so confoundedly beautiful and the children so endearing. It's going to be awfully interesting to watch them as recent migrants, their adjustment and the way the city treats them, with the effect of mass migration among my own people unforgotten and still very evident. There are quite a few landlords getting rich and fat."

Two deaths marred the fall. In October, after Ralph drove through a wickedly unseasonable blizzard to appear on a program at Bard College with Georges Simenon, he learned that his cousin May Belle DeWitt Johnston of Oklahoma City was dead. On August 21 Ralph had learned from her that she was going into the hospital for an operation. She never recovered from surgery. May Belle's death dealt a harsh blow to the sense of resurgent kinship inspired in Ralph over the summer with his visit to Oklahoma City. On October 13, just after his Town Hall lecture, Ralph left to attend his cousin's funeral in Oklahoma. At the Oklahoma City airport he found out that Zelia Breaux, too, had just died. Disheartened by these twin losses, Ralph did not linger in Oklahoma.

Once again, as in recent years, he made several trips to Princeton to attend a series of lectures in the Christian Gauss Seminars in Criticism, led in this instance by the British man of letters V. S. Pritchett on the subject of the comic element in the English novel. Here again Ralph saw his rise in prestige openly affirmed. In previous years, at such events in Princeton, he had listened from a distance and spoke not at all. Now he was escorted to the center and his opinions solicited. On November 28, he dined with Pritchett and other notable guests at the home of the director of the Gauss Seminars, E. B. O. Borgerhoff.

(In conservative Princeton, as elsewhere, Ralph's presence in such company often disturbed whites and blacks alike, even as he strove to maintain his rights and his dignity. Nancy Lewis, the wife of R. W. B. Lewis, recalled Ralph sleeping over one night on a sofa at their home. "We had a very good cleaning woman, a black woman," she said. "Just after Ralph's visit she suddenly stopped coming to work. When I asked her why, she said: 'Mrs. Lewis, I came in one morning and I saw a man sleeping on your sofa. He had bad hair.' ")

The repeated visits to Princeton and the cosmopolitan friendliness of several of its English professors made Ralph think again about the possibility of a teaching career despite the fact that, embarrassingly, he had no college degree. (He knew that R. P. Blackmur and Kenneth Burke also had none.) This idea grew further between November 30 and December 6, when he served as Centennial Visiting Professor at Antioch College. Visiting various classes, he also led one faculty seminar and delivered a well-received public lecture. Antioch, a bastion of white liberalism since the nineteenth century, seemed ready to hire him. "Don't laugh," he enjoined a skeptical friend, "I take this thing very seriously and I'll give them my best." America was changing swiftly, Jim Crow was on the run, and his authorship of *Invisible Man* made a university degree superfluous. When Ralph gave his public lecture, on "The Modern Novel and Its Development," the fact that the local white high school sent its juniors and seniors to listen to him created a stir. This was "quite a landmark," as Paul Bixler wrote to him. The village of Antioch not only had never hired a black teacher, it had even recently refused to allow a black education major from the college to train in its school system. Now the village seemed poised to accept change, especially if change came in the form of a man as polished and accomplished as Ralph Ellison.

No invitation came from Antioch College, but Ralph would never have moved to the small Ohio town except under extraordinary circumstances. New York City was now his home, and writing, not teaching, his métier. Besides, with Fanny ready to work to ensure his freedom to be an artist, he needed no regular job. That year, moreover, she found an ideal position when the fund-raising firm of Harold Oram Associates, long noted for raising money for humanitarian and philanthropic causes, including European refugee and American civil rights organizations, hired her to take charge of its office staff.

True, Ralph had not been doing much writing of late, or not much writing that seemed ready for publication. Questioned at Antioch about the status of his novel-in-progress, he was coy. "He declined to discuss it," according to the *Antioch Record,* "on the grounds that there might then no longer be any need to write it." As yet this coyness cloaked only petty anxiety about his future as a novelist. The year 1953, starting with the mysterious telephone call of congratulation and followed soon by the news of his triumph, had been undoubtedly thus far his *annus mirabilis.* After many years of laboring in the cold shadows, in a state of virtual invisibility, Ralph surely was entitled to laze awhile in the sunshine of sudden fame.

In good time—soon, quite soon, he knew—the germ of an idea would lead to his second, even more extraordinary book, just as the first rays of *Invisible Man* had flashed unexpectedly upon him in the summer of 1945. The main difference between then and now was that he was suddenly out in the open, glaringly visible in the wider world. That thought filled him with a profound sense of achievement, but also a measure of apprehension, as his miraculous year, 1953, drew to a close.

12

Second Act

1954–1955

And to think you won it for your first book. What will you win for your others?!   LUCILLE D. BROOKS (1953)

A few days after the first anniversary of the 1953 National Book Award, Ralph stepped off a plane at the Atlanta airport at the start of what would be his first extended venture in the region, lecturing and reading his work at colleges and universities. All the schools would be black, of course; as yet, no white Southern institution had invited him to its campus. In the Jim Crow terminal in Atlanta, with its stark signs separating whites from "colored," Albert Murray welcomed him. When Murray spotted the new Tuskegee president, Luther Foster, who had just arrived on another flight, he offered him a ride to the campus as well—thus sparing his president the indignity of using Jim Crow public transportation along the 135 miles to the institute.

During the drive, they discussed whether Jim Crow laws covering education were about to fall. The previous autumn, the Supreme Court had taken on five cases challenging school segregation in five separate geographical regions. At some point in the spring the Court was expected to hand down at least some decisions. Writing to Ralph the previous month, Murray despaired that Foster wouldn't ever understand the backwardness of Tuskegee and its need for radical change. On the campus itself, Murray wrote, "everybody knows it's a pile of shit." The founder's dream had atrophied into a regime of authoritarianism, fear, and docility among students and faculty alike. For Murray, as for Ralph, desegregation could not come too soon.

The next day, when Ralph faced the dark, upturned faces of students at a Vespers service in the chapel, where he had sat many a time listening in boredom to some great man, he was unsure how to read them. Perhaps the title of his lecture—"Literature and the Crisis of Negro Sensibility"—was too forbidding. Ralph decided to abandon his announced subject. Instead, he "spoke from the hip or heart or wherever it is that sincerity and desperation" are united. Still, the students remained "so quiet that I became truly desperate and found myself almost pleading with them to recognize that there was no longer any need to think of themselves as less than human." He spoke of a historical moment at hand in America, with forces locked in legal combat over Jim Crow. "We stand now at the crisis," he said. "There is no such thing as not being ready." In the Cold War the United States was trying to appeal to the world, but it could not be done "with a large segment of its population ignorant and bearing the stigma of second-class citizenship."

When he stopped speaking, for a second he was sure that he had lost his audience. Then the old chapel erupted in wild applause. After the service, he autographed more than a hundred copies of *Invisible Man*. Emboldened, in the next few days he spent much of the time "needling both students and teachers." He expressed dismay that Tuskegee offered no courses in American literature. After a long struggle in American colleges, the teaching of American literature had started to prevail in the face of English departments that were Anglophilic by definition and snobbish by nature. A similar change was needed at Tuskegee, especially with the end of Jim Crow in sight. "I asked them," he told Fanny about the teachers, "how they expect students to become integrated when they knew nothing of the society into which they were to be integrated? It hadn't occurred to them that literature had anything to do with us."

His complaints led directly to an invitation—quickly accepted—to return soon to Tuskegee to offer a weeklong course for teachers on American literature. This could be excellent preparation, Ralph believed, for his stint at the Salzburg Seminar in Austria later in the summer. The openness of the institute to his suggestions made this visit surprisingly reassuring. Around the Murrays he felt both relaxed and stimulated, and the same was true of other figures from his past, such as Mort Sprague and Mike Rabb, the latter of whom who had recently been appointed secretary to the board of trustees. At a dinner in Ralph's honor, when Mozelle Murray cooked corn bread, chitterlings, and waffles, Ralph had what he called "an uproarious time laughing about old times" with the Murrays and their other guests. He also dined at the homes of William Dawson, Bess Walcott, and Laly Charlton Washington, who were more optimistic than Murray about Tuskegee. At the Carver Research Center, where George Washington Carver had once explored the possibilities of the peanut, he now saw professors and students working on cancer cell research. "Carver was a conjure man," Ralph wrote Fanny, "but these guys and girls are scientists."

One night, taken by Al Murray to a dance at the Veterans Hospital that brought back poignant memories of his days as a Tuskegee student with his friend Julia "Chubby" Moore and her family, he impulsively borrowed a trumpet and joined the orchestra on one number. His playing was all rust. He would have stayed at Tuskegee longer but he had obligations elsewhere. Besides, he had hoped to do some writing (inspired by being at his old school) but got very little done "because I was being entertained too much" and "could not stay in my room at night when there was a chance to ride out to watch the country Negroes dance in their roadside night clubs."

On March 1, at a riotous little party with Murray and other friends, Ralph celebrated his fortieth (really his forty-first) birthday. The next day, hung-over, he reached New Orleans for an engagement at Dillard University. A fusion of two historically black schools that went back to the first decade after the Civil War, and church-affiliated, Dillard was well known in the black world for its academic rigor. At first nothing went right for him there. He discovered that he had arrived "right in the turbulence of Mardi Gras." In addition, he was distressed to find New Orleans, for all its reputation for cosmopolitanism, "a viciously jim-crowed city." At the airport, white cabdrivers refused to pick up black passengers. Black cabdrivers were few and hard to find. When he at last reached Dillard, which was two hours from the airport, it was shut down for the holiday. Hotel rooms were either barred to him or fully occupied. His cabbie finally found him a place to sleep.

The next day Ralph met his host, the young poet Saul Gottlieb, who took him to more respectable accommodations. With its gleaming white buildings and trim grounds, the Dillard campus was "quite handsome, and tropical," but New Orleans remained bizarre to him. "I've never been in a place like this city," he admitted. He found in the French Quarter, "for all its age and quaintness, a sucker-trap atmosphere like Broadway." Like something surreal out of *Invisible Man*, a mammy with electric bulbs for eyes grinned outside most of the joints: "Talking about weird! These things are worse than those little hitching post figures." Unlike at Tuskegee, he was now inspired to write. "I'm excited about the book," he wrote from New Orleans to Stanley Hyman, "though it's still little more than [an] idea and a few nebulous characters."

Gottlieb had alerted the English departments at Tulane, Loyola (also white), and Xavier, all universities located in New Orleans, about Ralph's visit. A few of these students and professors turned out for his main Dillard lecture, among them the respected Tulane scholar Richard P. Adams, who wrote to Ralph about reading *Invisible Man* and thinking, with a sense of awe, that "this man is not talking just about Negro experience, he's talking about human experience; in fact, he's talking about *my* experience." ("It's such letters as yours," Ralph replied, "which make me feel the effort to communicate is worthwhile.") He found the Dillard students far more spunky and smart than their country cousins at Tuskegee. "I'm told that they're stirred up. I hope so, they need a heapa stirring," he wrote Fanny. On March 17, when he spoke in Baton Rouge at Southern University, "it was the largest body of Negro students I had ever appeared before," he informed Gottlieb, "and it did go rather well."

Leaving Louisiana, he headed east to another version of the black South at Bethune-Cookman College in Daytona Beach, Florida. On the small, sunny campus, neatly kept and adorned with palm trees, poinsettias, and hanging moss, the main event was the celebration on March 19 of the school's fiftieth anniversary. In 1904, starting out with $1.25 as capital, Mary McLeod Bethune had founded the Daytona Normal and Industrial School for Negro Girls. Now president emeritus, Bethune was a revered figure in black America. Twice head of the National Association of Colored Women, she had forbidden segregation on her campus and championed the right of blacks to vote. Two presidents of the United States had appointed her to the National Child Welfare Commission, and three other presidents, as well as her good friend Eleanor Roosevelt, had drawn on her wisdom. The anniversary also attracted Ralph Bunche, who had won the 1949 Nobel Prize for peace, and Langston Hughes, who had known Bethune since 1931, when he and Zora Neale Hurston had driven through the South with her. Although Ralph was probably less sentimental than the others about schools founded on the Tuskegee model, as her school was, he obviously respected what Bethune had accomplished and her courage in the course of achieving it.

His tour almost over, on March 22 he reached Washington. Fanny met him there, after a month of separation. "Where you are is home," he had written her from New Orleans. "I love you." At Howard University he lectured on "The Humanities and Their Place in Today's World" and also gave a television interview. In addition, he reunited with some old friends from Tuskegee as his success continued to take him back into the past. Finally, on April 8, Ralph closed out his tour at yet another historically black school, Coppin Teachers College in Baltimore.

One result of his traveling through the South was a new interest in helping the organized civil rights movement—or, more accurately, the NAACP. That month, encouraged by Ralph, Fanny joined a membership drive that was a major part of the ambitious Fight for Freedom fund-raising campaign mounted by the association as it continued its costly legal challenges, mainly in the South. She sent letters to her fellow tenants at the Beaumont begging them to help the NAACP. "The least we can do is to contribute financial support," she insisted. "We all have friends in the South who risk their lives to do these things." A few months later, Ralph joined the Committee of 100 in support of the NAACP Legal Defense and Education Fund. Sidestepping the main organization, which he saw as bureaucratic, he pitched in to help Thurgood Marshall, William Hastie, Jack Greenberg, and other bright lawyers of the Legal Defense Fund. But he believed that his art, and the prestige that came with it, was to be his main contribution. As the walls of segregation fell, he also saw himself bringing a refined Negro presence to places of power hitherto reserved for whites. In joining the board of the Newport Jazz Festival, created by members of the wealthy Lorillard tobacco family, as he did about this time, he took one of those steps—although Ralph's ambitions were much higher.

He remained prickly about attempts, implicit or explicit, to confine him. Asked for an essay on black fiction by the magazine *Jewish Frontier,* he refused. The appearance of new novels by black authors spurred his anxiety about his own lack of production. That anxiety only increased when John Oliver Killens's *Youngblood* garnered some good reviews, because Killens had savaged *Invisible Man* in 1952. Finally, in April, Ralph's two-year drought ended when he published the weak short story "Did You Ever Dream Lucky?" in *New World Writing.* In the tale Mary Rambo (a character in *Invisible Man*) tells about an incident in which she and her young daughter swipe a mysterious-looking bag from the scene of a car wreck, only to discover that it holds not the fortune that they had dreamed of but tire chains. As Ralph admitted in an appended note, it was "an offshoot, a further elaboration, of one of the themes of [his] first novel."

On May 17, Ralph was alone at home, turning the pages of Bruce Catton's absorbing volume of history about the last year of the Civil War, *A Stillness at Appomattox* (earlier that year it had won a Pulitzer Prize), when a radio bulletin stopped him cold. As he listened, he felt his body tremble. Led by Chief Justice Earl Warren, the U.S. Supreme Court had just unanimously overturned the 1896 landmark decision *Plessy v. Ferguson*. In effect, the Court had declared racial segregation illegal across America. Bundling the five cases involving civil rights and education currently before it under the aegis *Oliver Brown et al. v. The Board of Education of Topeka, Kansas,* the Court had ruled that the infamous "separate but equal" doctrine of segregation had no place in the area of public education. The three cited words were the most infamous used in *Plessy v. Ferguson,* a case that involved public transportation but had led to almost sixty devastating years of Jim Crow for black America. Tears sprang to Ralph's eyes as he thought not simply about himself but also about the millions of other blacks, especially the young, about to enter a world transformed.

"It made for a heightening of emotion and a telescoping of perspective," he confessed to Mort Sprague, as well as "a sense of the problems that lie ahead." Ralph knew that his life had suddenly changed, including his life as a writer: "I could see the whole road stretched out and it got all mixed up with this book I'm trying to write and it left me twisted with joy and a sense of inadequacy." Shrewdly, he also sensed danger even as he and other blacks should be celebrating. "Why did I have to be a writer during a time when events sneer openly at your efforts?" he asked himself. "What a wonderful world of possibilities are unfolded for the children!" Astutely he saw his task as a writer suddenly become more challenging than ever. "For me there is still the problem of making meaning out of the past and I guess I'm lucky I described Bledsoe," he wrote Sprague, "before he was checked out." Sensing the threat, he made a gesture toward affirming the proud loneliness of the artist and his exemption from political definition. "Here's to integration," he offered as a toast, "the only integration that counts: that of the personality."

Later that year, he would recall the resentment and hurt he had felt as a child on seeing a sign outside the city of Norman (the seat of the University of Oklahoma) declaring that "no Negro Americans were allowed in the city after nightfall." Now such viciousness was outside the law. "Several of the boys hold graduate degrees," he wrote, and "a Negro newspaper from my hometown carried photographs of black and white children swimming together in a white pool." Integration would help whites as well as blacks. Although "one may expect resistance to desegregation," he believed, "the South is turning away from the mad task of trying to hold back the wheels of time which has drained away so much of its creative energy." If he had any reservation about the *Brown* decision, it had to do with the fact that the Court had relied in part on the findings of his friends Kenneth and Mamie Clark, whose psychology experiments using black and white dolls to "prove" the ill effects of Jim Crow on the self-esteem of black children were the core of arguments by NAACP lawyers opposed to segregation. Ever suspicious of psychology and sociology when applied to large populations, and especially to blacks, he wondered about the long-term effects of the argument that they lacked self-esteem as a result of Jim Crow.

Because Ralph needed the money, he had to return to Tuskegee that June. He was also eager to join the debate at Tuskegee about the *Brown* decision and its likely effect on black schools. On June 23, when he delivered the summer convocation speech, he did not equivocate. Nervous about losing their jobs, black teachers (many were enrolled at Tuskegee) nevertheless had to prepare their students for the new challenges. They had to "consciously explore those areas of American life which have been denied Negroes and evaluate them for the younger generation which will inherit an un-segregated way of American life." On guard against ingrained Negro reticence, the black teacher "must instill his students with a spirit of curiosity and encourage an attitude of aggressive social and political responsibility toward the total society." Striving to eradicate "the attitude of passive acceptance" that characterized most black education, teachers must set aside worries about their job after *Brown*. "The Negro teacher will endure," he insisted, "as long as America endures. He will endure because he has something vital to say. . . . He is the designated carrier of a rich folk wisdom, gained from our mixed position in American society, and which forms the fountainhead of all our contributions, past and future, to man's knowledge of experience."

In his seminar for teachers on American literature—the first at Tuskegee—he stressed its moral content, its creative use of vernacular speech, and its aesthetic power as seen in the work of writers such as Mark Twain, Melville, and Faulkner. He admired these novelists for their enlightened, dexterous rendition of the subject of race—or, as he wrote to Mort Sprague, for "their handling of the problem of value when confronted in the form of the Negro and the Indian." He also lectured on Stephen Crane's *The Red Badge of Courage,* Hemingway's *The Sun Also Rises,* and Eliot's *The Waste Land,* as well as criticism by Kenneth Burke and Constance Rourke, among others. Pleased to be freed from the alien majesty of British literature, his students responded well to the native texts and, in particular, the discussions of race and art.

At Tuskegee, preparing his invited application for a Guggenheim fellowship, he named as referees a powerful group including Alfred Kazin, Robert Penn Warren, and Robert K. Haas (the president of Random House). In response to a request for a blurb, he read the galleys of Richard Wright's new book, *Black Power,* an account of his visit to the Gold Coast (soon to be Ghana) in West Africa. Ralph was noncommittal about the American-educated Kwame Nkrumah, who was leading the Gold Coast and Africa in their march toward independence. On the whole, the African independence movement, thrilling to many blacks, failed to stir Ralph. While he was not for colonialism, he saw himself (as Wright saw himself) as first and foremost a Western intellectual. A rejection of Europe was a step backward. Given his experience in America, he (like Wright) also had reservations about the ability of suddenly empowered blacks to govern. "Whether we like the developments reported in *Black Power* or no," he wrote, "it is not a book that can be easily dismissed. Certainly it cannot be safely ignored."

Returning to New York, Ralph packed his bags for the trip to Salzburg. The idea of a long flight over the Atlantic scared him so much that he wrote a conciliatory but nervous letter to his brother, Herbert, whom he had not seen in sixteen years ("Doesn't time fly!"). He was now 198 pounds, he wrote, "not a little of it around my middle"; also, he joked, "I've started getting grey about the temples and very soon they'll start calling me 'Baldy.' Even my moustache has a few white hairs." On August 19, about an hour before heading for the airport, he admitted in a quick note to Stanley Hyman his fear that he and Fanny might perish in a crash. (Later, he and Fanny almost always flew separately.) "Should anything happen to the two of us," Ralph declared, "I've told Albert Murray that you and he could see what you could salvage from my papers—if you have the time or inclination—though I pity you both." At the airport he bought a life insurance policy. Fanny was his primary beneficiary, with Herbert next in line.

After stops in Ireland and Amsterdam, they reached Salzburg the next day. This was Ralph's first time in Europe since 1945, and Fanny's first visit. At the airport to smooth their way with officials were George Adams, the director of the seminar, and his wife, Mabel. Nine years after the end of World War II, but gripped by the Cold War, Austria was under military rule, with French, American, British, and Russian zones. Salzburg was in the American zone.

Settled on either side of the Salzach River, in a green valley spreading under the Alps, the city of Mozart's birth was even more beautiful than the Ellisons had imagined. Ever since the first Salzburg Seminar in American Studies was held in 1947, the program had met in the Schloss Leopoldskon, on the outskirts of the city. Built in 1736, the Schloss, or castle, had fallen into disrepair. The impresario Max Reinhardt bought it and began renovating it, but did not finish; now his heirs rented it out. Four stories high and facing its own lake, the castle boasted a spacious entrance hall, several large public rooms graced by porcelain stoves, an eighty-thousand-volume library, an extravagant staircase, marble fireplaces faced with blue-and-white Delft tiles, stately old clocks, and paintings covering ceilings and walls. Some were family portraits, others mixed Greek and Roman mythology with Christian motifs. On a terrace facing the lake were busts of Roman notables, including Marcus Aurelius.

On the top floor, where the faculty lived, Ralph and Fanny unpacked their bags in a spacious room with a superb view. Across the way was the Schloss Hohensalzburg, a gem atop Monk's Hill and the best-preserved walled fortress of its kind in Europe. "Most of it is hidden by the pine trees," Fanny wrote home, and "it certainly beats any regular view that I have in New York." But they had to share a bathroom with others; also, the top floor sagged, and both the plumbing and the electricity were fickle. Ignoring these problems, Ralph and Fanny joined gladly in the missionary role of the enterprise. Founded by Harvard students distressed by how misinformed young Europeans were about American culture, the seminars were funded not by the U.S government but privately, with strong support from the Rockefeller Foundation. "One reason the venture works," Max Lerner wrote, "is that no one can suspect it of being an engine of American propaganda. It is wholly free-wheeling."

For this session Ralph joined Lerner, a former war correspondent now a Brandeis University professor as well as a newspaper columnist known for his commitment to civil rights; a University of Chicago historian; a Cornell economist; and a young musicologist at Harvard. Sixty-four students from all over Europe attended. Like American graduate students in some ways, these students were much more likely to be older, married (some with children), and established as teachers, lawyers, artists, scientists, journalists, or writers. Although no grades or examinations were given, the professors worked hard. "Each session of the Salzburg Seminar," according to a faculty handout, is "a great conversation that goes from breakfast to bedtime, seven days a week." Fortunately for Ralph, Fanny was at hand and eager to help him. He needed help. With little teaching experience, he had to deliver a fifty-minute lecture on Monday, Wednesday, and Friday, and also conduct ninety-minute seminars on Tuesday and Thursday. Fanny read Ralph's required texts, attended every class, and recorded in shorthand and then on the typewriter much of what he said.

His lecture course, "The Role of the Novel in Creating the American Experience," stressed his favorite writers from Melville to Bellow. His seminar, "The Background of American Negro Expression—Folklore, Writing and Music," examined black American expressive culture from slavery to the present day. With special attention to Jimmy Rushing, Charlie Christian, Benny Moten, Count Basie, and Duke Ellington, he explored the spirituals, blues, and jazz. Lecturing from notes, improvising in the seminar, Ralph offered the young Europeans his sense of the moral, intellectual, and technical complexity of America. He knew that he was in an odd position, a Negro teaching American culture to Europeans skeptical about America and its often boastful claims about liberty and justice. Ralph made it clear that "I feel neither the necessity to attack nor defend" America before Europeans; "I am interested only in helping them to discover the complex truth of American reality."

As a black man, Ralph fascinated the Salzburg students. Most likely, few had ever come so close to one, much less one as accomplished as Ellison. All but four enrolled in his lecture course. "The great mystery to me is the students," Fanny wrote home in turn, "what they *really* think and what they *really* feel. The excessive deference and uninterrupted politeness toward the professors and their wives make the head swim and the back ache." Simone Vauthier, a student from Lyons, tried to capture the mood of the lecture class held in the ornate Venetian Room, with its harlequin figures on the walls between candelabras. The professor is a forty-year-old man "with a small, black moustache against the Negro skin." Dressed in faded blue jeans and an unbuttoned light gray blazer, he reflects on Mark Twain. The professor gives "a deep, contented chuckle" and "grabs his broad nose with a powerful thumb grip." Ever present, his wife is "a delicate, dark-skinned and very graceful woman; she looks up from her pad and laughs too."

At least once, Ralph shattered the students' passivity and sense of decorum. Because he alluded so seldom to racial injustice in America, Vauthier wrote, "the more startling the eruption that comes when a velvet-eyed Frenchman declares that 'Negro writers' ought to write in 'a Negro manner.' Ellison's voice then rises in a crescendo; with immense emotional power and polemically hard-hitting hammer-blows" he assaults "each and every 'mystical' attempt at defining the Negro characteristics." He grills the hapless Frenchman: "Are you suggesting that Negroes should create their own artistic novel form? That's nothing but European romanticism." However, "some of the embers" of this fiery attack "fall crackling onto the red carpet in the seminar room." After all, "what has attracted the group of listeners" to the class "if not precisely a good amount of infatuation with the Negro, with the addition of respect for the author?" Surely, Vauthier wrote, Ellison understood that white romanticism accounted in large part for his popularity there, just as white romanticism and guilt accounted for much of his success at home. This knowledge had to inspire in the professor a brew of pride, pleasure, and regret. "There is a kind of melancholic trust in Ralph Ellison."

Aside from giving a reading in the Russian zone of Vienna, Ralph stayed close to the Schloss. With his tough regimen of reading, teaching, and almost unrelenting conferences with curious students, he craved the arrival of early evening, when the Austrian staff served cocktails to the faculty and their guests. He countered the cool, damp weather with martinis made from Stroh, the popular Austrian gin. The local liquors, Fanny soon discovered, especially one made from juniper berries, "can heat you faster than a red hot stove." At student parties they watched the young Europeans loosen up to the strains of jazz or try to learn the jitterbug and other American dance steps. Occasionally the Ellisons and their colleagues dined in town, and at least once Ralph caught trout in a nearby canal.

The seminar passed too quickly for many of the young Europeans, who appeared to feel an extra tinge of sadness in bidding farewell to the charming, dynamic Negro "Herr Professor" and "Frau Professor." Ralph poured more emotion than usual into his closing classes. "I will never forget your wonderful last lecture," a student assured him. Vilgot Sjomar, a Swedish journalist, later wrote a warm account of his weeks with Ellison in Salzburg. "For me, privately," he assured Ralph about his classes, "they were a sort of initiation in the USA." At least one student cried. She was embarrassed by her torrent of tears, a Yugoslavian woman wrote to them later, but had no regrets. Ralph was proud to think that he and Fanny had made a positive impact both as Americans and as Negroes. Some people at home and in Europe were suspicious of the motives behind the Salzburg Seminar and skeptical of its value. Ralph and Fanny were not.

With lectures sponsored by his German publisher, S. Fischer Verlag, just ahead of them, the Ellisons now discovered to their dismay that they could not fly around Europe on their original tickets as their travel agent had assured them they could. Thus, when the European representative of New American Library, Lewis Ullian, offered to drive them part of the way into Germany, Ralph and Fanny packed hurriedly and, without any farewell, slipped out early one morning. Later, Ralph made an apology of sorts to Adams for this breach of etiquette. "Certainly it was worth it," he noted, "as I must somewhat selfishly admit."

Ullian drove them to Munich, where they spent two pleasant Oktoberfest days, then through the green farmland of the Necker Valley to the historic university town of Heidelberg. On September 20 they reached Ulm, the site of Ralph's first engagement. The event was disappointing. The next morning, after Ullian left them according to plan, Ralph and Fanny made their way by train to Frankfurt. The lecture there and the next one, in Cologne, were also letdowns. "We found it a completely anticlimactic experience and regretted it," they wrote to Ralph's student Vilgot Sjomar. Paired with a German writer in Cologne, Ralph read for ten minutes or so, the German author did the same, then the audience applauded and left. According to their hosts, this was the German style. The fact that Ralph's honoraria were pitiful did not help.

They returned to Frankfurt via Wiesbaden and a trip along the Rhine, expecting to fly on September 23 to Florence, to which Aldo Celli, one of the more outgoing seminar students, had invited them. They were delayed in Frankfurt for five dismal, rainy days while they waited for travel money to arrive from the American embassy in Spain, a country to which they had suddenly been invited. When the money arrived, on September 28, they quit Frankfurt and headed south. Reaching Florence, they took Celli's advice and stayed across the river in the Roman Catholic monastery Villa San Girolamo in Fiesole. They strolled on the Ponte Vecchio over the Arno, visited the Uffizi, gazed on the Duomo, and paid homage to Michelangelo's *David*. Then they hurried on to Spain, where the U.S. embassy in Madrid had urgently invited Ralph to join a symposium, "Coloquios Intimos de Estudios Norteamericanos," taking place between September 30 and October 3 in the Escorial. Twenty-five Spanish men gathered to discuss American culture, its architecture, theater, cinema, literature, and what the embassy delicately called—in Franco's repressive regime—"unresolved problems in the socio-economic scene."

Later Ralph would thank John Reid, the cultural officer at the embassy, for "those three magnificent days at Escorial." Ralph wrote that the conference was "very lively, and we found a freedom of speech we had not thought possible under the circumstances." Awaiting an honorarium from the embassy, they decided to stay on and were soon glad they had done so—"the warm, beautiful and dignified Spanish" people impressed them with "their élan, which one senses immediately." The cheeky children along the Castellana, the handsome, sensual women, the elegant shops, the treasures of the Prado, contrasted with the German gloom. Perhaps their most exciting evening was spent in a seedy building near the statue of Cervantes. There, a friendly poet led them past lounging prostitutes and desperate-looking men sipping brandy to a performance of authentic flamenco. Later, their friends at home squinted "a little suspiciously" when they raved about Franco's Spain. In response, Fanny insisted that "we have embraced nothing new but are simply responding to the Spanish people."

As soon as Ralph's honorarium arrived they took a bus to the airport and flew to Paris. Their stay started unpromisingly when, tired of traveling, they arrived at around one in the morning, made their way to the Studia, a small hotel near the Invalides that Lew Ullian had recommended, and were given a cold, tiny interior room. After Ralph woke up the next morning with a cold, he and Fanny were about to check out in a huff when they mentioned Ullian's name. Immediately, the proprietor of the Studia led them to a spacious, warm, corner room, where Ralph and Fanny stayed during their ten days in the city.

Luring them to Paris were the recent appearance of *Invisible Man* in French from Editions Denoël, a subdivision of the giant French publisher Gallimard, and, to a lesser extent, the presence of Richard Wright and his family. Unfortunately, the National Book Award meant little to the French. Ralph was nobody. Moreover, Editions Denoël had inexplicably titled its translation *Au delà du regard* ("Beyond the Visible"). The book itself was just about invisible. But Ralph and Fanny's reunion after six years with Richard and Ellen Wright at their home in the Latin Quarter was pleasant, at least at first.

Exactly how well Richard was doing was another matter. To Ralph, the wisdom of his self-exile was more than ever in doubt. The eight years between *Black Boy* and *The Outsider* suggested a stark deflation in Richard's creativity. Wright's compensatory turn to travel writing, as in *Black Power,* was not much of a substitute for fiction like *Native Son* or *Uncle Tom's Children.* A slender, all-white, psychological novel, *Savage Holiday,* also appeared in 1954, to little effect. When Richard let it be known that he was writing a book about Spain, Ralph's reservations grew.

At Leroy Haynes's popular—at least among African-Americans—restaurant in Rue de Martyrs in Montmartre, Ralph and Fanny supped on barbecued pork, red beans and rice, and other soul food. The evening was unremarkable until a Gypsy woman working the room read Ralph's palm. When he mentioned that he had just attended a flamenco performance in Madrid, she urged him to hear three celebrated artists now living in Paris—Vicente Escudero, Pepe el de la Matrona, and Rafael Romero. The result for Ralph was one of the most riveting evenings of his visit to Europe. He had assumed that Escudero, now past sixty, was dead. Instead he had rebuilt a version of his art in its prime that both respected and defied old age. "Dry, now, and birdlike in his grace," as Ralph would soon write in admiration in *Saturday Review,* Escudero "is no longer capable of floor-resounding vigor, but conveys even the stamping fury of the Spanish dance with the gentlest, most delicate, precise, and potent of gestures and movements."

This was the high point of the Ellisons' visit to Paris. The weather was cold and rainy, and (as they wrote to the Ullians) they were simply "too tired to take the city on." The black American expatriate colony, which included James Baldwin and Chester Himes, seemed to be a hive of intrigue that found its center in envy and resentment of Wright, who was himself sure that some of the others were U.S. government agents. Their lives seemed petty and pointless. "The lonely, down-at-the-heels American expatriates huddling in the cafes and idling up and down Blvd. St. Michel depressed us no end," Fanny wrote. "We began to think yearningly of home." She stressed that "Paris was a *business* trip." Visiting the offices of his French publisher, Editions Denoël, Ralph was pleased to meet Michel Chrestien, the charming young translator of *Invisible Man.* "Of all the people with whom we spent time in Paris," Ralph decided, Chrestien was by far the best. When Chrestien invited the Ellisons to meet his family at their home in Seine-et-Oise outside Paris, Ralph and Fanny found them a civilized relief from the company of the Negroes, who "had thoroughly depressed us."

To Ralph, the black expatriates had given up prematurely, in a sense almost treasonously, on America. With *Brown v. Board of Education,* the Supreme Court had righted the ship of state and asserted the same historic imperatives of morality that had led once to the Civil War and the crushing of slavery. To exalt France over the United States on the subject of race was grating: "I am getting a little sick of American Negroes running over for a few weeks and coming back insisting that it's paradise." Ralph felt Negro writers such as Baldwin and Himes appeared to forget that the crucial problem facing artists is almost always the struggle to master their art, not the fight against Jim Crow. "My answer to them," he continued severely, "is that, my problems are not primarily racial problems, that they are the problems of a writer and that if a trip across to France would solve those, I would make it tomorrow, but after seeing them I am reluctant to believe that any such magic exists. So many of them talk and act like sulking children and all they can say about France with its great culture is that it's a place where they can walk in any restaurant and be served. It seems rather obscene to me to reduce life to such terms."

Preparing to return home, Ralph accepted an invitation from young George Plimpton to sit for an interview for the English-language *Paris Review.* Co-edited by Plimpton (Harvard '48), Peter Matthiessen (Yale '50), and the poet Donald Hall, the review was their antidote to the spreading disease of dull literary criticism. They sought to "put criticism where we thought it belonged," Plimpton told *Time* "in the back of the book." With the journal a hit, Viking was planning to publish some of its interviews as a book. On October 22, at the Café de la Mairie du Vie, Ralph faced questions posed by the American writers Alfred Chester and Vilma Howard (he was white, she was black and a Fisk graduate). The café was another stop on the Paris literary bistro tour, like the Closerie des Lilas, Deux Magots, or Brasserie Lipp. (Its claim to fame was that Djuna Barnes had written most of *Nightwood* there.) To his interviewers Ralph seemed uncannily self-possessed. "The quiet steady flow and development of ideas were overwhelming," they reported. "To listen to him is rather like sitting in the back of a huge hall and feeling the lecturer's faraway eyes staring directly into your own. The highly emphatic, almost professorial intonations startle with their distance, self-confidence, and warm undertones of humor." He said *Invisible Man* wasn't an important novel. "I failed of eloquence and many of the immediate issues are rapidly fading away. If it does last it will be simply because there are things going on in its depths that are of more permanent interest than in its surface. I hope so."

Five days later, after Plimpton sent him a rough typewritten transcript of the interview to revise in the coming weeks, he and Fanny flew to New York.

Returning to 730 Riverside Drive after seventy days away, "we fell into bed," Fanny wrote to Ellen Wright, "and slept for three days." They awoke to the realization that they were also "broke and very far behind" on paying off their debts.

In addition, getting back to work on his novel proved more difficult for Ralph than he had anticipated, especially as their calendar filled up with stylish distractions such as a luncheon for the prime minister of Ceylon, Sir John Kotelawala, at the St. Regis Hotel. Ralph turned instead to smaller tasks. Overhauling the *Paris Review* text, he warned Plimpton to "draw a deep breath before you count the pages because there are a hell of a lot of them." (The interview would appear the following spring, 1955.) For his friend David Sarser he was the ghostwriter of a timely piece, "Tape, Disks and Coexistence," comparing the two major sound-recording media then emerging, for publication the following March in *High Fidelity* magazine. Drawing on what he had heard and seen in Madrid and Paris, he composed his essay "Introduction to Flamenco" for the December issue of *Saturday Review*. Here, assessing some new recordings, he artfully teased out the ignored similarities between slave songs, blues, early jazz, and cante flamenco. All of these forms, expressing "tragic, metaphysical elements of human life," illustrate the existence of "an esthetic which rejects the beautiful sound sought by classical Western music." On January 1, 1955, *Saturday Review* also published a tiny but lyrical vignette titled "February." Writing about the Dayton winter of 1938, Ralph recalled the bitter ordeal when "I had lived through my mother's death in that strange city," surviving for three months living "off the fields and woods by my gun; through ice and snow and homelessness. . . . Shall I say it was in those February snows that I first became a man?"

These pieces kept his hand in as he waited for narrative inspiration to flow again. He and Fanny felt recharged by their return home. "The city is truly fabulous this year," she wrote to one of the black expatriates in Paris. The rich windows at Macy's and the giant, bejeweled Christmas tree at Rockefeller Center spoke to the special vitality of American life. Lifted by a Christmas gift in the form of a glowing reference to *Invisible Man* in the cover essay by Robert Gorham Davis in the *New York Times Book Review* of December 26, Ralph returned with confidence to his main work-in-progress. Soon Fanny reported to the Ullians that Ralph "is now hard at work on his new novel in an enthusiastic and satisfying way—a mood too precious to risk putting aside." The fact that many people in the white South were resisting the integrationist spirit of the *Brown* decision was balanced by the fact that in the North—certainly in New York City—the spirit of *Brown,* which was the spirit of his novel-in-progress, seemed to be accepted. Of course there were exceptions. At the National Book Awards ceremony on January 25, 1955, at the Commodore Hotel, a member or members of the staff in some way humiliated Ralph despite his elegant clothing and aristocratic air. Suppressing his rage, he accepted a written apology (after the NBA protested) for "a situation which embarrassed you" and an earnest promise of decent treatment in the future.

Continuing honors partially offset such humiliations. Coming home after a lecture downtown at the New School for Social Research, he opened a letter and read that he had just won a Prix de Rome. Each year, the classics-based American Academy in Rome invited a fellow chosen and supported by the American Academy of Arts and Letters in New York (a separate organization) to join the scholars, musicians, painters, and sculptors who held annual residential positions at the academy headquarters in Rome. Successfully sponsoring Ralph were his admirers John Hersey and Robert Penn Warren, who described Ralph as "a slow and careful worker who needs freedom and time to refine his work."

For a brief while Ralph dithered over the decision. With its modest stipend, even with free lodging the prize could scarcely support him and Fanny. The award was "as much pain as prize," he complained to Hyman. He had "almost turned it down, but I understand no one *ever* does that." Fanny convinced him to accept it. "We leave for one year at the Academy," she wrote gaily to friends, "loafing or whatever we want to do." When the Guggenheim Foundation rejected his application on the grounds that he had just won a fellowship, she reluctantly began to look for work in Rome. "I'll need the job," she wrote, "but I can think of nothing worse than having to work when really I'll want to relax and see things."

Perhaps because of the news and its promise of disruption, Ralph lost ground on his novel. He also shared with Hyman, who was still his main literary advisor, a concern about his reliance on jazzlike improvisation and hapless "riffing" instead of a tight plot. In April, when he sent Stanley a sample excerpt, his covering letter was curiously manic. "I'm enclosing copies of some of my work sheets," he wrote, "so that you may see the drift of a certain section of my current madness. It's still quite crude but it might give you a laugh—or a shudder. Anyway, it's out of context. What is it? A fable on sacred and profane love? Don't ask me! Choc-drinking Charlie [one of his new characters] slipped in when I was typing up a copy for you and he's still too drunk to master his lines—or even tell me what they really should be. Somewhere deep in my mind I suspect that he was once one of a group of nine or *ten* tailors—but then the goddam[n] doctors were once little colored boys like me or maybe Indians."

Was he writing a novel or a "fable"? Why did characters enter his work out of the blue, and mainly so to riff entertainingly rather than advance the plot? Where *was* the plot? The clue to Cliofus, an increasingly dominant figure, Ralph ventured, "is in his name. I just wish the son of a bitch wouldn't run off with my book." Perhaps a clue to Ralph's crisis was itself in that clue. The name Cliofus (at times spelled "Cliophus" or "Cleophus" in the manuscript) suggests that he was investing much of his hope for success in allegorical and mythical conceits. Cliofus, who would persist in Ralph's novel-in-progress even after he overhauled the work around 1958, clearly plays on the name Clio, the Greek muse of history. Ralph then combines Clio with, probably, Rufus—a name associated with the fox (*rufus* is Latin for red, and the red fox is a classic embodiment of cunning) and with black Southerners (as in Brer Fox in Joel Chandler Harris's "Uncle Remus" tales from the 1880s). Also, the name Cliofus suggests that he is an oaf—someone large, clumsy, but probably harmless. Virgil Branam, Ralph's earthy friend since their boyhood in Oklahoma City, was most likely one model for Cliofus.

When Hyman's response came, Ralph sifted it for the positive and jived about the negative. "Good to know you feel something going on therein," he wrote back gratefully. However, what he wrote next was alarming, if not appalling. The excerpt was "a mere fragment and by no means an attempt at a story or even a formal whole; although clues lying earlier in the talk between the two characters provide its frame, its foreshadowing and its broader meaning." Invoking Joyce's name and radical example, he hinted that his own work might thus be exempt from criticism. He then offered a startling admission—"I simply numbered pages for your convenience"—and followed with a somewhat preposterous suggestion about the excerpt, "that its most effective connection with the plot lies exactly in its seeming incoherence." He linked this incoherence to the idea of history as chaos. The past, "for all the Marxists have to say, has no plot—certainly, that 'history' which evolves from the whirling of the earth through space, heating up and cooling down, storming and sunning and winding and raining, cracking and mending, moving and shaking—hasn't; it's only that men give it significance." Hence his aesthetic of anarchy, as "old See-oafus riffs out the past, and significance must wait to register in the consciousness of his listener—who, as things now stand conception-wise, is either the hero or the hero's son. Form and formalities arise from his mind." Ralph then invoked, perhaps as added justification for his surrender to chaos, a heartbreaking line from *Moby-Dick* (chapter 114): " 'Oh where is the foundling's father hidden?' "

Between anxieties over his novel and the Prix de Rome, by May Ralph was complaining of sundry aches, pains, and strains, especially in his stomach. However, he easily passed a complete physical examination. His weight was up to 198 pounds, but the doctor pronounced him "healthy as a pig," according to Ralph, who conceded that "all my aches and pains are psycho—all brought on by this go[d]dam[n] novel I'm trying to do." In May, when he attended the annual ceremony of the American Academy and National Institute two blocks from his home, Archibald MacLeish announced that Ralph had won that year's Prix de Rome. According to the citation, *Invisible Man* had "examined with unsparing honesty the inner life of a Negro in America and, through that life, some facets of the common experience of western man in recent years."

In June, shortly after he attended a PEN reception for novelist Jules Romains, a former president of the organization, he and Fanny drove to Brandeis University in Waltham, Massachusetts, near Boston, to take part in another symposium on the novel; Irving Howe, Delmore Schwartz, and Katherine Anne Porter (once married to Albert Erskine) also spoke. In Cambridge he had a pleasant reunion with Lucille and Fred Muhlhauser, the director of the Salzburg Seminar, who had visited when the Ellisons were there. Then Ralph drove to Bennington, where he enjoyed not only the fragrant Vermont spring but also the varied pleasures of commencement. Sitting in on Hyman's last classes of the year, he marveled at "how frightfully brilliant some of these girls are!" He was also moved by "the rather beautiful and simple graduation ceremony held under the morning sky. With sweet-voiced choir and concert of mellow hand-rung bell . . . on a lawn still perfumed by spring flowers. I was taken in like the stranger at the wedding feast, and my old bones quickened to the challenge of so much youth and I kept going and enjoying myself to the end."

But Ralph had gone to Bennington mainly to have one last discussion about his novel before leaving for Rome. In 1943, Ralph's breakthrough

short story, "Flying Home," had been finished with Hyman's vigorous
advice at his apartment in New York, and Stanley had been plainly indispensable on *Invisible Man*. To at least one observer, Hyman's influence
was not good for Ralph. "Stanley Edgar Hyman ruined Ralph Ellison,"
Saul Bellow declared long after both men had died. "Hyman encouraged
Ralph to be ponderous, to become a spokesman for certain positions, to
pontificate. In a way, Ralph could choose between the two of us, his
friends, as examples. Hyman was the good Jew, I was the bad. . . . Hyman
saw himself as the great intellectual, and Ralph fell into the trap of seeing
himself as an authority on this and that. He did not allow himself to be
free and grow." This is probably an overstatement. Stanley had encouraged
Ralph to study Kenneth Burke, and without Burke, as probably without
Hyman, there would have been no *Invisible Man*. Burke and Hyman
encouraged in Ralph a reverence for the guiding power of myth, symbol,
and allusion. Unfortunately, that reverence was becoming dogmatic. That
this development was Hyman's fault is questionable. Ralph was becoming rigid on his own.

On July 5, back in New York, Ralph and Fanny attended yet another
semi-diplomatic party at Dorothy Norman's, this time for U Nu, the
prime minister of Burma. Ralph enjoyed the martinis and the small talk,
but he had limited interest in the problems of emergent nations in the Far
East or anywhere else. In this way he deliberately foreclosed some of his
professional possibilities. Richard Wright would travel to Bandung, In-
donesia, for the historic meeting of nonaligned nations out of which came
the notion of the Third World. Ralph could have been an astute commentator on such matters, but he was unwilling to divert his energies away
from the art of fiction into a book of social commentary such as Wright's
The Color Curtain (about the Bandung gathering). Even when the State
Department asked him in July to visit Ghana for its independence celebrations, he said no. In fact, the proposal epitomized the problem of mixing art and politics, in that the State Department wanted Ralph to write a
novel about Ghana to be filmed "as a phase of the country's Independence Day's celebrations." He also rejected attempts by the government
to arrange private meetings for him with foreigners, including Japanese
and Africans. As he prepared to leave for Europe, he seemed to be turning
inward as an American.

He resisted other efforts to turn him into a soldier for noble causes.
When, in 1955, the NAACP asked him to write a biography of Walter
White, its recently deceased veteran leader, Ralph declined. (That year,

Langston Hughes published *Fight for Freedom,* an informal history of the organization.) Ralph put his fiction first, period. Visiting Max Lerner and his wife, Edna, for "two fine days in the country," he enjoyed talking about gripping events down south about which Lerner wrote zealously in his *New York Post* columns. But he was heading to Italy, not Mississippi or Arkansas. He believed that isolation in Italy, rather than standing at the barricades, was more likely to produce a fine novel.

As he struggled with his book, Ralph was still eager on July 26 to take part in a formal discussion in Manhattan on the timely subject "What's Wrong with the American Novel?" (The sponsor was *The American Scholar,* the journal of the Phi Beta Kappa Society, which expected to publish the transcript.) With him were Hiram Hayden, the editor of *The American Scholar;* Stephen Becker, an editor and a novelist; Simon Michael Bessie, the general editor of Harper & Brothers; Albert Erskine of Random House; and his fellow fiction writers Jean Stafford and William Styron, whose first novel, *Lie Down in Darkness,* set mainly in his native Virginia, had earned fine reviews. Eight years before, Lionel Trilling of Columbia University had issued a damning indictment of the American novel. To Trilling, the American novel had died some time ago—and was still dead. Echoing Henry James's notorious words on American cultural poverty in Hawthorne's day, Trilling had insisted in his 1947 lecture "Manners, Morals, and the Novel" (published in 1950 in his influential collection of essays *The Liberal Imagination*) that this same American cultural poverty still blocked the rise of a worthy novelistic tradition.

The symposium was a sometimes scrappy discussion in which, with hindsight, one sees Ralph's sober attempts to answer the main question and also an emerging apologia for his faltering record as an artist. If the American novel was in trouble, he declared, the blame belonged far more to the artist than to the audience or to such wicked new diversions as television. Expounding yet again on the moral vigor of pre–Civil War American (New England) writing, he tried to update his recurring thesis in the light of the rapidly changing national scene, including the civil rights struggle. He repeated some key words and terms. One was "chaos," which was still and ever, as in *Invisible Man,* the most burdened word in his cultural vocabulary. The American novelist had to accept the reality of chaos as a threat to social order. As a moralist, he or she had to recognize its deadly threat; as an artist, he or she had to give it form. On any day on 125th Street in Harlem, Ralph said, he could see signs of chaos existing alongside patterns of social order: "I can see people gesturing wildly on the street; I can see dope addicts; I can see people acting out wild fantasies." This world was challenging. "I see a whole chaotic world existing within the ordered social pattern," he declared, "and I can see a million contradictions to that order."

"Wonder" was another key term for him here, as in "a sense of wonder." Great nineteenth-century novels were superior in that they "expressed a sense of wonder which gave the audience . . . a grasp of contemporary change; a sense of wonder arising out of the multiplicity of events being reduced to form; a sense of discovery." Instead of respecting chaos and a sense of wonder, and delving into the myriad geographies, ethnicities, races, dialects, and traditions of the nation, too many American novelists were settling for pinched offices. Criticizing Hemingway and Wright on this score, he also addressed Trilling's thesis. Hemingway had chosen to write about atypical slices of American culture, notably its expatriates, after starting out with the far more American stories about Nick Adams. Seeking to carry out a "revolution of the word," he had chosen to place his emphasis "mainly upon technique." Other American writers (probably Wright was guilty here) had entered into unwise competition with sociologists and psychologists. With Trilling, "a kind of snobbery of style" had emerged, and the worship of "a Henry James type of technique" rather than an engagement with "that great mass of experience which will not be hammered into shape by such delicate subtleties."

Faulkner had been the supreme American novelist since the Civil War, Ralph said, with Bellow as his able successor. Bellow proved that America could sustain fabulous fiction and that it did not need the recherché values preached by Trilling. Citing Ursula Brumm's anti-Trilling essay "Fallacies of Legislative Criticism" (appearing that year in *Western Review*), Ralph endorsed her championing of Bellow's *The Adventures of Augie March*. "Perhaps Trilling has never forgiven himself," he suggested privately in writing to Brumm, "for not having been born on the same social level as Henry James; thus with all that glory gone to dust he sees no other life to celebrate, his own being unworthy, Lord; so very unworthy." Bellow's *Augie March* "was exactly the right example with which to refute his argument, for it does for that life of which Bellow writes exactly what James did for that which he knew; it defines it by depicting it, by reducing it to form. And by doing so Bellow makes it possible for us to possess it and through the possession to understand a little more of the nature of man and society."

Both Ralph and Bellow had taken their major artistic cues from Mark Twain, not from Henry James. The title of Bellow's *The Adventures of Augie March* paid explicit homage to Mark Twain. (In May, Bellow had scribbled a note to Ralph on a postcard from Hannibal, Missouri: "Thought you'd like to be remembered from this place.") A crucial difference existed, nevertheless, between Bellow and Ellison, one that time would only exacerbate. Ralph talked about the chaos of 125th Street in Harlem, but he was not writing (as he had written in parts of *Invisible Man*) as if he were an insider there. Bellow, on the other hand, was writing about the world he actually lived in, or he used that solid life as his runway for flights of the imagination as wild as those in *Henderson the Rain King*. Ralph, with a growing distance between himself and the black social reality about him, was finding it hard to turn that reality into fiction. The first words of Ralph's one published novel—"I am an invisible man"— testify that this growing sense of his own relative social amorphousness already leeched his vitality by 1945. To the contrary, the first words of Bellow's breakthrough novel—"I am an American, Chicago born"—testify to his social anchorage. Elsewhere, Ralph had conceded the existence of this contradiction in his own life. "This is America and our task is to explore it," he declared, "create it by describing it." At the same time, "you have all these great things happening; and on the other hand you have writers like me" who do not travel, who do not know the country first-hand. "So how am I really going to communicate?"

When the discussion at the *American Scholar* symposium turned to the frequent elusiveness in America of the second novel following the sparkling debut, he put some of the blame on "the fluidity of our society. Reality changes fast, and if you don't keep up with it, you are apt to fall into writing the same book." Albert Erskine then reflected on the "ballyhoo" of the flashy first success and the ensuing absence of a second act, in F. Scott Fitzgerald's requiem for his own career. "I think that is a thing," Erskine observed somberly, "which frequently destroys people." Ralph was even more specific, and more pessimistic: "Your integrity is destroyed."

13

Adventure in Rome

1955–1957

Home is where I would like to be.
RALPH ELLISON (1956)

On September 22, with a sense that they were embarking on the
grandest adventure of their lives together, Ralph and Fanny sailed
from New York for Naples. Sharing the eleven-day journey were seven
other new academy fellows. They docked at Cannes, then made a detour
to Antibes to visit an exhibition of Picasso's work. At Genoa, with its steep
hills, intriguing funiculars, and handsome homes, they strolled as a group
for the first time on Italian soil. At Naples to greet them officially—and
help them recover their considerable excess baggage—were Laurance and
Isabel Roberts, the academy's patrician director and his wife. Setting out
at once by car across Italy to Rome the party stopped now and then to
gape at sights such as the coastal town of Terracina, with its impressive
cliff and ancient temple and fortress. "The sun reflected on the cliff,"
Fanny wrote home, "made it glow as if it were burning from the inside."
The clear, dry air—fragrant with end-of-summer scents—the honest local
wines, the good food and company, left her, and Ralph, refreshed and
optimistic about their latest adventure by the time they reached Rome.

The main American Academy building, an imposing neoclassical structure, sat atop the highest of the famed Seven Hills of Rome. It looked out
over the heart of Rome and almost directly across the city at the Villa
Medici, the site of the far older and more venerable French Academy in
Rome. Assisted by cheerful members of the staff, Ralph and Fanny
unpacked in their assigned bedroom and small adjoining study in the
main building. When Ralph quietly protested the inadequacy of their
quarters, he was given one of the more charming spaces at the academy—

a secluded studio in a corner of the back garden, up against the Aurelian Wall that marked one boundary of the academy grounds.

The pros and cons of academy life soon became clear. The rooms were free, but the pieces of furniture rickety and drab. Maids cleaned the fellows' rooms daily, but the fellows shared bathrooms. To reach them, Fanny noted, they had to hike down a corridor as long and as cold as a Manhattan block in winter. "The food is excellent," she wrote home, just before Ralph began to complain about the effect of garlic on his tender stomach. Socializing with most of the sixty or more other residents at the public meals was taxing, too. The dinners, served by candlelight at long tables, demanded a level of diplomacy that Ralph (and some other fellows) could not always muster. Soon, at his urging, Fanny began to prepare breakfast and dinner in their rooms using an electric hot plate and an electric oven picked up at a flea market. They saved money this way, since residents had to pay for meals from the academy kitchen.

The director and his wife lived across the street in the Villa Aurelia, a seventeenth-century palace of red stucco walls and marble. Also in the villa were elegant quarters where distinguished visitors such as Leonard Bernstein, Bernard Berenson, Paul Hindemith, Gian Carlo Menotti, Rufino Tamayo, Serge Koussevitzky, Allen Tate, and Robert Penn Warren stayed on their visits to the academy. That year, the veteran cultural historian and critic Van Wyck Brooks, the official writer-in-residence, lived there, too. Of the fellows that year, the most prestigious group, as always, was that comprising the classics scholars. There were five architects, including young Robert Venturi of Philadelphia, and three musicians, five painters, and two sculptors. Although a few fellows were remote, the Ellisons would befriend many of their colleagues. Long after they had all left Rome, Ralph and Fanny still corresponded with the classicists William MacDonald and Brooks Emmons and the painters Walter Hahn, Leon Goldin, and Alfred Blaustein, as well as their wives.

Ralph enjoyed the distinction of being the only writing fellow that year, and only the fifth writer in its history. In 1951, the poet Anthony Hecht had been its first, followed by William Styron, Allen Tate (the first resident in writing), and the young poet Richard Wilbur. Proud to be the first black to hold a fellowship, Ralph was aware of the ways in which his uniqueness spawned certain anxieties and insecurities in him. Fortunately, Fanny was on hand as an excellent buffer between him and this new world. She was pleasant to one and all, while he was often nervous and reserved. She could negotiate smoothly the eddies of gossip, competition, and envy, but also create more intimate ties to the friendlier fellows and their wives.

While Fanny explored Rome, Ralph stayed put at the academy. First he worked "like hell," and successfully, on an essay for *High Fidelity*. "Living with Music" is short but charmingly captures his love of music from his early days in Oklahoma City, when he first wrestled with the trumpet, to his life in contemporary New York, in which the blossoming world of electronics competed more and more with live performances. Carefully he crafted his essay around his standing belief in the fluidity of American culture. The spirituals, he argued genially, were not so remote from Beethoven or Bach, nor was Armstrong so removed from Brahms or Chopin, that one couldn't love them all. "In the swift whirl of time," he reminded his readers, "music is a constant, reminding us of what we were and of that toward which we aspire. Art thou troubled? Music will not only calm, it will ennoble thee."

He had barely finished this essay when, ten days after their arrival, the Robertses led a group of new fellows and their spouses, including Ralph and Fanny, on a tour of Tuscany and Umbria. An annual event, the tour would take in a dozen hill towns, each possessing artistic treasures. Into the Robertses' Chevy station wagon and three smaller European cars the tourists packed their suitcases—together with picnic baskets, food, and bottles of wine—for what would prove a spectacular introduction to the cultural wealth of Italy. At Orvieto, where they picnicked on soup, ham, veal, cheese, fruit, and wine in the ruins of an ancient amphitheater, they began their visits to a succession of charming towns and cities, including Perugia, Urbino, Rimini, Todi, Assisi, Ravenna, Pisa, Siena, and Florence. Checking into small hotels in the evening, they drank martinis, dined at excellent local restaurants, and usually went to bed tired but contented. By day they saw stunning things, such as the pregnant Madonna of Piero della Francesca, dressed in a blue robe, her hand reaching toward her swollen stomach. This masterpiece had turned up only three years earlier in a small cemetery in Monterchi, where the artist's mother was buried. In Florence, where Ralph and Fanny had stopped the previous year, they visited the Uffizi; in Urbino, the Palazzo Ducale. "Did the art books come alive!" Ralph wrote home. Unfortunately, it soon seemed like a surfeit of caviar. "We feasted on gallery after gallery of great paintings and sculpture," Fanny recounted wearily, "on cathedrals, baptisteries, monuments, piazzas, ancient houses, interesting people, shop windows, and the glorious Italian countryside and seaside."

Nevertheless, Ralph liked what he saw. "The Renaissance has sent my imagination on a jag ever since I was shooting snipes in Oklahoma," he wrote to Al Murray, "but here it's all around you everywhere you turn, the same sky, earth, water, roads, houses, art. And not only that, it's all mingled with the Romans, the Greeks, the Greco-Christians." Stimulated, he raced through Marguerite Yourcenar's novel *Memoirs of Hadrian*. At meals he listened intently to the classicists as they discussed antiquity—"who did what when and why and where"—and felt lost in a world that "I've got to get with [or] die of frustration." He was certain that a surer command of the classical world would allow him to apply more brilliantly his knowledge of myth and ritual—"for here is where the myth and ritual business operates in a context not of primitive culture but beneath the foundation of the West." Unfortunately, the classicists didn't always admit him and other nonclassicists easily into their discussons. Some were "snobbish about this mess," he wrote; "but it belongs to anyone who can dig it—and I don't mean picking around in ruins, as important as that is." He began to put together a reading list "so that I can orientate myself in relation to the classical background."

On October 23, Fanny went with some trepidation to the headquarters of the Pontificia Opera di Assistenza, the central Roman Catholic relief organization in the world. At stake was a job with a subsidiary group, the Lampada della Fraternità, or the Lamp of Brotherhood, which had been founded in 1950 to serve the families of soldiers killed in Italy and abroad. Harold Oram Associates, her employer in New York, was negotiating to represent the Lampada in the United States. Impressed by her, a Lampada executive overlooked her shaky Italian and her Protestant roots and hired Fanny to work three days a week, from 9:30 a.m. until 1:00 p.m., for $30 a month. Her job was to translate bulletins into English. Fanny's coup astonished other spouses at the academy and delighted Ralph no end. After paying for meals they had only $25 left each month from his stipend; her income would make a huge difference in the way they lived. "It's a wonderful job," she assured her mother. Hers was "an unusually high salary" in economically depressed postwar Italy, where vendors often sold two or three cigarettes at a time, eggs singly, and bread by the slice.

Fanny's colleagues were kind to her, but she had to spend long hours after work puzzling over Italian passages. Still she was pleased. "Ever since my grandfather died in 1927," she wrote to Nina Bond, a colleague in New York who was subletting the Ellisons' apartment, "there's been an angel in my life." Fanny's joy bubbled in a letter to another friend (although she seemed to separate her opinion from Ralph's): "We, I, love this wonderful city; its wonders are endless." The following summer, she reassured a black friend nervous about coming to Rome: "I believe you would like the Italians; they're very much like Negroes . . . informal, voluble, warm."

Her success in supplementing what she called "the stingiest fellowship in existence" pleased Ralph but intensified his dependence on her. She learned Italian; he did not. The academy provided free lessons from an ancient Russian émigré countess but Ralph visited her only once. As a result, Fanny had to perform virtually every errand or task involving the use of Italian. He preferred to work on his novel, and Fanny fully supported him here and in his refusal to go sightseeing with her. "Ralph walks a narrow path, from our living quarters to his study and back," she wrote. Four years after finishing *Invisible Man,* he had made no true progress on its successor, although that October he assured a friend that he would be done with it in one more year.

Exacerbating his nervousness was the frequent presence as visitors to the academy of established and productive writers such as Allen Tate and his wife, the novelist Caroline Gordon, and Robert Penn Warren and his second wife, Eleanor Clark, also a novelist. Fond of their young children, Rosanna and Gabriel Warren, Ralph welcomed the chance to get to know Red Warren better. Warren's respect for Ralph had already led to certain generous gestures. Warren and Tate, both of them former Fugitives and ex-supporters of segregation, were inclusive with Ralph and Fanny in ways that left no doubt about their sincerity. Joking with Albert Murray, Ralph promised to ask the unpretentious Caroline Gordon, a Southerner, for some chitterlings "as soon as I know her better . . . cause as sure as hell she's going to come up one day wishing for some turnip greens cooked with a ham bone." On November 16 he and Fanny attended as honored guests Tate's lecture on modern American poetry at the American Library on the Via Veneto. Admiring the men as writers, Ralph also liked their style. Tate and Warren and their wives lived sometimes at La Rocca, a sixteenth-century fortress above Porto Ercole, about seventy miles from Rome, which Ralph and Fanny visited along with William Styron, another friend of Warren. Ralph felt pressure to compete with these men. The writers were "coming and going all the time," Ralph wrote timidly that fall. Their presence "doesn't seem to help me write any faster."

The truth is that, for all its pleasures, he was not very happy at the academy. He could never forget that he was different. He cut his own hair, for example, rather than venture into an Italian barbershop. Coming over on the ship, a seaman had spoken of a small black district in Rome, but Ralph would not seek it out. He was not inclined to make friends with a fellow black American, Frank Snowden, the cultural attaché at the American embassy and a bona fide classics scholar. The Snowdens invited the Ellisons to Thanksgiving dinner at their home, where they enjoyed excellent turkey, chestnuts, mincemeat pie, and biscuits. To Fanny, Snowden was "a very handsome and cultured man, and so is his wife." But Ralph was not charmed. "I'll bet money that he's an operator."

Unsuited to living in so much intimacy with many other people, white or black, Ralph was well mannered almost always but also developed a dislike for some of them—and blamed himself for having succumbed to the allure of prestige in coming to Rome. The following May, writing to Saul Bellow, he recalled wistfully that he had planned to spend more time in Oklahoma City. "So much of our stay here has been packed with trouble," he confided. He complained about adjusting "to the institutional ways of life; learning to live with prying paranoids, to avoid the burbling old maids and the academic bitching at breakfast."

By this time Ralph was just about boycotting the academy dining tables, even though Fanny, who actually liked the food, found it hard to both do her office work and prepare meals. He needed her to do both; he needed to feel comfortable in order to work. "I long ago began to understand," Fanny wrote about his eating, "that the deep center of all his irrationalism was in his pancreas. Did I say 'understand'? I don't understand but I try to respect it." He couldn't or wouldn't drink Italian coffee, which was too bitter. After a tiring search, Fanny found a place that sold American coffee, but at the steep price of $2 a pound. Once, feeling an urge to eat pigs' feet prepared Southern-style, he sent her to try to find the necessary spices and herbs. "You'd have laughed your ass off," he joked to Murray. "The poor girl walked her feet off trying to find them because she knew there'd be an evil [SOB] if I didn't get all the ingredients for this ceremonial dish, so that she came in late, with only some bay leaf and allspice. And just as she suspected I was fit to be tied."

Homesick, he relied on jazz—played loudly, perhaps even defiantly—to fill part of the void. Having brought with him an excellent reel-to-reel tape recorder, "I have the academy ringing with Duke and Count and Jimmy Rushing." Getting up before dawn on Sundays, long before Fanny, he indulged his love of the main Roman flea market. In January he bought two Etruscan amphorae for 10,000 lire and a bronze Etruscan warrior and a dancer for just over 16,000 lire. These prices were excellent, if the pieces weren't fakes. Still, academy life was a strain for him, and even for the normally tolerant Fanny. "There are all sorts of people here," she wrote home, "of all ages married, unmarried, provincial, sophisticated, nosey, malicious. . . . It's like the chilling discovery after marriage of what your mate is really like—except there is no love with which to rationalize." Fortunately, Christmas, celebrated joyfully throughout the city, made for a sweet diversion. The "spectacular and dramatic" Roman Catholic liturgy, the pungent incense, tall, thick candles, and heavy red brocades compelled Ralph, Fanny, and other academy newcomers when they attended midnight mass at Christmas and on New Year's Day. (At Easter, Ralph would be less reverent about a high mass at St. Peter's celebrated by Pope Pius XII. He found the ancient ceremony "very impressive," he wrote to Al Murray. Pius XII, however, was too staid. A Negro pope— "preferably one converted from one of the storefront cults" at home— would bring back "some of the old vitality to the Church. . . . Most of all, he'd have some real singing.")

As if the holidays were not enough of a distraction from his work, illness struck both Fanny and Ralph early in 1956. At four one morning she was stricken by abdominal pain so severe that Ralph summoned the academy doctor, who diagnosed "appendicular colic." She was recovering nicely when bronchial pneumonia felled Ralph. Injected with strong doses of penicillin and streptomycin, he stayed in bed for nine days while he reread *Great Expectations*, *The Idiot*, and *The Possessed*. He also planned to reread *Moby-Dick*. Dostoyevsky and Melville had assisted at the birth of *Invisible Man*. Now, he hoped, they would come through for him again.

Toward the end of Ralph's illness, the sun blazed suddenly over Rome and the locals announced that winter was well on its way out. By this point, he and Fanny absolutely had to have a vacation. "We both need to get away from the Academy," Fanny wrote to two Princeton friends living in Italy, Leslie and John Aldridge. The editor of a noted 1952 anthology of essays on the American novel, Aldridge was spending the year in Ravello, in the mountains above the Amalfi coast and the Bay of Salerno. The need to get away became even more urgent on February 3, when the Roman sun vanished and snow poured down on the city for the first time in years. At first the giddy citizens threw snowballs; then a biting chill sent them indoors. At the poorly heated academy, the inhabitants shivered through most of February. Rain falling almost without respite seeped through holes in the roof, and the academy's front cornice began to give way. The muddy Tiber plunged sullenly through the stricken city. Between the white folks and the cold, Ralph could barely stand it. "I'm homesick," he wrote to Murray, "for some moses [blacks] for one thing"; also, "I got no way to get any corn bread and these Romans think a chitterling is something to stuff sausage into. There is very little whiskey I can afford, *no* sweet potatoes or yellow yams, a biscuit is unheard of—they think it means cookie in this town—and their greens don't taste like greens. What's worse, ain't nobody around to speak the language."

The visit to the Aldridges in March lasted about ten days. Ravello indeed seemed "an enchanted town," as John had promised. Lemon trees hugged lean ledges, villages clung to the sides of stony cliffs, their white houses with green shutters stacked upon each other, "all looking bravely and precariously out across the bay of Salerno," Ralph noted mordantly, "—from whence came the Moors, the boats loaded with loot from the New World, and most recently the Americans." The two couples started off well together. At least once they went down to sunbathe on the beach at Positano. But when John and Ralph clashed about books and ideas, Ralph held little back simply because he was a guest. "I will eat a man's food," he declared, "and then give him hell if he thinks that a meal entitles him to my agreement to some crap[p]y ideas." In coming to Ravello, he judged, the Aldridges had "fallen for the old American escapist dream of romantic Italian isolation up on a hill, only to discover that they need people in the worst kind of way." Ralph was put off even more by the semi-precious Anglo-Indian writer Aubrey Menen, who lived near Ravello. Menen invited the Ellisons and the Aldridges to dinner but had done so, as Ralph saw it, mainly to bait them: "He's never been to America, the profits from his American sales allow him to live like a king in a harsh, badly off part of Italy—and he hates the United States!" Noting that the bachelor Menen lived with a male secretary, Ralph guessed that he probably had come to Ravello to be "in easy access of little boys."

Ralph might have questioned also his own self-imposed isolation up a hill in Rome among whites while at home the civil rights movement grew stronger. On December 1 the previous year, 1955, Rosa Parks had refused to give up her seat on a bus to a white man in Montgomery, Alabama. The resulting bus boycott, as yet unresolved, had brought Dr. Martin Luther

King, Jr., to prominence. Ralph seemed somewhat ambivalent about the new course of the movement. In private letters, he was proud of the leadership of black ministers. But at times he expressed himself in a satirical, even sardonic way that mixed pride with cynicism. Looking at photographs of some defiant black ministers, he saw them as "the old steady, mushmouthed, chicken hawk variety, real wrinkle headed bible pounders" who had just "caught some son of a bitch not only stealing the money, but sleeping with all their own private sisters!" Still, their success pleased him. "I'm supposed to know Negroes," he wrote, "being one myself, but these moses are revealing just a little bit more of their complexity. Leader is a young cat [who is] not only a preacher but a lawyer too, probably also a[n] undertaker, a physician, *and* an atomic scientist. And they're standing their ground in spite of threats, assassinations, economic reprisal, & destruction of property."

He was further surprised when William Faulkner, quoted in *Life*, asserted that he was ready to shoot blacks in the street, if necessary, to save the Old South. His outburst stunned Ralph, because he had long believed in the patrician Mississippi novelist's astute and brave moral penetration of Southern reality. Ralph voiced his disillusionment mainly in a letter to Murray: "Faulkner has delusions of grand[eu]r because he really believes that he invented those characteristic[s] which he ascribes to Negroes in his fiction and now he thinks he can end this great historical action just as he ends [*Light in August*], with Joe Christmas [a racially ambiguous and murderous figure] dead and his balls cut off . . . and everything just as it was except for the brooding, slightly overblown rhetoric of Faulkner's irony. Nuts!" In writing to a Random House editor he was more sober. Although Faulkner's statement was depressing, "I refuse to let his statement destroy the meaning which his works hold for me, but if the best can get so lost what the hell are the rest of us going to do?"

In June, when Irving Kristol of *Encounter* magazine asked him for an essay on the civil rights struggle, he noted that "from this distance some of the developments are ironic, to say the least," while others are "so strangely hopeful that I find myself laughing [at] the sheer unexpectedness of it." Robert Penn Warren, who had published a powerful essay on the subject in *Life* ("Divided South Searches for Its Soul"), had recommended him for the job. Thus sponsored, Ralph agreed to write the essay. Warren was so enthusiastic about Ralph's first draft that he urged him to think about writing a small book, just as he had expanded his own *Life* essay into *Segregation: The Inner Conflict in the South*. But Ralph seemed unable to wrestle the subject into submission. His essay had become "a monster of bastard form" with a "demented head" and "more *leit-motives* than a Wagnerian opera." He never finished the essay.

Passing up a chance to review James Baldwin's provocative book of essays *Notes of a Native Son*, Ralph refused to mount a bully pulpit from which to preach his own ideas. Instead, he concentrated on his novel. Gamely he assured Bellow that "I've been making headway with the book although it's far from finished." His slowness he blamed in part on Rome: "This place has little of the creative tension so typical of New York. You can see more art, hear more and better rendered music, and heaven help us, find more interesting writing, there in a day than you can in months here. . . . As you can probably tell, I'm a bit homesick for the big city, sub-ways and all."

Restless, Ralph indulged himself a bit by spending money. Coming to love the recorder because of Cecile Hebald, another fellow at the acad-emy, he ordered a splendid one of his own, a tenor instrument in C from Dolmetsch in England. Thrilled by the light in Italy, he bought a new Leica M3, plus a light meter. He made the transaction through Albert Murray, who could buy them with the benefit of his military discount at the PX on his base (he was now a captain in the U.S. Air Force stationed in Casablanca). The equipment cost $212—a remarkable sum, given the fact that in January Fanny had warned him that they had only about $200 in the bank. He made no attempt to justify these and similar purchases.

After exasperating delays, a translation of *Invisible Man* now finally appeared in Italy from the publisher Giulio Einaudi. When its translator, Carlo Fruttero, proposed to visit Ralph to introduce himself, Ralph was arch: "Indeed, you have been most 'invisible' and your name seemingly top secret." *Uomo invisible* appeared with a handsome dust jacket marred by the assertion that the novel had won Ralph the Pulitzer Prize. It also brought him little in the way of royalties. The same was true of all his European translations, as he complained to his German publisher, Brigitte Fischer of S. Fischer Verlag. European editions were "a mixed blessing, consisting of very beautiful books, warm critical reception, and much less money than seems justifiable."

All the same, being able to display the translation was pleasant, espe-cially so as spring brought a flock of migratory writers and artists to the academy. Some were familiar, others new; but Ralph found almost all stimulating. They included the painter Ben Shahn and the sculptor Alexan-der Calder; the poet and translator John Ciardi, who would become a

good friend; Archibald MacLeish and his wife, Ada, who took Ralph and
Fanny to lunch away from the academy; the poet Theodore Roethke; and
the Warrens. Ralph also finally met Ignazio Silone, for whose New York
publisher he had provided a blurb. Ironically, perhaps because of the
influx from America, Rome seemed to him "a rather provincial town"
compared with New York. "The present, with its irritating but creative
tension is there [in New York]; there, I believe, more than anywhere else
in the world. There is the new in art, in music; and, God help us, in
literature."

Curiously, instead of heading home, Ralph applied for a one-year renewal of his fellowship, which he soon won. The news came, he wrote to
the American Academy of Arts and Letters in New York, "when my work
was most recalcitrant and I was despairing that . . . I would soon be
undergoing the trauma of returning home and the resulting interruption
of my work." He seemed proud of the renewal, which "is setting a precedent." (The same day, nevertheless, he confided to Max Lerner that "the
events at home are of far more interest to me at the moment. . . . Home is
where I would like to be.") Asked about the state of his novel, he was
cagey. "Some of the incidents," he wrote to Arabel Porter at the New
American Library, "continue to be quite mad and I'm sorry that it isn't
convenient—just as a check on my sanity—to read them to you over the
telephone." A few months later he would write something similar to Harry
Ford of Knopf: "About the novel I'll only say that some of the scenes are
molto outrageous. If only I didn't require the gestation period of a[n] ele-
phant to bring forth my odd mice!"

A good job awaited him at home, but Ralph rejected the offer from
Abram L. Sachar, the president of Brandeis University, to join the faculty
at a salary of $6,500, with a job promised for Fanny as well. (Max Lerner
was behind the offer.) What had attracted him at first was the proximity
of Brandeis to Cambridge, he wrote to Al Murray: "I'd like to operate
among the Harvard brains a while so that I can see what they're really
putting down." But teaching would hurt his writing: "Whatever I do, my
main work will be writing novels." Fanny supported his decision. "His
function is to write," she told her grandmother. "Many people can teach
but not many can write as well as he." Defensively, Ralph later claimed to
Lerner that if Sachar had offered him $8,000, he would have taken the
job, but Sachar "thought he could get me for the same money that he'd
pay some kid fresh out of school." Perhaps it never occurred to Ralph to
ask for more money; perhaps he didn't want to beg; perhaps he really

didn't want to go home. He gave Lerner yet another reason for refusing the job. "As you'll recall," Ralph wrote, "we've been contemplating adopting a child." The Brandeis money would not offset "our loss of Fanny's earning power while she looks after a child." And yet, "frankly, I've been taking chances and living lean so long that the very prospect of security makes me feel insecure."

He was confused. "Maybe all I really want," he wrote Murray, "is a little house within quick driving distance of New York, good bird hunting cover and a trout stream." He also saw a college job as marking him as a genteel English professor when he needed to view himself as virile, even visceral. He wanted to be like the black boxing champion Jack Johnson. Modern boxers such as Joe Louis and Sugar Ray Robinson were fine models, but "that old dancing master, wit, and bull-balled stud, Jack Johnson, is really *my* mentor, because he knew that if you operated with skill and style you could rise above all that being-a-credit-to-your-race crap." Even with his white women, Johnson mastered the world about him and was thus a credit to the human race: "If he liked a woman he took her and told those who didn't like it to lump it—and that's the way the true studs have always acted." Ralph was not afraid of Brandeis or anyone. If black NAACP lawyers could manipulate the white U.S. Supreme Court into ruling for integration, "I dam[n] sure can run skull practice on the critics."

Carefully made plans to drive to Paris and back with the Murrays were threatened in May when James Putnam of PEN America wired Ralph asking him to attend, as a special American delegate, the twenty-eighth annual congress of PEN International, to be held in London in July. Pearl Buck, John Steinbeck, John Hersey, Elmer Rice, and Arthur Miller were also scheduled to attend (although Miller seemed preoccupied at the moment with his new wife, Marilyn Monroe). Ralph accepted at once. He and Fanny decided to forswear a planned visit to the Loire Valley, arrive earlier than planned in Paris, leave the Murrays there, and then fly to London.

On June 24, Al, Mozelle, and their twelve-year-old daughter, Michele, arrived in Rome bearing various treasures—Ralph's new Leica, plus other PX-purchased items such as Pond's skin cream, deodorant pads, American ground coffee, bourbon, and Kleenex. On June 27, the two families headed north. With Murray's meticulous planning, they made excellent time and missed few important sights along the way. The families traveled well together. "They are wonderful people and I am very fond of them,"

Fanny had written to her mother. "He is Ralph's very best friend." The friendship was strained neither by the confines of the car nor by Ralph's neediness. "We got along very well," Murray recalled decades later. "We kept on schedule but we also had a great time. To me Ralph wasn't demanding at all. We all made sure to remember we were on vacation."

The pleasure lasted to the end. "We found Paris charming," Ralph wrote Bellow. Strolling in the Tuilleries, they stumbled happily upon Alfred Kazin, his wife, and their baby daughter. Ralph thanked Kazin for praising him in the second edition of Kazin's *On Native Grounds*. At Richard and Ellen Wright's home they saw James Baldwin and Chester Himes. For the tortured Himes, Ralph now had mainly contempt. "I suppose he'll go through the rest of his life pimping off white girls while hating them for being white," he wrote to Horace Cayton. In turn, Ralph's optimism about America grated on Himes, who was "so in love with his vision of an absolute hell that he can't believe that the world has changed in twenty years. He would impose further madness on the world instead of increasing our capacity for reality."

On July 8, the Ellisons took an Air France flight to London. Proudly they registered at the Ritz Hotel, where PEN had reserved deluxe rooms for them. The Ritz, Fanny wrote her mother happily, was "all that the name implies." They had arrived in time for a reception at the Tate, the premier gallery for modern art in England. Thus began a succession of "the most amazing experiences since arriving here in London." The next day, they attended a reception by the lord mayor of London and later that evening the inaugural session of the PEN congress in the Great Hall of the Royal College of Surgeons. A day later, after a cruise in the afternoon on the Thames, they were among the special guests of the Old Vic at a performance of Shakespeare's *Richard II*. On July 11, the American ambassador hosted a buffet luncheon, and at four they sipped tea on the terrace of the House of Lords at the invitation of Lord Pethick-Lawrence of Peaslake. In the evening, forty special guests chosen from among the almost 750 delegates attended a reception at Clarence House hosted by Queen Elizabeth the Queen Mother (Elizabeth II was her daughter). As Ralph put it, "it was my very pleasant fate to meet the Queen Mother and the charming little Princess [Margaret] and to drink the Queen's champagne." Sadly for Fanny, spouses were not invited.

The next day, Ralph and Fanny enjoyed cocktails at the Savage Club, courtesy of the PEN Centre for Writers in Exile, before dining at the Savoy Hotel at the main formal banquet of the congress. At their table were Graham Greene, V. S. Pritchett, André Maurois, J. B. Priestley, and—most impressive for Ralph—T. S. Eliot, who in 1948 had won the Nobel Prize for literature. If Ralph and Eliot exchanged a significant word, Ralph didn't record it. Eliot would have had little interest in speaking with him. A British citizen since 1927 and a declared royalist, the Missouri-born and Harvard-educated Eliot had long ago ceased to betray any concern for the dynamics of American literature or culture, much less for the tawdry subject of race relations and American blacks.

As an official delegate, Ralph attended an executive meeting of PEN International. Otherwise, his task was simply to represent the American writer, which he did once again at a government reception at Lancaster House and at a mayoral luncheon in the resort town of Brighton. He also saw a crucial part of his job as countering anti-Americanism—"answering private snipings directed at the States by certain English leftists and certain writers from behind the Iron Curtain." When an East German delegate pointed out provocatively that Ralph had not been in the reception line of guests of honor, he refused to be provoked. Instead, he luxuriated in his hour of prestige in London, his chats with lords and ladies, a princess and a queen—even if he also adopted a jaded tone in writing to Bellow that he had been meeting or seeing "all the old farts and the younger English literary gangsters, fairies, floosies, and broken-down aristocrats." But his London visit ended with a thud. First came the revelation that PEN was paying for their room but not their other hotel expenses; then they learned that they had overstayed their reservation by one night. Shocked by their bill, they now saw that the "great and mighty first-class Ritz" was in fact "merely a gip joint in fancy dress." When they moved to a dowdy guesthouse elsewhere in London, "we were suddenly lost among strangers in a sprawling city."

On July 17, after ten days in England, they flew to Frankfurt and then to Munich, principally so that Ralph could buy a wide-angle lens for his Leica near the factory that made them. This time, unlike during their Oktoberfest visit to Munich in 1954, they found "the people were all so nice, treating us not as tourists but strangers whom they wished to feel welcomed."

In August, without air-conditioning but with mosquitoes galore, their rooms at the academy became almost intolerable. Broke, the Ellisons waited out the heat. Ralph accepted an invitation from Granville Hicks, the former Communist editor of *New Masses*, to contribute to a volume of essays on the state of the novel by top American novelists. Wiring his acceptance, Ralph promised to send what Hicks summarized as an essay on "the relation of the alienated novelist to the centers of power."

The past few years had seen a continuing debate among top critics on the future of the American novel. As a student of the form but also now as a troubled practitioner, Ralph enthusiastically started work on the piece but quickly found himself stuck. One problem was a gnawing, neurotic restlessness. "Ralph is always waking up," Fanny confided to her mother. "He's a night prowler, can't sleep most of the night." Drinking Coca-Cola—hardly a sedative—he stalked the rooms, munching on snacks, reading, and "talking out loud—to me or imaginary people. Between him and the mosquitoes I seldom dream in peace." Ralph was an insomniac, she wrote elsewhere, "who can't sleep soundly even when he is dead tired."

That fall, in his second volume of autobiography, *I Wonder as I Wander,* Langston Hughes reflected on the chronically unhappy people he knew and listed Ralph (and Wright) among them. "There are many emotional hypochondriacs on earth," he noted, "unhappy when not unhappy, sad when not expounding on their sadness." Ralph reacted badly to this wisecrack. Hughes had "as much talent for psychology as he has [for] writing a poetry of ideas," he wrote to Horace Cayton. "It probably doesn't occur to him that bad writing and phoniness and cheap sophistry and opportunism could possibly make one ill when one sees it in a former idol and an old friend." Ralph's anger sprang mainly from his natural dislike of being publicly ridiculed but also from his anxiety about his sense of distance from most other black writers, whether American, African, or West Indian. Invited by the American embassy in Rome to return to Paris in late September for a congress of writers organized by the editors of the magazine *Présence Africaine,* he declined. This was not his crowd.

On September 6, he was more comfortable when he wired news of his intention (he felt "quite honored to be asked") to attend a conference on "Cultural Freedom in the Western Hemisphere" later that month in Mexico City, sponsored by the Paris-based Congress for Cultural Freedom. His partners in the U.S. delegation would include John Dos Passos, the socialist Norman Thomas, and the founder of the American Civil Liberties Union, Roger Baldwin. Ralph made his acceptance contingent on the quick delivery of funds—at least $826.60—to pay for a round-trip, first-class ticket. On September 16 he left Rome for Paris. There he was taken to the headquarters of the Congress for Cultural Freedom for a briefing from Nicholas Nabokov, the secretary-general of the organization, on the Mexican event. He then flew on to New York for a flight connecting almost immediately to Mexico City. Checking into the conference hotel, he slept from four in the afternoon until seven the next morning.

He awoke rested but was soon agitated. The opening session, aside from a speech by Norman Thomas, was an almost concerted attack by delegates on the United States. As he informed Fanny, he found himself "almost drowned in the Latin rhetoric." Some of the Latin Americans obviously expected him, as a Negro, "to join them in blaming every evil in their countries on this country," but he would have none of it—or of them. Mainly he kept company with Dos Passos, Baldwin, and Thomas. Although he said he wanted to see more of Mexico City—"that most interesting city"—he ventured only a few steps from his hotel, and mainly to take photographs. Then and later, developing countries, no matter how rich in history or art or people, meant little to Ralph.

On September 27, he left Mexico for New York—which was surely the main reason for his decision to go to Mexico City. Although he would be away from the academy for six weeks, and at the start of the academic year—which sat poorly with the academy leaders—he was glad to be home. An annoying error in *Time* magazine on September 10 served ironically to underscore his pleasure in being home. Writing about advances in civil rights since 1954, *Time* regretted that Richard Wright and Ralph Ellison "both were living in Europe" as expatriates. Ralph shot off a letter of correction. *He* was no expatriate.

In New York, with his apartment sublet, he stayed with David Sarser, who was about to be married, before the current tenant at 730 Riverside Drive invited him to use the apartment. Disoriented, he wrote to Fanny about "being in the apartment and yet not in it . . . in New York and yet not here to stay, feeling the need to be working and being unable to do so." He missed his domestic routine in Rome. He missed Fanny as helper. He missed sex. When she wrote of her longing for him, he more than matched hers: "I hope to rest up the last weekend just to have some physical reserve when I get there. Perhaps part of my tiredness comes from the added weight of the old hammer as much as from all the hectic running around; so save it, pretty mama, save it!"

Hungry for the old familiar faces, he quickly telephoned a raft of friends and just as hungrily arranged to meet many, including Albert Erskine, Bea Steegmuller (Francis was in Rome), Saul Bellow (who was teaching at the New School), Max Lerner, and Kenneth and Mamie Clark. A private loan, along with a fellowship check from the academy, allowed him to buy a Dacron and cotton summer suit. He also visited a doctor, who pronounced him in great shape, and a dentist, who was less impressed.

On October 7 he went to Princeton as guest of honor at a dinner party that included R. W. B. Lewis, Nancy Lewis, the journalist Murray Kempton, and Francis Fergusson, a noted authority on drama and mythology. Back in Manhattan he visited Gordon Parks at *Life*, where Parks was now established as one of its star photographers. When Francis Steegmuller returned to New York, Ralph spent time with him and Bea. On October 18 he attended a cocktail party and the next day a dinner at Dorothy Norman's home, where he saw his friend the critic Harvey Breit, the sculptor Isamu Noguchi, and Elia Kazan's wife, who annoyed Ralph by pressing him to read a play she just happened to have with her. He guessed the reason before she told him. ("Seems there's a Negro son-of-a-bitch in it," Ralph told Fanny, "and I guess she wants me to tell her that it's O.K. But who knows, maybe I'll write a play some day and will need advice on its technique.") Out of touch with the details of the current presidential campaign between Eisenhower and Adlai Stevenson, he found both candidates hard to take. Stevenson was too burdened by the Democrats' traditional fealty to the white South, and Eisenhower was too limited a man: "Everyone in this gang is for Stevenson which I am not although I am a registered democrat," he wrote Fanny. "I can't stand American politics for the moment because I can no longer swoller the southerners and Ike is still a hick."

Lunching with Saul and Sondra Bellow, Ralph found him somber with grief about his boyhood friend Isaac Rosenfeld. Once immensely promising as a writer, Rosenfeld had just died in obscurity in Chicago. The good news was that "although Saul is sad with the world," he and Sondra were happy with each other as they awaited the birth of their child in February. Presenting him with a signed copy of his latest novel, *Seize the Day,* Saul mentioned that he had just bought a big old house in Tivoli, New York, with a small inheritance left to him by his father. When he returned from Italy, Saul said, Ralph was free to stay there anytime.

For Ralph, the only truly disturbing aspect of his brief trip to New York was the state of the apartment. Rented at first to one of Fanny's co-workers, Nina Bond, a trustworthy individual, it had then passed on to a succession of subtenants (all known to Fanny and Bond) who apparently were less considerate. Someone had "borrowed" books. During a break-in, as Ralph and Fanny called it, in April, someone had jimmied open a filing cabinet that held clippings, family pictures, and the like. Fanny and Ralph were aghast: "Could they have been looking *for papers, political 'documents'*?" Roaches infested the once fastidiously clean apartment. Grease marred several surfaces. Irate, Fanny held Bond accountable. (When she eventually returned to the apartment from Italy, she hired a man to clean all the windows. When Bond protested paying the $10 it cost, Fanny gave no ground. "I watched him and I know," she wrote Bond. He had washed ten windows at 75 cents a window, with a tip of $2.50. "So pay me my $10 and shut up.")

Leaving New York on October 26, Ralph stopped for two days in Paris to report to congress officials on the Mexico City conference before flying on to Rome. He had been away almost six weeks. He had neglected his novel during that time, but now was suddenly "anxious that I might have lost control—such as I ever have—of my book." Still he did not hurry back to his desk; he "required lots of rest and concentration to set things going again." While he rested, he worked through an enormous pile of mail. In New York, Diana Trilling (Lionel Trilling's wife and a fellow intellectual) had invited him to join the board of directors of the American Committee for Cultural Freedom, an affiliate of the Paris-based congress. This might be a crucial step toward entry at last into the elite circle of thinkers surrounding the Trillings. Fanny urged him not to accept. "Why this sudden cultivation of you?" she asked. "They seem to be lagging a bit, like the Negro colleges that discovered *IM* two years after." Nevertheless, Ralph informed Mrs. Trilling that he was "more than willing to contribute to the work." Similarly, he bolstered both his anti-Communist credentials and his New York base by signing a message organized by William Phillips and Philip Rahv at *Partisan Review* and directed at the Polish Writers' Association, urging writers, intellectuals, and students to join the struggle against "Stalinist terror and foreign domination."

He also joined a committee chaired nominally by Faulkner, whom the Eisenhower administration had inveigled into serving as head of the People-to-People program, yet another Cold War cultural project employing or co-opting writers. But he rejected a suggestion by Faulkner, Steinbeck, and Donald Hall to Eisenhower that he should free Ezra Pound, who was confined to a psychiatric hospital in Washington, D.C., after being found guilty of treason for anti-American broadcasts he had made from Italy during the war. "I do not . . . agree to the freeing of Ezra Pound," Ralph wrote Faulkner. Pound was a great poet, he said, "but I can't see this as a reason for freeing him any more than I could see

the Rosenbergs freed because of their particular professions . . . even
had they been the first in their fields." Pound had committed treason.
Although his work had helped Ralph as a writer, "nevertheless, you know
and I know that were I to wander into a situation where one of his more
irrational disciples . . . was beating the drums of hate, nothing (certainly
no quotation of Pound's poetry, not even the most eloquent) could save
me from a glimpse of death." Linking Pound to anti-Communism was a
bad idea: "Isn't it a bit incongruous that the Pound question with its problems of hate and genocide should be connected with our efforts to help
those who are trying to free themselves from that same type of evil, given
the authority of the State, which Pound encourages?"

Ralph could not see that even if Pound had committed treason, he did
not necessarily deserve to be sentenced for life. Similarly, the fact that
Pound's admirers might menace or even harm Ralph was no reason why
Pound himself should be punished or denied mercy. Ralph thought differently because the charge had been treason against the United States—an
unforgivable crime as he saw it.

In October 1956, along with friends from his original group such as the
painters Walter Hahn, Leon Goldin, and Stanley Hollingsworth, Ralph
began another year at the academy. The poet John Ciardi, whose translation of Dante's *Divine Comedy* would soon become a classic, joined Ralph
as a fellow in writing. The American painter Helen Frankenthaler, another
friend over the coming years, also arrived. Among the new classicists,
Ralph and Fanny liked William Arrowsmith, who was also a *Hudson
Review* editor, and Ann Freeman, a vivacious junior scholar. Sharing
the writer-in-residence position were Robert Penn Warren, who left in
February, and his successor, Archibald MacLeish. The Russian-American
"magic realist" Peter Blume, warm to Ralph and Fanny from the start, was
now the painter-in-residence. This was a welcome change. "The mainly
new people here at the Academy are mostly pleasant," Ralph wrote,
unlike the previous fall, "when I frequently felt that I had turned up at the
wrong church."

Ralph's sense of comfort at the start of his second year was not
matched by Fanny's. By the end of 1956—just after she passed her forty-
sixth birthday on November 27—certain pressures began to build dangerously. For Fanny, menopause was at hand. In the spring she had tinted her
hair black for the first time. ("It looks much better and perfectly natural,"
she reassured herself gamely. "Ralph likes it too.") In the fall she went to

night school to study Italian but restlessly gave it up. "I felt I'd better not continue," she wrote her mother, "because I was getting 'nerves' and am having nausea and stomach pains all too often." She blamed her ills on the urban anxieties of Rome, the snarling traffic, the "highly excitable people." She needed a change of scenery—a "sojourn on a desert island, with books and music and prepared meals, *and no social life*." And with Christmas approaching, she feared, "the madness will intensify."

At forty-six, she knew that her chances of becoming pregnant were now almost zero. Meanwhile, she and Ralph doted on Rosanna and Gabriel, the two beautiful children (aged three and one) of Robert Penn Warren and Eleanor Clark. Ralph found his own passion for a child whetted by the Warren kids, by various pregnancies at the academy, and by the birth of sons to the novelist John Cheever and his wife, Mary, and to Saul and Sondra Bellow. (The Cheevers, who were living in Rome, had befriended the Ellisons.) "It's enough to make a duffer like me think of giving up both the pen and the bed," he joked.

A crisis was at hand. Fanny looked forward eagerly to their leaving Italy. When the time came, she confided, "I will be as happy to return home as Ralph would have been any day since he first came here." She began to hunt for a freighter that would take them and their belongings home. Meanwhile, Ralph seemed like a new man. He saw much of R. P. Blackmur of Princeton, who, according to Ralph, had "a capacity for night-owling and drinking that is appalling." He also found Blackmur overwhelming as a conversationalist, dominating "even when he has nothing to say," but almost as amazing as the great jazz trumpeter Buck Clayton—"no straining and grunting, just smooth, hot sound." Spending many evenings with the Cheevers and the Tates, Ralph also delighted in his conversations with Red Warren and, to a lesser extent, Archibald MacLeish. These friendships boosted his sense of belonging to the topmost stratum of American writers. This elite group—Anglo-Saxon, Protestant, and white Southern—now saw him, it seemed, as one of their own.

On April 12, MacLeish gave an electrifying private reading of his new verse play, *JB,* a meditation on the book of Job that would soon be a Broadway hit. Afterward, joining the celebration, Ralph quizzed MacLeish about life in the 1920s in Paris with young Ernest Hemingway. Life in Rome was suddenly glamorous. On the last day of April—"a day that spoke of coming Spring"—he and Fanny lunched on a sunny balcony at the Palazzo Caetani with the Principessa Caetani, more than eighty years old but the dynamo behind the admired journal *Bottegha*

Oscura. Caetani invited the Ellisons to another lunch, this time with the MacLeishes and the Ciardis at Tre Scalini on the Piazza Navona. Along with the MacLeishes, Ralph and Fanny paid a three-day visit to the principessa and her husband, the duke, at their country home at Nympha, with its towering cypresses and profusion of rosebushes. Once a thriving Roman city, Nympha had been taken over by the Caetani family in the previous century.

Of all these writers, Ralph was happiest with Red Warren and his family. "We became quite fond of them and they of us," he wrote Al Murray. In different ways, a keen sense of the troubled racial history of their homeland cemented their friendship. Warren was an honest, principled, and shrewd white man. Ralph also found in their relationship a healthy competition. "I got to measure my mind against one of the best Southerners and it's just like we've been saying." If a black could master "his own sense of reality he doesn't have to step back for anybody." Whites could and would do the same. Warren had "lived and thought his way free of a lot of irrational illusions."

Working with greater confidence now, "Ralph has hit a high peak in his work," Fanny reported, "and the things coming out of it are brilliant and fine." He also was having more fun. Loaned a Volkswagen sedan for two months by his German publisher, he used the car as often as possible, despite gas rationing, and as aggressively as back home. (The Italian drivers were "wild and crazy," according to Fanny, and Ralph "loses his temper very quickly.") But his work didn't suffer—at least not his smaller projects. For *Preuves,* the Paris-based journal of the Congress for Cultural Freedom, he answered and edited a questionnaire on race and civil rights. Going through a bottle of Pernod, he interviewed Warren for the *Paris Review.* He corrected proofs of his 1944 story "Flying Home," to be reprinted in a collection from Viking Press. He also finished his long essay on the novel, promised to Granville Hicks, called "Society, Morality, and the Novel."

To complete the essay, he wrote Murray, he "had worked against a writer's block the size of Rockefeller Center." Only his novel was proving truly recalcitrant. He had set it aside, he explained, "to deal with the Novel and those [such as Lionel Trilling] who say the form is dead. Fuck Trilling and his gang. I know that a novel is simply hard to write, especially during this time when you can't take anything for granted anymore."

"Today is Ralph's birthday," Fanny wrote to a friend on March 1. "And when I wished him *auguri* this morning he groaned in remembering how swiftly the years are passing and I said, 'Forget them.' And he said, 'Do you mean they'd go away?' "

Early in March, as Ralph and Fanny thought about and then rejected going to Sicily with Walter and Maud Hahn, five fellows from the original group, including Leon Goldin and Stanley Hollingsworth, discovered that they had won a third year at the academy. Despite his gnawing homesickness, Ralph, too, had applied to his sponsors, the American Academy of Arts and Letters in New York, for a third year in Rome. At a wild celebration to which Ralph and Fanny contributed four bottles of champagne, Fanny was among the rowdiest revelers celebrating the five renewals. But her joking and drinking now masked constant pain. In March she confessed to her mother in Chicago about enduring "rough times personally and emotionally."

Three weeks later she could not hold back. "Over the past several weeks I've been very miserable," she confessed, "because of Ralph. There is a lovely young woman here." Ralph had begun an affair with a young married woman who belonged to the somewhat large American colony in Rome. With the woman a frequent guest at the academy, Fanny at times feared she would crack. Unsure about who knew what, she withdrew as best she could from academy life even as she lived within its walls. She traveled by herself out of Rome. She took up painting. Finally, on the verge of a breakdown, she consulted a psychiatrist, Dr. Alberto Giordano, at the Piazzale Medaglie d'Oro.

One of Fanny's friends had discovered the romance when she stumbled one day upon Ralph and the woman in an intense but muted conversation. "I said to myself right away," she recalled, "those two people are involved." Her main worry was about Fanny, who was "totally concerned with Ralph's welfare and success although she was also absolutely a fine person in her own right. Fanny was talented and active and obviously a very successful woman." But the woman also admired Ralph's lover: "She was stunning. She stood tall and had a wonderful, lustrous complexion. She was charming. It was difficult for her, too. She and Ralph had been struck by lightning. They really had no choice." The lovers enjoyed trysts in Ralph's secluded studio deep in a corner of the grounds, against the Aurelian Wall. To reach it without being detected one could enter the academy grounds by a service gate on a side street. More often, they met elsewhere in the city.

Looking back more than forty years later on the affair, Ralph's lover characterized him as a difficult, high-strung, and often clueless person who had swept her off her feet. "I was young. . . . He was a middle-aged

man who seemed even older than he was, and so much more sophisticated than me." He was often friendly—but "the more I got to know him,
the more I saw that he wasn't nearly as wise as he seemed from a distance." To her, Ralph had a brilliant mind but often lacked common
sense. His imagination would get the better of him. "If you told him
something," she said, "a week later you would hear it from someone else,
but it would be distorted. If he said he would fix something involving
other people—a misunderstanding, for example—he would usually end
up making it worse. And he was very angry a great deal of the time."

Ralph, according to her, thought of odd ways of gaining revenge when
he felt wronged. "I remember that some woman, one of the fellows' wives,
had done him something, or so he thought. He told me that he was going
to fix her. He would come on to her, get her really interested in him, and
then leave her dangling. He wanted to break her heart." Once, before
they became involved, another man had made a pass at her. "Ralph was
furious. He told the man's wife. She never spoke to me again. Ralph often
left things in a mess." She, too, recalled Ralph as not a womanizer—"he
was no John Cheever, that's for sure." He was "constantly offended by
things and incidents that no one else would notice." When a certain
employee slighted him, he threatened to have the man fired. "I'm sure the
guy slighted him," she decided, "but Ralph's response seemed over the
top." Usually he was controlled, but "several times I saw him storm out of
events, or walk away in disgust. Lots of people at the academy were not
likable. Most of us were polite to them. Ralph didn't always hide his feelings, or even try to."

Whether or not her memory is accurate, Ralph was of course hypersensitive about race. Many slights that white people didn't see gashed his
flesh. For example, after reading an essay by Ralph, Archibald MacLeish
raved in a note to the Ellisons about the quality of Ralph's intelligence ("it
is an artist's intelligence but it is also *intelligent*"). Miffed, Ralph pointed
out to Fanny "the unconscious condescension in [MacLeish's] remarks
about my intelligence. Why make a compliment out of the obvious, aren't
most writers intelligent?" Since he no longer needed MacLeish's contacts, he ignored him: "I decided months ago that I didn't want to stay
here another year and so didn't write to him."

About their affair, Ralph's lover believed—in hindsight—that Ralph
had taken it too seriously, too melodramatically (although there is evidence that she had once hoped that it might lead to a new life). She also
believed she knew what Ralph saw above all in her: "He wanted children.
He knew that *he* could have children, and that Fanny couldn't. I think

that's how we got together. He wanted to marry me. But I don't know how good a husband or a father he would have been. There was something there almost like a psychosis. He was scary, in the amount of emotion he brought to everything personal. He was much more than I had bargained for. It just wasn't rational." Also, his marriage was "really one-way. It was not a sharing marriage. Fanny did everything, and everything was for Ralph. She catered to his whims. He was egotistical. Just like with the lectures I heard him give—he was never prepared. He seemed to think he was doing enough just by being there."

As with his first wife and Sanora Babb, Ralph decided that he had to tell Fanny everything about the affair. In his mind, he was being honest, but a note on a calendar for April 9 suggests an element of obtuseness: "Excruciating Day & Night. FANNY magnificent in her generosity." Their marriage was in jeopardy, he briefed her. If this woman agreed, he would marry her and start the family that Fanny couldn't give him. Adding to Fanny's woes, on a bright, beautiful day she was walking through the front gate when the *portière* handed her a telegram from Chicago. Her maternal grandmother had just died. The news left her numb. Finally she unburdened herself to her mother about what life with Ralph was really like: "I remember when R[alph] was writing his first book there were no women in the picture but there were other very cruel, sadistic moments when I thought I would go out of my mind and about which I talked to no one and for which I always blamed myself. It was a bad start for our marriage and it crippled me in many ways. . . . I stuck it out all these years because in moments when he isn't in the throes of something he is a wonderful companion and I know that I love him and he loves me. If I had been able to have a child, I would have felt less inferior and been therefore a better wife and helped [him] through his bad moments."

Shortly afterward, Ralph left Rome for an eight-city lecture tour sponsored by the United States Information Service (arranged by none other than Archibald MacLeish). Starting on May 8 in Trieste, he spoke in Milan, Turin, Genoa, Florence, Naples, Bari, and Rome. While he was gone, Fanny decided she could take no more. On May 16 she gave notice at the Lampada. "For sudden and unexpected reasons" she needed to return as soon as possible to the United States. Later that month, she wrote to her mother: "I'm a little more mature but am paying for it with what little youth I have left and with my spirit." She would leave Italy in July. Ralph decided to stay behind until September at least, "even if I don't get a renewal for next year."

In early June, with her passage home set, Fanny took off for a short stay in Florence to get away from "the oppressive atmosphere of the Academy where it is impossible to escape seeing people one does not want to see." Later that month, Ralph's lover left Italy for at least two months. He expected that when she returned, they would decide that they belonged together. Then he learned that the academy in New York had not renewed his fellowship. Awaiting his lover's return, he played out the last few weeks with Fanny before she left for home. Early in July they drove ninety miles along the coast north of Rome to visit John and Mary Cheever. Without much success, they tried to enjoy the pleasant company, the food and drink, the warm blue water.

Fanny then took a business trip to Holland. The evening before leaving Rome, she had one of her worst fights with Ralph, who crushed her. "I lost under a hail of harsh, unqualified, violent words," she wrote to Dr. Giordano. When she returned from Holland, she said, Ralph was morose and tight-lipped: "He volunteered no information as to whether they had future plans." He let her know only that he was expecting a letter soon about his lover's decision. Fanny gave up the last vestige of hope for reconciliation. During the affair, she explained to Giordano, "my lack of control *and* wisdom has been due to the fact that I had no resources to sustain me. Had our marriage been a successful one, or rather had it not been harassed by the particular kind of anxieties that it has, I could have been the calm, objective person. But since I have always doubted that my husband really and truly loved me, naturally I could not believe that he loves me now in this situation. Thus the panic, the hysteria, the despair."

"I think at last I have 'thrown in the sponge,'" she wrote further. Something died in her following a session of hot sex with Ralph, when "he sat afterwards looking as though he had done something dreadful." She could not forgive him for the fact "that he allowed me to see his forlornness—indeed, he may have even wanted me to see it. Whichever it was, I think it uncharitable of him." On a walk together, Ralph also told her that he now understood the difference between the ethical and the moral—"that the ethical was what a person owed a situation, a social situation, but that the moral was what he owed to life, that is, one's commitment to continue life, meaning children of course. And every child we passed he looked at with great wistfulness and sentimentality. My feeling was one of embarrassment, and I even wondered then if I would want him the father of my child if there could be one."

On July 22, he and Fanny took a train from Rome to Naples, where a freighter would take her home. In Naples, they found a hotel room for her. Then they went to the station so that Ralph could catch the 6:30 p.m.

train back to Rome. Her last glimpse of Ralph, she wrote, was of him "sinking into your seat with an expression of anguish on your face as the train pulled away." The next day, she left Naples on the *Paolina*.

Back at the academy, Ralph was glad to play host to visitors from Oklahoma City. On July 28 he hosted a dinner for Saretta Slaughter Finley, her physician husband, Dr. Gravelly Finley, and their thirteen-year-old son, Tuffy. Born into money, as the daughter of Dr. Wyatt H. Slaughter and Edna Randolph Slaughter, Saretta had loomed over Ralph in his childhood like a princess to a pauper. Now Saretta had even more money, and Ralph had—prestige. His prestige did not make him forget his boyhood poverty, and Saretta's easy sense of superiority to him. In Rome, Tuffy called Ralph "Uncle," but, Ralph wrote dourly to Fanny, "I wonder how far she would have allowed him to get with that uncle business had I remained a local boy?" Still, the Finleys were "nice and unpompous" and brought "a bit of reality to the air of unreality which the academy has assumed since I've been alone."

Without Fanny or his lover, he endured the roasting August days unhappily. He wanted out, especially as the mail brought no letters from them. "Rome, for me, is already becoming a thing of the past," he wrote a friend. Forced to return home because his fellowship was over, he saw that his best option was reconciliation with Fanny. In his fashion, and despite her doubts, he loved her. He needed her emotionally, financially, and as the almost perfect ally as he scaled the heights of the white-dominated racial mountain above him. In turn, Fanny loved but also needed him. Without Ralph, she would slide back into the Philistine black middle class. He had lifted her into exclusive circles she would never see again if they parted ways.

Three weeks passed with Fanny silent. Ralph then wrote her a long letter disparaging his lover, who was displaying "much confusion and dashing around and conflict of emotion." Their plans were still uncertain, he told Fanny. However, he would rather talk about the future "in our old setting; perhaps that alone would clarify what the situation between us actually is, or at least, what led to it." He now offered his best defense of his infidelity: "There was, I admit, some shabby aspects to what I did but then passion makes its own rules when it has to; the question is what is hardest to forgive, the breaking of the rules or the existence of the passion itself? I can say that I miss you and that I do, and always have, realized how really good you've been to me. More than that I'm concerned about you and I hope you'll take care of yourself . . . at least until I return."

After receiving a cool telegram on August 18 from Fanny ("ALL IS

WELL YOUR LETTER RECEIVED WILL WRITE SOON"), Ralph
tried again. He had received her "wire and its abstract message," but he
was "annoyed that it wasn't a letter. I still am." He continued to mock his
lover. Apparently she had decided "not to be cruel, not to cause the family pain"; in short, he said, she was being bourgeois. About to leave for a
conference in Japan, he wished that he could go directly from Japan to
New York: "I just have no desire to prolong what would be a sterile and
painful situation." He had lost faith in the woman. For her, living with
Ralph would require "that she move into strange regions of existence, that
she violate one group of ties in order to embrace the unknown, give all for
passion—or what not." She belonged to his past: "I do know that I don't
want now what I wanted of her. . . . A rather sad story; still, what I desired
was good, and I wanted it badly enough to make the desperate attempt I
made. That is *my* way of living and I'll always be sorry that you had to suffer in the apparent madness of my lunge toward what might actually be
an abstract ideal." This ideal involved his wish for kids—"though children, once they're yelling their little heads off, are anything but abstract."

This seemed to be the closest thing to an apology that Fanny would
ever get from him. He both praised and blamed her for the disaster:

> Fanny, you just have to let some thing[s] work their own way
> out. If you have done all you can do, then you must not
> push the other fellow or fight him into stances of decision
> he might otherwise reject. What you are, and what you can
> do, what you have learned, are important values and anyone
> concerned with values, and I am, will recognize what you
> are and act accordingly. I say this now without changing one
> bit of my belief that you were partially responsible for what
> happened here. You are a good woman who helped create
> that which caused you pain, when you might have held
> yourself in reserve and overcome the situation without stir-
> ring up all the limitations of our relationship. The point
> here is not who is responsible, but that you are *you* and
> must have faith in you. Nor must you feel that I'm saying
> this after a defeat of my desires, it is not that simple for I
> haven't pressed or persuaded or tried to give courage in a
> decision where I feel the other person [his lover] must know
> her own mind; perhaps I could have helped, certainly I
> could have destroyed *his* [his lover's husband's] happiness.

No, I'm saying this after this brief separation, after missing
you, and out of a desire that you do no further harm to your
image of yourself. Right now I'm very tired and I don't like
this indirection of statement, so I'll only repeat what I told
you, that "if I find that I'm wrong, I'll come and tell you." So
now I'll tell you that the old ties still hold. Instinctively I
find myself shopping for the apartment—or at least looking
at things which would go well there.

When Fanny weighed in at last, she sent Ralph a three-page, single-
spaced, and superficially serene letter. Only at the end did she refer to the
affair. She hoped that nothing that happened to his lover would "interfere
with your plans. Certainly after the destruction and torment the situation
has caused, it should somehow bring itself into focus and fulfill some of
its promise. As for myself, I find that I only needed air in which to
breath[e]. It of course is too soon for me to know how I shall really feel
but at the moment I know that I feel good and what I see in the mirror is
a face without strain. So don't beat yourself over the head about me. It
may even turn out that you've done me a favor." Ralph had signed his
letters to her, "Love, Ralph." Fanny ended this one: "Good luck and Go
with God."

More confident now despite her tone, Ralph chided Fanny in a short,
handwritten note about sending "a needlessly dismal letter." Instinctively,
like a silverback, he tried to dominate her. "Your butt must be screaming like a child's for a good spanking," he suggested. If she was now happy,
he was content; but she should not report it in so dismal a fashion, as if
she expected him to resent it. "Fanny, it's shocking but I guess you'll
always be my child-wife—and what, beyond all the recent trouble, a
headstrong, willful, little bitch you are!" Nevertheless, "I can still write
Love and mean it, Ralph."

On August 28, Ralph left Rome with an Italian delegation to attend the
congress of PEN International in Tokyo and Kyoto. He loved what he saw
of the country. "Japan simply takes you over with its unique beauty," he
wrote Fanny. "I'd love to stay a year." He found enchanting the subtle aesthetic of restraint that was visible in ordinary houses or in wrapping pack-
ages, "or in the manner they bind up the wounds of an injured tree. I find
the country much more fascinating than Italy."

Hoping to spend four days in Calcutta, he was forced to fly to the

British colony of Hong Kong and wait three days when the Indian government delayed granting him a visa. Again Italy suffered in comparison. The
Chinese were exceptionally handsome, the women often "breathtakingly,
head snappingly, beautiful as they walk along the streets in sheathes cut
to the upper thighs for comfort in the hot climate. . . . They make these
Roman gals look artificial." Chinese politics he found less interesting.
Invited to visit the border to view the heavily armed Communist forces,
he instead went shopping. Low on funds, he nevertheless picked up a
new Burberry trench coat, a pair of cuff links, and a tie tack, as well as
some silk fabric and a gold chain, presumably for Fanny.

After Japan and Hong Kong, he abhorred impoverished Pakistan. On
September 19, when he lectured at Karachi University, he faced down a
Pakistani writer who lauded the superiority of his nation's alleged spiritual
values. "Spirituality got into culture through the efforts of men," Ralph
pointed out; "there might be just as much spirituality in a skyscraper as in
a sacred cow." As for the Pakistani people and their spirituality, "I only
hoped that they would be better able to feed and clothe their people,
and . . . get them off the sidewalks." The man continued in his "arrogant
high British wog style (pleasant to me of course) and left. I could have
kicked his butt till his nose bled." Calcutta in socialist India was even
worse. Ralph loathed the poverty and the pro-Communist posturing—
"the thousands of people sleeping on the sidewalks, the filthy cows roaming the busiest streets of a city of eight million, the squalor, the crowds
marching around behind the hammer and sickle. . . . Needless to say, I
was glad to get out the following morning and head for Rome." He refused to blame these conditions on European colonialism: "The British
simply couldn't have created all of that."

Meanwhile, in New York Fanny heard certain rumors, which she shared
with Ralph. A woman at the academy had announced: "I hear Fanny and
Ralph are washed up." Fanny did not assure Ralph that the woman was
wrong. "I've read and reread your letter many times," she wrote; "it seems
very contradictory but I nevertheless gather from it that you are tired,
quite unhappy, and want to come home." She saw through his attempts to
treat her as a child. "We've torn down most of what we built over the years
but maybe now we can build something better. It depends on the foundation of course, which we must examine together."

"My cup runneth over with disgust," Ralph replied quickly. He was
now avoiding his lover, who seemed to him "noticeably older, tense and
sad. . . . She does so need to grow out into her own life but I fear she

never shall." Finally he shouldered the blame. "If-if-if, if I'd been a better man this mightn't have happened. If it weren't so painful I too would be amused and when I laugh now the laugh is bitter. So much for this just now, I hurt but I'm coming home. I beg your patience; I would have at least you happy."

At home, Fanny knew that she had won this skirmish but perhaps lost the big war. "These are strange, unsettled days for me," she wrote him early in October. "I don't know where I'm going or what I want, am frequently depressed, finally had to get some sleeping pills." The next day, writing again, she tried to blame her melancholy on going back to her former employer, Harold Oram Associates. She had never liked backtracking in life. But she knew that her job was not the issue now. Almost overwhelming feelings of sorrow and loss were haunting her: "You say you and [his lover] have aged. So have I, as you will see, but what is more serious for me is that I've lost the spark." She wasn't bitter. In fact, "I am more compassionate towards you (and even her at this moment). . . . You acted badly but only in terms of my personality. Perhaps with another kind of wife, it all would have been admirable and your integrity would have been judged as integrity and not sadism." Nevertheless, she chastised him as she apparently had never done before, starting with his spending spree in Hong Kong: "Since I've known you you've never shown that you knew the value of money; you must always have what you have to have at the moment that you want it. This is something I've never said to you in all the years. I don't know if I'm braver or if it's just that you're not here to bite off my head. Your volatile nature and acid tongue have kept me from saying several things, which had I said them would have been better for the two of us."

Her charges stung Ralph—but he knew that Fanny now held the whip. "I got the impression," he replied meekly but not without some guile, "that you feel that . . . I have the notion that everything will go on with us as before. If so, then please understand that I know better and that I face the possibility that the basis of any lasting relationship might have been destroyed and that you might find it impossible to be near me for long; that all remains to be seen. Nor should you feel the need to be compassionate, since you have an honest right to rage, though I am grateful for it. Still, if you think that this thing I'm going through and have put you through is simple sadism, then you have been observing quite another drama indeed." As for her sense of inner loss, "I'm sure you still retain your spark and I can't imagine you without it though perhaps now it glows from the depths." On the subject of finance he was defensive. Her criticisms were "just the kind of barbs that bring acid to my tongue." True, he was bad with money; but he had never lived merely for wealth. In almost the same breath, he asked her for cash: "Do what you can about money if you still wish to; another hundred plus that you intend to deposit on the 15th should get me through and if you can't do anything about it I'll find another way."

Fanny applied for a bank loan. When the loan came through on October 23, she almost sternly informed him that he had $200 at his disposal and no more. After years of silent suffering she had scored some crucial points by speaking out. The air around them was still murky, but some of the smoke was starting to lift.

Now Ralph made preparations to leave Rome. Without Fanny to take charge, he did a sloppy job. Instead of sending his various arts-and-crafts purchases in the secure packing crates of his painter and sculptor friends, as was his option, he struggled to manage everything on his own. In the end, he left books for the academy to mail to him—and would dispute the charges for years to come. Nevertheless, on November 4, stowing his luggage and excess baggage into the academy station wagon, he headed for the docks at Naples. After two years and two months in Italy, he boarded the *Giulio Cesare* and headed home. He had come, he had seen, but he had not conquered.

14

The Pleasures of Home

1957–1961

It is not easy to find the right way. . . . You must manage your freedom or drown in it.   SAUL BELLOW (1957)

On November 14, 1957, after a miserable voyage on the *Giulio Cesare,* Ralph reached New York "dead-tired, broke, and scrambled up inside." Only a radio call at sea from NBC inviting him to take part in a one-hour show on the Negro question lifted his spirits.

Uncertain upon his arrival how Fanny would receive him, he in fact returned to her arms and their bed. Four days later, Ralph wrote to his lover in a way that startled her. "I'm haunted by the last evening we were together," he told her, "and despite my ambiguous position I miss you more than I care to say." But she recalled no ambiguous position. "I didn't really see how this could be," she answered. "I remember you and your words too clearly." He acted as though they had reached no understanding. A chatty letter addressed to both her and her husband further disturbed her. "My feelings haven't changed," she pleaded. "I meant what I told you that last evening and afternoon. . . . I love you, love you, love you. That has not changed, not a bit, nor ever shall."

By this time, unfortunately for her, Ralph and Fanny had reunited as man and wife. Staring down the world, Fanny reported only domestic felicity. "Ralph has been home hardly ten days and already it seems months," she wrote in a letter to Rome, knowing that these words would reach Ralph's lover, "so quickly have we slipped back into our old comfortable and pleasant pattern of life." But after life at the academy, she hated their three-room apartment: "The dull, restricted view is maddening and depressing." Accordingly, she had made changes. "The apartment is newly decorated," Ralph wrote to his lover, "and bright and pleasant."

Only his novel was suffering: "Alas, I've experienced none of that tremendous burst of energy which marked my trip [to New York] last year, the old metabolism just hasn't rev[v]ed up as yet."

Still, it was heavenly to be back in New York, where "the liquor's good, the steaks thick and juicy and I've been stuffing myself with ice cream and sweet potato pie!" After two years in Europe he and Fanny were elated to be among so many black folks. He was home only one day when they went to a benefit performance of the racially integrated and thus controversial musical drama *Jamaica,* starring Ricardo Montalban and Lena Horne ("that gal is simply good to hear and see," he decided, "even when you're tired"). He took part in the NBC television panel. The show reunited him with Max Lerner, whose columns on civil rights he still read avidly; the veteran Urban League leader Lester Granger; and Clarence Mitchell of the NAACP. To the *New York Times,* "the hour was consistently stimulating."

On September 3, the Arkansas National Guard, called out by the segregationist governor Orval Faubus, had prevented nine black youths from enrolling at Central High School in Little Rock. On September 23, after a federal court ruling against Faubus, the youngsters entered the school amid insults and obscenities from a mob of angry whites. The next day, Eisenhower took to the radio to denounce mob rule and anarchy. Asserting federal control of the Arkansas National Guard, he reinforced it with a thousand paratroopers from the 101st Airborne Division. All over Rome, Ralph had seen—thanks to anti-American radicals—a poster of whites spitting on one of the students. The poster had sickened him. Back home, he tried to catch up on two semi-lost years of civil rights history, starting with Rosa Parks's singular act of defiance in Montgomery. He had missed the rise to national prominence of Dr. Martin Luther King, Jr., and being at home for dreadful events such as the murder of fourteen-year-old Emmett Till in Mississippi, allegedly for whistling at a white woman. While he was away, one hundred white congressmen signed a manifesto opposing racial integration. More encouraging, Eisenhower had signed into law the Civil Rights Act of 1957, which allowed the Department of Justice to enforce the right of blacks to vote. That year, Dr. King, Bayard Rustin, and Stanley Levison formed the Southern Christian Leadership Conference (SCLC) to unite nonviolent protest groups across the United States.

Ralph had come back to a rapidly changing America. In fact, the entire world was swiftly changing, as was clear when he and Fanny attended a mayoral reception at the Waldorf-Astoria for Kwame Nkrumah, the prime minister of newly independent Ghana. In the words of the prime minister of Great Britain, Harold Macmillan, the winds of change were sweeping Africa. Pleased to attend the reception, Ralph declined, as before, to join the chorus of praise for Nkrumah, Ghana, or the burgeoning African independence movement. Skeptically he waited to see what Africans would make of their freedom. In any event, he was far more stirred by the civil rights struggle in America. Wanting to help the movement, he saw himself limited in his ability to do so except by advancing his novel-in-progress, occasionally taking part in discussions such as the NBC program, and sending token sums to the NAACP Legal Defense Fund. He couldn't afford to take his Chrysler out of storage or pay for the new battery, registration, and insurance it needed. (He saw now that paying to garage the car, instead of selling it, had been dumb. "I must be a fool," he declared. "I'm always parted from my dough.")

Ralph and Fanny had to subsist on cheap pleasures and the kindness of friends, as when they visited Saul and Sondra Bellow at their lovely if decrepit mansion in Tivoli, the birthplace of Eleanor Roosevelt, in Dutchess County, New York, about two hours from the city. They spent Thanksgiving with close friends from their Rome years—Al and Lottie Blaustein and Walter and Maud Hahn. They rekindled older friendships. A few were centered in Harlem, others further south in Manhattan, where they mingled with whites at various parties and dinners. Steadily they slipped back into old grooves. By December, though, the partying was seen as a threat to Ralph's creativity. "There'll be no more merry-go-rounds and fanfare, we're hoping," Fanny wrote to a friend. "Just quiet and work and wonderful music which pours through a thousand snarled wires in our front closet."

Bellow had been one of the few persons to whom Ralph had turned for advice during his Rome affair, when he wrote about "something eating my innards which I can't write about." Bellow had urged him to sever all ties to his lover. With the affair still unsettled in Ralph's mind in 1958, he turned again to Saul. "Things Rome-wise are still snarled up for me," he admitted, "and I guess there's nothing to change it. Time might dull the effect but I'll never forget it." Saul once more told Ralph to make a clean break. He also tried to help with Ralph's money problems and with what Ralph himself called his "writer's block as big as the Ritz."

Bellow had no such block. Since *The Adventures of Augie March* in 1953 he had brought out *Seize the Day* and was now deep into *Henderson the*

Rain King. As for money, he disputed Ralph's idea that college teaching would hurt his writing. Building his own career and family while teaching, he wanted Ralph to seek a position at Bard College, near Tivoli, where Bellow had once taught and had good contacts. That month, *The Nation* carried Bellow's essay "The University as Villain." "It is not easy to find the right way," he warned writers who believed that universities invariably damage the artist. "You must learn to govern yourself, you must learn autonomy, you must manage your freedom or drown in it," he advised. "You may strain the will after Experience because you need it for your books. Or you may perish under the heavy weight of Culture. You may make a fool of yourself anywhere."

If Ralph took a job at Bard, moreover, he could stay for virtually nothing in Bellow's "wreck of a house" on Kidd Lane in Tivoli. Away at the University of Minnesota, Bellow assured Ralph that "the house in Tivoli is open to you for as long a time as you like or need." These suggestions intrigued Ralph. His stint in Salzburg in particular had opened his mind to the idea of regular teaching, and the house was fantastic. Dating from the seventeenth century, it was so big it boasted a ballroom. Its problems included peeling paint, cracked plaster, sagging floorboards, a leaking roof, and an uncertain supply of water (until Bellow dug a well), but its charm was considerable. About his mansion, Saul liked to pretend that he'd been conned: "A couple of beguiling fairies sold us the place and lied about the water, the roof . . . and various other things." But its beauty trumped its defects. Ralph could concentrate on his novel. For a while, the Ellisons would live discreetly apart. This seemed to both parties possibly a good idea.

Bellow's advice and offer helped as 1958 unfolded. "I'm working on my book," he reported to a friend in Rome, "which elates me and depresses me as the days come and go." He was boosted further when he renewed the friendship he had forged in Italy with Robert Penn Warren. He and Fanny spent a rich weekend at the Warrens' home in Fairfield, Connecticut, then on January 12 attended their annual New Year's party, which attracted several writers and editors from New York. This friendship meant more and more to Ralph. "I like him better the more I see of him," Ralph wrote now to Al Murray. Egged on by Eleanor Clark, an expert, he even tried skiing for the first—and last—time.

Soon his novel-in-progress stalled again. Refusing to panic, especially after Bellow had secured for him the promise of a job at Bard, he wrote an essay that William Phillips at *Partisan Review* had requested on the advice of Stanley Hyman. Ellison and Hyman, meanwhile, were at odds. Writing about black folklore for the journal, Hyman had quoted liberally from *Invisible Man*—"but what he says the quotations mean," Ralph decided indignantly, "is so fantastic that I had to go back and look at the text." Happy to spark a critical controversy, Stanley suggested Ralph should write a rebuttal to be published alongside his essay. Ralph did so.

One of his most influential essays, "Change the Joke and Slip the Yoke," appeared in the Spring 1958 issue of *Partisan Review* (along with Hyman's forgettable "The Folk Tradition"). Ellison took issue with Hyman because of the differences between "our conceptions of the way in which folk traditions get into literature—and especially the novel; our conceptions of just what is *Negro* and what is *American* in Negro American folklore; and our conceptions of a Negro American writer's environment." To Ralph, much was at stake. Entranced perhaps by the vogue of "archetypal" criticism associated with Northrop Frye, Hyman had looked at modern black writers in relation to two key forms: the folktale and the blues. The folktale, he noted, is dominated by the archetype of the trickster, whom Hyman identifies as the " 'darky' entertainer"—the clever black man playing dumb to fool the white folk. Meaning to praise Ralph, he claimed that "the fullest development I know of the darky act in fiction is Ralph Ellison's *Invisible Man*, where on investigation every important character turns out to be engaged in some facet of the smart-man-playing-dumb routine."

These words incensed Ralph. "I think he's going to be hurt by my essay," he wrote to Al Murray, "but I'm just dam[n] tired of guys who are more interested in anthropology monkeying with the novel. These fucks are so impressed that Joyce used myth to organize *Ulysses* that they really can't believe that Bloom isn't Ulysses." As Ralph saw it, Stanley had reduced *Invisible Man* to the level of "Negro literature," and reduced Ralph's use of folklore to a single device. He had failed to give proper credit to Ralph's wide reading in Western literature, as well as to the depth and breadth of his cultural analysis. Where Hyman believed that archetypes determine fiction, Ralph insisted on the novelist as artist-creator of his world, which was bounded only by the almost infinite possibilities of the novel and the novelist's creative intelligence.

Ralph won this literary skirmish, but just as anxiety about the American novel continued to vex the current intellectual scene, so did it tax him in his aim to write a major second book. This general anxiety was clear in the critical response to *The Living Novel,* a symposium of essays written by novelists and edited by Granville Hicks that came out that April. This volume included Ralph's essay "Society, Morality, and the Novel," on which he had labored in Rome. Most critics loathed the book. Typical was Alfred Kazin's mocking review, entitled "Ten Young Novelists in Search of Pity," in *The Reporter.* In *Saturday Review,* David Daiches found Ralph's essay provocative and useful, although the volume itself achieved little. Robert Gorham Davis, always a fan of Ralph's work, wrote that "the collection is worth having for this essay alone." But Orville Prescott in the *New York Times* was harsh on Ralph and others. For "pretentious and sententious writing," Bellow and Ellison were the worst offenders. Ellison had "lost his way in a swamp of jargon expressions, sweeping generalizations and questionable statements."

With his essay, Ralph again thrust himself boldly into the current controversy surrounding the American novel, just as he had done at the *American Scholar* symposium in 1955. In fact, this essay drew heavily on what he had said at that gathering. Once again, Lionel Trilling was a major target of the nativist school to which novelists such as Ellison and Bellow belonged. According to Trilling, the lack of density and class division in American society prevented its writers from fulfilling (in Ralph's words) the novel's "classic intention . . . the investigation of the problem of reality beginning in the social field." Here Ralph again objected. Henry James's autopsy of young America's bulimic cultural body (as James defined culture), and Trilling's stretching of James's analysis to the present, seemed to Ralph to provide only the "reasons why American novelists cannot write French or English novels of manners." In a tradition born of Mark Twain, American writers had done other things. Faulkner's "The Bear" is a profound statement on slavery, racism, and America, although Malcolm Cowley, in his landmark volume *The Portable Faulkner,* had invited readers to skip the most "difficult"—that is, for Ralph the most morally complex—part of the story. Snobbishly, Trilling had dismissed Faulkner as provincial, but Ralph saw the Mississippi writer as expanding the moral inquiry "at the heart of Twain's fiction." Again Ralph held up as the proper model for the age Bellow's *The Adventures of Augie March,* which epitomized "the picaresque, many-leveled novel, swarming with characters and with varied types and levels of experience." (Of course, he was now trying to write precisely such a novel, as he had done with *Invisible Man.*) "We love the classics," he declared, but "have little interest in what Mr. Trilling calls the 'novel of manners,' and I don't believe that a society hot in the process of defining itself can for long find its image in so limited a form. Surely the novel is more than he would have it be, and if it isn't then we must make it so."

Praising Bellow and attacking Trilling and Cowley, Ralph had pushed his way further than ever before among the so-called New York intellectuals. He qualified for this club by virtue of his long residency in New York; his love-hate relationship with the radical left; his shrewd essays in magazines such as *The Nation, Partisan Review, Commentary,* and *The New Republic;* and, not to exhaust the list of qualifications, a degree of anxiety over his ethnicity in relation to America. In a real sense, he was one of them. He certainly seemed so in March, when he joined Trilling and the sociologists Sidney Hook and David Riesman (whose study *The Lonely Crowd* had become a classic) in petitioning the U.S. State Department on behalf of *Partisan Review* and against restraints placed on its distribution overseas. He performed again in this fashion in May, when he joined Hook, Arthur M. Schlesinger, Jr., and Roger Baldwin in sending an open letter to the people of France, organized by *Partisan Review;* and in December, when he joined a protest to the United Nations against Franco's suppression of the Catalan language and literature.

In another sense, Ralph did not belong in this world, and could not. So Fanny had intuited in September 1956, when she looked askance at Diana Trilling's invitation to Ralph to become a board member of the American branch of the Congress for Cultural Freedom, where he would be the sole black and a rare Gentile. "I'm sure you don't want to be caught on that board," she had advised Ralph. (Fanny seemed less willing than he was to have him used as a token.) Most of the New York intellectuals were Jewish, and perhaps a non-Jew could not belong properly to the group, even though the Jews were not monolithic. Some, like Lionel Trilling, said to be the first Jew to gain tenure in the humanities at Columbia, maintained an aloof style that some other Jews saw as designed mainly to obscure their Jewishness. Others, like Bellow, were defiantly writers first, Americans second, and Jews third. Still others, such as Alfred Kazin, explored the ecstatic tension between their Jewishness and the secular, nominally Christian stratum of high culture that had captured their artistic souls. Both Bellow and Kazin had fallen in love with the English language in part from reading the King James Bible, including the New Testament, after years of knowing the Old Testament laboriously in Hebrew.

In May, a splinter group of sorts formed when Ralph joined Bellow, Jack Ludwig, and Keith Botsford (all teachers at Bard at one time or another) in deciding to found a magazine. They expected its editorial board to include S. J. Perelman, Arthur Miller, and the novelist Herbert Gold, who lived near Ralph on Riverside Drive. Creative writers would provide its reviews and other literary criticism. Ludwig planned an essay on barbers, Bellow one on crime cases, and Ralph on unusual blacks such as Adam Clayton Powell, Jr. The journal would reflect America's diversity. Seeking, like Whitman, to celebrate their nation's "barbaric yawp," they would call it *The Noble Savage*.

Ralph's association with these and other white writers encouraged those critics who thought of him as dangerously conflicted about Negro culture. In March, for instance, a writer in *Time* magazine poked at him as a "jazzed-up, Joyced-up intellectual" who found his fellow Negroes revolting. Ralph reacted with a variation on one of his favorite lines. "I could have kicked his nose," he wrote Bellow, "till his ass bled." In November, *Time* provoked him again by listing him among black writers self-exiled in Europe. He shot off a note of protest. "While I sympathize with those Negro Americans" who lived abroad because of racism at home, "my own needs, both as a citizen and as artist, make the gesture of exile seem mere petulance. . . . Personally I am too vindictively American, too full of hate for the hateful aspects of this country, and too possessed by the things I love here to be too long away."

On May 17, *Saturday Review* published Ralph's essay "The Charlie Christian Story." Despite his extensive training in music, this was his first piece on American music. Inspiring the essay was nostalgia for his boyhood friend Christian and for Oklahoma City in general. It is steeped so deeply in Ralph's boyhood memories that he even supplied *Saturday Review* with a photograph of the first-grade class at Douglass in 1923 that included Christian and Ralph's brother, Herbert. Ralph's Christian is a tragic figure, in that he died young, but he was also doomed by his medium. Such is the lethal volatility of jazz, which, "like the country which gave it birth, is fecund in its inventiveness, swift and traumatic in its developments, and terribly wasteful of its resources. It is an orgiastic art . . . and many of its most talented creators die young." Pleased by the response to the essay, Ralph decided to try his hand at other pieces on music. In July, *Saturday Review* published "Remembering Jimmy," about the blues singer Jimmy Rushing, the other homegrown musical genius from Ralph's days in Oklahoma City. In September the *Review* offered his "As the Spirit Moves Mahalia," about Mahalia Jackson, who was taking black gospel singing to unexpected new heights of national popularity. Now Ralph began to think of writing a book of essays on music. While he "wouldn't be a jazz critic for love or money," he wrote, he would attend the Newport Jazz Festival that summer. He would also write for *Esquire* a retrospective essay on Minton's Playhouse in Manhattan, the place where bebop was born in the early 1940s.

Involvement in the 1958 Newport Jazz Festival, organized by the white impresario George Wein, exposed a new, agonized strain in his thinking about evolving black culture. The festival itself was a landmark event. According to *Down Beat* magazine, it was "the biggest, most financially successful jazz venture ever undertaken." The players were mainly black, the audience mainly white. This mixture had much to do with the strength of Ralph's reaction, in that he saw on display at Newport a kind of orchestration and performance of the influence on the nation of *Brown v. Board of Education* and the civil rights movement. The musicians included jazz makers old and new, as well as others representing blues, gospel, and even the latest craze, rock 'n' roll. Mingling with jazzmen such as Louis Armstrong, Benny Goodman, Duke Ellington, and Miles Davis were popular performers such as Ray Charles, Mahalia Jackson, and the rock 'n' roll sensation Chuck Berry.

This was a heterogenous stew of American, black-dominated expressive culture, and Ralph found some of the stew indigestible. His main objection was not to rock 'n' roll, as some might have expected, but to the new jazz. Coolly critical at a public symposium, privately to Al Murray he was blunt about his belief that "a hell of a lot of it was simply pathetic." The younger jazz musicians, including the internationally famous, were creating their new sound "by fucking up the blues." He looked down on "that poor, evil, lost little Miles Davis," on John Coltrane for his "badly executed velocity exercises," and on Horace Silver, whose group "went wanging away like a slightly drunken gospel group after announcing a blues." The late Charlie "Yardbird" Parker's influence, "as miserable, beat and lost as *he* sounded most of the time," had betrayed true jazz, and his epigones seemed to believe in "the witchdoctor's warning: If Bird shits on you, wear it." Evidently "Bird had crapped on most of the saxophonists, who try to see how many notes they can play in a phrase and how many 'changes' as they call their chord progressions." About the more cerebral, restrained jazz musicians (epitomized by the Modern Jazz Quartet) he was just as critical: "Taste was an item conspicuously missing from most of the performances; there was nothing worse than a half-educated jazz

modernist [who's] convinced himself that he's a genius, maybe next to
Beethoven, or at least Bartok, and who's certain that he's the only Mose
[Negro] jazzman who has heard the classics or attended a conservatory."
(Although less hostile, *Metronome* magazine judged that "it was not an
inspiring festival" and reported "many moments of really bad taste and
bad music.")

Ralph's temper was tested again when he started work in Harlem on
his piece about Minton's Playhouse. Again he was blunt in letters to Murray. He hated having to make nice to older performers in order to interview them—having "to talk to these screwed up musicians, drinking beer
so that I could listen to their miserable hard-bopping noise." Finally he
decided that he didn't need them but would rely on his memory, imagination, and lyric gifts as a writer. To Ralph, Duke Ellington was still *the* master. At a party given by Columbia Records at the Plaza Hotel, at which
Ellington, Miles Davis, Jimmy Rushing, and Billie Holiday performed,
Ralph loved the way (as he saw it) the Ellington players slyly scorned
Davis although he was now probably the most admired jazz instrumental-
ist in the world except for Louis Armstrong. (Reciprocating, Ellington
welcomed Ralph and Fanny to his going-away champagne party in September on board the *Ile de France* as he prepared for his first European
tour in a decade.)

Ralph's "The Golden Age, Time Past," which *Esquire* published in January 1959, was a triumph. With a kind of spectral elegance it conjures up
the swinging jazz scene in Harlem in the late 1930s. Scrupulously it has
nothing to do with invidious comparisons of the old and the new, but
seeks instead to paint in the chiaroscuro of the nightclub and amber-
tinted memory something of the dignity and manliness that he believed
was on its way out in jazz. His writing was so evocative that Jason Epstein
asked him to write two books for Doubleday, one on jazz in general, the
other a biography of Jimmy Rushing. Someone else begged him to write
the script for a documentary film about Mahalia Jackson. To these offers
he said no. He wanted to reserve his strength for his novel, which he
thought was now going well. In August 1958, taking a chance, he sent
some pages to Frederick Morgan of the *Hudson Review* after Morgan
asked to see a piece of the new book with a view to publishing it. But
Morgan rejected the excerpt.

The new novel had begun to take shape. At its center would be characters
named Hickman and Bliss. (In *Invisible Man,* a woman says to the shad-

owy Rinehart: "But Bliss, daddy—Rinehart! . . . Daddy, what did I do?")
Alonso Hickman in his youth had been a gambler and a trombone-playing
jazzman. One day, a red-haired white woman falsely accuses his brother
of raping her. Whites lynch him. Some months later, the woman, pregnant, visits Hickman in desperate search of a black midwife. Overcoming
his rage, he delivers the baby himself. The paternity of the boy, Bliss, is
a mystery. He looks white, but is he? (We never know for a fact.) Guilt-
ridden about the lynching, the woman gives Hickman the baby to take his
brother's place. When Hickman finds God and becomes a preacher, he
brings up the boy with help from the women in his congregation.

As a preacher, Hickman practices a theatrical trick that traumatizes
the boy. Bliss is concealed in a coffin in what appears to be a funeral, then
rises from the dead through the "miracle" of Hickman's preaching. Confined in the dark with only a teddy bear, an Easter bunny, and a white
leather Bible, Bliss fears suffocation. Eventually he runs away and makes
a new life for himself as a white man. A con artist at times, he eventually
surfaces as Adam Sunraider, a notoriously bigoted U.S. senator from New
England. Hickman knows that the senator is Bliss but loves him all the
same. When he learns about a plot to assassinate Sunraider, he tries to
warn him. In Washington, he and his followers are in the gallery of the
Senate, listening to one of Sunraider's orations, when a young black man
guns down the senator.

Rushed to the hospital gravely wounded, the senator calls for Hickman. At his bedside, the two men enter into a protracted "dialogue." The
main structural device of the novel, Ellison decided, would be the long
flashback, with narratives or reveries by both men. Some of the rhetoric is
conventional in style, but some of it involves varying degrees of surrealism
and stream-of-consciousness technique. Hickman and Bliss each preach
at least one long sermon. The history of their relationship emerges. Sunraider's narratives are sometimes only projections into language of his
subconscious; but sometimes they are projections into language of *Hickman's* subconscious, informed by his deep knowledge of the man who was
once his boy.

The primary mode of the narrative would be allegory, with its range of
meanings enriched by references and allusions, obvious or elusive, deriv-
ing from the vast midden of American racial history. Clearly Hickman
embodies black American historic culture. In his youth he is carefree,
illicit, secular, and musical; then he is religious, forgiving, and moral. The
women of his congregation are nurturing. Led by Hickman, they are

proud of their identities as Negroes descended from Africa. Bliss is more complicated. He is America, or white America—except that, as Ralph sees it, America is both black and white. Whites are part black and blacks are part white. And yet Bliss and most white Americans evade this truth.

In naming the infant Bliss, Hickman consciously mocks the myth of pristine white American innocence (a myth that Bliss himself reinforces as Sunraider, in naming himself Adam). Ignorance is bliss, Hickman says. Blacks nourished America into being, but then whites turned viciously on blacks, forsaking love, compassion, and humanity in favor of wealth, power, and the myth of racial supremacy.

The core historical analogy of the text is the gunning down of President Lincoln in the name of slavery; Hickman's group even repairs to the Lincoln Memorial to meditate before the attempted assassination. Lincoln's splendid vision of American unity is besmirched by those who practice racial hatred. The ideals of the Golden Day of New England or American moral culture in the mid-nineteenth century were corrupted by evil forces that sacrificed the ideal of unity and of spiritual and moral law.

The core *literary* analogy in American fiction is obviously *Adventures of Huckleberry Finn,* Mark Twain's tale of the kindly, moral slave Jim and the white boy Huck, who identifies with Jim, wrestles with his own conscience about slavery, then helps in Jim's humiliation before he flees civilization in disgust and sets out for the territory. For Ralph (as for Hemingway, if for sometimes different reasons) that novel is the original national text in fiction. The allegorical linking of white and black, or white and Indian, inspired the growth of American literature from James Fenimore Cooper to William Faulkner and beyond. But beneath almost every narrative of this type when written by a white author is the idea of the inability of white culture to assimilate blacks or Indians. Sunraider, born Bliss, stands for America in its original indebtedness to blacks but also in its inability or refusal to acknowledge, much less repay, this debt. To the making of America blacks had contributed labor, music, laughter, and the example of compassion and forgiveness. In return, whites vilify blacks in the name of racial supremacy. As a result, whites possess power and wealth but not happiness or spiritual depth.

The difficulties posed by Ralph's architecture and ideas are clear. The old black preacher had become an arthritic figure in fiction and drama, one that recalled stereotypes of black humility and passivity. Could Ralph breathe new life into this stock figure? Other aspects of the story were also unoriginal. The flaming red hair of Bliss's mother, for example, recalls the scarlet letter worn by Hawthorne's Hester Prynne. The Easter bunny in Bliss's coffin points awkwardly to the idea of the Resurrection. His beloved stuffed bear echoes one of Ralph's favorite slang expressions— "Bear"—for a tough, rugged black man. The color of his Bible—white— speaks for itself. Also challenging Ralph was his wish to create the novel around a variety of flashbacks. Here, he was perhaps in thrall to Faulkner, who was himself mortgaged to Joyce, for all his genius. In a sense, Ralph was writing a kind of *As I Lay Dying,* except that Faulkner had not only deployed there a gallery of narrators but also blended the comic with the grotesque while speaking to the humanity of the poor whites central to that novel.

Ralph's obsessive use of the flashback also echoes *Absalom, Absalom!* Like Ralph's novel-in-progress, *Absalom, Absalom!* is about miscegenation, pride, power, and violence; but it is as masterfully controlled as it is dense. Could Ralph maintain a similar mastery on the vast canvas that he was determined to fill? Or would he write, in the end, what Henry James had called, in warning against the native indulgence of the first-person novel, a "baggy monster"?

Long after Ralph's death, Toni Morrison would observe that this story was "not really a story anybody needed to hear again." She went on: "Ellison had tried to revive the senile 'tragic mulatto' genre. Faulkner had done it already and about as well as it could have been done. . . . If Ellison had turned it out quickly after *Invisible Man,* that would have been fine." But for all practical purposes, "the story was dead." The project, one of Ralph's scholarly friends would remark, was "part of an intellectual activity of long ago." Ralph's sometimes exuberant, sometimes mournful troping on old Oklahoma, his nostalgia for an ideal, interracial American history that really had never been, and his modish commitment to Joycean and Faulknerian narrative techniques brought with them key problems of clarity and organization. Bellow once wrote cruelly, if covertly, about Ralph's "powers of organization"—but the evidence Bellow then adduced was Ralph's finicky arrangement of the contents of his car trunk, which "with its tools and weapons announced that he was prepared for any emergency, could meet every challenge to his autonomy." The sprawling masterpiece he hoped to achieve could not be so easily mastered.

With the Bellows away, at the end of the summer of 1958 Ralph ensconced himself in their Tivoli mansion. He had accepted an offer to teach two related courses on American literature, one course each semester, at Bard College in nearby Annandale-on-Hudson. Bard would pay him $2,000 for the year, plus $200 in traveling expenses. He arrived in Tivoli ready to write. "I'm a little desperate about the book," he confessed; now he would have a good chance "to get it over with."

By mid-September, he was captivated by Dutchess County. "The country hereabouts is quite lovely," he wrote to a friend, "with mountains in all directions and rolling farmland in between." Near the house was "a large vineyard to remind one of Italy and such a wealth of peach and apple trees as Italy never knew. The trees have begun the first tentative turning to the colors of fall and red shades dazzle in the sumac trees." The only drawback was heavy pollen, which would plague him for a long time; "but that will go with the first frost—which will also bring the trees to the full glory of their fall color and all will be well. I shall work and hunt or simply walk in the woods."

Ralph would teach at Bard and live in the Bellow mansion while Fanny visited him on those weekends when he did not return to Manhattan. While Bellow was away (for two years, minus the summers) he watched over the house. The decrepit mansion needed constant work, for which Ralph, with his handyman skills, was well qualified. Saul charged Ralph no rent, and also paid for utilities and other expenses. Ralph knew that his friend was subsidizing his stay. "I now have some idea of what it costs to keep the place going during the winter," he wrote Saul later that year, "and I feel guilty that you've paid for so much of my comfort here."

At Bard, one day a week, he offered the first semester of his course, "Nineteenth- and Twentieth-Century American History in the American Novel." In it he would explore "the ethical structure" of the novel "from Melville to Faulkner," as well as its themes, techniques, forms, "and the state of the American ideal during the major phases of our national identity." His reading list included four novels by Faulkner, Gertrude Stein's *Three Lives,* Francis Parkman's *The Oregon Trail,* and R. W. B. Lewis's *The American Adam.* (He included no African-American writer.) American literature was popular and he presented it with flair. "When he lectured on *The Sun Also Rises* he drew an enormous crowd," Eric Werthman, a former student, recalled. "He seemed obsessed by Hemingway" and often "enthralled" the students. "He was an amazing teacher," Ivan Levison, another student, said. Ralph did almost all of the talking. "He did not try to engage students in debate. If you were there to listen, it was an extraordinary opportunity." Normally he was contained, professorial, but at least once he exploded, when a student asked why they were not reading any poets—Ezra Pound, for example. "I will not read Ezra Pound!" he thundered.

The looseness of his course description was right for Bard, an expensive, liberal private college attended mainly (or so it seemed) by bright, artistic, but sometimes neurotic kids from New York. Walter Winchell disparaged it once as "The Little Red Whorehouse on the Hudson." Written examinations were deemed an affront to the students. Grades had been abolished at one point, but the college had restored them in an inoffensive form that reflected the "special" quality of the Bard youth. Professors befriended students. To Ralph, the freedom was often excessive. "The college is a place to stay away from," he noted, "what with its aching blue-jeans, short-shorts, padded bras, and adolescent adventurism. This, as you know, is a progressive college and the kids really believe it." Elsewhere he was more graphic: "They wear beards and let their unwashed tits bounce around in their low-cut blouses and are still, literally, chewing gum."

"He didn't quite fit in at Bard, with his careful dressing and his thin, groomed mustache," Werthman recalled. In his classes, he sometimes asked tough, personal questions about race and civil rights. He was unpredictable. When Werthman got into trouble for picketing a store in nearby Kingston, New York, that had Jim Crow branches down south, Ralph urged him to continue to rebel. "For the first time he dropped the professorial mask and I saw real anger, a kind of electricity in him," Werthman said. Many of the kids were excited to be dealing with a black professor, probably for the first time in their lives. Idealists for the most part, many admired him. Ivan Levison was struck by his "transcendent nobility, his moral core. He was honest, self-effacing, serious. He was a great person, his own man in a magnificent, quiet way." In turn, Ralph worried about their preparation for life. "I know Bard is something of a special case," he reasoned, "but the picture I get of what the American whites who matured during the thirties are doing to their children is frightening."

George Lynes (whose father, Russell Lynes, the managing editor of *Harper's* for many years, would later become one of Ralph's closer friends) said that Ralph "tended to stutter or stammer. But all the same his class was fascinating—everyone seemed to be there every week. The two hours went by very quickly. His passion for the material, for literature, was evident." "I've been more than earning my pay there," Ralph wrote Bellow, "but I'm afraid that the place is so lax that little of it will mean anything."

He began to fraternize a little. "It was not unusual for us to have a class outside on the grass or even down at Adolph's" (a local bar), recalled Vera Gordon. On the whole he was disciplined, but one evening he drank far too much. "We had to help him home that night," Werthman remembered. The sight of a black man dancing with white coeds offended some locals, he noted, but he seemed to have no wish to sleep with students. In fact, "I felt he was scared by women," Werthman added. "He hardly ever talked about the women in the novels he taught. I always felt that women were 'The Other' to Ralph." Nevertheless, he counseled one young woman on her love life (she was thinking of marrying her boyfriend, an apparently troubled local fellow): "Enjoy your love, my dear friend. Glory in it. Only remember this: If you humiliate yourself too often . . . you might well lose that for which you sacrifice." He could be curt. Scrawling an F on one student's "criteria sheet," or report card, Ralph added: "In the future do not take any course you have no interest in."

The few Negro students seemed to avoid him. With forty kids in one class—a huge turnout for Bard—he was hurt that not one was black. He made no special effort to meet the relatively few black students. He was the professor. They should come to him.

In 1958, with Bard beset by financial woes and the faculty fighting its president, Ralph stayed clear of the struggle. He liked the head of the English Department, Ted Weiss, a poet and the editor, with his wife, Renée, of *The Quarterly Review of Literature*. Ralph felt less comfortable with some other faculty members. That he had no college degree bothered him. Confident in front of students, he was less so with faculty. Once, at a formal lecture organized by Weiss, "Ralph came to the podium almost drunk," Werthman said. "It was a disappointment." At faculty parties he was both welcome and the odd man. After a few drinks he could be combative. "Respectability is the very devil to escape these days," he wrote to Al Murray, "but I go on outraging quite a number of people just by being me." He so enraged a faculty wife from Arkansas, he said, she called him a nigger. Coolly he then asked her to kiss him. To Murray he conceded the fact that "I'd been pretty sadistic by remaining calm."

At the Tivoli manor, Ralph was both lord and laborer. "I'm used to cleaning the apartment in the city," he assured Bellow, "and have vacuumed and scrubbed and dusted and am quite concerned that the place be and remain shipshape." Briskly he dealt with local workmen, and he was vigilant about leaks when rain drenched the region. When high winds blew off a garage door, he replaced it himself. Fixing broken windowpanes, he also took care of a massive old tree out front that he knew Saul loved. Respectfully he left Bellow's bedroom and study untouched, and fixed up a guestroom for himself and set up his office in the ballroom.

He loved the peace. Although he knew that Bellow wanted to sell the house, he discouraged prospective buyers and other visitors. Indeed, he confiscated at least two keys, including one from the startled wife of Fred Dupee, a former Bard professor who lived in nearby Rhinebeck and wrote regularly for *Partisan Review*. "I'm not so anti-social as this all might sound," he assured Saul, "but I *do* have a thing about anyone coming into my lair, even if it's a loaned lair." He enjoyed, as he wrote to Albert Murray, "subjecting myself to the discipline of isolation." Isolation did not mean austerity. When the autumn chill set in, he built a crackling fire every day, sipped bourbon or wine, read book after book, and listened to music. "Like a nineteenth-century Englishman living in Africa," he joked to Murray, he insisted on many of the civilities of home. Donning an apron, he tried his hand at haute cuisine. He also took to wearing a long, striped Moroccan garment, with slippers curving upward at the toe. At peace in some ways, he often found it hard to sleep. Deep into the night he pottered about the many rooms, listening to jazz.

With the hunting good locally, Ralph joined the Rod and Gun Club of Red Hook, a nearby town. Chanler A. Chapman of Barrytown, the model for the eponymous, outrageous hero of Bellow's *Henderson the Rain King*, gave Ralph written permission to hunt on his estate. Refusing to shoot deer, he instead went after rabbits and ducks, although roaming the countryside was really enough for him: "It is so beautiful that I feel fully compensated." He needed good reasons to visit the city during the week, as when he drove to Columbia University after *Esquire* offered him $50 simply to stand by in case Leslie Fiedler, Wright Morris, Dorothy Parker, or Bellow failed to show up at its symposium on fiction. And he was at the Donnell Library on 53rd Street on February 5, 1959, as a member of the selection committee for the 1959 National Book Award in fiction. Here, as with the new jazz, he showed a certain congealing of taste. The book of the year was Vladimir Nabokov's *Lolita*. Deemed obscene when first offered to New York publishers, it had come out in France from Olympia Press, which was known less for its belles lettres than for its pornography. Finally published in America, it tested obscenity laws but prevailed against them. Lionel Trilling deemed it "unique in my experience of contemporary novels."

Apparently almost all of the NBA jury arrived at the Donnell Library prepared to crown *Lolita*. Not so Ralph, who wanted to honor Bernard Malamud for his short-story collection *The Magic Barrel*. Malamud was both a friend and a fellow member of the informal club of ethnic, American-born writers to which Nabokov had no wish to belong. *Lolita*, which is about the madness of love and one man's perverse desire for a sexy child, also disturbed Ralph. The fact that *Invisible Man* revels in one place about an act of incest between a man and his young daughter did not dispose Ralph to like *Lolita;* and Nabokov's view of America in his book as a stinky cultural landfill was anathema. He battled with Alfred Kazin in particular. Kazin liked Malamud but saw *Lolita* as a far superior work of art. "Most of the deliberations," Ralph wrote to Bellow, "broke down to my arguing Alfred out of his desire to be fashionable." Convinced, or worn down, by Ralph, the jury chose *The Magic Barrel*. (At the March 3 awards ceremony, the emcee embarrassed him by going on and on about the wonderful Mr. Ellison's many books, of which only the most famous, she said, was *Invisible Man*.)

Trips into New York and lectures at white colleges such as Hamilton in upstate New York and Middlebury in Vermont took their toll on his evolving novel. "Up until the trip in to New York for the book circus," he wrote to Bellow about the National Book Awards ceremony, "I was writing quite well, with new material flowing from the typewriter with that wild ease which makes me keep trying through the long periods of difficulty and uncertainty." The seclusion of Tivoli helped him, which explains in part why he was pleased when Ted Weiss invited him to teach two courses in the fall—one on the American novel, the other on the Russian novel—and two more in the spring.

Early in June, eagerly awaited by Ralph, Bellow reached Tivoli with his young son, Adam. His wife, Sondra, was driving out from Minneapolis. Ralph wanted to get Saul's response to his growing manuscript. "I guess I must be nearing the completion," he had alerted Bellow; "recently the typewriter has been drawing me like a magnet." He had read parts of the book to a gathering of Bard students and teachers, "and at the end of two hours they were still in a trance. . . . Old Hickman had them, man; the few Christians, the Jews and all."

To Ralph's relief, Bellow quickly read what he was offered and pronounced it fine. He then selected about fifty pages for inclusion in the first issue of *The Noble Savage*. In addition, he let Ralph know that the mansion would be his for the coming year.

. . .

Elated by Bellow's response, on July 17 Ralph returned to 730 Riverside Drive. To Murray he described his sojourn at Tivoli as "a most interesting year, full of irritations and discoveries; progress on the novel and a definite deepening of my perception of the themes which I so blindly latched on to." Nevertheless, he wanted a break. Thus, offered the chance to go to Europe, he seized it.

From July 22 to July 25, in Frankfurt, he attended the annual congress of PEN International in the United States delegation, which included the playwright Elmer Rice, the biographer Leon Edel, and John Cheever. Cold War tensions and issues dominated the gathering, with the major topic being the writer's fate under Communist dominance. Particularly vexing for PEN on this score was the status of its Hungarian chapter, with a lesser but related and potent topic the official vilification in Russia of Boris Pasternak for publishing his novel *Doctor Zhivago* abroad and then winning the Nobel Prize. In 1956, in Budapest, Soviet tanks had crushed a popular uprising against Communism. The following year, PEN International, meeting in Japan, suspended the Hungarian chapter. Now a special PEN committee had recommended that Hungary be readmitted.

After a hot debate, PEN readmitted Hungary by a vote of nineteen to nine, with eight abstentions. The American chapter had arrived with instructions to refrain from voting. Ralph made it clear that the decision disappointed him. Resolutely anti-Communist, he saw the readmission of Hungary as an act of appeasement. If it was incongruous to some that the brown-skinned American delegate was the one most opposed to Communism, he saw no incongruity. He was pleased, indeed, that his place in the delegation, despite all the bad news about Jim Crow in the South, reinforced American claims to being the world leader in democracy. Contemptuous of anti-Americanism, he ridiculed the shoddy level of discussions at the congress and deplored the pervasive sympathy for radical socialism. The level was abysmally low, he believed, "thanks to much repetition of politico-cultural theories discredited some thirty years ago." He was equally hard on writers who saw a major threat in the form of science and technology in the modern world. Many delegates "seemed to forget that it is the responsibility [of] the literary mind to keep pace with that growth, to dominate it, and to humanize it."

Suspicious of the so-called Third World, he kept away from it. Langston Hughes, helping to gather books to send to Ghana, noted that all "of the prominent contemporary writers of color in the U.S.A. to whom we wrote" donated volumes—except Ralph. He identified himself with the defense of Hungarians, Bulgarians, and other victims of oppression, but was quiet about Africa. Interviewed a year later in *Phylon: The Atlanta University Review of Race and Culture,* he was clearly proud of his response when the Department of State asked him to visit Ghana: "I said I had no interest in it." He had "no special emotional attachment to the place. I don't read much on Africa nowadays. It is just part of the bigger world picture to me." He was starting to collect pricey African art (especially after reading André Malraux on the subject) but did not embrace Africans as friends. With Africans he had met in Europe, "I never really got into contact. I won't have anything to do with racial approaches to culture." He went further: "The African content of American Negro life is more fanciful than actual." Blacks must accept the reality of America. "As long as Negroes are confused as to how they relate to American culture," he said, "they will be confused about their relationship to places like Africa."

(This trip to Frankfurt—paid for by PEN—would be the last time he saw Europe. He never visited Africa. His brief trip to Mexico City marked his only time in Latin America. In fact, Ralph and Fanny never once paid for a visit or vacation outside the United States.)

His attitude to Africa would soon baffle and enrage other blacks as they began to look beyond the United States for answers to questions about their identity. Ralph believed that the answers were already clear. On a panel discussion the following winter, he bravely took on the makers of a documentary movie called *The Cry of Jazz,* which identified jazz as a black phenomenon now largely ruined by whites. Addressing the co-author of the script, Mark Kennedy, and its director, Edward Bland, Ralph stressed his opposition to this idea. "They are some arrogant and most[ly] half-educated studs," Ralph wrote to Murray about Kennedy and Bland, "—the same who've done their damn[ed]est to kill off Louis [Armstrong] and to make Jazz middle class." When he attacked their "pitifully bad" film, they "wanted to cut my throat before it was over." He made a distinction between the "half-educated" black nationalists and true Negro culture as seen in the turbulence of Harlem, its summer flash and fury, its suffering but also its gaiety. Dropping in on the annual national convention of the NAACP in Manhattan, he felt little respect for the intellect of most of the (male) members but was reassured by their flair. "Fifteen minutes in a meeting with some of those studs," he wrote, "and I'd want to start a fight, but just seeing them walk and pose and talk and flirt and woof—that's damn pleasant."

.   .   .

Ralph's return to 730 Riverside Drive in the summer of 1959 allowed him
to look afresh at what his marriage had become after Rome. Its terms had
changed. For a year, he and Fanny had lived more apart than together.
Both seemed to prefer it that way. Fanny used to pine for him; now she
was willing to have him on weekends mainly. Their inability to have a
child still tainted their marriage. In March, a missed period had led her
into the fantasy that she was pregnant. Instead, she wrote sadly to Ralph,
she had to face the fact that menopause was starting, "and that my body
blossoming in its strange way was the beginning of its end. . . . I knew I
wanted children, but I did not really understand what not having them
meant. This last grisly joke on myself is almost too much." Now "I must
free myself from this thing in some way to make way for the life ahead,
which seems to me now for the first time very dark. Even having been my
own straitjacket all these years, I still moved around in an airiness of my
own. Now I give up the hope, I give it up willingly as I would a curse."

In August she and Ralph went to Middlebury, Vermont, for the thirty-
fourth annual Bread Loaf Writers' Conference. Although the gray eminence of Bread Loaf, Robert Frost, was in residence, the Ellisons had
much more fun with old friends, such as John Ciardi, and with certain
new friends, especially the handsome, young, but already acclaimed poet
and translator Richard Wilbur and his equally attractive wife, Charlotte.
In 1956, critics lavishly praised his elegant lyrics for *Candide,* with music
by Leonard Bernstein and a text by Lillian Hellman. In 1957, he won both
the National Book Award and the Pulitzer Prize for his volume of poetry
Things of This World. A sense of easy intimacy quickly developed between
Ralph and Dick Wilbur, who shared the same birthday, March 1. At Bread
Loaf, Ralph delivered three public lectures, led writing clinics, and met
individually with students. Most students were thrilled to work with him
but he also had his critics. An exchange with an admirer of Norman
Mailer led to the public accusation that, unlike Mailer, Ralph was leading
a self-deceiving life. Days later Ralph still smarted from the attack. "This
same character told me that I was harming myself because I no longer
lived with Negroes," Ralph reported to Murray, "and I hung around with
too many intellectuals." "You mean," Ralph had shot back, "that I've
stepped out of my place?" He had given the fellow hell "for trying to tell
me what my life was like and what Negro life was like. I'm damned sick of
these 'white Negroes' trying to tell me what it is to be a black Negro."

In fact, no fellow writer irked Ralph more now than Mailer, whose first novel, *The Naked and the Dead,* in 1948, had made him famous. His next two novels were less admired, but Mailer had strengthened his status as a celebrity by writing subversive essays on American culture after the end of World War II. Unlike Ralph, he cared little for decorum. In his long essay "The White Negro," he had shrewdly analyzed many of the key insecurities of white urban artists and thinkers in an age marked by fierce anxieties about issues such as nuclear war, the Holocaust, black civil rights, miscegenation, and sexual freedom. Although Ellison never stated it precisely, it disturbed him that in "The White Negro," as well as in the classic Beat novel by Jack Kerouac, *On the Road,* a quality in the American past that he loved to praise but also assumed was dead had now returned, but in a disturbing way. Once again, as in pre–Civil War America, the figure of "the Negro" was becoming both the focus of the nation's moral and artistic consciousness and its key metaphor. But instead of standing for the nobility of mankind, "the Negro" was now the symbol of America's sexual and social epilepsy. The untamable jazz- and blues-man, and increasingly even the rank-and-file black man, was now being seen as epitomizing the restless heart of a new America.

To Ralph, the Beat sense of freedom proclaimed in work by writers such as Mailer, Kerouac, Allen Ginsberg, and other white writers and artists was a kind of cancer that was threatening to metastasize into chaos. "These characters are all trying to reduce the world to sex," he wrote indignantly. "They have strange problems in bed; they keep score a la Reich on the orgasm and try to verbalize what has basically to be warmth, motion, rhythm, timing, affection and technique." He was pleased that Bellow (whose own fascination with the sexually obsessed psychologist Wilhelm Reich is reflected in *Henderson the Rain King*) saw the Beats as doing little more than thrashing about like prisoners trapped in Puritan stocks. "That's what's behind Mailer's belief in the hipster and the 'white Negro' as the new culture hero," Ralph decided; "—he thinks all hipsters are cocksmen possessed of great euphoric orgasms and are out to fuck the world into peace, prosperity and creativity. . . . It makes you hesitant to say more than the slightest greetings to their wives lest they think you're out to give them a hot fat injection. What a bore."

Mailer admired Ralph as a writer and also pitied him. That year, 1959, in his *Advertisements for Myself,* he praised but also denounced Ralph. "He is essentially a hateful writer," Mailer declared. "When the line of his satire is pure, he writes so perfectly that one can never forget the experience of reading him—it is like holding a live electric wire in one's hand.

But Ralph's mind, fine and icy, tuned to the pitch of a major novelist's madness, is not always adequate to mastering the forms of rage, horror, and disgust which his eyes have presented to his experience, and so he is forever tumbling from the heights of pure satire into the nets of a murderously depressed clown." Perhaps it took one "mad" major novelist obsessed by violence (the following year Mailer was arrested for stabbing his wife) to know another. Since Mailer had no access to Ralph's private life and unpublished writings, especially his novel-in-progress, his assessment of his character was astonishing in its audacity. And yet, erratically perhaps, he had placed his finger on some genuine elements in Ralph's psychology. Even Stanley Hyman was starting to see his old friend as a changed man. Stanley "recently accused me of having sold out to the movers and shakers of this world," Ralph complained. In a way Ralph conceded the charge even as he defended himself against it. The artist "is drawn to the impurities of life much as a homing missile to its target. Man just ain't no abstraction, he's mixed as a downhome stew and that's what makes him interesting. Some of the nastiest farts I ever had to smell bloomed during a solemn church service."

Despite Stanley's criticism of Ralph, he still loved and respected him, as did most of the people who knew Ralph well. When Stanley and Shirley drew up their wills they passed over their brothers to name Ralph and Fanny guardians of their children in the event of a catastrophe. A prime reason for this respect was Ralph's courage and honesty. Honesty was there in his concession, where many others lied to themselves, that he was now trafficking in some of "the impurities of life," that is, the desire for money, power, and social prestige. With the *Brown* decision opening the way for blacks to rise in the world, he was determined to do so. By dint of talent, ambition, and labor he had made himself into a formidable intellectual and artist. Thus he deserved any honor or privilege that society bestowed on him. Once upon a time, he had looked more frugally on himself and the world—as he was reminded at the end of August when Ida Guggenheimer, ninety-three years old, died. The anti-Communist politics of his novel had wounded Ida and they had parted ways. "Now she's gone and I'm sorry," he said, "for she was a tough-minded old lady with a tenacious sense of life and a true generosity of spirit." She had embodied a certain cultural spirit that was vanishing: "The old Jews who suffered the isolation of being Jews are worth millions of those who came after them and it's sad to see them go."

Back in Tivoli for the fall semester, Ralph got an offer from Paul Engle, the founder of the University of Iowa Writers' Workshop (the first college program in creative writing in the country), to be writer-in-residence. Ralph, though, was not yet tired of life in Dutchess County. Many students had signed up for his courses. The apple orchards near the old house on Kidd Lane were heavy with fruit. At twilight, deer gathered timidly on the meadow that stretched before the house. Late into the autumn he was still harvesting eggplants, peppers, squash, and tomatoes from the vegetable garden that Saul had put in that summer. The hunting was still good.

Around October that fall, life also improved at 730 Riverside after the owner of the Beaumont, Eugene Ramsey, finally decided to allow tenants to change apartments. Ralph and Fanny quickly secured an apartment one floor higher (8D), with five bright, airy rooms and a full view of the Hudson River. "Perhaps I'll write a couple or so of books," Ralph wrote mordantly to Stanley, "before I work out a good reason for not being able to write in *this* location." By November 1, Fanny had moved them. At about the same time, Bellow offered to sell the mansion to Ralph at a bargain price. Sondra was divorcing him, without offering a reason (she had been having an affair in Minnesota with his friend Jack Ludwig, who had been hired by the university there at Bellow's insistence). Ralph had no way of buying the mansion. Besides, his job at Bard wasn't permanent, and he also had doubts about living in an overwhelmingly white setting. Some local people liked and accepted him, but others did not. Some of the latter found Ralph too full of himself, and a few tried to provoke him. Renée and Ted Weiss heard Gore Vidal ask Ralph one day: "What's a jungle bunny like you doing in these parts?" According to the critic and editor Richard Poirier, "Fred Dupee and Gore Vidal thought he was pompous and overbearing, and they let him know it."

John Cheever, who lived with his wife, Mary, and their young children in the town of Scarborough-on-the-Hudson, was a good friend here as in Italy. Prolific, Cheever was then doing his best work as a writer. Between 1957 and 1964 Cheever published five books of fiction, including two novels. Unlike Ralph, Cheever was using his sojourn in Italy to fine effect, while in his own use of Italy Ralph might as well have spent two years on the moon. Ralph was drawn toward Cheever, who embodied the kind of white, Anglo-Saxon, high-toned style that Ellison admired. Like Ralph at this time, Cheever favored conservative Brooks Brothers clothing, and his speech was upper-class Eastern establishment even if his true origins were less aristocratic. For much of his life, also, Cheever was a cheerful drunk, a courtly womanizer, and a closet bisexual. Easygoing, he accepted Ralph as a professional and, within certain limits, as a social equal. When he applied for a Guggenheim fellowship that year, he asked Ralph for a letter of recommendation.

Ralph genuinely liked Cheever but he also courted him because of two specific goals that Cheever was well placed to help him achieve. One was election to the American Academy and National Institute of Arts and Letters, the self-anointed elite among American writers, with its headquarters, ironically, but a few blocks from Ralph's home in uptown Manhattan. The other was admission to the Century Association—or the Century, simply—which was the oldest and most prestigious social club for artists and lovers of art in America (the academy had been a sort of stepchild of the Century). The former had elected only one black in its history, when W. E. B. Du Bois, not yet smeared as a Communist sympathizer, joined the National Institute in 1943. The Century had never admitted a black member. These two were the most treasured and paradoxically benign "impurities of life" (his desire to achieve them was what made them, in this sense, impure) to which Ralph now aspired. Cheever belonged to both.

In early December, Ralph was in Iowa City for a two-day symposium on contemporary writing also attended by his bête noire, Mailer. Polite to his rival on the surface, privately Ralph told Al Murray of refusing "to turn myself into a clown like Mailer" (using Mailer's own image of Ralph as a "clown" against Mailer himself) and of loathing "the phony Mailer image of the outlaw." But compared with other writers on the program Ralph seemed almost housebroken. Mailer, living up to his reputation, loudly deplored the sheepishness and monotony of the times. The veteran intellectual Dwight Macdonald, ridiculing American anti-intellectualism, labeled as mediocre writers Archibald MacLeish, a three-time Pulitzer Prize winner; the Nobel laureate John Steinbeck; and Thornton Wilder, whose play *Our Town* was worshipped as an American classic. The young novelist Mark Harris also lashed out at the prevailing American values. In contrast to them, Ralph seemed tame and lame. Unlike the others, he spoke from notes, as usual. Fumbling for words and ponderous, he came across as academic. "Somewhat incongruously," *Newsweek* reported (pointing no doubt to his skin color), he was "the least ferocious of the speakers" and "painted a less dismal picture" in defense of a more democratic approach to art.

Ralph's restraint made him attractive to academics. At the University of Iowa, his popularity with faculty writers such as Paul Engle and Vance Bourjaily only grew when he went out hunting with a few of the locals— even if he did so with a borrowed gun and spiffy wear that included soft leather dress shoes, a rakish hat, and his Burberry trench coat. Later, Engle pressed him again about coming to Iowa, perhaps permanently, to teach fiction writing. Engle's offer was timely, given Bard's money problems. But Ralph did not want to leave New York City. Tivoli was also a sweet place to work, and his novel-in-progress was his top concern. On this score, he was heartened when Jack Ludwig praised the excerpt, "And Hickman Arrives," that Bellow had placed in *The Noble Savage*. "They give me a sense," Ralph said of Ludwig's comments, "that I really have hold [of] something"; they "serve to relieve some of the fog of uncertainty." But at times the fog was almost too thick. "I feel that I'm falling apart," he confessed to Saul early in 1960. "I find myself in strange places in my dreams." Hickman and Bliss "seem like people out of some faded dream of nobility. They need desperately to be affirmed while I seem incapable of bringing them fully to life."

Meanwhile, Fanny moved upward professionally when she became executive director of the American Medical Center for Burma, a direct consequence of her job with Harold Oram Associates, its main fundrasier. An internationally known project in medical philanthropy, the center was headed by the Burmese-born American physician Dr. Gordon Seagrave. Her main task would be to raise $100,000 annually for the center. At $5,600 a year, her salary was now more than double Ralph's income from Bard. Augmented by lectures and royalties from *Invisible Man*, his total annual income was around $4,000.

At Bard, Ralph's new course on the Russian novel attracted fewer students than his previous classes but was "intense and most useful to me," he admitted, "for I'm learning much more than the kids." Still, his was an essentially lonely life in Tivoli. He tried to fill the void with music— except that much of the new jazz continued to offend and baffle him. He often saw the crisis in sexual terms: "When so many musicians can stand up in public and make their horns sound so miserable and self-pitying, castrated and flat, something awful must be happening to the country; something no one has named or even begun to grasp. The stuff sounds gutless and homo." He guessed that the new jazz had something to do with the inability of many blacks to absorb racial integration. Instead of being set free, many jazz artists seemed "disorganized by a little acceptance." Many younger blacks, rebellious but aimless, were finding integration toxic: "It looks as though these guys are doing to themselves, out of self-hate and a child-like self assertion, exactly what all the years of slavery and second-class citizenship couldn't do—they've killed their own rich Negro sense of life and become zombies."

Ralph's own zest for what he saw as the good things in life, and in America, only grew with integration. He wanted only the best for himself. For example, early in 1960, when he bought a puppy, it had to have a fine pedigree. From a litter of Labrador retrievers bred by a friend of Cheever in Croton-on-Hudson, New York, he picked out a lively black male. "This little ball of devilment," he wrote to Cheever, soon won his heart; doting on its "throaty contralto voice," Ralph adored the fact that it loved "sleeping near my machine." Naming it Tuckatarby of Tivoli, he registered Tucka with the American Kennel Club. In this way, perhaps, Ralph acknowledged that Fanny would not be bearing him a son—ever.

That winter, 1960, with Bard still beset by internal disputes, Ralph drove an hour south of Manhattan to Rutgers University in New Brunswick, New Jersey, to deliver a lecture. A snowstorm led to a wretched turnout, but a few weeks later university officials offered him a position at $9,000 a year, more than what most full professors earned at Bard. Instead of signing up at once, Ralph set his sights on a far more prestigious target, the University of Chicago, which he visited about a month after his Rutgers lecture. In a four-day span, for a fee of $500, he lectured formally and informally, and also sat in on at least two writing classes. His visit encouraged him to think about a position there—although leaving New York would be a huge step. (Since the early 1940s, the university had employed at least one black professor.)

In Chicago, Bellow, who had attended the institution before transferring to Northwestern in nearby Evanston, Illinois, where he was now teaching, gave a party in his honor. But it was Richard Stern, an instructor in writing, who had secured Ralph's visit. Over the four days he was Ralph's escort and guide—except in black Chicago, which bordered the university. There Ralph (coached by Fanny) led. Stern liked what he saw in Ralph. Although "I was the junior by fifteen years," he wrote later, "Ralph didn't lean on me with years or accomplishments; he had the gift of equality." On May 11, when Stern interviewed Ralph, the feeling was so rich that a lightly edited version of the transcript would appear in Ralph's next book. Elegant in a double-breasted navy blue blazer, charcoal gray slacks, and a superb pair of shoes ("shoes, he taught me," Stern wrote, "were exceptionally important to blacks"), Ralph seemed at ease crossing the Quadrangle. He joked with the well-known black economist Abram Harris ("who, within sixty seconds, asked Ralph where he'd bought his shoes"), but was especially impressed by Nathan A. Scott, Jr., an erudite black associate professor in the Divinity School. At thirty-five, Scott was both an Episcopal priest and a critic of modern literature and religious thought who had published three books on modern writers such as Kafka, Silone, and D. H. Lawrence. Eventually he would publish about two dozen volumes. Ralph had probably never met a black man or woman who possessed Scott's range of learning in literature. Seeking to take the measure of Scott ("whom I found intriguing"), he was clearly a little intimidated. Nevertheless, Scott's presence made the idea of a job at Chicago even more attractive. Returning home, Ralph assured the chair of the English Department, Alan Simpson, that his visit had been "one of the most exciting times of my career as a lecturer" and that "*any* opportunity to return will be received with pleasure."

Long awaited by Ralph, the appearance of the first issue of *The Noble Savage* lifted his spirits. "And Hickman Arrives" was prominent in an issue that included the work of Arthur Miller and Wright Morris. The response to the new magazine and to Ralph's piece was, on the whole, favorable. Hailing the "Birth of a Lusty Biannual" in *Saturday Review*, Granville Hicks noted that although "a long time—eight years" had passed since *Invisible Man*, Ralph's excerpt "sharpens the anticipation" for its successor. The piece left "many questions unanswered, but it is full of dramatic power." The *Hudson Review*, which had rejected one section, now asked to look at another. Preparing the second issue of *The Noble Savage*, Ludwig demanded something from Ralph—even four or five pages "on any bloody thing you want to write about." The hubbub left Ralph pleased. "Although I'm damned disgusted with myself because of my failure to finish," he wrote to Al Murray, "I know nevertheless that it's better to publish one fairly decent book than five pieces of junk." Crazy things were still happening in the manuscript. Someone had just driven his Cadillac into a senator's lawn and set the car on fire (later this section would appear as "Cadillac Flambé"). Another character suddenly orders a case of bourbon and a white "cooch" dancer to come to his house and perform. "The only granny-dodger is so wild," Ralph told Murray, "that I'm not sure that he won't blow the book to hell. As you can see, deep down I'm as mad as ever—insane, that is, but it seems to be my only way."

The effect of his "only way" was seen again later that year, when Ted and Renée Weiss published a second fragment in their magazine, *The Quarterly Review of Literature*. Thirteen pages long, "The Roof, the Steeple and the People" is as intriguing as but also no more completely coherent than "And Hickman Arrives." Opening with Hickman and Bliss, the piece slides into an ungrounded dialogue between young Bliss and his friend Body, in which Bliss admits that "the landscape of [his] mind had been trampled by the great droves of galloping horses." It ends mysteriously, its meaning perhaps trampled under the hooves of those galloping horses of the mind, with Bliss and his mentor, Hickman, walking hand in hand into a darkened movie house.

The instability of Ralph's novel-in-progress perhaps reflected the sudden shudder of rebellion that overtook the civil rights movement in the South starting on February 1, 1961. On that day, four college students from black North Carolina A&T in Greensboro sat down on stools at a whites-only lunch counter at a local Woolworth's store. Denied service, they refused to move. Less than two weeks later, inspired by that event, Fisk students in Nashville began their own siege of a local Woolworth's lunch counter. Attracting blacks and whites, the sit-in movement began to spread across the country—first to other lunch counters and restaurants, then to public beaches, libraries, and even churches. Whites struck back. In Nashville, the home of the students' main lawyer was bombed, and police arrested almost two thousand students across the South. Despite these efforts, Jim Crow barriers began to crack and then fall apart. In addition to the NAACP, the SCLC and the Congress of Racial Equality (CORE) entered the fray on behalf of the sit-in movement. The nonviolent war against Jim Crow had begun.

The scale and speed of the resistance stunned and confused Ralph as it stunned and surprised many of the resisters themselves. The brutality of the white reaction further rocked his idealistic notions about the likelihood of voluntary change in the South as well as his faith in the white aristocrats of the South. Late in 1959, he had abruptly pulled out of a project organized by the University of North Carolina scholar Louis D. Rubin, Jr., in which Ralph would have joined ex-Fugitives including Allen Tate and Donald Davidson in writing a book of essays on Southern literature. Usually pleased to be invited to associate with Southern white men of substance, especially artists and intellectuals, he had misgivings about where this association would lead him. *His* South was a different South, he wrote to Rubin, who argued in vain that the book would be richer precisely because of that difference.

·   ·   ·

In May, about the time Ralph finished an introduction to the Dell edition of *The Red Badge of Courage and Four Great Stories of Stephen Crane* (for $500), Saul Bellow returned to Tivoli. After a tiring visit to Poland and Yugoslavia on behalf of the Department of State, Bellow had gone to Minnesota to see his wife, Sondra, and their son, Adam. To his dismay, Sondra barred him from the house and also from seeing Adam. On June 1, the marriage was legally over.

With Bellow in pain, the men grew closer. According to one of Bellow's biographers, "Ellison and Bellow became inseparable." Saul even joked that some people might see them as a gay couple. As he swung slowly in his hammock in the shade and brooded—to add to his sorrows, a nephew had committed suicide—he was grateful to have Ralph at hand. "The important thing was," Saul recalled, "that the gloomy house was no longer empty—no longer gloomy." Every day they met in the kitchen to prepare and have breakfast, went their separate ways, then met again at the cocktail hour to talk leisurely about their work or events of the day. In the U.S. presidential race, predictably, they found John F. Kennedy fascinating and Richard Nixon unattractive. After supper, which they prepared together, they drank and talked late into the night. Both men loved to play the recorder. On Ralph's last visit to Frankfurt, he had bought two fine recorders, a soprano and a tenor. They also listened to their favorite recordings of Bach, Scarlatti, and Poulenc, to *The Messiah* and *The Magic Flute*. They were happy together.

The biggest difference between them, as Ralph saw it, lay in Saul's facility in finishing ambitious works of fiction. But they were different in other ways, too. With his Ivy League clothes, Bellow recalled, Ralph was "never anything but well-dressed." Eyeing Saul's faded blue jeans and ragged chambray shirt, "he studied me, silently amused—deeply amused by my lack of consideration for my appearance." They also differed about casual sex. Bellow's bed had long been a kind of comfort station for passing women; Ralph's was not. Despite these differences, the two men got along well. Unfortunately, this season of harmony did not last. Tuckatarby of Tivoli became the snake in their Eden. Less than a year old, the black puppy often defecated indoors, sometimes on Saul's Persian rugs, or chewed on his furniture and books. Stubborn about his dog's rights, Ralph refused to discipline Tucka or even to clean up after him outdoors. Bellow began to seethe. One day, after he found a pile left by Tucka in his herb garden, he exploded at Ralph: "Can't you arrange to have him do his shitting elsewhere?" According to Bellow, "this offended Ralph greatly,

Fanny with Ralph and Langston Hughes,
Newport Jazz Festival, c. 1959 LIBRARY OF
CONGRESS

Saul Bellow, 1958—once a close friend of
Ellison's, but not always VICTORIA LIDOV,
© BETTMAN / CORBIS

R. W. B. "Dick" Lewis,
another Ellison favorite, 1976
RALPH ELLISON / COURTESY
OF NANCY LEWIS

Robert Penn Warren, Eleanor Clark Warren, the painter Robert Motherwell, Ralph, and Nancy Lewis (Mrs. R. W. B. Lewis), 1963 COURTESY OF NANCY LEWIS

The same day, Ralph and Fanny with their godson Nathaniel Lewis COURTESY OF NANCY LEWIS

The writer Amiri Baraka, with whom Ellison clashed, and his wife, Amina, Newark, 1967

The poet Richard Wilbur and Charlotte Wilbur, great friends of the Ellisons for many years COURTESY OF RICHARD AND CHARLOTTE WILBUR

The author and editor Irving Howe, an early champion of *Invisible Man* whose later criticism pushed Ralph to write perhaps his finest essay, 1962 JOSE MERCADO / STANFORD NEWS SERVICE

James Baldwin and Norman Mailer, who once called Ellison "essentially a hateful writer"
© BETTMAN / CORBIS

Presenting his friend John Cheever with the Howells Medal for Fiction of the American Academy of Arts and Letters, 1965
© BETTMAN / CORBIS

Friends Rose and William Styron, 1968
© BETTMAN / CORBIS

At the White House, with President Lyndon Johnson, Henry McPherson, Jr., special counsel to the president, and Attorney General Ramsey Clark, c. 1967 LIBRARY OF CONGRESS

At a Washington book party in 1968 with Lady Bird Johnson, who inscribed this photograph "To Ralph Ellison—whose time and talent helped make this book possible" LIBRARY OF CONGRESS

With Herbert Ellison at the award ceremony for the Chevalier de l'Ordre des Arts et des Lettres, Consulate of France, Manhattan, 1969 STÉPHANIE RANÇOU / LIBRARY OF CONGRESS

At the White House for an Arts Council event, December 14, 1966 FRANK HOY / WASHINGTON POST

At home, 730 Riverside Drive in Manhattan, c. 1972 © 2007 NANCY CRAMPTON

The writer Ishmael Reed,
one of Ralph's liveliest critics,
c. 1975 © CHRISTOPHER
FELVER / CORBIS

Albert Murray RALPH ELLISON / LIBRARY OF
CONGRESS

With Mary Humelsine, wife of Carlisle H. Humelsine, director of the Colonial Williamsburg Foundation LIBRARY OF CONGRESS

Charlotte and Nathan Scott, friends since Nathan's years as a professor of literature and religion at the University of Chicago in the 1960s. After Ralph's death, Charlotte, a professor of finance, became Fanny's most trusted advisor. COURTESY OF NATHAN AND CHARLOTTE SCOTT

At City College, New York, 1984, after the Langston Hughes Medal award ceremony, with professor Raymond Patterson, president Bernard Harleston (back to camera), Hale Smith of the University of Connecticut, and Marvina White of CCNY

(*top*) At the American Academy of Arts and Letters, 1992. Among Ralph's closer friends: back row, to his left, Alfred Kazin; middle row, third from right, Arthur M. Schlesinger, Jr.; front row center, Louis Auchincloss NIKKI BERG / TIME-LIFE

(*middle*) Fanny at home with John F. Callahan, one of the Ellisons' most beloved friends in Ralph's last years RALPH ELLISON / LIBRARY OF CONGRESS

(*bottom*) With John Callahan's daughters, Eve (left) and Sasha, 1984 JOHN CALLAHAN / LIBRARY OF CONGRESS

With their host Toni Morrison, State University of New York at Albany, 1987 COURTESY OF TONI MORRISON

With Rita Dove and Henry Louis Gates, Jr., at National Book Awards ceremony, 1991

(*top*) Eightieth birthday dinner at Le Périgord restaurant, Manhattan, March 1, 1994. With Silvia Fioretta Erskine (Albert Erskine's daughter), Joseph Mitchell of *The New Yorker* LIBRARY OF CONGRESS

(*middle*) Ralph at home, 1994 LIBRARY OF CONGRESS

(*bottom*) Ralph Ellison memorial, Riverside Drive at 150th Street. At left, 730 Riverside Drive. Created by Elizabeth Catlett for the Department of Parks and Recreation, New York City. Bronze, 15 feet by 10 feet. Dedicated May 1, 2004 COURTESY OF AVON KIRKLAND, NEW IMAGES, INC.

The invisible Man

"I am an no invisible man. No, I don't
mean a spook nor one of these Hollywood ectoplasms. I am a mong substance
of mass bulk and liquids. I'm invisible
to sight simply because people refuse
to see me. I am not complaining. It's
sometimes an advantage to be unseen
For instance, I have been carrying on
a fight with Consolidated Edison for
over a year now. I use their service
and pay them nothing at all and they
don't even know it. They've tried to
catch me, they know the power is
being drawn off. But they don't
know where all they know is that
it disappears somewhere safe into
the jungle of Harlem. But they don't
know that I still live there. Several
years ago, before I discovered
the advantages of being invisible

and he was outraged when in a fit of nastiness I took a swipe at the dog with a broom for fouling the terrace."

Indignant, Ralph took his complaints to John Cheever. The problem, he fumed, was that Bellow had grown up with mongrels. He could not appreciate the rights of a pedigreed dog. Tuckatarby of Tivoli was a *"chien du race,"* as an amused Cheever wrote in his diary, not some mutt to be smacked. (Cheever meant "chien de race," Bellow pointed out.) Such aristocratic dogs should shit wherever they liked. Cheever, who loved Bellow, as Bellow loved Cheever, perhaps noted the irony of a black man complaining to a WASP that their friend, a Jew, did not appreciate purity of blood—in a dog. (Details of the incident surfaced only after Cheever died, when some of his journals were published.) Ralph was glad when, near Christmas, Saul left for the Caribbean to teach for several months at the University of Puerto Rico.

Years later, after Ralph's death, Bellow published in *Partisan Review* a sometimes inaccurate and devious but amusing account of their time together. Bellow would end this vignette with an image of Ralph fastidious in brewing coffee, which was a way of suggesting that coffee-making lessons had been Ralph's main influence on him. "We did not form a great friendship," he insisted. "What we had was a warm attachment. He respected me. I admired him. He had a great deal to teach me; I did my best to learn. Since that time I have brewed my morning coffee precisely as he had taught me to brew it." Assessing Ralph as a novelist, he was also both full of praise and slickly backhanded: "In what he did, Ralph had no rivals. What he did no one else could do—a glorious piece of good fortune for a writer."

Speculating on Ralph's struggle to finish his second novel, Bellow recalled that Ralph was forever talking about his past in Oklahoma. In this way, Bellow judged, he had not been unlike the vain Robert Frost—but with a big difference. Frost had been "his own hagiographer," creating lovely poems that deliberately left an image of him as a kindly sage. Ralph returned to his own past "not in order to revise and gild it but to recover old feelings and also to consider and reconsider how he might find a way to write his story." Although Bellow did not explicitly say so, the hole that Ralph was digging for himself as a novelist by 1960 had much to do with his indenture of his fiction to an obsessive archaeology of the self that elided key aspects of the story. His deeper past, his more intimate sense of self, was becoming a site dank and dense with concealed or camouflaged treasures of history, mythology, folklore, and archetypes, out of which he sought to construct his epic narrative. No doubt Ralph could anchor these forms in his own mind by dreamy reference to the facts and incidents of his youth. But on the page, his ability to turn them into art was proving to be tentative.

The death in Paris on November 28 of Richard Wright put Ralph's life and career in a new perspective. At fifty-two, Wright had succumbed under odd circumstances in the second-rate medical clinic to which he had gone after a protracted, mysterious illness. (Some people in Paris blamed his death on a virus picked up in Africa, but others were sure that the CIA had poisoned him.) "We are shocked and grieved," the Ellisons wired Ellen. "Our deepest sympathy is with you and the children." The vagaries of life, and Wright's self-imposed, ill-advised exile in Europe, had driven a wedge between the two men. The last time they met, in 1956, they had found it hard to make casual conversation. One career was sinking as the other soared. To Ralph, all debts he had owed Wright were now canceled forever. With the death of his former mentor and friend, "a period of my own life has come to a definite end."

Civil rights crises across the South led to a dramatic jump in the demand on Ralph for appearances. In addition to his duties at Bard in the first few months of 1961, he lectured at Middlebury in Vermont, Swarthmore in Philadelphia, Coe College in Cedar Rapids, Iowa, and Boston College, where he appeared on a fiction panel with John Hawkes and Elizabeth Janeway. In May, he spoke to a class in American literature at Yale taught by R. W. B. Lewis. The events in the South were not destroying his idealism about America. If anything, his rhetoric reached new heights of patriotic fervor in response to what he saw as deepening cynicism about America as more and more blacks, in particular, were questioning the notion of white patrician authority and the obligations of citizenship. At Coe College, for example, he spoke again about "our forefathers" and their hallowed doctrines, which had "taken on a form of sacredness." He mourned the alleged moral abdication of modern American writers. "With this turning away, we have suffered," he complained. "It has created some shocking discoveries such as those now currently being faced in the South."

To some listeners, Ralph was solemnly touting the ideas of certain eighteenth-century white men of property, including Washington and Jefferson, who had owned slaves; and also the ideas of certain nineteenth-century white writers whose own values had been compromised. He seemed to believe too much in the transformative power of the writer as opposed to the activist. In his lectures, he usually refused to descend to the topical even as his young listeners hungered to discuss race and civil rights. He saw himself striking blows for both the artist and the Negro by hewing to this Olympian position. And, once again, reality challenged him.

In May, a party of blacks and whites led by CORE embarked on a bus ride from Washington, D.C., into the South in order to test the degree of its compliance with new rules about integration set by federal judges and the federal Interstate Commerce Commission. At several stops, enraged whites, tacitly supported by local police, beat or harassed the so-called Freedom Riders. In Jackson, Mississippi, police arrested most of them. On May 20, the U.S. attorney general, Robert F. Kennedy, ordered a force of six hundred U.S. marshals to protect the riders. The attacks enraged Ralph. When CORE held a fund-raising auction in New York, he donated the manuscript of an essay on New York City that he had written for a special issue of *Esquire* only to have it rejected as too radical. "I could have done the mood piece they wanted," he explained, "but I wanted them to look inside what makes a black Negro black." He had "used a switchblade on just about every thing they hold sacred—especially white women—and they dropped it like it was cancer."

He began to understand that the strife fomented by the civil rights struggle, and not the will to integration itself, was the main reason for the sudden increase in requests for Negroes like him to speak to white people. Still, he told himself, he had to accept the calls—"which I can't very well refuse to do, now that young Mose [blacks] is setting the pace for students all over the country." However, he and "young Mose" hardly knew each other. While black youths hungered for leadership, the most honored living black American novelist had no young black disciples, students, or friends. Asked urgently to nominate some younger Negro writers for university fellowships, Ralph was candid: "I am very, very sorry that I am not in touch with any young Negro writers these days and cannot be of assistance to you."

Ironically, he didn't know perhaps the most talented and visionary of all—the poet LeRoi Jones, later Amiri Baraka, who would soon personify for Ralph almost everything he deplored in the realm of race, art, and American culture. In 1958, after reading Ralph's *Partisan Review* essay "Change the Joke and Slip the Yoke," Jones wrote to Ralph praising that piece and also the Charlie Christian piece in *Saturday Review*. Living in

Greenwich Village, Jones was then editing *Yugen,* a Beat magazine, with his wife, Hettie Cohen, who was also a manager at *Partisan Review.* To Jones, the essay on Christian was "the finest piece of Jazz writing I have seen in quite a while." Sending Ralph the first number of *Yugen,* he asked to meet him. "Perhaps," he ended, "I can drop up to see you one afternoon when you are not too busy . . . whenever that is." Ralph never replied. Later, when Jones became the explosive, anti-white Amiri Baraka, Ralph would deride his views and his work and also rebuff Baraka's new attempts to get to know him. "I remember going over to see him one night without calling first and he wouldn't let me in," Baraka later recalled. To Baraka, Ralph was "a snob, an elitist."

As the spring semester of 1961 came to an end, Saul returned from Puerto Rico. The two men were still friends but would never again be as close as they once had been. Ralph was also preparing to leave Tivoli for good. In his new apartment overlooking the Hudson, he worked as well as he did in Tivoli—even if in both settings his novel was stagnating. ("Things go about the same with me," he wrote Hyman; "I'm still slugging and trying to make this mass of words mean something and am very weary.") But a bright new opportunity had also come his way. The Department of English at the University of Chicago, through Dick Stern, had successfully nominated Ralph for the most prestigious visiting lectureship in literature at the school. Although it would last only a quarter, it would pay handsomely and also allow the faculty to inspect Ralph closely. Perhaps this visit would lead to a regular appointment.

Before he left Bard in June, students and faculty alike gave him a rousing send-off when they packed the largest auditorium to listen to him deliver the annual John Bard Lecture. The president feted Ralph and Fanny at a formal dinner at his home. Shortly afterward, with Tuckatarby of Tivoli riding shotgun, Ralph pointed his Chrysler New Yorker toward Manhattan. His years in Tivoli had been enriching, and life in the Bellow mansion often a joy, albeit at times also lonely and melancholy. But he had arrived expecting to polish off his novel. He hadn't.

15

Hanging Fire

1961–1964

*I know by now that all my little triumphs are in reality
defeats.*   RALPH ELLISON (1961)

Late in September, Ralph and Fanny drove from New York City to
Chicago, their car burdened with Ralph's luggage. After helping him
unpack in a room at the Quadrangle Club, near the heart of the University of Chicago campus, she flew back to Manhattan, leaving Ralph to
settle in as Alexander White Visiting Professor.

Throughout the quarter, Ralph seldom felt at home at the Quadrangle
Club, or anywhere else on campus. Much was expected of him. Previous
Alexander White Visiting Professors included Julian Huxley, Isaiah Berlin, T. S. Eliot, and Arnold Toynbee. Ralph was the first person to take
part in the new Celebrities in Residence program at the college. Feeling
the pressure of expectations abruptly raised after the ultra-relaxed Bard,
he longed for Fanny and their apartment above the Hudson. "Your leaving
has left an emptiness," he wrote to her, "and I think I've had just about
enough of Chicago for a while."

He was to teach one undergraduate course and offer two public lectures, on familiar subjects. He was uneasy from the start facing his classes,
and his response was to talk and talk and talk. Fanny's family was no help
when he visited them on Sundays. Her mother lived in one of the seedier
sections of the city, and her stepfather was in pitiful condition in a hospital. He saw in the slums not the handiwork of capitalism but mainly the
decaying of traditional Negro character by people who lacked the will or
the vision to move beyond poverty.

Ralph saw a fair amount of Dick Stern and Nathan Scott, the urbane
scholar of literature and religion who had so impressed him on his previ-

ous visit. On a Saturday-afternoon visit to Scott's home, he met Scott's wife, Charlotte, a Barnard graduate and an economist at the Federal Reserve Bank of Chicago—the rare black holding such a position nationally—and their two children, Nathan and Leslie. The more he found out about the high-achieving Scotts, the more Ralph was impressed. Three years later Scott would become a full professor of theology and literature at Chicago. In 1966, he would also be appointed Canon Theologian of the Cathedral of St. James. While Ralph was uneasy at the university, the Scotts seemed clearly comfortable. On October 6, when they held a dinner party at their Hyde Park home in Ralph's honor, they did so with impressive elegance.

He missed Fanny: "Here, unlike in Tivoli, I find it terribly difficult to live and sleep alone." Now Fanny missed him, too. Since her return from Italy she had started drinking more and more, and sometimes lost control. During one evening telephone call, her slurred speech upset him. Al and Mozelle Murray's daughter, Michele, now a dance student at Juilliard and often at the apartment, noticed that Fanny often dressed in Ralph's bathrobe, puffed his cigars, and swilled hard liquor.

While Ralph refused to admit that his affair in Rome and his way of managing it (Fanny had called it sadistic) were the main cause of her decline, for her the wound remained raw. Sometimes when she drank she scribbled notes. One of them that survived reads: "I should murder her as the last rectifying act of my life." Further tearing at her was her infertility, as well as a cancer scare that fall. Ralph's decision to live more away from her than with her in the four years since Rome also hurt. He claimed that he needed isolation to write, she said, but "I have the feeling that you really prefer it this way." At one point she wrote to him about envying his freedom. "I don't refer to just your writing and your teaching," she explained, "but to your habits (including the bad ones), your mode, your quality, your pattern. All the things you do and say—which in the end lead to your work." In contrast, "I have rigor mortis of the soul. Meanness, disorganization, an illiterate intelligence, inflexibility, and an aversion to most people gave me [those qualities] when I was about seventeen."

When she flew to Chicago for a quick visit, she soon wished she hadn't. Ralph was nasty to her. She returned home to her work and her bottle— but also to her dependence on him. "Are you all right?" she asked after a few days of his silence. "Are you angry with me still? Is anything wrong?" Ironically, he seemed unaware that liquor was affecting *his* demeanor. Dick Stern, impressed by his sprightly knowledge of literature, classical music, jazz, electronics, and men's clothing, and by his grace and wit when he was sober, soon found out that "this confident, warm, and charming man" was in fact also "pocked with insecurity, anger, and bitterness," and that he chronically "countered these feelings with booze." That fall, the men met four or five evenings a week to unwind over martinis—in Ralph's case, several martinis. As Stern recalled carefully, Ralph "didn't get drunk, only easy and weary. Then he stuttered, fumbled for words, and occasionally turned sarcastic, angry." He refused to talk to Stern "about weakness, uncertainty, or difficulties. Even half-boffo, he was on top, or wanted to be—which didn't mean dominance, although we had small struggles which could get sharp. We'd walk up and down the side streets of Black and Jew, few holds barred; cleansing and revitalizing sessions."

As his first public lecture drew close, Ralph felt the pressure growing. "I lecture on Monday," he wrote to Fanny, "and I'm nervous as hell, constipated as hell, homesick as hell!" On November 21, before an audience that included the university chancellor, he delivered his first talk. Obviously wanting him to succeed, the crowd of more than one hundred greeted him with loud applause. Then, to the dismay of every professor in the hall, Ralph spoke, as usual, from notes only. Offering his well-worn reflections upon the nation's moral failure following the Civil War, he rambled when he should have been on point. "His model was jazz," Stern saw; "inspiration would arrive as needed, and, therefore, the lectures would be more powerful, fresh and true." Unfortunately, this was a world-class university, not a nightclub. "Ralph said good things, but he stumbled, repeated himself, went off on tangents, and then the tangents of tangents." The scholars in the audience were not impressed. Although he would always applaud Ralph's courage and integrity, "a refusal to drift in whatever way the wind happened to be blowing," Nathan Scott also saw a lack of "seriousness" and "penetration" in Ralph's way of talking about literature. "I was never persuaded," Scott said, "that he had read major works in any deep way. He always talked in loose generalities about Melville, Hawthorne, Fitzgerald, about Eliot, about Malraux."

Ralph had no clue that he had bombed. When Stern hinted that he should type up his second address, Ralph dismissed the notion: "He wouldn't; he thought the lecture had gone well." On December 7, the second lecture also flopped. Ralph didn't think so. "My last public lecture was a success," he assured Fanny, "and I think I managed to say a few things which I'd never managed before. Anyway its reception was good." At the same time, he revealed a visceral fear: "I'm holding on here, moving frantically and gabbily through my public and social days and feeling more and more melancholy when I'm alone at night. I don't know quite the source of it but I suppose it's because I know by now that all my little triumphs are in reality defeats. I'm not always aware of this but at night it comes down, especially after a talk or after an encounter with strangers over food and drink."

At Thanksgiving, faced with a choice of joining Fanny in New York or eating with her family in their blighted section of Chicago, he instead headed to Iowa City to spend time with his dog, Tucka (who was being boarded there), the Bourjailys, and the Engles.

Back in Chicago, he mourned the deadly social gap between blacks and whites, which seemed much starker than in New York. In November, after an invitation from one of the city's top hostesses, Lois Solomon (later Lois Weisberg), he ventured into the upper-class North Side for a party nominally in his honor attended by Dizzy Gillespie and Tony Bennett. He went to a Sunday luncheon at the home of Bertrand Goldberg, the main architect behind the landmark sixty-story Marina City project. He was dazzled there by sculptures by Degas and Arp, paintings by Albers and Klee, etchings by Braque and Picasso. But when he hustled off to the South Side to address blacks at the South Side Community Art Center, he found the audience on the whole pitiful. "It was very strange," he wrote Fanny, "with people still caught up in the old worn attitudes toward writing, with the old questions of whether I was a Negro writer or something else coming up like a phono record that has been caught in its groove for fifty years. I'm afraid that I didn't always control my irritation." He contrasted his black hosts to his white ones. "The distance between the two groups is just a matter of a few miles," he wrote, "but in terms of attitude, expectation, understanding the distance is heartbreakingly far. It's enough to make me sad."

By this point he understood that the University of Chicago would not make him an offer. He felt "the old pain which comes when I've been out of my regular paths for too long, because for all my activities here I feel that it isn't real, that my real life lies there." This failure led to a fresh strain on his friendship with Saul Bellow, who followed Ralph in the winter as a visiting professor at the university. When the English Department would not hire him either, Bellow's longtime friend Edward Shils of the Committee on Social Thought pressed Edward Levi, the university president, to appoint Saul to a five-year term on the committee. Thus began his long association with the university. Dick Stern believed that Ralph was "hurt and angry" to see "his old friend, housemate, and rival" succeed where he had flopped.

His sense of defeat wrecked Christmas 1961 for him and Fanny. Her failure to remember to send a Christmas card to Ralph's brother and his wife in Los Angeles triggered a vicious quarrel, despite the fact that Ralph had made little effort to see his brother in almost twenty-five years. Drinking heavily, he rained abuse on Fanny. To dull the sound of her voice, he told her, he needed a dozen bottles of bourbon in six days. Stung, Fanny protested sharply, "because I couldn't possibly be as ignorant and stupid of your needs (or my own) as you accuse me." His affair in Rome was behind this "precipitant ugliness," as it was behind much of their fighting. "If you could think just a little bit beyond yourself," she said, he might see the truth. Fomenting his rage was his failure to finish his book, which came from his being "too socially accessible." She warned him about living still as in "the post book-award days—the excitement, the flattery, that ended with a headache the following day and such a sense of waste." This pattern could go on for years, "and one day we'd wake up dead." He had to learn self-discipline. "It's no skin off my nose," she admitted, "to go out repeatedly and be admired and stared at. It's about the most I'll ever get from people. But with you it's a different story and you don't 'need' this." As for his lament "that our marriage was an ongoing disappointment," perhaps they should end it. If so, they should do it quietly. "It will be the end of me but I can hardly complain, for you have given me a very great deal, far far more than I've been able to give you. And it may be not too late for you to find in someone else all you have missed in me."

The squall passed. For a few months, he guarded his time carefully. Young authors seeking his advice met resistance. He received far too many requests, he told one: "If I complied, work on my own novel would come to a dead stop." He piled up some fresh pages over the winter before taking to the road in the spring. In the colleges, where he found a growing militancy among the black students, he mixed his admiration for their courage with warnings that militancy could be counterproductive. At Hampton Institute, as elsewhere, he stressed the need to keep politics and art separate, and warned of the dangers of political fantasy. Fiction exists for itself, not to advance the cause of civil rights. Many young black writers, he told a reporter, "are obsessed by a history that doesn't exist and never existed." About cruder strains of protest writing he was severe: "We create the meaning of our lives by recapturing them in the imagination, not by putting them down as a sociological description of 'I Been Buked,

I Been Scorned.' The sociologists and historians can do this sort of thing much better than the novelists."

The growing worship of Africa as the motherland of black America bothered him. Invited by the young South African writer Ezekiel Mphahlele to an international writers' congress in Kampala, Uganda, Ralph declined. Sticking by his beliefs, he was prepared to risk offending others. When he served as a selector for the Freedom House Bookshelf Committee, a conservative organization, only one book on the long list of American titles chosen by his committee for distribution in Africa was written by a black American: Booker T. Washington's *Up from Slavery.* Ralph's notable political acts now almost always advanced the cause of anti-Communism, not civil rights. Approached by William Phillips at *Partisan Review,* he signed open letters of protest against the repeated jailing of the dissident writer Milovan Djilas in Yugoslavia. He signed a similar protest against the Chinese invasion of India. Against racism in America he felt indignation but he signed practically nothing.

He was growing ever more self-conscious about his problems with his novel. To a journalist at Hampton he offered an inexplicably glowing report. The book "will appear in the fall [1962] probably," he predicted. "It's keeping me up at night and there's a great pile of manuscript." Determined to finish it, in April he rejected an offer from Purdue University of a half-time professorship at $10,000 a year. In May he turned down a year-long stint at the University of Massachusetts. A few days later, when Rutgers University in New Brunswick again offered him a position—this time as a visiting professor, at almost $14,000 a year—he again demurred. "I am at present at a critical point in my novel," he explained, "and rather hesitate to involve myself in teaching." Then Ralph realized that the money was too good, no teaching was expected, and the location—less than an hour by train from Manhattan—was almost perfect. He took the job.

In 1961 and 1962 Ralph's only significant publication was another essay on music in *Saturday Review.* Ostensibly a review of Robert George Reisner's *Bird: The Legend of Charlie Parker,* the essay is, at first glance, playful and satirical. But "On Bird, Bird-Watching, and Jazz" has a serious, even somber aspect. Ralph used the piece to comment on the function of the black artist in America. Born in 1920 in Kansas City, Kansas, Charlie Parker had died a heroin addict in New York City at thirty-five. His body was so ravaged that the coroner assumed he was in his fifties. By 1962 many people had come to regard him as one of the supreme jazz geniuses and avant-garde artists of the century. Although critics had been at first hostile to bebop—the music he helped to create—the growing eminence of his musical collaborators, including Dizzy Gillespie, Miles Davis, and the drummer Max Roach, made it clear now that his influence would likely continue for decades. To his many fans, Parker had made jazz into a premier medium for expressing some of the most complex, forbidding tensions of postmodern Western life.

To Ralph, this was nonsense. Although he sprinkled confetti-like compliments to Parker throughout his text, he portrayed him not as a genius but instead as a purveyor of chaos, a trickster like Rinehart in *Invisible Man,* a confidence man and a crook. The essay began with what seemed to be unambiguous praise. "One of the founders of postwar jazz," Parker had "as an improviser, as marked an influence upon jazz as Louis Armstrong, Coleman Hawkins or Johnny Hodges." But "for all the pathetic comedy of his living—and despite the crabbed and constricted character of his style," Ralph declared, "Parker was a most inventive melodist; in bird-watcher's terminology, a true songster." Urbane, learned, but also quietly sardonic, the essay chuckles over the ironies of Parker's nickname and its subversive associations, until even Ralph admits to the compulsively farcical nature of his own jiving and gibing: "Symbolic birds, myth and ritual—what strange metaphors to arise during the discussion of a book about a jazz musician!"

When he discusses Bird's legacy in its broadest implications, the laughter dies. The archetypal jazzman had always been something of a clown in facing white audiences, said Ralph, as in the example of the notoriously affable Louis Armstrong. All appearances to the contrary, the typical jazzman was no less a kind of clown when (under Parker's leadership) he morphed during the 1940s into the cerebral performer who developed a discordant, avant-garde form of music that defied dancing, which had been the basis of jazz from the start. And the jazzman had been no less an entertainer or a clown when, in the 1950s, following the lead of Parker and Miles Davis, he showed elaborate contempt for his mainly white audiences by often turning his back to them while playing or by spurning their applause. Puzzled and hurt at first, said Ralph, whites later came to expect and perhaps even like the displaying of contempt. Black disdain, seen by some observers as a form of political "resistance," had become mainly another part of the jazzman's shtick. When the performance was over the white man still possessed his power, while the black man, the jazzman, had lost his dignity.

To Ralph, Parker epitomized the corruption of values that threatened classic Negro culture in an integrated America for which too many blacks were not ready. A renegade and an outsider by virtue of being black, a junkie, and the "exponent of a new and disturbing development in jazz," Parker had become a truly woeful culture hero—"a suffering, psychically wounded, law-breaking, life-affirming hero—for post-war American rebels and sufferers." Ralph sympathizes only a little with these rebels who saw in Parker's agony "a ritualization of their own fears, rebellions and hunger for creativity." For Ralph, Parker's role was unworthy, a fact reflected in his weakness as a musician. Speaking heresy to many younger jazz lovers, Ralph criticizes Parker's music. "For all its velocity, brilliance and imagination," he judges, "there is in it a great deal of loneliness, self-deprecation and self-pity. With this there is a quality which seems to issue from its vibratoless tone: a sound of amateurish ineffectuality, as though he could never quite make it. It is this amateurish-sounding aspect which promises so much to the members of a do-it-yourself culture; it sounds with an assurance that you too can create your own do-it-yourself jazz." (Ralph might well have been writing about an abstract expressionist painter such as Jackson Pollock.) Parker's music reflects the immature, teen-centered nature of modern American art and life, said Ralph. His genius consists in the fact that he "captured something of the discordancies, the yearning, romance and cunning of the age and ordered it into a haunting art." In this sense, his art "blew him into the meaningful center of things."

So artful and witty was Ralph that probably few readers understood that he had come to the *Saturday Review* not to praise Parker but to bury him. Despite his fame, Parker had not mastered his age, according to Ellison, but had been enslaved by it. Bird was not like the mythical phoenix or the soaring eagle, but (as in the ditty Ralph uses in *Invisible Man*) more like the poor robin plucked clean of his feathers by the vicious world. The essay ends on a lighter note that deflected its rage against Parker, his admirers, and the seismic shift in the national temper that *Invisible Man* prophesied in 1952 but that Ralph deplored in 1962. In doing so, it only partly conceals the extent to which it reflects his own fears, anger, and frustration as an artist.

To Ralph, signs of the corruption of Negro artists and what he saw as classic Negro culture were sprouting everywhere. Late in June, at the Harlem nightclub Small's, when Dial Press gave a huge reception for James Baldwin to mark the appearance of his sensational novel of interracial sex and bisexuality *Another Country*, "almost every celebrity in town was included on the guest list," as Baldwin's friend Fern Marja Eckman wrote. Baldwin was attracting celebrities and many younger blacks alike with his combination of militancy and supplicating eloquence, his sensual hugging of America and, at the same time, his theatrical rejection of it. "I don't want to be fitted into this society," Baldwin told Eckman. "There's no difference between being fitted into this society and *dying*."

Another Country surged up the best-seller list with a speed rivaled that year only by William Golding's *Lord of the Flies*. Despite its shabby construction as art (Stanley Hyman called Baldwin's writing in it "bad by any standard") and its at times pornographic passages, the novel was hailed by many editors, publishers, reviewers, reporters, and agents. They praised *Another Country* as a prophetic commentary on race, miscegenation, homosexuality, and power in America. Toppling thick, old Puritan walls of hypocrisy, Baldwin seemed a modern, black Joshua. In *The New Republic* (to Ralph's indignation) Edmund Wilson hailed Baldwin as the greatest African-American writer ever.

If Ralph was upset, he also had to face the fact that Baldwin had built his literary career tenaciously. In 1952, while critics were hailing *Invisible Man*, Baldwin was correcting galleys of his first novel, *Go Tell It on the Mountain*. Since then, he had published two more novels, including *Giovanni's Room*, a landmark in gay American literary history although put together in an even more ungainly way than *Another Country*; two passionate collections of essays about race, *Notes of a Native Son* and *Nobody Knows My Name*; and a controversial play, *The Amen Corner*. Ellison did not envy Baldwin his success. He scorned Baldwin's technical weaknesses, his tortured engagement with the white world, his obsession with sex, and his championing of homosexuality. In a note about this time he reduced Baldwin's prophetic status to a pithy suggestion: "Perhaps what Baldwin is telling white Americans is: allow Negroes to sleep with your daughters or we homos will sleep with *you*." Displaying "the arrogance of a [Leslie] Fiedler, a Mailer," Baldwin was trying "to inflate his personal problem to the dimension of a national problem." Imagine, Ralph said, if Proust had done the same!

Meanwhile, Baldwin's reputation soared as he drastically altered the image of the black American writer. Stirring many younger blacks, he made a euphoric tributary tour of Africa. When he returned home, he seemed to donate, not merely to lend, his prestige to the civil rights cause, and in the process distended it. Helping to launch the impassioned black attack

on white liberals that, as Ralph saw it, would disfigure the civil rights movement, he was just as hard on the fervent liberal Robert F. Kennedy as on
the waspish (and WASP) conservative charmer William F. Buckley, Jr.
Overcoming their putative disdain of homosexuals, many blacks embraced
Baldwin as a brother and a hero. On May 17, 1963, he made the cover
of *Time*.

Baldwin seemed to personify one pole of black literary behavior, Ralph
the other. Ralph gave no thought to the idea of confronting white police
and their dogs and hoses. His admiration for black ministers and protesting students began to dissipate as responsible gestures began to give way
to rising signs of chaos. Enraged by racism, he became adamant about his
identity as an artist, and thus about steering clear of overt political action.
In the late 1930s he had been a radical joiner; now he reverted to an older,
more exclusive—or reclusive—self-display. "Ralph told me," one Ellison
scholar said about this will to stand apart, "that even as a youngster there
was a certain strangeness about him. He said, 'I was reading a lot, I was
interested in things that most kids were not interested in, I had the musician's special status. I was at Tuskegee not with a hoe and rake or brick-
layer's tools, but with my trumpet case, and people detected something
different about me. Something strange.' He was used to living within a
world he had created. 'I've been seeing by my own candle for a long time,'
he said proudly." (Nevertheless, Ralph was pleased in 1962 when Albert
and Mozelle Murray moved to Manhattan from California, where they
had been living. Now he had a black friend nearby with whom he could
speak as an intellectual peer.)

Even as he turned away from some blacks, he gave whites who wanted
to develop ties to black America a cultivated means of access. Eleanor
Clark and Red Warren, Dick Lewis recalled, "used to say of Ralph, with
ironic affection, 'he's every white man's favorite black man.'" Lewis and
Richard Wilbur and their wives, Nancy and Charlotte, became the Ellisons' intimate friends. Ralph later remembered black-tie parties for two
hundred in Connecticut at the Wilburs' "big rambling house," complete
with a dance band, "a lot of amusing academic and literary types—and
dam[n] good food." The Wilburs were "interesting enough and humorous
enough to make things swing." (Richard Wilbur taught at the University
of Connecticut at Storrs.) With both couples Ralph relaxed easily—almost
always. "I realized only long after I had met him," Dick Lewis said, "that
there was a lot of suppressed anger in him." Once, during a heated discussion at the Lewis home near Yale, where Lewis was now a professor,

"he got angry and stormed off. He drove all the way back to the city, I found out later. We were dumbfounded. The next morning his car was back in the driveway, and he was upstairs in the guest room. He got over whatever made him furious enough to leave and then he came back to us. We never found out what had made him boil over."

On June 20, 1962, in Dwight Memorial Chapel at Yale, Ralph became godfather to Dick and Nancy's son, Nathaniel Lindau Lewis, with a gala celebration afterward attended by the Warrens, Dan Aaron, Robert Motherwell, Helen Frankenthaler, and other friends. The fact that a growing number of the Ellisons' friends were WASPs was no accident. To be sure, Ralph still felt a personal and intellectual bond to Jews. On March 29 he appeared gladly with Philip Roth at Yeshiva University in New York. In May, he spoke at a local Jewish community center. But as he floated upward into the social empyrean, his inevitable turn toward WASPs suggests that, like even the best Americans, he could not fully emancipate himself from caste and class preference. Even for many Jews, the platinum card of social credit was acceptance by rich, cultured WASPs. Ralph was often caught in the middle. Jewish critics such as Alfred Kazin and Irving Howe respected Ralph, the black editor Charles Harris observed, but "on the other hand he wasn't one of them. He was just about the only black person invited by the *New York Review of Books* or magazines with that kind of prestige to respond to people like Kazin or Howe, yet Ralph knew that most people in that crowd did not consider him a true equal." The price he paid for easy association with like-minded whites was a measure of insecurity only heightened by the knowledge that to many fellow blacks this delight was a form of racial betrayal.

That fall, Ralph moved upward in the academic world when he became a visiting professor of writing and comparative literature and the first writer-in-residence at Rutgers University. Two friends spearheaded his appointment: John Ciardi and William Sloane, a lanky New Englander with a mordant wit who ran the university press. Ralph's appointment was a small part of a vague plan to lift the prestige of the state university of New Jersey, which existed regionally in the shadow of Princeton, the University of Pennsylvania, and Columbia University. Compared with renowned state universities such as Michigan, Wisconsin, or California, Berkeley, Rutgers was mediocrity itself. "The literati are at Princeton, not Rutgers," Sloane admitted to Ralph. In New Brunswick, the sense of inferiority was pervasive. A press release joked that with Ralph's appointment the university—located on the Raritan River—was "trying to shore up its 'left bank.' "

The wonder was, he wrote modestly to a friend, that "any respectable university would allow a degree-less character like me within ten miles of its campus." The job was ideal for his writing, in that it included no class-room teaching. Two days each week he made himself available to students or faculty. Few called on him. Most professors, perhaps disapproving of his cushy job, all but ignored him, as did the English Department, which had been fighting a turf war with Comparative Literature. His office was not plush. It also housed a graduate student, who was disturbed by the reception Rutgers was giving this fine writer. "I was shocked that he had to share an office with me," Alan Cheuse, a future novelist, recalled. "In fact, I was irate—but Ralph was absolutely sweet about it, always charming and generous to me." Two days a week, Ralph drove up in his car, unloaded his typewriter, sat down at his desk, and worked away. Once every week, Cheuse and the poet Jay Wright, a friend and fellow student, cooked dinner for Ralph in Cheuse's basement apartment. "As a reward," Cheuse said, "he would read to us from his novel-in-progress. After dinner, he would light a big cigar, sip his liquor, and read to us in a wonderful, affable way. He showed a lot more interest in me as a young, ignorant writer than he had to, given how famous he was. Ralph was wonderful."

Wright, an African-American, found Ralph less embracing, although Wright's core ideas about race and literature were close to Ralph's. (He would ask Ralph to help him resist an attempt by Langston Hughes to include his work in an anthology of younger black poets.) Perhaps Ralph was less interested in poetry than in fiction. Whatever the reason, Wright saw a gap that Cheuse crossed but that he didn't. Henry Dumas, a black writer and friend of Cheuse and Wright, had an even harder time with Ralph. Once, when Ralph heard Dumas's voice downstairs, he acted quickly to avoid a meeting. "You tell that Vachel Lindsay nigger that I'm not in," he told Cheuse, alluding to the bombastic verse of the white author of *The Congo* (1914).

In the office next to Ralph's was Joseph Frank, the future biographer of Dostoyevsky, who was then beginning to think about taking on a task that eventually would run to five volumes. "Ralph was very enthusiastic about Dostoyevsky and the project," Frank said. "He pulled down a book of essays on Dostoyevsky from a shelf and gave it to me. I think he understood Dostoyevsky. Ralph was lively, vibrant, warm, and friendly—if he liked you." The two men would remain friends long after Ralph left Rutgers University.

In the fall, Ralph's easy schedule allowed him to speak at various places, including Dartmouth and a Princeton University conference on "The Negro Community in the United States," where he joined C. Vann Woodward of Yale, a highly regarded white historian of the South whom Ralph would soon call a friend; Benjamin Quarles, a Harvard-trained black historian and biographer of Frederick Douglass; and the Harvard urban sociologist Nathan Glazer. At Nathan Scott's invitation he returned briefly to Chicago to address a gathering of liberal white Baptist ministers. Elsewhere he appeared with Philip Roth to talk about the novel.

On December 17, at Rutgers, he read a section from his novel-in-progress that featured the antics of his comical three-hundred-pound character Cliofus. The piece evoked some laughter, according to a polite reporter, from "the small but interested audience." Some days later he let *Partisan Review* have another section, "It Always Breaks Out," for its Spring number. This piece, too, had extremely broad comedy. In it, a raving white racist spews out on page after page his absurd ideas about the new kind of (post-*Brown*) "Nigra" who scorns whites as ridiculous. The white man closes the excerpt by pondering the notion that the black waiter serving him and his friends just might "regard all whites through the streaming eyes and aching muscles of one continuous, though imperceptible and inaudible, belly laugh?" This piece exemplifies a kind of thigh-slapping, black barbershop style of comedy that Ralph wished to explore as part of his quilting of American rhetorical modes in his novel.

In 1963, his only other piece of published fiction also fell flat. Ralph seemed to be almost daring the reader to dislike his work. This story, "Out of the Hospital and Under the Bar," appeared in *Soon, One Morning,* an anthology of writings by Negroes between 1940 and 1962. He admitted in a note that the story had come from an earlier version of *Invisible Man,* but he defended its provenance. "Reading it now, almost ten years after it was put aside," he claimed, "I have the feeling that it stands on its own if only as one of those pieces of writing which consists mainly of one damned thing after another sheerly happening." Defiantly he told those readers who "desire more than the sheer narrative ride, who hunger and thirst for 'meaning,'" to be creative and "take this proffered middle, this agon, this passion, and supply their own beginning, and if an ending, a moral, or a perception is needed, let them supply their own. For me, of course, the narrative is the meaning."

Meanwhile, Ralph moved closer to admission to the Century. In addition to his onetime editor Frank Taylor, he found a sponsor in Marvin Halverson, a former dean at the Chicago Theological Seminary who was trying to launch an ambitious project later called the Society for the Arts, Religion, and Contemporary Culture. Thus far he had gained at least the nominal support of the theologian Paul Tillich, the architect Louis Kahn, the mythologist Joseph Campbell, and the poet W. H. Auden. When Halverson incorporated the foundation in 1962, Ralph was on its governing board. Halverson would help him get into the Century. Poring over the little book that identified its almost two thousand members, Ralph compiled two lists. The first set ("if not friends, quite friendly") comprised twenty-three men. (The Century did not admit women.) They included John Cheever, Robert Penn Warren, Malcolm Cowley, Van Wyck Brooks, George Plimpton, and Arthur M. Schlesinger, Jr. On the other list ("these I know but not too well") were ten men, including Henry Kissinger and Archibald MacLeish. With this beginning, aided by Warren in particular, Halverson pressed forward.

On January 7, a committee interviewed Ralph at the "clubhouse" on West 43rd Street. He did well. The Century placed his name on its long waiting list.

Separately, as a spokesman for blacks or "the Negro," he was also rising in certain official circles. In February, he was in Washington as a guest of the Panel on Educational Research and Development. The focus of this meeting was the education (or lack of education) of "underachieving" students, "the difficult 30 percent of the school population," as one official put it. The panel invited him although he had little or no training or expertise in the field of education. He was a Negro, he was superbly accomplished, and he was moderate.

On February 12, 1963, Ralph had his first taste of White House glamour when he joined John F. Kennedy and several hundred other guests at a buffet reception to mark the centennial of Lincoln's Emancipation Proclamation. The presence of the first Negro cabinet member, Robert C. Weaver, and the first Negro ambassador to a European country (Finland), the journalist Carl Rowan, dramatized progress in American race relations. But the walls weren't exactly tumbling down. On that same day the U.S. Commission on Civil Rights presented Kennedy with a copy of *Freedom to the Free,* its 246-page report on the state of civil rights in America. Unwittingly mocking the glitter and glamour of the reception, it warned that " 'the last battle for equal rights' for the Negro may have to be fought in the North." Southern progress had been painful, slow, and steady even as Governor George Wallace of Alabama, at his inauguration, promised "segregation now, segregation tomorrow, segregation forever." However, according to the report, Northern opposition to racial justice was far more subtle "and the more difficult to eliminate." Accepting it, Kennedy conceded that there was still "some length to go" to achieve justice for blacks across the nation.

On February 23, at the meeting in Washington of the Panel on Educational Research and Development, which met at the Executive Office Building, Ellison joined experts in sociology, education, public policy, and philanthropy from various universities, the Ford Foundation, the American Council of Learned Societies, and some of the government agencies involved in urban affairs. With pride he noticed that, apart from Arthur Miller, he was the only creative writer present. In what probably struck some who knew him as a surprise, he was also almost alone in defending the main target of this liberal project: black youth. Ralph's inveterate suspicion of sociology as a discipline was on view once again as he deplored what he saw as its pessimism about black youth. No elitist on the topic of education and black youths, he had almost always identified as his main antagonist the Negro middle class, what he saw as its shabbily run institutions, its materialism and Philistinism, its snobbery and self-hatred.

Ralph had no such quarrel with the masses of blacks. Impressed by his observations, leaders of the panel invited him to take part in further deliberations that involved black youngsters. That summer, in Cambridge, Massachusetts, he met with its steering committee to plan a gathering of almost seventy experts, including a large number of blacks, to be held under the auspices of the Bank Street School of Education. Inviting two black friends, the physicist Herman Branson (then at Howard University) and Allison Davis, an expert on psychology and black leadership at the University of Chicago, he promised to help them "search for new ways to educate children who, because of segregation, poverty, or both, are failing to gain an adequate education."

His role in the seminar showed again how ready he was to defend the emerging whipping boy of American urban life, the young black male. Of the many speeches delivered over two weeks in September in Dedham, Massachusetts, where the panel met, Ralph delivered what was commonly seen as its most provocative. In fact, only his speech was included in its entirety in the official seminar report. Speaking off-the-cuff, he startled listeners with his attacks on key liberal assumptions. "There is no such thing," he declared, "as a culturally deprived child." Negroes did not survive slavery and Jim Crow without having developed a culture rich in music, religion, and linguistic mastery. Yes, Negroes lose much of that cultural richness in migrating to Northern cities, but they also adapt and stay strong. "To fail to recognize this," he argued, "is to expect far too much of a human being while crediting him with far too little humanity."

No one, Ralph went on, should seek to erase those core black values honed in the South, including "the group discipline, the patience, [and] the ability to withstand ceaseless provocation without breaking down or losing sight of their ultimate objective." Young urban blacks could be invaluable to America. "We need aggressiveness," he declared. "We need daring." If we would only concede the "phony" nature of much American life, we would look more favorably on those so-called "culturally disadvantaged." Black youth needed teachers "who can convey to them an awareness that they do, indeed, come from somewhere, some place of human value, and that what they've learned there does count in the larger society." At Bard, the wealthy young students had been as culturally confused as any young people could be. "If you can show me how I can cling to that which is real in me," he ended, "while teaching me a way into the larger society, then I will not only drop my defenses and my hostility, but I will sing your praises and I will help you to make the desert bear fruit."

Moved by his sense of Negro America standing at a major intersection of history, Ralph made perhaps as eloquent a defense of black youth as anyone had done in some time. In the process, he may have underestimated the importance of protest and the assertion of race pride, when such gestures seemed necessary to these young people. Perhaps he was underestimating the psychological need among blacks for a form of catharsis. In any case, he was preaching a sermon that few young blacks would heed in the coming years.

Against a backdrop more chaotic than anything in *Invisible Man,* more than ten thousand public demonstrations against racism took place that year, 1963, along with the arrest of several thousand black youths and their white, Northern sympathizers. In Birmingham, Alabama, the notorious police chief Eugene "Bull" Connor arrested and jailed Dr. King. Someone bombed the black-owned Gaston Motel, King's headquarters. On a Sunday in September, a bomb exploding under the 16th Street Baptist Church in Memphis killed four black girls.

Each new level of violence disturbed Ralph but also raised his stock as a public speaker, especially on college campuses. Within a few weeks, turning down several other invitations, he spoke at Yale, Harvard, Duke, and

McGill in Montreal. In a gesture that pleased him, Tuskegee Institute awarded its best-known dropout an honorary doctorate. At a PEN America monthly dinner he spoke on the problems of the Negro author. Discussing Mark Twain on educational television, he opposed the expurgation of the word "nigger" from *Adventures of Huckleberry Finn,* which some blacks, in the increasingly self-righteous political climate, now demanded. He gave no thought to join the March on Washington, where Dr. King delivered his celebrated "I Have a Dream" oration, but soon took part willingly in a public panel discussion of the event.

On such occasions Ralph's voice, like his message, was not oracular but softly modulated. Yet he very much wanted to be heard. In July, for the first time in many years, he attended Henry Kissinger's annual International Seminar at Harvard. As always, he was careful to stick to his core beliefs, and to the limits of his expertise. At Harvard, he spoke about literature, not international politics. Asked to sign an open letter to President Kennedy calling for a tougher stand on racism and civil rights, he declined to do so although a wide range of artists and religious figures endorsed the statement. He wanted less and less to do with signing open letters. As criticism grew about the NAACP's lack of radical zeal, he did not desert the organization. That year and the next he helped to choose the annual winner of the Spingarn Medal, its top honor. Still an admirer of the Legal Defense Fund, he served, albeit in a token capacity, on its fund-raising Committee of 100.

The civil rights struggle continued to spawn lucrative opportunities for him. In March, when Rutgers invited him to come back for another year, an official praised him lavishly: "You have been a very great asset indeed." Ralph knew better. William Sloane, who had helped to bring him to New Brunswick, was much more honest when he lamented the university's "failure to make adequate use of you, or, indeed, to pay much attention to your very existence." Aware that he was a token, Ralph was not so self-righteous as to walk away from the job. Once poor, he was now prosperous, and he preferred the latter.

With a combined income of just over $20,000 in 1963, he and Fanny were doing very well. Adorning Ralph and Fanny's apartment now were abstract oil paintings, a lithograph signed for Ralph by Robert Motherwell, collages by Romare Bearden, pieces of sculpture old and new, examples of traditional African art, and kachina dolls from Oklahoma. The living room favored modern furniture: chairs by Mies van der Rohe and Marcel Breuer, a glass-topped coffee table, an austere metal-and-glass desk designed by Ralph himself. A cart of African violets growing under fluorescent lights added a touch of natural beauty ("It was from him that I learned all that I know about house plants," Saul Bellow revealed). Tucka, sleek and adoring, lounged at his master's feet while a whimsical parakeet chirped in its cage. "The luxurious effect of the three front rooms (the living room and study) is overpowering," Richard Kostelanetz marveled in print, "as well as somewhat surprising; it is not the sort of elegance that most people, their minds cluttered with stereotypes about Negroes, 'ghettos,' and writers' homes, expect to find on the edge of Harlem."

Nevertheless, the social problems funding this elegance were taking their toll on the neighborhood and beyond. The Beaumont had decayed since the Ellisons had moved in eleven years before. Prostitutes trolled the streets outside and at times even the lobby, vandalism was rife, mailboxes were jimmied open in search of checks, the elevators often stuck, and maintenance was poor. Muggings and purse snatchings were commonplace. But although the Ellisons could afford to move to a safer section of the city, they liked their roomy, riverfront apartment and its city-controlled rent. Their marriage slowly began to right itself. On May 15, 1963, Fanny lost her mother. Drinking much less now, she mourned with dignity.

Early in 1963, Ralph joined Nathan Scott in sending to Doubleday an outline for a proposed anthology of essays by black writers to be called "Perspectives on the American Experience." Doubleday was interested, but when some of the writers they wanted, including Gwendolyn Brooks, Horace Cayton, and James Baldwin, were less enthusiastic, they gave up the idea. Ralph faced other small setbacks. When "It Always Breaks Out" (from his novel-in-progress) appeared in March in *Partisan Review,* the response was a yawn. The same month, William Shawn rejected another section that he had solicited for *The New Yorker.* Reluctantly taking on some smaller jobs, Ralph agreed to write an essay about Tuskegee for *Holiday* magazine, an essay on big-band music of the 1930s and 1940s for *Saturday Review,* and a review of Edmund Wilson's acclaimed study of Civil War literature, *Patriotic Gore,* for *The New Leader.*

He finished none of these essays. Instead, in the fall of 1963 he agreed readily when Albert Erskine at Random House suggested that the time was right for a book of his essays. Baldwin had shown that year, with his explosive *The Fire Next Time,* that a book of essays on race could become a best seller. Ralph signed a contract, negotiated by Helen Strauss at the William Morris Agency, which gave him an advance of $5,000 for the book. By mid-November, Erskine and a colleague had made a preliminary selection, and Ralph further sifted this material. He had to answer two important questions. What, if anything, could be chosen from his pro-Communist years of writing for journals such as *New Masses*? And how could the book achieve a sense of coherence and unity when the material ran from short pieces on music to lengthy interviews?

That fall, his duties remained light at Rutgers University. The English Department now and then reached out to him, as when Paul Fussell asked him to address some honors students. Otherwise he was mainly on his own or on the road making money. At McGill University in Canada he delivered a lecture but also sat for a thoughtful interview with Allan Geller that *Tamarack Review* later published. Making the rounds of the Philadelphia area, he appeared at Swarthmore College, Temple University, and the Art Alliance. He spoke at Wesleyan University in Connecticut. With white schools in the South at last seeking black speakers, he traveled to Duke (along with the poet W. D. Snodgrass and the cartoonist Jules Feiffer) and to Washington and Lee University in Virginia. Almost everywhere, he attracted young whites eager to feel the heat of Negro indignation and young blacks who expected black speakers to fan the fire. But Ralph declined to pander to what he saw as inappropriate desires. He stuck to what he truly knew, literature and especially American literature; or he read something from his novel-in-progress. He would not exhort or denounce even though he continued to speak, as a preacher would, without a finished text before him ("I find it almost impossible to write a talk," he explained to a professor at Duke).

He also refused to leap at every bone tossed his way, no matter how prestigious. Asked to teach in the 1964 Harvard University summer school, he said no. He wanted to rest over the summer. Besides, the money wasn't good. He was interested in serving institutions that had altruistic purposes, as long as their needs didn't hurt his writing schedule. Reflecting his new interest in African art, he joined the board of consultants of the Center for Cross-Cultural Communication, an organization led by Warren M. Robbins, whose ambition was to create a National Museum of African Art in Washington, D.C. Saul Bellow, a former anthropology student and one of Robbins's consultants, may have recruited him. The men were on cordial terms again. On October 12, in Bellow's absence but at his request or with his consent, he read aloud a meditation by Bellow on the evil of the Holocaust at a Manhattan conference on the status of Jews in the Soviet Union.

. . .

The horror in Dallas on November 22 shocked Ralph and Fanny as it shocked America and the world. The evening before, they had attended a gala reception at the home of Ronald Tree, a wealthy British business-man, and his wife, Marietta Peabody Tree, a member of an illustrious New England family, in honor of the American Place Theatre. Ralph was at home when the news broke. Admiring Kennedy for his evident fond-ness for art and artists, he had refused to criticize him publicly over the issue of civil rights. "He's certainly paid more attention to writers," Ralph had noted, "than any other president in a long time . . . except for Presi-dent Roosevelt." In the next few days he and Fanny fixed their attention on the bulletins, newscasts, and images of the dreadful event and its aftermath. They watched the return of the president's body to Washing-ton; the hasty swearing in of the drawling Texan Lyndon B. Johnson, who seemed at first to be an appalling successor to Kennedy; the arrest of Lee Harvey Oswald and his murder on live television; the state funeral; the grieving Jacqueline Kennedy and her small son's heartbreaking salute.

The assassination seemed to be an obvious watershed in American his-tory. But Ralph also saw in it a horrific intervention by real life in his novel-in-progress, which itself turned on an attempted political assassina-tion by gunfire. The decade of violence that followed Dallas would include the assassinations of Malcolm X, Dr. King, and Robert F. Kennedy. The savagery of the Vietnam War and the bitterness of the antiwar movement would be accompanied by the rise of Black Power, an epidemic of race-related urban riots on a scale unseen in America since 1919, and what he saw as the degradation of American moral values. About ten years after Dallas, Ralph would confess to John Hersey that "one of the things which really chilled me—slowed down the writing—was that eruption of assas-sinations, especially the first. Because, you see, much of the mood of this book [his work-in-progress] was conceived as comic." (The core of the book was never comic.) But "suddenly life was stepping in and imposing itself upon my fiction. . . . I managed to keep going with it, I guess, be-cause there was nothing else to do. I know that it led me to try to give the book a richer structuring, so that the tragic elements could contain the comic and the comic the tragic, without violating our national pieties—if there are any left." The comic tone and often serendipitous structure of his manuscript to this point suddenly seemed shockingly inappropriate. The triumph of chaos, as Ralph saw it, had radically changed things.

The tragic events of late November overlapped with a serious literary

controversy over Ralph's right to define himself as a writer. The trouble
began when Irving Howe, a loyal socialist committed also to his Jewish
immigrant heritage, offended Ralph with an essay, "Black Boys and Native
Sons," that his magazine, *Dissent,* published in its Autumn number. In his
essay, Howe praised, at the expense of Ellison and Baldwin, the radical
passion of Richard Wright. "The day *Native Son* appeared," he declared,
"American culture was changed forever." Flawed by the dogmatic Stalin-
ism of the 1930s, *Native Son* was nevertheless far superior as fiction by a
Negro to Baldwin's misguided *Go Tell It on the Mountain* and *Giovanni's
Room.* In his more recent work, such as the aggressive *Another Country*
and *The Fire Next Time,* Baldwin had redeemed himself. Not so Ralph
Ellison. Although as art *Invisible Man* verges at times on the miraculous
(Howe had voted for it to win the National Book Award), the novel is
haunted by "the ideological delusions" of the 1950s, with the Communists—the "Brotherhood"—depicted in gross caricature. The epilogue,
especially when Invisible asserts that "my world has become one of infinite possibilities," is "vapid and insubstantial." Wright wrote fiction as a
Negro should. Ellison had shirked his responsibilities.

Initially, Ralph did not respond. In mid-November, when Howe invited
him to reply to his charges, he declined to do so. He changed his mind
only after speaking with Myron Kolatch of *The New Leader:* "He suggested that I put down my ideas and I agreed." For this particular duel,
The New Leader was ideal turf. Founded in 1923, it was mainly an organ
for immigrants (many of them Jewish) fleeing Soviet totalitarianism. It
had a proven interest in race and civil rights. Dr. King's crucial essay "Letter from Birmingham City Jail" had first appeared there.

In his rejoinder, "The World and the Jug," which *The New Leader*
hailed as "a major statement on the role of the Negro writer in the continuing Negro revolution," Ralph posed three vital questions to Howe and the
readers in general. First, why do critics "suddenly drop their advanced
critical armament" when confronting black America and "revert with an
air of confident superiority to quite primitive modes of analysis?" Second,
why do "sociology-oriented critics rate literature so far below politics and
ideology" that they would rather trash a novel than accept it on its own
terms? And finally, why do people who write about black America "never
bother to learn how varied it really is?"

Mocking Howe's tribute to Wright's "clenched militancy," he quoted
from the catalogue of the failings of Negro culture that comes early in
Wright's autobiography, *Black Boy.* Thus he showed that Wright was, in

fact, perhaps as militant against black America as he was militant against capitalism or white America. Ralph insisted that he had no aesthetic or intellectual indebtedness to Wright. "No, Wright was no spiritual father of mine," he said, "certainly in no sense I recognize." He refused to believe that "unrelieved suffering is the only 'real' Negro experience, and that the true Negro artist must be ferocious." Negro life, he explained, is a *discipline*—just as any human life which has endured so long is a discipline teaching its own insights into the human condition, its own strategies of survival. There is a fullness, even a richness here; and here *despite* the realities of politics, perhaps, but nevertheless here and real. Because it is *human* life."

Because Ralph was at times vehement, many readers saw his *New Leader* response as a personal attack on Howe. He thus saw fit to send Howe a note assuring him that "my disagreement is with some of your ideas and not with you personally." The men agreed to a rematch. On February 3, 1964, *The New Leader* printed a reply by Howe, following which Ralph published a rejoinder. In his socialist zeal, Ralph said, Howe had made Negro culture what it was not; it did not embody "a will to historical forgetfulness." It was not a super-force that left no room for the accidents—a harelip, a stutter, or epilepsy—that shape character and history. Despite the somber attitude of Howe (and Wright and Baldwin), Ralph declared himself happy to be a Negro: "Who wills to be a Negro? I do!" A division of labor existed among members of the tribe. Some people agitated for rights. His job was to publish more novels, he said demurely— "and here I am remiss and vulnerable perhaps."

Probably for the first time in modern American history, a black intellectual had fought a public duel against a white intellectual and won. At one point Ralph even humiliated Howe by showing that he had plagiarized himself in his second essay, into which he had spliced a section taken from a much earlier essay. Many blacks probably took pleasure in this besting of a white man, but several prominent Jews, including Nat Hentoff, Alfred Kazin, Bernard Malamud, Sidney Hook, Daniel Aaron, and Stanley Hyman, were also glad to see Ralph pummel Howe in public. They saw Howe's praise of "clenched militancy" as an extension of his quarrel with those Jewish writers who refused to be defined first by their Jewishness. Kazin wrote Ralph that he had never seen "the artist's dignity in the face of all the usual abstractions so joyously assert itself." To Malamud, Ralph's statements were "beautifully and nobly written." Hook called them "*inspired* good sense."

"The World and the Jug" is probably Ralph's richest apologia for his life as a writer who happened to be black, as well as for the Negro culture that had made him. (The title alludes to Schopenhauer's remark that, in life, one must take the jug with the water.) As such, it also defends all American writing that seeks to move beyond ethnicity and toward national or universal values.

His brave refusal of coarse, destructive forms of militancy, his eloquent embrace of a studied moderation, and his complex patriotism cost Ellison some potential admirers but also brought him new rewards. On January 6, for example, in Washington he delivered a prestigious lecture at the Library of Congress under the auspices of the Gertrude Clarke Whittall Poetry and Literature Fund. "I take the invitation as a high honor," Ralph had replied early in 1963, "and I accept with pleasure." (The $1,000 honorarium was his highest to date.) As the first black to deliver such a lecture at the library, Ralph carefully prepared "Hidden Name and Complex Fate," a charming venture into autobiography that allowed him to return in time to his father's act of naming him in honor of Ralph Waldo Emerson, and then to move more purposefully toward the dangerous present. Again he mourned the loss of moral authority in America between the days of Emerson and the present. The turmoil of the age was, in large part, moral confusion masquerading as radical thought.

He refused chances to associate with radicalism even on his own terms. When John Henrik Clarke, an old adversary linked to both Marxism and black cultural nationalism, asked him for a piece on Harlem for a special number of *Freedomways* magazine, Ralph coolly rebuked him: "If I appeared in your journal it would constitute an act of opportunism on the part of both of us." And for a while he seemed to be prevailing against the enemy. In February, as Signet reprinted 130,000 copies of *Invisible Man* to meet the surging demand for the book in colleges and elsewhere, he also published a stinging essay in the fledgling *New York Review of Books* in which he took to task the enfant terrible of black letters, LeRoi Jones, whose searing one-act play *Dutchman* reverberates with a hatred of whites. In his latest book, *Blues People,* Jones tried to explore in prose some of the sociological, anthropological, and historical aspects of the blues, which he defined mainly as an acute form of political resistance. He also believed that, as with jazz, whites had compromised the purity of this classic Negro form. These theses offended Ralph. Jones had ignored "the intricate network of connections which binds Negroes to the larger society." Moreover, the blues speak to us "simultaneously of the tragic and the comic aspects of the human condition," and thus "any effective study of the blues would treat them first as poetry and as ritual." Instead, Jones had stressed politics and ideology.

Unfortunately for Ralph, he was unwilling to be friendly with writers whose ideas or art offended him. At best he was prepared to be polite, but he saw too much at stake for him to agree to help, much less embrace, many promising younger Negro writers. Asked by young Toni Cade, later Toni Cade Bambara and the author of the praised works of fiction *The Salt Eaters* and *Gorilla, My Love,* for a letter of support in applying for a Eugene Saxton fellowship, he ignored her. When Kristin Hunter asked for a blurb for her first novel, *God Bless the Child,* Ralph apologized seven months later for failing to read the galleys, then did so only after meeting and liking her. "We are pulling for you, and we wish you the best," he then assured "Christine" Hunter. Returning unread another novelist's manuscript, he archly advised the man to try any publisher since "most publishers consider anything about Negroes highly salable as of this historical moment." Asked by *The New Republic* to review Langston Hughes's anthology *New Negro Poets: U.S.A.,* he refused. In October, when Hughes telephoned Ralph to ask him to join a BBC discussion on race along with Baldwin, Jones, and Lorraine Hansberry, the young author of the landmark play *A Raisin in the Sun,* he said no. Hughes's compulsion to help younger writers (as he had once helped Ralph) mattered little to Ralph, who now saw him as a shallow sentimentalist. "I don't think you missed anything," he wrote to a friend who lamented being unable to attend a recent lecture by Hughes in Paris. "He probably had to tell the French, under the guise of discussing the problems of Negro writers, how difficult it is for Negro writers to be served hamburgers in Mississippi."

Ralph was surely under no obligation to help anyone, but he was stirring up a growing dislike of him among younger blacks that added to his sense of isolation and made the task of creating art more difficult than it already was. He wanted his core principles and ideas to be known accurately, rather than allow the impression to flourish that he lived by half-truths. This Olympian position offered its rewards. On January 31, 1964, he was summoned to the American Mount Olympus when the American Academy and National Institute of Arts and Letters informed him that the National Institute had elected him a member. Entering with him were Truman Capote, Bernard Malamud, John Updike, Hannah Arendt, Horace Gregory, Leon Edel, and James Baldwin. Among Ralph's main champions for this important honor was Lewis Mumford (ironically, given Ralph's lampooning of his book *The Golden Day* in *Invisible Man*).

On April 1, when he attended the welcoming dinner for new members, Ralph savored this latest proof of his success as a writer. Before dinner, cocktails were served in the Childe Hassam Room. On its walls hung many paintings by Hassam donated by the artist early in the century. After dinner, when it was time for the formal introduction of the newcomers, each was expected to make brief remarks. When Ralph's turn came, he was succinct. Although he knew full well that few persons present had produced a book more acclaimed than *Invisible Man,* he modestly poked fun at himself for being "the least productive person in the room." He had learned so much, he said, from the works of many of the men and women in attendance. Obliquely he addressed the unspoken topic of his skin color by lauding the democratic essence of the world of art: "It is a world that is available to any individual whose consciousness has become sensitized to its power." His blending of affability and solemnity were in sharp contrast to James Baldwin's offhand remarks that let everyone know that he had little time for the elite organization. That dinner might have been the last Baldwin attended at the Academy and National Institute. To Ralph, however, this was almost the equivalent of consecrated ground. For the rest of his life, the academy and institute constantly affirmed and reaffirmed for him his standing as one of the greatest living writers in America.

A few days later, a trip to Los Angeles to deliver the Ewing Lectures under the auspices of the Department of English at UCLA gave Ralph the chance to reunite with his brother. Ralph and Herbert had not seen each other in twenty-six years. Herbert had made a decent life for himself and his wife, Ada. The intellectual, cultural, and economic gap between the brothers was now unbridgeable, but Ida's children began to mend the rift that had opened with their mother's death in 1937.

The mending buoyed Ralph as he approached one of the crowning events of his life. In 1947, as a nobody, he had attended for the first time the annual May ceremonial of the Academy and National Institute. Now, on the afternoon of May 20, 1964, he was inducted into the institute before a crowd of about a thousand members and their guests. In addition to Fanny, he had invited Albert and Mozelle Murray; Ida Guggenheimer's daughter, Clara Binswanger; and Francis Steegmuller, who had recently married the Australian-born writer Shirley Hazzard, following the death in 1961 of Bea Stein. Nor did he forget the neighborhood folk, including

Eugene Ramsey and his wife, the owners of 730 Riverside Drive, and Alma Arter, an old friend of the Ellisons who lived in Harlem. As always, the annual ceremonial was a lengthy affair. When it was over, Ralph headed for the bar, secured a drink of hard liquor, and blushingly accepted many hearty backslaps and handshakes. Unfortunately, a pesky fly—his unfinished novel—hovered near the rim of his glass. Approached by the journalist Dick Schaap, who was writing an article on one-hit wonders of the American literary world such as Harper Lee, Joseph Heller, Henry Roth, and Ralph Ellison, he was frank. "I've got the central concepts," he said of his novel. "But I haven't written it in order, and I'm still doing continuous writing and rewriting."

If life was mainly good for him in 1964, it was a time of terror and sorrow for the nation as a whole. In March, riots erupted in Jacksonville; in July, in Harlem, Brooklyn, and Rochester, New York; and in August, in Chicago, Philadelphia, Jersey City, and Paterson, New Jersey. After generations of Negro humility and passivity, militant younger black men and women were turning to leaders such as the Black Muslim minister Malcolm X, once a pimp and a thief but now transformed into a crusading prophet by Elijah Muhammad and the Nation of Islam. Random, vengeful violence against whites (unsanctioned by Malcolm) became one feature of this irregular but often lethal rebellion. The South remained a dangerous place for reformers black or white. In Mississippi, Michael Schwerner and Andrew Goodman, white and Jewish from New York, and James Chaney, black from Mississippi, were abducted and murdered for their efforts at black voter registration. In the North, the white backlash against hastily imposed desegregation led many white voters, in a presidential election year, to throw their support in Wisconsin, Indiana, and Maryland primaries behind George Wallace. Moving toward the far right, the Republican Party rejected the moderate governor of New York, Nelson Rockefeller, and instead nominated the conservative Barry Goldwater of Arizona.

Almost uncannily, certain dramatic features of *Invisible Man*—the character and deadly fate of the black nationalist West Indian Ras the Destroyer; the death of the handsome but doomed black organizer Tod Clifton; the rioting near the climax of the action; the imminent threat of total chaos—now seemed to be not so much a fictional world created by Ralph as his inspired prophecy. "Now people are reading it," Ralph told an interviewer about his novel, "and they think that I invented Malcolm X." He offered himself, though, as no hot gospeler but instead as a dedicated, disciplined artist and intellectual. "I try to vote responsibly," he said, even as he alluded impatiently to the menacing style that seemed to him to be making the culture of younger blacks a sour affair, without access to peace, harmony, and the joy of life. "I contribute whenever I can to efforts to improve things," he said about resistance to racism. "It's a more complex problem than that of simply thrusting out your chin and saying 'I'm defiant.' That's all right, but defiance has to have a real role."

Ralph was not uninvolved. Unwilling himself to write about politics and race, he sat for a long interview with a close friend who was. Robert Penn Warren was doggedly preparing his own tract for the explosive times, the book *Who Speaks for the Negro?* The next day, June 18, Ralph spoke on a charged but ultimately confused and impotent panel (as he saw it) at Columbia University on the subject of the arts in the current national crisis. Later that summer, although he passed up a chance to speak at a *Partisan Review* symposium on the meaning of Goldwater's nomination, which many people on the left saw as almost diabolical, Ralph signed a public letter of support for Robert F. Kennedy, the brother of the slain president, that appeared in the *New York Times* as Kennedy challenged the respected incumbent, Kenneth B. Keating, for a U.S. Senate seat in New York. He attended a last-minute rally for Kennedy, who had become a zealous defender of black civil rights, and was pleased when Kennedy won. On August 20, at the Town Hall in Manhattan, he joined yet another panel discussion, this time organized by the Student Nonviolent Coordinating Committee (SNCC), that featured in addition to himself Judge Constance Baker Motley, a former NAACP lawyer, and his friend the Southern historian C. Vann Woodward. Led by the activists Ella Baker and Bayard Rustin, SNCC had emerged as a more confrontational group than either the NAACP or Dr. King's SCLC, but Ralph was now willing to be publicly identified with their efforts.

Although he delivered two or three lectures that summer, including yet another at Kissinger's Harvard seminar, his main excitement was shepherding his new book through production at Random House. By this time it had acquired a jazzy title: *Shadow and Act* (taken from a line in Eliot's *Four Quartets*). He was also pleased by the news that he had won a year-long fellowship that, starting in September, would affiliate him with Yale. With his Rutgers appointment expiring, he was on the brink of taking a job at the State University of New York at Stony Brook when he heard the welcome news about the fellowship. Once again, his benefactor behind the scenes was Robert Penn Warren, for some years a professor at Yale. At

Warren's urging, the Rockefeller Foundation, through a relatively new—
and relatively short-lived—program, gave Yale University the sum of up to
$14,000 "to enable Mr. Ralph Ellison, Visiting Fellow, to work full time on
his second novel." "My thanks to you," Ralph saluted Red Warren, "for
this unexpected piece of good luck."

That fall, even as the summer fires at last were dying out across the
country, Ralph slipped smoothly into the genteel culture of the colleges,
or residential complexes, at Yale. With no formal teaching duties, he was
one of many distinguished guests at Yale called upon to do little more
than grace the senior common room or share an hour or two with awed
undergraduates. He also served as living proof, if proof were needed, of
Yale's racial liberalism. He had very good friends on the campus other
than Warren, especially Dick Lewis and his wife, Nancy. Although he had
time to travel he did so only modestly, as when he joined Granville Hicks
and the poet Karl Shapiro on a program at the University of Wisconsin. At
all times he kept his eyes on the gestation of *Shadow and Act.* Thus he
seized on a chance for some good advance publicity, at least among the
more intellectual Jewish readers, when Norman Podhoretz of *Commentary,* the leading journal dedicated to Jewish intellectual interests, asked
for the right to publish Ralph's introduction to the book. Ralph's "On
Becoming a Writer," which appeared that fall in *Commentary,* so impressed
Wallace Stegner, the founder of the creative writing program at Stanford
University in California, that he invited Ralph to teach there for a year.
(The idea intrigued Ralph, but he begged off for the time being.) More
valuable advance publicity came when the Library of Congress published
Ralph's Gertrude Clarke Whittall lecture, "Hidden Name and Complex
Fate," in a series of occasional pamphlets called *The Writer's Experience.*

Shadow and Act, with blurbs by Warren and Daniel Aaron, reached the
bookstores in October. Probably the most startled early reader was Ralph's
pivotal English teacher at Tuskekee Institute, Morteza Drexel Sprague, to
whom he dedicated the book—"A Dedicated Dreamer in a Land Most
Strange." (Why he passed over Fanny once again is unknown.) Almost all
the major reviews were excellent. *Time* and *Newsweek* hailed *Shadow and
Act* as brilliant, absolutely important in the context of the controversial
age. Although the *New York Times Book Review* found some essays better
than others, it judged all of them good and the best indispensable. A
widely syndicated appraisal, originating in *Saturday Review,* took note of
the consuming rage of many contemporary Negro writers even as it hailed
Ralph as being above them all in quality. While too many Negro writers

offered mainly jeremiads, Ralph Ellison was an authentic American visionary.

As with *Invisible Man* in 1952, virtually all the reviewers were white. Unlike in 1952, the black far left, which had flayed Ralph then, was now virtually mute. Communism had been eviscerated as a political and cultural force. Two reviews were clearly hostile, at least in places. One, by the white jazz critic and former English professor Martin Williams, attacked Ralph for his contemptuous attitude—in his essay "Sound and the Mainstream"—to modern jazz and especially to the iconic Charlie Parker. The other, more forceful dissident was, ironically, Norman Podhoretz. Citing Daniel Aaron's blurb to the effect that *Shadow and Act* has "the same eloquence and humor and wisdom" to be found in *Invisible Man,* Podhoretz insisted that eloquence, humor, and wisdom are "precisely what *Shadow and Act* for the most part lacks.*"* Because Ralph had never bothered to master the art of the essay, he said, most of his pieces are "awkwardly composed, marred by pompous locutions, clumsy transitions, and sometimes even by bad syntax." Podhoretz then helpfully provided a sample sentence that is bad by almost any standard (although the sentence is not characteristic of Ralph's writing in *Shadow and Act*). As for the structure of Ralph's longer essays, they indeed are not tightly planned but depend instead on the kind of natural expansiveness that Podhoretz deplored but many readers found attractive. Surprisingly vitriolic, Podhoretz perhaps attacked Ralph as aggressively as he did out of resentment at what he saw, not without reason, as Ellison's glee in humiliating Irving Howe. (Several years after Ellison's death, in his essay "What Happened to Ralph Ellison," Podhoretz reversed course. Admitting that he had penned a "wrongheaded negative review," he now praised Ralph's "moral luminosity.")

Shadow and Act sold decently for a book of essays—about 6,500 copies in its first six months—but certainly was no match for Baldwin's best seller of the previous year, *The Fire Next Time.* Nor did it fare nearly as well as Saul Bellow's latest novel, *Herzog,* which rode atop the best-seller list when *Shadow and Act* appeared and remained there for many more weeks. Nevertheless, from the moment of its publication Ralph's second book anchored his reputation as a man of letters. Its blending of polemics, reflection, retorts, assertions, and engaging, often lyrical essays showed off his high intelligence, his intricately loving feel for the realities of Negro mass culture, his love of learning, and his love of America. In *Mademoiselle,* Paule Marshall, author of *Brown Girl, Brownstones* and other novels, would deem it even more invaluable to her than *Invisible*

Man. For a rising generation of black writers, *Shadow and Act* would become a Bible as they sought to reconcile their love of literature and art with a nation that too often tried to excuse or exclude Negroes from the ranks of true humanity. Virtually all books by blacks venturing into this subject can either trace their main ideas back to Ellison or find themselves in alignment with his insights. In these respects, *Shadow and Act* has no superior except for Du Bois's *The Souls of Black Folk,* published sixty-one years before. For the artist, it would outlive virtually all of the books of essays by James Baldwin, or Eldridge Cleaver's *Soul on Ice,* another book that became a big best seller while *Shadow and Act* sold modestly.

For many sympathetic whites as well, the book illuminated the complexity of black culture as never before. It did so in large part because of the mature, civilized, sophisticated, learned, playful, and sympathetic voice of its "hero," Ralph Ellison. Mary Hemingway, Ernest's widow, wrote Ralph to say that her late husband "would have been so pleased by your references to his work" in this "wise and wonderful book." (In fact, Ernest never cared much for American Negroes. When the integrated Brooklyn Dodgers visited Cuba, he invited the white players to his home, Finca Vigía, but quietly barred their black teammates. Nevertheless, a friendship grew between Mary Hemingway and the Ellisons.)

Crowning a superb year for Ralph, in late November the Century voted at its annual general meeting to admit him. Delighted, Ralph dispatched a check for $262 to cover the entrance fee and other costs. The sixty-eight new members included M. H. Abrams, a leading literary scholar; the journalists Joseph Kraft and Clifton Daniel; and the writers S. N. Behrman and Ved Mehta.

Founded in 1847 as an "Association of Gentlemen engaged in Letters and the Fine Arts," the club had admitted young Henry James in 1875 (Whistler's portrait of him as a young man hung on a wall). The grand, multistoried "clubhouse" offered a tiny but well-stocked, heavily used bar; elegant sitting and dining rooms with russet-leather armchairs and sofas and fine old Persian rugs on the floor; an abundance of books and magazines. The Whistler painting was only one piece in a notable art collection. On the ground floor was a major billiards area. The kitchen was decent, and the staff, including several blacks, loyal and skilled. A Manhattan counterpart to the renowned social clubs of London, the Century exuded a beguiling air that blended artistic and professional distinction with the accoutrements of social privilege. One key rule was that no business (except club matters) was to be conducted on the premises. This rule reflected less the high tone of the Century than its tax-exempt status as a purely social club. It was also all male. Already a few members were looking for change, but Ralph cherished this aspect, mainly because he was sure that introducing white women would set off certain tensions and inhibitions that otherwise would not exist.

Now he had a splendid second home. A renting tenant uptown in an increasingly raunchy district, he became a gentleman among gentlemen once he stepped into the foyer of the Century and was greeted by name by the staff. With confidence, he sat down to dine, ready to join or even to dominate the conversation, at the polished long table reserved for members only, or he lounged in a comfy armchair or on a plush leather sofa, a martini in one hand and a fat cigar in the other. He quickly became known as a fine fellow, one who could be counted on to add spicy wit and a manly, boisterous charm to conversations.

At fifty, he was atop that part of the world about which he cared the most. America was rumbling with social discord, belching fire, and his second novel was not under control. But overcoming the many handicaps and setbacks of his life, Ralph had secured a place for himself near the top of his Mount Parnassus.

16

Tell It Like It Is, Baby

1965–1967

*In the middle of a Negro rebellion . . . Ralph Ellison's
voice is a lonely one.*   NEW YORK *Newsday* (1967)

On February 21, 1965, at the Audubon Ballroom in Washington
Heights, north of Harlem, two black gunmen assassinated the most
charismatic and militant African-American political and religious leader
of the age, Malcolm X. The death of Malcolm would reverberate throughout black America. At Malcolm's funeral, the black actor Ossie Davis (in
a scene reminiscent of Tod Clifton's funeral in *Invisible Man*) eulogized
him as "our own black shining prince, who didn't hesitate to die, because he loved us so." Malcolm "was our manhood, our living black manhood. . . . Harlem has no braver, more gallant champion than this
Afro-American who lies before us now—unconquered still." Three years
later, in their best-selling study *Black Rage,* two black psychiatrists identified Malcolm as "the only universal black hero. In his unrelenting opposition to the viciousness in America, he fired the imagination of black men
all over the world."

In the wake of this murder, committed apparently by fellow Muslims,
1965 saw unprecedented turmoil over civil rights. Within days of Malcolm X's assassination, and following mass arrests in connection with a
voter registration campaign in Selma, Alabama, Dr. King and John Lewis
of SNCC led a march from Selma to the state capital, Montgomery. At
the Edmund Pettus Bridge in Selma, television and newsreel photographers recorded the marchers' bloody encounter with state troopers and
policemen using tear gas, whips, and clubs. These images shocked many
Americans, black and white, into a commitment to the civil rights movement. Intensifying black rage and the will to revolt, the images also stiff-

ened the resolve of liberal whites. A few days later, President Johnson seized control of the Alabama National Guard and ordered it to protect demonstrators marching from Selma to Montgomery.

Later that year would come the first clear enunciation of the doctrine of Black Power, which aimed to sweep aside the pieties of the civil rights movement and assert for blacks the explicitly economic and political goals of all their agitation. First mentioned almost casually by Adam Clayton Powell, Jr., in a speech at Howard University, then picked up by militant SNCC leaders, Black Power swept aside talk of integration or even the need for a complex dialogue about racism. Now the overriding goal was the acquisition of power, which was to be achieved, in words commonly attributed to Malcolm X, "by any means necessary." Black Power seemed to scorn white liberals even more than it opposed outright white racists. As such, it threatened the future of all the leading civil rights organizations. Under its most dramatic leader, the twenty-four-year-old, Trinidad-born Stokely Carmichael, SNCC adopted Black Power as its absolute, incontestable goal.

Ralph did not admire Malcolm. At a public forum three years later, he would be elliptical about the slain leader but also express his skepticism about the aura of heroic sanctity surrounding his legacy. "I wouldn't dare to tell the truth about him," Ralph told a man who wondered whether Ralph might ever use the figure of Malcolm in his fiction. "It would destroy the same myth, and this myth is a valuable myth." All the same, "I don't want Malcolm telling me what American history is, and I don't want him to tell me what my experience has been." Malcolm's death, following the assassination of President Kennedy, reinforced Ralph's dread that the novel he was writing, which began with an attempted assassination, prophesied the truth about modern America. "One reason Ralph was having so much trouble with his novel," his friend Richard Wilbur said, "was that history was interfering with him. The succession of assassinations in the real world made it necessary for him to revise and keep revising so as to keep his novel from portraying some particular historical event."

The real assassinations challenged the critical but finally optimistic and benevolent view of America at the core of his novel-in-progress. In the aftermath of Malcolm's slaying, as a generation of angry blacks attempted a revolution of spirit and psychology, he held fast to pacifist beliefs and attitudes even as he sought to capture, in his evolving narrative, the essence of the American experience.

.   .   .

Two days after Malcolm's death, Ralph accepted an honor that left little doubt about the distance between him and Malcolm's most ardent followers. In Washington, D.C., President Johnson named him among the twenty-four founding members of the National Council on the Arts. Chairing the council was Roger L. Stevens, a wealthy real estate developer and Broadway producer who was now the president's main advisor on the arts and would become one of Ralph's major sponsors in upper-class Washington. Gregory Peck, Agnes DeMille, Isaac Stern, and Leonard Bernstein also sat on the council, which Johnson saw as a crucial part of the Great Society that he envisioned following his sudden accession to the presidency. The council would give birth to the National Endowment for the Humanities (NEH) and the National Endowment for the Arts (NEA), which sought to place the federal government in direct service to art and humanistic knowledge in America. To radical blacks, these were examples of a black man colluding with white power. But Ralph saw himself serving the American liberal tradition that he loved and revered.

Earlier in January, Ralph had gone to Washington to take part in a meeting to plan the council. Exactly who invited him is not clear, but he had already identified himself publicly with certain Democratic Party leaders. He had served on that committee on the arts in support of Robert F. Kennedy's election to the Senate, and he also knew Jacob Javits, the state's other senator and a major supporter of Johnson's arts initiative. While in Washington, Ralph had spoken at a *Washington Post* literary luncheon. He used the occasion to proclaim the need for racial unity: "We live separated but, culturally and in terms of ideals and hopes, are united."

Consistent with this approach, he rejected appeals for help from black separatists. When LeRoi Jones urged support for a black arts repertory theater and school to be established in Harlem, his aim to have a theater "where the most meaningful dramas of our time can be staged, in repertory, in this largest of Negro ghettoes," did not move Ralph. "Ralph saw the low, agit-prop nature of LeRoi Jones's work as showing contempt for black people," Stanley Crouch, a friend and admirer of Ralph later commented. "He knew that after 200 years of being unable to express themselves freely, blacks were susceptible to anyone among them who spouts off. He disliked the cheap demagoguery." Jones saw a different America. Malcolm's murder had accelerated his flight from Greenwich Village (and from his white wife and their children) to Harlem. That year, he staged two of his most contentious one-act plays about race, *The Toilet* and *The Slave*. (His theater flourished for a while before authorities discovered a cache of firearms in its basement and shut it down.)

In contrast, Ralph's public protests were mild. He joined an amicus curiae legal brief in support of Ralph Ginzburg, who had been charged with obscenity in connection with his magazine, *Eros*. In racial matters, in February he took part in a six-hour discussion at the Carnegie Endowment International Center in New York on the civil rights movement, SCLC, and its future. He became involved in an NAACP Legal Defense Fund program, chaired by Ralph Bunche, to construct a five-year plan for legal action against Jim Crow in the South. Speaking on the meaning of Selma, Ralph made a profound impression. According to the director of the fund, Jack Greenberg, "it contributed a quality to the events of that day which we have not had before." But when politics or even social science seemed to impinge on art, Ralph was touchy. At a meeting in February at which PEN worked on plans for its 1966 world congress, he offered as one possible focus "the apparent surrender on the part of literature to the social sciences in describing personality, reality and value."

Because of the racial turmoil—and both as a celebrity and as a moderate—he found himself in growing demand on white college campuses. At Stanford University, a school that had barred blacks for most of its existence, all freshmen now had to read *Invisible Man*. Princeton, with an equally exclusionary history, asked him to teach as a visitor (he declined). On February 22, the day after Malcolm's assassination, he began a week of lecturing to students, teachers, and librarians in Philadelphia and at nearby Swarthmore College. Early in April, lured by a fat honorarium, he endured the long plane ride to Fairbanks, Alaska, and the presence of Norman Mailer to take part in the annual Festival of Fine Arts at the University of Alaska.

Proud of his appointment to the new National Council on the Arts, on April 9 Ralph was in the Cabinet Room at the White House for the mass swearing-in ceremony. Never had he imagined that he would one day stand so close to the very center of national power. He listened carefully as President Johnson stressed his hope that civilization—by which he surely meant his administration—would be judged "by our contributions in the arts rather than our conflicts and hostilities." Unpleasant thoughts about the Vietnam War were set aside as the council celebrated its launching. A cocktail party later that day, hosted by the National Trust for Historic Preservation, was followed by a black-tie dinner at the splendid

Georgetown home of Roger Stevens and his wife, with the majority leader of the Senate, Mike Mansfield, and a number of cabinet members in attendance. For Ralph and Fanny, the day confirmed their faith in the rising tide of American democracy inspired by Johnson. "Fanny especially," Richard Wilbur recalled, "was always glad of Ralph's taking on or being offered these things. She was aware of Ralph's being the first of his race to be asked, and proud of it."

The next day, at the first of five meetings that year at which the council organized itself, he spoke on the future of American fiction. Above all, he hoped that the council would seek to stimulate the American artist's knowledge of the nation in all its complexity. ("Ralph was ever so fond of the word 'complexity,' " recalled Wilbur. "I think that his favorite expression was the 'complexity of the American experience.' This is what Ralph wanted to expose, especially in the essays devoted to racial matters, where there is complexity upon complexity.") "America is no longer a provincial nation," Ralph told a reporter, "and it is time for the American artist to know as much about the United States as he knows about England, Italy, or Greece." He agreed completely that the council should proceed slowly and build solidly.

Its importance grew in September when Johnson signed into law a bill establishing the National Foundation for the Arts and the National Endowment for the Humanities, with both organizations to be overseen by the council. That day, Johnson asked Congress for just under $18 million to initiate the crucial grant-in-aid programs of the two foundations. For the rest of his life, Ralph would look back with pride on his role in founding the NEH and what soon became the National Endowment for the Arts.

Brimming with confidence, he became even more assertive than in the past. At the National Institute, put in charge of the committee to choose the winner of the William Dean Howells Medal, which went every five years to the author of the best work of fiction during that time, he seized control. As with the fight over the candidacy of Nabokov and *Lolita* for the National Book Award, he spoke against the overwhelming majority. While most members wanted Saul Bellow to win for *Herzog*, Ralph instead backed John Cheever for *The Wapshot Scandal*. In the end he won, but even Cheever questioned the wisdom of the decision. Although he declared himself "deeply grateful" for the award, privately he found it "very embarrassing because the only reason I got it is because Saul Bellow and Ralph Ellison had a fight and Ralph wouldn't let them give the thing to Saul." Perhaps there were other reasons. In any event, Ralph's praise of Cheever at the May award ceremony seemed to include a possible slap at Bellow as a novelist and certain of his heroes when he decried the age as "a time in which it has become fashionable to glorify the slob and to project the perverse and infantile as metaphors of the human condition."

Following the ceremony, about two dozen guests repaired to the Ellison apartment nearby for a buffet dinner ostensibly in honor of Robert Penn Warren and his wife, Eleanor Clark. It was really much more Ralph and Fanny's coming-out party among the American cultural white elite. With Harlem's top caterer supplying the food (except for the black caviar, which Fanny bought), as well as a bartender and two servers, their guests sat down at the Ellisons' oversize dining room table or ate off trays elsewhere. Among the guests, including the Warrens, were John and Mary Cheever; Stanley Hyman and Shirley Jackson; Kenneth and Libby Burke; John and Barbara Hersey; Helen Frankenthaler and Robert Motherwell; Albert and Marisa Erskine; Mary Hemingway; Bea Roethke, the widow of the poet Theodore Roethke (who had killed himself); William and Rose Styron; and the poet Stanley Kunitz and his wife, Elise. Albert Murray was the only black guest.

"That was a stupendous party you gave, really great," Warren said, thanking the Ellisons. Writing to Shirley Jackson (who died in her sleep about three months later), Libby Burke admitted her surprise that the Ellisons had spared no expense. When the last guests were gone, Ralph and Fanny congratulated themselves on the success of their pricey debut at a social level entirely new to them as hosts. But they could afford it now. Fanny began to think of retiring from her job. She hired a housekeeper to come in five days a week, six hours a day.

Ralph found his links to Lyndon Johnson thrilling. On June 8, after speaking at a conference in Boston on "The Negro in America" organized by *Daedelus,* the journal of the almost two-hundred-year-old American Academy of Arts and Sciences, he visited the White House again for the presentation of medals to young Presidential Scholars of 1965. Closeness to Johnson had its dangers. So Ralph soon found out when he attended a one-day, thirteen-hour Festival of the Arts and Humanities intended to celebrate Johnson's commitment to art and learning. Just before the opening, Robert Lowell, with his impeccable Boston Brahmin roots and his many honors as a poet, shattered the decorum of the White House by withdrawing in order to signal his opposition to the Vietnam War, although his intensely polite letter mentioned no specific conflict. (In World War II, Lowell had been jailed as a conscientious objector.) He was not alone in opposing the war and, by implication, Johnson. A group of twenty-seven painters, writers, sculptors, musicians, and theater people, including friends of Ralph such as Stanley Kunitz and Nat Hentoff, appealed for help in order to publish an antiwar statement in the *New York Times*.

Lowell's letter forced every invitee to declare his or her position on mixing art and politics, which was the same as declaring the depth of their opposition to the war. Twenty artists, including Robert Penn Warren, Alfred Kazin, Bernard Malamud, and William Styron, backed Lowell in a signed letter (although none had been invited to the event). Bellow and John Hersey said that they would attend but also voiced their opposition to what America was doing in Vietnam. Ralph was among those who did not waver. At the festival on June 14, when Dwight Macdonald circulated a petition in support of Lowell, he refused to sign it. "It's adolescent; he's boring from within at the White House," he told a reporter. As for Lowell, he said, the president wasn't telling him how to write his poetry, and Lowell shouldn't be telling the president how to govern. Deploring the "herd" mentality of many artists, he connected it to America in the 1930s, when socialism was the fiery idea. "Some of my best friends are mixed up in it," he confessed about the antiwar movement, "which leaves me all the more amazed."

At a meeting of the American Academy of Arts and Letters that year, Lewis Mumford spoke passionately of "a rising tide of public shame and private anger" against the "moral outrages" of the government. Ralph never opposed the Vietnam War. He felt a keen attachment to President Johnson. On March 15, addressing a joint session of Congress on behalf of a historic voting rights bill, Johnson had woven into his speech the very title of the anthem of the movement, "We Shall Overcome." On June 4, speaking at Howard University, he had offered by far the bravest backing of black economic, political, and cultural goals ever ventured by a president. Johnson, Ralph insisted, "is far ahead of most of the intellectuals—especially those Northern liberals who have become, in the name of the highest motives, the new apologists for segregation." (He was referring to liberals who endorsed the separatist goals of black radicals.)

The summer of 1965 was like nothing America had seen since the "Red Summer" of 1919, when white and black mobs clashed in several Northern cities. The worst uprising in 1965 took place in Watts, a predominantly black section of Los Angeles. Over five days, blacks looted and burned stores and buildings as the death toll reached thirty-four, with more than a thousand injured and almost four thousand arrested. With the spectacular events in Watts sparking explosions in Chicago and elsewhere, Ralph and Fanny did not travel much that summer. When he got away, it was to drive to Cambridge, Massachusetts, for the third straight year to speak at Kissinger's annual international conference. There he was the soul of moderation and reason. "You were an enormous success, as always," Kissinger said, thanking Ralph, "to nobody's surprise." While radicals railed against big business, he flew to Northfield, Minnesota, where on July 21 he spoke to a gathering of AT&T management trainees at Carleton College on the role of Negroes in American society.

That summer Ralph worked with National Educational Television in New York on a two-part series on jazz. When the first session was recorded on August 27 at the celebrated Village Gate nightclub in Greenwich Village, Ralph's partner as a commentator was Martin Williams, the jazz critic who in 1964 had criticized *Shadow and Act* for its disdain of Charlie Parker. The first program, featuring the progressive Dizzy Gillespie Quintet, was "Jazz Goes Intellectual: Bop!" The second, more avant-garde part, "Jazz: The Experimenters," came on September 10, also at the Village Gate. This program featured the Charles Mingus Quintet, the Modern Jazz Quartet, the saxophonist Ornette Coleman, and the pianist Cecil Taylor. Barely tolerating the bebop pioneer Gillespie, Ralph showed his strong disapproval of the avant-garde. While the NET producer and others were ecstatic about his conservative commentary ("You are a superb anchor man and I am grateful"), Williams found it scandalous. He was appalled both by Ralph's evident dislike of bebop music and by the way Ralph's script set up Williams as a cerebral mouthpiece for the decadence that now passed for jazz. (Ralph was perhaps taking revenge for William's review of *Shadow and Act*.) For example, Ralph spoke about "the cult aspects, the empty imitation of the personal styles of Dizzy Gillespie and Charlie Parker, the banality of hip conversation, the snobbery based on knowing more titles than the fellow at the next table in a night club." In the second show he was equally caustic. "Jazz exists today in a climate wherein a certain piety has developed towards the goals of so-called serious music," he declared. "For some Negro musicians it has become a musical route to social respectability, and to wide acceptance among the cult of jazz intellectuals."

In December, in a long letter to Ralph, Williams blasted his constant belittling of the major musicians after 1940. Worse, "I think you did a great deal of it," he wrote, "out of ignorance of the facts and ignorance of the music." Williams challenged him: "I don't believe you know John Coltrane's work." Moreover, Ralph would never have spoken "so strongly on any other subject or other artistic activity from so little knowledge. And that's what surprises me." Ralph did not respond to these charges. To him, jazz seemed no longer to be anchored in dance and song, to lyrical and rhythmic values, but had moved instead toward ever more abstract and abstruse, and obtuse, standards and practices. (Ironically, this criticism was not far from that of some reviewers, black and white, who in 1952 had found *Invisible Man* murky and faddish.)

Ralph could afford to ignore Williams. On American Negro culture, he was authority for many observers. That summer, *Esquire* chose him from among many political leaders, artists, scientists, thinkers, and athletes as one of the one hundred "best people in the world" by "virtue of what they have done or are or both." The publication of Robert Penn Warren's book on the current racial crisis, *Who Speaks for the Negro?,* only added to his reputation. Thirty pages in it offered an excellent statement of Ralph's ideas about race in America. Warren presented Ralph as someone who stressed not revolution but repose, not indignation but wisdom. "The whole effect of his smoothly modeled face," Warren noted, "is one of calmness and control; his gestures have the same control, the same balance and calmness." This calmness came from habitual "self-conquest and hard lessons of sympathy learned through a burgeoning and forgiving imagination"— and yet it did not preclude "the possibility of a sudden nervous striking-out, not entirely mastered." Ellison had a curious habit, "the utterance of a little sound—'ee-ee'—breathed through the teeth, a humorous, ironical recognition of the little traps and blind alleys of the world, and of the self."

The most intense black voices of the age stressed the agony of black life under whites. Blacks must hate whites, without exception. Instead of embracing the gospel of love, forgiveness, and nonviolence preached by Dr. King, blacks must be militant. Ralph challenged these ideas. He warned Warren: "The danger lies in overemphasizing the extent to which Negroes are alienated, and in overstressing the extent to which the racial predicament imposes an agony upon the individual. For the Negro youth this emphasis can become an excuse and a blinder, leading to an avoidance of the individual assertion." Although in 1948 he had asserted the bleakness of much of the black life about him in his essay "Harlem Is

Nowhere," now he stressed—as he had stressed for years—the integrity of black culture. Unlike the hot new radicals, the black masses accepted and loved their "blackness," with its moral and aesthetic values.

Not only was Negro culture moral, its internal value system insisted that it should use mainly humility and self-discipline to defend itself. "There is a great power in humility," Ralph told Warren. "Dostoevsky has made us aware—in fact, Jesus Christ has made us aware. It can be terribly ambiguous and it can contain many, many contradictory forces, and most of all, it can be a form of courage." Too many people were cashing in on the idea of black pain. The psychologist Dr. Kenneth Clark, in stressing the power of racism to destroy blacks, "misses the heroic side of this thing—perhaps he has an investment in negative propaganda as a means of raising funds with which to correct some of the injustices common to Negro slums." Other radicals were even less scrupulous: "Where Negroes are concerned, the *open sesame* to many of the money vaults in this country seems to be a description, replete with graphs, statistics, and footnotes, of Negro life as so depraved, hopeless, and semi-human that the best service that money could perform would be to stuff the mouths of the describers so that the details of horror could stop." A pluralistic view of American culture ("without any racial judgments, negative or positive") was the essence of Ralph's national vision.

To militant blacks, such views made him a traitor. To many whites (and to black moderates), he was integrity itself. "When the smoke of battle begins to clear," Allen Tate wrote to Warren, "he will be there as the authentic culture-hero." Ralph took on Hannah Arendt as someone who misread the signals of black culture. In a *Dissent* article in 1959 about the children asked to integrate Little Rock High School in 1956, she had deplored the parents' willingness to send their children into danger in the name of integration. Those black parents, like so many civil rights activists, had confused the political sphere with the social sphere. Strenuously objecting to Arendt, Ralph pointed out that behind the parents' actions (although some students had volunteered for the task) was neither negligence nor pushiness but a nobility of ideals involving "self-confidence, self-consciousness, self-mastery, insight, and compassion." The parents recognized "the overtones of a rite of initiation" in their children's suffering. They expected a son to "face the terror and contain his fear and anger *precisely* because he is a Negro American." (Arendt conceded privately to Ralph that "you are entirely right: it is precisely this 'ideal of sacrifice' which I didn't understand.")

In September, *The Nation* carried Ralph's superb "Tell It Like It Is, Baby." Part autobiography, part dream, it blends subjects such as his traumatic memory of his father's death, Oklahoma City in his youth, his two years in Rome, the civil rights movement, and American history. Anchoring these elements is Ralph's confession of his failed attempt in Rome to write an essay about anti-black violence at home, and also his revulsion at Southern white senators and congressmen for defying the U.S. Supreme Court over Jim Crow. Appearing in the special centenary issue of the magazine, the piece showed the richness of his imagination even as he was becoming isolated as a spokesman on race.

His prestige received a remarkable and unexpected boost on September 26, when in a special issue the syndicated *New York Herald Tribune* literary magazine *Book Week* published the results of a poll of "two hundred prominent authors, critics and editors" about American fiction from 1945 to 1965. Of the ten thousand works of fiction published in the past two decades, the magazine had asked, which was the most distinguished, the one most likely to endure? *Invisible Man* was the winner. *Lolita* came next, then J. D. Salinger's *The Catcher in the Rye*. Bellow took the next three places, followed by works by Mailer, Warren, Malamud, and Hemingway.

The news of Ralph's triumph went far beyond the regular readers of *Book Week*. Although the fact that the book is the story of a black man and was written by one probably played a major role in the voting, this aspect only underscored Ralph's powers of social prophecy. *Invisible Man* now seemed almost immortal. The following year, 1966, in a tough-minded look at American fiction since the war, Alfred Kazin called *Invisible Man* "in many ways the strongest American novel of the period, the one most genuinely expressive of the unconscious, primitive, and 'religious' feelings to which the literary mind now pines most."

Ralph sought to explore in miniature these primal feelings in "Juneteenth," an excerpt from his big manuscript published at the end of 1965, in the twentieth-anniversary number of *The Quarterly Review of Literature*. Here, Bliss and Hickman engage in a swinging, rhythmic, revivalist conversation, a duet in which Hickman celebrates "slipping off the chains." Hickman ventures to interpret the deeper significance of the Negro's exile from "the loins of Africa," his slavery in the New World, and his emancipation, or "illusion of emancipation." True emancipation will come, Hickman cries, when the scattered bones of the dead slaves and their persecuted descendants, buried in American soil, come alive ("this land is ours because we come out of it, we bled in it, our tears watered it, we fertilized it with our dead") and grow into their almost sacred stature as God's chosen children. From the bodies of dead Africans moldering in American soil arose a new Negro identity: "We were rebirthed from the earth of this land and revivified by the Word. So now we had a new language and a brand new song to put flesh on our bones." Ralph's integrationist but race-proud vision was seldom more exuberantly expressed. Robustly, the story celebrates the history of Negroes prevailing in the face of injustice: "We learned to bounce back and to disregard fools."

After his *Book Week* triumph, Random House quickly signed him to a contract that would bring him $50,000, paid over three years, as an advance on his next novel. This contract made him more cautious than ever in guarding his time and his literary reputation. He declined an invitation to join the Harlem Cultural Council, an organization led by Frederick O'Neal, the black president of the Actors' Equity Association. He resisted overtures from the American Council for African Culture, in which the novelist John Oliver Killens, an old adversary, was prominent. He declined to attend a conference called by the leftist Harlem Writers Guild at the New School for Social Research. Partly as a result, he became its prize scapegoat, attacked by writers such as Killens, John Henrik Clarke, and Herbert Aptheker.

Rejecting such links, he spent more time at Yale, where he was attached to Silliman College as a Rockefeller Foundation fellow in American Studies. Other fellows included Willie Morris and William Styron, as well as the former U.S. ambassador to India Chester Bowles and the eminent black legal scholar A. Leon Higginbotham, Jr. Ralph found Yale congenial. He liked the solidity of its intellectual culture in the humanities, the faux-Gothic elegance of the campus. He spent little or no time in the slums not far away, where New Haven's depressed blacks lived in an altogether different atmosphere. He would probably have jumped at the chance to join the faculty in English. But the department was not ready to hire a black.

On October 21, in Chicago, the poet Gwendolyn Brooks—still a moderate, but moving closer to radical nationalism—introduced him before his lecture on "American Pluralism from the Negroes' Side of the Line." This was the concluding address of the annual conference of the conciliatory National Association of Intergroup Relations Officials. This umbrella organization served the disparate interests of the NAACP, the National

Urban League, the Catholic Interracial Council, the Anti-Defamation League, and the American Jewish Committee. The purpose of inviting Ralph was explicit: to counter the fiery influence of James Baldwin. ("At previous conventions, our membership has been frequently 'Baldwinized,'" an official explained.) Many other groups now wanted to hear Ralph. A few days later, at Philharmonic Hall for the New York Orchestral Society, he discussed the "Future of Arts in New York" with Lillian Hellman, the dancer and choreographer José Limón, the painter Larry Rivers, and the writer and critic Marya Mannes. Two days later, on October 27, at New York University, he appeared with Alfred Kazin and others under the auspices of PEN to talk about "The Writer and the City." He was the subject of one of four programs in the series *USA: The Novel,* produced by National Educational Television. At his apartment he was interviewed for a BBC profile by the American writer Richard Kostelanetz. The editorial board of *The American Scholar,* the magazine of Phi Beta Kappa, elected him a member. He was also elected to the American Academy of Arts and Sciences.

Ralph also accepted, with unusual eagerness, an invitation to join the Carnegie Corporation's ambitious Commission on Educational Television. This fifteen-member group aimed to study television programming in America and to create a detailed report with recommendations for future action. The industry had never lived down Newton Minow's devastating comment in 1961 to the National Association of Broadcasters that if they were to watch a day of television without interruption, "I can assure you that you will observe a vast wasteland." This was an extraordinary opportunity for Ralph. Out of this effort would come what Americans would call public television (following the release of the Carnegie report two years later).

The last few days of 1965 brought to a glamorous end arguably the most successful year of his life. On December 20, the Ellisons joined the Johnsons at the White House for a black-tie dinner of lobster and roast duckling in honor of Ludwig Erhard, chancellor of the Federal Republic of Germany. Two days after Christmas, he was off to Chicago to appear with John Cheever and Norman Mailer before a packed auditorium of professors and graduate students at the annual convention of the Modern Language Association. Now Ralph could almost look down on both authors, although Mailer's fame, or notoriety, had soared with his colorful acts in opposition to the Vietnam War. Appearing first, Cheever read a story that cleverly, perhaps frivolously, satirized the hero of Mailer's *An American Dream.* In response, Mailer read a harshly critical essay, "The Dynamic in

American Letters," in which he took to task both the superficial American novelist of manners, such as Cheever, and the earthier, more democratic, but apolitical sort, such as Ellison. When it was his turn, Ralph was aloof, magisterial, and bland. While Mailer flailed away at political power and Cheever mocked it, he seemed to embody it confidently.

In some respects, 1965 marked the high phase of what Ralph's future friend the short-story writer James Alan McPherson would call with regret his "institutionalization" (astutely, Kenneth Burke had warned about it in 1953). "When you get institutionalized," McPherson said, "you become an extension of the institution and you are constantly called upon to justify yourself in those terms."

On the civil rights barricades, the year 1966 began badly. On January 3 in Tuskegee, Sammy Younge, Jr., a young member of a local family well known to Ralph, was shot dead trying to use a restroom at a Texaco service station. The killer was an ornery, older white man from a village some distance away. A week later, Vernon Dahmer, a leader in black voter registration, died after white vigilantes firebombed his grocery store and home in Mississippi.

Such events disturbed Ralph, but only from a distance. He was now living a different kind of life. On January 18, 1966, he and Fanny, along with Vice President Hubert Humphrey, Senator Jacob Javits, and Mayor John V. Lindsay of New York City, accompanied by their wives, attended a reception at the home of Lucia Chase, the wealthy co-director of the American Ballet Theatre. Then the party went on to the gala opening of the twenty-seventh season of the company, where members of the National Council on the Arts were the guests of honor (not surprisingly, since the council had given it matching grants totaling $350,000, thus saving its season, if not its life). Two years after his election to the National Institute of Arts and Letters he became a vice president. On February 1, when NET broadcast the film *Ralph Ellison on Work-in-Progress* as a part of its *USA: The Novel* series, hundreds of thousands of viewers in six major cities from coast to coast heard him speak on the subject. Later that month, L. Quincy Mumford, the librarian of Congress, invited him to serve a three-year term as honorary consultant in American letters. Accepting, Ralph now held the most prestigious official position in American literature. In that capacity he would select the consultant in poetry, which was then the nearest thing the nation had to a poet laureate. Ralph would serve two consecutive terms.

On the heels of such unusual recognition, Ralph found himself beset by wooers of one kind or another from organizations such as the University of North Carolina, the Center for Advanced Study in the Behavioral Sciences at Stanford, MIT, and the University of Utah. His television consultancy also kept him busy. In March he attended a black-tie dinner given by the Carnegie Commission at the Regency Hotel in Manhattan, then flew to Boston for a three-day meeting attended by Dr. Frank Stanton of CBS, which had given $1 million to the commission.

As for his novel-in-progress, he still asserted that he was close, very close, to finishing. "I am hard at work on the novel," he assured the Rockefeller Foundation, his sponsor at Yale, "and am beginning to see the end in sight." To his brother, Fanny wrote: "Ralph has decided that he really is going to get the book to the publisher and has begun assembling [the] manuscript for me to type." Yet he would not stop traveling. On April 18, for example, in Washington, he delivered a touching address to the National Committee for Support of the Public Schools about his teachers in Oklahoma who had "represented a continuity of that stream of New England education which had as its carriers those young people who went South during the Reconstruction to staff the schools for Negro children." On a higher academic level, at the University of North Carolina he joined C. Vann Woodward in discussing the topic of myth, regional beliefs, and folkways in the South. In Iowa, on April 30, he was the luncheon speaker at the annual meeting of the Midwest Modern Language Association.

By this point, Fanny had retired from her position at Harold Oram. Free now at fifty-five to travel with Ralph, she often did so. While she listed her occupation as "housewife" in filing taxes, she was now also, with his new prominence, his travel agent, bookkeeper, office manager, stenographer, and filing secretary. Whether he always or often recognized her excellent work is not clear. Writing to Rose Styron, Fanny noted with approval an article in a national magazine that mentioned Bill but also praised Rose. "Ever[y] now and then," she noted archly, "a woman is duly credited."

Ralph also took seriously his eminence as a leader in the National Council on the Arts. With $8 million of federal money, the NEH had begun to make grants and awards, set policies and procedures—and spark controversy. When critics mocked the council's standards, Ralph struck back sharply. "The criticism of the Council so far," he told *Newsweek*, "has been mostly cocktail-party criticism, uninformed intellectuals getting off in corners and complaining." The council had standards—"there is pretty high taste on the Council"—and also a sense of purpose. He was absolutely loyal to its chairman, Roger Stevens. "He doesn't make the kind of brilliant speech intellectuals like to hear," Ralph said, "but where it counts he gets the information across." In September, he complained to the *Wall Street Journal* about new criticism of the council.

Such loyalty made him valued in certain powerful circles. Going off the National Council on the Arts on schedule after one year, at the end of 1966 he became a director of the Associated Councils of the Arts, a non-profit private organization funded in part by the Rockefeller Foundation to serve community and state arts councils and commissions. Here, too, his personal link to Roger Stevens was key. Capping his rise in Washington, Ralph was appointed to the board of directors of the projected John F. Kennedy Center for the Performing Arts. Congressional funding for a national cultural center had started under President Eisenhower in 1958. Stevens, chairman of its board since 1961, steered Ralph into this coveted position. Going to the White House was becoming almost a habit. In late September he attended a stag luncheon for the poet-president of Senegal, Léopold Sédar Senghor.

His ideas, and the clarity and dignity with which he expressed them, were deemed important. Appearing before a U.S. Senate subcommittee that included Robert Kennedy, Jacob Javits, and Abraham Ribicoff of Connecticut, he answered with a studied calm their questions about the current crisis in American cities, where violence, crime, and poverty had become identified overwhelmingly with blacks, especially black youth. The contrast was stark between him and Claude Brown, whose autobiography, *Manchild in the Promised Land,* about growing up poor in Harlem and a reform school, had become a sensational best seller. (Ralph had refused to provide a blurb for the book.) While Brown shocked his listeners with talk of having watched his father slit a man's throat when Brown was five years old, and decried Harlem as a kind of war zone, Ellison suavely described it as a place "where the Southern Negro can transform himself into the man of his dreams." Listeners were left to reconcile the two reports. Brown spoke "in the raw language and raw philosophy of the streets," the *Washington Post* wrote, while Ellison made "slow, considered statements." Negroes, he said, "want to transform Harlem, the Harlems of their country. These places are precious to them. These places are where they have dreamed, where they have lived, where they have loved, where they have worked out life as they could. . . . A slum like Harlem isn't just a place of decay. It is a form of historical and social memory."

Annoyed by reports that described his approach as supine, he was pleased when Myron Kolatch's *New Leader* published his and Brown's testimony in full. In some respects, here was Ralph at his finest. Quizzed by senators fearful of cities on fire, he was calm, factual, analytical, probing. Prodded about the Vietnam War, he offered a startling perspective. "As much as I dislike warfare," he told Javits, the status of blacks had always improved with major wars and crises, including the Civil War and the Great Depression. "When there is a breakdown of the structure, democracy spreads." The current urban violence was often overstated, he said. In New York, it did not begin to match the 1943 Harlem riot. The core of the crisis was not fierce blacks but what the city itself had been allowed to become, and also what it could become—not "an instrumentality for making money, but . . . a place for allowing the individual to achieve his highest promise" and "a more gracious sense of human possibility."

If Ralph failed to convince many people, he stood by his views. In October, when he took part in a television program sponsored by the Harvard Center for Research and Development on Educational Differences, his task was to comment on a study of the differences in the reactions of black and white youths in a Boston housing project to questions about their future. Asked to name their heroes, the white boys offered well-known public or historical figures. The black boys tended to name family members, usually male; the black boys also joked more than the whites. Ralph looked for the positive in what others saw as a lack of ambition and seriousness. The choice of male relatives challenged the fixation of certain sociologists on the alleged matrilineal nature of black culture. As for the blacks and joking—yes, "non-seriousness is exactly a mark of their culture," but "there are goals, there are social forms that are Negro. They might be humble, they might not be high style, but they do give structure to Negro ambitions, to a Negro's sense of himself, to a Negro identity." Many "experts" really knew little about black culture. In making policy "it would be a good thing to have a few Negroes sitting around even if they don't say a thing, because they would be reminders of what problems really exist."

Here, Ralph was warming up to attack the highly controversial 1964 report by the sociologist Daniel Patrick Moynihan (then assistant secretary of labor) to the president on the Negro family. Warning of a disintegrating Negro family structure, Moynihan pointed to its growing matrilineal core (caused mainly, he said, by the harsh conditions imposed on black men by a racist society). The previous year, his and Nathan Glazer's

Beyond the Melting Pot had antagonized Ralph with its statement by Glazer that the Negro was "only an American." In saying so, Glazer meant that unlike other ethnic groups, such as the Italians or Poles, American blacks had no direct historical connection to a foreign nation from which their ancestors had come. Ralph considered this beside the point. The report, seen at first as a brilliant intervention, was soon under attack, not always reasonably. Although it criticized racism, its critics read it as mainly an attack on blacks. The older civil rights groups, besieged by Black Power activism, dared not support its premises and conclusions. Ralph, too, did not support them. To the debate he brought his inveterate suspicion of sociology. To him, sociology typically reduces, compresses, and distorts knowledge. Intrinsically it lacked what it claimed to possess, a capacity for deep human understanding. Above all, he loathed references to black culture as isolated and incapable of assimilation into American culture.

In November 1966, Ralph finally made public his opposition to Moynihan's work in the *New York Times Magazine*. "Moynihan looked at a fatherless family," he complained, "and interpreted it not in the context of Negro cultural patterns, but in a white cultural pattern." Within black culture, grandmothers look after kids; mothers work or go on welfare; kids identify with stepfathers, uncles, even the mother's boyfriends. "How children grow up," he said, "is a cultural, not a statistical pattern." This was the defensive "race man" in Ralph speaking, confusing a love of blacks with the social results of the poor conditions imposed on blacks by racism. He brushed aside the idea of the deforming effects on boys, even more than girls, of growing up poor and without fathers. He was perhaps defending his own upbringing after the death of his father. Like the kids in Boston, he fell back on jokes. "The Moynihan Report complained that Negroes don't strut anymore," he said, laughing. "Why, Negro faggots are the struttingest people I know." Too smart and honest to miss the irony of his position, he repeated a joke Al Murray had cracked about him and a lazy black housemaid resentful of Ralph's criticism. One black was not supposed to be hard on another black. "She saw the books and the furniture and the paintings, so she knew you were some kind of white man," Murray explained, but "what she didn't stop to notice was that you're a *Southern* white man."

In October, a trip to Los Angeles for the Carnegie Commission allowed Ralph a chance to visit Oklahoma City (with Fanny) for the first time since 1953. He feared what he might find. Fanny, buying their plane tickets, left possible a quick return "if Okla. City doesn't live up to Ralph's imagination."

Reaching Oklahoma City, they checked into a leading hotel in a city now desegregated, at least in its public areas. In Deep Second, at Jim Randolph's drugstore, a crowd as excited as Ralph welcomed him home. Wyatt Slaughter took them to see Edna Randolph; en route, they passed by the office of Jimmie Stewart, a boyhood friend now a city councilman and a key black leader. That evening, at Stewart's home, a wealth of old friends and teachers welcomed the Ellisons with a party attended also by the white mayor of the city. By two in the morning, when he returned to their hotel, all of his worries had vanished. "Urban renewal" had destroyed much of the old Second Street, but left enough intact to make this visit richly satisfying. At City Hall, the mayor presented him with a certificate declaring him an ambassador-at-large for Oklahoma City. With Fanny, he visited his father's grave. The blankness of the space disturbed Ralph. (The following month, he arranged for a gravestone that read "Lewis Alfred Ellison, March 4, 1877–July 19, 1916. Father of Ralph and Herbert." Oddly, he did not mention his mother. Since her death in Ohio in 1937, he apparently had never visited her grave.)

A month later he was back in Oklahoma to take part in the inauguration and first festival of the state's Arts and Humanities Council. The governor gave gold medals to Ralph, the Native American prima ballerina Maria Tallchief, and the composer Roy Harris, fellow stars from Oklahoma. In the spring, the city asked Ralph for permission to name a housing project after him. Modestly, he recommended that instead they should honor older folk such as the musicians Jimmy Rushing and Charlie Christian or civic pioneers such as J. D. Randolph and the journalist Roscoe Dunjee. "I know that I stand on their shoulders," he explained, "and thus I'd be embarrassed to receive an honor which is more deservedly theirs."

Oklahoma moved and inspired him, but he could never live there again. New York was art and money and power and style, and the Ellisons were now most comfortable near its topmost echelons. They thrilled to be able to join Mary Hemingway at the Broadway premiere of *The Taming of the Shrew,* after which they dined on pheasant and trout in aspic at her home on East 65th Street. Adoring the Ellisons, Mary had "one profound regret," she wrote Fanny (echoing an earlier piece of wishful thinking), which was "that Ralph and Ernest never knew each other. . . . In the old days they might have been in the same room listening to Fats Waller." On November 28, they attended Truman Capote's sensational Black and

White Ball at the Plaza Hotel, in part a coming-out celebration in New York for *Washington Post* publisher Katharine Graham. "People are practically committing suicide," someone confided to *Life,* "because they didn't get an invitation." Ralph and Fanny (suitably masked) joined the almost five hundred other guests representing appropriate levels of glamour. Rose Kennedy was there along with Jackie Kennedy's sister, Lee Radziwill; Mrs. Henry Ford II; the president's daughter Lynda Bird Johnson; Teddy Roosevelt's daughter Alice Roosevelt Longworth; the Maharaja and the Maharani of Jaipur; and Frank Sinatra and his young bride, Mia Farrow. Norman Mailer, Marianne Moore, and Ralph, in addition to the puckish host, were perhaps the best-known writers on hand. Waiters poured Taittinger with the midnight supper. Then the dancing began, with music provided (in keeping with the theme) by the all-white, ultra-fashionable Peter Duchin Orchestra and the all-black, super-hip, if also outré Soul Brothers ensemble. Finally, at four in the morning, to the strains of "Good Night, Ladies," the last of the guests stole away.

As invitations poured into 730 Riverside Drive and select acceptances went out, Ralph's novel suffered more than ever. He kept that fact to himself. "Yes, I think I am near the end of my new novel," he assured Secker & Warburg, the London publishers of *Shadow and Act,* "but it is yet too soon to know just when I'll reach completion."

Nineteen sixty-six ended with two tragic events. In Tuskegee, a friend found Morteza Drexel Sprague sitting in an armchair at home, dressed for work but dead of a heart attack. And on New Year's Eve in Oakland, California, after Virgil Branam's wife had taken their fifteen-year-old son to a party, a boy playing with him in a back room pulled the trigger of a gun he thought was empty and blew a hole in young Branam's head. Horrified, Ralph and Fanny saw this tragedy as a token of both the fickleness of fate and the unspeakable violence of the age.

In contrast, their life was now at its splendid apogee. Ralph, who had not regarded himself as having a talent for public service, now thought otherwise. With his work on the Carnegie Commission on Educational Television and the National Council on the Arts, and his multiple visits to the White House, he reevaluated his powers. Early in 1967 President Johnson appointed him to yet another prime position, on the American Revolution Bicentennial Commission. Here he slipped smoothly into a different circle of the powerful, including General Lauris Norstad, once supreme Allied commander in Europe and now the president of Owens-

Corning Fiberglass Corporation; Whitney North Seymour, the former president of the American Bar Association; and Charles Thornton, the head of Litton Industries. On January 27, he was in the inner circle when the Carnegie Commission released its long-awaited report. It ended on a historic note by arguing that "a well-financed and well-directed educational television system, substantially larger and far more pervasive and effective than that which now exists in the United States, must be brought into being." Using for the first time the term "public television" (rather than the deadly "educational television"), it asked Congress to establish "a federally chartered, nonprofit, nongovernmental corporation, to be known as the 'Corporation for Public Television.' " Later that year, Lyndon Johnson signed the Public Broadcasting Act of 1967.

Ralph then became one of the five trustees, including Newton Minow, of the National Citizens' Committee for Public Television. One prime position led to another. Carlisle H. Humelsine, the chairman of the American Revolution Bicentennial Commission, on which Ralph served, was also president of Colonial Williamsburg, the eighteenth-century American village restored and reconstructed through the foresight and largesse of John D. Rockefeller, Jr., starting in the 1920s. Ralph joined its board of directors. Here, Ralph was once again the token Negro. He seemed proud of that fact. He saw himself as eminently qualified for these positions, as indeed he was, but he also believed that very few other blacks were. He was gatekeeper to both blacks and whites. When John Hammond, the famed musical scout and executive, asked Ralph to help him get into the Century, Ralph could only marvel at the wonders that time had wrought in America. Hammond had been born into wealth and privilege.

One mark of success in Manhattan, as elsewhere, now seemed appropriate and within their means. "We've begun to think desperately of a place in the country near New York," Fanny wrote to Ralph's family in Oklahoma. The house was mostly her idea, she admitted. She made it clear that she and Ralph would never totally abandon the city, which "never loses its possibilities." Richard and Charlotte Wilbur had their own summer place, a fairly modest one at that time, in Cummington, Massachusetts, in the Berkshires. Through the Wilburs, Ralph and Fanny reached a local real estate agent.

A quick visit by Fanny to sparsely populated Plainfield, near Cummington, confirmed that this was indeed the place. Ralph drove up with her to look for himself. The price, $34,000, seemed a bit of a stretch to the Ellisons, who had never owned a house. Finally they decided to take the plunge. In March, accompanied by Tucka, they drove to Plainfield for the closing. Paying $15,000 in cash, they assumed a mortgage of $19,000. The estate consisted of a house and some outbuildings, along with three adjoining tracts of land totaling about ninety-seven acres on Lincoln Hill Road. The house was "246 years old," Fanny wrote to a friend, but also had been renovated many times in its long history. On this trip, a thick coverlet of lovely snow draped almost everything in sight.

His public obligations growing, Ralph became even more guarded than ever with other writers looking for help. He wrote a blurb for the young novelist Cormac McCarthy, but McCarthy was a fellow Random House writer admired by Red Warren and Albert Erskine—and, indeed, by Ralph himself. It was noticed when he stayed away from a reception for the Guyanese novelist E. R. Braithwaite, whose *To Sir, with Love,* about a black schoolteacher in England, would become a popular movie starring Sidney Poitier. Asked to endorse Ishmael Reed's novel *The Free-Lance Pallbearers,* he did not reply. Ralph did allow his work to appear in the anthology *The Best Short Stories by Negro Writers,* edited by Langston Hughes. (Not long afterward, following a fairly routine operation, Hughes died unexpectedly at sixty-five in a midtown hospital. On May 25, the Ellisons attended his funeral in Harlem.) When the avant-garde poet N. H. Pritchard, after chatting amiably with Ralph at a party, sent him some poems and asked for help in applying for a fellowship, Ralph's somewhat frigid response—that Pritchard should send nothing "until you've heard from me what my circumstances are since I am heavily committed"— baffled and wounded Pritchard. Ralph was doubtless sincere when, in declining to contribute to a book of essays on blacks in America, he pleaded that "I write slowly and it would not be practical for me to accept additional writing assignments." But to others involved in the project, he seemed to regard himself as exclusive.

Given a chance to explain and defend himself, he did so quite well. A major opportunity came in March 1967 in *Harper's,* when the magazine published "A Very Stern Discipline: An Interview with Ralph Ellison." This piece was a buffed version of the text of an interview conducted over three sittings in 1965 with Lennox Raphael, Steve Cannon, and James Thompson, who were key members of a black literary workshop on the Lower East Side attached to *Umbra* magazine (a journal founded by Thomas C. Dent). The fact that Ralph agreed to the interview indicates that he remained willing to exchange ideas with brighter representatives of the new generation, especially if the young black lions came to his den. In fact, many of the *Umbra* group admired *Invisible Man* and *Shadow and Act*. Their main difficulty was in reconciling Ralph's ideas to the real changes overtaking black America. (The title of the interview reflected his core belief that Negro life, at its best, required vigilance in order to maintain black humanity in the face of dangers and temptations.) Even with younger blacks who admired him, Ralph was often wary, even tense. "Ellison greeted us courteously," Dent noted, "but seemed extremely reserved." He "looked like any professor or lawyer, only, in his polo shirt, more relaxed" and "surprisingly youthful." He answered questions "with short, well-formed statements; everything he said had the ring of knowledge, of scholarship."

Here Ralph ranged with nervy brilliance in response to questions about white and black writers, the Harlem Renaissance, Lyndon Johnson, civil rights, the Vietnam War, radicalism and the function of literature, and Black Power. *Harper's* was a bully pulpit. Bravely he attacked what he saw as the new compulsion among black leaders and writers to denounce whites without debating the ideas involved in race-rooted tensions. In particular he objected to one unnamed writer (almost certainly Amiri Baraka) "who rants and raves" against society but in fact "challenges nothing" and lives by "countering lies with lies." After all, Jewish writers had learned much from Gentile artists such as Pound even as Jews rejected most of his political ideas. Too often, blacks were "in such haste to express our anger and our pain as to allow the single tree of race to obscure our view of the magic forest of art." He found fault with black hate-mongers and also "some of our Jewish critics" (Irving Howe, probably) who want black writers to emphasize suffering rather than life's pleasures: "That's where assumptions of white superiority, conscious or unconscious, make for blindness and naiveté." Blacks needed "a corps of artists and intellectuals who would evaluate Negro American experience from the inside, and out of a broad knowledge of how people of other cultures live, deal with experience, and give significance to their lives."

Praising the interview, many whites now saw Ralph, as one man put it, "in the unique position of being perhaps the only Negro intellectual who is party-free." White Southerners such as Walker Percy, Allen Tate, James Dickey, Harper Lee, and Reynolds Price (each of whom wrote a letter about the piece) made sure to thank him. If any black writer sent a similar letter, he did not save it. The lack of a response pushed him toward sympathetic whites such as the Mississippi-born Willie Morris, who recently had become the editor of *Harper's.* Meeting at a cocktail party given by the *Paris Review* at an Upper East Side art gallery, Morris at once saw in Ralph "his distinctive *Southernness.*" Morris had come a long way from his racist roots. Later that year, in his memoir, *North Toward Home,* he would recall beating up a three-year-old black child when he himself was twelve. A regenerate Confederate in New York, Morris lived near 730 Riverside Drive and dined there sometimes or with Ralph and Fanny at the Red Rooster restaurant in Harlem.

For two or three years, Morris, Ralph, Murray, and their wives rang in the new year with a down-home dinner of pigs' feet, hog maws, and chitterlings. With pleasure Morris would recall the shared ease in telling stories, "the congenial social manner, the mischievous laughter, the fondness of especially *detail* and the suspicion of the more grandiose generalizations about human existence, the distrust of European Intellectualism." Ralph brimmed with laughter "and ironic funny stories, and there was a twinkle in his eye at such moments, and a good feeling for all things in their passing. I thought him a very great man." Nevertheless, "I always sensed in his core an ultimate self-protective distance breached by only the very few."

If white Southerners liked "A Very Stern Discipline," it offended the main critic of *Shadow and Act,* Norman Podhoretz. He denounced as "a calumnious falsehood" a remark by Ralph that "some of the *Commentary* writers" were among the "new apologists for segregation." Podhoretz demanded an apology. Flatly refusing to provide one, Ralph instead prepared a fourteen-page typewritten rebuttal, "I Do Not Apologize," that quoted from essays damaging to blacks by Podhoretz and by Nathan Glazer. Soon he also attacked Daniel Patrick Moynihan's essay "The President and the Negro" (published in *Commentary*) and, again, the Moynihan Report on the decline of the Negro family. The *Harper's* interview fed the distrust of Ralph among some blacks. In *Liberator* magazine the South African–born poet Keorapetse Kgositsile charged that "at times Ellison seems unable to distinguish the America of his imaginative projection and pressing hopes from the America we know. . . . Ellison might very well be the 'original' displaced man." The essay sported a devilish title: "Ralph Ellison: Shadow or Act?"

Getting Ralph out of Manhattan and into their new country retreat proved no easy task for Fanny. He felt the allure of the city, the Century, the Academy, board meetings, and lordly lectures. "I sense a deep hesitancy in Ralph," Fanny wrote to Mary Hemingway. "It's as if we were going to the Samoa Islands."

Finally, on June 13, they reached Plainfield. With the ivory cover of winter long gone, their hundred acres gleamed in the sun. The main dwelling offered two upstairs bedrooms, two baths, a living room, and a separate dining room. The living and dining rooms each had their own fireplace. Near the house stood a two-room structure that Ralph decided to use as his study, as well as an enclosed tool shed. Preferring a more modern look—glass, stainless steel, and leather—he took a few days to adjust to living in the old house. Not so Fanny. "Oh, how beautiful it is," she wrote to a friend, "—wild flowers, birds and acres & acres of woods we've not even had time to explore." Arriving too late for planting, they still could prune, weed, and clear brush. To reach their cool ponds, now spilling over thanks to spring rains, they had to hack out paths. This kind of work excited Ralph. He soon paid $1,250 for a new tractor, as Fanny reported, and "mowed acres and acres of ground with the enthusiasm of a boy on his first bike." In July, helped by a local workman, he replaced the roof on his studio.

The local folk were friendly. Founded in 1785, Plainfield supported one place of worship, the Plainfield Congregational Church, whose minister stopped by to welcome the newcomers. The Wilburs shared with them their local circle of friends, including Calvin H. Plimpton, the president of nearby Amherst College, where Richard had been an undergraduate, and Plimpton's wife. The Ellisons and the Wilburs now became closer than ever. "Dick and Charlee are great people," Fanny wrote, "vibrant, energetic, goodlooking, forthright and gifted. . . . They are responsible for our having bought up here, and we *are* grateful." Looking back, Charlotte was struck by how quickly the couples had clicked: "There was a mutual attraction, mutual liking, mutual liveliness. Everyone liked to talk, drink, stay up late, and be in each other's company." "He and I had such clear similarities," Dick Wilbur recalled, "in the way we had pulled ourselves together. We had both bummed around on freight trains and we both had the kind of feeling for America that you get from seeing it from a hobo's point of view. I liked Count Basie and could sing any James Rushing song or whistle any solo, and Ralph could do the same. As we gelled, we decided that we belonged together in the world of modern art and writing. But it was much more a coming together of people who found each other good company."

Over the Fourth of July holiday, their first visitors from New York arrived—Al and Mozelle Murray. This ability to host city friends at their Berkshires estate added to the Ellisons' happiness at having taken this bold step. Only Ralph's recalcitrant novel disturbed their bliss. "I regret to say, Ralph has gotten very little writing done," Fanny wrote. "The distractions are irresistible." The distractions in the Berkshires were surely preferable to what was happening elsewhere in the summer of 1967. While Ralph rode his tractor or eased his car down sleepy arterial roads looking for bargains on antiques, the civil rights movement, suborned to some extent by the overexuberance of Black Power, was enduring another fierce summer. In June, SNCC boycotted a White House conference on civil rights. CORE, too, disparaged President Johnson and his goals. The NAACP seemed to be growing feeble. While the CORE leader Roy Innis backed Black Power, the aging Roy Wilkins, the head of the NAACP, denounced it at the annual convention that summer as "the father of hatred and the mother of violence." Black Power would lead to black death, he said: "It is a reverse Mississippi, a reverse Hitler, a reverse Ku Klux Klan." The same month, James Meredith, who had dared to try to integrate the University of Mississippi, was shot during a civil rights march. In July in Chicago, a force of some four thousand National Guardsmen ended nights of looting, arson, and assaults. When Cleveland exploded, Guardsmen again had to quell the violence. Insurrections also occurred in Waukegan, Illinois; Lansing and Benton Harbor, Michigan; Omaha; Dayton; and Atlanta.

With Fanny determined not to return too soon to New York, Ralph nevertheless slipped away in the early fall for college lectures made more lucrative by the summer violence. The higher honoraria did not seduce him into compromises. On September 7, while a young, mostly female audience at Douglass College in New Jersey sat expecting at least a few comments on Black Power, he resolutely lectured about literature. A week later, at the University of Illinois, he spoke yet again on "The Function of the Novel in American Democracy." His visit was front-page news for the student newspaper, but other items diminished it. One was the threat of mob violence against the Black Power zealot H. Rap Brown, who was in jail in Virginia on charges of inciting riot and arson in Cambridge, Maryland. Another news item reported that "a group described as black power advocates" in New York had trapped a top school official in his office as part of a bitter teachers' strike. After a struggle, the newspaper reported, the police "seized six men and five women. All were Negroes."

Olympian in his style, Ralph sometimes found himself in almost bizarre situations, as when certain old white men seemed more indignant about racism than he was. On October 6, when the University of Michigan in Ann Arbor conferred an honorary degree on him, he shared the stage with the former secretary of state Dean Acheson, the pioneering heart surgeon Michael DeBakey, and the Swedish sociologist Gunnar Myrdal, whose *An American Dilemma* had so vexed him in the 1940s. In Myrdal's presence, Ralph warned against accepting too readily the findings of sociologists. "In treating people as abstractions rather than individuals," he said, "sociology has ignored the complexity of human life." Worse, "sociologists have created young Negroes who believe the sociological definitions of themselves." He cited the perhaps apocryphal words of a thirteen-year-old black boy, after a riot in New Jersey, to the effect that "women dominate our families and I'm culturally deprived." Myrdal struck back. Yes, he said sternly, sociology had its limitations. Nevertheless, social evil was a reality, and "we must have radical reforms and rational information to cement them to."

Meanwhile, the Michigan campus was alive with antiwar student agitation urged on by other visiting professors in town for a teach-in called "America in Crisis." The popular radical academic Staughton Lynd, formerly of Yale University, warned that Vietnam was no isolated event. American society "is racist, imperialist and proto-fascist, and will go on producing wars until you or I stop it." The black leader Rev. Albert Cleague of Detroit pointed out indignantly that about one quarter of the American soldiers killed in Vietnam were black. "It would be better," he argued, "if they were to fight and die" on American city streets, because "the black man has no stake in the white man's Vietnam War. The Vietnamese are our friends since all non-whites have the same enemy." Ralph would have none of this talk. He paid for this aloofness. In an essay in *Newsday* (the influential Long Island daily newspaper), a journalist reported from Ann Arbor that "this past week I have heard angry young Negroes here call Ellison 'an uncle Tom' and 'a house nigger' and, in rare moments of comparative civility, 'a man 10 years behind the times.'"

Such responses wounded Ralph. Nevertheless, he neither endorsed Black Power nor openly opposed the war. Loyal to Johnson, he joined the Citizens Committee for Peace with Freedom in Vietnam. Heading this elite pro-war group were Paul Douglas, the former U.S. senator from Illinois, who had asked Ralph to join, and Omar Bradley, the much decorated World War II general and former chairman of the Joint Chiefs of

Staff. Harry Truman and Dwight Eisenhower were also members. Ralph was pleased to be in such fine company, but his expressions of fealty sometimes went too far. Earlier that year, thanking Johnson for a signed photograph and a brief audience, Ralph probably showed in his baroque syntax a superfluity of gratitude. "But for the opportunity which you granted me," Ralph wrote, "I would still be unaware of certain capacities for constructive action which I was thereby to discover." Johnson's attention to him was "almost unbelievable. But then, perhaps, a broad capacity for making the unbelievable a reality is a mark of your personal style, and the nation is fortunate that this is so."

"There was a profoundly conservative streak in Ralph," Bill Styron believed. "He simply wasn't going to go along with the peaceniks and with antiwar slogans. Instead, he fell into a trap and turned into a hawk." Nevertheless, Styron quickly pointed out, "among intellectuals it was perversely brave to be for the war. It was both an act of heresy and a mark of extreme independence."

At Plainfield, struggles with his manuscript were affecting him. According to Fanny, she "could hear Ralph up at 5 or 6 in the next room, talking to his characters. I think he may have talked to them all day long." Such colloquies were not unusual as he worked on his fiction, but they were now more frequent. Perhaps it meant real progress, Fanny thought. "He is writing intensely," she informed Rose Styron at one point. "The phone seldom rings and about the only person we see each day is the mailman at a distance." Perhaps she was bluffing a little.

In October he quit his typewriter to return to the road. He did so disastrously. His main stop was Grinnell College, in Iowa, where he took part in a panel discussion titled "Urban Culture and the Negro" as one of several celebrities who received honorary degrees, spoke publicly, and also met with students. Among the group, in addition to Ralph, were Willie Morris, Martin Luther King, Jr., Fred Friendly (the president of CBS), the artist Robert Rauschenberg, the philosopher Marshall McLuhan, and the semanticist and later U.S. senator S. I. Hayakawa. "The students were aggressive in wishing to expose all the hypocrisies of the day," Morris remembered about the panel and its reception. "They were especially hard on Ralph Ellison."

Worse was to come. The next day, at a party crowded with students conversing earnestly with some of the visitors, including Ralph, a motorcycle roared up suddenly outside. Moments later, Morris wrote, "in came a big, rousing figure, a young black man in his mid-twenties in a black leather jacket and a black beret." This fellow, either a genuine or wannabe militant, had just arrived from Chicago. Cornering Ralph, he and another black youngster got into "a vehement argument" with him about *Invisible Man.* Suddenly the black-jacketed man turned on Ralph. "You're an Uncle Tom, man," he shouted. "You're a sell-out. You're a disgrace to your race." Conversations stopped in mid-sentence as everyone turned to watch Ralph. "The whole set of his features was transmuted, the muscles of his body tensed," Morris wrote. "I resent being called an Uncle Tom," Ralph responded, visibly controlling his emotions. "You don't know what you're talking about. . . . What do you know about my life? It's easy for you. You're just a straw in the wind. Get on your motorcycle and go back to Chicago and throw some Molotov cocktails. That's all you'll ever know about."

A black student leader, Henry Wingate (later a federal judge), broke up the confrontation. Ralph's accusers roared off. As Morris (and, separately, Wingate) recalled, Ralph then lost control. Putting his head on Wingate's shoulder, he broke down in tears. "I'm not a Tom, I'm not a Tom," he sobbed. Later, he sat outside the building under the soft stars. "I'm sorry about that," Morris said to him. "Why be sorry?" Ralph replied. "I've heard that kind of thing for a long time. I'm used to it."

Chastened, he headed back to Plainfield. The benefits to body and soul of owning a country retreat were never clearer to the Ellisons. On November 15 they drove to nearby Pittsfield to try to resolve a small but nagging problem about their house. Months before, on May 28, they had written to their insurance company, Allstate, asking for an increase in the coverage on the premises from $30,000 to $50,000. Curiously, no one had replied. Now, in Pittsfield, they heard that an official in the regional office claimed that he had written to them explaining that because their house was not worth $50,000 (after all, they had just paid far less for it), Allstate would not increase their coverage. The next day, November 16, Fanny wrote to their lawyer, Alfred Rice (he was also Mary Hemingway's lawyer), in Manhattan. "What is your advice?" Fanny asked. They lived in a remote area, she informed him, and "if the house ever caught fire it could hardly be saved unless the volunteer fire department of Plainfield has facilities for transporting adequate water." Would he investigate the matter for them? "Meanwhile," she joked, "may we not go up in smoke."

Rice then discovered that Allstate was unaware that the property in Plainfield was occupied only seasonally, which actually disqualified Ralph and Fanny from holding a homeowner's policy on it. On November 27, over the telephone, he ordered Allstate to convert that policy to one that covered fire damage. The next day, Allstate informed the Ellisons in a letter that "your new Fire Policy has been issued November 27, 1967, the date your attorney instructed us to convert your Homeowners Policy to a Fire Policy."

November 29 was a sunny day. Two local men were on the grounds, hanging new doors on the toolshed. At about 1:30 p.m., Ralph and Fanny drove off to run some errands in the nearby town of Adams. At two o'clock, the men finished the job, packed up their tools, and drove away.

At about 2:45 p.m., Ralph and Fanny returned to Plainfield. Approaching their house on Lincoln Hill Road, they saw what looked like steam rising from the roof, black smoke billowing from the chimney. Dense smoke filled the rooms downstairs. Pushing open the front door, Ralph ran into the kitchen for a fire extinguisher. When he approached the door leading to the living room, he saw flames glowing underneath it. The fire extinguisher was useless. Freeing Tucka, he drove frantically to the nearest house, which was about a half mile away. He found no one at home. He then raced about two miles to the Plainfield post office, where the postmistress called out the all-volunteer Cummington Fire Department.

While the brigade was assembling, Ralph rushed back to the house. He found it now engulfed in flames. When the firemen finally arrived a half hour later, they were too late. Except for a washing machine dragged away from the fire, everything was gone.

Appalled and distraught, Ralph and Fanny lingered in a daze at the smoldering site of their catastrophe. Dusk fell and the stars began to come out. Without a hotel or guesthouse nearby, they were at a loss what to do next. Finally they telephoned friends in Worthington, some miles away, and asked to spend the night. As darkness covered the chilly Berkshires, Ralph and Fanny, with Tucka, drove slowly away from Plainfield and the smoldering ruins of their summer home.

17

A "Lone-Star" Negro

1968–1970

Why scapegoat me? Like the little boy who soiled his britches and said his brother did it.

RALPH ELLISON (c. 1968)

A year after the fire in Plainfield, Fanny recalled sadly how she and Ralph had been "very much traumatized over our loss." Watching the old house burn down, she told another person, "is a nightmare image we will long, long see." The Wilburs tried to console her but found it hard to do so. "Fanny reacted to the fire as if she had lost a child," Charlee said. "Friends had given them nice things for the house—an early American handmade quilt, for example. She had lost everything." The fire marshal ruled that faulty electrical wiring had caused the fire, but almost thirty years later, deeply depressed after Ralph's death, Fanny would scrawl: "R. knew, I'm sure, that it was arson but he made no complaint to the town." She believed (at least when she wrote the note) that some local person or persons had deliberately burned them out. Whatever its cause, the fire loomed as a cruel symbol. For Ralph, owning a home in New England placed him in what once had been the center of American artistic and moral glory, to Emerson and Melville and abolitionism. Now a mysterious fire had turned his New England dream into sorrow and a sense of rejection.

Six years would pass before the Ellisons returned to live in Plainfield. Now and then they drove out to inspect the ruins but those melancholy hours sapped the urge to rebuild. On the first Sunday following the fire, the church program extended to them the "deep sympathy of the entire Plainfield community" and expressed the hope that by spring they would "again be a part of the community." Several individuals wrote them letters. The most moving gesture occurred early in 1968 when "your Plain-field friends and neighbors," after passing the hat, sent the Ellisons a check for $205 "to get something for your new home." Fanny responded graciously if perhaps ambiguously, too: "We had no idea how much we were welcome until the fire."

Allstate wasn't as friendly. It settled only the following May, after frustrating delays. But the Ellisons made money from the fire. The settlement paid off their mortgage, refunded them their investment of $15,000, and left them the land and the outbuildings. True, Allstate could not restore Ralph's work on his second novel—but how much of it had he lost? About five weeks after the fire, he wrote about a modest setback: "I lost part of my manuscript—the revisions over which I had labored [in] the summer and valuable notebooks. But since returning to N.Y. I've been hard at work and am gradually reconstructing." During the summer he had done little work on the book. He hadn't lost anything written before he reached Plainfield, except for certain notebooks. Writing to Nathan Scott just after the fire, Ralph assured him that he "fortunately had a full copy of all that he had done prior to that summer." In March, less than four months after the blaze, Fanny promised that Ralph would deliver the manuscript "early next year." By October, the story was changing. To a reporter in Charlotte, North Carolina, Ralph mourned the loss of 365 pages, a neatly symbolic figure to which he would cling for many years. Fire or no fire, he knew that the book was in trouble in 1968 when he told Richard Kostela-netz that it "has become inordinately long—perhaps over one thousand pages—and complicated." In any event, finishing had become a painful topic. "He has become so embarrassed about his inability to finish the book," according to Kostelanetz, "that he gets visibly upset whenever acquaintances ask about it."

Ralph's discomfort became so intense, so suppurating, that both he and Fanny soon fell back reflexively on the fire when asked about the delay. In 1979, she told an inquiring stranger that "the fire all but trauma-tized us; Ralph lost the manuscript of a new novel that he would have handed the publisher that September. No words can explain such a loss." Elsewhere she spoke about having to be restrained by firemen from rush-ing into the burning house to rescue the manuscript, which she could see clearly, so very clearly, through a window as the flames closed in.

Back in New York, devastated, Ralph plunged deeper into other work. In December, he gamely attended a trustees' meeting of the National Citizens' Committee for Public Television, the successor to the Carnegie Commission on Public Broadcasting. Murmuring their condolences to him were some powerful American men: Thomas Hoving, the director of the Metropolitan Museum of Art; Ralph Lowell, a trustee of almost every important civic and cultural institution in Boston; Devereux C. Josephs, the president of the Carnegie Corporation and a major figure in several global corporations; and Newton Minow of the Federal Communications Commission. Asked about the fire, Ralph offered a stoical expression. Asked about his novel, he smoothly changed the subject. Urbane, ironic, intelligent, weathered, he spoke even without speaking. A living, breathing artist set down among philanthropists, businessmen, and administrators, he both embodied black masculinity and challenged the gestures of black activists.

Glad to be prominent (as in becoming a trustee of Channel 13, the main public broadcasting station in New York), he also wanted to reflect his sincere lack of interest in power. So he tried to make clear at the official residence of Arthur Goldberg, the U.S. ambassador to the United Nations, when he joined William Styron, Marianne Moore, John Ciardi, and Robert Penn Warren, among others, to discuss the relationship between art and politics (with bloody Vietnam on everyone's mind). Here he gladly endorsed Plato. "When poets try to be legislators," Ralph warned, "then we are in trouble." And yet he also wanted to improve his standing with the Johnson administration. Early in 1968, with Johnson's reputation besmirched by Vietnam, Ralph agreed to write an essay on him for a book containing tributary essays by some of his major political appointees, to be edited by the political scientist James MacGregor Burns. A part of Johnson's reelection strategy (although Burns and the essayists pretended otherwise), it was scheduled to come out just before the Democratic National Convention that summer.

Proud to be included, Ralph supported Johnson even as his policies in Vietnam made many artists and intellectuals hate him. On March 6, at the National Book Awards ceremony at Lincoln Center, Ralph was incensed when the poet Robert Bly delivered a searing attack on the president. He stayed loyal to his most powerful patron even as the rebellious Mailer's long antiwar piece "Steps of the Pentagon" filled almost an entire number of *Harper's*. "I don't see us withdrawing from the war," he said to Richard Kostelanetz in an interview. "We have certain responsibilities to the Vietnamese and the structure of power in the world. It's too bad, but that's the way it is." Thus he was shaken when Johnson, after a weak showing in a primary in New England, announced on March 31 that he would not seek reelection. The Ellisons wrote at once to the White House to express their "shock and regret" about the news. "We admire the President," they declared, "for his courage and the guidance he has given our Nation."

With Johnson leaving, Ralph consolidated his place among the powerful. On the board of the Associated Councils of the Arts he became friends with philanthropists such as the North Carolina garment tycoon R. Philip Hanes, Jr. The Authors Guild reappointed him for a three-year term on its top council. He was made a trustee of the body officially charged with advising the developers of the proposed experimental school, Hampshire College, in the Amherst Valley of Massachusetts. Joining the former U.S. attorney general Ramsey Clark and Rodman C. Rockefeller, among others, he became a trustee of the New School for Social Research, an institution he had admired since his first year in Manhattan. He attended meetings of the Hudson Institute for Policy Research in the Public Interest in Croton-on-Hudson, New York. "Ralph had a deep-seated need to be a member of the establishment," William Styron believed. "He was trapped in needing to belong, to perhaps compensate for something." Because he often seemed confident and self-possessed, affable and modest, few knew what that "something" could be.

Ralph did not shut out black institutions but found them dowdy in comparison. In February, attending a conference in Washington sponsored by the venerable Association for the Study of Negro Life and History, he offered only lukewarm support to an initiative in Congress, led by Representative James H. Scheuer of New York, to found a federally supported Commission on Negro History and Culture. (The bill failed.) He lent his name, but little else, to a call to rescue the neglected Schomburg Collection of African-American materials at the New York Public Library in Harlem. He was more comfortable with prosperous folk, as when the Century, where he had become one of the more dependable members, appointed him to its committee on literature. This was a minor position, but one he accepted with "a deep sense of pride."

As the year 1968 spread a plague of destruction, each terrible event meant, perversely, more prestige and more money for Ralph. "Things are flying!" his lecture agent happily informed him. Or, as one jaded university official put it, "many might cringe at another program on the Negro," but such programs had to be endured. A more earnest or hypocritical official spoke of the need for "speakers to better inform us of the revolution." Ralph maintained his bedrock values. While many students looked for fire, he offered his tried trio of topics: American diversity, the American novel, and the Negro and American literature. When the African-American Society of Dartmouth College sponsored a "Black Arts Festival" in keeping with a "Black Power Focus," he asked to be excused. He shied away from "Black America Week" at the University of Maine and would not support a plan to honor the memory of W. E. B. Du Bois on the centenary of his birth in Great Barrington, Massachusetts, in 1868.

Meanwhile, he jacked up his lecture fees so sharply (to a minimum of $1,500, plus expenses) that his alarmed agent hoped that "Mr. Ellison does not over-price himself." There seemed to be no such danger, not with Armageddon at hand. The official National Advisory Commission on Civil Disorders—the so-called Kerner Commission—warned grimly that "our nation is moving towards two societies, one black, one white—separate and unequal." In Orangeburg, South Carolina, when local black college students marched in protest against a Jim Crow bowling alley, three of them were killed and forty or more wounded. On March 28, national attention turned to Memphis, Tennessee, where Dr. King had gone in order to lend his personal support to a strike by the city's garbage collectors, almost all of them black. Again the result was violence and looting, severe injuries, hundreds of arrests, and deaths.

On April 4, at a black-owned motel in Memphis, a white gunman assassinated Dr. King. His death touched off riots in over 120 cities, with more than sixty thousand federal troops called out to stop them. About fifty people died, thousands were injured, and almost $50 million in property was lost. Ralph was at the University of Notre Dame in Indiana when news of the assassination broke. A state of shock and mourning froze the campus as grim stories spread about cities burning across America. He was one of a constellation of stars, including Norman Mailer, Joseph Heller, Kurt Vonnegut, Granville Hicks, Wright Morris, and William F. Buckley, Jr., there to take part in the annual Sophomore Literary Festival. On this conservative, Roman Catholic campus, the organizers gave Ralph the prime speaking spot, 8 p.m. on April 6, the last full day of the festival.

As Ralph rose to speak, the audience stood up and applauded wildly. Whatever it expected of him, he did not talk about King's death. Instead, speaking calculatedly on "The Function of the Novel in American Democracy," he left his listeners to link the past to the present. With dignity he answered some questions before leaving the stage to another standing ovation. In a disintegrating America he seemed to his admirers the picture of morality and order. His response to King's murder would remain muted. His admiration for the minister had been mixed, and especially so after King criticized Johnson's Vietnam policies. He did not disparage King in public. At a meeting of the advisory committee of the National Book Award, he approved of two new prizes in his name. On November 1, at a memorial service at the Museum of Modern Art in Manhattan, he joined in the tributes to the slain leader.

With Johnson's withdrawal, Ralph backed the candidacy of Vice President Hubert Humphrey. In doing so, he rejected the passionate Robert F. Kennedy, who enjoyed strong support among blacks, and also the more cerebral Eugene McCarthy, the main choice of artists and intellectuals. He crossed old friends such as Bellow, Kazin, Styron, Murray Kempton, C. Vann Woodward, Edward Albee, Arthur Miller, Elizabeth Hardwick, and Dwight Macdonald. Ralph became a founding member of Citizens for Humphrey, as well as co-chairman (with Sol Hurok and Isaac Stern) of the Committee on Arts and Letters for Humphrey. After Kennedy's murder in June, Humphrey announced a "Task Force on Arts and Letters"; Ellison joined the pianist Eugene Istomin and the architect Philip C. Johnson as co-chairs of this electioneering ploy. But Ralph made it clear that Humphrey had to keep blacks in mind after he had their votes. "I take it that the Humphrey Administration," he insisted, "will recognize the demands of the Negro minority, not only because of their moral justification, but because of the faith in the reality of the American promise which their demands embody." (The report of his "task force" mentioned blacks only once.)

By this time his essay in defense of Johnson, "The Myth of the Flawed Southerner," was out, published in Burns's collection *To Heal and to Build: The Programs of Lyndon B. Johnson.* Early in May, Douglas Cater of the White House staff wrote to say how that piece had "greatly pleased" Johnson. Ralph identified Johnson's pronounced Southern character as at the root of both his greatness and his unpopularity in the North; but Ralph believed, as he had for some time, in the redemptive power of white Southern leadership. In Washington, at a convention of book publishers, he was pleased to join Lady Bird Johnson when she stood in for her husband to sign copies of the book. A few weeks later, at a state dinner in the same city, he was seated with Mrs. Johnson and the Shah of Iran. That was to be his last taste of preferment with Lyndon Johnson or the White House, but when Ralph reflected on sitting with the president, or escorting the first lady, he shook his head in wonderment. "I suppose that Mama would feel that some of her sacrifices for us are paying off," he mused in a letter to his brother, Herbert.

Turning down an invitation to teach in the 1968 Harvard summer school, he cited his need to "devote my energy to my own writing." Nevertheless, early in July he and Fanny, along with Tucka, went to Rhode Island for the increasingly popular annual Newport Jazz Festival. That year the festival reflected the vicious racial tensions testing the nation, as when the black *New York Amsterdam News* deplored "the presence of so many mediocre white bands and groups" and accused the white founder and veteran director, George Wien, of "exploiting African-American art."

Whatever those judgments, this was a delightful chance for a holiday in New England with Fanny, his friend Charlie Davidson, to whom he had been introduced by Al Murray, and Davidson's wife, Terry. Along with his brother, Davidson owned three fashionable men's clothing shops in New England, including the Andover Shop on Harvard Square in Cambridge. He had become Ralph's main purveyor of shoes (size 9E) and clothing. An energetic, engaging man of many interests, including jazz, Davidson had an array of friendships so diverse that *The New Yorker* once remarked on it. It was Davidson's doing when a black limousine pulled up outside his shop door and James Conant, a former president of Harvard, stepped inside to meet Ralph. He and Ralph enjoyed discussing not only jazz and politics but also the texture of various gabardines, the subtle changes in Burberry's trench coats, or the success of an olive-colored chambray shirt against Ralph's brown skin. Ralph stocked conservative suits for his board meetings and other encounters with the rich and powerful. (Richard Kostelanetz noted that "when he dons a dark suit and black Homburg, encases himself in a dark overcoat, and climbs into his black Chrysler, he looks more like a prosperous banker than a novelist.") To Davidson, Ralph was a man "full of kindness and thoughtfulness. He was a perfectionist but he was also grounded. In part he liked me because he liked people who could do and make things with their hands. But you couldn't pin him down. Ralph was like a drop of mercury under your thumb. Just when you thought you knew him, he showed you something else, something more."

From merry Newport, where they stayed at the Davidsons' summer home, Ralph and Fanny drove to the funereal ruins on Lincoln Hill Road in Plainfield. "It was dreary as hell," Ralph confessed to Charlie. "Not the weather but the sheer devastation of what had been a quite lovely old house and grounds now reduced to a scene of desolation. A forlorn chimney standing stark and crumbling above a cellar-hole full of crushed and rusting appliances, broken crockery, ashes." Jonquils were in bloom, but the water pump was gone. The chimney had to be toppled, debris trucked away, the cellar hole filled. Staying with the Wilburs, the Ellisons talked over the wisdom of rebuilding and decided that they weren't ready to come back.

In New York, Ralph moved carefully as raw antagonisms pushed apart blacks and whites. He failed to reply when Vincent Harding, a bona fide scholar of black American religion, asked him for help in planning a journal that was to be a cross between *Présence Africaine* of Paris and the muckraking *Ramparts*. He strongly disapproved of a project, supported by a philanthropic group, to found a racially exclusive Black Academy of Arts and Letters. (Established, the academy soon withered away.) Carefully he chose to visit that fall only eight college campuses, where he finally began to air some of his views on the racial crisis. He did so at the elite Davidson College in North Carolina, where he was the first black person appointed Reynolds Distinguished Lecturer. Marking Davidson's history of segregation as a thing of the past, he criticized Black Power supporters for promoting new forms of separatism. "If the continent couldn't hold two nations," he remarked (alluding to the Civil War), "it certainly can't hold two separated races." At Brandeis University, where he spoke at a conference on the role of black students at a white university, he deplored the growing habit, disheartening to many people who had fought Jim Crow, of black students segregating themselves as much as possible in otherwise integrated schools.

Ralph was en route to the University of Texas, where he would lecture, on November 4, on "The Negro in American History," when he found out to his dismay that Richard Nixon had narrowly defeated Humphrey. Two days later, he was in New Orleans to share a stage at a national convention of historians with C. Vann Woodward, Warren, and Styron. Their topic, "The Uses of History in Fiction," thrust Ralph into perhaps the most vitriolic controversy involving race and art in America since the appearance in 1915 of D. W. Griffith's pro–Ku Klux Klan film *The Birth of a Nation*. Central to the dispute was Styron's best-selling *The Confessions of Nat Turner,* a novel based on the life of the leader of the bloodiest American slave rebellion, in Virginia in 1831. Although it won Styron a Pulitzer Prize, the novel outraged many blacks. With scant historical evidence, as they saw it, Styron had re-created Turner as a cowardly slave hungry for white women, a masturbator, and perhaps latently homosexual. While several major white scholars and critics, including Eugene Genovese and Alfred Kazin, backed Styron's rights, many more blacks assailed the book as a slander on a historical hero. In *William Styron's Nat Turner: Ten Black Writers Respond,* Styron was flogged without mercy.

As a result, the mood was tense in the convention auditorium in New Orleans. Because the four speakers were old friends, they seemed to have a common cause, but in his opening statement Ralph appeared to censure Styron without naming him. He named Faulkner and Warren, but not Styron, as notable challengers of traditional racist Southern history. In *All the King's Men,* Ralph said, Warren had used history to make fiction but without pretending to be writing history. He seemed to imply that Styron had not been so scrupulous. Beyond asserting that Styron was no bigot, Ralph left him to fend for himself. Unlike Warren, who also did not defend Styron, Ralph seemed amused at times during the contentious question-and-answer period by what he called "Bill's personal problem." He also made a startling confession. "I haven't read his book," he said. "Our house burned down so I didn't get to read it at first, and after the controversy I deliberately did not read it." He did not explain the last remark.

Ralph's attitude baffled and hurt Styron. "Naturally, I was disappointed," he admitted. "I thought maybe something of the hostility of *Ten Black Writers* had rubbed off on him and he didn't want to be associated with me. Maybe he was burying his head in the sand in a curious way to avoid being seen on the 'wrong' side. I know that Vann Woodward was quite put out by Ralph that day. I remember him saying that something troubled him about the way Ralph had acted." The reasons for Ralph's equivocating about Styron are hard to pin down. On September 1 of the previous year, 1967, Ralph's agent, now Owen Laster of William Morris, had sent him a copy of *Nat Turner* along with an offer of $1,000 from *Vogue* if Ralph would write an essay on Styron. Ralph declined the offer. Although he cited the pressure of work, perhaps he saw the invitation as an indignity. Also, while a Hollywood company reportedly had paid Styron $600,000 for the screen rights, a producer had recently offered Ralph only $55,000 for *Invisible Man.* Writing to Rose Styron, Fanny had been gracious: "We are enormously happy about the success of your book and its fine promotion." Whether Ralph felt the same way is unclear.

Perhaps his ambivalence went back to an incident that took place before 1967, when the Ellisons cheerfully visited the Styrons at their home in Roxbury, Connecticut. Ralph and Fanny liked the Styron children, Tommy and Susanna, and Tucka and the Styron pooch had gone swimming together in a pond behind the house. Encouraged by the Styrons, Ralph and Fanny decided to look for a home in Roxbury. "I called our own agent," Rose Styron recalled, "the man who had sold us our house. He assured me that he had several properties to show them in Roxbury. I told him exactly who the Ellisons were. I arranged for Ralph and Fanny to drive up, look over some houses, and then lunch with us. The broker came by and he was very polite. He went off with the Ellisons in their car. Then the hours passed, and they were gone so long that Bill and I were sure that they had found their dream house." They hadn't. When they returned, Fanny stayed in the car while Ralph stalked in alone. Instead of showing them houses in Roxbury, the broker had taken them some miles away to Seymour, a dull industrial town. He didn't want them to buy in Roxbury. "Ralph was furious, he was indignant, as he should have been," Bill Styron said. "It was a calamitous insult. We were deeply embarrassed."

The Ellisons never returned to Roxbury. The following week, a petition posted on the door of the local Episcopal church demanded that the broker be punished. According to Rose Styron, he soon fled Roxbury. "True, Roxbury had never had a black homeowner," she said, "but it was not a racist town." The pain of the insult evidently lingered. "Ralph was always friendly to us after the incident," Bill Styron added, "but it remained something that we always regretted." Perhaps it irked Ralph that Styron had produced a best-selling, acclaimed novel (a pattern he would repeat with *Sophie's Choice*) while he himself remained stalled. Whatever the reason, Styron tested Ralph's desire to be embraced by elite white Southerners. His friendship with Allen Tate, Red Warren, Willie Morris, and C. Vann Woodward meant much to him, and the same month as the New Orleans symposium he agreed to write an essay on Eudora Welty for *Shenandoah* magazine. Ralph continued to think of himself as a sort of brother to genuine Southern aristocrats. But in his mind, Styron failed to measure up to this group. In some scattered notes for a proposed essay on Faulkner, he scribbled: "Faulkner was truly an aristocrat. . . . Red Warren is a poor white. Bill Styron is worse." (In fact, Styron had enjoyed a prosperous childhood and was a Duke graduate.) Lyndon Johnson, he added, was a leader in the mold of Thomas Jefferson.

·   ·   ·

Ironically, a day later it was Ralph's turn on the spit. Appearing at black Tougaloo College in Mississippi, he listened intently in Woodworth Chapel as the school choir intoned first Bruckner's "Tantum Ergo," then a Negro spiritual. After an introduction, he rose to deliver his remarks. He had barely opened his mouth when a drunken man interrupted him with loud, irrelevant comments. When nobody made a move to usher the man out, Ralph became icy with indignation. He lost his audience. Later, a student publication would comment on the famous visitor's "somewhat dry but well-organized talk" but also on his divorce from reality. Ellison's political vision, expressed "fuzzily," was that "everything will be all fine in the end if we all just do our thing and stretch the system enough to make some of us a little more comfortable than we were before." Since *Invisible Man,* Ellison had become something of a lost soul; in his speech he had omitted "any mention of legitimate or observable black-white schisms." Ellison, "a 'lone-star' negro," saw progress in mere tokenism. "Prosperity has made the rags-to-riches dreams within the system come true for him," the essay went on. "He seems to us soft, and passive."

The same criticism of him appeared that year in an afterword by Larry Neal to *Black Fire: An Anthology of Afro-American Writing,* edited by Neal and LeRoi Jones. While *Invisible Man* is "a profound piece of writing," Neal wrote, it was also "the kind of novel which, nevertheless, has little bearing on the world as the 'New Breed' sees it." As for younger blacks, "we know who we are, and we are not invisible, at least not to each other. We are not Kafkaesque creatures stumbling through a white light of confusion and absurdity." (Later, Neal would reappraise Ralph positively.) In his collection of essays *Soul on Ice,* Eldridge Cleaver dismissed Ellison as merely "a noisy writer." In turn, Ralph continued to show little respect for most black students, professors, and writers. Disdaining militants, he mourned their "vast incomprehension of the complex situation in which we find ourselves." But his sense of hurt was clouding his vision. The erudite Nathan Scott was "catching the same kind of thing" from militants because, as he said, he "was not one specializing in what is called the black experience"; nevertheless, Scott recalled feeling sad because he "never heard Ralph speak with admiration of any black writer." R. W. B. Lewis had a similar reaction. The fact that Ralph ridiculed the folk comedy of Zora Neale Hurston puzzled Lewis, because "I would have thought they were made to get along."

Somewhat brusquely Ralph rejected an invitation to work on a children's book with the head librarian at Fisk University, Arna Bontemps. A respected poet and novelist from the Harlem Renaissance, Bontemps had steadily published books since then, including co-authored or co-edited volumes with Langston Hughes. Ralph was even more dismissive when a publisher asked him to write a book about James Baldwin. Invited to contribute to the founding of a magazine, to be called *Renascent,* which hoped to reach "the long neglected black masses," he was discouraging in his response. If the brothers and sisters of Omoja, a self-styled Black Power cultural group in Boston, really expected help from "Dear Brother Ellison," they did so in vain.

Occasionally he took up a younger black writer. About this time, he showed some fondness for the work of Ernest Gaines (they met in April 1969 at the home of the agent Dorothea Oppenheimer). Gaines, who had published his first short story in 1956, had worked long and hard at his craft; his 1968 collection, *Bloodline,* showed that he now possessed a distinct voice. But if Ralph liked Gaines, he continued to imply that he knew of few or no other accomplished younger black writers. Meanwhile, writing in *Harper's,* Irving Howe published a long essay on recent fiction by William Melvin Kelley, John A. Williams, Sarah Wright, Hal Bennett, Carlene Polite, James Alan McPherson, and Ishmael Reed—all of them black. Howe knocked some writers, admired others, but called all of them serious and disinterested in racial separatism.

Under intense pressure, Ralph often lost his poise. That fall, when he left the board of *The American Scholar* after a three-year term, his ill temper marred his farewell. Writing to him later, Hiram Hayden (the editor) called him "a valuable, if fiery" board member. He ruined his last meeting by insisting that Nathan Scott be voted onto the board. With three places at stake and a long list of nominees, Scott came in fourth. Perhaps Scott lost because, as Jerry Watts would report, Ralph "commandeered the entire discussion and harangued the board for over an hour and a half." Having too often seen this side of Ralph, whom he otherwise admired and liked, Hayden pitied him. Ralph's loss of control was "one manifestation of the lonely burden that certain black men of a transitional generation have carried." Scorned by militants, too liberal for conservatives, lionized by liberal or calculating whites, and "yet always aware of that one difference, these aristocrats of the mind and spirit . . . have belonged to no community except the small one of their peers."

Relaxing at private dinner parties or with friends at the Century, he was charming and liked but also tended now to pontificate, to try to dominate conversations. "Ralph had a great thing about making proclamations, making speeches," Shirley Hazzard said. "He could become obnoxious fairly quickly." Liquor had a lot to do with these episodes. Richard and Charlee Wilbur recalled a time in their lives when "everybody got quite drunk." With two or three drinks Ralph's voice often became the loudest. Increasingly, he needed to be at the center of discussions occurring in his presence. "A kind of Visiting Writer's role was thrust upon him," Dick Wilbur said, "and people were forever asking him the same questions." For Ralph the interviewing never stopped: "We'd be sitting around and talking of an evening, and at a certain point he would say, 'Well now, returning to your second question.' Well, we hadn't asked him a question. I think he was obsessed by the subject of how people shape their lives and find their version of humanity in America." Wilbur added: "Ralph came close to thinking that it was the only American subject worth discussing. I think he sometimes felt that people who were talking about, say, baseball were off the subject, and he would insist on lecturing them."

Improvising in public lectures made him oracular—and, like any self-respecting oracle, in need of deciphering. Nathan Scott recalled listening to a lecture Ralph gave one evening in which he "spoke with unfaltering fluency for an hour on the vernacular and I sat there listening carefully to every word, and my goodness, at the end of that lecture, had my head depended upon it, I couldn't have told you the gist of what he said! I absolutely couldn't get hold of anything, except the vernacular and the marvelous capacity it had for capturing 'complexity.' There was loud applause at the end and people thought it had been a great performance. Well, it was a great performance, but I couldn't really tell you what he had just said."

Of his black friends, Ralph probably saw only Scott and Albert Murray as his peers. He admired Romare Bearden and Gordon Parks, but one was a painter, the other a photographer. Ralph had to respect the learning of Scott, who by 1970 had published a dozen books about religion and modern writers such as Hemingway, Camus, and Beckett. Scott, however, never lived in New York.

Ralph sometimes seemed close to violence. He was cordial at first with the young editors of a new periodical in book form called *Amistad,* published by Random House (only one number appeared), where Charles Harris, its co-editor along with John A. Williams, worked. However, Ralph was not cooperative when the first, attractive issue came out in 1970 to good reviews. "Ellison should have said something about *Amistad* and how important it was," Harris believed. What Harris did not remember, perhaps, is that in an interview with Williams in *Amistad,* Chester Himes had said some caustic things about Ralph ("I think he's gotten a bit pompous," for example). After the project folded, Harris simmered when, at a party for Ernest Gaines, Ralph seemed to be taunting him about it. Ralph stiffened. "Do you know what riffing is?" he asked Harris. "We ought to get together sometimes to do a little riffing." When Harris lit into Ralph, he did not back down. "You know I carry a knife," he warned. Ralph could be gracious, Al Murray said, "and also potentially violent, very violent. He was ready to take on people and to use whatever street corner language they understood. He was ready to fight, to come to blows. You really didn't want to mess with Ralph Ellison." James Baldwin called him the angriest man he knew. Stories circulated that he had pulled a knife on this person or that. Richard Wright wrote about an enraged Ellison once pulling a knife on Himes. In a telephone call to his young friend Horace Porter, Ralph would set the record straight: "Horace, it never happened."

Guarding his time, Ralph turned down an offer of $2,500 from Willie Morris at *Harper's* for a short essay about going back to visit Tuskegee. However, he agreed to join the progressive Columbia University sociologist Herbert Gans, as well as Whitney Young, Jr., of the National Urban League, in preparing a pamphlet, *The City in Crisis.* That Ralph would collaborate with a sociologist was a sure sign of the troubled times. He was on firmer ground when called upon to write his first essay on painting, for the catalogue of an exhibition of collages by Romare Bearden that opened on November 25, with Ralph and Fanny present, at the State University of New York at Albany. (He also was a co-sponsor of the first major commercial gallery exhibition of works by black artists, with the opening night at the Lee Nordness Galleries in New York a benefit for the NAACP.) A friend of Ralph since the 1930s, Bearden was the most widely respected black artist in America. Ralph was bashful at first about writing the essay, "out of the fear that I'd only produce something quite empty and pretentious." His fears were unjustified. The response was so enthusiastic that Ralph saw it "as something of a miracle."

With Bearden's ideas about race and art much like his own, Ralph reiterated with elegant twists and turns the key points in his opposition to anyone—radicals or sociologists—who, in his eyes, reduced black humanity to statistics and pathologies. He wrote of "that imbalance in American society which leads to a distorted perception of social reality, to a stubborn blindness to the creative possibilities of cultural diversity, to the prevalence of negative myths, racial stereotypes and dangerous illusions about art, humanity and society." Here he aimed his attack at the propaganda in much "black" art. Genuine art demands discipline and humility, he believed. The artist does not "tell it like it is," in the cant of the day, but aims at "revealing that which has been concealed by time, by custom, and by our trained incapacity to perceive the truth." Ralph touched on all the European influences—from Giotto to Mondrian—that Bearden had absorbed in searching for his own race-related but not race-defined identity. Meanwhile, lesser artists "clung with protective compulsiveness to the myth of the Negro American's total alienation from the larger American culture." In doing so, they "allowed the realities of their social and political situation to determine their conception of their role and freedom as artists."

About this time, Ralph scored some tantalizing artistic points of his own when he published in *The Quarterly Review of Literature* probably the strongest single section of his novel-in-progress to appear in his lifetime. Entitled "Night-Talk," it came, according to Ralph's own prefatory note, "from a novel-in-progress (*very* long in progress)." In a hospital room in Washington, the delirious Senator Adam Sunraider (born Bliss, and white-skinned, although his racial ancestry is unknown), gunned down on the Senate floor by someone in the visitors' gallery, communes as best he can with Alonzo "Daddy" Hickman. The old black minister had brought him up, but Sunraider had repudiated him in fleeing into the white world, where he would become a supremacist. The technique in "Night-Talk" is fundamentally surreal, a mélange of Joyce and Faulkner that Ellison sought to manipulate for his own fictional ends. "Sometimes they actually converse," Ralph notes about the men, but "sometimes the dialogue is illusory and occurs in the isolation of their individual minds, but through it all it is antiphonal in form and an anguished attempt to arrive at the true shape and substance of a sundered past and its meaning." Picking up the plot roughly where "And Hickman Arrives" left off nine years before in *The Noble Savage,* the excerpt addresses in quite impressive fashion the core question of the novel when projected as an allegory of American culture. How and why did the white-skinned boy Bliss, brought up so lovingly by Daddy Hickman and the adoring black churchwomen, come to desert them and transform himself into a rabid racist? That is, why did white America reject its innate bond to black America?

Sunraider as young Bliss, his spirit roiled both by his painful sense of deracination and by abandonment, tells of wandering among white folk in Atlanta, looking desperately for the white parents he never knew. His act was both treacherous and full of genuine pathos; the author clearly feels for him in his ordeal. In a movie house for whites only, lonely and forlorn, Bliss had pined for the movie star Mary Pickford, with whom he associated the mother he has never seen but desperately wants to find. Bliss also negotiates the colorful black world of Atlanta, where he is attracted and repelled alike by its remarkable flair and its compelled subordination. He encounters (as Sunraider tells us in a duly italicized reverie) a jumbled cast of characters, black and white, who perform the kaleidoscopic variety and vitality of the American experience. At some point in Atlanta, Hickman finds and reclaims Bliss after a desperate search—but only temporarily. Slipping back into the narcotic, fantastic white world symbolized by the flickering images on the movie screen and, in particular, by Mary Pickford's alluring face, Bliss begins his emotionally lethal morphing into the character of a supremacist. His vision clarified by the imminent threat of death in the hospital, Sunraider indicates by his narrative that he might be on the verge of a harrowing but redemptive final self-awareness.

Ralph's often sensational but also at times uneasy mixing of originality and obvious indebtedness to Joyce and Faulkner is both effective and defective. In one Joycean reverie, Sunraider (and Ellison) riffs effortlessly and yet also sometimes irritatingly on topics such as American industrialism, agrarianism, and race: *"And how do they feel, still detroiting my mother who called me Goodrich Hugh Cuddyear in the light of tent flares then running away and them making black bucks into millejungs and fraud pieces in spectacularmythics on assembly lines?"* In homage to Faulkner, the prose is often lovely, yet dangerously close to unintended parody, as when Sunraider flashes forward from his childhood to his days as a (white) scam filmmaker, seducing a country girl: *"On the hill the cattle tinkled their bells and she said, Mister Movie man, I have to live here, you know. Will you be nice to me and the blossoms were falling where the hill hung below the afternoon and we sprawled embraced and out of time that never entered into future time except as one nerve cell, tooth, hair and tongue and drop of heart's blood into the bucket."* Anchoring "Night-Talk," despite these problems, is the somber severity of the question at the core of the novel. Sunraider muses in his delirium: *"Oh, if only I could have controlled me my she I and the search and have accepted you as the dark daddy of flesh and Word—Hickman? Hickman, you after all. Later I thought many times*

that I should have faced them [the white world] *down . . . and said, Look,
this is where I'll make my standing place. . . . But how make a rhyme out of
a mystery?"*

Thus (in a rhetorical maneuver typical of the piece and the novel) the
author makes his hero-villain surreptitiously echo the words of "Dixie"
("In Dixie land I'll take my stand"), the anthem of the reactionary South.
Ellison as novelist veers from insight into imitation, from superb improvising that showed off his amazing imagination and literary gifts on the
one hand, and, on the other, a patently scholastic indenture, perhaps
even enslavement, to the very literary tradition he was trying to conquer.

More honors came. Just before Christmas 1968, Ralph learned that
France had decided to appoint him a Chevalier de l'Ordre des Arts et des
Lettres. Soon afterward, the board of trustees of Bennington College in
Vermont elected him to a seven-year term. On January 19, 1969, a few
days before Lyndon Johnson left office, he conferred on Ralph and eighteen other Americans the Presidential Medal of Freedom, the highest
honor that could be conferred by a president on a citizen. "Ralph Ellison
is a writer," his presidential citation read, who had "inspired the white
American not just to understand the black American's problems, but to
stand up and fight to eliminate them. His vision of our Democracy has
helped Americans to a new determination to bring equality to the lives of
all our people." (In his own two-page tribute to Johnson, included in a
bound volume given to the president at a farewell dinner and ball in New
York that month attended by some five hundred admirers, Ralph praised
him for pursuing "his goals and options" on the subject of civil rights
"more strenuously than any President since Abraham Lincoln.")

For Ralph, the ceremony at the French consulate on Fifth Avenue,
where he was the sole honoree, had an appeal and charm all its own. The
painter Helen Frankenthaler, calling it "a beautiful moment," marveled at
"that scene, the honor, the history." He sent invitations to more than 150
guests from all over the country, including Tuskegee and Oklahoma City.
Presiding at the ceremony, Edouard Morot-Sir, the cultural attaché, made
a pretty yet grave little speech. For Ralph, the fact that André Malraux,
whose novels had helped to change his life in the trying late 1930s, had
decided on the honor as minister of culture was a major source of pride.
Later, Ralph wrote to Morot-Sir that the award led him "to believe more
fervently than ever in the power of art to impose a certain ennobling sym-
metry upon the lives of men."

These recent honors helped to offset the demoralizing effect of certain incidents that month. At Oberlin College in Ohio, the black student "caucus," which he had agreed to meet, received him rudely. One "sister," addressing Ralph directly, curtly dismissed *Invisible Man* because of its harsh portrayal of the ultra-nationalist Ras the Destroyer. When Ralph would not apologize for the character, she snapped, "That just proves that you're an Uncle Tom!" Other students were equally disrespectful. Ralph "just accepted it very calmly," one observer noted, but he was hurt. When Ohio State planned a Black Heritage Week celebration dedicated to him, he would not attend. "I am totally involved in my own writing," he told Purdue University in turning down another invitation. In March, he spoke safely from his home, on closed-circuit television, to students at six black colleges, including Grambling in Louisiana and Langston in Oklahoma.

A call for "black studies" had now risen on campuses across America. In a letter to the University of Pittsburgh Press, Ralph showed his distrust of the idea: "So-called black studies are really no refuge from the searching eye of criticism." His attitude reflected the spirit of "The New Black Myths," an article (not by him) in the May 1969 issue of *Harper's*. "The rush is on," the piece began derisively. "Come and get it: Afro-Americanism, black studies, the Negro heritage. From Harvard to Ocean Hill [in Brooklyn], from Duke to Madison Avenue, they are trying, as they say, to restore the Negro to his rightful place in American history and culture; black (and white) intellectuals, scholars, teachers, politicians, hustlers busy with black restoration." This cynicism ignored the potential of such study, the wrongs it sought to address, and the patient efforts of many academics and their institutions. And yet the actions of many angry students encouraged such scorn. Once, according to a report, students booed Ralph off a stage at Yale. He himself spoke of visiting Calhoun College at Yale (headed by R. W. B. Lewis) and having to dress down two ill-mannered black students from another Yale residential complex who had come to hear him. "Those people were so rude to their hosts," Ralph recalled indignantly, "that I had to tell them 'For God's sake, what is this? Are we going to fight the race war here? When I came up to say something about literature?' And so on. They were pretty nasty."

His most successful lecture of 1969 was probably at the U.S. Military Academy at West Point, New York. On March 26, with the Vietnam War still raging, he addressed the nine hundred members (or plebes) of the freshman class, for whom *Invisible Man* was a required text. His escort at

West Point was a young English instructor, Captain Emory Elliott, who had prepared a meticulous lesson plan for use in every class. Meeting Ralph turned out to be a major turning point in his career, if not his life. A scholar of seventeenth-century English literature, Elliott discovered through his engagement with Ralph and *Invisible Man* that his true interest was in American literature and American Studies, in which he would become a national figure. "I peppered Ellison with all sorts of silly, naive questions about the book," Elliott recalled. "And he simply astonished me by his complex ways of thinking, the many levels of his responses and his commentary on any topic that came up. I really felt—for the first time in my life—that I was in the presence of a genius." Moreover, Ralph was modest and funny. Asked why he hadn't finished another novel, he mentioned the 1967 fire. "You see, Captain Elliott," he drawled, "I'm not burned out. I'm just burned up."

In Thayer Hall, where the excited plebes greeted him with a standing ovation, he first disarmed them with self-deprecating remarks about assigned texts, then held them with a lecture that stressed the universality of his novel. In the question-and-answer period, one inquiry stilled the hall: "Mr. Ellison, sir, why did you include a scene involving sex between a black man and a white woman?" Quietly, Ralph explained that his novel was built around themes, rituals, and taboos important to American culture. Interracial sex involving black men and white women was the most reviled of American taboos, and so "it had to be in my book." When he was done, the plebes rose again to applaud him. Obviously he had touched many of them. As he and Elliott were leaving the lecture hall, a black cadet suddenly blocked their path. "Mr. Ellison, sir," he demanded, "tell me, what should I be doing with my life?" Obviously the cadet had been thinking about the war, Black Power, and his privileged place at the Point. Ralph looked at him. "What's the highest achievement you can attain here?" he asked. "Commandant of the Point, sir!" the cadet replied. "Then that is what you should be aiming for—to be commandant of West Point."

Soon he was relaxing over food and liquor at the Officers Club with other leading faculty members, including Major Frederick Franks and Lieutenant Colonel Jack Capps, who had approved the assignment of *Invisible Man*. Capps asked Ralph to return to speak to the class of '73, who would also be reading the novel. Relishing his success—and thinking perhaps about his court-martialed father—Ralph loosened up and took command of the table. He had strong political views, Elliott noted, but views more conservative than those of the officers. Not everyone was charmed. A visiting black sociologist seethed as Ralph, praising American democracy, recalled attending a dinner party in Rome while at the American Academy there. Across the table during that dinner sat the friendly American wife of an Italian count. "You don't remember me, do you?" she asked Ralph. He didn't. She was the daughter of one of the Lewisohn brothers, owners of the clothing store where he had worked in Oklahoma City. One of his tasks had been to fetch the little Lewisohn girls from school to the store. "This is why America is the greatest country in the world!" Ralph exulted, according to Elliott. "Here was the daughter of an Oklahoma City businessman, a Jew, who had become a countess; and there I was, a black man who had once worked for her father, when I was poor, and now I was sitting across from her at a fancy dinner in Rome." What a wonderful nation! "Mr. Ellison, you are the exception!" the sociologist exploded. "You cannot offer yourself as representative of the United States!" But Ralph refused to yield an inch on the subject of the glory of American democracy.

On Vietnam, too, he still pitched his own tent far from the protesters, many of whom felt betrayed by President Nixon and by Henry Kissinger, who now dominated American foreign policy. Ralph remained a member of the essentially pro-war Citizens Committee for Peace with Freedom in Vietnam. Perhaps his sole antiwar gesture came when he signed a one-sentence statement to be published in *Esquire*: "I believe that Muhammad Ali, Heavyweight Champion of the World, should be allowed to defend his title." Ali had been stripped of his title after refusing to fight in Vietnam because of his beliefs as a Muslim. Returning the petition to Irwin Shaw, who had sent it, Ralph stressed: "The encircled statement is the limit of my endorsement."

He was bolder in opposing the persecution of Jews, as when he signed a statement condemning the murder in the Soviet Union in 1952 of twenty-four Jewish writers, artists, and intellectuals. Here he associated himself with Bellow, Howe, and the Jewish Labor Committee. Along with Bellow, Elie Wiesel, Lionel Trilling, and the black civil rights activist Bayard Rustin, he joined the board of directors of the new Institute for the Study of the Holocaust. (Invited to inaugurate a visiting lectureship at Hebrew University in Jerusalem, he declined; he would not leave the United States.) He made other calculated gestures. Later that year, he was a sponsor of a dinner in New York in Rustin's honor. A former conscientious objector and a homosexual jailed for "indecent" behavior, Rustin was now involved in an ugly struggle in New York City. The mainly white

United Federation of Teachers had gone on strike to protest the expulsion by a black administrator of some white teachers in a largely black and Latino district. A dedicated union supporter, Rustin had aligned himself publicly with the UFT. With some blacks smearing Rustin as an Uncle Tom, Ralph was proud to stand by him.

The spring of 1969 was perhaps the most militant season of student protest against the war and for Black Studies. Storming buildings and issuing "nonnegotiable" demands became commonplace. Deploring such developments, Ralph quietly defended his ideas when he ventured onto campuses. Different places received him in different ways. Students at the predominantly black Central State University in Wilberforce, Ohio, listened politely to his description of America. Kids at the mainly white Lafayette College in Pennsylvania were much more restive. Recent speeches by the anthropologist Margaret Mead, famously an apostle of freedom, had roused the youths, who barely tolerated Ralph's plea for unity. As an inspiration, he did not compare well with Mead or with another visitor, the exuberant poet Allen Ginsberg. The name Ralph Ellison had become synonymous with ultra-conservatism. The future National Book Award–winning black novelist Charles Johnson, then a student at Southern Illinois University, remembered asking a librarian in the new Black Studies program for a copy of *Invisible Man*. "We don't carry it," she told him. "Really? Why not?" "Because Ralph Ellison is not a black writer."

At Amherst College in Massachusetts, where Ralph spoke on May 14, a two-day campus-wide protest against the war led black students to demand their own day, when the entire campus would discuss racism. At the behest of the president (his good friend Calvin Plimpton), and for a fee of $1,000, Ralph ended a day of seminars by faculty members with a lecture before a huge audience. Again he was brave. Conceding the virulence of racism, he stressed instead the fruitful effects of racial difference in creating the national culture. "Race is a factor in American life," Ralph insisted, addressing the black students in particular, "but it is also an excuse . . . for not seeing ourselves as we really are, for not becoming what we thought we would become, for not creating what we promised to create." His message was unequivocal: "Let's stop being victims."

Despite the turmoil, Ralph sought to maintain not only his dignity and intelligence but also his zest for life. To celebrate the publication of Richard Wilbur's collection *Walking to Sleep*, the Wilburs invited two hundred guests for a black-tie dinner and also dancing, to the music of a live Dixieland combo, at their home in Portland, Connecticut. Arriving in style with Fanny, a bounce to his step, Ralph joined the festivities with gusto. When the jazz band played its first notes, he needed no encouragement to hit the dance floor. In April he and Fanny joined Plimpton and his wife, Ruth, at a gala performance of the New York City Ballet. Four days later they dined comfortably at Marietta Peabody Tree's luxurious Manhattan home, where the guest of honor was Errol Barrow, the premier of Barbados, where the Trees owned a magnificent vacation home on the Sandy Lane beach. Ralph and Fanny gladly attended a lunch, co-sponsored by him, in honor of Hubert Humphrey. And in May, at the Waldorf-Astoria, the Ellisons graced a lively testimonial dinner, which Ralph also co-sponsored, to celebrate A. Philip Randolph's eightieth birthday. Fanny co-sponsored a salute to the actress Lillian Gish (ironically, a star of *The Birth of a Nation*) at Columbia University. The Ellisons that month also attended a gala luncheon at the Commodore Hotel, for which they were co-sponsors, to mark the thirtieth anniversary of the NAACP Legal Defense Fund.

Meanwhile, Ralph and Fanny maintained gallantly that the end of his second novel was at hand. "He is about to complete a new novel and another book of essays," she wrote to a relative in November. Ralph did not have "writer's block," she made clear; for him, "writing is his way of life and he does that as any other man would perform the work of his choice." Unfortunately, he was not writing very well. Agreeing in 1969 to compose an essay of fifty to sixty pages on the American language for *Encyclopaedia Britannica,* he surrendered after deciding that his draft lacked authority and was unlikely to gain it. Although he formally proposed to a publisher writing a book on Negro life, to be illustrated with photographs, he lost interest in it.

Ralph had better luck with an affectionate trifle, "Homage to Duke Ellington on His Birthday," commissioned by the Sunday *Washington Star* newspaper in Ellington's native Washington to mark his seventieth birthday. And yet even this trifle presented problems. Writing slowly as usual, to meet the deadline he had to dictate it over the telephone to the *Star.* Ralph had been delighted when President Nixon gave a state dinner at the White House, which the Ellisons attended, in honor of Ellington's birthday. There, "years ago, Duke's father, then a butler, once instructed white guests from the provinces in the gentle art and manners proper to such places of elegance and power." At the American Academy, he sought to have Ellington admitted to the National Institute. His music, Ralph declared, was proof that integration is a basic principle both of democracy and of art. Influential with his peers, Ralph succeeded. One day after he and Fanny attended an NAACP benefit at Madison Square Garden in honor of Duke, the National Institute voted him in as a member. Ellington entered with Philip Roth, Cleanth Brooks, and C. Vann Woodward, among others.

Money was certainly no problem for Ralph now. In addition to the excellent insurance settlement, he was making good money. His total income in 1969, as reported to the IRS, was about $37,000, a sum higher than the annual salary of the best-paid professor in the arts and sciences at Harvard. Although Boston College complained that his requested lecture fee of $300 was larger than the combined sums it had paid to W. H. Auden and Robert Lowell, he could have earned even more. Scrupulous, and cautious, he declined an invitation from the Black Students Union at the University of Delaware, where "Black Awareness Week" was being organized "to pinpoint the Black Man's achievements in the anthropological, historical, sociological, psychological, political and cultural area." Similarly, he passed up an invitation to lecture extended by the troubled Afro-American Cultural Center at Harvard. He turned down a request from the organizers of a writers' conference at Fisk University the following year, 1970. He knew that Robert Hayden, the cosmopolitan poet, had been heckled at a recent conference there.

Fresh topics could draw him out. Thus, in October, he visited Carnegie Mellon University in Pittsburgh to speak on "The Novelist and the City" at a symposium on the humanities and urban affairs. His talk led directly to an offer from Carnegie Mellon of a visiting professorship for the following year. He fielded (but rejected) offers of visiting professorships from the State University of New York at Buffalo and at Purchase; from Smith College in Northampton, Massachusetts, not far from Plainfield; and from Fresno State University in California. At this point, Ralph still wanted to avoid a regular teaching job. He had also become aware that the right one could make his life a great deal easier.

Early in December 1969, Ralph was looking forward to attending a dinner at Rodman Rockefeller's home when a telegram from Oklahoma announced that Edna Randolph Slaughter had died. Canceling his appointments, he flew west to attend the funeral of the woman whose friendship with his mother had blessed his childhood following his father's untimely death. Then, in January, his longtime friend Horace Cayton died in Paris. Considered at one time a major sociologist, the co-author with St. Clair Drake of *Black Metropolis*, a study of Chicago, Cayton had drifted into obscurity. A recent grant to write a biography of Richard Wright had brought him to Paris. At sixty-seven, in a lonely hotel room in a strange land, Cayton succumbed to a heart attack. Even after Michel Fabre, the young French scholar who was also writing a biography of Wright, spread the word, nobody claimed the body. Instead, on February 3, only Fabre and an undertaker were present when Cayton's body was cremated at Père Lachaise.

Sadly, Ralph read the letter from Fabre telling of Cayton's end. He may well have reflected on the fact that of the promising young black writers and intellectuals on the scene around 1940, he was one of the few—along with Gwendolyn Brooks and Chester Himes—still visible. And he had surpassed them all. Only his failure to finish his second novel, as well as the pain caused by his refusal to kneel before anti-intellectualism, separatism, and cynicism, still challenged him. He could do little about them except to soldier on. He would not resign his vocation as an artist, and he would not give in to what he saw as the lunacy of the age.

The latest published excerpt from his novel, "A Song of Innocence," appeared in the *Iowa Review*. It only added to the view that he was in trouble as a fiction writer. The excerpt seemed mainly an attempt to justify incoherence by linking it to genius. As the excerpt opens, the hugely mythic Cliofus is slipping into one of his "bad spells," when words come out of him "so fast that while I could hear them inside me I couldn't connect up with them." Stumbling along in this somewhat drunken manner, the narrative appears to flee, rather than engage, the sonorous theme that announces itself in an unconscious parody of the kind of Faulknerian rhetoric that was often empty even when Faulkner himself wrote it. Thus the narrator intones about "all that lonesome rising and falling of sound like singing has you by the short hair and dragging you out into the ole calcified night of loneliness toward the unsayable meaning of mankind's outrageous condition in this world."

His inspiration flagging, Ralph pecked away at the book most mornings, then devoted many afternoons to rambles in the wonderful city. Visiting its museums, he saw fewer and fewer black patrons. Black Arts and Black Power rhetoric, he believed sorrowfully, was driving them away from artistic resources almost as precious as life itself. He stopped in at commercial art galleries and specialty shops, or attended his various board meetings. He could also depend on the sweet relief from grit and grime offered by the Century, by his jolly fellow members, and by the lubricious bar where he had taught the staff precisely how to make a martini. (At one time Ralph even carried about with him an eyedropper in order to regulate the correct, minute infusion of vermouth into his gin.) That his fellow members respected and liked him became clear (if he ever doubted it) in January 1970, when they elected him to the admissions committee. There he took charge of the writers' section. As a committee member he couldn't nominate new members, but he could quietly expedite, or delay, or deny entry. Gripping the front doorknob tightly, he did little to admit other blacks or to facilitate the admission of women, who were still barred from membership.

Hibernating in the snowy months, he headed out in the late winter and spring of 1970 on a demanding tour that took him to Buffalo, Wisconsin, Iowa, Kansas, Oklahoma, and Mississippi. Despite the large crowds, almost everywhere he noted a depressing trend. When he addressed an assembly of some 2,700 students at Iowa State in Ames, he gazed upward to see the handful of blacks in attendance huddling in an upper balcony, as in the days of Jim Crow when blacks had to sit in the "Crows' Nest" or "Nigger Heaven," as blacks then mordantly called the balcony. "Ralph could never understand what they were thinking," Stanley Crouch noted about self-segregating students. "He had not endured segregation and its indignities and broken free of it in order to surrender then to a new, reverse segregation. He was very disappointed and impatient with them." At a reception, when he found the black students clustering once again, he tried to draw them out. Although he brought up names such as Amiri Baraka and Malcolm X, "they do not say much." A student reporter marveled later that "whether to the formal audience, or the informal group, or to the individual, Ellison paints the same picture. He doesn't change his story or its sincerity in its presentation."

This fitful wrestling with young people was no fun. Another sweep of colleges found him "bone weary and disgusted," especially after a blizzard stranded him in Chicago. But lecturing in Oklahoma was a pleasure. Speaking at the state university in Norman allowed his family and friends to see him in command of a large audience, at a place that used to bar blacks. He joined Willie Morris at elite Millsaps College in Jackson, Mississippi. Staying at the top hotel in town, he had proof that integration had reached even Mississippi. And yet when the flowers bloomed in the spring of 1970, the nation seemed more divided than ever by race. The paramilitary Black Panther Party, founded in California, intensified the violent undertone of much black protest. The white backlash took various forms. Probably none dismayed Ralph more than the suggestion by Daniel Patrick Moynihan to President Nixon (in a memorandum leaked to the press) that "the time may have come when the issue of race could benefit from a period of 'benign neglect' " (the two deadly words came from a British government report in 1839 about Canada).

Almost as discouraging to Ralph was an essay on Richard Wright in *The Atlantic Monthly* by his old friend Stanley Edgar Hyman, in which Stanley stated what now seemed axiomatic: "There can be no doubt that Negro hatred of whites is close to universal." The words tore at Ralph's soul. "I do not believe this," he scribbled in the margin of his copy of *The Atlantic;* "there is too much of human complexity missed." In a long letter he scolded Stanley for using terms such as "Negro artists" and the "Negro American experience"; such terms made "our Negro American attitudes and emotions towards whites far too simple." The Negro American style "has been shaped by a determined will to control violent emotions (we seldom run amuck) as a life-preserving measure against being provoked into retaliatory actions by those who desire only to destroy us." Stanley had not allowed for more complex Negro reactions. He had allowed for "no contempt—a quite different emotion than hate—no irony, no forbearance, no indifference, no charity, no mockery, no compassion, no condescension—not to mention . . . ambivalence of emotion and attitude which you so readily see in the Blues." One's racial identity, Ralph insisted, "does not dominate individual culture so absolutely as you would seem to believe."

Eager to continue this challenge to the doctrine of mass Negro hatred of whites, in March he jumped at an invitation from Henry Grunwald of *Time* to write an essay for a special issue on black America. On April 6, the magazine carried his provocative "What America Would Be Like Without Blacks." Here Ralph confronted "the fantasy of an America free of blacks," which was "as old as the dream of creating a truly democratic society." (Even Harriet Beecher Stowe and Abraham Lincoln at one time had backed the idea of "repatriating" blacks to an Africa their parents and even grandparents had probably never seen.) Without blacks, he declared, "something irrepressibly hopeful and creative would go out of the American spirit," something that began with the American language. "The American nation is in a sense the product of the American language," he argued. Racial difference had inspired the best of American folklore and the best of American literature, as in the work of Mark Twain, Stephen Crane, Ernest Hemingway, and William Faulkner.

"Materially, psychologically and culturally," Negroes were embedded in America. "The nation," he concluded in *Time*, "could not survive being deprived of their presence because, by the irony implicit in the dynamics of American democracy, they symbolize both its most stringent testing and the possibility of its greatest freedom." To illustrate that freedom, Ralph told Stanley Hyman an anecdote: "Said a young white professor of English to me after a lecture out in northern Illinois, 'Mr. E., how does it feel to be able to go to places where most black men can't go?' Said I to him, 'What you mean is, how does it feel to be able to go places where most white men can't go.' "

Kudos greeted his piece in *Time*. Soon thereafter, a sneak attack in *Life*—then a magazine with a circulation of over five million—almost leveled him. An essay by one Clifford Mason (identified as a teacher and a critic) exalted Richard Wright while denouncing Ralph Ellison and, to a lesser extent, James Baldwin. "History has a way of vindicating art," Mason declared of *Native Son*. "The problem of Bigger Thomas is the problem of our times. The cities are burning, almost as if inspired by Wright's three-decades-old prophecy." Instead of revering Wright as a prophet, Ellison and Baldwin had helped to create the false image of him as a writer "too much given to social protest, too preoccupied with one level of black society and too constrained by the limitations of his brutish protagonist really to qualify as a master." Mason likened Ralph's politics to the "obsequious bleatings of white appeasement." Thus Mason sought to counter "the great disservice white critics have done to all black literature over the years by praising Ellison at the expense of Wright."

The printing of this essay up front in *Life* gave it the look and force of a sanctioned editorial. Enraged, Ralph fired off an eleven-page salvo to the editor. In it, he blasted the "editorial shoddiness" that thus had damaged *Life*'s prestige and also "my reputation both as a writer and a man of integrity." Providing evidence of his many personal links to Wright, Ralph's letter cites almost every comment by him in print about *Native Son* to prove that he had not once disparaged it. (Here, his extensive files, tended by Fanny, proved invaluable.) Moreover, *Native Son* had enjoyed extraordinary white support from the moment the Book-of-the-Month Club selected it in 1940 up to the moment of Irving Howe's glorification of it in his duels with Ralph in 1963 and 1964 in *Encounter* and *The New Leader*. Bitterly Ralph wrote of "a smell about this enterprise, an odor rank of enclosed rooms of the mind, a stench revealing a fear to face up intellectually to the complications of literature no less than to those of a multi-racial, pluralistic society."

Through Alfred Rice, his attorney, Ralph threatened to sue *Life* and Clifford Mason. When advised that the First Amendment would prohibit his winning, he accepted an offer by *Life* to publish a rejoinder. Vacationing with Fanny at the home of friends in Worthington, Massachusetts, he tried to boil down his response—which was not Ralph's strength. He gave up. The silliness in *Life* had no effect on his reputation where it mattered most to him. On June 7, Williams College in Massachusetts awarded him his fifth honorary degree. At Hollins College in Virginia, where he joined Dick Wilbur, James Dickey, Shelby Foote, and William Manchester at an annual conference on creative writing, he found his reputation as a major artist untouched and, indeed, reaffirmed.

While in Worthington, Ralph had received a letter that a sometimes ditzy housekeeper failed to give him for some days. From New York University, Dean R. Bayly Winder had written to offer him one of the most prized academic positions in the state, if not the nation. Winder asked Ralph to consider accepting one of the ten academic chairs set up recently by the state of New York and named in honor of the humanitarian Albert Schweitzer. Private and public universities across the state competed for the positions. Nominating Ellison as its candidate, New York University had won a chair for him. The terms were grand for an academic. Altogether, his annual salary and benefits, plus secretarial, research, and discretionary funds, would add up to $100,000—much more than Ralph had ever earned annually. Some teaching was required, but the professorship also offered ample time for research and writing.

Wasting little time, on June 23, 1970, Ralph accepted the offer. His appointment, and his new life, would start on the first day of September.

But for one man who had been of incalculable value to Ralph as he struggled in the 1940s to create *Invisible Man,* that summer was his last. In North Bennington, Vermont, on July 29, Stanley Hyman suffered a heart attack and died. Hyman was fifty-one. Although Stanley and Ralph had not been quite as close as in the distant past, the news shook Ralph. As with the passing of Richard Wright, another key friend and intellectual mentor, ten years before, a major chapter of his life came to a close.

18

Professor in the Humanities

1970–1973

*Slowly, slowly—and too often not so slowly—we all go
into the dark.*   RALPH ELLISON (1971)

On the sunny morning of September 18, 1970, settling into his new
rented offices on the fifth floor at the privately owned building at
One Fifth Avenue, Ralph officially assumed his duties as Regents Professor and Albert Schweitzer Professor in the Humanities at New York University. In historic Washington Square, a green space associated in the
minds of book lovers with the genius of Henry James, the trees were still
in their late-summer splendor. Denizens of Greenwich Village leaned and
loafed about the park as students hustled by. All signs seemed propitious
as Ralph began his new life.

Although the Schweitzer professorship was technically a year-to-year
appointment, Ralph joined the faculty with tenure and a degree of freedom beyond the reach of most professors. Belonging to no department,
he reported directly to the dean. Thus he had no department meetings
and no obligatory committee meetings. He would serve on committees at
his pleasure. Whereas almost all other professors in the humanities
taught at least four courses each year, he needed to teach only two. Neither of these had to be in the fall. He could devote many uninterrupted
months to his writing.

In terms of prestige, New York University in 1970 was neither Harvard
nor Yale. To Kenneth Silverman, the future Pulitzer Prize–winning biographer and a faculty member since 1964, NYU then was "a dowdy unimpressive place, faintly bohemian. There was no pretense of trying to catch
up to Columbia. There was no sense of a center, of having a campus, or
even a focus. There was no real library." The faculty was uneven in qual-

ity, the students even more so. A few academic stars, such as the political theorist Sidney Hook, the biographer Leon Edel, and the literary critic M. L. Rosenthal, shone, but many professors seemed to lack ambition. The school's major asset was its location on Washington Square, where russet townhouses from another age had coexisted easily with the other charms of Greenwich Village. But by 1970 the park had also become a haven for idlers, panhandlers, and petty drug dealers.

With the Schweitzer professorship, plus his international reputation, Ralph arrived as perhaps the brightest light in the humanities. He had his personal secretary, a suite of offices, a research assistant, and a hefty charge account for books, journals, entertainment, and other professional expenses. He had money to invite distinguished visitors or to fund conferences. He immediately announced a plan to invite four visiting lecturers that year: Stanley Edgar Hyman, R. W. B. Lewis, Kenneth Burke, and the Oklahoma-born historian of America Daniel Boorstin.

He was now free of the need to accept invitations to lecture or to consider requests from publishers other than his own. (He brushed aside a large advance dangled before him by a rival publisher for a biography of Joe Louis or Bessie Smith, whichever he preferred.) For its part, NYU had scored a coup. When most colleges were begging for black professors, it had snapped up, free of charge, the most famous black writer in the world. At the same time, Ralph made it clear that he would not teach courses in black literature. "I made the mistake of broaching the subject one day, some time after he'd been here," his colleague John Maynard said, "when I was directing undergraduate studies in English. After all, we had a course in the Jewish novel. But he said no. He wanted no part of such teaching." He wouldn't teach creative writing either. "He could easily have taught writing," Maynard recalled, "but he did not want to do so." Showing perhaps his sensitivity about lacking even a bachelor's degree, Ralph solemnly stated his overall teaching goals. "We will be exploring," he announced, "the relationship between sophisticated and vernacular culture in the United States. . . . I feel that this is one of the abiding phenomena in this country starting from our British and American background. We have always been in the position of transforming earlier techniques, recreating them in terms of the American experience." Race would be a key factor because European cultural traditions had come "into ceaseless contact with the imaginations of Negro Americans who have been in the unique position of being inside the society and yet outside."

That fall, a series of gestures made his positions clearer than ever. In

September, he declined an invitation to attend a cocktail party for the new Black Academy of Arts and Letters—an elegant ghetto, he perhaps felt, that he did not want to enter—although it attracted respected scholars such as C. Eric Lincoln in religion, John Hope Franklin in history, Martin Kilson in government, and St. Clair Drake in sociology. He would not help in the founding of the New York–based Black Film Foundation despite the presence on the project of actors such as Diana Sands, Brock Peters, and James Earl Jones. He ignored a request to contribute to a new Pittsburgh-based magazine, *Black Lines: A Journal of Black Studies.* He was positively indignant when the cultural nationalist Hoyt Fuller, preparing a special Ralph Ellison number at *Black World* (formerly *Negro Digest*), which he edited, wrote "asking if I cared to contribute to the issue!" Fuller mentioned that it would include essays by Larry Neal, John A. Williams, and John Henrik Clarke, but Ralph did not see such people as his friends or allies. "Needless to say," he wrote, alluding to the fact that all three had criticized him in one way or another, "he got no reply, unless he was able to hear me." (After the issue appeared, with some words of praise for him, he made it known that "as a whole [it] was not pleasing.") When Nathan Hare of the magazine *Black Scholar* asked Ralph to contribute to an issue in which some "young black militants" would comment on black literature, "what it is and what it ought to be," Ralph was again mute.

The sense that he was on the other side of a wall was now widespread among black writers. In his interview of Chester Himes for the premier issue of *Amistad,* John Williams mentioned the blurb that Ralph had recently written for James Alan McPherson's short-story collection *Hue and Cry.* "He says that this kid is great, this is real writing," Williams told Himes. "The implication is that a lot of black writers whom he considers 'obscenely second-rate' use their blackness as a crutch, as an excuse for not learning their craft." Himes criticized Ellison for being obsessed with the idea that black writers were not good craftsmen. "I remember when he was imitating Richard Wright," Himes remarked. Ralph's position on black craftsmanship "appeals more to the white community than the black community." As with his opposition to the Black Academy, Ralph ran the risk of seeming self-righteous. He was ready to run that risk. He would not abandon his beliefs, even in dealing with people who praised him. That fall, when the journal of the historically black (because of white exclusionism) College Language Association devoted a special issue to his work, he thanked its respected editor, Therman B. O'Daniel, condescendingly: "Some of the interpretations I found to be quite serious."

And yet, as Irving Howe and others had noted, most talented young black fiction writers or intellectuals were Ellisonian to one degree or another, even if they had also developed indelible sympathy for black cultural nationalism. In February, a reviewer in the *New York Times Book Review* identified Joyce and Ellison as the obvious main sources of inspiration behind Cecil Brown's somewhat scandalous new novel, *The Life and Loves of Mr. Jiveass Nigger.* "Ellison was a literary radical," the film and culture critic Clyde Taylor judged. "With *Invisible Man* he gave us a novel way of seeing our literary and social possibilities. He was like a grandfather to us, like a wise guru or leader, and then when we became active, he looked back as if to say, like Eliot in Prufrock, 'that's not what I meant at all.' " Ralph had no interest in being seen as an activist. "I always felt," the historian John Hope Franklin said, "that Ralph was an artist in the purest sense, and this precluded his rolling up his sleeves and getting into the action that was necessary to reform our society."

Prominent among these young admirers late in 1970 was James Alan McPherson, a graduate of Harvard Law School. Encouraged by the leading figures then at *The Atlantic Monthly*—Michael Janeway, Edward Weeks, and Robert Manning—the twenty-seven-year-old McPherson (a contributing editor) began work on a piece on Ellison that grew and grew. "I told them that Ellison was the living writer I admired above all others, and they gave me a free hand and every encouragement," McPherson said. "Starting in the spring of 1970, I interviewed and corresponded with Ralph, but I also traveled to attend some of his lectures, to hear what he had to say and how he interacted with people. He was very good to work with, respectful but independent." The result, "Indivisible Man," cosigned by the men, was probably the richest portrait of Ellison since Warren's *Who Speaks for the Negro?* The cover of the December 1970 issue of *The Atlantic* sported a stunning photograph of Ralph taken by Gordon Parks. Dressed in a rain-sprinkled Burberry trench coat, its tan shade setting off his nut-brown skin, his fedora (covering his baldness) deftly tilted, Ralph seemed the epitome of mature, masculine grace and power.

The response was a flood of cheering letters. "All kinds of people from all kinds of places have called us," Fanny wrote happily. The letters and calls came not only from friends such as Robert Hayden, John Hope Franklin, Mary Hemingway, and Nathan Scott but also from younger writers now enlisting as irregulars in the Ellison brigade. *America,* a magazine published by the United States Information Agency, distributed an excerpt throughout Soviet Russia. That Ralph as a black man could command an *Atlantic Monthly* number in so virile and polished a fashion counted for much in a culture riddled with insecurities. Not everyone was impressed, of course. The following year, 1971, the wildly popular, spunky young poet Nikki Giovanni, in her volume of autobiography *Gemini,* spoke for many of her peers in dismissing Ralph. "I never wanted to be Ralph Ellison," she insisted. *The Atlantic Monthly* cover story "was pitiful. He's not worth it." Although *Invisible Man* is a good book, "as a writer Ellison is so much hot air, because he hasn't had the guts to go on writing." A year later, in *Time,* she hadn't changed her mind: "He can put us down and say we are not writers, who are persistently exposing our insides and trying to create a reality."

Closing out 1970, Ralph joined the poet John Hollander and the art critic Harold Rosenberg on a featured panel at the annual convention of the Modern Language Association, with "The Artist and the City: The New York Experience" as their topic. The New York experience indeed needed explicating. Whatever one might say of its storied, glamorous past (eliding its darker patches, including slavery), the current reality of the city was forbidding. More than ever, stark differences divided rich from poor, white from black and brown. Ralph straddled both worlds. Just before Christmas, shopping at Gucci on Fifth Avenue, he picked up a pricey leather handbag for Fanny. Returning home to 730 Riverside Drive, he had to watch his step. A flyer urging the residents of his building to unite against crime also dubbed his neighborhood "the fastest deteriorating area in New York City." The buildings at 740 and 745 Riverside Drive were "the worst center of dope distribution, crime and violence in our whole area." A recent police operation had netted over 150 arrests. Muggers pounced on tenants in the lobby, the elevators, and even the upper hallways of the Beaumont "at various times during the day and night." Before Ralph led Tucka out into the dark on his nightly walk, he donned a rough jacket and slipped a knife into his pocket.

Nevertheless, Ralph and Fanny—Ralph, certainly—were determined not to move. Rent was cheap, the view of the Hudson almost priceless. In fact, they coveted the eight rooms of apartment 11C, where one of the few remaining white tenants, an aged lady, held on. In May, with the death of Eugene Ramsey, the black West Indian–born owner of the Beaumont since the early 1950s, some tenants began to discuss buying the building from the widow Ramsey and converting it into a cooperative venture. Fanny was among the leaders in this move. Unfortunately, most tenants could not afford to buy their apartments. Even with a guarantee of a loan of $50,000 from Ralph's friend Roger Stevens, the conversion effort died.

A brave man, Ralph loved where he lived. He cherished its proximity to Harlem (to many people it *was* Harlem); the majestic river, fogbound on some days like Huck and Jim's Mississippi; the passing boats and ships; Riverside Park, leafy green for much of the year, its trees austere in winter but revealing even more of the river; and certain subtle elements that reminded him of his family's deep past. "One reason I live here," he told the journalist Hollie West, "is that there's a railroad track right down there. I've got a river, a highway and a railroad track. I like to hear those cars bumping along there." During Reconstruction his father's people had built railroad trestles, and his cousin Tom Brown of Oklahoma had put in almost fifty years as a fireman on the Santa Fe Railroad. Folklore was an essential part of Ralph's literary vision and practice, and "so much of folklore is mixed up with traveling, with freight trains, with the sounds of trains and so on. That's the advantage of having lived close to the railroads."

For Fanny, the situation was less romantic. "Don't ever live in New York," she warned the sculptor Tex Schiwetz, a friend from their Rome years who now lived in rural Georgia, unless one was "prepared to be the target along with 7 million other people of bomb threats, blackouts, disastrous fires, muggings, and strikes which invade your very home." Gotham life was tough—"but would we move away from here? No!" But with the security of his NYU job, and three years after the fire, she began to push quietly toward reclaiming their Plainfield life. With her retirement, Fanny's life had become an uneasy blending of privilege and despair. She had risen in the world with Ralph, if mainly as a dependent. She could see that Ralph knew now that he needed her, but the wounds sustained in 1957 in Rome had not healed completely. She was, though, in far greater control of her emotions, just as Ralph had become more considerate, more solicitous. "We have an awful lot of fun and the years are flying by," she wrote cheerfully to Schiwetz. "I'm never bored," she said to another friend. She claimed "a full and harmonious life" with Ralph and Tucka and two parakeets, her time spent mainly on "house chores and keeping his papers and correspondence in order."

Feeling her age—sixty late in 1970 (although she now claimed fifty-six in order to match Ralph)—Fanny saw herself on a downward path. She took Geritol to boost her energy. She slept late, and let the chores pile up. "Ralph, on the other hand," she noted freely, "is working better than he has for years—he works on the novel in the morning and on essays in the afternoons . . . every day!" Ralph, replenished by success after success, seemed at the height of his powers. She was fading. At Christmas she got her Gucci bag but gave Ralph nothing. She waited until Christmas Eve before rushing out guiltily to look for Ralph's gift. She found a shiny espresso machine, but the hour was too late to have it delivered and it was too heavy to lug home. As always, she put up Christmas window lights, but did so on December 26.

Early in 1971, Ralph taught his first class at NYU, in a course on "The American Vernacular as Symbolic Action." "Dr. Ellison" listed on his syllabus old favorites by Constance Rourke and Kenneth Burke, as well as more recent criticism by Richard Bridgman, Leo Marx, Howard Mumford Jones, and John A. Kouwenhoven, whose *The Beer Can by the Highway: Essays on What's American About America* was one of Ralph's favorites on the gumbo of American culture.

Attendance was encouraging at first before lethargy set in. Ignoring Socrates, he lectured relentlessly, and often from mildewed notes. Some students listened; others slipped into a mild torpor. As at Bard, few blacks enrolled in his courses. "There were very few black undergraduates and almost no black graduate students at NYU then," Amritjit Singh, an alumnus, recalled. "There is no doubt in my mind that he could have been a great teacher, if he wanted to. It's just that he refused to dwindle into becoming a mere college professor." He didn't mix and mingle with students. "He seemed not to want any more students than he had." Eventually some of the graduate students and even some colleagues started calling him, behind his back, "the invisible man."

Avoiding the lecture circuit, he spent more time than ever at the Century, or on committee meetings among the elect at the American Academy, or on the advisory committee of the increasingly moribund National Book Award. The main excitement that year came from the Yale classicist Erich Segal's *Love Story,* a dish of warm syrup set mainly at Harvard. Ralph agreed with Bill Styron, who damned the outrageously popular novel as "a banal book which simply doesn't qualify as literature." Then, early in the year, he added significantly to his already striking list of board memberships. Two years after they had first inspected Ralph, the trustees of the Colonial Williamsburg Foundation in Virginia elected him a member. Behind the appointment was almost certainly its director, Carlisle H. Humelsine, who had served with Ralph both on the American Revolution Bicentennial Commission and on the Kennedy Center board.

Ralph would look forward eagerly to the May and November meetings in Virginia, as Colonial Williamsburg joined the Century Association and the American Academy of Arts and Letters to form his golden triangle of institutional commitments. For him, the rare appeal of Colonial Williamsburg was the way it blended American colonial history with the ancestral culture of the South, and also the extent to which it brought him into further contact, as equals nominally, with wealthy, powerful, educated whites. In his mind, this was proof of his distinction but also of the decline of racism in America. He was thrilled that his fellow trustees included Winthrop Rockefeller and Abby Aldrich Rockefeller, the granddaughter of John D. Rockefeller, Jr., the pillar of American capitalism who in 1926 had launched this project in historic reclamation. Also on the board were scholars and cultural critics with whom he felt comfortable, including Edgar Shannon, a former English professor now president of the University of Virginia, and the popular historian Daniel Boorstin of the University of Chicago, who had also served with Ralph on the American Revolution Bicentennial Commission.

As the first black trustee, Ralph stood out. The truth about slavery in colonial times was a touchy subject, one represented only in fleeting glimpses in the restored and simulated village of Colonial Williamsburg. With his appointment the white trustees were heeding inevitable political pressures and also taking a step toward historical truth. And here, as elsewhere, Ralph made no particular effort to encourage more racial integration, to raise the profile of blacks. He was sure that in the fullness of time, and inspired quietly by his own stellar influence, the board would elect other qualified blacks if and when it found them. In the meantime, he represented the race by making friends with his fellow trustees, enjoying the rich dinners (usually with Fanny), and adding to the conversation at board meetings without asserting any sort of pushy agenda.

For many sensitive blacks, the unacknowledged scent of slavery fouled the air at Colonial Williamsburg as it did at Monticello, Thomas Jefferson's home, where tour guides spoke of "servants" or "dependents" and never of slaves. Ralph and Fanny knew that to some extent they were complicit in this suppression of history in the name of progress. Fourteen years after their first visit, she would write to a friend about that visit and, in particular, a reception on the back veranda of Bassett Hall, the refined period building where at least two Rockefeller families stayed from time to time. The autumn sun was sinking as she and Ralph, the only blacks present who were not servants, ventured where, most likely, no black couple had ever been allowed. A cold drink in her hand, and with the chatter of rich white folks in her ears, Fanny looked out over a green grove of trees and plush meadows eddying down to the water's edge. The past that Colonial Williamsburg embalmed so exquisitely—a history of massacred English settlers, of dispossessed and eventually exterminated Indians, and of black slaves sweating in the cotton fields—seemed to come alive. "And there we all were with drinks in hand," she recalled, "choosing for the moment not to remember."

If to some observers Ralph's pride in passively serving Colonial Williamsburg eluded easy understanding, its significance to him is clear in a letter he would write in 1978 to the University of Virginia in support of James Alan McPherson, who was then up for tenure in the English Department. Ralph hailed the proposed appointment (it's possible that he didn't know that three other blacks, one with tenure, had fled the department four years before), especially "because in its quiet way it aroused hopes for the reconciliation of issues that have long flawed America's drama of social hierarchy." The tenuring of McPherson was "dramatic." In addition to being "an *educational* event, it was also vibrant with that power to stir the depths of emotion and memory that is released by deeply meaningful symbolic actions. Would but that our professional dramatists could tap such lodes of drama which lie so near the surface of our daily affairs! But then the real drama of American society has seldom found its way to the stage." This appointment (which McPherson won but soon gave up) and Colonial Williamsburg were part of his idyll of the South, of Huck and Jim on their raft, of white aristocrats and their black counterparts, whose nobility could not be erased by Jim Crow.

On March 22, on spring break from NYU, Ralph and Fanny went on a special vacation. (Aside from their Plainfield ventures, this is the only major vacation on record for which they actually paid their way.) They broke their rule against flying together after sending their lawyer an "in case of death" letter that left most of their estate to Herbert. Passing through Savannah, they went to Ossabaw, Georgia, one of the largely unspoiled but threatened islands on the Atlantic coast off the Carolinas and Georgia. (The main threat was real estate developers, who envisioned condominiums and golf courses built for whites on vast tracts of land virtually untouched since the days of slavery.)

On Ossabaw their host was Tex Schiwetz. Aged and gray-bearded, Schiwetz was a near-recluse in love with this landscape. In Rome he had worked mainly in marble, but here on Ossabaw he found inspiration in the fantastic shapes sculpted by nature out of driftwood, the white skeletons of trees, the subtly shifting dunes of sand along the island's eight miles of Atlantic beach. Liked by local blacks and whites alike, Schiwetz was a committed conservationist. For eight days the Ellisons lived the simple life. With Schiwetz as their guide they walked about the island, learning about its flora and fauna, as Ralph snapped photographs of egrets, wild turkeys, alligators, otters, seductive flowers, lowering clouds, and haunting sunsets.

Returning to New York, Ralph agreed to join artists including Samuel Barber and Aaron Copland on the advisory board of Schiwetz's conservation project. This proved to be yet another token involvement. Although he appreciated the efforts of visionaries like Schiwetz, ecology was not of major concern to him. (Eventually, much of Ossabaw Island would become a nature conservancy.) Urban pleasures were much more to his liking, as when he took part in what he affectionately called "the yearly Academy riot" and "that much too wordy brawl" that drew the cultural elite on May 26 to Audubon Plaza and the headquarters of the American Academy and National Institute of Arts and Letters. The annual "riot" and the Ellisons' post-ceremony buffet supper meant so much to him that he refused to attend the dedication of the Lyndon Baines Johnson presidential library in Austin, Texas, held on the same day. Not even a handwritten note from the ailing Johnson ("you are still very much wanted") that guaranteed him a seat on a chartered jet leaving and returning to New York on the same day could change his mind.

But escaping New York City in the summer of 1971 was very much on his and Fanny's agenda. Much worse than the heat was the continuing rise in crime spawned by the sale and use of illegal drugs. In August, the cover of *New York* magazine showed the face of a young black man with a golden nose. This image illustrated the lead story, about the return of King Cocaine to the city, and the close links between drug addiction and blacks. Simmering tensions over racism and Black Power also continued to disrupt and corrupt American lives, especially in the cities. The fate of the Soledad Brothers (named after Soledad State Prison in California) haunted their many sympathizers across the nation. Young Jonathan Jackson had killed a white guard in Soledad. During an alleged attempt to escape, a white guard in San Quentin killed Jackson's brother, George. In February 1971 three Black Panthers, with their trademark black berets, expansive Afro hairstyles, and dark glasses, glared at readers from the cover of *Newsweek*. In August, the trial of nine Black Panthers in New Haven on the charge of murdering a fellow party member focused attention on

the Panthers, the police, and the judiciary. The president of Yale, Kingman Brewster, then shocked much of the nation by publicly expressing
doubt that the Panthers could get a fair trial almost anywhere in America.

In October, the Coalition for the Defense of the Panthers, linking sympathetic students, professors, and the NAACP, asked Ralph to speak at
a rally in New Haven. He declined. He supported neither Brewster's
skepticism about American justice nor black political radicalism linked
to violence and separatism. This refusal did not mean that he was politically inert. Along with notables such as Jackie Robinson, Representative
Shirley Chisholm, and Roy Wilkins, he signed a petition condemning the
New York Real Estate Board for obstructing efforts to achieve racial integration in housing. Given his lack of interest in Africa to this point, it was
remarkable when he joined Alfred Kazin, Diana Trilling, and Kurt Vonnegut, among others, on a committee aiding the novelist Kofi Awoonor,
clapped in jail in his native Ghana on flimsy political charges.

In July, he revisited his relationship with Richard Wright when he went
with Fanny to deliver a lecture in Iowa at a two-week summer institute on
Afro-American culture, the first week of which was devoted to Wright.
The conference brought together almost every important Wright scholar,
old and young, black and white, American and European. They included
Donald Gibson, Edward Margolies, Keneth Kinnamon, Nick Aaron Ford,
and Michel Fabre, who was still at work on his biography. Ralph was
pleased to meet Fabre, who in the fall would co-edit "A Bibliography
of Ralph Ellison's Published Writings" in the journal *Studies in Black Literature*. Organizing the gathering was Charles T. Davis, the director of
the Institute for Afro-American Culture at the University of Iowa. A cultivated, affable man, Davis had been probably the first black assistant
professor at Princeton. Shortly he would move to Yale, where he would
create a racially integrated, intellectually rigorous African-American Studies program that would produce many future leaders in the field. Without
fanfare or fuss, Davis would seek to fuse Ralph's pluralist and yet integrationist vision of America to the rebellious spirit of younger blacks
within the framework of an elite American university. The Iowa gathering
was Ralph's introduction to what Black Studies could become in steady
hands.

Welcomed as the keynote speaker on July 18 (and paid an honorarium
of $1,500), Ralph delivered a sinewy lecture based on his intimate knowl-
edge of Wright. In New York, Wright had been his first model of the dedicated black writer. Wright had also asked him to compose his first review

and his first short story. Ralph also wanted his audience to know that, despite this help, his own intellect hadn't been a blank slate in those days. He had already read many major texts. Impressed by the manuscript of *Native Son,* he nevertheless would soon be on a literary course altogether different from Wright's. This moving lecture, well received in Iowa, was later published as "Remembering Richard Wright."

A vacation on Long Island Sound was so refreshing that Fanny freely admitted on their return that "the grubbiness of the neighborhood is pretty much of a shock." Graffiti, the latest indignity, was spreading unimpeded, and she knew exactly whom to blame. "The Puerto Ricans have scrawled on every building front," she noted, "between the southern side of 150th and 145th streets." (The Ellisons lived on the north side of 150th Street.) Rebuilding in Plainfield now seemed necessary, and financing was no problem. In addition to his salary, raised to $36,500 in his second year, Random House agreed to pay him $125,000 over four years as an advance against royalties from the Vintage paperback editions of *Invisible Man* and *Shadow and Act.* By 1972 *Invisible Man* was selling about 125,000 copies annually. That year, a poll of one hundred leading critics by two Penn State professors listed it once again as the post–World War II American novel most likely to endure. (Saul Bellow was deemed the most important novelist.)

This new level of prosperity showed itself in fancier clothing for both Fanny and Ralph. To many of his colleagues, who made do with aging tweed jackets, nondescript ties, fraying cuffs, and sensible shoes, Ralph was the most elegantly garbed professor at the university. "I was in awe of him, although he was always pleasant," Ken Silverman recalled. "His clothes seemed tasteful and expensive. He was always beautifully barbered, his thin mustache trimmed precisely, with the pleasant aroma of aftershave lotion trailing him. He was always very done-up, formal, but he carried it off well. You noticed his shoes, too. They were often sporty, like saddle shoes; sometimes two-toned, and always made of what looked like very fine leather."

Unfortunately, his teaching did not measure up to this finery. The course he offered in the fall of 1972 differed only slightly from what he had offered in the spring. John Maynard loyally called it an "omnibus course, for undergraduates and graduates," but others saw it as mere repetition. This was not the way to attract students. Robert Raymo, a medievalist who had been Ralph's colleague and friend at Rutgers almost a decade before, recalled him as attracting "very few students. I found this very sad and discouraging, and he did, too. He was reclusive— he reacted to the students by becoming reclusive. The black students wouldn't have anything to do with him, and the white students were few. Ralph wanted to be popular, but on his own, decent terms."

Intriguingly, as well as perhaps amusingly, his first major use of his Schweitzer chair was to hire to teach postwar American fiction a "white" man Ralph knew to be black. This near-incarnation of Ralph's character Bliss, who is brought up black but later becomes the racist Senator Sunraider, was Anatole Broyard, a staff book reviewer for the *New York Times.* His darker-skinned sister Shirley was married to Franklin Williams of the NAACP. Born in New Orleans, Broyard had moved to New York to become a writer. He then decided to pass for white. His children by his wife, who was white, apparently would find out the truth about him only after his death. In the 1970s he was one of the few readers and critics of Ralph's novel-in-progress. ("Albert [Murray] and Anatole's objections to proliferations of dreams miss their function as revelations of psychic states," Ralph complained in a note.) Philip Roth would use Broyard as the main inspiration for the hero of his novel *The Human Stain,* published in 2000. As for Broyard, perhaps he, too, enjoyed the joke. He named his only daughter Bliss.

And when Ralph acquired a doctoral student, he was neither Negro nor white but a Sikh from India. Amritjit Singh had come from Delhi to NYU on a Fulbright scholarship, expecting to work on Hemingway. Instead, he soon gravitated toward African-American literature. The novels of the Harlem Renaissance became the topic of his doctoral dissertation. On the advice of his thesis director, who knew nothing about the subject, Singh sent Ralph a copy of his prospectus. After a while, word came that, yes, Professor Ellison would see him. "Behind a door I found a large room," Singh recalled, "where his secretary worked." Behind her was another closed door, then another large, dark room with bookshelves, "and sitting behind a big desk was the great man himself." Waving Singh into a seat, Ralph was blunt in his first question. "Mr. Singh," he asked, "how do you justify calling people 'black' when all of their lives they had called themselves Negro?" The question astonished Singh. "I guess when he saw the look on my face, how incredulous I was, he dropped the matter," Singh said. "He relaxed a little, and pretty soon he assured me that he would work with me."

As he pushed forward on his dissertation, Singh found Ralph helpful.

"I would get a postcard from him," he remembered, "telling me to call him on the telephone at such and such a time—so *I* would pay for the calls—and he would be there, at home, when I called. Sometimes he spoke to me for about an hour, going over various points in the chapter I had sent him. He was always courteous, polite, encouraging." As for Ralph's first, dismaying question to him, Ralph perhaps liked to challenge students, but had deeper reasons for calling himself Negro. "My grandmother and grandfather were Negroes," he explained. "My father and mother were Negroes; my friends, teachers, ministers, physicians were Negroes. I'm pretty close to black, but I'm pretty close to brown, too. In a cultural sense, the term 'Negro' tells me something about the mixture of African, European, and native-American styles which define me. . . . Black, in America, connotes a certain ideological stance. In that sense, I am not black. I am a Negro-American writer. I emphasize Negro because it refers specifically to American cultural phenomena."

Singh may well have been the only graduate student on whose dissertation committee Ralph served. He was doing little of a public nature with his chair. Despite his announced plans, he hadn't brought any lecturers to NYU. Some of the money simply went back to the state. Reporting to a budget-conscious state assemblyman in 1971, he ingeniously defended his record. "Not only does it take time to assemble men of the insight and stature I have in mind," Ralph wrote, "I am also aware of the responsibility that should be exercised in the handling of public funds." For his "program," which was "interdisciplinary," he had "approached" notable men such as Kenneth Burke, John Kouwenhoven, Harold Rosenberg of the University of Chicago, and Gordon Parks. From France would come, he expected, André Malraux, who had stepped down as minister of culture, and Maurice Couve de Murville, the former premier. He also hoped to do something with public television. In fact, it was not until April 1972 that the first speaker (Kenneth Burke) sponsored by Ralph's Schweitzer professorship came.

Ellison remained active with small projects, such as joining the Bicentennial Fellowship Committee of Phi Beta Kappa to help screen candidates in its fellowship competition. For a book of essays on Wright that Charles Davis was editing, he revised the transcript of "Remembering Richard Wright." He claimed to be planning a book of short stories. "It has been my plan to publish a collection," he wrote, "but not until I write more stories. I'm hoping that will be soon." This project went nowhere. As it turned out, Ralph's only volume of short stories, *Flying Home,* appeared posthumously, with not one piece in it written after 1956. He continued to hint that his novel would appear soon. Declining to take part in a major symposium on civil rights at the Johnson Library in Texas, he cited the need to meet a "deadline from my publishers."

He often gave in perhaps too easily to the demons of success. Some notes scribbled by Fanny one evening late in 1972 offer a peek at the demons in action. After going alone to see *Lady Sings the Blues,* a movie about Billie Holiday, and loving it, she had returned home around 6:30 p.m. Ralph was waiting, "hungry but nice." Out all afternoon, first at a board meeting and then at the Century, he "came home in drenched rain soaked shoes, & drunk." Apparently, arriving home inebriated from the Century was not unusual for Ralph. Fanny saw many of Ralph's downtown engagements as a waste. Although she enjoyed some of the socializing, she believed that he was at his best as a human being when he was writing. She deplored the hobnobbing with "all big muckity mucks whom I wish would drop dead. Because when R is away from his typewriter for 64 consecutive hours he becomes a tortured man."

For Ralph, escaping the "big muckity mucks" was hard. Honors still came his way, driven mainly by his reputation as an artist and as a man of integrity who was fearless in a trying time. Ralph saw danger in precipitous social change but wanted nonetheless to be part of genuine change. Such was the case in May, when the board of visitors of Wake Forest University of North Carolina, a respected, historically white Southern school, elected Ralph a member. An old friend, Harold Hayes of *Esquire* magazine, had vouched for his suitability as the first black. For the next fifteen years, he would serve proudly on the board.

A similar conquest came on June 4 when, in accepting an honorary degree from the College of William and Mary in Williamsburg, he also delivered the commencement address. The second-oldest American college, William and Mary was an exclusive state school in Virginia, where resistance to racial integration was a burning issue in a state proud of its past and the culture that had produced Washington and Jefferson. Ralph carried the day. His overwhelmingly white audience heard little that rebuked the status quo, except that Ralph's dark-skinned body, keen mind, and eloquent speech effectively challenged the deadly myth of black inferiority. When he was done speaking, the ovation was loud and long.

These victories on distant campuses tended to belie the fact that he was still less than settled at NYU. In September 1972, Ralph returned there to find his stature diminished. With the state in sudden financial trouble, the legislature in Albany had slashed the budgets of the Schweitzer professorships. Ralph's allotment was now $50,000, half its original size. Chipping in to subsidize it, NYU imposed economies. His private secretary and suite of rented rooms were in jeopardy. None of his projects as Schweitzer professor was, because he had planned none. His salary was untouched.

That year he made nearly $100,000, or about ten times the salary of a starting assistant professor. In the fall he spent almost $3,500 on new stereo equipment, cameras, photographic accessories, and the like. At a cost of $2,400 he swaddled Fanny in her first mink coat. He and Fanny stepped up their annual giving to charities. The largest donation, $1,500, went to the fund at Bennington College in honor of the late Stanley Edgar Hyman. Ralph continued to send money to the NAACP Legal Defense Fund. He also signed an advertisement in September in the *New York Times* soliciting funds for the Emergency Campaign for Social Justice run by the Legal Defense Fund. With the fund now fighting over one thousand cases across the nation, he joined the executive committee of the campaign. Although he attended few meetings, he didn't want to hold himself aloof from the issue of civil rights, even if his main sympathies were with the old guard. Early in 1972, at the New York Hilton, he was eloquent when he joined Vernon Jordan of the National Urban League, the Harlem businessman and political leader Percy Sutton, and other black leaders in paying tribute to Roy Wilkins at the annual fellowship dinner of the NAACP. To many young black activists, Wilkins epitomized the sickly spirit of compromise. Ralph saw the disorganized Black Power movement as a disruptive force that depended on insult, rage, and antagonism. This disruptive quality was on painful display that fall when movement leaders such as Jordan, Wilkins, Julian Bond, and Roy Innis joined an ailing Lyndon Johnson at the formal opening of the civil rights archives at the Johnson Library in Austin, Texas. Out of loyalty to Johnson, who had survived a stroke some months before, Ralph attended the gathering. He was present during its ugliest moment, when Innis threatened to break it up unless those present allowed him to speak at length. The meeting was in an uproar until a tired, trembling Johnson took to the podium to call for peace.

Regretting this turn of events, Ralph bade goodbye to the former president and Lady Bird Johnson and returned home. The following year, 1973, after Johnson's death, the Ellisons became charter members of the

Friends of the Johnson Library. In the presidential elections of 1972, with the incumbent Richard Nixon campaigning against the Democrat George McGovern, Ralph took no active role in support of the antiwar McGovern, whom he perhaps found too liberal. After McGovern's landslide defeat, Ralph was asked to become a founding sponsor of the Coalition for a Democratic Majority, along with Jeane Kirkpatrick (later a conservative Republican stalwart), Norman Podhoretz, Bayard Rustin, and others. This organization hoped to move the Democrats closer to the center. Sympathetic to the centrist aims of the coalition, Ralph was now non-committal about the party. Lyndon Johnson's dramatic actions in the 1960s to advance civil rights legislation had sparked his interest in electoral politics. With protective laws now firmly in place by 1972, he gave up on this interest.

He was an artist above all, Ralph reminded himself and others. He was therefore pleased in the fall of 1972 to begin a five-year term on the advisory board of the National Portrait Gallery in Washington. No doubt other black academics, trained in the field, knew more about art; but no black American brought to the boardroom table anything like Ellison's cultural authority, and few matched his experience developed over the years through his membership in pioneering organizations such as the Kennedy Center in Washington, the Commission on Public Broadcasting, the Bicentennial Commission, and the Council for the Humanities—to name only a few.

Quite apart from such connections, he continued to attract, albeit slowly, talented and persistent younger black writers and intellectuals. Dr. Harry Edwards, a controversial professor of sociology at the University of California, Berkeley, known for his caustic critiques of racism in American sports, wrote to Ralph praising him and asking to meet him. Edwards did so after reading a piece on Ralph in an unlikely place, the December 15 issue of *Muhammad Speaks,* the weekly newspaper of the Nation of Islam, or the Black Muslims. The editor of *Muhammad Speaks*— a periodical not known for its interest in belles lettres—was Leon Forrest, a promising fiction writer living in Chicago. Interviewing Ralph at 730 Riverside Drive, Forrest had made a good impression. "Leon adored Ralph," Toni Morrison recalled. Ralph's response to Forrest was a wary mixture of generosity and withholding.

Forrest had come to New York mainly to meet with Morrison, a young editor at Random House, which was about to publish his first novel, *There Is a Tree More Ancient Than Eden.* Ralph had played no part either in the signing of Forrest or in the hiring of Morrison, who was one of no more than three black editors working at a major book publisher in Manhattan. Nor would Ralph have wanted, apparently, any part in her hiring. "At Random House," Morrison said, "he was unhelpful when I tried to enlist him on behalf of new or younger writers. Leon Forrest was the exception." Morrison courted black writers. "I published white writers mainly but I always looked out for black talent—people like Gayl Jones, Henry Dumas, Toni Cade Bambara, Lucille Clifton, June Jordan. Unfortunately, Ralph had no interest in rallying for such writers"—or for black editors. "I have no doubt," she said, "that if Albert Erskine, who was quite friendly to me, or anyone else at Random House had asked him if he wanted to meet me, he would have said no." At Morrison's urging, nevertheless, Ralph wrote a three-paragraph foreword to Forrest's *There Is a Tree More Ancient Than Eden*. "He said, 'I don't normally do this sort of thing.' 'Yes, I know,' I told him. 'That's why it would be so helpful.'"

Invited to President Nixon's inauguration, Ralph didn't go but was in Washington on January 30 to take part in a writing conference with Wallace Stegner, John Barth, Ernest Gaines, and, from Ralph's deep past, Margaret Walker, who had published a popular historical novel, *Jubilee*, set in the slave South. Reflecting a pluralistic vision of America, the panels included women, men, blacks, whites, and a Kiowa writer from Oklahoma, N. Scott Momaday (a protégé of Stegner at Stanford), who would win the Pulitzer Prize in fiction for his *House Made of Dawn*. America was now speaking with many voices, and Ralph probably saw the event as a vindication of his faith in a united pluralism.

The following month he published "Cadillac Flambé," the seventh section of the novel in print thus far. Appearing in Ted Solotaroff's *American Review*, "Cadillac Flambé" is perhaps the most realist of the eight excerpts to appear during Ralph's lifetime. At its heart is a black musician, Minifees, who commits one of the most outrageous acts imaginable in the black world as conjured up by Ralph. Offended by Senator Sunraider's racist rantings, the musician drives his fine white Cadillac onto Sunraider's lawn and, in protest, sets the car on fire in a drama narrated by a white reporter.

"Cadillac Flambé" provoked the interest of some readers by its comic exuberance and tricky range of allusions. At the very least, it reassured Ralph's admirers that he was still capable of writing bright fiction. It relieved, for the moment, the growing anxiety of those who had begun to doubt that the master was still in command of his craft.

· · ·

Early in March, at the Century, Ralph introduced Robert Penn Warren when he read some of his poetry at a "literary afternoon" to which ladies were invited. Slowly, pressure was building to admit them as members, an idea toward which Ralph remained unsympathetic. He seemed almost as opposed, in practice, to admitting other blacks. Morrison, one of the first women to be offered a membership at the Century, remembered that Ralph made no attempt to make her feel welcome, and never said hello when they met. "My suspicion was that he considered himself an exception. He got to speak for us but he did not like to be identified with us." Early in 1973 the widow of a former member complained about the situation to Ralph. Why didn't the Century have more blacks? She wanted to get to know more blacks. She had met the acclaimed artist Jacob Lawrence at dinner once, and he seemed a lovely man. "Why shouldn't he be a member of the club?" she asked. "Why shouldn't you put him up? . . . You may be very lonely in the club." But Ralph saw no point in pushing for change based on racial reasons. He had earned his way in. Let other blacks do the same.

The blacks he cherished the most were those figures, many of them now spectral, from his deep past in Oklahoma. Thus he was hit hard in March when Virgil Branam died unexpectedly. After thirty years at sea, Virgil had retired but taken a part-time job as a crossing guard, shepherding schoolchildren in Berkeley, California. One day, agitated by a minor traffic accident, he suffered a massive, fatal heart attack. To Ralph, Virgil had been one of the heroic figures of his youth, an irrepressible comedian, a rowdy, sexy smasher of rules and taboos. In later years, mainly through postcards from distant ports, but also when he lived in New York, he had been for Ralph a prime connection to his youth. Two years before, Ralph had written lovingly to a mutual childhood friend about "the Great Big Black One," as Virgil was known among his pals. "I lived during a most painful part of my adolescent confusion in the reflected light of his outrageous glory."

"Well, let's face it," he mused, "we were told that you can't go home again and it's true—except in dreams, memory, and through the recollections one shares with friends." His infrequent trips back to Oklahoma City were inevitably bittersweet. Meeting old friends, some now infirm, "and reminiscing with them over drinks, helps kill some of the pain of times lost and scenes vanished, and even restores some of the ghosts from the past. Everyone remembers vividly something that has grown dim for the rest and the talking brings the old days alive again." Branam had made the old days live again, and now he, too, was gone. "Slowly, slowly—and too often not so slowly—we all go into the dark."

This was a momentary expression of sadness, not despair. Strong-willed, he looked resolutely to the future. He still had work, important work, to do. The major task remained clear. Early in June, he denied a request from National Public Radio "because both my agent and my publisher" wanted him to do no more interviews "until the publication of my next novel." Among the lesser tasks, he agreed to join a visiting inspection committee at Hampshire College. The Authors Guild Foundation elected him a board member. He joined the national council of the new Museum of African Art in Washington. In Manhattan, Whitney North Seymour, the former head of the American Bar Association and a member with Ralph of the Bicentennial Commission, talked him into joining one of his organizations, Citizens for a Sensible Landmarks Law.

In the spring of 1973, Ralph and Fanny were at last ready to return to Plainfield. Contacting a local contractor, and using deliberately modest plans drawn up by a friend in the Berkshires, they arranged for the construction of two rooms, with a kitchen and a bath, to be added to the old "studio," an outbuilding that had survived the fire. One room would be large enough for them to entertain guests. The other, much smaller, would be their bedroom.

When they reached Plainfield, they expected to find the work done. It wasn't. After hammering and sawing furiously for two or three days, the workers usually vanished as they juggled jobs to keep their income flowing. Their plumber provided water for the bathroom, but a new stainless-steel sink, a dishwasher, an electric range, a freezer, and a water heater remained uninstalled for several weeks. Fuming, Ralph and Fanny washed their dishes in their bathtub. Complaining was almost pointless. A novice painter showed up, Ralph said, ineptly tried his hand at staining the new cabinets, "and has thus produced a color that makes me want to puke."

Nevertheless, in the sweet summer air of New England, Ralph felt renewed and recharged. Taking his tractor out of storage, he cut paths to their ponds and trimmed the green meadows. Breaking the soil for the first time in years, he and Fanny watched with pleasure as tomatoes, basil, and parsley took root. Next year, Ralph swore to Herbert, they would arrive in the late spring and plant rows of carrots and lettuce and, above all, greens—"Turnip greens! Mustard greens!" Tucka, now almost fourteen, seemed bewildered by this return to the land, but Ralph and Fanny relished it. "I haven't gotten as much work done," he wrote Herbert, "but I have a feeling that my mind is a lot clearer and I know that I've had more exercise than I've had for years." At times, he and Fanny seemed nonchalant about having come back ("it's fun and we feel lucky to be out of the city"), but they also believed that the horrendous wound opened by the fire had healed at last. The fire had come like a divine trial, a fitting symbol of what Ralph saw as the destructive civil disorders of the 1960s. They had survived the ordeal and had emerged not unscathed but more finely tempered than ever.

In August, the *Washington Post* ran a long, three-part interview with him that accurately summed up his role in the preceding decade. The Oklahoma-born journalist Hollie West started with a blunt question: "How do you feel about the criticism you sometimes get from black students who feel you haven't been militant enough?" "I say," Ralph replied, "you be your kind of militant and I'll be my kind of militant." Yes, the militants had caused him pain. But something fundamental was changing in America, even if not everyone recognized it. Many who had attacked him in public, he revealed, now assured him in private of their admiration. Although nasty skirmishes were still being fought, he was sure that people like him were winning the war by staying true to the ancient, tested Negro values and virtues. As for the black militants, "where are they today? Many of them are in exile. Many of them are exhausted." They had lost because "they were not rooted in what they could have been rooted into, which by inheritance they should have been rooted into." And he had won without compromising his core beliefs. "I am not a separatist," he stressed. "The imagination is integrative . . . and I'm unabashedly an American integrationist."

Most advocates of militant Black Power, Ralph said, were now discredited. As a West Indian, the fiery Stokely Carmichael had been unaware of certain truths of American life. (In 1969, Carmichael moved to Guinea, in West Africa, and became Kwame Ture.) Among these truths were the fierceness of the white will to violence and also, therefore, the crucial need for blacks to work out an accommodation with whites. In the long haul, defeating whites isn't really a possibility. Despite their moaning about brutal conditions below the Mason-Dixon Line, he noted, many of the former militants "are going back South to live." Blacks and whites alike needed to remember these primal truths about violence in America. The previous November, police had shot to death black students at

Southern University in Louisiana. In 1970, the National Guard had killed four white students at Kent State University in Ohio, and police had shot dead two black students at Jackson State University in Mississippi. Young people had to learn "that it's one thing to use violent rhetoric and it's another to deal with the violence which is released by the rhetoric." They had to learn "that Americans, when they get panicky, will kill you." The slaves had created Negro culture out of this core fact. "There never was a simple matter of frightening the white man," Ralph told West. "It was always a question of what to do when he got frightened, and our history has taught us he gets frightened awfully easy." Nonviolence had achieved the major goals of the civil rights movement. Radicals had then built their militancy on the same nonviolent resistance that they then claimed to despise.

Even of the nonviolent civil rights movement, Ralph was critical. Martin Luther King, Jr., was now a revered martyr, but while he lived many blacks had opposed or ignored him. "It's another instance," he pointed out, "of martyrdom endowing the martyr with a hell of a lot more following than he had during his struggles." As for King's opposition to the Vietnam War, he should have become a politician, "because he was moving in that direction—at least events were moving him in that direction." When West spoke of Dr. King possessing a dynamic unity of morals and ethics, Ralph commented dryly, "So it seems." Yes, King was moral, but "his morality was too simplistic." Morality is different when the state is involved, "because a state is based upon power and the exercise of power and that involves violence. There's always some violence in the offing— whether it's day-to-day stress between man and nature or between armed contingents of the various interests and aspects of authority."

Here Ralph was speaking not altogether unlike Dr. Bledsoe, the power-loving head of the college in *Invisible Man* who punishes and betrays the young narrator. For some time Ralph had been defending Bledsoe, if mostly in private, although for many readers he is an arch-villain. To him, Bledsoe was not evil but the epitome of Negro psychological and even spiritual ingenuity in response to white terror. Over the centuries they had developed a philosophy of life forged from those conditions and possessing its own morality, ethics, and aesthetics shaped in large part by that terror. In turn, the black lives shaped by that philosophy, such as Bledsoe's, had helped to shape American reality.

Ralph had seldom lost touch with these truths he held dear. While so many other people, in the sometimes harrowing past decade, had given in to sentimentality, despair, rage, or hatred, he had kept his poise. He agonized at times over his tense relationships with so many other blacks, and his mixture of mature self-confidence, on the one hand, and the core insecurity that kept him stuck so close to home even as he preached liberal universalism, on the other. For the moment, restored at last with Fanny to his acreage in New England, he was proud that he had kept the faith when many others had strayed, and was flourishing while so many others had perished.

19

The Monkey on His Back

1974–1979

How does one untangle the snarl of fate?

RALPH ELLISON (1975)

Early in 1974, to his embarrassment, Ralph found himself mentioned in an amusing *New York Times* essay about slowpoke American writers. Linked to the likes of Henry Roth, the reigning king of procrastinators (his only novel to this point, *Call It Sleep,* had come out in 1934), Ralph thickened the smoke rising from the 1967 fire. "When you lose 365 pages of a novel," he explained, in a major inflation of his real loss, "you just can't reclaim the subtleties, the abstract ideas, the rhythm, even punctuation, and you undergo a traumatic experience, even though you tell yourself you don't." The manuscript was now so long that "my editor says it's three books." Its theme was unusually challenging. "The book has to do with memory. I'm writing about what happens when people don't remember where they come from, and how this affects their loyalties."

Despite such explanations, Ralph's failure to produce the book, his lack of involvement in campus life, and financial problems at NYU combined to weaken his faculty position. He lost his personal secretary. In other ways, his prestige was reaffirmed. When the Modern Language Association elected him an honorary fellow, he became one of forty internationally known writers, including Beckett, Borges, and de Beauvoir, so honored. At Princeton, his former Rutgers colleague Joseph Frank, at work on a multivolume biography of Dostoyevsky, hinted that Princeton might soon offer Ralph a job. The University of Virginia formally invited Ralph to join its English faculty. In February, in another show of kinship with white Southerners, he and Fanny attended the Eudora Welty Award dinner in New York as "honorary members," or so he put it, "of a rather small committee of Eudora's friends."

Harvard, too, was interested in hiring him. It had made a mess of its dramatic venture into Black Studies shortly after students seized University Hall in the spring of 1969. During a faculty meeting that spring at which, according to one report, "some black students arrived carrying meat cleavers" (in fact, one student speaker had flashed a meat cleaver), the worried faculty had voted to create a full-fledged Department of Afro-American Studies, and not a subsidiary program. Students would take part in voting to select faculty. When John Hope Franklin and other major black scholars refused offers, Harvard had asked Ewart Guinier, a former trade unionist and a lawyer who had attended Harvard, to chair the department. Soon Guinier was struggling not only with whites such as the university president, Derek Bok, and Henry Rosovsky, dean of the Faculty of Arts and Sciences, but also with the few black professors hired by Harvard, including the young Jamaican sociologist and novelist Orlando Patterson. At one point, Guinier publicly denounced Patterson as "a patronized, colonized slave," while Patterson responded that Guinier was "a madman." Now Harvard wanted to appoint in English, entirely free of the Afro-American Studies Department, the most eminent black American writer.

On December 1, 1973, when Ralph joined Harold Cruse (whose 1967 study, *The Crisis of the Negro Intellectual,* he admired), Al Murray, and Nathan I. Huggins of Columbia University for a symposium at Harvard, he was in effect giving a job talk. Key black members of the faculty and administration, notably Martin Kilson of the Department of Government and Archie Epps, the dean of students, had also helped the students to shape it. To Kilson, the conference was "the only serious intellectual endeavor" undertaken at Harvard on the subject of race "after 7 years of a lot of strident black nationalism." Ralph was a genuine hero. "Without your own courageous example," he wrote Ellison, "in holding to a universalistic-cultural ground over [the] past decade of separatist mania among the brothers," little good would have been achieved. For Ralph to join the Harvard faculty would be a "God-send." At least one student shared this view. "He was a hero to me," Cornel West (Harvard '74) said. "Ellison was cosmopolitan, he was wise, he had the ability to connect the high brow with so-called low brow. I was thrilled to see him in the flesh." The second step came on January 31, 1974, when President Bok informed Ralph that Harvard's governing board would award him an honorary doctorate of letters. "Although I am overwhelmed by their gracious invitation," he replied, "I, nevertheless, am delighted to accept it." This boost was well timed. On February 14, at NYU, Dean R. Bayly Winder chided Ralph gently about "the lack of students" in his courses. Ralph then agreed to give four public lectures. Amritjit Singh recalled that the first was a success: "People came out in droves to see the 'invisible man.' "

Pressing forward, Henry Rosovsky came to Manhattan for dinner with Ralph at the Harvard Club. Then, on April 11, Ralph arrived in Cambridge. At five o'clock in University Hall in Harvard Yard, he sat down in a room hung with portraits of university luminaries to chat with Rosovsky, who let him know that Harvard was ready to hire him and could be "very flexible about the terms." Ralph savored the moment but did not commit himself. Later that evening, over cocktails and dinner at the faculty club, several professors of English inspected him while he inspected them. The department had never had a black faculty member, although over the years it had trained a few black graduate students. In 1969, under pressure, Harvard had offered its first course in African-American literature, taught by a popular, adventurous assistant professor, Roger Rosenblatt. Since then, the department had denied him tenure. Ironically, when Ralph visited Harvard he was in the middle of reading the manuscript of Rosenblatt's book *Black Fiction,* with a section on *Invisible Man,* for Harvard University Press. Admiring the study, he had telephoned a startled Rosenblatt to joust with him a little, then provided a blurb for his book.

The following day, perhaps even before Ralph left Cambridge, Rosovsky wrote a letter to Ralph offering a professorship with tenure. Matching Ralph's pay at NYU, he offered a salary of $37,000 a year. This sum, Rosovsky told him, would make Ralph the highest-paid member in the Faculty of Arts and Sciences at Harvard.

Picking among various offers of honorary degrees, on May 12 Ralph spoke to a crowd of over fifteen thousand at the University of Maryland commencement. "The dark underside of our history," he told the gathering ominously but also optimistically about America, "is now being projected into the light." Later that month, Wake Forest University in North Carolina, where he was a trustee, also awarded him a doctoral degree *honoris causa.* In between these two events he traveled with Fanny to his beloved Colonial Williamsburg, where the affection was mutual, for the annual spring meeting of its trustees. That month he joined its executive committee. Still the only black board member, he took pleasure in the various friendships with the wealthy and powerful, as well as the simply gifted, that membership brought him. At Christmas that year, for example, he and

Fanny exchanged cards with U.S. Supreme Court Justice Lewis F. Powell, Jr., and his wife, Jo.

Unquestionably, the most glittering event of the spring of 1974 was his return to Cambridge on June 12 to receive his Harvard degree and also address the class of '49 on its twenty-fifth anniversary. On this visit, with Harvard wooing them, he and Fanny stayed at 17 Quincy Street, the official home of President Bok and his wife, the writer Sissela Bok (her father was Gunnar Myrdal, whose *American Dilemma* had provoked Ralph in 1944). To Ralph, his alumni address was almost as important as the degree. Almost providentially, as he told his audience, he was now standing in the place where his namesake, Ralph Waldo Emerson, had delivered his revolutionary, cultural nationalistic address of 1837, "The American Scholar." Keenly aware of this ancestral figure, Ralph sought to link the mysteries of the American past to the present national chaos over the issues of race and social justice. He had approached the event, he admitted, as a black freshman "entering an Ivy League college for the first time" might have approached it, with a sense that he was "in the presence of a mystery—Please! Not that of race, but of the mystery of social hierarchy; that mystery which arises from strangeness and from the differences in life-style and experience existing between individuals and groups occupying different regions, neighborhoods and levels of the social pyramid." Those differences could be intense, "and a great deal of our misunderstanding springs from our failures of communication."

By accident, he said, he had stumbled into his own epiphany about America when the light of understanding at last broke for him. In the summer of 1953, wandering in Memorial Hall after taking part in a symposium, he had suddenly looked upward. For the first time he noticed engraved rows of the names of Harvard's Civil War dead. The list had shocked him into a climactic sense of the moral core of American, or New England, culture. In language that echoed Lincoln's Gettysburg Address, Ralph pondered the tragic fate of the Harvard men's sacrifice. Americans had either forgotten or ignored it. "A discontinuity had been imposed by the living," he noted sadly, "and their heroic gestures had been repressed along with the details of the shameful abandonment of those goals for which they had given up their lives." Setting aside as so much fluff the idea of intrinsic American "innocence," he spoke instead of "hubris" and "nemesis," which explained more accurately for him the current moral crisis. And yet Ralph was also optimistic. Since the *Brown* decision, riots and assassinations had stripped away the self-delusions of American life.

Now the chance for a national regeneration was at hand. Invoking Emerson's prescription against despair—"conscience and consciousness, more consciousness and more conscientiousness"—Ralph exhorted his listeners to fight for America. "Let us not be dismayed, let us not lose faith," he urged, "simply because the correctives which we have set in motion, and you have set in motion, took a long time. It took strong stomachs, it took strong arms, it took our capacity for violence and for humor to get us to this point. I say this to you, as one who believes that the difficulties which we face today are indeed minor."

This affirmative message from a black man moved many of the alumni, although the graduating seniors themselves were electrified by the Class Day address of Elliot Richardson, the former U.S. attorney general. Richardson had resigned rather than fire the special prosecutor, Archibald Cox, in the Watergate scandal that forced President Nixon to leave office later that year. The next morning, escorted by Professor Alan Heimert, class of '49, who was both Harvard's premier scholar of New England religion and a leader in the campaign to establish Black Studies peacefully at the university, Ralph entered Harvard Yard with other distinguished honorees. These incuded the cellist Mstislav Rostropovich, the soprano Beverly Sills, and the anthropologist Clifford Geertz. He was the only African-American. "Out of experience proudly inherited and thoughtfully observed," his citation read, "this deeply American writer asserts with clarity and power man's eternal search for his humanity."

Finally, he decided against Harvard. Although vigorous at sixty, he was too old for such a big move. Moreover, Harvard was asking him to intervene in a domestic dispute when he wasn't a family member. Years later, Henry Rosovsky said that Ralph had wanted to take the job but "it was a time of harsh words and threats of violence, and I think that he became scared of the situation. At NYU he didn't face any militant organization prepared to embarrass and humiliate him; but he couldn't be so sure about Harvard." Although he had more and more young black supporters, Ralph still had his enemies. In the June 1974 issue of the influential *Black World*, the novelist and poet Ishmael Reed pummeled him about his alleged habit of granting interviews "in which he puts down younger [black] writers for lack of 'craftsmanship'—no specifics, 'craftsmanship.'" According to Reed, although Ellison wrote "sly attacks" against black writers, his idea of craftsmanship "is merely giving the synopsis of a Hemingway or Fitzgerald novel he's read." This was only "rhetoric, the kind of thing his friends accuse younger Afro-American writers of indulging in."

Such criticism did not intimidate Ralph. "He saw the enormous jealousy that many black people had for other blacks who had succeeded,"
Stanley Crouch said. "He thought that Ishmael Reed was envious, and he
really had no respect for Reed's half-baked ideas." He was as tough with
offending whites. Commenting on a tribute to Malcolm Cowley planned
by the American Academy of Arts and Letters, he shared with his friend
Marchette Chute, one of the organizers, his disappointment with recent
academy actions. Her work on behalf of Cowley reassured him that
"those who seem inclined to embrace political positions that are more
fashionable than wise and who champion artistic modes that are more slick
than transcendent haven't completely taken over the place." She had restored "something of that pride that *I* felt in being a member and fellow of
those whom I considered the guardians of continuity and high standards
in character as well as in the arts."

After a quiet Plainfield summer in 1974, Ralph returned to NYU intend-
ing to step up his teaching activity there. He did some writing, but only
brief essays. As a member of the American Revolution Bicentennial Commission, he composed an elegantly phrased two-page notice about James
Armistead of Virginia. Born a slave, Armistead had joined Lafayette's army
around 1781. He had then served with such distinction as a spy on various
dangerous missions that the General Assembly of Virginia later paid for
his emancipation. Ralph contributed this piece of black and American
history to *Profiles of Patriots,* a volume that included essays by the major
historians Samuel Eliot Morison and Henry Steele Commager as well as
one by Chief Justice Warren Burger.

In November, with its annual dinner for new members, the Century
welcomed its second black member, Albert Murray. Ralph telephoned his
regrets, although it was not clear why he was unavailable. Nor is it certain, despite their long friendship, that he was one of Murray's sponsors.
(As he had done for Ralph, Robert Penn Warren was among Murray's
main champions.) A discordant note now sounded in their relationship.
Perhaps it had something to do with a measure of envy due to Murray's belated blossoming as a writer. Beginning in 1970 with *The Omni-Americans*
(a collection of pieces on African-American culture), every year he had
published one or two books, including the novel *Train Whistle Guitar* in
1974. It's clear, though, that Ralph didn't want Murray, or any other black
person for that matter, on the Colonial Williamsburg board. When his
colleagues there pointedly asked him to suggest two new trustees, he

offered up Albert Erskine and Richard Wilbur, even though the nominating committee had noted that some members believed that the board should be "more intersexual and interracial."

Ralph was now consolidating his resources and conserving his efforts. At home, Fanny spent much of her time in a mighty effort to put their voluminous archives in order. "It's a traumatic thing for me to do," she wrote, "since both Ralph's and my tendency is to keep, keep, keep. But something has to give and I have rationalized that if I close my eyes and just toss it out, it will never be missed since I've long ago forgotten what it was." Ralph did not help much or perhaps even join in the effort. Besides his writing, his cameras, his bourbon and cigars, his fine clothes, and his books and magazines, he was happier at home tending to other chores, such as taking care of the aged Tucka or tending his large flower cart full of African violets. Clipping dead leaves and repotting plants had become part of his Sunday routine, along with working his way through the dense thicket of the Sunday *New York Times*. They did not attend church.

Life was good—if one forgot the recalcitrance of his novel-in-progress, the tensions with other black writers, the inherent difficulty for a black man in feeling genuinely accepted by the whites among whom he moved as a putative equal. He had money to spend. In 1975, as a board member, Ralph pledged $5,000 to the Kennedy Center for the Performing Arts. He and Fanny bought more pricey African art. To a reliable dealer on West 77th Street Ralph paid $700 for a wooden female doll from Upper Volta. The following year he spent $3,000 on an Eshu cult figure from the Yoruba and $1,700 for a Shango cult figure. Two years later, he paid $3,000 for another mask. In 1977, an appraiser valued the Ellisons' entire art collection at $90,000, with the African pieces the most valuable. But despite this collecting, Ralph and Fanny still showed no interest in knowing Africa or Africans. "I am not a Pan-Africanist," he told the young black poet Quincy Troupe. "I love the art for itself. Nor am I anti-Africa." (If Ralph ever wrote to or was visited by an African, the evidence apparently doesn't exist.) He began an informal association with the Museum of Primitive Art in New York. Citing that link, the Metropolitan Museum of Art made Ralph and Fanny "complimentary" members.

If some people saw collecting art objects as a bourgeois affectation, Ralph now defiantly spoke of bourgeois values as important to black America. He made this point early in 1975 in a concise essay in the *Los Angeles Times* after the U.S. Census Bureau reported that, despite the protests of radicals, most blacks now belonged to the nation's middle-income group. He also noted that having a middle-range income was not necessarily the same as being middle-class. The latter bespoke a sense of aspiration and responsibility. "A large and expanding middle-income group is a precondition for social progress," he argued. "The existence of a middle class—with its intellectual, political and social sophistication—is the most reliable sign of any group's qualitative growth and development." In spurning middle-class values in favor of Black Power rhetoric, black society had knifed itself near its heart, so that "black Americans may never transcend the valueless and directionless void in which we now find ourselves." He knew personally black professors and even college presidents whose homes "were devoid of books or serious art." How could such a group ever lead the people?

His bookshelves rose from floor to ceiling. Also on display were bronze medals of Emerson and Lincoln; a photograph of Faulkner and Malraux; a postcard showing Botticelli's *Birth of Venus;* a figure of Hercules; a porcelain head of Eros. Ralph deliberately set a framed photograph of Mark Twain against a dark background to show off the picture's gray scale, thus "introducing what I hope is a not too intrusive symbolism of blackness. For after all, didn't he discover the proper literary use of Afro-American folklore, and didn't he feel rather darkly about human nature? And didn't he balance his pessimism with good bourbon and fine cigars? What *lares!* What *penates!*" These objects were indeed his household gods. And, after ten years of struggle, his gods were winning. The Black Power and Black Arts movements were now in retreat, so Ralph believed, in the erratic swing toward Marxism-Leninism and Maoism taken by certain of its leaders, including Amiri Baraka. According to the *New York Times,* the emphasis now was on "economic class struggle and the overthrow of capitalism and imperialism." Opposing those gone leftward was a much larger group of steadfast cultural nationalists including Don L. Lee, now Haki Madhubuti, a Chicago poet whose collection *Don't Cry, Scream,* published in 1969 by a small black press, had reputedly sold about 100,000 copies. To Ralph, this conflict was proof of the failure of black extremism. Still touchy about using the term "black" instead of "Negro," he protested when the public library of Albany, New York, asked him to take part in Black History Week. "As a Negro American," he responded, "I was trained to study and observe Negro American history; therefore I cannot accept an act which would designate even symbolically the identities of my parents and grandparents as non-existent." His key message extolled the Constitution and the Founding Fathers—"for when we take the long, backward view of history we can see that there has been continuing fulfillment."

Clarifying his ideas about race, art, and culture, on May 10, 1975, he delivered the commencement address at the Curtis Institute of Music in Philadelphia. Here he offered the first version, then titled "The Little Man Behind the Stove," of what would become "The Little Man at Chehaw Station," one of his finest essays. (The final, more charming title would come from Joseph Epstein, the editor of *The American Scholar,* where the piece first appeared.) At a recital at Tuskegee once, he had played a trumpet solo that disappointed his teachers. The concert pianist on the faculty, Hazel Harrison, had then offered him advice that seemed corny. "You must *always* play your best," she warned, "even if it's only in the waiting room at Chehaw Station [the train station that served the institute], because in this country there'll always be a little man hidden behind the stove." The little man will "know the *music,* and the tradition, and the standards of *musicianship* required for whatever you set out to perform." Only in time did he understand the wisdom in her words; the little man "has come to symbolize for me no less than the enigma of artistic communication in American society." At once both "a focus of insight and a threat to stale perception," the man was also "a metaphor for those individuals we sometimes meet whose refinement of sensibility cannot be explained" in the usual ways, such as education or social status. In *The American Scholar* he added that, whatever else may have shaped them, "culturally and environmentally such individuals are products of errant but sympathetic vibrations set up by the tension between America's social mobility, its universal education, and its relative freedom of cultural information."

His own experience of such tensions, which had started in his youth, came to a head, in some respects, on June 21, when he was honored in Oklahoma City at the opening of the Ralph Ellison Branch Library. The news of this coming honor had almost overwhelmed him. "So exhilarating was its effect," he told his sponsors there, "that I dared not dwell upon it lest I awaken to find that I had either misread, misheard, or been beguiled by a mischievous dream." Chief among the sponsors was Jimmie Stewart, a boyhood friend who was now perhaps the foremost black civic leader in Oklahoma City. Because the fourteen-thousand-square-foot library was built to serve the black community, Stewart wanted it named after the city's most respected author, black or white. In Ralph's youth, when the public library barred blacks, Ralph and his enterprising friends had pooled their books. Then white officials tired of black protests had dumped a disorganized collection into two rooms in the Slaughter Building. Now Governor David L. Boren had proclaimed him an "Outstanding Oklahoman," and the combined 1931 and 1932 graduating classes of Douglass High School assembled in his honor. Herbert, silent and pensive, flew in from Los Angeles for the occasion. Trailed by Jervis Anderson, a Jamaican-born staff writer for *The New Yorker,* Ralph melted before all this love and praise. He also amazed Anderson with the acuteness of his memory of people he had known in his youth. "I dream constantly of Oklahoma City," he explained. "My childhood is there. . . . You tend to dream, can't help dreaming, of your early experiences and the people you first knew. Old faces and old things are always turning up. As a result my early life stays fresh."

"His classmates monopolized him for virtually the entire weekend," *The New Yorker* noted. A "Sip and Dip" party filled Stewart's home and spilled over onto his moonlit back lawn. With both awe and affection, black Oklahomans welcomed the celebrity from New York who was also one of them; "there were classmates, friends of classmates, and families of classmates, exchanging anecdotes of the old days." Relaxed but elegant, Ralph wore to this party a double-breasted navy blue blazer with gray flannel trousers, a blue shirt, a polka-dot necktie, a matching breast pocket handkerchief, and "a sensational pair of black-and-white shoes." Anderson also noted the few strands of hair induced by Ralph across an otherwise denuded pate, and a thin, razor-sharp mustache that pointed to a touch of vanity. He was, indeed, a somewhat fizzy mixture of pride and vulnerability, joy and despair. "His eyes expressed a mixture of skepticism, gentleness, resignation, inner strength, and pain," Anderson wrote. "Many bright surprises are hidden behind his melancholy exterior. There may break out, at any time, a sudden burst of joyous laughter, a long stream of excited chatter, a flash of street swagger and savvy, a swift slash of sarcasm, a gracefully understated piece of wit, or a coolly self-deprecatory remark—followed by laughter." Ralph seemed to exude a quality of "ease and self-possession" that was clearly "not consummate." One felt "a continuous effort to retain discipline and control over himself, to keep a lid on the volcanic parts of his personality." Attacked, he often gives a chuckle that is "not to be taken for mirth, however. It is merely a diversionary tactic. It means . . . that he is reeling from a blow, that he is concealing the pain, and testing its depth. But it is at just such a moment that he is at his most dangerous." Usually "he rebounds off the ropes with a deadly counterpunch that ends the contest."

Introduced by Hannah Atkins, a poised young black state representative, Ralph read a prepared speech. "I dare not try to do as I usually do: from the head," he admitted. "It's too emotional a period." He praised those who had stayed behind when others had gone off into the wider world, and also the older generation, men and women such as Roscoe Dunjee and the Episcopal priest, Father Fitzpatrick, who had fought Jim Crow. He acknowledged the key role of the city in shaping him, "a bookish boy" who had labored to learn music, failed, and then succeeded as a writer. "How does one untangle the snarl of fate?" he asked dreamily. "How does [one] grasp the fortune in one's fateful fall?" Pride, self-reliance, and faith in America had been the keys. One of those who had stayed behind, Dr. Melvin Todd, would note that "Ralph made a decision early on that he wasn't going to let racism consume him and that he wanted to be treated as a man and an American, and that he had as much right to have that treatment as anyone else and he wasn't going to rely on the crutch of his color." Oklahomans admired Ralph for his belief that "I'm going to do what I'm going to do and I'm going to do it my way and come hell or high water I'm not going to let anyone sway me for popularity."

Earlier, at a brunch, Ralph had reflected on those older blacks like himself who had seen Oklahoma at its worst. "We were taking chances; we had no idea how it was going to turn out," he told the gathering. "But you all came through. And you inspire me. You affirm my sense of life. You are testimonies to the faith of your fathers and mothers—especially the mothers." With Herbert listening to him, he doubtless couldn't help but think of his mother and her years of sacrifice for her boys. "To have had some recognition in my town, in her town, and her not being here—that is the sad part," he said to *The New Yorker*'s Anderson one night in his hotel room. "I don't feel any sense of triumph. As a novelist, I'm much too disciplined to irony."

He and Fanny left New York early for Plainfield, to spend the summer of 1975 there. "We love the garden and the grounds, which we are constantly laboring over," Fanny wrote to friends, "and we are gradually dressing up the cabin." At their only dinner party, their guests were old friends with homes in the area—Russell Lynes, a former publisher who was chairman of the MacDowell artists' colony and also president of the Century, and his wife, Mildred (Ralph had taught their son George at Bard); the scholar-critic John Kouwenhoven and his wife, Joan; and, still their best friends in the Berkshires, Richard and Charlee Wilbur. Ralph tapped away at his novel but also agreed that summer to join a Pushcart Press project to publish an annual anthology of work offered by the best small presses in America and to award the annual Pushcart Prize for poetry— although he had paid scant attention to poetry for most of his life. Ralph thus joined older writers, including Anaïs Nin, but also welcomed the chance to work with several brilliant younger figures, including the poet Daniel Halpern and the novelists Joyce Carol Oates and Reynolds Price.

They returned to New York and NYU, but came back to the Berkshires to celebrate Thanksgiving with the Wilburs in Cummington. In December, John Hersey, who was then secretary of the American Academy of Arts and Letters, informed Ralph that the academy had elected him a member. Richard Wilbur, supported by Robert Penn Warren, Malcolm Cowley, Allen Tate, and Stanley Kunitz, had proposed Ralph for an honor he had craved—promotion from the larger National Institute to the elite, fifty-member academy. Anticipating the objection that he had only two books to his name, his friends pointed out that he had been working for twenty years on "a massive fiction that now nears completion. [But] why should we wait for that? Should this Academy be the last to recognize work that already claims international recognition?" To Warren in Florence, the news was "a word too long delayed." Others agreed. From Brown University, the poet and professor of English Michael S. Harper alerted Ralph about a special number of *Massachusetts Review* that, Harper said, Ralph "must be in." Praising him, Stanley Crouch let him know that he was writing a book about *Invisible Man* tentatively entitled "Tracking the Fox."

The Ellisons' friendship with the Wilburs paid off again when Charlee and Dick invited them to join a venture that promised them a place in the sun that was also an excellent business opportunity. Fanny, who was more concerned than ever about money as she and Ralph approached old age, seized the chance. Guided by a friend from the Colonial Williamsburg group, she had started to invest in mutual funds. For the first time in her life, as she told the man, "the mystery of the symbols and jargon of the stock exchange, due to your careful explanations, is disappearing." In the historic Old Town section of tropical Key West, Florida, a lawyer was renovating a dilapidated set of eleven houses, plagued by termite damage, cracked masonry, and peeling paint, for sale as condominiums. Charlee Wilbur, the leader in helping to sell units at Windsor Grove, hoped that fellow writers and their spouses would fill the entire complex. Only six square miles in size, Key West supported both a year-round population and a growing body of transients. Hemingway had once owned a home on the island. With the warm surrounding sea, lush vegetation, and gorgeous sunsets, Key West had much to offer. The community was beyond liberal. Its social tolerance, especially of homosexuality, was remarkable.

Fanny persuaded Ralph that they should join the Wilburs, John Hersey, John Ciardi, Alison Lurie, and other friends and buy a unit. Ralph gave her a free hand. On December 17, accordingly, she put down $1,000 on a four-room unit of 950 square feet at 727 Windsor Lane. A few months later she closed on the unit, in her name only, for $19,610. The monthly mortgage payment was $120, but at the height of the tourist season the unit could be rented out for several times that amount. Although Ralph let Fanny make the purchase, some time passed before he set foot in the compound. He was obviously uncomfortable with so much tropical freedom. On one visit, when Charlee arranged a meeting between him and a local friend—a black man—who wanted to meet him, "Ralph showed up dressed in an Abercrombie and Fitch hunting outfit. I think it was an exact copy of what Hemingway wore on safari, bought in the same shop in New York." The local man was bemused. "Nice guy, your friend," he told her later, "but what the hell is he doing wearing clothes like that?" In a place where people actually gathered to applaud sunsets, Ralph was seldom at ease. He was liberal, but exuberant gay culture offended him.

At sixty-three, Ralph had long ago lost all interest in adventures. With his riverside apartment in Manhattan, his acres in the Berkshires, and his dark forest of Oklahoma memories, he needed no adventure. He had not left the United States in almost twenty years. Invited by the scholar Per Seyersted to address the Nordic Association for American Studies in Sweden, he said no to Scandinavia. He also said no to India when Amritjit Singh arranged an invitation to the American Studies Research Centre in Hyderabad. That year, 1975, he passed up a chance to teach again in the Seminar in American Studies in Salzburg.

Tired of teaching, Ralph applied for a paid sabbatical leave from NYU for the academic year 1976–1977. When the administration balked in response, he found a champion in James W. Tuttleton, the chair of the English Department. The men had come to respect and like each other. In February, Ralph had proposed Tuttleton for membership in the Century. Using his influence, Tuttleton secured the sabbatical for Ralph. He also pressed him about joining the Department of English starting in the fall of 1977.

Ralph was ready for a year off. "Just the amount of reading papers keeps me tied up," he complained to Robert B. Stepto, an assistant professor at Yale and the author of a study of African-American fiction, including *Invisible Man,* which Ralph liked. The students were often poorly prepared, their essays weak. "I am unhappy with the numbers who can't write." Although he and his boyhood friends had "a fairly poor education," several of them had been much better writers. At one point Ralph grew irate about "one black girl who got a C+ and is bitching about it! . . . She should have been thrown right out of [the] university, for she is not ready for the work."

Some students of course enjoyed studying under him. In 1976, one auditor in "Fiction and Democracy" was Ron Welburn, a poet of mixed Native American and African-American ancestry who had come to NYU from all-black Lincoln University to work in American Studies. "It was a great course," Welburn recalled of his main encounter with Ellison. Yes, some students were "befuddled" by Ellison's lectures and turned off by his remoteness; but the graduate students in American Studies "enjoyed it much, much more." Welburn found Ralph a riveting lecturer, "like no one I'd previously encountered." His knowledge, like his analyses, "seemed to have Olympian origins. He knew so darn much and it all made sense!" *Pudd'nhead Wilson* and *Adventures of Huckleberry Finn* were central to the course, but Kenneth Burke's ideas and books such as Robert Toll's scholarly *Blacking Up* (about minstrelsy), Hugh Dalziel Duncan's *Symbols in Society,* and John Kouwenhoven's *The Beer Can by the Highway* were also crucial. "His lectures were a mixture of homespun lore, years of reading and thinking, Midwestern erudition, and urban savvy." Ellison was both friendly and detached. "He didn't tarry much after class and wasn't terribly accessible before it started," Welburn conceded. "He was outwardly patient with questions about the term paper and so on, but you could sense he was trying to move along." Always he was poised. "He wasn't rattled by questions that seemed to challenge his opinions, but he listened carefully and by golly he had a way of looking right at you that seemed to look through you."

The increase in the number of his black students, although relatively modest, was a token of an improvement in his ties to younger blacks. A sometimes contentious but mainly genial interview that winter brought Ralph together with Ishmael Reed, Quincy Troupe, and Steve Cannon—although this was mainly a duel between Ralph and the iconoclastic Reed. Already Reed had published three novels, including *Mumbo Jumbo,* which had been nominated in 1972 for the National Book Award in fiction along with another book by Reed in the poetry section. He believed he had good reason to dislike Ralph. The previous year, when the American Academy had given him a prize at its May ceremony, Ralph had loudly insulted him in front of Robert Penn Warren, the playwright Edward Albee, and the composer Roger Sessions. "Ishmael Reed!" Ralph had shouted on spotting him. "Ishmael Reed! You're nothing but a gangster and a con artist!" "I was stunned," Reed said. "I looked around, embarrassed, and people were watching us, people whose work I admired. He didn't care. I'm sure that he was drunk." "I was there and saw it happen," Quincy Troupe said. "I liked and admired Ralph, but when he drank he could be a mean drunk. I remember once at a party on Park Avenue, or Fifth Avenue, Ralph asked me loudly, 'How did you get here?' 'The same way you did,' I told him. He couldn't believe that we could have rich friends in common. Or that I didn't want to fight with him or put him down. I still admired him and his work."

Ralph saw his interlocutors as, most likely, crude black nationalists. "Where on earth did the notion come from," he asked, "that the world, and all its art, has to be reinvented, recreated, every time a Black individual seeks to express himself? The world is here and art is here, and they've been here for a long, long time." When Reed attacked the American Academy, Ralph defended it. After all, W. E. B. Du Bois, Langston Hughes, Jacob Lawrence, Romare Bearden, and Gwendolyn Brooks either had been or were members. When Reed criticized the attitudes of certain Jewish intellectuals toward blacks, Ralph saw only "a cultural lag" that would be closed. He deplored the popularity of black "demagogues" and the habit of idolizing ex-pimps and ex-prisoners (almost certainly he meant Eldridge Cleaver, and perhaps also Malcolm X), which "gave many kids the notion that there was no point in developing their minds; that all they had to do was to strike a militant stance, assert their unity with the group and stress their 'Blackness.' If you didn't accept their slogans, you were dismissed as a 'Neegro' Uncle Tom." For many blacks, too often, "just give the most banal statement a rhyme and a rhythm, put a little strut into it, and we'll grab it like a catfish gulping down a piece of dough-bait."

But a revealing moment came when Ralph tried to answer questions about younger writers such as Jayne Cortez, Calvin Hernton, Al Young, Sonia Sanchez, Lorenzo Thomas, Don L. Lee, Stanley Crouch, Nikki Giovanni, and Amiri Baraka. ("When did Baraka become *young*?" Ralph quipped.) Obviously he knew little about these writers. Crouch was "a very intelligent guy." Lee's "ideological emphasis got in the way of my really getting to his poetry. Maybe it's a case of [a] generation gap. . . .

I don't think very much of what Miss Giovanni does, but that doesn't mean anything; it's a matter of taste." (Asked in 1979 to vet a list of over three hundred American books selected for exhibition at the Moscow Book Fair, he cut only Giovanni's book of poems *Cotton Candy on a Rainy Day*.) "Toni Morrison's work I know," he said. "She's a good novelist." He had a copy of a Gayl Jones novel, "but I haven't read it." About Charles Johnson he admitted, "I've never heard of him." Satisfied not to know the younger writers, he saw no obligation to help them. Some months later, when the *New York Times Book Review* asked him to write about Reed's novel *Flight to Canada,* he declined.

Ralph and Fanny seemed much more comfortable with academics who openly admired his ideas and work, especially the scholar Robert Stepto of Yale and the poet Michael S. Harper of Brown University. Interviewing Ralph on March 7 for a special "black" number of *Massachusetts Review,* Stepto and Harper saw themselves as leaders of a movement opposed to black cultural nationalism, as Ralph was. "We are really about the business of taking on the Black Aestheticians," Harper assured Ralph. "We are interested in redressing this business." Stepto saw the present moment as a watershed. Having watched sadly as Ralph suffered "the ravages and taunts" of the late 1960s, "in my own inadequate way I wish to offer evidence of a new day before us." As always, Ralph asserted his independence. Told that Leon Forrest had remarked that James Alan McPherson, Toni Morrison, and Albert Murray might constitute, along with Ellison, a "crowd" opposed to the Black Arts admirers, Ralph laughed ("Ha, ha, ha") at the idea. "I'm a loner," he said. Perhaps "I share certain sensibilities with people, black and white, who operate in the arts," he conceded, "but schools, that sort of thing—no. In the first place, I don't think it's necessary. And . . . when people get together that way they tend to control one another's ideas."

Another devoted Ivy League fan was Horace Porter, now an assistant professor of English at Dartmouth College. Several years before, as an undergraduate at Amherst College, he had met Ralph following his first reading of *Invisible Man.* The novel "had changed the way I saw myself in relation to America and the world [and] had shaken my mind with the force of an earthquake." Listening to Ralph speak at Amherst, "I was swept up by the wonder and intensity of the occasion." Giving up the social sciences, he turned to literature, because "Ellison had unleashed in me whatever demon or angel tells a young man or woman to take a shot at becoming a writer." Porter went on to complete a doctorate at Yale. Sending Ralph an autobiographical essay he had published, and expecting no reply, he received in return a three-page, single-spaced letter. In February 1977, at Ralph's invitation, he visited 730 Riverside Drive. The Ellisons, he recalled, "looked youthful and relaxed and genuinely pleased to see me." "Horace," Ralph asked, "when did you become interested in writing?" As Porter rattled on nervously in response, Ralph said little. Then he offered his visitor a glass of wine, lit a pipe, and chatted amiably with him for two hours or more. Ralph seemed especially curious about Porter's years growing up in South Carolina, where Ralph's father was born. Entranced, Porter lost track of the time, but Ralph ended the visit gently. "Horace," he asked suddenly, "when are you coming back?" Before seeing him out, he inscribed Porter's first-edition copy of *Invisible Man*: "For Horace Porter, with hopes that he'll write a much better novel than this one." Thus began a solid friendship between the Ellisons and Horace, spoiled only a little by the fact that while Fanny was polite and even gracious, "I felt embraced by Ralph but I never felt embraced by Fanny. She would stay in the background, smoking her cigarettes. I couldn't tell what was wrong. I don't think that it was old-fashioned racism, having to do with skin color, but it was something like that."

Not every Ivy League visitor fared as well. On May 8, 1976, young Robert G. O'Meally, a Stanford graduate who had written his doctoral dissertation at Harvard on Ellison under Ralph's longtime friend Daniel Aaron, came to 730 Riverside Drive to interview him. After a favorable reading of the manuscript by Albert Murray, Harvard University Press had given O'Meally a contract to publish what would be the first book on Ellison's life and work. The press then sent a copy of the manuscript to Ralph. He did not enjoy reading it. Unimpressed by its critical insights, he also noted certain errors of fact. Coolly pointing out the latter, he was stonily silent about the former with O'Meally, from whom—realistically or not—he had expected far better work, given his elite education. Despite the fact that O'Meally revered Ellison and almost worshipped *Invisible Man* and *Shadow and Act*, Ralph refused to hold him to a lower standard than that to which he held anyone else approaching his work. He was indifferent to O'Meally's gentle manner, softness of speech, and humility. Indeed, he chose to see O'Meally, for some years, as embodying much of what was wrong with younger blacks and the opportunities opened up after the *Brown* decision. Unaware of the depth of Ralph's resentment, O'Meally left the apartment with fresh resolve. "The discussion was extremely profitable," he later wrote to Ellison. He would be "extensively revising my manuscript. Without your assistance some serious errors could not have been avoided." But his troubles with the Ellisons had only just begun.

To Ralph, the Bicentennial celebration of 1976 was an excellent opportunity for him to speak out about the meaning of America. For an ambitious CBS television series, *The Transformation of American Society,* he interviewed Roy Wilkins. Agreeing to join the National Citizens Emergency Committee to Save Our Public Libraries, he also delivered a formal Bicentennial lecture, based on his "Little Man Behind the Stove" speech, for the Society for the Libraries in New York. His most significant lecture came on April 30, when he spoke about the "Perspective of Literature" at a conference on the law at New York University. Discussing Melville, Twain, and his own familiar ideas about myth, ritual, and the Negro, he then turned to the turbulence involving the law "going back to 1954 and coming through the measures passed during the sixties." Following *Brown,* Ralph declared, the nation had indulged a sense of good intentions and rectified many past injustices; but "with our usual American innocence, we failed to grasp that it was going to cost us something." When blacks became "symbolic of so many other issues in American life," their freedom had an unfortunate effect on young whites. "It was as though the word had gone out, that the outsider, the unacceptable, was now acceptable. . . . They translated it to mean that all of the repressed psychological drives . . . were now fair game. 'Let it all hang out,' they said. 'We have all become black men and women.'" The challenge was now clear. "This projection, this identification of the socially unacceptable with the blacks, must be raised to consciousness." Only then "will we be able to reassume that optimism so necessary for living and dealing with the many problems of this diverse pluralistic society."

Under the leadership of Carlos Baker of Princeton, Ralph joined the board of advisors of a project to publish a one-hundred-volume collection of American literary works. The project brought together the American Revolution Bicentennial Commission, of which he was still a member, and the Franklin Library, the publishing division of the private Franklin Mint. He urged the inclusion of not one but two Bellow novels—but did not recommend any novel by a black writer. Modesty forbade his choice of *Invisible Man,* which was included anyway. Among autobiographies he backed the inclusion of Wright's *Black Boy,* Washington's *Up from Slavery,* and Du Bois's *Dusk of Dawn* (perhaps the sole example of Ellison praising

Du Bois's work). He did not support the inclusion of the sensationally influential *Autobiography of Malcolm X.* While he passed over the poetry of Langston Hughes, he nominated Hughes's collection of comic fiction *The Best of Simple.* He had once derided the quality of these popular stories about a Harlem barfly in a letter to Wright, after Hughes asked Ralph for help in making a book out of them, but he had come to appreciate them. Striking a separate deal with the Franklin Library for a Bicentennial edition of *Invisible Man,* he earned at least $65,000 from the sale of deluxe leather-bound copies individually signed and with a foreword by him.

The glory of the American Revolution and the vitality of American democracy were affirmed for him on May 19, when the American Academy of Arts and Letters formally inducted him. At the same time, the National Institute inducted the black poet Gwendolyn Brooks. Having won the Pulitzer Prize in 1950 for poetry based on high-modernist principles lovingly applied to the Negro culture of her Chicago, Brooks was now reinventing herself as a black cultural nationalist. Nevertheless, she gladly entered the Institute.

Ralph and Fanny left for Plainfield shortly after his induction. Supported by his sabbatical, this would be their longest stay there ever. As Fanny put in rows of tomatoes, cabbage, celery, green peppers, and herbs, Ralph tried to find inspiration in the Bicentennial as he worked on his novel. He ignored or rejected many invitations. Some refusals came easily, as when the Black Panther Party asked him to join celebrities including Jane Fonda, Ossie Davis, Dr. Benjamin Spock, and Noam Chomsky in sponsoring a Committee for Justice to oppose the FBI in its harassment of the Panthers. He ignored the plea of James Farmer, once a major civil rights figure, for help finding a job or money. He made a few mildly activist gestures. He joined Hubert Humphrey and other prominent leaders in signing an open letter to the board of trustees of the NAACP demanding that the embattled Roy Wilkins remain head of the organization. In September he served as a vice chairman for a gala seventy-fifth birthday celebration of Wilkins held at the New York Hilton. Not in attendance himself, he composed a ten-minute narrative praising Wilkins, which the actress Cicely Tyson read to the audience.

On walks or long drives in the Berkshires he gloried in the iridescent turning of the leaves in autumn but tried not to stray too far from his desk. Perhaps he was jolted on October 22, when Saul Bellow won the 1976 Nobel Prize for literature, joining Faulkner, Hemingway, Steinbeck,

O'Neill, Eliot, and (more dubiously) Sinclair Lewis and Pearl Buck, as the modern immortals of American writing. Ralph must have been pained by the sad difference between his own record and that of someone whose breakthrough as a writer had come after *Invisible Man*. Bellow had mined, or plundered, the lives of several of his friends for the sake of his stories. The result had been an extraordinarily complex multi-novel exposition of modern American life. If Ralph, comparing himself with Saul, took any satisfaction in the idea that (as at least two major polls had asserted) Bellow had created no single work as powerful as *Invisible Man,* he must have also known that this was so mainly because *Invisible Man* engages probably the most harrowing element in American culture: the specter of race as embodied in black life. But while Bellow fed aesthetically on the world he lived in, Ralph seemed unable to use *his* life in the same way. Instead, he seemed trapped in the vines and tendrils of the past and by the unwieldy power of Oklahoma and African-American folklore and folkways, classical myths, and often awkward comedy.

Speaking to Reed, Troupe, and Cannon, Ralph had unwittingly illustrated the problem. "When you put a detail in its proper place in an action," he said, "it gathers up associations and meanings and starts speaking to the reader's sense of significance. . . . Place[d] in the right context, and at the optimum stage of an action, it vibrates and becomes symbolically eloquent. . . . It's symbolic action." Joking even as he alluded thus to Kenneth Burke, Ralph then illustrated this point by referring to the sensational moment in Bellow's *Mr. Sammler's Planet* when a black pickpocket exposes himself grotesquely to Sammler. "The thing sets up all kinds of reverberation in the narrative," Ralph said, laughing. "It becomes damn nigh metaphysical." But what he said next was in part a confession of his inability now to maintain the structure of his fiction without slipping and sliding into messiness. "If I had written the scene," he insisted, "I would have tried to make it even more eloquent by having the pickpocket snatch it [his penis] out and hit the hero over the head with it. I would have further physicalized the metaphysic—soma to psyche!" The four men guffawed, but the real joke was on Ralph. In *Henderson the Rain King*, Bellow had taken this mixture of metaphysics and reality, social realism, surrealism, and slapstick about as far as a novelist could go safely. In his next novel he had returned to earth. Meanwhile, Ralph was bedeviled by too rigid ideas about culture and art, myth and symbol, allusion and leitmotif. His inability to create an art that held a clean mirror up to "Negro" life as blacks actually led it, especially at or near his own social level, was disabling him as a writer. As a novelist, he had lost his way. And he had done so in proportion to his distancing of himself from his fellow blacks.

A sad example of this loss of control is "Backwacking, A Plea to the Senator," a scrap of the manuscript of the novel-in-progress dated (by Ellison, apparently) November 22, 1976, which takes the form of a letter of complaint written allegedly in 1953 by a barely literate white Alabaman, "Norm A. Mauler, A Concern Citizen" (presumably a gibe at Norman Mailer). The letter is addressed to the major character Senator Sunraider. (Ralph was still nursing his animus against Mailer. Asked by him in 1977 to sign a protest against the decision by the House of Representatives to end its investigation of the murders of Martin Luther King, Jr., and Robert F. Kennedy, Ralph ignored him.) The letter is a long, racist complaint about the latest example of hypersexuality in the black male. "Here is what he is doing," Mauler writes: "HE *and his woman have taken to getting undressed and standing back to back and heel to heel, shoulderblade to shoulderblade, and tale to tale with his against her's and her's against his, and then after they have horsed around and manuvered like cats in heat and worked as tight together as a tick to a cow's tit,* HE *ups and starts in to* HAVING AFTER HER BACKWARDS!" Outraged, Norm A. Mauler insists that blacks be stopped. These days, instead of "the nigger" living by the old pious maxims, *"he is coming up daily with all* KINDS *of new minds and new notions, most of them nasty, radical and* UNGODLY." And so on. Perhaps as telling is the startling amount of time and labor that Ralph expended on this crude piece of "humor." Although the letter is only nine pages long, he saw fit to type, or have Fanny type, at least fifteen drafts.

"He took a sort of jazz musician's attitude to writing," Bellow said some time after Ralph's death. "He was always very happy when he was blowing a riff on the typewriter. And his feeling for the language was such that there was nothing paradoxical or kinky about the transfer from music to the page and back again." As a result, the quality of his work stayed inconsistent. In February 1977, after years of begging Ralph to offer him some material, the fiction editor of *Esquire* magazine, Gordon Lish, rejected two sections of the novel. Almost certainly, one section was "Backwacking." The piece appeared in the far less competitive *Massachusetts Review* in its Autumn 1977 issue.

In November, Ralph and Fanny did not bring home to Manhattan a finished novel, as he had hoped, yet he continued to prosper professionally. On November 22 *The New Yorker* published Jervis Anderson's long profile of him and his return to Oklahoma City. Although elements of vanity and a suppressed rage flash through it, Ralph emerges mainly as sensitive, elegant, sophisticated, and heroic. The response was highly positive, with messages of praise reaching him from all over the country. At the Century, the Academy, and New York University, his stock rose. After a few days, he thanked Anderson, but patronizingly. He showed surprise at Anderson's skills as a writer. Admitting his earlier "doubts about your project," Ralph said that he had not thought of himself as an interesting subject. More likely, he had doubted the black journalist's ability. Despite their days together, he addressed his letter "Dear Jervis Anderson." He was glad that Anderson had done such a good job. A "white Virginia banker," he wrote, had found in the essay "an affirmation of his own American faith" and had discovered also "certain unities of American experience which exist beyond the obvious divisions of race, class and geographical region."

At home, Ralph worked hard at editing his interview with Reed, Troupe, and Cannon. (As with his interview with Stepto and Harper, he both altered his answers and asked himself new questions. "He was always meticulous, always a craftsman," Stepto recalled.) "I saw that many of my answers were banal," he told Reed; "therefore I've tried to offer extensions and addenda." He had been "wordy as hell" and "long-winded," but "since once an interview is committed to print it becomes a piece of 'literature,' I don't think of this as cheating."

His sunbursts of publicity did not prevent a somewhat humiliating turn at NYU. Stopping by his offices, he discovered that the university, crying austerity, had stripped his suite of most of its furniture. When James Tuttleton pressed him again to join the Department of English as a protection against such indignities, he gave in. His income was not reduced. If NYU was financially strapped, he was not. For 1976, the Ellisons reported earning the considerable sum of about $68,000 to the Internal Revenue Service.

Well before the end of spring 1977, Ralph and Fanny were back in Plainfield as his pleasure in his country home deepened. Now a more mellow man, he joined Fanny in adding dahlias and other flowers. That summer he made an attempt to close the gap between himself and Herbert, who came from Los Angeles to stay with them in Plainfield for about two weeks. Intensely closemouthed and reflective, as Jervis Anderson had noted, Herbert had just suffered two grievous losses. His wife's son, Lewis, died; then she died. The invitation to Plainfield had everything to do with these events. It didn't go well. More at ease with Fanny, Herbert joined her in painting the main dwelling while Ralph worked at his desk. When he joined them, he offered comments that often came across as snide criticism. By the time the men and Fanny headed to the city to prepare for Herbert's flight home, Ralph was in a foul mood. "Wish I hadn't come," she scribbled.

In September, Ralph and Fanny returned to New York for his baptism as a member of the English Department. He surrendered his suite of rooms at One Fifth Avenue for a typical professor's snug office at 19 University Place. He tried to blend in. When he met his colleagues in the mailroom or the corridors, he was polite and even genial. Most of them, seeing him as a celebrity, didn't expect intimacy. Some kept their distance. "I was told that they saw a sort of black cloud hanging over him," recalled Ulrich Baer, a professor of German, many years later. "Looking at him, they saw mainly an extreme case of writer's block. The younger ones in particular couldn't be sure that the disease wasn't contagious."

Ralph was unperturbed. "We stay well and occupied," Fanny wrote to friends from Manhattan, "doing most of the time what we want to do and not what others want us to do." Politely he fended off invitations to lecture or to teach at the University of Alabama, Wesleyan, Howard, and other schools. When Roy Wilkins was finally deposed at the NAACP, Ralph pulled away from the organization. He rebuffed an invitation to write for its main magazine, *Crisis*. His interest in the Legal Defense Fund waned. Mary Hemingway's presence kept him involved, as her co-chairman, in fund-raising for black Meharry Medical College, though this kind of involvement was largely titular and token. Ralph was still unsentimental about historically black colleges. He looked toward the future. Reviving memories of his role in the rise of the NEH and NEA, he testified in Boston before a congressional committee in connection with federal support for scholarship and art. Ralph spoke with authority about the earliest days of the National Endowment for the Humanities, before it even had a name.

The Ellisons made the most of their more glamorous outings. In February they gladly attended a gala dinner and dance given at the New York Armory at East 67th Street and Park Avenue to honor the posthumous appearance of James Jones's novel *Whistle*. The event attracted Jackie Onassis and also Lauren Bacall, who sat at their table and delighted Fanny with her "plain-spoken, irreverent, sort of don't-give-a-damn" attitude. But as more and more young people, especially blacks, sought to meet Ralph, he and Fanny kept down the number of visitors. "This takes a lot of doing," she noted, "since we don't wish to offend people . . . want-ing assistance of some kind in their artistic projects." They did little assisting. When Kristin Hunter asked Ralph to support her application for a Guggenheim fellowship, he begged off. He no longer wrote such let-ters, Fanny explained, "because too many novelists, poets, artists, photog-raphers were asking him for reference[s]." When one hapless young man sent a manuscript and a self-addressed envelope, Ralph demanded an additional $1.20 in postage. "I do not think forty-five cents—even at book rate—will guarantee delivery of a typescript," he explained. "We will hold it until we hear from you again."

As for his own projects, following some suggestions by Joseph Epstein of *The American Scholar*, Ralph expanded and buffed his engaging essay "Little Man at the Chehaw Station," first delivered at the Curtis Institute of Music in Philadelphia, for publication in the prestigious journal. To celebrate the appearance of the essay Ralph invited Epstein to lunch at the Century. Although they sat down at 12:30 p.m., it was almost 5:00 when the two men left the club after hours of eating, drinking, and rous-ing talk. But Ralph was having more and more trouble meeting deadlines for even small jobs. For an edition of essays by his once crucial friend and advisor Stanley Edgar Hyman, now dead almost a decade, he offered some wise and touching words—but sent them too late for use in the volume.

He was also leisurely about his comings and goings at the American Academy or the Century. And yet if some members found him from time to time hectoring, especially when liquored up, they also valued his lead-ership. He took on the position of secretary of the National Institute of Arts and Letters (a post usually held by a member of the academy). Serv-ing on the National Medal of Literature committee at the academy, he battled with his usual vigor in support of his candidate, Archibald MacLeish, over the rival claims of Elizabeth Bishop, Lillian Hellman, and Isaac Bashevis Singer. He was less successful trying to secure its Distin-guished Service to the Arts award for his mentor Roger Stevens. Some-times he was too relaxed. At the annual May ceremonial in 1978, he was expected to speak for three minutes but rambled on for at least fifteen as he ad-libbed his introduction of new members, including Robert Rau-schenberg, Donald Barthelme, and Joyce Carol Oates. His sense of belong-ing showed also in his and Fanny's annual post-ceremonial supper. For the first one, in 1965, they had hired help and offered catered food and black caviar. For this one he helped Fanny cook up a big pot of chili.

The admission of other blacks into the academy and the Century remained a problem for him because his standards were so high. He used little of his extensive credit in either place to get more admitted, although he was happy to see his old friend Romare Bearden, as well as another painter, Jacob Lawrence, inducted into the institute. (He had been much less enthusiastic about Lawrence joining the Century.) The fact that since Duke Ellington's death the music division had included no blacks seemed not to bother him much, although members were ready to bring in topflight popular musicians, black or white. At the Century, when A. Walton Litz of Princeton and John William Ward, the president of Amherst, sought to put up for election Charles T. Davis, head of the African-American Studies program at Yale, Ralph was slow to reply—if he ever did. One year he backed the nomination of Romare Bearden, and on another occasion of Nathan Scott. Otherwise he was mostly silent.

Race remained both the subject of some of his greatest insights and a petard on which he now and then hoisted himself. He still cherished the notion of a fair-minded Southern aristocracy with whom blacks could and should work for their mutual benefit, if implicitly with the black masses down south in a lesser role. He was thrilled accordingly to travel in 1978 to Charlottesville to deliver a lecture at the University of Virginia, where Scott and his wife, Charlotte, were now on the faculty. He held an endowed chair in Religious Studies and English, and she had an equally prestigious position teaching finance and economic policy. In the English Department was James Alan McPherson. The two men had kept in touch over the years, as McPherson worked on a volume of short stories. (Later that year, he won the Pulitzer Prize in fiction for the volume, *Elbow Room*.) Introducing Ralph before his public lecture, the president of the university, Edgar Shannon, stressed Ralph's almost unique powers as an American cultural visionary. The lecture itself was, of course, on—as McPherson put it—"the very complex . . . nature of American reality." By this time, Ralph essentially had no other topic.

He would probably not have expounded on any other topic in a place where the past was not only not dead, to paraphrase Faulkner, but hadn't yet passed, and where local whites routinely referred to "Mr. Jefferson" as if the founder were still alive. As a result, the public reception for the Ellisons at the Colonnade Club on the historic Grange was part genuine welcome and part racial charade, with the few blacks and the many whites mingling uneasily. If Jim Crow was officially dead at the university, it was still alive close by. Membership in the Farmington Country Club, where Faulkner had ridden to the hounds in the years when he taught at the university, was still forbidden to blacks. Indeed, members were dis-couraged from bringing them as guests. But Ralph preferred to dwell on the signs of progress as Shannon slowly emancipated his university. Under his leadership, blacks and Jews were gaining strength on the campus.

Almost all of the Ellisons' sympathy in such matters was with men like Shannon. They reserved much less for the black victims of Jim Crow who were now attending schools like Virginia and for the trickle of young black professors hired by hitherto white universities. Affirmative action in edu-cation did not appeal to Ralph and Fanny. Their distrust of the younger professors continued to find its focus in the person of Robert O'Meally, who was still preparing his manuscript on Ralph's life and work. While Ralph was merely chilly to O'Meally, Fanny was sure that the latter and his manuscript seriously upset her husband—"but, as with most annoy-ances and situations which are very disturbing, he buries them deep and says nothing." The problem was much bigger than one scholar, she said. Harvard University Press, which was to publish the book, was "over-accommodating O'Meally out of that spurious philosophy of the sixties when too many universities hired black men because they were black and graduated black students for the same reason—ability and performance discounted." This indictment was delivered in a letter to a white librarian, Stewart Lillard, who had done some valuable research on Ralph's ances-tors in South Carolina. It expressed the Ellisons' shared lack of respect for what younger black scholars (supported by sympathetic white scholars like Daniel Aaron) were doing to establish the formal study of black Ameri-can writers in colleges, universities, and professional organizations from which blacks and their writings had been barred or ignored for generations.

On June 3, 1978, President Leon Botstein of Bard College, where Ralph had learned to be a teacher almost twenty years before, presented him with an honorary doctorate. He and Fanny attended a chic dinner and dance for almost two hundred supporters of the Museum of the City of New York, where Ralph was still on the board of trustees. His member-ship on this board and others like it remained important to him even though his contributions in terms of time or money had become, like his presence as a black on such boards, token. When his membership on the National Portrait Gallery Commission ended that month, the director of the gallery, Marvin Sadik, was restrained in his expression of thanks. "I fully appreciate how difficult it was for you to attend Commission meet-ings," he wrote.

Back in Plainfield, a little poodle, Tiger, amused them but also sadly reminded Ralph and Fanny of the loss of the marvelous Tuckatarby of Tivoli, who had been put down. Once again, they seemed genuinely to believe that this time, this summer, this year, Ralph would finish his novel. "Ralph is bearing down," Fanny assured a friend, "trying to get the monkey off his back." They were now mellow and comfortable with each other—although Ralph still had his dark moods and a sharp edge to his tongue. On sunny days Fanny stayed outdoors as much as she could, leaving him alone with his moods, his genius, and his now senile monkey. On rainy days "we close ourselves into one of the back rooms and tiptoe about."

The end of Ralph's career as a professor at New York University came suddenly. Returning at the start of the 1978–1979 academic year, he found financial support from the state for the Schweitzer professorships, including his own, again diminished. By then, the total cost of his position—salary, benefits, and more—well exceeded the sum of money provided by the state legislature. One day in March, he was browsing through the student daily newspaper when one item made him sit up straight. Ralph Ellison, the Albert Schweitzer Professor in the Humanities, was retiring from the university at the end of the summer. Shocked and upset, Ralph marched into his chairman's office to demand an explanation. He left deflated. The faculty handbook was explicit that retirement at age sixty-five was mandatory for all faculty and staff. He had turned sixty-five (really sixty-six) on March 1.

On May 16, the Department of English gave a pleasant little farewell cocktail party for him, organized by his colleague Ken Silverman, at the university's La Maison Française. He was thanked for his nine years of service and, generously, for the prestige he had added to a university in need of prestige. Later that year, he would become professor emeritus, a title that brought only a few vestiges of privilege.

Within a few days of his party, Ralph began the dispiriting business of moving his books, papers, pictures, plaques, and other *penates* out of his office. When he turned in his keys, the truly active part of his life was over.

20

The Uncanny Penetration of the Past
1979–1986

Ralph Ellison's words seemed almost like those of a voice from another time and space.
KIMBERLY COLEMAN (1979)

Near the middle of June 1979, with the ominous sense of having reached a critical point in their lives, Ralph and Fanny settled in for their longest stay in Plainfield since the fire of 1967. Weeks away from his official retirement from NYU, they were thinking now of even longer stays in the Berkshires. "If the cabin doesn't collapse next winter," Fanny assured a friend, "we'll come back and try to have something more substantial built." No travel was planned. "We don't move around much," she wrote another friend; "it isn't good for Ralph's work." For the sake of his novel-in-progress Ralph turned down most of the invitations that came to lecture or teach. He insisted that he had "a publisher's deadline which, in view of my retirement, has now become absolute."

For him as a writer, it was a time of nearly final stocktaking, but under strangely altered circumstances. The situation of the black writer in America had changed remarkably since the publication of *Invisible Man* in 1952, and even since *Shadow and Act* in 1964. The 1960s and 1970s had produced an astonishing vitality in black writing, a second outpouring to far surpass that of the Harlem Renaissance of the 1920s. As a creative artist, as distinct from an intellectual, had he seen time pass him by? Some people answered no, but with implicit reservations. The previous December, in a special issue of *The Nation* devoted to "Black America," the white literary historian Robert Bone had hailed Ralph as a tower of integrity in an era that had produced more than its share of shady characters. But had Ellison, in standing apart, missed out on the protean vitality of the age? "Simply put, the 1960s were a time of *divergence,*" Bone judged, and "the 1970s of *convergence.*" While the Black Arts movement had been "part media event and part hustle," as Bone put it, "something deadly serious" had taken place. The younger writers had transformed the quality and quantity of published black American writing. For all his nobility, where was Ralph Ellison in this new age?

Gwendolyn Brooks, Ann Petry, William Denby, Robert Hayden, James Baldwin, and Albert Murray, among others, had adapted and produced as the world about them changed. A richly diverse group of younger writers had emerged, too. Leon Forrest had followed his 1973 novel, *There Is a Tree More Ancient Than Eden,* with *The Bloodworth Orphans* four years later. After Ishmael Reed's first novel, *The Free-Lance Pallbearers,* in 1967, and in addition to a praised book of poetry, he had published *Yellow Black Radio Broke-Down* in 1969 and *Mumbo Jumbo* in 1972. John Edgar Wideman, having launched his career in 1970 with *Hurry Home,* had published *The Lynchers* in 1973. After the appearance of *Faith and the Good Thing* in 1974, Charles Johnson was gaining further recognition as a writer of fiction and an essayist. Black women writers had emerged as a literary force. Alice Walker had published the novel *The Third Life of Grange Copeland* in 1970 and *In Love and Trouble: Stories of Black Women* in 1973. Her novel *Meridian* would also attract attention, and her astonishingly successful *The Color Purple* would win her a Pulitzer Prize in 1983. From Toni Morrison had come *The Bluest Eye* in 1970, *Sula* in 1974, and *Song of Solomon* in 1977. Edited by Morrison, Toni Cade Bambara's startling collection of short stories, *Gorilla, My Love,* had come out in 1972. Maya Angelou, a national celebrity since 1970 with the publication of *I Know Why the Caged Bird Sings,* had published other volumes of autobiography. The poet June Jordan, whose *Things That I Do in the Dark* had won acclaim in 1977, was rising in stature as an essayist and the author of children's books, plays, and a novel. These writers were only among the vanguard of a literary outpouring unprecedented among black women.

Where was Ralph? For Robert Bone, he was nothing less than the hero of the decade, "the most eloquent opponent of revolutionary nationalism" despite his thin publishing record. "Stressing his American identity," Bone wrote, "and insisting on the highest standards of his craft, Ellison has functioned as a center of moral energy and model of artistic integrity for all serious black writers." The published excerpts from his novel-in-progress suggested to Bone that "his long silence will be viewed in retrospect as a prolific gestation period." This prediction was largely wishful thinking on Bone's part. Moreover, it seemed to some observers that, as a novelist, Ralph had lost more than he gained by keeping away from younger black writers. So confident in his vision of black culture, his friend Anatole Broyard of the *New York Times* wrote, Ellison "tends to resist certain revisions of it." He was stubborn. " 'When the word changed from "Negro" to "black," ' he once said to me [Broyard], 'an element of mysticism slipped in that I've never felt comfortable with.' " He also saw no link between his idealism and his frustrations as a novelist.

In the summer of 1979, his most valuable writing turned out to be in service not to his second novel but to the Franklin Library, which specialized in high-quality, high-priced productions and reproductions. For the deluxe, signed edition of *Invisible Man*, the United Parcel Service delivered to Plainfield six thousand sheets of vellum and a box of special pens. Each volume would bring Ralph a royalty payment. Turning away from his new novel, he compiled more than forty drafts of the opening section alone. This was further evidence, perhaps, of the perfectionism that was clogging his arteries as a writer. Zealous about preserving his reputation for excellence, he was ready to labor over these drafts rather than toss off a loose statement about a book with which he had lived for over thirty years.

New honors and appointments made him less able to see his situation clearly. That summer he agreed to join the television journalist Walter Cronkite, Representative Albert Gore, Jr., and important scholars including John Morton Bloom on the advisory council of Open Channels, a new NEH-sponsored educational program connected to the Museum of Broadcasting in Manhattan. He proudly accepted an invitation from Douglas Dillon, the chairman of the board of trustees of the Metropolitan Museum, to serve on the advisory board of the Department of Primitive Art of the Museum of Modern Art in New York City; the following year, 1980, he also began a long, formal association with the Department of Primitive Art at the Metropolitan Museum. That year he helped in the launching of "Treasures of Ancient Nigeria," perhaps the most spectacular public showing to that time of African art in America. But he still made it clear that his interest was in African art, not in Africa's problems. When the Phelps Stokes Fund, which concentrated on Africa, asked him to join a commission to publicize the plight of over four million refugees from war, oppression, or drought, he scrawled on the letter of invitation a note that he was "over-committed."

Fortunately for him, his admirers persisted in celebrating him despite his aloofness. On September 19, he and Fanny arrived at Brown University in Providence for a three-day festival in his honor. The first academic conference devoted exclusively to his life and work, it was the result of a special effort by the poet Michael S. Harper, who was now directing the creative writing program at Brown, and his colleague Barry Beckham, a young black novelist. Apprehensive at first about how the students would receive him, Ralph found himself embraced. The festival turned out to be, as he informed a friend, "serious, exhilarating and . . . somewhat historical." Exhilaration started for him in Rockefeller Library with the unveiling of a watercolor portrait of Inman Page, the first black graduate of Brown University (class of 1877). Improbably, Ralph had been thrust backward into his distant Oklahoma past—Inman Page had been the principal of the Douglass School for most of the time Ralph had been a student there. In a charming speech, Ralph recalled the incident at school when he had punched Page by mistake and then had toppled with him off the stage in the school auditorium. Recovering, Page had then chased him out of the hall, insisting loudly all the while that Ralph was never to return. This episode of comic disgrace seemed now to Ralph invested with an archetypal magic that linked glowing elements of history, comedy, violence, dignity, and mercy in a uniquely American fashion. Never had he imagined that one day he would speak not only about, but also in a sense *for,* Page at the same Ivy League university that had trained him. History had come full circle. "It is as though a preordained relationship has been violated," Ralph told his listeners, "and as a result my sense of time has begun leaping back and forth over the years in a way which assaults the logic of clock and calendar, and I am haunted by a sense of the uncanny."

Ralph and Fanny later listened as Jervis Anderson, R. W. B. Lewis, James Alan McPherson, and Leon Forrest, in a session moderated by Charles Nichols, a black professor of English at Brown, delivered papers written in Ralph's honor. After a formal dinner, Nathan Scott addressed a large gathering of faculty and students on the subject of "Ellison and *Communitas.*" The next day brought more lectures, this time by Robert Stepto of Yale; Michel Fabre, who had finally published his scholarly biography of Richard Wright; and John F. Callahan, a young professor at Lewis and Clark College in Oregon who, in addition to being a close friend of Michael Harper, had published a book on F. Scott Fitzgerald and, more pertinently, an outstanding scholarly essay on Ralph's work.

Dinner was at the president's home, after which everyone proceeded to Sayles Hall, where the audience was said to be larger than the one that

T. S. Eliot had attracted during his visit to Brown. Ralph's lecture elaborated on his whimsical, yet charged, memory of tumbling off the stage with Page. All of history, he reminded his audience, is not written down in books. "Thank God for that," he declared, "because if it were, the democratic promise would come to a standstill." Volatility was part of the process and promise of American democracy. "We live by contention," he insisted, "and this is our good fortune." Contention is creativity. The "random contacts of people," the interplay of mere chance and serendipity, the years between the event and the moment when its core meaning reveals itself, this is what history means. As for American history, "the unceasing pressure on our American principles and beliefs by our equally American blindness and greed—such is the stuff of American reality, and our obligation is to listen and to learn, to remember and to honor our contentions and our diversities." From these, "the American character and truly American art" have sprung.

This elderly man's emphasis on American principles and ideals, his appeal to the wisdom of the Founding Fathers, might have turned off most of the students. It did not. Ellison's speech, one of them wrote, "challenged opinions that for many have characterized the last decade." And yet his young listeners "allowed the words of Ralph Ellison to trickle into their thoughts." Then "the rate at which the meanings were digested increased as the evening progressed past the doubts/realities of the seventies." To many of the youths, his words may have "seemed almost like those of a voice from another time and space." But after his speech, as Sayles Hall emptied, many of the students gathered around him, unwilling to let him go. Clearly they had valued his attempt to resuscitate "the optimism lost in this decade."

Ralph filled up those hours once claimed by NYU mainly by putting in more time than ever at the Century, where he was now a distinctive presence. He was vigilant about the quality of new members. In September 1980 Ralph gladly supported the nomination of Nathan Scott, "one of my most esteemed friends," as a "non-resident" member (resident members lived either in or close to New York City). Scott was "a marvelous conversationalist," he assured his fellow Centurions, "a connoisseur of good food and drink (he makes an excellent Martini), and an intellectual whose curiosity ranges from the vernacular forms of our culture to the more abstract levels of philosophy and theology."

In some respects, Ralph was talking about himself as most Centurions saw him. "Ralph was always a very popular member," Arthur M. Schle-singer, Jr., recalled. The two men had met for the first time around 1956 on the Spanish Steps in Rome. "Aren't you Arthur Schlesinger?" Ralph had asked. "Aren't you Ralph Ellison?" Schlesinger had countered. The novelist and the historian and public servant were good friends who met regularly both in midtown at the Century and uptown at the American Academy. "Ralph had no self-consciousness at all about being a Negro," Schlesinger said, "as he insisted on calling blacks long after it was the thing to do. He was very confident; but I never saw him as pompous or overbearing, at the Century or the academy. He was almost always friendly and charming. Yes, he drank, and then he might become insistent, perhaps, but never obnoxious. I never saw him drunk." Schlesinger added: "I know it's a cliché, but Ralph had *gravitas*." This mixture of seriousness and a love of fun drew many people to him. They admired his passion for dancing. Anatole Broyard of the *New York Times* recalled a 1980 New Year's Eve party, where there was at least one person out on the polished floor "who did not dance awkwardly or ambivalently. . . . Ralph dances the way he writes, both with the beat and against it. He does more different steps than other people, more figures, you might say, as in figures of speech. Though he works in a traditional framework of the Lindy, the two-step and the rumba, he achieves more variety, expression and spontaneity than those people who conceive of dancing as an entirely uninhibited or improvised activity."

At the Century, Ralph continued to be among those opposing the admission of women. The presence of women, he believed, would spoil the old fraternal spirit and encourage snootiness and stuffiness. He hadn't been happy in 1976 when the Century had voted to allow ladies into the dining room in the evenings. He had accepted the change as many other members did—as a welcome boost to the club's coffers—but was distressed when a few members insisted that the time had come to change the rules. The debate became public knowledge. In February 1982, eight members called openly for change. They included Roger Angell of *The New Yorker;* Michael Sovern, the president of Columbia University; John Hammond, the revered music producer; and Paul Goldberger, the architecture critic of the *New York Times*. Ralph refused to sign their petition. In January 1983, the news broke in the *New York Times,* where several Centurions worked in its upper echelons. *Time* magazine, which boasted its own cadre of members, embarrassed the club by reporting that it had refused to consider two prominent, highly respected women, Joan Ganz Cooney of Children's Television and Betty A. Prashker, the head of Crown Publishers. Still, Ralph was determined not to surrender without a further struggle.

In June, he was back at Brown, this time to receive an honorary degree. The next day, Wesleyan University in Connecticut gave him another. His main sponsor at Wesleyan was his admirer Robert G. O'Meally, the assistant professor whose book on Ralph was finally about to appear. Still suspicious of the project, Ralph accepted the degree but was cool to O'Meally. When he read *The Craft of Ralph Ellison* that fall, he became truly unhappy. Certain errors had slipped past copy editors. For example, the president of Invisible's college, A. Hebert Bledsoe, had become "Julian" and then "Julius" Bledsoe. (Jules Bledsoe had been a celebrated black opera singer.) But the most serious error was a misquotation of some of Ralph's published words about Richard Wright in *Shadow and Act*. According to O'Meally, Ralph had called Wright "too driven or deprived or depraved." In fact, Ralph had written "too driven or deprived or inexperienced." Also upsetting to Ralph was the claim that he had stammered or stuttered as a child. O'Meally, he protested, thus "imposes upon me a childhood speech defect that I, having been cursed with a hair-trigger verbal articulateness which was a constant source of trouble, never possessed." Of course, many people heard Ralph stammer or stutter at times, so he probably also did so as a child.

The Craft of Ralph Ellison left Ralph, "to put it mildly, pissed off and resentful, both at the author and at the university press which published his book." Despite his anger, he did not lash out at O'Meally. Only in 1982, two years later, did he finally unburden himself. When O'Meally asked him for help in compiling a Ralph Ellison bibliography, he spoke up. "I think you should know that I was quite unhappy," he wrote to O'Meally, to find the book "full of inaccuracies," notably the attribution to him of the word "depraved." "Understandably," he concluded, "this all makes me most reluctant to be involved with your continuing project." O'Meally apologized for "the blunders of a young scholar who has tried his best to avoid error."

With its analyses of Ralph's work, its biographical facts, and its bibliography, *The Craft of Ralph Ellison* stimulated new scholarship about its subject. More and more academics were turning their attention to Ralph's work. One such venture was a fat volume of critical essays and other material to be edited by a young white graduate of Yale University, Kimberly Benston. At first, Ralph was cool to Benston. Like Werner Sollors of Columbia University, he had published a book on Amiri Baraka. When Ralph learned that Benston's proposed book would include essays by Kenneth Burke and Joseph Frank, the Dostoyevsky scholar he had met during his time at Rutgers, he began to relent. A full conversion would come when he finally met Benston at the madhouse of a Modern Language Association annual convention in New York in December 1983. A few months later, when Ralph wrote about "the mind-blasting noise" and the brevity of their meeting, he was warmer to Benston than before ("still, it was a beginning and next time we'll go on from there"). Although they never became close, Benston, who had witnessed at Yale and elsewhere what he called "the headier competitions for entrance into the Ellisonian *sanctum sanctorum*," and had "lamented the bruises" some of his ambitious friends had suffered in jostling for Ellison's attention, recalled that he himself was treated by Ralph "with great kindness and good humor."

By this time, Ralph and Fanny had also begun an acquaintance with the young scholar John F. Callahan. It would prove to be one of the most significant friendships of their later years. The fact that Callahan was white was probably of some importance; Ralph found in his friendship with admirable whites an emotional satisfaction born of his faith in interracial democracy. More important than Callahan's white skin, of course, was the fact that he was witty, lively, well read, honest, and increasingly devoted to the aging Ellisons. Fanny took to him at once. He thus joined the tight circle of Ralph's younger friends who were admitted from time to time at 730 Riverside Drive, or who were welcome to telephone him at almost any time of the day. This circle comprised mainly Michael Harper, Robert Stepto, John Wright of Minnesota, James Alan McPherson, and Stanley Crouch. That it included no women, and especially no young black women, was to be expected. Ralph seemed unable to sustain relationships of this kind.

Tall, slender, intense, but fun-loving, Callahan was a New England Irishman with working-class roots who had broken out of his community, in the classic American fashion, to earn a doctorate in English. He had entered the Ellisons' lives through his close friendship with Harper. Admiring the quality of Callahan's first book, a study of F. Scott Fitzgerald published in 1972, Harper convinced a skeptical Callahan to send Ralph a copy. Ralph's response was silence. Late in 1977 Callahan mailed Ralph a copy of an essay he had recently published in the preeminent journal of African-American literary criticism, Joe Weixlmann's *Black American Literature Forum* (later called *African American Review*). Callahan's essay,

"Chaos, Complexity and Possibility: The Historical Frequencies of Ralph Waldo Ellison," which argues that Ralph's essays form an indispensable lens through which to view not only *Invisible Man* but also other major American fiction, astonished Ralph by what he saw as its penetration into the more complex mysteries of his mind and work. Although many articles on *Invisible Man* had appeared by this point, Ralph found none shrewder and more brilliant than Callahan's.

In January 1978, he sent Callahan a glowing letter of praise. Later that year, by invitation, Callahan arrived at 730 Riverside Drive for his first meeting with Ralph and Fanny. Over a bottle of Irish whiskey, which Ralph had puckishly bought for the occasion, reserve soon faded away. When Callahan persisted in calling him Mr. Ellison, Ralph commanded him to call him by his first name. Eager to help Callahan's career, early in 1980 Ralph wrote a letter of support when John applied for a Guggenheim Foundation fellowship. When the public policy division of the Ford Foundation asked Ralph to nominate someone for a fellowship in "contemporary trends and issues," he chose Callahan. This was not really a stretch, since Callahan's passion for progressive politics had led him to run, albeit unsuccessfully, for Congress (among those supporting him was Eugene McCarthy). Callahan won neither fellowship, but the Ellisons' affection for him only grew as the years passed. So, too, did Callahan's regard for them, and Ralph especially. "Ralph Ellison was a wonderfully complex man," he said. "He was playful, he was boyish, he was mischievous, he was austere, he was serious, he was fierce, he was tender, he was affectionate, and he was very, very smart."

Now Ralph began to develop an even more serious interest in his archives and in scholarship about his life and work. He had a high regard for researchers such as the white librarian Stewart Lillard, who had recovered, without any expectation of reward, about as much of the historical record concerning Ralph's paternal family roots as still existed. (Ralph apparently never indicated any interest in his mother's roots.) In 1982 Ralph corresponded with the historians James L. Roark and Michael P. Johnson, who were writing a book about William Ellison, a freedman from South Carolina. Scrupulously he corrected the erroneous notion that he belonged to that Ellison family. At home, in bulging boxes and full filing cabinets that clogged passageways, he and Fanny continued to accumulate as much evidence about Ralph as they could find. At times, when she wondered about the value of all of this hoarding, ordering, filing, clipping, and pruning, Fanny reminded herself of the answer: "Because they will link up in some useful way for scholars and would be scholars." She sought to preserve the complete evidence, unflattering as well as flattering, that went with Ralph's greatness. She spared neither Ralph nor herself.

Early in 1981, Ralph seized on a novel, exciting chance to help a few of his fellow artists and intellectuals, especially younger people. In Chicago, the immensely wealthy John D. and Catherine T. MacArthur Foundation had set up a program of five-year fellowships awarded annually to promising individuals in the humanities, sciences, and social work, almost unprecedented in its generosity except for the Nobel Prizes. Soon known misleadingly as the "genius" award, the MacArthur fellowships were supposed to free the fortunate winners from mundane duties and allow them to explore their favorite projects without worrying about money. The foundation asked Ralph to help nominate individuals for the first class.

When he chose his nominees, all were men—four were black, four white: Cormac McCarthy, the freelance journalist Donald Katz (a former student of Ralph's at NYU), the scholar Lawrence Levine (his *Black Culture and Black Consciousness* was "a brilliant study of American cultural history," Ralph wrote), Leon Forrest, Robert Stepto, John Wright, Michael Harper, and John Callahan. In nominating them, Ralph stressed their ethnicity: "Katz and Levine are Jewish; Harper, Forrest, Stepto and Wright Afro-American [he was no longer wedded to the term 'Negro']; Callahan is an Irishman from New Haven; and McCarthy is white, Southern and from rural East Tennessee." His descriptions indicate the fine differences Ralph saw concerning class, caste, ethnicity, and race in America. McCarthy was not Irish but a white Southerner; Katz and Levine were not white but "Jewish."

In selecting nominees, Ralph had not looked beyond his own backyard. McCarthy was a protégé of Robert Penn Warren and edited by Albert Erskine at Random House. Forrest, Callahan, Stepto, Harper, and Wright had promoted his work in some way. He very much admired Wright's "Shadowing Ellison," an outstanding essay that appeared in the Winter 1980 *Carleton Miscellany*. ("Ralph was also impressed by the fact that I came from an old black frontier family in Minnesota," Wright said, "and also that I had started out successfully in science before turning to literature.") Neither Wright nor Katz had published a book. Ralph ignored promising young black writers such as Alice Walker, Toni Morrison, Gloria Naylor, Ishmael Reed, John Edgar Wideman, Charles Johnson, and James Alan McPherson—writers who among them would win one National Book Award, three Pulitzer Prizes, and a Nobel Prize.

Noticeably absent from Ralph's list was McPherson. He had given up his tenured position at the University of Virginia. His marriage, to a white woman, had failed. McPherson, caught up in a wrenching emotional crisis, seemed to Ralph too vulnerable and variable as a man and an artist. Accordingly, he warned the MacArthur Foundation against supporting him. Gentle and considerate, McPherson nevertheless now seemed to embody for Ralph the threat of chaos facing the nation and blacks especially. Praising the young writer as someone who was "not only talented but a serious American artist," he also noted with disapproval his "current restlessness." Certain personal events in Charlottesville had left the man "not only emotionally upset but unpredictable in his personal relationships." He had lost his way. McPherson's early success, instead of helping him to grow, "has led instead to what might be called a condition of hierarchical disorientation or, say, a condition of shock brought on by a long-delayed social mobility suddenly achieved." Integration, Ralph believed, had unhinged McPherson as it had unhinged many younger blacks. "For them," he wrote, "each venture into new areas of possibility became an initiation into new mysteries of social relationships, and these were mysteries for which our society provided no discernible rites of passage." Adopting the language of the theater, he offered a critique of the younger generation: "The old stage directions which had structured their actions in the old drama of social hierarchy were no longer so clear as guides to action, the old antagonists were no longer so easily identifiable; the traditional etiquette and gestures no longer conveyed the same messages, and the old stage lighting which had once illuminated areas of blackness and whiteness had dimmed to a sometimes baffling chiaroscuro."

The letter, for all its stylish turns and its element of truth, is in some respects a complex version of the seven Bellerphonic letters of "recommendation" Bledsoe gives to the hapless young hero of *Invisible Man*. Over the years, Ralph continued to sympathize more and more with the tough-minded if also ruthless A. Hebert Bledsoe. While "I by no means intend to imply a lack of faith in McPherson's ability," was it really wise to trust McPherson with a fat, five-year fellowship? "I can't help but wonder," he ventured, "if it wouldn't be more to his best interest that he remain where he is and work out his present problems before launching himself into a new scene of activity."

In a way Ralph was saying, as in the horrid dream of the narrator in

Invisible Man, "Keep This Nigger-Boy Running." No doubt he believed that McPherson deserved to be disciplined, just as he also believed that he was obliged to be unsentimental and frank in his evaluation. Clearly he was not prepared to give the young writer the benefit of the doubt about his ability to overcome his personal problems. Ralph did not bother to be subtle about the lack of qualifications of Amiri Baraka. No longer a radical black cultural nationalist, he observed, Baraka had apparently undergone "a series of ideological metamorphoses," but "in each instance . . . he has ended up an evermore fantastic reincarnation of [Eugene O'Neill's] the Emperor Jones." Having put away "his African regalia and, *he* says, his anti-Semitism," Baraka now called himself a Marxist-Leninist. Scathingly Ralph expressed surprise that Baraka was "being considered for what I'm sure he'd think ill-gotten capitalist gains. Unless, of course, like the famous emperor, he is searching for the wherewithal to fashion a silver bullet." (Three years later, responding to a request from the State University of New York at Stony Brook for an evaluation of Baraka's work, he marveled at his "considerable success at boring from within the groves of academe." Ralph had been "under the false impression that he [Baraka] had become a born-again Christian—or was it a Titoist?" Obviously he possessed a "general ignorance of your candidate" and no "firm grounds on which to respond.")

Cormac McCarthy and Larry Levine were in the first class of MacArthur fellows announced that September. The foundation also awarded a fellowship to McPherson, as it did to Stepto's colleague and, in the minds of some people, archrival at Yale, Henry Louis Gates, Jr., who admired Ellison and his work but was never invited to visit him. "Somehow Ellison got into his head," Gates said, "that I had been one of the black undergraduates at Yale who had heckled and booed him one day. Of course I never did any such thing. I found out later that he asked a friend whose daughter was graduating from Yale to take a photograph of me at Commencement. He must have remembered clearly the faces of the black students who had heckled him, and he realized from the photograph that I hadn't been there. All the same, we never became friends."

In the late spring of 1981 Ralph and Fanny made one of their infrequent visits to their condominium in Windsor Grove on Key West. The property had become a good investment. (In 1983, the rent for two winter months alone exceeded the mortgage payments for the entire year.) Ralph had begun to appreciate its charms, although not sufficiently for him to stay there often. "The grounds which we share with our friends and neigh-bors are landscaped with lovely tropical plants, trees, and flowers," he informed a friend, "though the thump of oranges and avocados on one's roof can be quite shocking."

On this trip, his neighbor John Hersey formally interviewed him for the second time. Hersey intended to publish the transcript in a Festschrift planned in honor of Charles T. Davis, the inspirational leader of African-American Studies at Yale, who had died of cancer in March that year. This interview sheds light on Ralph's hopes and fears now about his second novel. "I'm trying to make it a single work," he assured Hersey, although Albert Erskine now believed "it might be a trilogy." Since 1958 he had written much but "was never satisfied with how it connected." Unity remained a problem, as did the basic narrative approach: "I'm finding myself having to try first-person narration, and then try it again as third-person, in an effort to stay out of it as narrator myself. It's exasperating. . . . One of the challenges for a writer who handles the kind of material I'm working with is to let the people speak for themselves, in whatever way you can. Then you draw upon more of the resources of American vernacu-lar speech." The tone was an issue: "I said the book is comic," Ralph told Hersey. "Maybe ultimately what I write always turns out to be tragi-comedy, which I think has proved to be the underlying mode of American experience. We don't remember enough; we don't allow ourselves to remember events, and I suppose this helps us to continue our belief in progress."

(Later, Norman Podhoretz had a much simpler and not implausible explanation for Ralph's problems. "From large elements like the cadences of the italicized interior monologue," he said of the novel edited from the massive manuscript and published posthumously as *Juneteenth,* "to smaller stylistic details like the omission of quotation marks in the dialogue and the heavy reliance on gerunds, the voice is the voice of William Faulkner." Ralph struggled "for forty years to get Faulkner's sound out of his head.")

On March 1, 1982, his birthday, Ralph got out a tape measure, opened a metal file cabinet, and actually measured the manuscript for Herbert Mitgang of the *New York Times.* At nineteen inches, "it looks long enough to be a trilogy," he said, smiling proudly. "It all takes place in the twentieth century," he revealed, but "I'm convinced that I'm working with abiding patterns. . . . I'm dealing with a broader range of characters, playing with various linguistic styles." He didn't know when it would be done, but "if I'm going to be remembered as a novelist, I'd better produce it soon."

Ralph wanted to capture the dual reality of American history and American daily life. With regard to religion (hardly mentioned in *Invisible Man*), which had emerged again as a political force in American culture in the person of leaders such as Dr. King and the other ministers, priests, and rabbis who opposed the Vietnam War, Ralph suggested that he had instinctively captured this force in the novel. He seemed to overlook the fact that the black ministers of the civil rights movement, at work before he started writing the novel in 1958, probably had helped to inspire his creation of a hero who was a black minister-hero, and also that those same ministers tended therefore to make his hero predictable. His ideas about creating fiction seemed almost formulaic. "The fiction writer abstracts from the flow of experience certain abiding patterns, and projects those patterns as they affect the lives and the consciousness of his characters. So fiction allows for a summing up. It allows for contemplation of the moral significance of human events." Writers often "don't consider what a powerful effect vividly projected images of symbolic actions can have upon readers. . . . I believe writers might think a little bit about the implications of what they project, and of the kind of heroes or anti-heroes they project." He caught himself in time: "Of course, I'm not offering formulas. Everyone has to work out his writing for himself."

In an October 1982 *Playboy* interview he voiced his sense of futility: "Part of what's taken so long is that so many things have changed so fast in our culture that as soon as I thought I had a draft that brought all of these things together, there would be another shift and I'd have to go back and revise all over again." This interview showed also that the emergence of right-wing American political power dismayed him and subverted his idealistic vision of America. He saw Ronald Reagan as trying to destroy the very force, Roosevelt's New Deal, which had sustained and inspired Ralph in the late Depression. Sobered by this political sea change, in the spring of 1982 he became, at the urging of the liberal black mayor of Atlanta, Andrew Young, a national sponsor of the Emergency Black Survival Fund. This was a significant step for Ralph. He deplored what Young called "the Reagan administration's attack on this country's poor, which is threatening to deprive blacks and other minorities not only of their civil and economic rights, but of their very survival." Reagan, Ralph complained later that year, "is dismantling many of the processes and structures that made it possible for me to go from sleeping on a park bench to becoming a writer. And he is assuring people, in the most charming way, that this is good for us."

He blamed excessive liberalism for the rise of conservatism under Reagan. Behind that excess was the false idea, propagated in "the philosophy of 'let it all hang out' that emerged in the early Seventies," that total freedom is possible. *"There is no goddamned total freedom,"* Ralph insisted. "It's always relative." Radical sexual freedom, the core of the infamous *Playboy* philosophy, had precipitated the peculiar decay of America under Reagan. Self-discipline was crucial. Accordingly, Ralph called for the formation of a kind of compulsory national service, in which youths could choose either military or civilian involvement.

To celebrate the thirtieth anniversary of *Invisible Man,* Random House published a special edition of the novel, with a foreword by Ralph. In the *Washington Post Book World,* Jonathan Yardley's essay "30 Years on the 'Raft of Hope'" saluted the event by pointing to Ralph's links to Mark Twain and the ideal of racial respect and understanding in *Adventures of Huckleberry Finn.* Pleased by the edition, Ralph sent out copies to a long list of friends and acquaintances. Interest in making a movie of the novel persisted. The successful playwright Charles Fuller wrote a screenplay (the proposed cast included Sidney Poitier, the comedian Richard Pryor as Ras the Destroyer, and Howard E. Rollins, Jr., as Invisible). Nothing came of it, but the next few years brought inquiries from Roy Campanella, Jr., and a screen treatment by the novelist Trey Ellis. The powerful Hollywood-based musician Quincy Jones met with Ralph and Owen Laster, Ralph's agent, for several hours at the Stanhope Hotel in Manhattan, but to no avail. In truth, he would not have cared for any screen treatment of *Invisible Man.*

"What with that hubbub and various board meetings," Fanny noted unhappily, they reached the Berkshires in early June 1982 in "a fractious mood." She was determined to protect the summer months, "which he must keep private if he is to get any writing done." They had no sooner reached Plainfield than news came of the death of John Cheever. Traveling to Ossining, New York, for the funeral, Ralph listened with sympathy as Saul Bellow, who loved Cheever, delivered a heartfelt eulogy.

Despite Fanny's wishes and efforts, various events lured him back to the city. There was the retirement dinner at the Waldorf-Astoria for Joseph F. Cullman III of the Philip Morris tobacco company, a major philanthropist. Colonial Willamsburg also drew them away. That year, he wrote to James Randolph in Oklahoma City about his ease in associating there with rich and socially prominent whites. "By now we've become accustomed," he said of Fanny and himself, "to working out problems with the likes of old Virginians and the heads of major corporations with whom I'd never dreamed I'd even come within speaking distance. You should see Fanny by candlelight during a formal dinner in what was once a great plantation mansion! She looks like she was to the manor [manner] born—only it took a hell of a time to get her there." In November, he agreed to serve on two of its committees. He would step down unwillingly from the board two years later, after reaching its mandatory retirement age of seventy, but continue a lesser association with it for several more years. To Charles Brown, the chairman of the board of AT&T, Ralph confessed he revered the foundation because it "provides men and women of good will (but disparate backgrounds) an unhampered opportunity for working together in the interest of a transcendent cause. . . . I've never felt so American as when doing whatever I could to further the effort." He was certain that his courage many years before in exposing himself and Fanny to the traditional hostility of the white South to blacks had helped to change the region. In 1985, he reflected on how far Virginia had come since the days of "massive resistance" to the election of a black lieutenant governor (and future governor), Douglas Wilder. "I don't know how it all fits together," he admitted, "but the climate of racial relations is quite different than it was when we became affiliated with Colonial Williamsburg, and I suspect that Fanny and I have played a minor role in that change."

In truth, his effect was mixed. "What strikes me as most curious of all," one veteran official of Colonial Williamsburg, Cary Carson, said about Ralph, "is how little an impression he left behind. He is remembered here as Ralph Ellison, the famous American novelist and the first African American to serve on the board. But no one recalls anything he said at those meetings, any opinions he might have formed about CW's interpretation of American history, or whether he used his special credentials to argue for a more honest portrayal of slavery in the eighteenth-century." Several people had called for a fresh, more honest approach to the subject. A former historian employed at Colonial Williamsburg, according to Carson, "could recall no pet projects or special points of view that Ellison championed."

When Wake Forest University offered him another four-year term on its board of visitors, he quickly accepted. By this point, Ralph could also be relaxed and ironical, in the right company, about the main reason these boards wanted him. Louis Auchincloss, a fellow novelist and loyal Centurion, remembered asking Ralph—"I was terribly, terribly fond of him"—if he would consider joining the board of the Museum of the City of New York. "Ralph looked at me with that smile of his," Auchincloss recalled. " 'Lou-ee,' he said, very loudly for everyone to hear, 'do you want a *nigger* on your board of trustees?' 'Yes, I do, Ralph,' I told him. 'I really do.' Ralph just roared with laughter, wonderfully rich laughter. 'Well then, I accept, Lou-ee, I accept!' " Auchincloss recalled Ralph as always pleasant, never drunk or obnoxious despite his passion for martinis. (Actually, Ralph once apologized in a letter to Auchincloss for a "garbled telephone message" he had left "in a drunken, spur-of-the-moment reaction" after he had "imbibed more than my usual number of martinis.")

Always, if not always successfully, he aimed to blend in, to be a good citizen. In 1982, for example, when he joined Toni Morrison, Bernard Malamud, Henry Kissinger, and Isaac Bashevis Singer among the twenty-one "Literary Lions" honored at a black-tie, fund-raising dinner at the New York Public Library, he was the soul of modesty. "I am not much of a lion," Ralph wrote to Andrew Heiskell, the library chairman, "but it is a rare privilege." The following year, he joined an effort led by Vartan Gregorian, the dynamic president of the library, to restore and expand the faltering institution. Signing an appeal in the *New York Times* calling for gifts to the library to meet a matching grant from the NEH, he also became part of the Minerva Awards program honoring valedictorians of the 102 public high schools in the city. In May 1984, he gave the televised main address to the students, then helped the television journalist Barbara Walters hand out certificates. The next evening, at a black-tie dinner in Bryant Park behind the library, along with Walters and the philanthropist Brooke Astor, who had made rebuilding the library her major charitable goal, he celebrated the reopening of a beautifully restored exhibition hall at the library.

Yet sometimes he showed a different side under self-inflicted pressure, and his underlying rage erupted. Jonathan Fanton, who took over as president of the New School in 1982, had known Ralph from his Yale days. One day, he witnessed Ralph's explosive, less than rational side. "Someone on the board, one of our strong fiscal types, was going on and on about how the board members had to make a much greater effort to give more money to the school," Fanton recalled. Suddenly Ralph leaped to his feet. Defending the extent of his giving, he vented his resentment at being insulted. Everyone else was stunned. "No one expected certain board members to give a lot of money," Fanton said. "Certainly no one expected Ralph to do so. Somehow he got it into his head that people resented him and were criticizing him. He stormed out of the meeting. I don't believe I ever saw him again."

Retrospection became more and more appealing. On March 1, 1983 (his sixty-ninth or seventieth birthday), he was pleased to take part in a program about the WPA sponsored by the FDR Centennial Commission. With President Reagan's continuing assault on the New Deal, Ralph was eager to defend the Federal Writers' Project. Following a lecture by Jerre Mangione, once its coordinating editor and now its main historian, Ralph joined Ellen Tarry (a former colleague in the Negro unit), the poet David Ignatow, the playwright Lionel Abel, and Arthur M. Schlesinger, Jr., for a panel discussion. He made clear his gratitude to the Writers' Project, which had enabled his writing career and all of his many honors and awards.

His pleasure in the past was evident again later that month when he delivered the annual Morton Globus Distinguished Lecture at Baruch College of the City University of New York. His address, "On Becoming a Writer," attracted hundreds of students and faculty members. A student reporter, struck by "the energy of the audience's excitement and anticipation," noted Ralph's serenity as he talked about Oklahoma City and Tuskegee, about coming to New York and deciding in the late 1930s to try to become a writer. His face was "smooth, yet marked by deepened laugh lines around the corners of his mouth," she reported. To him the 1930s "seemed like a golden age," one rich in authors and intellectuals "who would talk to you." Ralph tried to convey both the excitement of those years and the constancy of effort needed to succeed as an author. "The matter of becoming a writer," he insisted, according to the reporter, "is tied up with the possibility and the availability of experience. It's not a matter of being optimistic, but moving toward that which has caught your eye, that which promises to test you to the point wherein you will transcend yourself and become something of which you had never dreamed." Here he paused. "I was transformed." Drifting to the side of the stage, he ended his lecture with words that seemed not unlike those of Tennyson's Ulysses: "The secret lies in that old frontier experience, that spirit of adventure, that willingness to test ourselves against that which seems impossible."

He was brilliant again a few days later at his third appearance in the Gertrude Clarke Whittall lecture series at the Library of Congress. Instead of lecturing, he read from his novel-in-progress. As at Baruch, he commanded his audience. "You would have thought it was Mark Twain," according to the *Washington Post.* The composition of the audience was also extraordinary given the ugly skirmishes he had fought only a few years back. Introduced by his old friend Anthony Hecht, now the consultant in poetry to the Library of Congress, Ralph read to an audience "of mostly young, mostly black fans who had filled the place a half-hour early and stood six deep in the hall outside watching on television." The heart of the reading was a section with "one Cleothus [Cliofus], at 300 pounds the biggest kid in the first grade." Starting coolly, Ralph "gradually warmed up as the laughter washed over him." By the end "he was laughing, too, stopping in mid-sentence, choking over some bit of description, each one wilder than the last." His audience, "which had been leaning forward, eyes alight, whooping with laughter at his descriptions—many of them scatological—almost wouldn't let him go. When they did leave the auditorium, it was to line up to shake the man's hand."

According to the *Post,* the story actually "never made much progress but meandered from one hilarious episode to the next." Inevitably, the reporter asked about the long-delayed novel. He had lost "some 500 pages" of the novel, Ralph said, "but he still had another 1,000." And he was slaving away. "Working steadily seven hours a day, he has amassed what he calls an enormous manuscript. That's about all he will say." Ralph never did stop piling up pages. "I knew for a fact that he was always writing," said R. W. B. Lewis. "We could see piles of manuscript on and around his desk. I think that his favorite term for what he was doing was 'knit.' Everything in the book had to be 'knitted' well together. In some respects the knitting was more important than actually finishing the job. I was never sure that he wanted to finish the book." Writer's block wasn't the problem. "The trouble was that Ralph would suddenly introduce a character with a certain purpose in mind," Al Murray recalled. "Then the character would develop a mind and life of his own, and before you knew it Ralph was backing up and he had a novella going." He had faced the same problem with *Invisible Man,* but one crucial element was missing now. "I thought Stanley Hyman was instrumental in helping Ralph pull the material together for *Invisible Man,*" Ted Weiss, Ralph's friend since his years at Bard, said. "Hyman helped him find the shape of the book, trimmed it, and gave it form and order. On the second novel, he had no one to help him in the same way."

If the Whittal reading was a triumph, Ralph also knew failures in public. In May 1983, his prominent role at the annual ceremonial of the academy and institute led to a small disaster. He came to the microphone after the large audience had squirmed through about two hours of speeches and presentations in sticky weather. Told to praise Bernard Malamud and then hand him the Gold Medal in literature, he instead held forth for what seemed to some listeners almost half an hour. Onstage behind Ralph, the historian Barbara Tuchman began to mutter in protest. A revolt began, to which Ralph seemed oblivious. According to Tobias Wolff, the author of *This Boy's Life* and other books, "at least once, Arthur Schlesinger tugged on Ellison's trouser leg to get him to stop. Ellison just shook him off—slapped at his hand—and kept on going. I admired Ellison deeply as a writer, and it was sad to see this happen."

By the time Ralph was done, the audience was abuzz with disapproval, and he was hot with rage. Dispatching a polished version of the text to the academy office for its *Proceedings,* he noted angrily that he had spoken from a draft, "which I hoped would allow for flexibility." Unfortunately, "due to the pressure of time, the squirming of the audience before me, and the mumbling of B. Tuchman to my rear (she seemed to feel that the audience preferred getting drunk to hearing what I had to say about Malamud), I edited my remarks quite drastically." A writer of Malamud's stature surely deserved more than "the usual clichés that are spun out on such occasions." In the future, the academy should instruct presenters to "go through the motions as quickly as possible out of regard for the audience's desire for free liquor." After all, "on any given occasion," the crowd "might consist of more low-grade idiots than of those seriously concerned with our promotion of artistic excellence." (Some people believed Ralph himself was tipsy.)

Over the year that followed, Ralph boycotted the academy. Eventually the academy president, John Kenneth Galbraith, begged him—"I make a personal plea"—to return to the fold despite his "discontent" with the academy. Malamud himself appreciated what Ralph had tried to do for him. He made sure that Nicholas Delbanco, the director of the annual writing workshop at Bennington, invited Ralph to join Malamud in addressing the students. On that occasion the Ellisons stayed with the Malamuds.

(Shirley Hazzard also recalled another unfortunate moment for Ralph at the Academy. Giving a toast for some reason, he was rambling on, obviously with too much to drink, when he suddenly looked at her husband and said: "'I see Francis Steegmuller there, shaking his head and I know what you're thinking, Francis: 'Well, Ralph, you were something once but you've just become a silly little fellow.' It was awful. People were shocked beyond words. Of course, Francis denied it on the spot.")

In fact, despite his lapses, most of his peers held him in high esteem.

At the Century, he became one of the sixteen trustees of the board of management. In late December, when he delivered an address marking the centenary of the Modern Language Association, its president, Joel Conarroe, pointed out that only Ellison among all living authors had been the subject of as many as three articles in its elite journal, *PMLA*. About this time, Albert Erskine and Ralph agreed that the publication of another collection of Ralph's essays and interviews was in order. Scheduled to appear in 1986 (twenty-two years after *Shadow and Act*), the book brought him an advance of $25,000 from Random House. Ralph began to buff his smaller pieces. For example, he reworked "Remembering Richard Wright," a speech delivered from notes in 1971 at the University of Iowa. Working with a mangled transcript, he eventually sent a polished revision to Michel Fabre in Paris for inclusion in a special Ralph Ellison edition he was preparing for *Delta*, a French journal devoted to the literature of the South. "Something is lost in the process," Ralph admitted of his many changes, "but, let's face it, we're dealing with two distinct forms of communication."

This reworked lecture would be perfect for his new book, *Going to the Territory*. The collection would look backward for the most part. This was true both of the Wright piece and "An Extravagance of Laughter," an essay begun by Ralph to honor the novelist Erskine Caldwell on his eighti-eth birthday. The essay opens in 1936, when Langston Hughes takes young Ralph, fresh from Alabama, to see his first Broadway play, *Tobacco Road*, adapted from Caldwell's best-selling novel. In the theater, Ralph embarrasses himself—and Hughes—by guffawing far too loudly and uncontrollably at the antics of Caldwell's "poor white" characters. Back in Alabama, blacks didn't find poor whites funny. Up north, however, Ralph's explosions of laughter (as he wrote to Caldwell in 1983) had been both exhilarating and cathartic, "for by giving artistic sanction to a source of comedy which in the interest of self-protection I had been forced to deny myself you had released me from three turbulent years of self-restraint." Expanding on this episode, Ralph's essay is a fertile exploration of black people, their politics and psychology, their art and humanity, united by his peculiarly independent point of view. Adding here, cutting there, he enjoyed the process of revision. However, this pleasure routinely led to excess. The surfeit of drafts of "An Extravagance of Laughter" added up to more than five hundred typewritten pages, suggesting the compul-sively repetitive nature of Ralph's evolved way of writing.

"An Extravagance of Laughter" and "The Little Man at Chehaw Sta-

tion" would form the vibrant core of the new book. They mix gravity and
wit with a rambling but amiable style that captures and releases Ellison's
literary personality at its richest. Unlike the anger visible in parts of *Shadow
and Act,* reconciliation is the emphasis of the new book. This spirit of reconciliation was becoming more and more important to Ralph. In March
1984, when he took part in a Ford Foundation seminar on Mahatma
Gandhi and nonviolence with the psychologist Kenneth Clark and the
owner of *The Atlantic Monthly,* Morton Zuckerman, he was friendlier to
Clark than he had been in years. Disagreeing with Clark's emphasis on
black self-hatred as a product of segregation, Ralph had kept his distance
for some years. Nevertheless, the heat of Black Power had seared both
men. Now Ralph was ready to concede the strength of Clark's core ideas.

But he wasn't quite ready to make peace with everyone. In 1980, the
publication of a book of letters between Langston Hughes and his close
friend Arna Bontemps had revealed Hughes's bitterness at his sense that
Ralph, having risen in the world, had been shunning him. Ralph also
seemed quick to sign petitions about injustice in Europe but slow to show
a similar concern for Africa. Annoyed, Hughes sometimes resorted to gibes
in writing to Bontemps about Ellison. "Ralphie is getting real baldheaded,"
he quipped once, "—further proof that he is an intellectual." The book of
letters stung Ralph, who nursed the grudge. In April 1983, he was chilly
when he finally admitted to his apartment a professor from California
who had begged him for three years for an interview about Hughes, whose
biography the professor was writing. Ralph made no effort to hide his
contempt for Hughes. "Hadn't Hughes dedicated *Montage of a Dream
Deferred* to him and Fanny?" the visitor asked. "Yes, yes," Ralph replied;
"one of those books—I really don't remember which." The visitor tried
again. Hughes, he said, had traveled all over the world. "That's right,"
Ralph drawled. "He traveled almost as much as some Pullman Car porters."
Langston, he said, was a lazy thinker who pandered to the masses. He
had taught Ralph little or nothing. (Many years later, the professor was
amused to discover that the Ellisons, who had offered him no refresh-
ments, reported to the IRS an expense of $25 to entertain him.)

A year later, when Ralph decided to accept the Langston Hughes
Medal, awarded annually to a major black writer by the City College of
New York in Harlem, he did so with trepidation. So he let on to Raymond
Patterson, the main organizer of the annual event. "Ray discussed with us
the possibility of bringing in extra security," one of his junior colleagues
said. Ellison "thought that he might be openly insulted, and even that some

students might throw things at him." In fact, no security was needed on April 11 when the president of CCNY, Bernard Harleston, jubilantly welcomed Ralph at Aaron Davis Hall. James Alan McPherson (who knew nothing of Ralph's destructive letter to the MacArthur Foundation about him) paid tribute to Ralph in his introduction. A standing ovation greeted him as he accepted the award, after which he read from his novel-in-progress. Listening intently, his audience, many of whom hadn't been born when *Invisible Man* was first published in 1952, chuckled and laughed loudly throughout his rambling, comic narrative. Then, when he was done, they rose again for another standing ovation. To them, Ralph was a giant—as Langston Hughes, too, had been.

In 1989, after the Stanford professor's two-volume biography appeared, Ellison sent him a letter that was charitable about the books and Hughes himself. "Learning the details of Langston's life of which I was unaware," he admitted, "is both illuminating and saddening, for no matter to what extent Langston was the author of his fate, such a generous man deserved much better."

Ralph's neighborhood remained a source of annoyance. Now it had become a cacophony of boom boxes: "Here we are, assailed by the new style portable jukeboxes which every little bastard within miles appears to own, and which they love to share with us deprived ones, even if it's four in the morning." But noise was not the main problem. By 1984, the once proud Beaumont had struck bottom. In winter, the heating system broke down. Busted water pipes flooded floors. A succession of incompetent or crooked building superintendents let the lobby grow shabby, the intercoms and doorbells fall silent. To save on polishing, to Ralph's horror, one of them painted over the brass railings. With many tenants unable to pay for a private guard service, all had to be vigilant. One resident was assaulted and robbed at the entrance on 150th Street. Muggers beat another tenant so badly that she had to be hospitalized. The cocaine market was flourishing in nearby Washington Heights, where whites with money sought out drug dealers. The corners at 174th and Amsterdam formed a cocaine supermarket, where drivers rolled down their windows and handed over cash for packets of powder. In the 34th police precinct—Manhattan north of 155th Street—officers in two months made more than a thousand drug-related arrests.

Besieged, the American Academy and National Institute operated nervously within its neoclassical buildings and ferried members downtown in hired limousines after events. When the Ellisons entertained whites, who might be special targets of muggers, Ralph almost always saw them into a cab, doors clicked shut, before saying goodbye. And yet Ralph refused to leave New York. As he had explained to an Oklahoma friend, "it's the 'getting place' of my profession." He stressed to the new owners of 730 Riverside Drive that he and Fanny intended to stay put. "We live here *not* because we could not have found living quarters elsewhere," he said, "but because we like our building and wish to remain."

He continued to be critical of the national leadership and the Reagan administration's attacks on federal funding for education and social services, especially for the poor. Reagan's threats against the National Endowment for the Arts and the National Endowment for the Humanities, which Ralph had helped to found, appalled him. (His contribution was recognized in 1985 when he wrote the introduction to *Buying Time,* an anthology to celebrate the twentieth anniversary of the NEA, and he was an honored guest when Mayor Ed Koch gave a formal reception at City Hall to mark the anniversary.) In the presidential election of 1984, Ralph's dislike of Reagan's policies led him into a sudden fascination with the candidacy of a brash black Chicago-based civil rights activist and ordained minister, Jesse Jackson. Once a lieutenant of Dr. King, and present at his assassination, Jackson had formed a grassroots organization in Chicago called Operation Breadbasket and preached fervently about leading the Rainbow Coalition. The Ellisons gathered a rich trove of newspaper and magzine clippings on Jackson, who must have seemed to Ralph like a character out of his novel-in-progress. They also gave money to support Jackson's 1984 (and 1988) presidential campaign. His candidacy combined for Ralph American courage and conviction about American democracy with the exuberant style of black self-assertion.

Nevertheless, Ralph still avoided political controversy if he could do so. Asked to join Jackson and others on television to discuss the future of black colleges, he declined. Fearing the politicization of PEN by Norman Mailer, the president of PEN America, he declined to be a special guest at the forty-eighth Annual International Congress of PEN, held in New York. When Bayard Rustin asked him to join an anti-apartheid effort, Project South Africa, Ralph offered only sympathy. Such discretion brought rewards. Ironically, the most prestigious award came from President Reagan. On April 1, 1985, he was among the first group of citizens, and the only writer, named to receive the new National Medal of the Arts created by Reagan. Would Ralph accept the award despite Reagan's controversial upcoming visit to the cemetery at Bitburg in Germany, where the dead included forty-seven members of the Nazi secret police? "This has nothing to do with politics," Ralph responded. "This is an expression of the American people and it will go on, I hope, some time after present political divisions are healed." At the White House for the presentation, he joined recipients who included Martha Graham, Louise Nevelson, Georgia O'Keeffe, and Leontyne Price. Addressing about a hundred guests, Reagan appeared to single out Ralph for praise. "Ralph Waldo Ellison is said to be greatly misunderstood," he said. "It's my hope that today will go some way to tell the great artists here in this room that I think we finally understand you." But Reagan's praise did not turn Ralph into a Republican—or even a political admirer of the president.

The medal was continuing proof of his vitality at a time when death was closing in on people dear to him. In Oklahoma, his cousin Tom Brown died. Tom's widow followed soon after. Then it was Jim Randolph, who had given Ralph his first real job, at Randolph's Drug Store some sixty years before. In the summer of 1985 he wrote from Plainfield to Camille Randolph Rhone about the continuing vividness of his memory of Oklahoma. "I can visualize the house where you lived on the corner of Third and Phillips," he assured her. Moved by the splendor of the Berkshires, with "the light made golden as it falls through the leaves of the . . . ancient, towering sugar maples outside my study window," he knew that his heart still belonged to Oklahoma. "We have many friends there," he wrote about New York, "but none whom I've known so long and well as those at home. Nor are its streets and buildings so full of personal associations and memories. Therefore the memories and knowledge of people that support my writer's imagination are for the most part back in Oklahoma. I often wonder what life would have been like had I been able to return to Oklahoma after college, but then I have to face the possibility that if I had I wouldn't be the 'me' I am today. So as it is I thank the stars that I had what I now realize was a rich and varied experience, and to that experience and to those who shared it I try to be true."

He tried to stay busy. In April 1986, for a fee of $3,000, he gave a heavily attended reading at the West Side YMCA in Manhattan. Later that month, he joined fifty other writers and hundreds of guests celebrating the sixtieth anniversary of the Book-of-the-Month Club. Still sociable in the right company, Ralph fretted a little about "a rather tame spring season" and was thus particularly happy to attend a dinner party at Louis Auchincloss's home on Park Avenue. "What a fine way," Ralph told his old friend, "to be roused out of the familiar doldrums[s] to which we'd become more or less resigned."

But the deaths of dear comrades continued, and kept him aware of his age. In March 1986, Bernard Malamud died at the age of seventy-two, Ralph's own (alleged) age. And on Easter Sunday, at the age of seventy, John Ciardi passed away at his home in New Jersey. Such losses distressed Ralph, even if he believed he still had much life ahead of him. In May, *Going to the Territory* appeared. Heralded by an excerpt in *Esquire*, his third book drew reassuring early reviews. To *Publishers Weekly*, Ellison's latest book "reaffirms one's respect for so perceptive and balanced a literary artist and critic." *Kirkus* flashed words such as "judicious" and "meticulous" in hailing a "magisterial performance."

This auspicious start pleased him, but success of this kind wasn't a worthy substitute for a second novel after one as mighty as *Invisible Man*. He was adamant about not giving up the struggle. Writing to Bill Ferris of the Center for the Study of Southern Culture in Oxford, Mississippi, he offered himself as one "who has long tried to follow the example" of his hero Faulkner, not least of all in his warring "with my own unruly demon." But time was running out. Early in the summer of 1986, as *Going to the Territory* appeared in bookstores, Ralph vowed to make one last effort to strive, to seek, to find a way to that second triumph in fiction of which he had been dreaming now for almost thirty-five years.

21

Flying Home

1986–1994

Today, alas, the time of such parties has come to an end . . .   RALPH ELLISON (1989)

The summer of 1986 started pleasantly. For the first time in twenty-two years Ralph had a book of his own to discuss with journalists and critics for newspapers and magazines, on radio and television, as well as a trove of reviews to parse. On July 4, America's birthday, a day of splendid sunshine, he and Fanny watched as a flotilla of tall ships from around the world, flags and banners fluttering, passed magnificently up the Hudson to the George Washington Bridge, turned, and sailed downriver into New York Harbor. Delighted by the procession, Ralph "watched and took photographs for hours," he recalled, "and ended the day with a feeling of having relived a graceful moment of a not always graceful past."

Near the end of July, after he had done all that Random House had asked to promote *Going to the Territory,* he and Fanny left for Plainfield. "It's a good place for Ralph to work," Fanny wrote optimistically to Vance Bourjaily, "and he has been working very, very well on his new novel."

The reception of his new book seemed to endorse Ralph's doggedly optimistic view of the nation. In 1964, when *Shadow and Act* appeared, whites wrote almost every review (just as they had done with *Invisible Man* in 1952). In 1986, several blacks had their public say. Moreover, in contrast to the scorn heaped on Ralph by black radicals in the years following *Shadow and Act,* almost all of these reviewers hailed him as one acutely tuned to the realities of African-American life and culture. In the *New York Times Book Review,* even as John Edgar Wideman, who would win a Pulitzer Prize, pointed out that "there is little in this volume that has not been published before," he also praised "the subtle, jazzlike changes Mr. Ellison rings against the steady backbeat of his abiding concerns as artist and critic." In the *Los Angeles Times,* David Bradley (whose novel *The Chaneysville Incident* was widely praised) marveled not only that Ellison's essays "never fail to be elegantly written, beautifully composed and intellectually sophisticated," but also that he was consistently "witty, literate, endearingly modest, delightfully puckish." White reviewers agreed with these assessments. To Louis Menand, *Going to the Territory* continued Ellison's noble, lifelong project, which was "the articulation of an enormously valuable view of American culture." "In only three books," Jonathan Yardley wrote, Ralph had "accomplished more than most writers can hope to do in dozens."

Nevertheless, three factors weakened his influence. First was the widening emotional gap between Ralph and black women writers. Second, most of the younger black writers, male or female, valued black cultural nationalism to an extent that seemed to set them still further apart from him. Finally, Ralph's perceived lack of regard for younger writers seemed heartless. Challenging traditional male cultural authority, the black feminist, or "womanist" (as Alice Walker preferred to call it), movement did not seek permission to act from any man, not even Ralph Ellison. In a variety of forms, Walker, Toni Morrison, Audre Lorde, June Jordan, Sonia Sanchez, Nikki Giovanni, Maya Angelou, Gloria Naylor, Lucille Clifton, and Ntozake Shange, among others, had created a literary country Ralph seemed to have little interest in visiting. To him, feminism was mainly another needless form of social division. For most of the women, some form of assertive feminism had become essential. The depiction of black women in *Invisible Man* did not recommend Ralph to them, nor did the absence of tenderness between men and women in general. In person, Ralph epitomized, at best in a courtly way, the essential indifference to them that they had come to associate with their "brother" writers.

The younger artists, male and female, felt on the whole a therapeutic need to express their outrage at racism, their skepticism about almost all whites, and their love for the black masses. Their modulated black cultural nationalism formed a discipline different from "that very stern discipline" (Ralph's phrase) that he saw as the backbone of "Negro" culture. While he stressed self-control, they felt the need to express rage *and* exuberance. And yet both sides had much in common. Reading essays such as "The World and the Jug" or "Change the Joke and Slip the Yoke" in *Shadow and Act,* the serious younger artists could hardly mount a more subtle yet dynamic defense of black American culture. None of them would publish a book of nonfiction prose even close in brilliance to *Shadow and Act*. Sooner or later, most thoughtful, honest black cultural nationalists found inspiration in Ralph's essays and interviews. "I thought [*Shadow and Act*] not only the best collection of nonfiction prose by a black writer," Ernest Gaines said later, "but the best collection period that I had ever read. I didn't care for *Invisible Man*. I read it once and then couldn't read it again, much as I tried. It's a cold book. It's more a collection of essays than a novel."

Although most black writers were probably as interested as Ralph was in material success, few wished or dared to show what seemed to be his excessive comfort with privilege. His appearance of supreme self-satisfaction in a white-dominated world grated on some blacks. Five years after Ralph's death, Houston A. Baker, Jr., the author of several frequently cited books of literary and cultural criticism, and also the first black president of the Modern Language Association, would assail what he took to be his self-appointed role in that milieu. "When Civil Rights and Black Power became American—indeed global—realities," Baker wrote, "Ellison reclined in butter-soft seats at exclusive Manhattan clubs, explaining to whites why he could not take any active part in the Liberation Politics of black Americans. America's industrial, democratic, lobotomizing machine—like the sleep of reason—had produced a clubbable monster in Ellison."

But in the late 1980s and early 1990s, Ralph could argue that many, if not most, of the best younger writers were in a sense his artistic progeny. In some ways, he was perhaps the cold, fearsome father, or the absent but haunting father, that some of them knew only too well. Many were Ralph's offspring all the same in their common belief in the importance of literary craft and in their experiments with form—whether in the retrospective epistolary style of Walker's *The Color Purple* or in the stylishly jazzy, parodic rhythms of Ishmael Reed's *Mumbo Jumbo* or Charles Johnson's *Oxherding Tale*. They were his progeny, or his younger relatives, when they explored the surreal, or revealed, despite their frequent scowling, almost as much faith in cosmopolitanism as he did. When Charles Johnson, with a longtime interest in subjects such as phenomenology and Zen Buddhism, accepted the 1990 National Book Award for his novel *Middle Passage,* his acceptance speech seemed to be one long tribute to Ralph. Johnson's gesture moved Ralph almost to tears. "Ralph said, 'I didn't know that people remembered what I had done,'" John Callahan recalled. "He was surprised that no one was knifing him when, in fact, everyone was praising him."

To the cultural and political critic Shelby Steele, who praised *Shadow and Act* as comprising "the most penetrating essays ever written on the relationship between black American culture and the broader American identity," Ellison was a hero and a prophet who would be vindicated. "Even today, there are prison cells around the world occupied by writers who have somehow threatened a politics or religion that their people or their leaders feel served by. And very often it is the spurned writer who wins the debate in the long run. So the hostility of many blacks toward Ellison is unexceptional in itself; and if history is any indication, the future will likely belong more to Ellison than to his accusers." Cornel West could see both sides of the man. Deploring the fact that "Ellison became such an American nationalist," he also praised the extent to which Ralph remained committed to the life of the mind even as his contradictions exacted a toll on him. To West, the toll was obvious. "He reminded me of what T. S. Eliot said once about Matthew Arnold: 'He had no real serenity, only an impeccable demeanour.' But for all of his problems Ralph was a formidable intellectual and a challenge and inspiration to all of us."

Toni Morrison went further. Ralph's career had produced a "spectacular novel; elegant essays; international respect," she said a decade after his death.

> And yet one is tempted to say also that it is tinged with tragedy, because expectations of much more fictional work were never realized. But tragedy is not the right word; it requires grandeur. The better word is melancholy. One contrasts the largeness of *Invisible Man* with its broad canvas and its wide range of effects, of insight, with the narrowness of his public encounters with blacks. The contemporary world of late twentieth-century African Americans was largely inaccessible, or simply uninteresting to him as a creator of fiction. For him, in essence, the eye, the gaze of the beholder remained white. But if the ideal white reader made sense for *Invisible Man* in 1952, he or she made less sense for the black writer by the seventies and eighties. And I don't think Ellison ever saw the need to revisit or redress anything he had done or not done, or to challenge his obvious level of success with more demanding ones. He saw himself as a black literary patrician, but at some level this was a delusion. It was simply his solution to that persistent problem black writers are confronted with: art and, or ver-

sus, identity. I don't see tragedy in his predicament. I see a
kind of sadness instead.

But Horace Porter, the former Amherst and Yale student who was now
a professor of English, and who kept in touch through cards, letters, and
occasional visits, knew a warmer Ellison. When he and his wife, Carla,
had a son born on Ralph's birthday, they named him Zachary Ellison
Porter. After Porter wrote a novel, he sent the manuscript to Ralph,
expecting a brief response. Instead, after reading it twice, Ralph sent him
a twenty-six-page document. "The length and form of his commentary, let
alone its characteristic profundity," Porter wrote, "was stunning." He marveled at the fact that "a phenomenal and talented novelist of seventy-one
had been sufficiently caring to take his precious time and write so sensi-
tively and at such length about an unpublished first novel of uncertain
direction and dubious value."

As in Porter's case, those people who stayed close to Ralph had to work
at it. He could be accommodating, but he also remained doggedly unsentimental. Stanley Crouch, a man of formidable energy, often telephoned
Ralph at home to engage him in long, rich conversations that he evidently
enjoyed. Nevertheless, Ralph criticized Crouch when he believed his
admirer deserved it, even if such criticism could deprive Crouch of invaluable support. In January 1987, writing in support of Stanley's application for a fellowship to write a book about Charlie Parker, he referred
without hesitation to the danger of "an unintended pretentiousness; a
temptation to place too much of a load of cultural, sociological, and historical analysis upon the slender reed of Parker's saxophone as upon the
brief and narrow social range of his turbulent life."

The resilient Crouch remained a friend. In 1990, Ralph wrote a blurb
for his iconoclastic book of essays *Notes of a Hanging Judge,* in which
Crouch tried to string up Toni Morrison as an artist and dismissed her
masterpiece, *Beloved,* as so much melodramatic propaganda. Crouch
sometimes took Wynton Marsalis, the jazz and classical trumpet virtuoso,
to Ralph's apartment. There, according to the scholar David Yaffe,
Marsalis, "with his trademark southern charm, would attempt to disabuse
Ellison of his notion that Thelonious Monk did not have technique." As
another writer judged, Ellison ended up being more influential on Marsalis,
who "worked tirelessly . . . to build a bully pulpit" from which to speak "as
advocate, spokesman, teacher and musical implementor" of Ralph (and
Albert Murray's "aesthetic notions of continuity and inclusiveness").

Thus armed, Marsalis and Crouch undertook the deliberate upgrading in prestige of jazz in New York City. Aided by Alina Bloomgarden of Lincoln Center, they convinced powerful civic and cultural leaders that jazz should have an equal status, nominally at least, with the Philharmonic, the Metropolitan Opera, and the New York City Ballet. Jazz at Lincoln Center was born. First it rented space at Lincoln Center, but then it secured its own home, at a cost of over $130 million, in the glistening new Time Warner Center nearby at Columbus Circle.

Crouch was himself a cool observer of Ellison's failure to get *his* biggest job done. "Bellow told me once," he said, "that Ralph's problem was that he had this ethnic desire, on behalf of black or Negro people, to have a black writer create literature at the level of Faulkner, Hemingway, or even Melville." Unfortunately, Crouch added, Ralph had decided to give *himself* the assignment. The result was, to some extent, tragic. "The tragedy lies in the weight Ralph put on himself. He created this grand tower in his mind, with a priceless penthouse at the top, which was virtually impossible to climb. There were stairs, but he hadn't built them well. Ralph wasn't wary enough of the dangers that come with the magnification of things by one's own imagination. Well, the greater the ambition, the greater the failure. The longer the book remained unfinished, the more excruciating the pain. And for a long time, sadly, he lived with a constant, debilitating sense of having failed."

Ralph continued to manage his prestige, if not his publications, well. With his lecture fee set at $4,000, fewer colleges and universities called him than in the past—but many still did. He picked and chose carefully. Once in the spotlight, he usually shone, as at Seton Hall University in New Jersey in December 1988, when he spoke at a two-day celebration in honor of Kenneth Burke. Ralph was pleased to pay tribute, in Burke's home state, to arguably the single most efficacious American influence on *Invisible Man.* Looking far ahead, he settled one important matter. When Dr. Howard Dodson, the head of the main Harlem branch of the New York Public Library on 135th Street, tried to acquire Ralph's papers, Ralph deflected the approach. "The Library of Congress, in Washington, D.C., is the nation's library," he told John Callahan. "I want my papers there."

Tired of travel, he was ready now to give up certain old connections. In 1988 he decided against going to Tuskegee to receive a medal as its most distinguished living alumnus. Instead, the medal came in the mail. (At this point, Ralph withdrew his ancient grievances against the school. Through "the mysterious processes of time," as he wrote to the Tuskegee president, he now saw that his years there had exposed him to the "transcendent vision" of Booker T. Washington.) Asked to lecture at Harvard on the occasion of the 150th anniversary of Emerson's revolutionary, ultranationalist Phi Beta Kappa address of August 31, 1837, "The American Scholar," Ralph at first saw the invitation as a chance to tie up a crucial loose end in his life. "I can't forget Emerson's powerful force in the life of my father," he asserted privately, "or the spiritual and intellectual support he provided several of my teachers and community leaders. . . . Emerson's voice rang loud in Negro communities and influenced my own elders' decision to seek a broader freedom out in the Territory." Never before had Ralph heaped so much praise on Emerson as an influence on blacks. But in the end, he found the task too arduous. Alfred Kazin delivered the address. In 1989, Ralph drove to Camden, New Jersey, to make peace with another giant of the American literary and moral tradition, Walt Whitman, whose "Calamus" poems, often seen as advocating gay life, he had mocked in *Invisible Man*. Lured in part by a fee of $4,000, Ralph appeared at the Whitman Center there and praised the author of *Leaves of Grass*.

Despite his reluctance to travel, he was still drawn to Oklahoma City. In November 1986 he starred at a black-tie dinner in honor of his boyhood friend Jimmie Stewart. Governor David Boren, a future U.S. senator and president of the University of Oklahoma, declared November 16 Ralph Ellison Day throughout the state. Ralph and Fanny loved this visit. "We're still reliving our exciting experiences in Oklahoma," he wrote to Walter Grey, a white friend who owned the local Grapevine Gallery, where Ralph bought many of the rugs, prints, and Indian dolls that imparted to his home something of the rustic atmosphere of old Oklahoma. Such visits had a painful side, of course. *"Tempus fugit,"* he wrote to Grey, "and in the process so many people whom we hold dear turn up missing." For the first time in his life, Ralph faced the "disquieting fact" that not a single member of his extended family, the Randolph and the Slaughter clans, had been there to greet him. All of them who had mattered to him were dead or had left the city. So-called urban renewal exacted a price as well—he felt "dismay over finding so much of the city in which I grew up destroyed."

Slowing down, Ralph and Fanny still enjoyed the fancy dinner party with fine china, sterling silver, crystal stemware, and cultured accents that reassured them that they were still welcome on the slopes of Mount Parnassus. For Ralph, the Century remained a joy even after, to his regret, women elbowed open its doors as members. About the American Academy and National Institute he was less sanguine. Cherishing the faded leather seat that was his own in the room reserved for conclaves of the super-fine fifty who constituted the academy, he defended its rules, regulations, and sense of decorum. Certain raffish new members were lowering its tone. To the composer David Diamond, he mourned the fact that "Time is cutting such a swath that the place is beginning to show signs of a discontinuity that it can ill afford." One by one the giants were falling. Malcolm Cowley was growing feeble, and charming Glenway Wescott had just died. With other deaths and signs of dotage, the patina of gold was fading away. Ralph shook his head to think how "so many who gave tone to [the] organization are being replaced by those who have little respect for its traditions."

His relationship to Toni Morrison was telling. Morrison would eclipse him in fame, fortune, and honors among black writers just as he had eclipsed Richard Wright, but in 1987, several months before the arrival that year of *Beloved,* she had not yet done so when she telephoned to invite him to visit the State University of New York at Albany, where she was now an Albert Schweitzer Professor in the Humanities. His initial reluctance did not surprise her. Perhaps only once, and then in passing, had he alluded to her in print. About her novels *The Bluest Eye, Sula, Tar Baby,* and *Song of Solomon* he was silent. "He seemed almost annoyed," she said about his response to her call. "He told me that he was busy, very busy. He was writing. Albany was so far away. He had no fresh material." Morrison was ready for him. "First I said that he truly would honor us simply by reading from his work-in-progress. Then I mentioned the fee— $5,000. Last of all, I spoke the magic words: 'We will send a car for you. We will pick you up at your front door and drive you to Albany. Then, after your reading, the car will take you from Albany back to your front door.' He agreed to come."

Ralph's visit with Fanny on April 21, 1987, was a bright success. Delighted by their reception, he was charming to one and all. "This was the closest I had ever come to them," Morrison said, "and I liked their company. He was witty; she was very easy to be around. His reading drew a crowd, well beyond what we'd expected—with whites and blacks alike. On stage he was modest, generous, gracious, amusing. The audience was mesmerized and laughed a great deal with him—and he seemed to enjoy himself immensely." But Morrison's courtesy seemed to mean little to him the following year. When she came up for membership at the Century, he was not one of her sponsors. Ralph also didn't help in her election to the American Academy and National Institute of Arts and Letters.

"When I was inducted," she noted, "I was never sure if Ralph voted for me, but I do know that he made no attempt to make me feel welcome. At the first meeting I attended, he . . . never said hello." Over the years "he never mentioned any of my books to me, or complimented me as a writer, as I did him. My assumption was that he thought very little of them."

In January 1988, following the publication of *Beloved,* he would not support the action of forty-eight black writers who published a letter in the *New York Times* after the National Book Award selectors passed over Morrison's novel in favor of Larry Heinemann's Vietnam novel, *Paco's Story.* On March 31, when Morrison won the Pulitzer Prize, he revealed to a *New York Times* reporter his annoyance "with some of the stuff that's been boiling about her not getting recognition." Now, challenged by the reporter, he was generous. "Toni doesn't need that kind of support," he said. "She can compete with the best writers anywhere." Luck often played a role in deciding these prizes, he said. "I never won a Pulitzer. I think that an artist like Toni who has talent leaves it to the book or product." His lack of solidarity with rival black writers was evident again after James Baldwin died of cancer in November 1987. Although Ralph praised Baldwin when a *New York Times* reporter called with the news, he shed few tears for a man whose life was the opposite of his own in many areas, including aesthetics, politics, and sexuality. At the academy, where its *Proceedings* included a short tribute to each recently deceased member written by another member, he declined to eulogize Baldwin, even after Margaret Mills, the executive director, declared that "it would be disgraceful" if Baldwin's death went unnoticed. After her election, Morrison wrote the tribute.

Ralph's last years were marked in no way by the kind of descent into reactionary views about American youth and culture that had overtaken, for example, Saul Bellow. In fact, Ralph's old faith in liberalism flowered anew. In October 1988, a few days before the U.S. presidential election, and at the behest of Arthur Schlesinger, Jr., he co-signed a statement of protest (his first against a sitting president) condemning Ronald Reagan's artful besmirching of American political liberalism. "He made sport of 'the dreaded L-word,' " the statement read, in a parody of the Declaration of Independence, "and continues to make 'liberal' and 'liberalism' terms of opprobrium." Ultimately successful, Reagan's aim was to associate the word "liberal" in the minds of American voters with the kind of fear and loathing that once stuck like tar to the word "Communist."

At home, he also showed more kindness than ever before. Ralph and Fanny now knew how much they needed and loved each other, and also loved what Ralph called "this crowded old nest where we've lived for over thirty years" amid "the bitter-sweet attractions of the city." To the end he kept close to the old nest. "Fanny would have traveled more," said John Callahan, "but even preparing to leave for Plainfield was sometimes too much of a burden for Ralph." New York City was the best of all worlds, and the only truly rewarding travel for Ralph was into the past. Not only Oklahoma but also his father's South Carolina meant more to him now than visiting exotic places. In 1987, when he accepted an invitation from Louis D. Rubin, Jr., of the University of North Carolina to join the Fellowship of Southern Writers, a new literary academy, he saw his induction as part of the completing of a circle that brought him back to the land of his most important ancestors.

At home he enjoyed old pleasures—reading, music, cigars, liquor, and television. He liked PBS, which he had helped to launch. An instructional series, *The Story of English,* captivated him, but so, too, did *Masterpiece Theatre,* although the "masterpieces" were often high-toned soap operas and never American. He watched sports, in which the growing presence of blacks confirmed his faith in the nation. He was enthralled by *The Cosby Show,* which starred the gentle, humane black comedian Bill Cosby as an affluent obstetrician and delved humorously into the domestic problems of his upper-middle-class family, members of an extremely thin slice of black America never before seen on television. He loved *Barney Miller* but was unimpressed by many other sitcoms because they lacked a tragic element. "If you forget the tragic underlayer of comedy," he told *TV Guide* in 1988, "then the comedy becomes trivialized." (The article about him, written by a former student at the University of Chicago, at last made him a celebrity to many of his neighbors: "Now they smile, make comments on such matters as the weather, the condition of the neighborhood, [Mayor Ed] Koch's arrogance and Reagan's bull," he wryly informed the writer. "Thanks to you I now have status!")

Fanny assured friends that Ralph was still working well, but if he was indeed writing, he wasn't sharing many of the results with the world. In the eight years after *Going to the Territory* he published only two short pieces. He wrote an introduction for a reprint of his friend John Kouwenhoven's 1961 collection, *The Beer Can by the Highway.* Then, in April 1989 in the *New York Times,* he published the last piece of "new" writing to appear in his lifetime. Predictably, it returned him to his boyhood. Composed in the second person, "On Being the Target of Discrimination" is perhaps Ralph's only extended public reference to wounds inflicted on him by racism in Oklahoma City. The piece links three unhappy moments in his childhood. First he discovers that he can't attend the school nearest his home because it is for whites only. Then, at the city zoo, he, his brother, and their mother are kicked out by a white man because of Jim Crow. Last of all, he watches and listens in excitement as a white marching band passes below his upstairs window. Playing his cornet, he joins the music. When he misses a cue, the baying of his horn shatters the silence. The band stops. A man points up at him and says, "I'll be damn, it's a little nigger!" The words devastate him: *Next thing you knew, you were up the stairs and on your bed, crying away in the dark your guilt and embarrassment. You cried and cried, asking yourself how could you have been so lacking in pride as to shame yourself and your entire race by butting in where you weren't wanted."*

Linking the moments is the joke born at the zoo with the white man's nastiest words to Ida (as told here): "When that car comes you be sure you get on it, you hear? You and your chillun too!" Hurt and humiliated, the three leave but soon turn the words into a comic cue, a salve to apply to wounds inflicted by Jim Crow. As he cries in bed, the boy remembers the words "You and your chillun too!" He starts to laugh, and his laughter leeches the poison of Jim Crow. So, too, had "Negro" laughter, like "Negro" music, triumphed as a feature of "that very stern discipline" out of which blacks had made their unique, marvelous culture.

Ralph lets the end of the piece collapse into farce. Perhaps it is therefore both a touching memento and a mocking suggestion of what might have been if Ralph had managed his career differently. One or two books of autobiography, two or three collections of short stories, his two published books of essays, and his masterpiece *Invisible Man,* even without a second novel, might have given his career a sense of wholeness and removed his burden of failed expectations. "The man is far too composed, too regal, to betray the weight of it," one interviewer noted about the burden, "but the soul must weary of its persistence." In 1986, on the *Today* show, when Bryant Gumbel suddenly jabbed him in the side with a question about the novel-in-progress, Ralph seemed to wince. Stammering, he once again stoked the 1967 fire in Plainfield.

Even so, articles and books about his body of work continued to grow in number. One day in 1986, a new volume of essays on his work arrived, without notice, edited by the renowned Yale scholar and critic Harold

Bloom (as part of Bloom's mammoth series of editions for Chelsea Press). Ralph was ecstatic. "I couldn't have anticipated such a development during even the wildest whirls of my imagination," he wrote giddily to Bloom, whom he knew from Yale. "Truly, Harold, . . . I am still spinning like a top." He also welcomed Kimberly Benston's substantial edition of essays and related material about him, *Speaking for You* (the title adapted from the last words of *Invisible Man*), and Alan Nadel's *Invisible Criticism: Ralph Ellison and the American Canon,* a sophisticated scholarly study in which astute references link his work to a range of writers from Mark Twain to Mikhail Bakhtin. "I think that you've produced an excellent, thought-provoking work of criticism," Ralph wrote in a long letter to Nadel, "and I'm proud that you picked my small body of writing as your subject."

Bloom, Benston, and Nadel were white. When he praised Robert G. O'Meally (despite his earlier hostility to *The Craft of Ralph Ellison*) for his introduction to his edited volume *New Essays on Invisible Man,* Ralph couldn't resist slapping at black "pseudo-intellectuals." "Perhaps after reading your introduction," he suggested, "some of our lazy would-be critics will realize that we don't inherit our ancestral lore through skin and genes but must pay it the respect of research and study." O'Meally appreciated the compliment but not the attack on black scholars—or, earlier, on himself. His last meeting with Ralph went badly. When he tried to introduce Henry Louis Gates, Jr., Ralph and Fanny seemed affronted. "I was very glad to get away from BOTH of the Ellisons, out of their clutches," he recalled about this meeting, which followed a memorial service at which Ralph had spoken. When O'Meally brought up the subject of his earlier troubles with them, they were utterly icy, he said. "Looking back, they remind me of the damned Bellegarde family in James's novel *The American:* suspicious, corrupt, decadent, and evil. Perhaps in that sense, too, Melvillean—miserable and perhaps mad." Their disapproval of him, and their lack of what O'Meally regarded as elementary racial sympathy, turned him against them—but not against what he saw as Ralph's wonderful books.

On March 1, 1989, Ralph quietly observed what he called his seventy-fifth birthday. He genuinely appreciated the calls, cards, and letters that arrived. He loved the fact that Michael Harper had asked each member of his creative writing class at Brown to send Ralph individual greetings. With unusual zest, he spent most of the morning working on his novel.

Reading some of his lines aloud and then listening with vast amusement to a tape recording of this reading (a habit he often indulged), he pushed on with the mighty task that had now consumed almost half of his life. "The story keeps writing itself," he assured his publicist, "and I'm racing along trying to keep up with it." He was glad to know he was still robust. In 1994, a journalist would estimate that he seemed "fifteen years younger than he is." Fanny, too, was trim, and few people could guess her real age.

Friends kept falling. On April 6, 1988, at Romare Bearden's memorial service in the Cathedral of St. John the Divine near Columbia University, Ralph spoke wistfully of his early days in New York and his first encounter with the ever generous Bearden. In their love of tradition and modernist originality, the men were to some extent intellectual brothers. An avid reader, Bearden knew many of the works admired by Ralph. He was perhaps the only African-American artist of whom Ralph spoke with unconditional respect. On this occasion he praised Bearden for teaching him much about how "color became space, space became perspective, and color became form." Bearden's work comforted and inspired Ralph. By 1988 the Ellisons had hanging on their walls at home at least a half dozen of his pieces.

In September 1989, Robert Penn Warren died after a struggle with cancer. "Just about the last thing Father said before he died," his daughter, the poet Rosanna Warren, recalled, "was something about having to go with Ralph to buy a car. He was delirious, but Ralph was on his mind." Quietly, graciously, starting in 1953, Warren had led Ralph to one honor and opportunity after another, as well as to a variety of important relationships with other leading whites in Rome and at the Century, the American Academy of Arts and Letters, Yale, and elsewhere. "Father never gave a sign that he thought that he was helping Ralph unduly," Rosanna Warren added. "He was a gentleman, and he saw Ralph as an equal who deserved every honor." Ralph knew his indebtedness here. Quoting Nathan Scott, he summed up what he saw as Warren's essence. "Red is indeed a man of 'grateful reverence,' both in his person and in his poetry," he declared in a tribute in the present tense although Warren was dead. "He celebrates the complexity of humanity in word and in deed, and for that I am most thankful."

At winter's end, in 1990, Ralph's first wife, Rose Poindexter, who also lived at the Beaumont and was on good terms with the Ellisons, died. May saw the death of William Dawson, the composer who had lured Ralph to Tuskegee in 1933. In June, Vivian Steveson, Ralph's first true sweetheart, died in Oklahoma City. In 1991, Paul Engle, the founder of the University of Iowa Writers' Workshop and perhaps the first nationally known literary figure to assert Ralph's excellence as a fiction writer, also passed away. September of that year saw the death of Russell Lynes, a good friend of many years both as a leader at the Century and, in the summer, as a fellow seasonal resident of the Berkshires. In February 1993, Albert Erskine, Ralph's editor of almost fifty years, with whom he had enjoyed an excellent relationship, died. To Ralph's chagrin and embarrassment, he missed the funeral. "There was a mix-up," John Callahan said, "and Ralph and Fanny sat in their apartment, all dressed up, waiting for the doorbell to ring and their chauffeur [hired by Random House] to call them downstairs. But the driver thought the job had been canceled and never showed up. In their younger days Ralph and Fanny would have swung into action and got there somehow. But now they were old. Much of their resilience was gone." In March, John Hersey of Yale and Key West, a prolific and respected writer, who had twice published key interviews with Ralph, died. In May, Irving Howe, Ralph's most vital literary antagonist, as attested by arguably the most important essay in *Shadow and Act,* also died. Howe had also been one of the four judges who had changed the course of Ralph's life in 1953 by passing over Hemingway and voting the National Book Award to a young black writer and his first novel.

The piling up of losses took its toll on Ralph's morale. To some friends he and Fanny seemed to be withdrawing. One of his dearest friendships foundered in 1987. In Key West, the Ellisons had let their condominium to Frank Taylor, the man who had signed Ralph as a novelist for Reynal & Hitchcock in 1943. Married for many years but now openly gay, Taylor had moved in with his partner. A dispute with the Ellisons about the state of the condominium soon followed. When Ralph heard that Richard and Charlee Wilbur had spoken of him and Fanny as disliking gays (Fanny had written to Charlee that her condo had been "dirtied by Frank Taylor and his lover"), he sent a six-page letter to the Wilburs that explained his position, and his definition of friendship, in a formal style that implicitly reprimanded the Wilburs. "Neither Fanny nor I are prejudiced against homosexuals," he insisted. Although he had been "hounded out of college" by a "homosexual dean of men," he was certain that "the experience did nothing to prevent my associating with or being a friend of homosexuals who did not, as you say, force one to be aware of their sexuality."

This letter came after a silence on the part of the Ellisons that the

Wilburs couldn't help but notice. It also followed a touching letter from Charlee Wilbur to the Ellisons reminding them of "the fun we had together, the closeness, many shared experiences, both happy and painful (especially the time of the fire)." The Ellisons were polite but did not respond in kind. They continued to rent out the Windsor Grove condo, then sold it in 1993 for a nice profit. To Charlee Wilbur, they were almost "pathologically isolated." Troubled, Richard again wrote soothingly to Ralph, who was only slightly warmer. "He didn't say," Wilbur said, " 'I'm retreating in order to finish my novel,' but we have always supposed that was the reason." The couples continued to exchange notes and cards, but now met infrequently. The same was true of Ralph's links to other veteran friends. Nathan Scott believed that Ralph's pride, as much as anything else, accounted for "his disinclination in the last years to maintain involvements with old friends who were still productive." And indeed Horace Porter recalled that one otherwise happy visit in 1991 was dampened for a while by an ill-advised question about the second novel. When Porter told Ralph that he was thinking of writing another novel, but confessed that he wasn't sure he could write a good one, Ralph smiled and said, " 'I'm not sure I can write one either.' We both laughed."

To the end, Ralph never lost his passion for books and reading. In 1992, a reporter from Chicago observed that "thousands of books are crammed into floor-to-ceiling bookcases, stacked on floors, in chairs, on desks." He defended this excess. "I don't know what they are going to stir," he confessed to the reporter, "but they give you a sense of a thickness of the life in which you are involved and remind you, even unconsciously, of the many dimensions of literature. They are all pertinent whether you write or not." Proud to be associated with his nation's literary heritage, in 1991 he accepted an invitation to join the electors of the new Poets' Corner at the Cathedral of St. John the Divine. Every year, electors would choose two American writers (not only poets) for induction, with a simple stone tablet marking this honor. In this way the vast, unfinished Episcopalian cathedral on Amsterdam Avenue would serve one of the splendid functions of Westminster Abbey in Great Britain. As Ralph started a four-year term, his first votes, written in a hand now somewhat shaky, were for Warren and Hemingway.

If his hand wavered easily, his mind did not. In April 1992, along with Saul Bellow, Joseph Brodsky, and Czeslaw Milosz, each a Nobel Prize–winner, he did well at a three-day *Partisan Review* conference organized at

Rutgers University. Several hundred listeners heard speakers discuss the fate of former Communist writers and also the likely impact of the collapse of the Soviet Union on American culture. Gloomy about America, Bellow inveighed against the rising influence in colleges and universities of Marxist theory, often expressed in jargon. He foresaw "a dark age coming over America" and a "new barbarism" in the corrupting influence of commercial television and the other media. Ralph was more optimistic. American culture was intrinsically conflicted, but this conflict had not stunted its growth. Offering himself as an "inside-outsider," he suggested that the former Soviet writers, now disoriented by their sudden freedom, could learn some key lessons from America. Here, glorious ideals had been constantly violated, but "it was the tenacity of our belief in those ideals that allowed the individual citizen to make choices and give creative thrust to his energies." Pain was inevitable. The duty of the writer is to speak truth to power but also to accept "the punishment that goes with telling the truth." Thus Ralph gave glimpses of the degree to which his mind had opened, or reopened, to more radical and even militant views, relatively speaking, of American history. At one point he even praised W. E. B. Du Bois and African-American studies. Citing a reissue of Du Bois's sometimes awkward but landmark Marxist study *Black Reconstruction in America,* which in 1934 had assailed racist views of Reconstruction, he defended such revisionist history. It "has allowed us to face some of the complexities of the past, especially things that occurred during slavery," he said.

Two months later, he was impressive again when he accepted the 1992 Chicago Public Library Harold Washington Literary Award. On April 19, facing some two hundred persons at the new Harold Washington Library Center on South State Street, he seemed to a *Chicago Tribune* reporter old yet sprightly. "Cashew-brown, with long limbs and an infectious grin," Ralph strolled easily to the podium, although "his steps have slowed" and his physique was now "sunken somewhat." To the many blacks watching him Ralph was a rare gift, a writer of genuine prestige being honored in the name of the first black mayor of their sadly Balkanized city. (A savvy leader, Washington had died of a heart attack while in office.) Instinctively Ralph stressed the positive and unifying aspects of Washington's legacy. "We have a tremendous way to go," he conceded, "but we have come a long way, too." Although in the 1930s Chicago segregated its libraries, "now you have this magnificent building in honor of a black mayor." He wanted nothing to do with Balkanization. Racial integration was "inevitable. We have to . . . stop fighting the inevitable." By meeting and talking about your common problems, "you gain understanding." His listeners applauded wildly. Fielding questions, he was witty. "Do you think black people are still invisible?" the last questioner asked. With a sly grin Ralph replied: "Some is and some ain't." Then, to thunderous applause, he strolled insouciantly off the stage.

In 1993, he enjoyed a few other flashes of the old glamour. Raising his glass at a formal dinner in April, he toasted the future of the fully merged (after many years of debate) American Academy of Arts and Letters, with the National Institute now dissolved into it. In his little speech he was by turns droll and solemn, colloquial and formal, democratic and elitist. Whatever the organization now called itself, names by themselves "don't mean a thing" if they "ain't got that swing." The glorious national "swing" came from the fact that in America "the pursuit of artistic excellence involves making art out of the complexities imposed by the diversity of our cultural heritage, our race, religions, and regions." He believed in excellence, not in mediocrity heated up by invectives about social injustice. The key challenge facing the American artist was still "to create something absolutely new out of the arts to which we're dedicated." The following month, Ralph's identification with the idea of excellence was confirmed again when the Graduate Center of the City University of New York, located in mid-Manhattan across the street from the New York Public Library, awarded him an honorary doctorate.

Anticipating Ralph's eightieth birthday on March 1, 1994, *The New Yorker* asked David Remnick to prepare a story about him. In February, Remnick visited Ellison at home for a long interview. Seated comfortably in what Remnick described appropriately as "a modest apartment overlooking the Hudson," Ralph lit a big cigar, savored the curling, pungent smoke, and talked quietly at first about his daily routine. He rose early and, after a brief uphill stroll along 150th Street to Broadway to buy a copy of the *New York Times,* he usually ate a simple breakfast of coffee and toast as he leafed through the newspaper. Near seven o'clock he turned on the *Today* show on NBC. Later, with a flick of the power switch on his IBM desktop computer, he returned most mornings to his Sisyphean task. "The hardest part of the morning is the first hour, just getting the rhythm," he admitted. First he read what he had written the previous day. Sometimes he liked what he read. Sometimes he saw that "it ain't worth a damn."

Listening carefully, intently watching Ralph's lined face, Remnick sought to catch the subtler meanings latent in his speech. Ellison, he decided, was "polite in the high style, careful in conversation almost to the point of deliberate, if ironic, dullness." Gently the journalist probed Ralph's "peculiarly modern burden, the burden of a second act" to follow the mighty *Invisible Man*. But Remnick did so only after waiting patiently while "Ellison skated amiably, and elliptically, around various questions of the day." Hearing the question, Ralph seems "a little startled." Then, haltingly, he offered his perennial excuse. "There was, of course," he drawls, "a traumatic event involved with the book." Exactly how much time had Ralph lost? Ellison is "quiet for a while, and then he said, in a tone that suggested we were talking about someone else and the question was merely *interesting,* 'You know, I'm not sure. It's kind of blurred for me. But the novel has got my attention now. I work every day, so there will be something very soon.' " Although Ralph's readers "can be greedy and ask for more," Remnick writes summarily, "what's done is done and, in a sense, is more than enough." Moreover, "it becomes clearer than ever" that *Invisible Man, Shadow and Act,* and *Going to the Territory* "are the urtexts for a loose coalition of black American intellectuals who represent an integrationist vision of the country's history and culture." Remnick names Charles Johnson, John Edgar Wideman, Leon Forrest, James Alan McPherson, Shelby Steele, Henry Louis Gates, Jr., Stanley Crouch, and Michael S. Harper as sharing that vision. In fact, Remnick might also have named almost every black American artist, male or female, of any consequence and complexity, including many who, viscerally offended or simply turned off by what they saw as Ralph's elitism, did not wish to be identified with him.

On March 1, Remnick was present when Random House hosted a birthday dinner for Ralph at the distinguished restaurant Le Périgord, on 52nd Street at Sutton Place. Also there were Al and Mozelle Murray and their daughter, Michele, then with the Alvin Ailey dance company; John Callahan, cherished as an intimate friend by the Ellisons; Albert Erskine's widow, Marisa, and their daughter, Silvia Erskine; Joseph Mitchell of *The New Yorker;* Harry Evans of Random House; Joe Fox, Ralph's editor at Random House since Erskine's death; and Owen Laster of the William Morris Agency, Ralph's longtime agent. During the meal, Ralph genially commanded the table as he told amusing tales about the road he had traveled to this elegiac moment. With affection he spoke about Oklahoma City and Tuskegee and New York City in 1936, when he arrived as a virtually penniless young man without a clue that he would settle there for the rest of his life and also become one of its most celebrated writers. He talked about the blues and jazz and poked fun at himself for brazenly trying to play the trumpet recently in the presence of Wynton Marsalis. He talked about the poetry of Robinson Jeffers. He laughed at the comic wonder of the black church.

After the fine food and "not a little wine," as *The New Yorker* reported two weeks later, Albert Murray rose to offer a toast. (With prodding from friends, Ralph had reconciled with Albert while Murray was in the hospital with a serious illness.) Taking his listeners back to Tuskegee and his first meeting with the intensely ambitious, serious youth at the front desk in the school library, he recalled (in Remnick's words) "the nascent elegance of Ellison, a slender concertmaster in his two-tone shoes, bow tie, contrasting slacks, and whatever else the best haberdasher in Oklahoma had to offer." Perhaps unaware of it, Murray glossed over Ralph's urgent sense of desperation in those Tuskegee years. He only hinted at Ralph's youthful rage to succeed, the fury of his deliberate refashioning of himself, the ruthlessness made obligatory by his devotion to art. Playfully, Murray also recalled the wisp of a poem written by Ralph at Tuskegee, with a copy left behind by him in the pages of one of the several books that Ralph had read just before Murray himself borrowed them: "Death is nothing. / Life is nothing. / How beautiful these two nothings!"

When Murray was done, Ralph rose to thank him and all who had come to celebrate his birthday. Looking around the ornate room he took in the American wonder of it all. Here were blacks and whites, Jews and Gentiles, Northerners and Southerners, the high-born and the grandchildren of slaves, all linked by a love of art and literature and an uncommon appreciation of the joyful but sometimes also painful complexities of American life. Ralph said that he thought not infrequently about the humble circumstances of his birth in Oklahoma City; about the trials his mother and father had faced; about the untimely death of his father and the ensuing years of poverty for his mother and her sons; and about his eventual, astonishing triumph over poverty and shame. Once again he stressed the complex wonder that is America. "There are a lot of subtleties based on race that we *will* ourselves not to perceive," he noted, "but at our peril. The truth is that the quality of Americanness, that thing the kids invariably give voice to, will always come out."

Two weeks later, John Callahan "kept calling, calling from Oregon to talk about the article" in *The New Yorker*, "but no one answered the telephone in the apartment. It rang and rang." Suddenly Ralph had begun to feel poorly. Several times at night he stumbled to the bathroom. Then he became too weak to go out for the morning paper. Fanny began to worry about him. One night he fell in the bathroom. Rushing to his side, she found that he couldn't get up. Unable to lift him, she dialed 911 and waited for help.

He was admitted to the New York Hospital–Cornell Medical Center, one of the premier hospitals in the city. Laboratory tests confirmed the presence of pancreatic cancer, an aggressive, deadly scourge. An operation was pointless. Determined not to die in the hospital, Ralph came home. By this time Callahan had arrived from Portland, ready to help in every way he could. They needed him. Pushing and pulling, he and Fanny managed to set up a hospital bed in the living room. From there, propped up on cool pillows, Ralph could see his beloved shelves of books, his and Fanny's paintings, photographs, sculptures, and other memorabilia. Through the windows, he saw the green boughs of trees in early springtime bloom along the Hudson.

As Fanny plunged into the depths of a sorrow and despair from which she would never fully recover, Ralph mainly remained in bed, speaking more and more softly until he couldn't speak at all. Instructed by Fanny, Callahan barred almost all visitors. When neither he nor Fanny could solve the mysteries of Ralph's complicated stereo system, with its tangled wires, tricky connections, and studio-quality reel-to-reel tape recorder, Callahan strode up the hill to raucous Broadway and bought a boom box and some audiocassettes. Following Fanny's preference, he found one with music by Prokofiev and another that featured Louis Armstrong. Hearing Prokofiev, Ralph nodded his head in somber appreciation. When Armstrong came on, with his gravelly voice, jazzy rhythms, and vital trumpet, Ralph slowly raised his right hand and made a circle with his thumb and forefinger. Louis Armstrong was perfect. Later that afternoon, John's daughter Eve, a student at Barnard, played her violin.

On Saturday, April 16, with the music of Bach playing softly, and with Fanny snuggled tightly against Ralph on the hospital bed, Callahan saw a single tear roll slowly down his cheek. Then he was gone.

Almost helpless in her grieving, Fanny told Callahan her wishes for the funeral. The service could have taken place at the Cathedral of St. John the Divine, with hundreds of mourners and the trappings of a state funeral, but Ralph hadn't wanted a cathedral, or a church, or any display of religion at all. An open casket at a funeral home, with a long line of gawkers, was out of the question. Ralph had talked of wanting to be buried in Trinity Church Cemetery, near their apartment, across the street from the American Academy of Arts and Letters. This is historic ground, the site of fierce fighting during the Battle of Washington Heights in the Revolutionary War. John James Audubon and John Jacob Astor are buried there. The plots were all taken, but the cemetery offered a vault in its ten-story mausoleum.

The cemetery is a subdued yet seemingly untamed piece of Manhattan. Hilly and studded with rocky outcroppings, it interrupts the unsteady flow of buildings on the side of Broadway heading downtown, and looks out on the Hudson from its western slopes. Its chapel is small, with room for only thirty persons. Heeding Fanny's wishes, Callahan and Joe Fox of Random House telephoned invitations. Callahan also stood guard between her and the many people she did not want to see. Many friends who waited for an invitation were disappointed. Bitter and in pain, Fanny sharply vetoed various names. Some who were invited did not attend. Robert Stepto was on his way from New Haven to Chicago to bury his father. Al Murray was kept away by a doctor's appointment. James Alan McPherson, who had flown in from Iowa City, showed up with a friend who was not on the list, and chose to stand with her outside the chapel when she was not admitted. Inside, R. W. B. Lewis spoke, as did William Styron, Leon Forrest, and John Callahan. Michael Harper read poems.

Pallbearers carried the coffin outside to a wall of burial vaults. There, Nathan Scott, an ordained Episcopalian minister, who had come from Virginia with his wife, Charlotte, moved forward. "I had with me a pocket edition of *The Book of Common Prayer* and read from the Committal in the burial service." When Scott was done, a mechanical lift slowly raised two cemetery workers and the coffin high into the air, up to the mouth of the vault. The workers had a hard time maneuvering the heavy coffin into place. For a chilling moment Callahan feared that the box might crash to the ground. Then, settling one end on the edge of Ralph's crypt, the workers caught their breath before sliding its wooden bulk into the space in the wall.

BOOKS BY RALPH ELLISON

Invisible Man

Shadow and Act

Going to the Territory

Conversations with Ralph Ellison
(MARYEMMA GRAHAM AND AMRITJIT SINGH, EDS.)

The Collected Essays of Ralph Ellison
(JOHN F. CALLAHAN, ED.)

Flying Home and Other Stories
(JOHN F. CALLAHAN, ED.)

Juneteenth: A Novel
(JOHN F. CALLAHAN, ED.)

Trading Twelves: The Selected Letters of Ralph Ellison and Albert Murray
(ALBERT MURRAY AND JOHN F. CALLAHAN, EDS.)

Living with Music: Ralph Ellison's Jazz Writings
(ROBERT G. O'MEALLY, ED.)

NOTES

The abbreviation RWEP, LC refers to the Ralph Waldo Ellison Papers, Manuscript Division, Library of Congress.

1   *In the Territory*

4 "**When I get there**": RWE to Harold Calicutt, Feb. 3, 1971, RWEP, LC.

5 "**a wee bit Creek!**": RWE to Mamie and Mitch Rhone, June 22, 1986, RWEP, LC.

5 "**What will you be if you stay**": George O. Carney, "Historic Resources of Oklahoma's All-Black Towns: A Preservation Profile," *Chronicles of Oklahoma* 69:2 (Summer 1991): 118.

6 "**fat little blob of blubber**": RWE to Camille Randolph Rhone, March 18, 1985, RWEP, LC.

6 "**I rem[em]ber toys**": RWE, "After Effects of the Dance," ms., n.d., RWEP, LC.

6 "**my father had two passions**": Ibid.

6 "**the first song taught me**": Ron Welburn, "Ralph Ellison's Territorial Vantage," in Maryemma Graham and Amritjit Singh, eds., *Conversations with Ralph Ellison* (Jackson: UP of Mississippi, 1995), p. 303.

6 "**patiently, lovingly**": RWE, "Leaving the Territory" [a memoir], ms., n.d., RWEP, LC.

6 "*I could see his long legs*": RWE, " 'Tell It Like It Is, Baby,' " in *The Collected Essays of Ralph Ellison,* ed. John F. Callahan (New York: Modern Library, 1995), p. 35.

7 "**Ulcer of stomach**": Death Certificate C 526: Louis Albert [Lewis Alfred] Ellison, July 19, 1916, Oklahoma State Board of Health, Bureau of Vital Statistics.

7 "**often warned us against**": RWE to Lowry Ware, draft, Sept. 7, 1990, RWEP, LC.

7 "**quite vividly**": Ibid.

7 "**into which I could walk**": RWE to Stewart Lillard, Aug. 28, 1973, RWEP, LC.

8 "**By way of entertaining**": RWE, "Leaving the Territory."

8 "**the Democratic party means to carry**": Cited in Stewart Lillard, "Alfred Ellison of Abbeville," ms., n.d., p. 7., RWEP, LC.

8 "**If you're going to kill me**": Ibid., p. 10.

9 "**Big Alfred**" Ellison: Ibid.

10 "**we must provide the means**": Jimmie Lewis Franklin, *Journey Toward Hope: A History of Blacks in Oklahoma* (Norman: U of Oklahoma P, 1982), p. 40.

10 "much worry and much grief": Lewis Ellison to Ida Ellison, April 1912, RWEP, LC.

11 "Your baby is sorry": Lewis Ellison to Ida Ellison, May 8, 1912, RWEP, LC.

11 "thick anthology of poetry": RWE, "Leaving the Territory."

11 "I can't forget Emerson's powerful force": RWE to Alfred Kazin, Nov. 4, 1987, RWEP, LC.

11 "hidden name and complex fate": RWE, "Hidden Name and Complex Fate," *Collected Essays of Ralph Ellison*, p. 189.

12 "After I began to write": Ibid., p. 195.

12 *"What quality of love"*: RWE, " 'Tell It Like It Is, Baby,' " *Collected Essays of Ralph Ellison*, pp. 35–36.

12 "bemused by a recurring fantasy": Ibid., p. 42.

12 "an impulse to keep the painful details": RWE, "Richard Wright's Blues," *Collected Essays of Ralph Ellison*, p. 129.

14 "He was also a ladies man": RWE to Muriel Spence, draft, n.d. [1985], RWEP, LC.

15 "the task we had": RWE to Camille Randolph Rhone, March 18, 1985, RWEP, LC.

15 "more Anglo-Saxon": RWE, "Leaving the Territory."

15 "intimately loved books": Ibid.

15 "old J.D.": RWE to Edna Slaughter, n.d. [c. 1955], RWEP, LC.

16 "the highly-pitched, somewhat nasal timbre": RWE, "Leaving the Territory."

16 "For you": Ibid.

17 "Through her": Ibid.

17 "You existed in the security": Ibid.

17 "Rearing and pitching": Ibid.

18 "I was very quiet at first": RWE, ms., n.d. [c. 1935], Box 110, RWEP, LC.

18 "prized baby chicks": RWE, "After Effects of the Dance."

18 "straight up the aisle": RWE, "Portrait of Inman Page: A Dedication Speech," in *Going to the Territory* (New York: Random House, 1986), p. 118.

18 "was constantly fighting": In Robert Penn Warren, *Who Speaks for the Negro?* (New York: Random House, 1965), p. 325.

18 "I loved her very much": RWE, "Going to the Territory," *Going to the Territory*, p. 135.

18 "Your father's death": RWE, "Leaving the Territory."

18 "Ralph told me": John F. Callahan to author, interview, Jan. 27, 2003.

19 "there is hardly a week that passes": RWE to Edna Slaughter, n.d. [c. 1955], RWEP, LC.

19 "How often did I hear my mother insist": RWE to James "Jimmie" Stewart, June 26, 1980, RWEP, LC.

19 "Well," the guard retorted: RWE, "On Being the Target of Discrimination," *Collected Essays of Ralph Ellison*, p. 824.

19 "You'll have to go now": Ibid., p. 825.

20 "Ralph also told me": John F. Callahan to author, interview, Jan. 27, 2003.

20 "Mama was a wonderful woman": Herbert Ellison to RWE, n.d. [1942], RWEP, LC.

20 "my brother and I": RWE, ms., June 19, 1992, at Harold Washington Library, Chicago, RWEP, LC.

21 "a magnificent carriage": RWE, "Leaving the Territory."

21 "I realize now": RWE to Hester [Cook] Holloway, Nov. 28, 1961, RWEP, LC.

21 "Descending the mountain": RWE, "Leaving the Territory."

22 "not a single white Tulsan": Hannibal B. Johnson, *Black Wall Street: From Riot to Renaissance in Tulsa's Historic Greenwood District* (Austin: Eakin, 1998), p. 62.

22 "I remember the others too": RWE, n.d. [1961], RWEP, LC.

24 "a kind and tolerant boss": RWE to Mamie and Mitch Rhone, June 22, 1986.

25 "My newspapers may be for sale": Anita Arnold, *Legendary Times and Tales of Second Street* (Oklahoma City: Black Liberated Arts Center, 1995), p. 11.

25 "He was a great man": RWE to Hobart Jarrett, n.d. [1976], RWEP, LC.

25 "did not approach events": Hollie West, "Through a Writer's Eyes," *Washington Post,* Aug. 21, 1973.

25 "*did* get into my imagination": Ibid.

25 "the hero of my childhood": RWE, "Bearden," *Collected Essays of Ralph Ellison,* p. 832.

25 "I terrorized a good part": RWE, "Living with Music," in *Shadow and Act* (New York: Random House, 1964), pp. 190–92.

26 *"Oh busy squirrel"*: RWE, "Leaving the Territory."

26 "It was Mrs. Breaux": Ibid.

26 "For more than ten years": Ibid.

27 "and through him": RWE, "Portrait of Inman Page," p. 116.

27 "He was a model": *Brown University Alumni Monthly,* Nov. 1979, p. 40.

27 "I had been caught": RWE, "Living with Music," p. 190.

27 "Jazz was regarded": RWE, "The Charlie Christian Story," *Collected Essays of Ralph Ellison,* p. 270.

28 "gave expression to attitudes": RWE, "Remembering Jimmy," *Collected Essays of Ralph Ellison,* p. 275.

28 "With Christian": RWE, "The Charlie Christian Story," p. 272.

28 "were members of the same first-grade class": Ibid., p. 267.

28 "a compact, debonair young man": RWE, "Remembering Jimmy," pp. 273–74.

28 "upset the entire Negro section": RWE, "The Charlie Christian Story," p. 269.

29 "Race prejudice is no trouble": *Black Dispatch,* Sept. 10, 1931.

29 "several of the Colored boys": *Black Dispatch,* March 14, 1921.

29 "put in some shelves": Hollie West, "Through a Writer's Eyes."

29 "the so-called boys book[s]": RWE to Linda G. Morris, Sept. 22, 1983, RWEP, LC.

30 "Now isn't that right": Misc. ms., draft, n.d., RWEP, LC.

30 "Cooper was a great writer": Misc. clipping, n.d., RWEP, LC.

30 "no one paid any attention": Ms., n.d., Richard Kostelanetz typescript, LC 175, RWEP, LC.

30 "He looked at me": Ibid.

31 "I was a very poor English student": *Denver Post,* n.d. [1952], Box 174, RWEP, LC.

31 "One day": RWE, "Leaving the Territory."

32 *"Hey, baby"*: RWE to Harold Calicutt, Feb. 3, 1971, RWEP, LC.

32 "the hell we raised in school": Harold Calicutt to RWE, n.d. [c. 1940], RWEP, LC.

32 "we held secret": RWE, "On Becoming an Unintentional New Yorker," ms., n.d., RWEP, LC.

33 "a beat-up yellow Stutz Bearcat": RWE, "Leaving the Territory."

33 "Treat people as individuals": Ibid.

33 "There was never a time": Hollie West, "Through a Writer's Eyes."

34 "It was a nasty, depressing situation": RWE, "Leaving the Territory."

34 "I was all over Oklahoma City": *Daily Oklahoman*, Jan. 11, 1993.

34 "With you": RWE, "Leaving the Territory."

34 "For a lil' ole": Ibid.

34 "when your mouth was running": Ibid.

35 "for the most part hidden": Ibid.

35 "vulnerable to unwelcome laughter": Ibid.

35 "the outrageous disparity": Ibid.

2   *Leaving the Territory*

37 "more wary of all contradictions": RWE, "Leaving the Territory," ms., n.d., RWEP, LC.

38 "I have no law for this": *Black Dispatch*, May 4, 1933.

38 "we were an isolated community": Zethel Chamberlain to author, interview, July 9, 2001.

38 "Jim Crow was very harsh": Pauline Vivette to author, interview, July 12, 2001.

38 "in those days": Dr. Gravelly Finley to author, interview, July 10, 2001.

38 "During my Oklahoma boyhood": RWE, "On Becoming an Unintentional New Yorker," ms., n.d., RWEP, LC.

39 "Jewbaby": Fanny Ellison, note, April 28, 1987 ["R. called him 'Jewbaby.'"], RWEP, LC.

39 "Here's a Jew Bet": *Black Dispatch*, Sept. 10, 1931.

39 "He was Jewish": RWE, "Leaving the Territory."

40 "She was my best friend": Pauline Vivette to author, interview, July 12, 2001.

40 "What are you doing about school?": Vivian Steveson to RWE, Feb. 14, 1933, RWEP, LC.

40 "the little girl": RWE, "Apex" Notebook, n.d., RWEP, LC.

40 "If someone other than Vivian": Ibid.

41 "Gee but I'd like": Ibid.

41 "Success comes to th[ose] who wait": RWE, "The Charlie Christian Story," in *The Collected Essays of Ralph Ellison*, ed. John F. Callahan (New York: Modern Library, 1995), p. 269.

42 "He offered to give me lessons": RWE, Misc. notebook, n.d., RWEP, LC.

42 "Made it alright": RWE, "Apex" Notebook.

43 "I was horrified": Ibid.

43 "We have tomorrow": Langston Hughes, "Youth," in *The Collected Poems of Langston Hughes,* ed. Arnold Rampersad (New York: Alfred A. Knopf, 1994), p. 39.

43 "one of the best poets": *Black Dispatch*, March 12, 1932.

43 "the greatest living Negro poet": *Black Dispatch*, March 19, 1932.

44 "a splendid recital": *Black Dispatch*, March 31, 1932.

44 "During the long silence": RWE, "On Becoming an Unintentional New Yorker."

44 "Oh what a beautiful city": RWE, "Apex" Notebook.

45 "The Fisk choir appears": Ibid.

45 "sang the songs": *Black Dispatch*, March 9, 1933.

45 "always just beyond the horizon": RWE, "Apex" Notebook.

45 "this quiet, unassuming musical genius": *Black Dispatch*, Jan. 5, 1933.

45 "William L. Dawson has me all excited": RWE, "Apex" Notebook.

46 "teach some of the dumb guys": RWE to Ida Ellison Bell, March 23, 1933, RWEP, LC.

46 "I'm here at Classen": RWE, "Apex" Notebook.

47 "if you will get up as much money": Tuskegee Institute (Alvin Neely) to RWE, June 10, 1933, RWEP, LC.

47 "It was like a bad joke": RWE, "On Becoming an Unintentional New Yorker."

47 "an almost instinctive reluctance": RWE, "Leaving the Territory."

48 "a powerful and degrading motive": Ibid.

48 "Because you, sir": Ibid.

48 "They, as the old saying held": Ibid.

49 "plans for committing suicide": Ibid.

50 "Keep away from thieves": Ibid.

50 "Look the bastard straight in the eye": Ibid.

50 "If you would see me now": RWE to Ida Ellison Bell, June 22, 1933, RWEP, LC.

50 "it looked like an excursion train": RWE, "Leaving the Territory."

51 "full of readings": RWE, "Perspective of Literature," *Collected Essays of Ralph Ellison*, p. 769.

51 "I saw with despair": RWE, "On Becoming an Unintentional New Yorker."

51 "I had no idea": RWE, "Perspective of Literature," p. 773.

3   *In a Land Most Strange*

52 "This is a beautiful place": RWE to Ida Ellison Bell, June 25, 1933, RWEP, LC.

53 "The wisest among my race": Booker T. Washington, *Up from Slavery: An Autobiography*, in *Three Negro Classics*, ed. John Hope Franklin (New York: Avon, 1965), p. 149.

54 "It is an exhibition": Tuskegee Institute *Student Manual* (Tuskegee: Tuskegee Institute, 1933), p. 37.

54 "Captain Drye was a true military type": Louis "Mike" Rabb to author, interview, Aug. 15, 2000.

54 "our hands, arms": RWE to Ida Ellison Bell, June 23, 1933.

55 "some hair grease": Ibid.

55 "going out with another boy": John Bell to RWE, June 29, 1933, RWEP, LC.

55 "I have wanted to come home": RWE to Ida Ellison Bell, July 23, 1933, RWEP, LC.

55 "I find them dull": RWE to Ida Ellison Bell, July 16, 1933, RWEP, LC.

55 "Vivian writes": RWE to Ida Ellison Bell, Dec. 4, 1933, RWEP, LC.

55 "You must understand": RWE to Ida Ellison Bell, June 1, 1936, RWEP, LC.

55 "There are too many girls": RWE to Ida Ellison Bell, Aug. 4, 1933, RWEP, LC.

56 "doing everything to make things pleasant": Ibid.

56 "He told me to tell you": RWE to Ida Ellison Bell, July 16, 1933.

56 "owe the school later on": RWE to Ida Ellison Bell, Aug. 4, 1933.

56 "This *does not include the uniform*": RWE to Ida Ellison Bell, Aug. 24, 1933.

56 "You could have pushed me over": RWE to Ida Ellison Bell, Oct. 1, 1933, RWEP, LC.

57 "a personality of steel": *Tuskegee Messenger* 11:10 (Oct. 1935): 8.

57 "a big yellow woman": RWE to Ida Ellison Bell, Nov. 5, 1933, RWEP, LC.

57 "and now they are on me": Ibid.

58 "my old suit was so dirty": RWE to Ida Ellison Bell, Nov. 11, 1933, RWEP, LC.

58 "to present certain aspects": Program Notes, *The Green Pastures: A Fable by Marc Connelly*, Nov. 11, 1933, Logan Hall, Tuskegee Institute, RWEP, LC.

58 "Here, you will find every phase": *Student Manual*, p. 3.

58 "Pick up your feet": Ibid., p. 45.

58 "Tuskegee is a vast workshop": Ibid., p. 11.

58 "I don't fit in well": RWE to John Bell, July 4, 1933, RWEP, LC.

59 "My mother was born": Carolyn Walcott Ford to author, interview, Aug. 18, 2000.

59 "scholastics were important": Laly Charlton Washington to author, interview, Aug. 18, 2000.

59 "I liked Ralph a lot": Louis "Mike" Rabb to author, interview, Aug. 15, 2000.

59 "In the cinema": Ibid.

59 "my mother was always called Mrs. Walcott": Carolyn Walcott Ford to author.

60 "I don't want you": Ida Ellison Bell to RWE, July 27, 1933, RWEP, LC.

60 "Things look bad for me": RWE to Ida Ellison Bell, Dec. 14, 1933, RWEP, LC.

60 "My stomach still bothers me": RWE to Ida Ellison Bell, Jan. 10, 1934, RWEP, LC.

60 "because it might get him into trouble": RWE to Ida Ellison Bell, Feb. 1, 1934, RWEP, LC.

61 "brought down to something practical": *The Booker T. Washington Papers*, vol. 2, ed. Louis R. Harlan (Urbana: U of Illinois P, 1972), pp. 260–61.

61 "I have found a new friend": RWE to Ida Ellison Bell, Feb. 1, 1934.

61 "a short man": Carolyn Ford to author, interview, Aug. 18, 2000.

61 "It's a hard go": RWE to Ida Ellison Bell, Oct. 1, 1933.

61 "You should know": RWE to Richard Wilbur, Feb. 24, 1987, RWEP, LC.

61 "In the case of Cap'n Neely": Albert Murray, *South to a Very Old Place* (New York: McGraw-Hill, 1971), p. 107.

62 "certain books": RWE, "On Becoming an Unintentional New Yorker," ms., n.d., RWEP, LC.

62 "honors student at Harvard": RWE, ms., n.d. [Sept. 29, 1971], RWEP, LC.

62 "in the destruction of that book": RWE, "On Becoming an Unintentional New Yorker."

62 "A Dedicated Dreamer": RWE, dedication of *Shadow and Act* (New York: Random House, 1964).

62 "How shall we sing": *The Bible Designed to Be Read as Living Literature*, ed. Ernest Sutherland Bates (New York: Simon & Schuster, 1965), p. 659.

63 "My trip to Tuskegee": RWE, "Note for Autobiography," n.d., RWEP, LC.

63 "I spend my time reading": RWE to Ida Ellison Bell, Feb. 6, 1934, RWEP, LC.

63 "really too nice": RWE to Ida Ellison Bell, Feb. 26, 1933 [1934], RWEP, LC.

63 "Don't get discourage[d]": Ida Ellison Bell to RWE, Feb. 6, 1934.

64 "I have stopped worrying": RWE to Ida Ellison Bell, Feb. 14, 1934, RWEP, LC.

64 "I have been admitted": RWE to Ida Ellison Bell, March 21, 1934, RWEP, LC.

64 "I have no razor": RWE to Ida Ellison Bell, May 2, 1934, RWEP, LC.

64 "Say, do they still sell liquor": RWE to Harry Brooks, March 23, 1939, RWEP, LC.

65 "Things are dull here": RWE to Ida Ellison Bell, May 2, 1934, RWEP, LC.

65 "School has been like a nightmare": RWE to Ida Ellison Bell, May 27, 1934, RWEP, LC.

65 "We spent each day": RWE to Ida Ellison Bell, June 15, 1934, RWEP, LC.

65 "At last I think": RWE, "Diaries 1934–36," RWEP, LC.

66 "I am getting ragged": RWE to Ida Ellison Bell, June 15, 1934.

66 "I intend to study there": RWE to Ida Ellison Bell, July 18, 1934, RWEP, LC.

66 "I paid for the trip": RWE, "Diaries 1934–36."

66 "that if I left": RWE to Ida Ellison Bell, Aug. 13, 1934, RWEP, LC.

67 "providing that this negro": RWE to Ida Ellison Bell, Aug. 28, 1934, RWEP, LC.

68 "Your breadth of interests": Walter B. Williams to RWE, March 6, 1934, RWEP, LC.

68 "artificial and alien": Harold R. Isaacs, "Five and Their African Ancestors," *Phylon: The Atlanta Review of Race and Culture* (Fourth Quarter, 1960): 320.

69 "You are so far": Ibid.

69 "half asleep or growling": Walter B. Williams to RWE, June 23, 1935, RWEP, LC.

69 "I have tasted ecstasy": Walter B. Williams to RWE, Nov. 16, 1944, RWEP, LC.

69 "I had a wonderful time of it": RWE to Ida Ellison Bell, Nov. 11, 1933.

70 "dramatic feeling": *New York Times,* Nov. 21, 1934.

70 "you had the sense": RWE, "Homage to William Dawson," in *The Collected Essays of Ralph Ellison*, ed. John F. Callahan (New York: Modern Library, 1995), p. 436.

70 "making this a lonesome place": RWE to Ida Ellison Bell, Dec. 23, 1934, RWEP, LC.

70 "Every one that say": Ida Ellison Bell to RWE, Jan. 7, 1935, RWEP, LC.

71 "I think both of us": Ida Ellison Bell to RWE, March 19, 1935, RWEP, LC.

71 "a gift from God": RWE to Ida Ellison Bell, Jan. 13, 1935, RWEP, LC.

71 "He is the only person": RWE to Ida Ellison Bell, Oct. 1935 [Feb. 1935], RWEP, LC.

71 "that beautiful and memorable": RWE to Hazel [Harrison], n.d., RWEP, LC.

71 "I had outraged": RWE, "The Little Man at Chehaw Station," in *Going to the Territory* (New York: Random House, 1986), p. 3.

72 "I am convinced you can write": Note by "MLB," in RWE, English 102 course paper, RWEP, LC.

72 "The spring is beautiful": RWE to Ida Ellison Bell, April 27, 1935, RWEP, LC.

72 "I want to see you so much": Ida Ellison Bell to RWE, May 11, 1935, RWEP, LC.

73 "Saretta liked him more": Dr. Gravelly Finley to author, interview, July 10, 2001.

73 "Though they have the brain power": RWE to Joe Lazenberry, Aug. 21, 1935, RWEP, LC.

73 "When I asked you": "Sue" to RWE, Aug. 20, 1936, RWEP, LC.

73 "I haven't forgotten": "Sue" to RWE, Sept. 6, 1936, RWEP, LC.

73 "My dear friend Ellison": Frank L. Drye to RWE, July 10, 1935, RWEP, LC.

74 "to the Tuskegee pattern": *Tuskegee Messenger* 11 (Nov.–Dec. 1935), p. 8.

74 "hypocrisy, meanness": Walter B. Williams to RWE, Aug. 20, 1935, RWEP, LC.

74 "was reading the books": Louis Edwards, "Albert Murray on Stage: An Interview,"

in Roberta S. Maguire, ed., *Conversations with Albert Murray* (Jackson: UP of Mississippi, 1997), pp. 85–86.

74 **"Death is nothing"**: David Remnick, "Visible Man," *New Yorker* (March 14, 1994): 38.

74 **"He was straight out of *Esquire*"**: Albert Murray at RWE symposium, City University of New York Graduate Center, May 8, 1999.

75 **"It was a bitter pill"**: RWE to Herbert Ellison, April 4, 1936, RWEP, LC.

75 **"Teachers of English"**: *Tuskegee Messenger* 10 (Feb. 1934): 3.

75 **"I loved Mr. Sprague"**: Laly Charlton Washington to author, interview, Aug. 18, 2000.

75 **"He was an honest teacher"**: Richard Kostelanetz, "An Interview with Ralph Ellison," in *Conversations with Ralph Ellison,* ed. Maryemma Graham and Amritjit Singh (Jackson: UP of Mississippi, 1995), p. 87.

75 **"most of the teachers"**: RWE, "What These Children Are Like," *Collected Essays of Ralph Ellison*, p. 547.

76 **"to illustrate how free"**: Murray, *South to a Very Old Place*, p. 109.

76 **"the wrenching that I went through"**: RWE, "What's Wrong with the American Novel," *Conversations with Ralph Ellison*, p. 44.

76 **"While I was reading"**: RWE, ["Back in the thirties . . ."], ms., n.d., RWEP, LC.

76 **"This work, a first novel"**: RWE, "English 409," ms., n.d., RWEP, LC.

76 **"although I was then unaware of it"**: RWE, *Shadow and Act*, p. 161.

77 **"I had been made furious"**: RWE, misc. notes, n.d., RWEP, LC.

77 **"is primarily an artist"**: Robert E. Park and Ernest W. Burgess, *Introduction to the Science of Sociology* (Chicago: U of Chicago P, 1919), p. 136.

77 **"inalienable coefficients of his blood"**: *Tuskegee Messenger* 11 (May–June 1935): 3.

78 **"There is a school of thought"**: RWE, "Sociology 406," May 13, 1936, RWEP, LC.

79 **"My shoes are all worn out"**: RWE to Ida Ellison Bell, Jan. 12, 1936, RWEP, LC.

80 **"I want to go to New York"**: RWE to Ida Ellison Bell, May 18, 1936, RWEP, LC.

80 **"Oh Ralph"**: Ida Ellison Bell to RWE, May 20, 1936, RWEP, LC.

80 **"a better class of people"**: Ida Ellison Bell to RWE, July 23, 1936, RWEP, LC.

4   *A Shock of Transition*

81 **"I confronted the city"**: RWE, "On Becoming an Unintentional New Yorker," ms., n.d., RWEP, LC.

81 **"moving like one hypnotized"**: Ibid.

83 **"Be nice to people"**: RWE to Langston Hughes, July 17, 1936, Langston Hughes Papers, Beinecke Library, Yale University.

83 **"it helps so very much"**: RWE to Langston Hughes, n.d., Langston Hughes Papers, Yale.

83 **"the bread of freedom"**: RWE, "On Becoming an Unintentional New Yorker."

83 **"*I was never her student*"**: RWE to Robert G. O'Meally, Sept. 28, 1979, RWEP, LC.

83 **"I fell in love"**: RWE to Richmond Barthé, draft, n.d., RWEP, LC.

83 **"one of the most sincere people"**: RWE to Hazel Harrison, Oct. 23, 1936, RWEP, LC.

84 **"to my surprise and joy"**: RWE to Langston Hughes, July 17, 1936, Langston Hughes Papers, Yale.

84 "too nasty and took up too much time": RWE to Ida Ellison Bell, Sept. 3, 1936, RWEP, LC.

84 "It is a very pleasant job": Ibid.

84 "When he asked me to read": RWE, "On Becoming an Unintentional New Yorker."

84 "impressed me as intelligent": Harry Stack Sullivan, letter of recommendation for RWE, Sept. 15, 1937, RWEP, LC.

85 "My, how you have improved": Hazel Harrison to RWE, Oct. 15, 1936, RWEP, LC.

85 "I feel I knew his best work": RWE to Langston Hughes, Aug. 24, 1936, Langston Hughes Papers, Yale.

85 "During the long extent": RWE to Richard Wilbur, Feb. 24, 1987, RWEP, LC.

86 "What I prophesied": Walter B. Williams to RWE, July 17, 1936, RWEP, LC.

86 "nasty": Ida Ellison Bell to RWE, Oct. 28, 1936, RWEP, LC.

86 "THOUGH FAR AWAY": RWE to Ida Ellison Bell, Dec. 25, 1936, RWEP, LC.

86 "I must settle my own affairs": RWE to Ida Ellison Bell, June 1, 1936, RWEP, LC.

86 "I must admit": Ida Ellison Bell to RWE, n.d. [May 1936], RWEP, LC.

87 "the scene of the folk-Negro's death agony": RWE, "Harlem Is Nowhere," in *Shadow and Act* (New York: Random House, 1964), p. 296.

87 "I used to stand on Sunday nights": Ibid.

88 "I did *not* come to New York": *Conversations with Ralph Ellison*, ed. Maryemma Graham and Amritjit Singh (Jackson: UP of Mississippi, 1995), p. 121.

88 "with a European accent": RWE, "An Extravagance of Laughter," in *The Collected Essays of Ralph Ellison,* ed. John F. Callahan (New York: Modern Library, 1995), p. 159.

88 "I laughed and laughed": Ibid., p. 186.

89 "I was testing myself": RWE, "On Becoming an Unintentional New Yorker."

89 "moved inevitably toward": Ibid.

89 "The roommate situation": Margaret Vendryes to author, Aug. 18, 2002.

91 "For the first time": RWE, ["Address at Langston Hughes Festival,"] City College of New York, April 11, 1984.

91 "It has a value": RWE to Langston Hughes, April 27, 1937, Langston Hughes Papers, Yale.

91 "He tells me there is no use": RWE to Ida Ellison Bell, April 20, 1937, RWEP, LC.

91 "Patience is not your forte": Hazel Harrison to RWE, March 19, [1937,] RWEP, LC.

91 "Sometimes I wish": RWE to Ida Ellison Bell, April 20, 1937.

92 "a national concentration point": Mark Naison, *Communists in Harlem During the Depression* (Urbana: U of Illinois P, 1983), p. 95.

92 "had Party membership": Ibid., p. 193.

93 "an appendage of his race": Claude McKay, *Harlem: Negro Metropolis* (New York: Harcourt Brace Jovanovich, 1968), p. 254.

93 "it was really easy": Herbert Aptheker to author, interview, June 25, 2001.

93 "I was in some of the first sit-ins": RWE, ms., n.d., RWEP, LC.

93 "to raise their voices": *Daily Worker*, July 2, 1937.

93 "I must drive the bombers": Langston Hughes, "Song of Spain," in *The Collected Poems of Langston Hughes,* ed. Arnold Rampersad (New York: Alfred A. Knopf, 1994), p. 197.

94 "The bastards waited until the morning": RWE to Joe Lazenberry, draft, April 18, 1939, RWEP, LC.

94 "one of us": "Charlie" to Evelyn Ehrend, n.d. [1937], RWEP, LC.

95 "People come in at all hours": RWE to Ida Ellison Bell, Aug. 30, 1937, RWEP, LC.

95 "You must not try to send me anything": Ibid.

95 "I told him to stay": Ida Ellison Bell to RWE, May 26, 1937, RWEP, LC.

95 "I don't want to see him again": Ida Ellison Bell to RWE, Aug. 10, 1937, RWEP, LC.

95 "and try and get yourself straight": Ibid.

95 "Your comrade, Mike Gold": Inscription in RWE's copy of Abner W. Berry et al., *The Road to Liberation for the Negro People* (New York: Workers Library, 1937).

96 "I often wonder": RWE to Ida Ellison Bell, Sept. 30, 1937, RWEP, LC.

96 "Langston Hughes tells me": RWE, "Remembering Richard Wright," *Collected Essays of Ralph Ellison*, p. 661.

97 "I'd become fascinated": Ibid., p. 659.

97 "after the habit of reflection": Richard Wright, *Black Boy (American Hunger)* (New York: Library of America, 1991), p. 37.

98 "For me": RWE, "The World and the Jug," *Collected Essays of Ralph Ellison*, pp. 166–67.

99 "re-writing but also reporting": Lewis Allan, letter of recommendation for RWE, May 3, 1938, RWEP, LC.

99 "To one who had never attempted": RWE, "Remembering Richard Wright," p. 663.

99 "prim and decorous ambassadors": Richard Wright, "Blueprint for Negro Writing," *New Challenge* 1 (Fall 1937): 53.

99 "the first attempt": RWE, "Creative and Cultural Lag," *New Challenge* 1 (Fall 1937): 90.

99 "in order to transcend it": Richard Wright, "Blueprint for Negro Writing," in *Richard Wright Reader*, ed. Ellen Wright and Michel Fabre (New York: Harper & Row, 1978), p. 42.

100 "was between anguish and joy": Constance Webb, *Richard Wright: A Biography* (New York: G. P. Putnam's Sons, 1968), p. 146.

100 "I am very disgusted": RWE to Ida Ellison Bell, Aug. 30, 1937.

101 "such a sad letter": Ida Ellison Bell to RWE, Sept. 8, 1937, RWEP, LC.

101 "I can't walk yet": Ibid.

101 "Tuberculosis of left hip joint": Certificate of death, Oct. 16, 1937, RWEP, LC.

101 "This is the end": RWE to Richard Wright, Oct. 27, 1937, Richard Wright Papers, Beinecke Library, Yale University.

102 "and then has not mastered": *Daily Oklahoman*, clipping, n.d., RWEP, LC.

102 "I feel very sorry": RWE to Richard Wright, Oct. 27, 1937.

102 "Gee but it's swell": RWE to Richard Wright, Nov. 8, 1937, RWEP, LC.

102 "I walk along thinking": RWE to Richard Wright, Oct. 27, 1937.

103 "Remembering Shooting-Flying": Ernest Hemingway, "Remembering Shooting-Flying: A Key West Letter," *Esquire* (Feb. 1935): 21.

103 "Where in hell": RWE to Richard Wright, Nov. 8, 1937, Richard Wright Papers, Yale.

103 "He was a man of great curiosity": RWE to Mamie Rhone, Dec. 3, 1985, RWEP, LC.

103 "the Dayton Youth Movement": Herbert Ellison to RWE, July 4, 1938, RWEP, LC.

104 "I shall never forget his kindness": RWE to Mamie Rhone, Dec. 3, 1985.

104 "WORKERS OF THE WORLD": RWE to Richard Wright, Nov. 8, 1937, RWEP, LC.

105 "**that I turned my full attention**": RWE, "Who Speaks for the Negro," ms. [1964], RWEP, LC.

105 "**that the light of magic suggestiveness**": Joseph Conrad, Preface to *The Nigger of the Narcissus* (New York: Collier, 1962), p. 19.

105 "**Funny she had to go do me**": RWE, "Goodnight Irene," ms., n.d., RWEP, LC.

106 "**I had to give that up**": RWE, "The Black Ball," in *Flying Home and Other Stories*, ed. John F. Callahan (New York: Vintage, 1998), p. 117.

106 "**The girl was very lovely**": RWE, "A Hard Time Keeping Up," *Flying Home*, p. 104.

107 "**I came back**": RWE to Joe Lazenberry, April 18, 1939, RWEP, LC.

108 "**You have absolutely no sense**": Nina Naguid to RWE, Nov. 30, 1937, RWEP, LC.

108 "**regaining faith in human nature**": Ibid.

109 "**The Communist Party**": *Daily Worker,* Feb. 25, 1938.

109 "**This is my story**": Constance Webb, *Richard Wright: A Biography*, p. 146.

109 "**kept it and kept it**": John Hersey, " 'A Completion of Personality: A Talk with Ralph Ellison," *Conversations with Ralph Ellison*, p. 294.

110 "**not an intellectual by any means**": Ibid.

110 "**all the bright Negro men**": Claude McKay, *Harlem: Negro Metropolis*, p. 232.

111 "**These rich bastards here**": RWE to Ida Ellison Bell, Aug. 30, 1937.

112 "**All I remember about him**": Wayne F. Cooper, *Claude McKay: Rebel Sojourner in the Harlem Renaissance* (Baton Rouge: Louisiana State UP, 1987), p. 362.

112 "**the drudgery was good for me**": Jerre Mangione, *The Dream and the Deal: The Federal Writers' Project, 1935–1943* (Boston: Little, Brown, 1972), p. 256.

113 "**its analysis of religious and mystical experience**": RWE, "Practical Mystic," *New Masses* (Aug. 16, 1938): 25.

5   *The Recognition of Necessity*

114 "**It took nerve**": RWE to Joe Lazenberry, April 18, 1939, RWEP, LC.

115 "**nice, if insipid bitches**": RWE to Richard Wright, April 22, 1940, Richard Wright Papers, Beinecke Library, Yale University.

115 "**image of woman's thought process**": RWE to Richard Wright, May 11, 1940, Richard Wright Papers, Yale.

115 "**full of piss and vinegar**": RWE to Richard Wright, April 22, 1940, Richard Wright Papers, Yale.

115 "**They thought I should**": John F. Callahan to author, interview, Sept. 28, 2002.

115 "**To open the old box**": RWE to Harry Brooks, March 23, 1939, RWEP, LC.

117 "**I was a Communist**": Richard Wright to Edward Aswell, Aug. 21, 1955, in Michel Fabre, *The Unfinished Quest of Richard Wright* (New York: William Morrow, 1973), p. 230.

117 "**ignorant of black institutions**": Ben Burns, *Nitty Gritty: A White Editor in Black Journalism* (Jackson: UP of Mississippi, 1996), p. 56.

117 "**His vision need not be simple**": Richard Wright, "Blueprint for Negro Writing," in *Richard Wright Reader*, ed. Ellen Wright and Michel Fabre (New York: Harper & Row, 1978), p. 44.

117 "**ferocious despair**": John Strachey, *Literature and Dialectical Materialism* (New York: Covici, Friede, [c. 1934]), p. 43.

118 **"The philosophy of Communism"**: Granville Hicks, "The Future of Proletarian Literature," in *Granville Hicks in The New Masses,* ed. Jack Alan Robbins (Port Washington, N.Y.: Kennikat, 1974), p. 64.

118 **"For more than one radical"**: Ibid., p. 102.

118 **"so hard and deep"**: Richard Wright, *Early Works: Lawd Today! Uncle Tom's Children, Native Son* (New York: Library of America, 1991), p. 874.

118 **"I read most of *Native Son*"**: RWE, "Remembering Richard Wright," in *Going to the Territory* (New York: Random House, 1986), p. 210.

119 **"the world's foremost novelist"**: *Time* 32 (Nov. 7, 1938): 59.

119 **"Malraux's real theme"**: Jack Alan Robbins, ed., *Granville Hicks in The New Masses,* p. 378.

120 **"By converting as wide a range"**: RWE to Joe Lazenberry, April 25, 1939, RWEP, LC.

120 **"the tragic soul-life"**: W. E. B. Du Bois, *The Souls of Black Folk* (New York: Bantam, 1989), p. 134.

121 **"a man of substance"**: William E. Cain to author, Nov. 1, 2002.

121 **"no more remarkable man"**: "The Landscape Garden," in *The Complete Poems and Stories of Edgar Allan Poe,* vol. 1, ed. Arthur Hobson Quinn and Edward H. O'Neill (New York: Alfred A. Knopf, 1964), pp. 389, 393. For these references to Unamuno and Poe I am indebted to Professor William E. Cain of Wellesley College.

121 **"He assumed that I hadn't read"**: Robert B. Stepto and Michael S. Harper, "Study and Experience: An Interview with Ralph Ellison" [1976], in *Conversations with Ralph Ellison,* ed. Maryemma Graham and Amritjit Singh (Jackson: UP of Mississippi, 1995), p. 323.

121 **"plunging headlong into chaos"**: John Hersey, "'A Completion of Personality': A Talk with Ralph Ellison" [1974], *Conversations with Ralph Ellison,* p. 288.

121 **"I never wrote the official type"**: Steve Cannon, Lennox Raphael, and James Thompson, "A Very Stern Discipline: An Interview with Ralph Ellison" [1967], *Conversations with Ralph Ellison,* p. 124.

122 **"forms of literary editorship"**: Walter Sutton, *Modern American Criticism* (Englewood Cliffs, N.J.: Prentice-Hall, 1963), p. 72.

123 **"The only thing I can do"**: Langston Hughes to Noel Sullivan, Jan. 29, 1936, Noel Sullivan Papers, Bancroft Library, University of California, Berkeley.

123 **"widespread sabotage and wrecking"**: RWE to Joe Lazenberry, April 18, 1939.

124 **"If we are ever to attain"**: RWE to Joe Lazenberry, April 25, 1939.

124 **"the moonlight and mockingbirds"**: Ibid.

124 **"I am mapping a novel"**: Ibid.

125 **"enthusiastic, bright-eyed"**: RWE, "An Extravagance of Laughter," in *The Collected Essays of Ralph Ellison,* ed. John F. Callahan (New York: Modern Library, 1995), p. 625.

125 **"Life in the United States"**: RWE, ["Negroes & Jews"], ms., n.d., RWEP, LC.

126 **"one of the most dramatic incidents"**: *New York Times,* June 5, 1939.

126 **"Man, you have to fall out of love"**: RWE to Horace Cayton, interview, Sept. 8, 1968, cited in Hazel Rowley, *Richard Wright: The Life and Times* (New York: Henry Holt, 2001), p. 176.

127 **"Every effort is being made"**: RWE, "Judge Lynch in New York," *New Masses* (Aug. 15, 1939): 16.

127 " 'No!' I shouted": Alfred Kazin, *Starting Out in the Thirties* (New York: Little, Brown, 1965), p. 139.

127 "Jesus Christ": Leah Levenson and Jerry Natterstad, *Granville Hicks: The Intellectual in Mass Society* (Philadelphia: Temple UP, 1993), p. 119.

127 "a brilliant and necessary diplomatic move": Harry Haywood, *Black Bolshevik: Autobiography of an Afro-American Communist* (Chicago: Liberator Press, 1978), p. 495.

128 "None of the people": RWE to Herbert Ellison, Feb. 6, 1940, RWEP, LC.

129 "To help my people": Mark Naison, *Communists in Harlem During the Depression* (Urbana: U of Illinois P, 1983), p. 268.

129 "a subtle piece": RWE, "Javanese Folklore," *New Masses* 34 (Dec. 26, 1939): 25.

129 "stressing the jim-crow": Len Zinberg to RWE, n.d. [Jan. 3, 1940], RWEP, LC.

130 "some of the most disgusting war propaganda": RWE, ms., n.d., RWEP, LC.

130 "Let no one fool you": RWE to Herbert Ellison, Feb. 6, 1940.

130 "turn his attention from": RWE, "Camp Lost Colony," *New Masses* (Feb. 6, 1940): 19.

130 "notable for its avoidance": RWE, "TAC Negro Show," *New Masses* (Feb. 27, 1940): 29–30.

130 "American culture was changed forever": Irving Howe, "Black Boys and Native Sons," in *A World More Attractive: A View of Modern Literature and Politics* (New York: Horizon, 1963), p. 100.

130 "more copies than any novel": Hazel Rowley, *Richard Wright: The Life and Times*, p. 191.

131 "I have talked about the book": RWE to Richard Wright, April 14, 1940, Richard Wright Papers, Yale.

131 "a terrific indictment": *Daily Worker*, March 23, 1940.

131 "It is no exaggeration": *Sunday Worker*, March 31, 1940.

131 "sounded like a broad scholar": RWE to Richard Wright, April 22, 1940, Richard Wright Papers, Yale.

131 "How far can the Marxist writer go": Ibid.

132 "These bastards here": RWE to Richard Wright, April 14, 1940, Richard Wright Papers, Yale.

133 "whose very presence here": RWE to Richard Wright, May 11, 1940, Richard Wright Papers, Yale.

133 "the wild river": Richard Wright, "Joe Louis Uncovers Dynamite," *New Masses* 17 (Oct. 8, 1935): 18.

133 "the 'river' is harnessing": RWE to Richard Wright, May 11, 1940.

134 "We drove all night": RWE, "A Congress Jim Crow Didn't Attend," *New Masses* 35 (May 14, 1940): 5.

134 "Not only did Randolph leave": Mark Naison, *Communists in Harlem During the Depression*, p. 297.

134 "We are running three pages": RWE to Richard Wright, May 15, 1940, RWEP, LC.

134 "I think there will be": RWE to Richard Wright, May 11, 1940.

135 "a people's war": Harry Haywood, *Black Bolshevik*, p. 498.

135 "As for Hitler": RWE to Richard Wright, May 26, 1940, Richard Wright Papers, Yale.

135 "This Trotsky business": Ibid.

136 **"played his own cards first"**: Hazel Rowley, *Richard Wright: The Life and Times*, p. 199.

136 **"only a bloody mound"**: RWE, "The Birthmark," *New Masses* (July 2, 1940): 16.

136 **"Her voice had been like a slap"**: RWE, "Afternoon," in *Flying Home and Other Stories*, ed. John F. Callahan (New York: Vintage, 1998), p. 42.

137 **"an acute attack of Hepatitis"**: Dr. Robert V. Sager to RWE, July 17, 1940, RWEP, LC.

137 **"You've been a grand wife"**: RWE to Rose Poindexter Ellison, July 25, 1940, RWEP, LC.

137 **"caught up in events"**: RWE, "The Golden Age, Time Past," *Collected Essays of Ralph Ellison*, p. 239.

138 **"Only through portrayal"**: *Daily Worker*, Oct. 27, 1940.

139 **"You've taken my blues"**: Langston Hughes, "Note on Commercial Theater," in *The Collected Poems of Langston Hughes*, ed. Arnold Rampersad (New York: Alfred A. Knopf, 1994), p. 215.

139 **"Just how much culture"**: Langston Hughes to Maxim Lieber, July 9, 1940, Langston Hughes Papers, Beinecke Library, Yale University.

139 **"In the style of *The Big Sea*"**: RWE, "Stormy Weather," *New Masses* (Sept. 24, 1940): 20.

139 **"ambassador"**: Richard Wright, "Forerunner and Ambassador," *New Republic* 103 (Oct. 24, 1940): 600.

139 **"prim and decorous ambassadors"**: Richard Wright, "Blueprint for Negro Writing," p. 37.

139 **"the dead-end utopia of Africa"**: RWE, " 'Big White Fog,' " *New Masses* (Nov. 12, 1940): 22.

140 **"is able to go with a Marxist understanding"**: RWE, "Negro Prize Fighter," *New Masses* (Dec. 17, 1940): 26.

140 **"every genuine anti-fascist struggle"**: "Writers and the War," *New Masses* (Aug. 5, 1941): 23.

141 **"March on Washington"**: Mark Naison, *Communists in Harlem During the Depression*, p. 310.

141 **"ignored the existence of Negro folklore"**: RWE, "Recent Negro Fiction," *New Masses* (Aug. 5, 1941): 22.

142 **"It is no accident"**: Ibid., p. 25.

6   *The Numbed and the Seething*

143 **"May I again suggest"**: RWE to Tenants of Apartment #4, Dec. 14, 1941, RWEP, LC.

144 **"Each day when you see us"**: Richard Wright, "*12 Million Black Voices*," in *Richard Wright Reader*, ed. Ellen Wright and Michel Fabre (New York: Harper & Row, 1978), p. 145.

144 **"magnificent in its simplicity"**: Horace Cayton, "Wright's New Book More Than a Study of Social Status," *Pittsburgh Courier*, Nov. 15, 1941.

144 **"a lacerating experience"**: RWE to Richard Wright, Nov. 3, 1941, Richard Wright Papers, Beinecke Library, Yale University.

145 "I am sure now more than ever": Ibid.

146 "to Negro slave stories": RWE, "Mister Toussan," *New Masses* 41 (Nov. 4, 1941): 19.

146 "There is the drama": RWE to Richard Wright, April 12, 1941, Richard Wright Papers, Yale.

146 "as the best piece of brief fiction": RWE, "Between Ourselves," *New Masses* (Nov. 25, 1941): 1.

146 "an outstanding Negro League member": "Who's Who," *Direction* 4 (Summer 1941): 2.

147 "Never before had I worked closely": Frank Marshall Davis, *Livin' the Blues: Memoirs of a Black Journalist and Poet*, ed. John Edgar Tidwell (Madison: U of Wisconsin P, 1992), p. 248.

147 "What rotten luck": *New York Times*, Jan. 10, 2006.

148 "I am filled with doubts": Sanora Babb to RWE, n.d. [Nov. 1941], RWEP, LC. For written permission to quote from her letters, I am indebted to the late Sanora Babb.

148 "you consider your marriage gone": Sanora Babb to RWE, n.d. [Jan. 1942], RWEP, LC.

148 "I am not a Negrophile": Ibid.

148 "the way you smiled": Sanora Babb to RWE, Feb. 7, 1942, RWEP, LC.

149 "I did not get into racial problems": Sanora Babb to RWE, n.d. [Dec. 1941], RWEP, LC.

149 "I kept remembering": Ibid.

149 "You said to me": Sanora Babb to RWE, Feb. 7, 1942.

149 "Darling, why don't you write": Sanora Babb to RWE, n.d. [Jan. 1942], RWEP, LC.

149 "You may tell me": Ibid.

149 "Your nationality was mentioned": Sanora Babb to RWE, n.d. [Dec. 1941], RWEP, LC.

150 "Did you know these things": Sanora Babb to RWE, Feb. 7, 1942.

150 "I think I will always hear": Ibid.

150 "After all these things": Ibid.

151 "one of the best critical pieces": John Stuart to RWE, Nov. 27, 1941, RWEP, LC.

151 "into a catalogue": RWE, "The Great Migration," *New Masses* (Dec. 2, 1941): 23. See also RWE's revision, "Transition," *Negro Quarterly* 1 (Spring 1942): 90.

153 "to treat critically all aspects": "Statement of Policy," *Negro Quarterly* 1 (Spring 1942): 3.

153 "I was a functioning editor": RWE to Mrs. Robert Polsgrove, Jan. 9, 1969, RWEP, LC.

153 "Jazz, like the country": RWE, "The Charlie Christian Story," in *The Collected Essays of Ralph Ellison*, ed. John F. Callahan (New York: Modern Library, 1995), p. 266.

154 "a most fruitful relationship": RWE to Frederick Clayton, April 30, 1942, RWEP, LC.

154 "The biggest literary project in history": Monty Noam Penkower, *The Federal Writers' Project: A Study in Government Patronage of the Arts* (Urbana: U of Illinois P, 1977), p. 237.

155 "deprived of their distinctive roles": Harry Slochower, "In the Fascist Styx," *Negro Quarterly* 1 (Fall 1942): 227.

155 "I viewed German culture": RWE to Fredric Kroll, April 8, 1985, RWEP, LC.

156 **"This is as it should be"**: RWE to John W. Barnes, May 2, 1942, RWEP, LC.

156 **"Negro writing awaited the emergence"**: "David Wilson" [RWE], "Treasury of Negro Literature," *Sunday Worker*, March 8, 1942.

157 **"we got to fight"**: RWE, "The Way It Is," *New Masses* (Oct. 20, 1942): 11.

157 **"during 1942 I found it necessary"**: RWE to A. B. Magil, Dec. 29, 1947, RWEP, LC.

157 **"It is our purpose"**: RWE to Eugene Holmes, May 2, 1942, RWEP, LC.

158 **"the genius of the Negro spirit"**: L. D. Reddick, "Publishers Are Awful," *Negro Quarterly* 1 (Summer 1942): 189.

158 *"this is a peoples' war"*: "Editorial Comment," *Negro Quarterly* 1 (Summer 1942): i.

158 **"a great gap"**: Abner W. Berry, " 'The Negro Quarterly,' A Vigorous Journal," *Daily Worker*, Sept. 15, 1942.

158 **"I went into it"**: RWE to Sanora Babb, July 4, 1943, RWEP, LC.

159 **"The thing to do"**: Stanley Edgar Hyman, "No Roots at All," *Negro Quarterly* 1 (Fall 1942): 274.

159 **"I have known of your work"**: RWE to Stanley Edgar Hyman, June 22, 1942, Stanley Edgar Hyman Papers, LC.

160 **"musical illiterate"**: *New Leader* 46 (Feb. 18, 1963): 21.

160 **"Feel free to send us anything"**: Stanley Edgar Hyman to RWE, July 12, 1942, Stanley Edgar Hyman Papers, LC.

160 **"No, I am not at all surprised"**: RWE to Stanley Edgar Hyman, n.d. [Aug. 1942], Stanley Edgar Hyman Papers, LC.

161 **"It is the first time"**: Michel Fabre, *The Unfinished Quest of Richard Wright* (New York: William Morrow, 1973), p. 240.

161 **"not reality in reverse"**: Ibid.

161 **"indeed, I felt"**: Richard Wright to Edward Aswell, Aug. 21, 1955, in Michel Fabre, *The Unfinished Quest of Richard Wright*, p. 230.

163 **"Guess you have been wondering"**: Angelo Herndon to RWE, April 9, 1943, RWEP, LC.

163 **"my job as managing editor"**: RWE to United States Selective Service, Local Board 58, March 3, 1943, RWEP, LC.

163 **"a fear and uncertainty"**: "Editorial Comment," *Negro Quarterly* 1 (Winter–Spring 1943): 295.

165 **"alone with the noise"**: RWE to Sanora Babb, July 4, 1943, RWEP, LC.

165 **"Wonderful country this"**: RWE to Stanley Edgar Hyman, June 2, 1943, Stanley Edgar Hyman Papers, LC.

165 **"Why the 'hell' don't you write?"**: Rose Poindexter Ellison to RWE, n.d. [May 1943], RWEP, LC.

165 **"You were always easy"**: RWE to Sanora Babb, July 4, 1943.

166 **"the poorer element's way"**: RWE, "Harlem 24 Hours After—Peace and Quiet Reign," *New York Post*, Aug. 3, 1943.

167 **"Ralph Ellison paints the picture"**: Mike Gold, "Change the World," *Daily Worker*, Aug. 6, 1943.

167 **"the pathetic and naïve nature"**: RWE, "Harlem 24 Hours After."

167 **"a dream deferred"**: Langston Hughes, "Harlem [2]," in *The Collected Poems of Langston Hughes,* ed. Arnold Rampersad (New York: Alfred A. Knopf, 1994), p. 426.

168 "was born in Oklahoma City": Affidavit from James L. Randolph of Oklahoma City, Sept. 11, 1943, RWEP, LC.

168 "In September Rose left me": RWE to Sanora Babb, Aug. 18, 1944, RWEP, LC.

168 "I like what your story says": *Harper's Bazaar* (Mary Louise Aswell) to RWE, Oct. 5, 1943, RWEP, LC.

168 "because I am a profound admirer": Henrietta Buckmaster to RWE, Oct. 9, 1943, RWEP, LC.

169 "being neither scholarly nor responsible journalism": RWE, "New World A-Coming," *Tomorrow* (Sept. 4, 1943): 67.

169 "particularly interested": William Morris Agency to RWE, Dec. 13, 1943, RWEP, LC.

7   *A Mighty Book, a Mighty Theme*

170 "It is the most democratic": RWE to Malcolm Whitby, Jan. 28, 1944, RWEP, LC.

170 "I love them": RWE to Sanora Babb, Aug. 18, 1944, RWEP, LC.

171 "some of the most expert": RWE, "The Red Cross at Morristown, Swansea, SW," ms., n.d., RWEP, LC.

171 "These here is some": Ibid.

171 "They, like the Russians": RWE to Sanora Babb, Aug. 18, 1944.

173 "an augury of wider recognition": Ida Guggenheimer to RWE, May 25, 1944, RWEP, LC.

173 "Well, I went to heaven": RWE, "Flying Home," in *Flying Home and Other Stories*, ed. John F. Callahan (New York: Vintage, 1998), pp. 147–73.

174 "a very remarkable story": *Chicago Tribune*, June 4, 1944.

174 "very nice to me": RWE to Ida Guggenheimer, June 26, 1944, RWEP, LC.

174 "white-hot protesting story": *New York Herald Tribune Weekly Book Review*, May 28, 1944.

174 "the Joycean interior monologue": *New Masses* (Sept. 26, 1944): 25.

175 "just sat there looking": *Oklahoma City Times*, Nov. 26, 1966.

175 "her husband's cruelty and extravagance": Fanny McConnell, ms., n.d. [1931], RWEP, LC.

175 "What has bothered me": Fanny Ellison to RWE, Oct. 1, 1958, RWEP, LC.

176 "a revolutionary effect": Fanny Ellison, ms., n.d., RWEP, LC.

176 "Between you and me": Fanny McConnell to Willie Mae Warren, Sept. 11, 1932, RWEP, LC.

176 "my old Alma Mater": Fanny Ellison to Stanley Edgar Hyman, Dec. 9, 1959, RWEP, LC.

177 "self-confident so much": Rodney G. Higgins to Fanny Higgins, June 29, 1937, RWEP, LC.

177 "How is the pretty": Lawrence C. Jones to Ligon Buford, July 25, 1938, RWEP, LC.

177 "It is no such thing": Fanny McConnell to Negro People's Theatre, March 20, 1938, RWEP, LC.

178 "marks the first time": Fanny Buford to Ligon Buford, March 8, 1944, RWEP, LC.

178 "accept our friendship": Ligon Buford to Fanny Buford, June 1, 1944, RWEP, LC.

178 "the lonely young man": Fanny Ellison, ms., n.d., RWEP, LC.

178 "There was a time": RWE to Ida Guggenheimer, June 26, 1944, RWEP, LC.

178 "the most ambitious": Ibid.

179 "a typical Babbitt watering place": RWE to Ida Guggenheimer, July 13, 1944, RWEP, LC.

179 "I am flat broke": Ibid.

180 "I did hear the rumor": RWE to Richard Wright, Sept. 5, 1944, RWEP, LC.

180 "latest ravings": Ibid.

180 "ridiculously uninformed": *Daily Worker*, Aug. 6, 1944.

180 "shameful manner": *Daily Worker*, Sept. 5, 1944.

180 "deep feelings of humiliation": RWE, "Statement of Plan of Work," n.d. [1944], RWEP, LC.

181 "Interned Fliers Got Set": *New York Sunday News*, Sept. 3, 1944.

181 "a mess of loose ends": RWE to *Antioch Review* (Paul Bixler), Nov. 30, 1944, RWEP, LC.

181 "This rather brash review": RWE, ms., n.d. [1964], RWEP, LC.

182 "What a kick in the teeth": RWE to Stanley Edgar Hyman, June 7, 1945, RWEP, LC.

182 "YOUR SILENCE PREVENTING WORK": RWE to Fanny Buford, Oct. 5, 1944, RWEP, LC.

182 "NOTHING HAS CHANGED": Fanny Buford to RWE, Oct. 5, 1944, RWEP, LC.

182 "Like a lovesick fool": RWE to Fanny Buford, Oct. 6, 1944, RWEP, LC.

183 "it was while writing": Jerre Mangione, *The Dream and the Deal: The Federal Writers' Project, 1935–1943* (Boston: Little, Brown, 1972), p. 256.

183 "He only felt the dull pain": RWE, "King of the Bingo Game," *Tomorrow* 4 (Nov. 1944): 33.

184 "The most promising": *Chicago Sun Book Week*, Dec. 3, 1944.

184 "wondering if Ralph would keep his word": Constance Webb (Mrs. Edward Pearlstein) to RWE, Jan. 7, 1966, RWEP, LC.

184 "What a horrible life": RWE to Fanny Buford, March 10, 1945, RWEP, LC.

185 "work and petty quarrels": RWE to Fanny Buford, March 1, 1945, RWEP, LC.

185 "the country where I've always desired": RWE to Fanny Buford, draft, March 5, 1945, RWEP, LC.

185 "And you see many of our Negro boys": RWE to Fanny Buford, March 10, 1945, RWEP, LC.

186 "what are the symbols": RWE to Richard Wright, Aug. 18, 1945, Richard Wright Papers, Beinecke Library, Yale University.

186 "Even the negative symbols": RWE to Fanny Buford, March 10, 1945.

186 "the stupidity and chauvinism": Ibid.

186 "a minor operation": Ibid.

186 "when I came home": Fanny Buford to RWE, March 30, 1945, RWEP, LC.

186 "I love you enough": RWE to Fanny Buford, March 1, 1945.

186 "Bobbins told me": Fanny Buford to RWE, Feb. 22, 1945, RWEP, LC.

187 "Truly you bear out the theory": Fanny Buford to RWE, March 17, 1945, RWEP, LC.

187 "Love, Rose": Rose Poindexter to RWE, July 2, 1945, RWEP, LC.

187 "I have been at work": RWE to Rosenwald Fund (Dorothy A. Elvidge), July 8, 1945, RWEP, LC.

187 "much different from what": RWE to *Antioch Review* (Paul Bixler), May 14, 1945, RWEP, LC.

188 "The blues is an impulse": RWE, "Richard Wright's Blues," in *Shadow and Act* (New York: Vintage, 1995), p. 78.

188 "forget that human life": Ibid., pp. 80–81.

189 "overrated": RWE to Richard Wright, Aug. 5, 1945, Richard Wright Papers, Yale.

189 "If he never yields": Kenneth Burke to Stanley Edgar Hyman, Dec. 4, 1945, Stanley Edgar Hyman Papers, LC.

189 "should be obvious": RWE, "Richard Wright's Blues," p. 93.

189 "I am so ashamed": Ida Guggenheimer to RWE, Aug. 9, 1945, RWEP, LC.

189 "We have become the fathers": RWE to Richard Wright, July 22, 1945, Richard Wright Papers, Yale.

190 "All in all": Ibid.

190 "the greatest joke": Ibid.

190 "So you and Wright": RWE to Richard Wright, Aug. 5, 1945, RWEP, LC.

190 "France is in ferment": RWE to Richard Wright, July 22, 1945, RWEP, LC.

191 "By becoming a part": Ibid.

192 "Beyond the mountains": RWE to Ida Guggenheimer, Aug. 13, 1945, RWEP, LC.

192 "It is truly no land": Ibid.

192 "This country was hewn": Ibid.

193 "I'm told that there is quite a lot": Ibid.

193 "an anemic fox-trot": RWE to Richard Wright, Aug. 18, 1945, Richard Wright Papers, Yale.

194 "In the summer of 1945": RWE, "The Art of Fiction: An Interview," *Shadow and Act,* p. 176.

194 "a cheeky, snobbish": Stanley Edgar Hyman, *The Armed Vision: A Study in the Methods of Modern Literary Criticism*, rev. ed., abridged (New York: Vintage, 1955), p. 125.

194 "What will they think": Fanny Buford to RWE, March 17, 1945.

194 "down upon paper": RWE to Ida Guggenheimer, July 13, 1944, RWEP, LC.

195 "I have considered the possibility": RWE to Richard Wright, Aug. 5, 1945, Richard Wright Papers, Yale.

195 "I am an invisible man": RWE, "The invisible Man," ms., n.d. [1945], RWEP, LC.

196 "One often hears of writers": Herman Melville, *Moby-Dick,* ed. Alfred Kazin (Boston: Houghton Mifflin, 1956), p. 350.

196 "There was a time when": RWE to Richard Wright, Aug. 18, 1945, Richard Wright Papers, Yale.

196 "I think our destiny": Ibid.

197 "intuition" to reject: Ibid.

197 "Fanny is reading Kafka": RWE to Stanley Edgar Hyman, Aug. 21, 1945, Stanley Edgar Hyman Papers, LC.

197 "Perhaps I like Louis Armstrong": RWE, *Invisible Man* (New York: Modern Library, 1952), p. 6.

198 "This section of the novel": RWE to Stanley Edgar Hyman, Aug. 21, 1945.

8   *The Agon of Writing*

199 **"enter the hell"**: RWE to Stanley Edgar Hyman, Aug. 21, 1945, Stanley Edgar Hyman Papers, LC.

199 **"an eminently distinguished piece"**: *English Journal* (Sept. 1945): 399.

199 **"I don't expect"**: RWE to Ida Guggenheimer, Aug. 14, 1945, RWEP, LC.

199 **"Negro books, of course"**: RWE to Stanley Edgar Hyman, Aug. 21, 1945.

199 **"literary program"**: Viking Press (Pascal Covici) to RWE, Sept. 5, 1945, RWEP, LC.

200 **"a nightmarishly 'absurd' situation"**: RWE, "Beating That Boy," *New Republic* 113 (Oct. 22, 1945): 535.

200 **"underground of the American conscience"**: Ibid.

200 **"profound"**: Thomas Sancton, "Unfinished Business," *New Republic* (Dec. 3, 1945): 770.

200 **"too superficial, too vague"**: Stanley Edgar Hyman to RWE, Oct. 27, 1945, RWEP, LC.

201 **"the broader conceptional framework"**: RWE to Bennington College (Sonia Grodka), Oct. 23, 1945, RWEP, LC.

201 **"Today, most Negro writing"**: *Bennington Evening Banner*, Nov. 2, 1945.

202 **"Welcome, O life!"**: James Joyce, *A Portrait of the Artist as a Young Man* (Harmondsworth: Penguin, 1992), pp. 275–76.

202 **"The Negro writers must know"**: RWE, "Joyce and Wright," ms. [transcript of lecture], Nov. 2, 1945, RWEP, LC.

202 **"Negro Writer Gives Lecture"**: *Bennington Evening Banner*, Nov. 2, 1945.

202 **"fell completely in love"**: RWE to Bennington College (Sonia Grodka), n.d. [Nov. 1945], RWEP, LC.

202 **"teasing and provoking Ralph"**: Michael S. Harper to author, interview, March 16, 2000.

203 **"a sea of prose"**: Dust jacket of Chester Himes, *If He Hollers Let Him Go* (New York: Doubleday, Doran, 1945).

203 **"the school perhaps founded"**: *Chicago Defender*, Dec. 22, 1945.

203 **"the *agon* of writing"**: RWE to Maxwell Geismar, March 10, 1946, RWEP, LC.

204 **"the heir of Abolitionists"**: RWE, "The Booker T," *New Republic* (Feb. 18, 1946): 262.

204 **"the nice patient guys"**: Russell & Volkening, Inc. (Henry Volkening) to RWE, March 8, 1946, RWEP, LC.

204 **"I have great misgivings"**: RWE to Russell & Volkening, Inc. (Henry Volkening), n.d., RWEP, LC.

204 **"I myself know only this"**: Ibid.

205 **"playing a game with myself"**: RWE, ms., untitled, n.d., RWEP, LC.

205 **"was moved to adopt you"**: RWE to Kenneth Burke, n.d., RWEP, LC.

205 **"the unification of every discipline"**: Stanley Edgar Hyman, *The Armed Vision: A Study in the Methods of Modern Literary Criticism*, rev. ed., abridged (New York: Vintage, 1955), p. 360.

206 **"the process embodied in tragedy"**: Kenneth Burke, "The Tactics of Motivation," *Chimera* 1 (Spring 1943): 27.

206 **"One of the most important things"**: RWE to Kenneth Burke, n.d., RWEP, LC.

206 "about two-thirds": RWE to Julius Rosenwald Fund (William C. Haygood), April 22, 1946, RWEP, LC.

207 "for another 12 months": *New York Amsterdam News*, April 27, 1946.

207 "Harlem is killing me": RWE to Richard Wright, Aug. 18, 1945, Richard Wright Papers, Beinecke Library, Yale University.

208 "a feeling of responsibility": James B. Reibman, "Ralph Ellison, Frederic Wertham, M.D., and the LaFargue Clinic: Civil Rights and Psychiatric Services in Harlem," *Oklahoma City University Law Review* 26 (Fall 2001): 1044.

208 "Not only is it the sole mental clinic": RWE, "Harlem Is Nowhere," in *Shadow and Act* (New York: Vintage, 1995), p. 295.

208 "money, the table": RWE to Richard Wright, June 24, 1946, Richard Wright Papers, Yale.

208 "He has aged visibly": Ibid.

208 "a serious contribution": RWE, "Stepchild Fantasy," *Saturday Review of Literature* (June 8, 1946): 26.

209 "You must know": Ida Guggenheimer to RWE and Fanny Ellison, Aug. 29, 1946, RWEP, LC.

209 "We promised you": RWE and Fanny Ellison to Ellen Wright, Sept. 23, 1946, RWEP, LC.

210 "How is it": RWE, "Twentieth-Century Fiction and the Black Mask of Humanity," in *The Collected Essays of Ralph Ellison*, ed. John F. Callahan (New York: Modern Library, 1995), p. 83.

210 "For one thing": RWE to *Survey Graphic* (Paul Kellogg), Dec. 29, 1946, RWEP, LC.

211 "hear something of your novel": Reynal & Hitchcock, Inc. (Mrs. Curtice [Margaret] Hitchcock) to RWE, April 15, 1947, RWEP, LC.

212 "I can only be useful here": Anaïs Nin, *The Diary of Anaïs Nin, 1944–47* (New York: Harcourt, Brace, 1971), pp. 212–14.

212 "Harlem is a ruin": RWE, "Harlem Is Nowhere," *Shadow and Act*, pp. 295–96.

213 "one of the kindest": RWE to Ida Guggenheimer, Aug. 16, 1947, RWEP, LC.

213 "much larger than our apartment": RWE to Langston Hughes, Aug. 25, 1947, Langston Hughes Papers, Beinecke Library, Yale University.

213 "There are no cats": Ibid.

214 "and there she lay": RWE to Fanny Ellison, Sept. 24, 1947, RWEP, LC.

214 "Down in Bennington": RWE to Ida Guggenheimer, Oct. 8, 1947, RWEP, LC.

215 "I have known it": RWE to Fanny Ellison, Oct. 13, 1947, RWEP, LC.

215 "My dear, all my former lovers": Fanny Ellison to RWE, Oct. 15, 1947, RWEP, LC.

215 "It's lonely here": RWE to Fanny Ellison, Sept. 20, 1947, RWEP, LC.

215 "It's as if my breath": Fanny Ellison to RWE, Sept. 29, 1947, RWEP, LC.

215 "Preparing for you": Fanny Ellison to RWE, Oct. 15, 1947.

215 "I'm very excited": RWE to Fanny Ellison, Sept. 17, 1947, RWEP, LC.

216 "we now have the Steins": Fanny Ellison to RWE, Sept. 29, 1947.

216 "I glory in knowing you": Ida Guggenheimer to RWE, Oct. 8, 1947, RWEP, LC.

216 "the most extraordinary and moving work": *Harper's Bazaar* (Pearl Kazin) to RWE, Oct. 27, 1947, RWEP, LC.

216 "by far the most remarkable piece of writing": *Irish Times*, Oct. 25, 1947.

216 "Hooray! Hooray!": Frank Taylor to RWE, n.d., RWEP, LC.

216 "the erection which projected from": RWE, "Invisible Man," *Horizon* (Oct. 1947): 108.

217 "exceptionally fine": *'48: The Magazine of the Year* (Richard E. Lauterbach) to RWE, Jan. 29, 1948, RWEP, LC.

217 "All in all": RWE to Richard Wright, Feb. 1, 1948, Richard Wright Papers, Yale.

217 "the color of a baboon's butt": RWE, *Invisible Man* (New York: Modern Library, 1952), p. 16.

218 "Would that all of my readers": RWE to Kenneth Burke, n.d., RWEP, LC.

218 "to be read as a near-allegory": RWE to *'48: The Magazine of the Year* (Walter Ross), March 1, 1948, RWEP, LC.

219 "Personally I was disappointed": RWE to Richard Wright, Feb. 1, 1948.

219 "your recent work": Ibid.

219 "I am working on a piece": Ibid.

220 "Who is this total Negro": RWE, "Harlem Is Nowhere," *Collected Essays of Ralph Ellison*, p. 321.

220 "life becomes a masquerade": Ibid., p. 322.

221 "a thousand Lafargue clinics": Ibid., p. 327.

221 "I've worked out a scheme": RWE to Richard Wright, Feb. 1, 1948.

221 "The article developed into": RWE to Edward Weinfeld, Sept. 29, 1948, RWEP, LC.

222 "the days when Ralph and I": Fanny Ellison to Langston Hughes, April 2, 1952, Langston Hughes Papers, Yale.

222 "but has studiedly refused": RWE to Richard Wright, Feb. 1, 1948.

222 "My permission is hereby denied": RWE to A. B. Magil, Dec. 19, 1947, RWEP, LC.

223 "would want to disdain": *New Masses* (Charles Humboldt) to RWE, Dec. 23, 1947, RWEP, LC.

223 "I'm getting some of the same reactions": RWE to Richard Wright, Feb. 1, 1948.

9   *In the Home Stretch*

224 "You must be in the home-stretch": Frank Taylor to RWE, Oct. 18, 1948, RWEP, LC.

225 "about eighty-five years ago": RWE, *Invisible Man* (New York: Modern Library, 1952), p. 13.

229 "It's time we here": RWE to Stanley Edgar Hyman, Feb. 21, 1949, Stanley Edgar Hyman Papers, LC.

229 "normal in every respect": Margaret Sanger Research Bureau to RWE, Nov. 16, 1948, RWEP, LC.

229 "Ralph told me one day": Charlotte Wilbur to author, interview, May 11, 2000.

230 "I had moved on": Sanora Babb to author, interview, Feb. 18, 2003.

231 "grounded in the past": Ibid.

231 "Dear Ralph": Sanora Babb to RWE, May 17, 1948, RWEP, LC.

232 "He told me he had picked up": Harriet Davidson to author, interview, Dec. 10, 2005.

232 "One of my sisters": Martha Bernard to author, interview, May 10, 2001.

233 "Our quarters are very small": Fanny Ellison to Adam Clayton Powell, Jr., April 16, 1948, RWEP, LC.

234 "I get the feeling": RWE to Albert Murray, Jan. 24, 1950, RWEP, LC.

234 "I talked with one of the editors": RWE to Richard Wright, Oct. 12, 1949, RWEP, LC.

234 "previous editorial commitments": RWE to *Harlem Quarterly* (Miss Barnes), June 19, 1950, RWEP, LC.

235 "I was amused": RWE to Stanley Edgar Hyman, Oct. 27, 1949, Stanley Edgar Hyman Papers, LC.

236 "a little black man": RWE, *Invisible Man* (New York: Random House, 1952), p. 559.

237 "Interestingly enough": RWE, "Introduction to *Invisible Man*," in *The Collected Essays of Ralph Ellison*, ed. John F. Callahan (New York: Modern Library, 1995), p. 472.

237 "With some": RWE to Stanley Edgar Hyman, Aug. 13, 1948, Stanley Edgar Hyman Papers, LC.

237 "had I not been consciously concerned": RWE, "Introduction to *Invisible Man*," p. 472.

237 "Now that nigger *there*": Ibid., p. 473.

238 "If Shirley does anything else": RWE to Stanley Edgar Hyman, Aug. 13, 1948.

238 "the ancestry of their techniques": Stanley Edgar Hyman, *The Armed Vision: A Study in the Methods of Modern Literary Criticism*, rev. ed., abridged (New York: Vintage, 1955), p. 360.

238 "I know that it is fast becoming": RWE to Stanley Edgar Hyman, Aug. 13, 1948.

238 "Ralph and I": R. W. B. and Nancy Lewis to author, interview, May 12, 2000.

239 "You missed a fine party": Stanley Edgar Hyman to RWE, April 5, 1949, Stanley Edgar Hyman Papers, LC.

239 "It was, 'That Shirley Jackson's' ": Judy Oppenheimer, *Private Demons: The Life of Shirley Jackson* (New York: G. P. Putnam's Sons, 1988), p. 181.

239 "One misses any conception": RWE, "A Journalist Considers the Position of the Negro in American History," *New York Star*, Dec. 12, 1948.

240 "I do get myself into": RWE to Stanley Edgar Hyman, Feb. 21, 1949, Stanley Edgar Hyman Papers, LC.

241 "Why should a man deliberately plunge": RWE, *Invisible Man*, pp. 438–39.

241 "the uncreated conscience": James Joyce, *A Portrait of the Artist as a Young Man* (Harmondsworth: Penguin, 1992), p. 276.

241 "the splendid photographs you took": Howard Nemerov to RWE, n.d. [1948], RWEP, LC.

242 "I did some ambulance chasing": RWE, transcript of interview, National Educational Television, Nov. 4–18, 1965, RWEP, LC.

242 "to get the dam[n] thing ready": RWE to Stanley Edgar Hyman, Feb. 21, 1949.

243 "I have become so disgusted": RWE to Richard Wright, Feb. 1, 1948, Richard Wright Papers, Beinecke Library, Yale University.

244 "the most important thing happening": *Chicago Defender*, Feb. 5, 1949.

244 "Red Visitors Cause Rumpus": *Life* 26 (April 4, 1949): 39.

244 "It got my back up": RWE, interview, National Educational Television.

245 "My grandmother not only stuck by": Martha Bernard to author, interview, May 10, 2001.

245 "a very advanced philosophy": RWE, "A Journalist Considers the Position of the Negro in American History."

246 **"I have made further cuts"**: RWE to Stanley Edgar Hyman, Oct. 27, 1949, Stanley Edgar Hyman Papers, LC.

10   *Finish Line*

248 **"forged the twin screen image"**: RWE, "The Shadow and the Act," *Reporter*, Dec. 6, 1949.

248 **"I reject Faulkner"**: RWE to Peter D. Bunzel, April 3, 1950, RWEP, LC.

249 **"through playing the obscene game"**: RWE, "Collaborator with His Own Enemy," *New York Times Book Review*, Feb. 19, 1950.

250 **"Ralph in Bed All Day"**: Fanny Ellison, note in 1950 "Day Book," RWEP, LC.

251 **"Just all of a sudden"**: Fanny Ellison to Elsa and Kuno Brandel, Jan. 17, 1952, RWEP, LC.

251 **"I asked him at once"**: David Sarser to author, interview, Feb. 10, 2000.

251 **"It was while I was there"**: Ibid.

252 **"He was always for anything new"**: Ibid.

252 **"he had been taught"**: Saul Bellow, "Ralph Ellison in Tivoli," *Partisan Review* 65:4 (1998): 526.

252 **"When the radio isn't playing loud"**: Fanny Ellison to Elsa and Kuno Brandel, Jan. 17, 1952.

253 **"and all week Ralph has been walking"**: Fanny Ellison to Beatrice Steegmuller, Aug. 1, 1950, RWEP, LC.

253 **"Forget him"**: RWE, *Invisible Man* (New York: Modern Library, 1952), p. 346.

253 **"quite exciting"**: RWE to Stanley Edgar Hyman, Feb. 21, 1949, RWEP, LC.

253 **"Outside the Brotherhood"**: RWE, *Invisible Man*, p. 377.

254 **"It is such a good book"**: Fanny Ellison to Elsa Brandel, Sept. 25, 1950, RWEP, LC.

254 **"great invisible waves of time"**: RWE, *Invisible Man,* p. 428.

255 **"Here, at least"**: Ibid., p. 571.

255 **"The end was in the beginning"**: T. S. Eliot, *Four Quartets,* in *The Complete Poems and Plays, 1909–1950* (New York: Harcourt, Brace & World, 1962), p. 123.

256 **"After failing to hear"**: RWE to Ellen Wright, March 26, 1952, RWEP, LC.

256 **"we hereby relinquish all rights"**: Russell & Volkening, Inc. (Henry Volkening) to RWE, Nov. 2, 1951, RWEP, LC.

256 **"a man's feelings"**: RWE, *Invisible Man*, p. 433.

256 **"I want you to overcome"**: Ibid., pp. 13–14.

256 **"my world has become"**: Ibid., p. 435.

257 **"I'm coming out"**: Ibid., p. 438.

257 **"Who knows but that"**: Ibid., p. 439.

258 **"we all had enough to drink"**: Judy Oppenheimer, *Private Demons: The Life of Shirley Jackson* (New York: G. P. Putnam's Sons, 1988), p. 157.

258 **"The damn baby"**: Ibid.

259 **"an extremely powerful story"**: *Virginia Kirkus Bulletin*, Feb. 1952.

259 **"You've created a work of such stature"**: Chester Aaron to RWE, n.d., RWEP, LC.

259 **"I think it beautifully conceived"**: Morteza Drexel Sprague to RWE, March 29, 1952, RWEP, LC.

259 **"We feel these days"**: Fanny Ellison to Langston Hughes, April 2, 1952, Langston Hughes Papers, Beinecke Library, Yale University.

259 **"You must gonna be great"**: Langston Hughes to Fanny Ellison, n.d. [March 1952], Langston Hughes Papers, Yale.

260 **"you are carried forward"**: *Saturday Review of Literature* (April 12, 1952): 33.

260 **"remarkable first novel"**: *Time* (April 14, 1952): 112.

260 **"a sensational and feverishly emotional book"**: *New York Times*, April 16, 1952.

260 **"rather murky"**: *New York Herald Tribune*, April 16, 1952.

260 **"the young dark Ulysses"**: *New York Herald Tribune Book Review*, April 13, 1952.

260 **"The geography of hell"**: *New York Times Book Review*, April 12, 1952.

261 **"but it is an immensely moving novel"**: Saul Bellow, "Man Underground," *Commentary* (June 1952): 608–9.

261 **"Of course 'Invisible Man' "**: Irving Howe, "Ralph Ellison's *Invisible Man*," *Nation* (May 10, 1952): 454.

261 **"For the most part brilliantly written"**: *New York World-Telegram*, April 16, 1952.

261 **"I am stewing"**: RWE to Harold Calicutt, April 21, 1952, RWEP, LC.

261 **"a new and startling revelation"**: Fanny Ellison to Marjorie Greene, May 13, 1952, RWEP, LC.

261 **"the scornful power"**: *Washington Post*, April 20, 1952.

261 **"a very formidable"**: *Nashville Tennessean*, April 27, 1952.

261 **"extremely unpleasant reading"**: *Charleston* (South Carolina) *Gazette*, July 19, 1952.

262 **"The book's fault"**: *Baltimore Afro-American*, May 10, 1952.

262 **"a bright and shining new Negro literary star"**: *Jet* (April 17, 1952).

262 **"conforming exactly to the formula"**: *Masses & Mainstream* (June 1952): 62–64.

262 **"Ellison's work manipulates"**: *Daily Worker*, June 1, 1952.

262 **"The Negro people need"**: Cited by Larry Neal in *Black World* (Dec. 1970): 36.

262 **"only made members desire"**: RWE to Richard Wright, Jan. 2, 1953, RWEP, LC.

262 **"and has used every opportunity"**: RWE to Richard Wright, Jan. 21, 1953, Richard Wright Papers, Beinecke Library, Yale University..

263 **"has literally been stormed"**: Rabbi Kurt L. Metzger to RWE, July 31, 1952, RWEP, LC.

263 **"finally get around to reading"**: Richard Wright to RWE, May 27, 1952, RWEP, LC.

264 **"His face is firm"**: *New York Times*, May 4, 1952.

264 **"It has been very amusing"**: RWE to Richard Wright, Jan. 21, 1953, RWEP, LC.

264 **"very real success"**: Mrs. R. Lloyd Douglas to Fanny Ellison, June 7, 1952, RWEP, LC.

264 **"The joke, of course"**: RWE, *Invisible Man*, p. 5.

265 **"apartment houses on Riverside Drive"**: Fanny Ellison to Renée Petersen, n.d. [July 1951], RWEP, LC.

265 **"I always thought of Riverside Drive"**: Stanley Edgar Hyman to RWE, Nov. 21, 1952, RWEP, LC.

265 **"Brother Wolf is at the door"**: Stanley Edgar Hyman to RWE, Jan. 12, 1953, RWEP, LC.

266 **"a novel which demands"**: RWE to Richard Wright, Jan. 21, 1953.

267 **"Now my instincts tell me"**: Ibid.

11   Annus Mirabilis

268 "Congratulations": *Twin City Sentinel* (Winston-Salem, North Carolina), March 17, 1953.

268 "a work of near-genius": *Observer* (London), Jan. 25, 1953.

268 "I spent the next 24 hours": *Twin City Sentinel*, March 17, 1953.

268 "This is absolutely on the q.t.": Ibid.

268 "I thought something was wrong": Ibid.

269 "possibly the languishing Pulitzer nominations": *Saturday Review of Literature* (Feb. 7, 1953): 17.

269 "just about the biggest literary event": Program notes, National Book Awards presentation ceremony, Jan. 27, 1953.

269 "Watch out for Bellow's novel": RWE to Richard Wright, Jan. 21, 1953, Richard Wright Papers, Beinecke Library, Yale University.

269 "With a positive exuberance": "Statement by the Fiction Jury," National Book Awards, ms., n.d. [Jan. 1953], RWEP, LC.

270 "it took me five days": *Twin City Sentinel*, March 17, 1953.

270 "the most literary": *Washington Star*, Feb. 1, 1953.

270 "the chief significance": RWE, "Brave Words for a Startling Occasion," Address, National Book Awards presentation ceremony, Jan. 27, 1953, RWEP, LC. In *The Collected Essays of Ralph Ellison*, ed. John F. Callahan (New York: Modern Library, 1995), p. 151.

271 "A small graying man": *Washington Star*, Feb. 1, 1953.

272 "I look back frequently": Robert Penn Warren to RWE, Jan. 12, 1953, RWEP, LC.

272 "this hell of a schedule": RWE to Robert Penn Warren, Feb. 6, 1953, RWEP, LC.

272 "to be faring quite well": Kenneth Burke to Stanley Edgar Hyman, n.d. [Jan. 1953], Stanley Edgar Hyman Papers, LC.

273 "how you want me to behave": RWE to Mrs. Joseph Mueller, May 20, 1953, RWEP, LC.

273 "Usually such awards": Theodore Roethke to RWE, Jan. 29, 1953, RWEP, LC.

273 "was not, I believe": *Bridgeport Sunday Post* (Connecticut), Feb. 1, 1953.

273 "a worthy prize winner": *Cleveland News*, Feb. 3, 1953.

273 "While applauding Mr. Ellison's sincerity": *Christian Science Monitor*, Feb. 5, 1953.

273 "now another ubiquitous Negro": *New York Amsterdam News*, March 14, 1953.

273 "I did not want my wife to read it": *Pittsburgh Courier*, April 4, 1953.

274 "For the first time": RWE to Richard Wright, Jan. 21, 1953, Richard Wright Papers, Yale.

274 "any application": John Simon Guggenheim Memorial Foundation (Josephine Leighton) to RWE, June 17, 1953, RWEP, LC.

274 "an almost direct link": "Faulkner, 'The Bear,'" transcript of radio broadcast, Feb. 8, 1953, RWEP, LC.

274 "Folklore is concerned only": *Dayton Journal*, April 30, 1953.

275 "sometimes strained and fumbling": *New York Herald Tribune Book Review*, March 22, 1953.

275 "was quite unfair": RWE to Stanley Edgar Hyman, April 1, 1953, Stanley Edgar Hyman Papers, LC.

275 "I have lost the delight": RWE to Richard Wright, Jan. 21, 1953, Richard Wright Papers, Yale.

276 "a splendid piece of work": C. L. R. James to RWE, April 30, 1953, RWEP, LC.

276 "For several weeks": Fanny Ellison, ms., n.d., RWEP, LC.

276 "Man must discard": RWE, notes for class visit, City College of New York, March 5, 1953.

276 "I am not trying": *CCNY Main Events*, March 23, 1953.

277 "courage, a cold, hard eye": *Greensboro Daily News* (North Carolina), March 16, 1953.

277 "No man for literary finery": *Twin City Sentinel*, March 17, 1953.

277 "that I found myself carried back": RWE to May Belle DeWitt Johnston, April 2, 1953, RWEP, LC.

278 "opened up vistas": RWE to Alexander and Juanita Morrisey, April 9, 1953, RWEP, LC.

278 "Ralph Ellison, the young Negro author": *Greensboro Daily News*, March 16, 1953.

278 "as I would like to sneak in": RWE to May Belle DeWitt Johnston, April 2, 1953.

278 "They're calling me Rinehart": RWE to Alexander and Juanita Morrisey, April 9, 1953, RWEP, LC.

279 "There is no racial novel": *Nashville Banner*, April 24, 1953.

279 "I think the great problem": Ibid.

280 "After a man makes $10,000": *Time* 61 (May 11, 1953): 58.

280 "I addressed my book": RWE to *Chicago Defender* (John Sengstacke), Jan. 15, 1953, RWEP, LC.

280 "upholding those highest traditions": National Newspaper Publishers Association to RWE, April 1, 1953, RWEP, LC.

280 "Few things during this most eventful period": RWE to National Newspaper Publishers Association, May 4, 1953, RWEP, LC.

281 "always admired": RWE to [Gwendolyn Brooks?], Dec. 23, 1963, RWEP, LC.

281 "the deficiency immediately declares itself": *New Yorker* (June 21, 1953): 93.

281 "*Is Mr. Norton*": "Lecture Notes: Hunter College, Marshall Stern's [Stearns] Class—the Novel," May 27, 1953, RWEP, LC.

282 "I am to be asked formally": RWE to Fanny Ellison, July 2, 1953, RWEP, LC.

283 "who, before I knew him": RWE, inscription in William L. Dawson's copy of *Invisible Man*, Robert W. Woodruff Library, Emory University.

283 "There is so much": RWE to May Belle DeWitt Johnston, April 2, 1953, RWEP, LC.

283 "where I spent some of the happiest years": RWE to Fanny Ellison, July 2, 1953, RWEP, LC.

283 "Did very well too": RWE to Othello "Bert" Brown, June 8, 1954, RWEP, LC.

284 "The city has changed": Ibid.

284 "As far as he will let me know": RWE to May Belle DeWitt Johnston, April 2, 1953.

284 "we ha[d] such wonderful times": RWE to Herbert Ellison, Aug. 12, 1954, RWEP, LC.

284 "a wonderful write up": May Belle DeWitt Johnston to RWE, March 5, 1953, RWEP, LC.

284 "because I thought": *Daily Oklahoman*, July 10, 1953.

285 "everyone who saw Ralph": May Belle DeWitt Johnston to Fanny Ellison, July 27, 1953, RWEP, LC.

285 "Already I can see": RWE to Fanny Ellison, July 2, 1953.

285 "My skin has burned": Ibid.

286 "looking younger and very handsome": Fanny Ellison to Random House (Ethel Greenberg), n.d., RWEP, LC.

286 "and we will be talking": Fanny Ellison to May Belle DeWitt Johnston, July 21, 1953, RWEP, LC.

286 "If we ever have a boy": RWE to James L. Randolph, Sept. 18, 1953, RWEP, LC.

287 "And it was then": RWE, "Address to Harvard College Alumni, Class of 1949," *Collected Essays of Ralph Ellison*, p. 419.

287 "Upon them a discontinuity": Ibid., p. 420.

287 "once we began the discussions": RWE to James L. Randolph, Sept. 18, 1953.

288 "your violent reaction": Karl E. Nyren to RWE, Sept. 30, 1953, RWEP, LC.

288 "making a mockery of everything": RWE to Francis Ames Randall, Aug. 31, 1953, RWEP, LC.

288 "I am most eager": Henry Kissinger to RWE, Aug. 11, 1953, RWEP, LC.

288 "one of the high points": RWE to Henry Kissinger, Aug. 13, 1953, RWEP, LC.

288 "one of the most mixed": Fanny Ellison to Richard and Edith Weaver, Aug. 25, 1953, RWEP, LC.

289 "I began to think": Ibid.

289 "It was not until the morning": Ibid.

289 "You know how he can't bear": Ibid.

290 "The whole experience": Ibid.

290 "We live in Puerto Rico": Fanny Ellison to Mrs. Sidney Mintz, June [July] 1, 1953, RWEP, LC.

291 "We had a very good cleaning woman": Nancy Lewis to author, interview, July 1, 2006.

292 "Don't laugh": RWE to Melvin B. Tolson, Nov. 24, 1953, RWEP, LC.

292 "quite a landmark": Antioch College (Paul Bixler) to RWE, Dec. 16, 1953, RWEP, LC.

292 "He declined to discuss it": *Antioch Record*, Dec. 4, 1953.

12   *Second Act*

293 "everybody knows": Albert Murray to RWE, n.d. [Jan. 1954], RWEP, LC.

294 "spoke from the hip": RWE to Fanny Ellison, Feb. 23, 1954, RWEP, LC.

294 "We stand now at the crisis": *Tuskegee Institute Herald*, Feb. 23, 1954.

294 "needling both students and teachers": RWE to Fanny Ellison, March 4, 1954, RWEP, LC.

294 "I asked them": RWE to Fanny Ellison, Feb. 23, 1954.

294 "an uproarious time laughing": RWE to Fanny Ellison, March 4, 1954.

295 "Carver was a conjure man": Ibid.

295 "because I was being entertained": Ibid.

295 "right in the turbulence": RWE to Fanny Ellison, Feb. 23, 1954.

295 "quite handsome, and tropical": RWE to Fanny Ellison, March 4, 1954.

296 "I'm excited about the book": RWE to Stanley Edgar Hyman, March 12, 1954, Stanley Edgar Hyman Papers, LC.

296 "this man is not talking": R. P. Adams to RWE, March 12, 1954, RWEP, LC.

296 "It's such letters as yours": RWE to R. P. Adams, March 31, 1954, RWEP, LC.

296 "I'm told that they're stirred up": RWE to Fanny Ellison, March 16, 1954, RWEP, LC.

296 "it was the largest": RWE to Saul Gottlieb, March 31, 1954, RWEP, LC.

296 "Where you are is home": RWE to Fanny Ellison, March 16, 1954.

297 "The least we can do": Fanny Ellison to Mrs. Ralph Cooper, April 27, 1954, RWEP, LC.

297 "an offshoot": Ralph Ellison, "Did You Ever Dream Lucky?" *New World Writing* 5 (April 1954): 134.

298 "It made for a heightening": RWE to Morteza D. Sprague, May 19, 1954, RWEP, LC.

298 "no Negro Americans were allowed": RWE, "A Statement on the Problem of Desegregation in the United States," Salzburg Seminar in American Studies, 1954, RWEP, LC.

299 "consciously explore those areas": "Address at Tuskegee Institute," press release issued by Division of Public Relations, Tuskegee Institute, July 1954, Tuskegee University Archives.

299 "their handling of the problem": RWE to Morteza D. Sprague, May 5, 1954, RWEP, LC.

300 "Whether we like the developments": RWE, ms., n.d., endorsement of Richard Wright, *Black Power: A Record of Reactions in a Land of Pathos* (New York: Harper & Brothers, 1954).

300 "Doesn't time fly!": RWE to Herbert Ellison, Aug. 12, 1954, RWEP, LC.

300 "Should anything happen": RWE to Stanley Edgar Hyman, April 19, 1954, Stanley Edgar Hyman Papers, LC.

301 "Most of it is hidden": Fanny Ellison to "Ann," Sept. 14, 1954, RWEP, LC.

301 "One reason the venture works": Max Lerner, *New York Post*, Sept. 20, 1954.

302 "Each session of the Salzburg Seminar": "Information for Faculty, Salzburg Seminar [in American Studies]," n.d. [1954], RWEP, LC.

302 "I feel neither the necessity": RWE to Salzburg Seminar in American Studies (Dexter Perkins), Jan. 28, 1954, RWEP, LC.

302 "The great mystery to me": Fanny Ellison to "Ann," Sept. 14, 1954.

302 "with a small, black moustache": Simone Vauthier, ms., n.d. [1954], RWEP, LC.

303 "the more startling the eruption": Ibid.

303 "can heat you faster": Fanny Ellison to Frances and James Curry, Aug. 27, 1954, RWEP, LC.

303 "I will never forget": Goran Palm to RWE, Sept. 1, 1955, RWEP, LC.

303 "For me, privately": Vilgot Sjomar to RWE, Jan. 17, 1955, RWEP, LC.

304 "Certainly it was worth it": RWE to Salzburg Seminar in American Studies (George Adams), Sept. 26, 1954, RWEP, LC.

304 "We found it a completely anti-climactic experience": RWE and Fanny Ellison to Vilgot Sjomar, Dec. 12, 1954, RWEP, LC.

305 "unresolved problems": Notes issued by the United States Embassy, Madrid, Sept. 3, 1954, RWEP, LC.

305 "those three magnificent days": RWE to United States Embassy, Madrid (John T. Reid), Dec. 8, 1954, RWEP, LC.

305 "very lively": RWE and Fanny Ellison to Vilgot Sjomar, Dec. 3, 1954, RWEP, LC.

305 "the warm, beautiful": RWE and Fanny Ellison to Mr. and Mrs. Robert Burton, Casa Americana, Madrid, Dec. 9, 1954, RWEP, LC.

306 "Dry, now, and birdlike": RWE, "Introduction to Flamenco," *Saturday Review* 37 (Dec. 11, 1954): 38.

306 "too tired to take the city on": Fanny Ellison to Lewis and Edith Ullian, Dec. 30, 1954, RWEP, LC.

306 "Of all the people": RWE to Michel Chrestien, April 4, 1955, RWEP, LC.

307 "I am getting a little sick": RWE to Richard Wright, Jan. 21, 1953, Richard Wright Papers, Beinecke Library, Yale University.

307 "put criticism where we thought": *Time* (Aug. 11, 1958): 57.

307 "The quiet steady flow": *Paris Review* 8 (Spring 1955): 56.

307 "I failed of eloquence": Transcript of interview, ms., n.d. [Oct. 1954], RWEP, LC.

308 "we fell into bed": Fanny Ellison to Ellen Wright, Nov. 23, 1954, RWEP, LC.

308 "broke and very far behind": Fanny Ellison to Lewis and Edith Ullian, Dec. 30, 1954.

308 "draw a deep breath": RWE to George A. Plimpton, Nov. 22, 1954, RWEP, LC.

308 "tragic, metaphysical elements": RWE, "Introduction to Flamenco," pp. 38–39.

308 "I had lived through": RWE, "February," *Saturday Review* 38 (Jan. 1, 1955): 25.

308 "The city is truly fabulous": Fanny Ellison to "Sheba," Dec. 14, 1954, RWEP, LC.

308 "is now hard at work": Fanny Ellison to Lewis and Edith Ullian, Dec. 30, 1954.

309 "a situation which embarrassed you": Commodore Hotel (J. C. Egan) to RWE, Feb. 9, 1955, RWEP, LC.

309 "a slow and careful worker": Ms., n.d. [1955], Archives of the American Academy of Arts and Letters.

309 "as much pain as prize": RWE to Stanley Edgar Hyman, April 12, 1955, Stanley Edgar Hyman Papers, LC.

309 "We leave for one year": Fanny Ellison to Lewis and Edith Ullian, April 21, 1955, RWEP, LC.

309 "I'm enclosing copies": RWE to Stanley Edgar Hyman, April 12, 1955.

310 "is in his name": Ibid.

310 "Good to know": RWE to Stanley Edgar Hyman, April 27, 1955, RWEP, LC.

311 "healthy as a pig": RWE to Stanley Edgar Hyman, May 24, 1955, RWEP, LC.

311 "examined with unsparing honesty": Archives of the American Academy and National Institute of Arts and Letters, May 25, 1955.

311 "how frightfully brilliant": RWE to Stanley Edgar Hyman, May 24, 1955.

312 "Stanley Edgar Hyman ruined": Saul Bellow to author, interview, March 15, 2000.

312 "as a phase": U.S. Department of State (Mary Stewart French) to RWE, July 12, 1955, RWEP, LC.

313 "two fine days": RWE to Max and Edna Lerner, Aug. 2, 1955, RWEP, LC.

314 "I can see people gesturing wildly": *Conversations with Ralph Ellison*, ed. Maryemma Graham and Amritjit Singh (Jackson: UP of Mississippi, 1995), pp. 25–26. See also Hiram Hayden, ed., "What's Wrong with the American Novel?" *The American Scholar* (Fall 1955): 464–503.

314 "expressed a sense of wonder": *Conversations with Ralph Ellison,* pp. 25–26.

314 "Perhaps Trilling has never forgiven himself": RWE to Ursula Brumm, July 28, 1955, RWEP, LC.

315 "Thought you'd like to be remembered": Saul Bellow to RWE, May 2, 1955, RWEP, LC.

315 "This is America": *Conversations with Ralph Ellison,* pp. 52–53.

315 "the fluidity of our society": Ibid., p. 49.

315 "I think that is a thing": Ibid., p. 50.

315 "Your integrity is destroyed": Ibid.

13   *Adventure in Rome*

316 "The sun reflected": Fanny Ellison to Willie Mae Warren, Sept. 28, 1955, RWEP, LC.

317 "The food is excellent": Ibid.

318 "like hell": RWE to Random House, Inc. (Harry Ford), Oct. 23, 1955, RWEP, LC.

318 "In the swift whirl of time": RWE, "Living with Music," in *The Collected Essays of Ralph Ellison,* ed. John F. Callahan (New York: Modern Library, 1995), p. 236.

318 "Did the art books": RWE to Random House, Inc. (Harry Ford), Oct. 23, 1955.

319 "The Renaissance has sent my imagination": RWE to Albert Murray, Oct. 22, 1955, RWEP, LC.

319 "It's a wonderful job": Fanny Ellison to Willie Mae Warren, Nov. 7, 1955, RWEP, LC.

319 "Ever since my grandfather died": Fanny Ellison to Nina Bond, Nov. 10, 1955, RWEP, LC.

320 "We, I, love this wonderful city": Fanny Ellison to Georgia Craven, Jan. 8, 1956, RWEP, LC.

320 "I believe you would like": Fanny Ellison to Anne Arter, Aug. 14, 1956, RWEP, LC.

320 "the stingiest fellowship": Fanny Ellison to Rosemary Newcomb, Feb. 13, 1956, RWEP, LC.

320 "Ralph walks a narrow path": Fanny Ellison to Georgia Craven, Jan. 8, 1956.

320 "as soon as I know her better": RWE to Albert Murray, Oct. 22, 1955, RWEP, LC.

320 "coming and going": RWE to Charles Justice, Nov. 20, 1956, RWEP, LC.

321 "a very handsome and cultured man": Fanny Ellison to Willie Mae Warren, Nov. 23, 1955, RWEP, LC.

321 "I'll bet money": RWE to Albert Murray, Oct. 22, 1955.

321 "So much of our stay here": RWE to Saul Bellow, May 16, 1956, RWEP, LC.

321 "I long ago began to understand": Fanny Ellison to Nina Bond, Jan. 27, 1956, RWEP, LC.

321 "You'd have laughed": RWE to Albert Murray, April 12, 1956, RWEP, LC.

321 "I have the academy ringing": RWE to Albert Murray, Oct. 22, 1955.

322 "There are all sorts of people here": Fanny Ellison to Nina Bond, Dec. 30, 1955, RWEP, LC.

322 "spectacular and dramatic": Fanny Ellison to [Willie Mae Warren], Jan. 11, 1956, RWEP, LC.

322 "very impressive": RWE to Albert Murray, April 5, 1956, RWEP, LC.

322 "preferably one converted": RWE to Albert Murray, April 1, 1956, RWEP, LC.

322 "appendicular colic": Fanny Ellison to Willie Mae Warren, Feb. 4, 1956, RWEP, LC.

322 "We both need to get away": Fanny Ellison to John and Leslie Aldridge, Jan. 26, 1956, RWEP, LC.

323 "I'm homesick": RWE to Albert Murray, March 16, 1956, RWEP, LC.

323 "an enchanted town": John Aldridge to RWE, Nov. 7, 1955, RWEP, LC.

323 "all looking bravely": RWE to Albert Murray, March 16, 1956.

323 "I will eat a man's food": Ibid.

323 "He's never been to America": RWE to Random House, Inc. (Harry Ford), March [n.d.], 1956, RWEP, LC.

323 "in easy access": RWE to Albert Murray, March 16, 1956.

324 "the old steady, mush-mouthed": Ibid.

324 "Faulkner has delusions": Ibid.

324 "I refuse to let his statement": RWE to Random House, Inc. (Harry Ford), May 15, 1956, RWEP, LC.

324 "from this distance": RWE to *Encounter* (Irving Kristol), June 23, 1956, RWEP, LC.

325 "a monster of bastard form": RWE to Random House, Inc. (Harry Ford), Jan. 17, 1957, RWEP, LC.

325 "I've been making headway": RWE to Saul Bellow, May 4, 1956, RWEP, LC.

325 "Indeed, you have been most 'invisible' ": RWE to Giulio Einuadi Editore (Carlo Fruttero), March 1, 1956, RWEP, LC.

325 "a mixed blessing": RWE to S. Fischer Verlag (Brigitte B. Fischer), April 22, 1956, RWEP, LC.

326 "a rather provincial town": RWE to Random House, Inc. (Harry Ford), March [n.d.], 1956, RWEP, LC.

326 "when my work was most recalcitrant": RWE to American Academy of Arts and Letters, April 23, 1956, Academy archives.

326 "is setting a precedent": RWE to Brandeis University (Abram L. Sachar), April 23, 1956, RWEP, LC.

326 "the events at home": RWE to Max Lerner, April 23, 1956, RWEP, LC.

326 "Some of the incidents": RWE to Mrs. John Porter, April 22, 1956, RWEP, LC.

326 "About the novel": RWE to Random House, Inc. (Harry Ford), Jan. 17, 1957, RWEP, LC.

326 "I'd like to operate": RWE to Albert Murray, May 18, 1956, RWEP, LC.

326 "His function is to write": Fanny Ellison to [Grandma Brock], Jan. 28, 1957, RWEP, LC.

326 "thought he could get me": RWE to Fanny Ellison, Oct. 26, 1956, RWEP, LC.

327 "As you'll recall": RWE to Max Lerner, Dec. 24, 1956, RWEP, LC.

327 "Maybe all I really want": RWE to Albert Murray, April 12, 1956.

327 "that old dancing master": RWE to Albert Murray, May 18, 1956.

327 "They are wonderful people": Fanny Ellison to Willie Mae Warren, Aug. 16, 1955, RWEP, LC.

328 "We got along very well": Albert Murray to author, interview, Aug. 8, 2000.

328 "We found Paris charming": RWE to Saul Bellow, Aug. 15, 1956, RWEP, LC.

328 "I suppose he'll go": RWE to Horace Cayton, n.d. [June 1956], in Michel Fabre to Fanny Ellison, Nov. 20, 1994, RWEP, LC.

328 "all that the name implies": Fanny Ellison to Willie Mae Warren, July 10, 1956, RWEP, LC.

328 "it was my very pleasant fate": RWE to Congrès pour la Liberté de la Culture (John Hunt), Aug. 14, 1956, RWEP, LC.

329 "answering private snipings": Ibid.

329 "all the old farts": RWE to Saul Bellow, Aug. 15, 1956.

329 "great and mighty first-class Ritz": Fanny Ellison to Mozelle Murray, July 31, 1956, RWEP, LC.

329 "we were suddenly lost": Fanny Ellison to Jack Ludwig, Jan. 31, 1968, RWEP, LC.

329 "the people were all so nice": Fanny Ellison to Mozelle Murray, July 31, 1956.

330 "the relation of the alienated novelist": Granville Hicks to RWE, Aug. 25, 1956, RWEP, LC.

330 "Ralph is always waking up": Fanny Ellison to Willie Mae Warren, Aug. 12, 1956, RWEP, LC.

330 "who can't sleep soundly": Fanny Ellison to Willie Mae Warren, Sept. 26, 1956, RWEP, LC.

330 "There are many emotional hypochondriacs": Langston Hughes, *I Wonder as I Wander* (New York: Hill & Wang, 1993), p. 120.

330 "as much talent for psychology": RWE to Horace Cayton, n.d. [1956], RWEP, LC.

330 "quite honored to be asked": RWE to Congrès pour la Liberté de la Culture (Nicholas Nabokov), Sept. 6, 1956, RWEP, LC.

331 "almost drowned": RWE to Fanny Ellison, Sept. 28, 1956, RWEP, LC.

331 "both were living in Europe": *Time* (Sept. 10, 1956): 124.

331 "being in the apartment": RWE to Fanny Ellison, Oct. 6, 1956, RWEP, LC.

332 "Seems there's a Negro": RWE to Fanny Ellison, Oct. 19, 1956, RWEP, LC.

332 "although Saul is sad with the world": Ibid.

333 "Could they have been looking": Fanny Ellison to Nina Bond, April 2, 1956, RWEP, LC.

333 "I watched him": Fanny Ellison to Nina Bond, Nov. 1, 1957, RWEP, LC.

333 "anxious that I might have lost control": RWE to Jean Douglas, Jan. 17, 1957, RWEP, LC.

333 "Why this sudden cultivation": Fanny Ellison to RWE, Sept. 29, 1956, RWEP, LC.

333 "more than willing": RWE to Diana Trilling, Nov. 20, 1956, RWEP, LC.

333 "Stalinist terror and foreign domination": *Partisan Review* (William Phillips and Philip Rahv) to RWE, Nov. 6, 1956, RWEP, LC.

333 "I do not . . . agree": RWE to William Faulkner, Feb. 22, 1957, RWEP, LC.

334 "The mainly new people": RWE to John Hunt, Nov. 19, 1956, RWEP, LC.

334 "It looks much better": Fanny Ellison to Willie Mae Warren, April 7, 1956, RWEP, LC.

335 "I felt I'd better not continue": Fanny Ellison to Willie Mae Warren, Dec. 5, 1956, RWEP, LC.

335 "It's enough to make a duffer": RWE to Saul Bellow, April 9, 1957, RWEP, LC.

335 "I will be as happy to return home": Fanny Ellison to Ursula Arnold, Jan. 4, 1957, RWEP, LC.

335 "a capacity for night-owling": RWE to Albert Murray, April 4, 1957, RWEP, LC.

335 "a day that spoke": Fanny Ellison to Nina Bond, April 30, 1957, RWEP, LC.

336 "We became quite fond": RWE to Albert Murray, April 4, 1957.

336 "Ralph has hit a high peak": Fanny Ellison to Fred and Lucille Muhlhauser, Jan. 26, 1957, RWEP, LC.

336 "wild and crazy": Fanny Ellison to [Grandma Brock], Jan. 28, 1957, RWEP, LC.

336 "had worked against a writer's block": RWE to A. L. Hart, April 19, 1957, RWEP, LC.

336 "to deal with the Novel": RWE to Albert Murray, April 4, 1957.

336 "Today is Ralph's birthday": Fanny Ellison to Dale MacDonald, March 1, 1957, RWEP, LC.

337 "rough times personally": Fanny Ellison to Willie Mae Warren, March 15, 1957, RWEP, LC.

337 "Over the past several weeks": Fanny Ellison to Willie Mae Warren, April 6, 1957, RWEP, LC.

337 "I said to myself": The identities of both women are concealed at the request of interested parties.

338 "it is an artist's intelligence": Archibald MacLeish to Fanny Ellison, June 16, 1957, RWEP, LC.

338 "the unconscious condescension": RWE to Fanny Ellison, Aug. 24, 1957, RWEP, LC.

339 "Excruciating Day & Night": RWE, note in appointment book, April 9, 1957, RWEP, LC.

339 "I remember when R[alph]": Fanny Ellison to Willie Mae Warren, April 26, 1957, RWEP, LC.

339 "For sudden and unexpected reasons": Fanny Ellison to Col. W. Ch. J. M. van Lanschot, May 16, 1957, RWEP, LC.

339 "I'm a little more mature": Fanny Ellison to Willie Mae Warren, May 30, 1957, RWEP, LC.

339 "even if I don't get a renewal": RWE to Congrès pour la Liberté de la Culture (John Hunt), June 12, 1957.

340 "the oppressive atmosphere": Fanny Ellison to Willie Mae Warren, May 30, 1957.

340 "I lost under a hail": Fanny Ellison to Dr. Alberto Giordano, July 4, 1957, RWEP, LC.

340 "I think at last": Ibid.

341 "sinking into your seat": Fanny Ellison to RWE, Aug. 21, 1957, RWEP, LC.

341 "I wonder how far": RWE to Fanny Ellison, Aug. 12, 1957, RWEP, LC.

341 "Rome, for me": RWE to Congrès pour la Liberté de la Culture (John Hunt), Aug. 16, 1957, RWEP, LC.

341 "much confusion and dashing around": RWE to Fanny Ellison, Aug. 12, 1957.

341 "ALL IS WELL": Fanny Ellison to RWE, Aug. 18, 1957, RWEP, LC.

342 "wire and its abstract message": RWE to Fanny Ellison, Aug. 24, 1957, RWEP, LC.

343 "interfere with your plans": Fanny Ellison to RWE, Aug. 21, 1957, RWEP, LC.

343 "a needlessly dismal letter": RWE to Fanny Ellison, Aug. 28, 1957, RWEP, LC.

343 "Japan simply takes you over": RWE to Fanny Ellison, n.d. [Sept. 1957], RWEP, LC.

343 "or in the manner": RWE to Fanny Ellison, Sept. 29, 1957, RWEP, LC.

344 "breathtakingly, head snappingly, beautiful": RWE to Fanny Ellison, n.d. [Sept. 1957].

344 "Spirituality got into culture": RWE to Congrès pour la Liberté de la Culture (John Hunt), Sept. 27, 1957, RWEP, LC.

344 "the thousands of people": RWE to Fanny Ellison, Sept. 29, 1957.

344 "I hear Fanny and Ralph": Fanny Ellison to RWE, Sept. 17, 1957, RWEP, LC.

344 "My cup runneth over": RWE to Fanny Ellison, Sept. 29, 1957.

345 "These are strange, unsettled days": Fanny Ellison to RWE, Oct. 4, 1957, RWEP, LC.

345 "You say you": Fanny Ellison to RWE, Oct. 6, 1957, RWEP, LC.

345 "I got the impression": RWE to Fanny Ellison, Oct. 9, 1957, RWEP, LC.

14   *The Pleasures of Home*

347 "dead-tired, broke": RWE to Albert Murray, Feb. 6, 1958, RWEP, LC.

347 "I'm haunted": The name of the recipient of this letter is omitted at her request.

347 "I didn't really see": Ibid.

347 "Ralph has been home": Fanny Ellison, Nov. 25, 1957, RWEP, LC. The name of the recipient of this letter is omitted at the request of interested parties.

347 "The dull, restricted view": Fanny Ellison to RWE, Sept. 17, 1957, RWEP, LC.

347 "The apartment is newly decorated": The name of the recipient of this letter and the date of the letter are omitted at the recipient's request.

348 "the liquor's good": Ibid.

348 "the hour was consistently stimulating": *New York Times*, Nov. 18, 1957.

349 "I must be a fool": RWE to Leon and Meta Goldin, Nov. 18, 1957, RWEP, LC.

349 "There'll be no more merry-go-rounds": Fanny Ellison to "Anne" [Ann] Freeman, Nov. 25, 1957, RWEP, LC.

349 "something eating my innards": RWE to Saul Bellow, April 9, 1957, RWEP, LC.

349 "Things Rome-wise": RWE to Saul Bellow, Feb. 26, 1958, RWEP, LC.

349 "writer's block as big as the Ritz": Ibid.

350 "It is not easy to find": Saul Bellow, "The University as Villain," *Nation* 185 (Nov. 16, 1957): 363.

350 "wreck of a house": Saul Bellow to RWE, Sept. 7, 1956, RWEP, LC.

350 "the house in Tivoli": Saul Bellow to RWE, May 27, 1957, RWEP, LC.

350 "I'm working on my book": RWE to "Dmitri," April 14, 1958, RWEP, LC.

350 "I like him better": RWE to Albert Murray, Feb. 6, 1958, RWEP, LC.

351 "but what he says": RWE to Saul Bellow, Feb. 26, 1958, RWEP, LC.

351 "our conceptions of the way": RWE, "Change the Joke and Slip the Yoke," *Partisan Review* 25:2 (Spring 1958): 212.

351 "the fullest development I know": Stanley Edgar Hyman, "The Folk Tradition," *Partisan Review* 25:2 (Spring 1958): 200.

351 "I think he's going to be hurt": RWE to Albert Murray, Feb. 6, 1958.

352 "the collection is worth having": Robert Gorham Davis, "In Search of What Matters," *New York Times Book Review*, (Dec. 8, 1957), p. 6.

352 "pretentious and sententious writing": Orville Prescott, "Books of the Times," *New York Times*, Dec. 30, 1957.

352 "classic intention": RWE, "Society, Morality, and the Novel," in *The Living Novel: A Symposium,* ed. Granville Hicks (New York: Macmillan, 1957), p. 83.

353 "I'm sure you don't": Fanny Ellison to Diana Trilling, Sept. 26, 1956, RWEP, LC.

354 "jazzed-up, Joyced-up intellectual": *Time* (March 3, 1958).

354 "I could have kicked his nose": RWE to Saul Bellow, Feb. 26, 1958, RWEP, LC.

354 "While I sympathize": RWE, "Letter to the Editor," *Time* (Feb. 9, 1959): 2.

354 "like the country which gave it birth": RWE, "The Charlie Christian Story," *Saturday Review* (May 17, 1958): 42. See *The Collected Essays of Ralph Ellison*, ed. John F. Callahan (New York: Modern Library, 1995), pp. 266–72.

355 "wouldn't be a jazz critic": RWE to Albert Murray, Sept. 28, 1958, RWEP, LC.

355 "the biggest, most financially successful": Don Gold and Dom Cerulli, "The Newport Festival," *Down Beat* 25 (Aug. 7, 1958): 15.

355 "a hell of a lot of it": RWE to Albert Murray, Sept. 28, 1958, RWEP, LC.

356 "it was not an inspiring festival": Bill Coss, "The Newport Jazz Festival," *Metronome* 75 (Sept. 1958): 34.

356 "to talk to these screwed up musicians": RWE to Albert Murray, Sept. 28, 1958.

357 "But Bliss, daddy": RWE, *Invisible Man* (New York: Modern Library, 1952), p. 373.

359 "not really a story": Toni Morrison to author, n.d. [July 9, 2004].

359 "part of an intellectual activity": Robert B. Stepto to author, interview, Dec. 13, 2000.

359 "powers of organization": Saul Bellow, "Ralph Ellison in Tivoli," *Partisan Review* 65:4 (1998): 525.

360 "I'm a little desperate": RWE to Albert Murray, Sept. 28, 1958.

360 "The country hereabouts": RWE to "Dmitri," Sept. 17, 1958, RWEP, LC.

360 "I now have some idea": RWE to Saul Bellow, March 18, 1959, RWEP, LC.

360 "the ethical structure": RWE to Bard College (Elsie L. Quinn), Aug. 26, 1958, RWEP, LC.

360 "When he lectured": Eric Werthman to author, interview, May 29, 2004.

360 "He was an amazing teacher": Ivan Levison to author, interview, April 3, 2004.

361 "I will not read": Ibid.

361 "The Little Red Whorehouse": Eric Werthman to author, interview.

361 "The college is a place": RWE to "Dmitri," Sept. 17, 1958.

361 "They wear beards": RWE to Albert Murray, June 27, 1959, RWEP, LC.

361 "He didn't quite fit in": Eric Werthman to author, interview.

361 "transcendent nobility": Ivan Levison to author, interview.

361 "I know Bard": RWE to Albert Murray, June 27, 1959.

361 "tended to stutter or stammer": George Lynes to author, interview, April 18, 2004.

361 "I've been more than earning my pay": RWE to Saul Bellow, March 18, 1959, RWEP, LC.

362 "It was not unusual": Vera Gordon to author, n.d. [May 2004].

362 "We had to help him": Eric Werthman to author, interview.

362 "Enjoy your love": RWE to "My dear Sylvia," Jan. 22, 1959, RWEP, LC.

362 "In the future": Richard Kagle to RWE, Jan. 15, 1961, RWEP, LC.

362 "Ralph came to the podium": Eric Werthman to author, interview.

362 "Respectability is the very devil": RWE to Albert Murray, June 27, 1959.

362 "I'm used to cleaning": RWE to Saul Bellow, Sept. 21, 1958, RWEP, LC.

363 "I'm not so anti-social": Ibid.

363 "subjecting myself to the discipline": RWE to Albert Murray, June 27, 1959.

363 "Like a nineteenth-century Englishman": Ibid.

363 "It is so beautiful": RWE to Saul Bellow, Nov. 27, 1958, RWEP, LC.

363 "unique in my experience": *New York Herald Tribune*, March 5, 1959.

364 "Most of the deliberations": RWE to Saul Bellow, March 18, 1959, RWEP, LC.

364 "Up until the trip in to New York": Ibid.

364 "I guess I must be nearing": Ibid.

365 "a most interesting year": RWE to Albert Murray, June 27, 1959.

365 "thanks to much repetition": RWE to James Putnam, Jan. 28, 1960, RWEP, LC.

365 "of the prominent contemporary writers": Langston Hughes to RWE, Dec. 8, 1959, RWEP, LC.

366 "I said I had no interest": Harold R. Isaacs, "Five Writers and Their African Ancestors," *Phylon: The Atlanta University Review of Race and Culture* (Fourth Quarter 1960): 317.

366 "They are some arrogant": RWE to Albert Murray, April 2, 1960, RWEP, LC.

366 "Fifteen minutes in a meeting": RWE to Albert Murray, June 27, 1959.

367 "and that my body blossoming": Fanny Ellison to RWE, March 16, 1959, RWEP, LC.

367 "This same character": RWE to Albert Murray, Sept. 17, 1959, RWEP, LC.

368 "These characters are all trying": RWE to Albert Murray, Sept. 28, 1958, RWEP, LC.

368 "He is essentially a hateful writer": Norman Mailer, *Advertisements for Myself* (New York: G. P. Putnam's Sons, 1959), pp. 431–32.

369 "recently accused me": RWE to Albert Murray, Sept. 28, 1958.

369 "Now she's gone": RWE to Albert Murray, Sept. 17, 1959.

370 "Perhaps I'll write": RWE to Stanley Edgar Hyman, Nov. 17, 1952, Stanley Edgar Hyman Papers, LC.

370 "What's a jungle bunny": Ted and Renée Weiss to author, interview, Dec. 14, 2000.

370 "Fred Dupee and Gore Vidal": Richard Poirier to author, interview, Aug. 12, 2002.

371 "to turn myself into a clown": RWE to Albert Murray, April 2, 1960, RWEP, LC.

371 "Somewhat incongruously": *Newsweek* (Dec. 28, 1959): 65.

372 "They give me a sense": RWE to Jack Ludwig, Dec. 13, 1959, RWEP, LC.

372 "I feel that I'm falling apart": RWE to Saul Bellow, Jan. 19, 1960, RWEP, LC.

372 "intense and most useful": RWE to Albert Murray, n.d. [c. Nov. 1959], RWEP, LC.

373 "This little ball": RWE to John Cheever, March 18, 1960, RWEP, LC.

373 "I was the junior": Richard Stern, "Ralph Ellison," in *What Is What Was* (Chicago: U of Chicago P, 2002), p. 23.

374 "whom I found intriguing": RWE to Richard Stern, May 23, 1960, RWEP, LC.

374 "one of the most exciting times": RWE to University of Chicago (Alan Simpson), n.d [1960], RWEP, LC.

374 "a long time": Granville Hicks, "Birth of a Lusty Biannual," *Saturday Review* (May 14, 1960): 14.

374 "on any bloody thing": *The Noble Savage* (Jack Ludwig) to RWE, April 9, 1960, RWEP, LC.

374 "Although I'm damned disgusted": RWE to Albert Murray, April 2, 1960, RWEP, LC.

375 "the landscape of [his] mind": "The Roof, the Steeple and the People," *Quarterly Review of Literature* 10 (1960): 115–28.

376 "Ellison and Bellow became inseparable": James Atlas, *Bellow: A Biography* (New York: Random House, 2000), p. 301.

376 "The important thing was": Saul Bellow, "Ralph Ellison in Tivoli," p. 525.

376 "never anything but well-dressed": Ibid., p. 526.

376 "Can't you arrange": Ibid., p. 527.

377 *"chien du race"*: Ibid.

377 "We did not form": Ibid., pp. 527–28.

377 "his own hagiographer": Ibid.

378 "We are shocked and grieved": RWE and Fanny Ellison to Ellen Wright, Dec. 2, 1960, RWEP, LC.

378 "a period of my own life": RWE to Horace Cayton, July 15, 1961, RWEP, LC.

378 "our forefathers": *Cedar Rapids Gazette*, April 14, 1961.

379 "I could have done the mood piece": RWE to Albert Murray, April 2, 1960.

379 "which I can't very well refuse": Ibid.

379 "I am very, very sorry": RWE to Gorham Munson, May 24, 1961, RWEP, LC.

380 "the finest piece of Jazz writing": "Roi" [LeRoi] Jones to RWE, n.d. [1958], RWEP, LC.

380 "I remember going over to see him": Amiri Baraka to author, interview, May 4, 2003.

380 "Things go about the same": RWE to Stanley Edgar Hyman, March 10, 1961, RWEP, LC.

15   *Hanging Fire*

381 "Your leaving has left": RWE to Fanny Ellison, Oct. 10, 1961, RWEP, LC.

382 "Here, unlike in Tivoli": Ibid.

382 "I should murder her": Fanny Ellison to RWE, Dec. 13, 1961, RWEP, LC.

382 "I have the feeling": Fanny Ellison to RWE, Dec. 11, 1961, RWEP, LC.

382 "I don't refer": Fanny Ellison to RWE, draft, Oct. 17, 1961, RWEP, LC.

382 "Are you all right?": Fanny Ellison to RWE, Nov. 8, 1961, RWEP, LC.

383 "this confident, warm, and charming man": Richard Stern, "Ralph Ellison," in *What Is What Was* (Chicago: U of Chicago P, 2002), p. 25.

383 "I lecture on Monday": RWE to Fanny Ellison, Nov. 15, 1961, RWEP, LC.

383 "His model was jazz": Richard Stern, "Ralph Ellison," p. 25.

383 "a refusal to drift": Charlotte and Nathan Scott to author, interview, June 20, 2000.

383 "He wouldn't": Richard Stern, "Ralph Ellison," p. 25.

383 "My last public lecture": RWE to Fanny Ellison, Dec. 11, 1961.

384 "It was very strange": Ibid.

384 "the old pain": Ibid.

385 "hurt and angry": Richard Stern, "Ralph Ellison," p. 25.

385 "because I couldn't possibly be": Fanny Ellison to RWE, Jan. 1, 1962, RWEP, LC.

385 "If I complied": RWE to Rozell Leavell, March 19, 1962, RWEP, LC.

385 "are obsessed by a history": *Norfolk-Portsmouth Virginian-Pilot*, April 22, 1962.

386 "will appear in the fall": Ibid.

386 "I am at present": RWE to John L. Swink, May 12, 1962, RWEP, LC.

387 **"One of the founders"**: RWE, "On Bird, Bird-Watching, and Jazz," *Saturday Review* 45 (July 28, 1962): 47.

389 **"almost every celebrity"**: Fern Marja Eckman, *The Furious Passage of James Baldwin* (New York: M. Evans & Co., 1966), p. 165.

389 **"bad by any standard"**: Stanley Edgar Hyman, "No Country for Young Men," *New Leader* (June 25, 1962): 23.

389 **"Perhaps what Baldwin"**: RWE, note, n.d., RWEP, LC.

390 **"Ralph told me"**: Robert G. O'Meally to author, interview, Dec. 15, 1999.

390 **"used to say of Ralph"**: R. W. B. Lewis to author, interview, May 12, 2000.

390 **"big rambling house"**: RWE to Charlie D[avidson], Aug. 10, 1968, RWEP, LC.

391 **"on the other hand"**: Charles Harris to author, interview, Feb. 11, 2000.

391 **"The literati are at Princeton"**: Rutgers University (William Sloane) to RWE, Nov. 5, 1962, RWEP, LC.

392 **"trying to shore up"**: Rutgers University, press release, n.d.

392 **"any respectable university"**: RWE to Hannah Atkins, n.d., RWEP, LC.

392 **"I was shocked"**: Alan Cheuse to author, interview, Sept. 17, 2003.

392 **"Ralph was very enthusiastic"**: Joseph Frank to author, interview, Nov. 15, 2000.

393 **"the small but interested audience"**: Alan Cheuse to author, interview.

393 **"regard all whites"**: RWE, "It Always Breaks Out," *Partisan Review* 30 (Spring 1963): 13–28.

393 **"Reading it now"**: RWE, "Author's Note," in *Soon One Morning: New Writing by American Negroes, 1940–1962*, ed. Herbert Hill (New York: Alfred A. Knopf, 1963), pp. 243–44.

394 **"if not friends"**: RWE to Marvin Halverson, Sept. 27, 1962, RWEP, LC.

394 **"the difficult 30 percent"**: Executive Office of the President, Office of Science and Technology (Joseph Turner) to RWE, Feb. 7, 1963, RWEP, LC.

394 **" 'the last battle' "**: *New York Times*, Feb. 13, 1963.

395 **"some length to go"**: *Wall Street Journal*, Feb. 13, 1963.

395 **"search for new ways"**: *Education of the Deprived and Segregated: Report of a Seminar Conducted by the Bank Street College of Education at Dedham, Massachusetts, September 3–15, 1963* (New York: Bank Street School of Education, 1963), p. 5.

395 **"There is no such thing"**: RWE, "What These Children Are Like," in *Education of the Deprived and Segregated*, p. 45.

396 **"the group discipline"**: Ibid.

397 **"You have been a very great asset"**: Rutgers University (Richard Schlatter) to RWE, March 13, 1963, RWEP, LC.

397 **"failure to make adequate use"**: Rutgers University (William Sloane) to RWE, Oct. 17, 1963, RWEP, LC.

398 **"It was from him that I learned"**: Saul Bellow, "Ralph Ellison in Tivoli," *Partisan Review* 65:4 (1998): 525.

398 **"The luxurious effect"**: Richard Kostelanetz, "Ralph Ellison: The Novelist as Brown-Skinned Aristocrat," *Master Minds: Portraits of Contemporary American Artists and Intellectuals* (New York: Macmillan, 1969), p. 48.

399 **"I find it almost impossible"**: RWE to Duke University (William J. Nichols), Nov. 6, 1963, RWEP, LC.

400 "He's certainly paid more attention": Allen Geller, "An Interview with Ralph Ellison," in *Conversations with Ralph Ellison*, ed. Maryemma Graham and Amritjit Singh (Jackson: UP of Mississippi, 1995), p. 71.

400 "one of the things": John Hersey, "'A Completion of Personality': A Talk with Ralph Ellison," *Conversations with Ralph Ellison*, p. 278.

401 "The day *Native Son* appeared": Irving Howe, "Black Boys and Native Sons," in *A World More Attractive: A View of Modern Literature and Politics* (New York: Horizon, 1963), p. 100.

401 "He suggested that I put down": RWE to Irving Howe, Dec. 13, 1963, RWEP, LC.

401 "a major statement": "Between Issues," *New Leader* 46 (Dec. 9, 1963): 2.

401 "suddenly drop": RWE, "The World and the Jug," *New Leader* 46 (Dec. 9, 1963): 22.

402 "No, Wright was no spiritual father": Ibid., p. 30.

402 "my disagreement is with some": RWE to Irving Howe, Dec. 13, 1963.

402 "a will to historical forgetfulness": RWE, "A Rejoinder," *New Leader* (Feb. 3, 1964): 15–22.

402 "the artist's dignity": Alfred Kazin to RWE, Feb. 8, 1964, RWEP, LC.

402 "beautifully and nobly written": "Bern" [Bernard Malamud] to RWE, Feb. 12, 1964, RWEP, LC.

402 "*inspired* good sense": Sidney Hook to RWE, Feb. 4, 1964, RWEP, LC.

403 "I take the invitation": RWE to the Library of Congress (Roy P. Basler), March 20, 1963, RWEP, LC.

403 "If I appeared in your journal": RWE to *Freedomways* (John Henrik Clarke), March 13, 1964, RWEP, LC.

403 "the intricate network": RWE, "Blues People," *New York Review of Books* 1 (Feb. 6, 1964), in *Shadow and Act* (New York: Vintage, 1995), p. 253.

404 "We are pulling for you": RWE to Kristin Hunter, Nov. 23, 1964, RWEP, LC.

404 "most publishers consider": RWE to Rush W. Greenlee, Nov. 23, 1964, RWEP, LC.

404 "I don't think you missed anything": RWE to Joseph Frank, Nov. 23, 1964, RWEP, LC.

405 "the least productive person": "Dinner Meeting Addresses of the National Institute of Arts and Letters," n.d. [1964], Archives of the American Academy of Arts and Letters.

406 "I've got the central concepts": Dick Schaap, "Behind the Lines," *New York Herald Tribune Book Week*, May 24, 1964.

406 "Now people are reading it": Allen Geller, "An Interview with Ralph Ellison," *Conversations with Ralph Ellison*, p. 85.

408 "to enable Mr. Ralph Ellison": Rockefeller Foundation to Yale University (Kingman Brewster), Aug. 17, 1964, RWEP, LC.

408 "My thanks to you": RWE to Robert Penn Warren, Aug. 9, 1964, RWEP, LC.

409 "the same eloquence": Norman Podhoretz, "The Melting-Pot Blues," *Book Week* (Oct. 25, 1964): 1.

409 "wrongheaded negative review": Norman Podhoretz, "What Happened to Ralph Ellison," *Commentary* (July–Aug. 1999): 58.

410 "would have been so pleased": Mary Hemingway to RWE, Nov. 14, 1964, RWEP, LC.

16   *Tell It Like It Is, Baby*

412 **"our own black shining prince"**: Eulogy delivered by Ossie Davis at the funeral of Malcolm X, Faith Temple Church of God, Feb. 27, 1965.

412 **"the only universal black hero"**: William H. Grier, M.D., and Price M. Cobbs, M.D., *Black Rage* (New York: Bantam, 1969), p. 168.

413 **"I wouldn't dare"**: "The Uses of History in Fiction: Ralph Ellison, William Styron, Robert Penn Warren, C. Vann Woodward," in *Conversations with Ralph Ellison*, ed. Maryemma Graham and Amritjit Singh (Jackson: UP of Mississippi, 1995), p. 170.

413 **"One reason Ralph"**: Richard and Charlotte Wilbur to author, interview, May 11, 2000.

414 **"We live separated"**: *Washington Post*, Jan. 15, 1965.

414 **"where the most meaningful dramas"**: LeRoi Jones to "Dear Friend" [RWE], Feb. 4, 1965, RWEP, LC.

414 **"Ralph saw the low"**: Stanley Crouch to author, interview, Jan. 27, 2005.

415 **"it contributed a quality"**: NAACP Legal Defense and Educational Fund, Inc. to RWE, June 7, 1965, RWEP, LC.

415 **"the apparent surrender"**: Minutes of meeting of Committee on Theme for 1966 PEN Congress, Feb. 11, 1965, RWEP, LC.

415 **"by our contributions"**: *Washington Post*, April 10, 1965.

416 **"Fanny especially"**: Richard and Charlotte Wilbur to author, interview.

416 **"Ralph was ever so fond"**: Ibid.

416 **"America is no longer"**: *Daily Oklahoman*, Oct. 21, 1966.

416 **"very embarrassing"**: John D. Weaver, ed., *Glad Tidings: A Friendship in Letters: The Correspondence of John Cheever and John D. Weaver, 1945–1982* (New York: HarperCollins, 1993), pp. 180–81.

417 **"a time in which it has become fashionable"**: RWE, "Presentation," ms., May 19, 1965, RWEP, LC.

417 **"That was a stupendous party"**: Robert Penn Warren to RWE and Fanny Ellison, July 2, 1965, RWEP, LC.

418 **"It's adolescent"**: *New York Post*, June 15, 1965.

418 **"a rising tide"**: John Updike, ed., *A Century of Arts and Letters* (New York: Columbia UP, 1998), pp. 185–86.

418 **"is far ahead"**: Steve Cannon, Lennox Raphael, and James Thompson, "A Very Stern Discipline: An Interview with Ralph Ellison," *Conversations with Ralph Ellison*, p. 122, reprinted from *Harper's* (March 1967): 76–95.

419 **"You were an enormous success"**: Harvard University (Dr. Henry Kissinger) to RWE, July 1965, RWEP, LC.

419 **"You are a superb anchor man"**: National Educational Television (Jerome Toobin) to RWE, Sept. 1965, RWEP, LC.

419 **"the cult aspects"**: RWE, "Jazz Goes Intellectual: Bop!," ms., Aug. 27, 1965, RWEP, LC.

419 **"Jazz exists today"**: RWE, "Jazz: The Experimenters," ms., Sept. 10, 1965, RWEP, LC.

420 **"I think you did a great deal"**: Martin Williams to RWE, Dec. 10, 1965, RWEP, LC.

420 **"best people in the world"**: *Esquire* (Aug. 1965): 64–65.

420 "The whole effect": Robert Penn Warren, *Who Speaks for the Negro?* (New York: Random House, 1965), p. 326.

420 "The danger lies in overemphasizing": Ibid., p. 328.

421 "There is a great power": Ibid., p. 341.

421 "When the smoke of battle": Cited in Robert Penn Warren to RWE, June 13, 1965, RWEP, LC.

421 "self-confidence, self-consciousness": Robert Penn Warren, *Who Speaks for the Negro?*, p. 343.

421 "you are entirely right": Hannah Arendt to RWE, July 29, 1965, RWEP, LC.

422 "two hundred prominent authors": *Washington Post*, Sept. 26, 1965.

422 "in many ways the strongest": Alfred Kazin, "Imagination and the Age," *Reporter*, May 5, 1966.

422 "slipping off the chains": RWE, "Juneteenth," *Quarterly Review of Literature* 4 (1965): 262–76.

424 "At previous conventions": National Association of Intergroup Relations Officials (John L. McKnight) to RWE, Aug. 6, 1965, RWEP, LC.

424 "I can assure you": Newton Minow to National Association of Broadcasters, May 9, 1961, cited in *Chicago Tribune*, April 24, 2001.

425 "institutionalization": James Alan McPherson to author, interview, June 1, 2003.

426 "I am hard at work": RWE to Rockefeller Foundation (Gerald Freund), March 8, 1966, RWEP, LC.

426 "Ralph has decided": RWE and Fanny Ellison to Ada and Herbert Ellison, Sept. 15, 1965, RWEP, LC.

426 "represented a continuity": RWE, address to National Committee for Support of the Public Schools, ms., April 18, 1966, RWEP, LC.

426 "Ever[y] now and then": Fanny Ellison to Rose Styron, Oct. 17, 1967, RWEP, LC.

426 "The criticism of the Council": *Newsweek* (July 18, 1966): 58.

427 "where the Southern Negro can transform": *New York Times*, Aug. 31, 1966.

427 "in the raw language": *Washington Post*, Aug. 31, 1966.

427 "want to transform Harlem": "Harlem's America," *New Leader* 49 (Sept. 26, 1966): 26.

428 "As much as I dislike warfare": Ibid., p. 27.

428 "non-seriousness is exactly": RWE, "The World Across the Street," transcript, ms., n.d., RWEP, LC.

429 "Moynihan looked": John Corry, "An American Novelist Who Sometimes Teaches," *New York Times Magazine* (Nov. 20, 1966): 180.

429 "She saw the books": Steve Cannon, Lennox Raphael, and James Thompson, "A Very Stern Discipline: An Interview with Ralph Ellison," *Conversations with Ralph Ellison*, p. 133, reprinted from *Harper's* (March 1967): 76–95.

430 "if Okla. City doesn't": RWE to Nancy [Hanks], n.d., RWEP, LC.

430 "I know that I stand": RWE to Oklahoma City Housing Authority (Tolbert E. Elliott), April 11, 1967, RWEP, LC.

430 "one profound regret": Mary Hemingway to Fanny Ellison, Dec. 11 [1966], RWEP, LC.

431 "People are practically committing suicide": *Life* 61 (Dec. 9, 1966): 117.

431 "Yes, I think I am near": RWE to Secker & Warburg Ltd. (Frederick J. Warburg), Dec. 16, 1966, RWEP, LC.

432 "a well-financed": "A Summary of the Commission's Report," *Public Television: A Program for Action*, Jan. 26, 1967, report of the Carnegie Commission on Educational Television.

432 "We've begun to think": Fanny Ellison to Tom and Bert Brown, Jan. 21, 1967, RWEP, LC.

433 "246 years old": Fanny Ellison to Peter "Tex" Schiwetz, April 3, 1970, RWEP, LC.

433 "until you've heard from me": RWE to N. H. Pritchard, Sept. 16, 1967, RWEP, LC.

433 "I write slowly": RWE to Howard University Press (Lewis H. Fenderson), May 31, 1967, RWEP, LC.

434 "Ellison greeted us courteously": Thomas C. Dent, "Notes on the Interview," *Harper's* (March 1967): 79.

434 "who rants and raves": Steve Cannon et al., "A Very Stern Condition," *Harper's* (March 1967): 77.

434 "in the unique position": Holt, Rinehart & Winston, Inc. (Arthur A. Cohen) to RWE, May 22, 1967, RWEP, LC.

435 "his distinctive *Southernness*": Jervis Anderson, "Profiles: Going to the Territory," *New Yorker* (Nov. 22, 1976): 55.

435 "the congenial social manner": Willie Morris, *New York Days* (Boston: Little, Brown, 1993), p. 276.

435 "a calumnious falsehood": "Letters," *Harper's* (May 1967): 10.

435 "at times Ellison seems unable": Keorapetse Kgositsile, "Ralph Ellison: Shadow or Act?" *Liberator* (May 1967): 11.

435 "I sense a deep hesitancy": Fanny Ellison to Mary Hemingway, April 27, 1967, RWEP, LC.

436 "Oh, how beautiful it is": Fanny Ellison to "Libo" [Ford?], July 24, 1967, RWEP, LC.

436 "mowed acres and acres": Fanny Ellison to Rose Styron, Oct. 17, 1967, RWEP, LC.

436 "Dick and Charlee are": Ibid.

436 "There was a mutual attraction": Richard and Charlotte Wilbur to author, interview.

437 "I regret to say": Fanny Ellison to Rose Styron, Oct. 17, 1967.

437 "the father of hatred": Peter Bergman, ed., *Chronological History of the Negro in America* (New York: Harper & Row, 1969), p. 596.

437 "It is a reverse Mississippi": *New York Times,* July 6, 1966.

437 "a group described": *Daily Illini*, Sept. 15, 1967.

438 "In treating people as abstractions": *Michigan Daily*, Oct. 5, 1967.

438 "is racist, imperialist": Ibid.

438 "It would be better": Ibid.

438 "this past week I have heard": *Newsday* (Long Island, N.Y.), Oct. 28, 1967.

439 "But for the opportunity": RWE to Lyndon Baines Johnson, March 21, 1967, RWEP, LC.

439 "There was a profoundly conservative streak": William Styron to author, interview, Nov. 23, 2003.

439 "could hear Ralph up": Richard Wilbur to author, interview, May 11, 2000.

439 "He is writing intensely": Fanny Ellison to Rose Styron, Oct. 17, 1967.

439 "The students were aggressive": Willie Morris, *New York Days*, p. 277.

439 "in came a big, rousing figure": Ibid., p. 279.

440 "I'm not a Tom": Ibid., p. 280.

440 "I'm sorry about that": Ibid., p. 278.

440 "What is your advice?": Fanny Ellison to Alfred Rice, Nov. 16, 1967, RWEP, LC.

441 "your new Fire Policy": Allstate Insurance to RWE and Fanny Ellison, Nov. 28, 1967, RWEP, LC.

17   *A "Lone-Star" Negro*

442 "very much traumatized": Fanny Ellison to Mr. and Mrs. Sanford, Dec. 3, 1968, RWEP, LC.

442 "is a nightmare image": RWE and Fanny Ellison to Thomas T. Packard, Dec. 10, 1967, RWEP, LC.

442 "Fanny reacted to the fire": Richard and Charlotte Wilbur to author, interview, May 11, 2000.

442 "R. knew, I'm sure": Fanny Ellison, ms., n.d. [1995], RWEP, LC.

442 "deep sympathy of the entire Plainfield community": "Order of Morning Worship, Plainfield Congregational Church, United Church of Christ," Dec. 3, 1967, RWEP, LC.

443 "your Plainfield friends": Frederick R. Tirrell to RWE and Fanny Ellison, Feb. 18, 1968, RWEP, LC.

443 "We had no idea": Fanny Ellison to Mr. and Mrs. J. R. Dufreese, Dec. 10, 1967, RWEP, LC.

443 "I lost part of my manuscript": RWE to Jack Ludwig, Jan. 5, 1968, RWEP, LC.

443 "fortunately had a full copy": Nathan and Charlotte Scott to author, interview, June 20, 2000.

443 "early next year": RWE to "Mrs. Hopper," n.d., RWEP, LC.

443 "has become inordinately long": Richard Kostelanetz, "Ralph Ellison: The Novelist as Brown-Skinned Aristocrat," in *Master Minds: Portraits of Contemporary American Artists and Intellectuals* (New York: Macmillan, 1969), p. 45.

443 "He has become so embarrassed": Ibid., p. 46.

443 "the fire all but traumatized": Fanny Ellison to Lucy Golsan, July 27, 1979, RWEP, LC.

444 "When poets try to be legislators": *New York Times*, Dec. 13, 1968.

444 "I don't see us withdrawing": Richard Kostelanetz, "Ralph Ellison: The Novelist as Brown-Skinned Aristocrat," p. 55.

445 "shock and regret": Fanny Ellison to the White House (Douglas Cater), April 1, 1968, RWEP, LC.

445 "Ralph had a deep-seated need": William Styron to author, interview, Nov. 23, 2003.

445 "a deep sense of pride": RWE to Century Association, Feb. 23, 1968, RWEP, LC.

445 "Things are flying!": Adult Education Council of Greater Chicago to Fanny Ellison, Sept. 11, 1968, RWEP, LC.

445 "many might cringe": University of Rochester (Andrew Weissman) to RWE, n.d. [1968], RWEP, LC.

445 "speakers to better inform us": Park College (Kansas City) to RWE, March 15, 1969, RWEP, LC.

446 **"Black Power Focus"**: Afro-American Society of Dartmouth College to RWE, Nov. 9, 1967, RWEP, LC.

446 **"Mr. Ellison does not over-price"**: Adult Educational Council of Greater Chicago (Beryl Sacks) to Fanny Ellison, March 12, 1968, RWEP, LC.

446 **"our nation is moving towards"**: Governor Otto Kerner, chair, *Report of the National Advisory Commission on Civil Disorders* (Washington, D.C.: U.S. Government Printing Office, 1968).

447 **"I take it"**: RWE, "Statement," ms., n.d. [1968], RWEP, LC.

447 **"greatly pleased"**: The White House (Douglas Cater) to RWE, May 3, 1968, RWEP, LC.

447 **"I suppose that Mama"**: RWE to Herbert Ellison, n.d., RWEP, LC.

448 **"devote my energy"**: RWE to Harvard Summer School (Thomas E. Crooks), Aug. 18, 1968, RWEP, LC.

448 **"the presence of so many"**: *New York Amsterdam News*, July 13, 1968.

448 **"when he dons a dark suit"**: Richard Kostelanetz, "Ralph Ellison: The Novelist as Brown-Skinned Aristocrat," p. 47.

448 **"full of kindness"**: Charlie Davidson to author, interview, June 10, 2002.

448 **"It was dreary as hell"**: RWE to Charlie Davidson, Aug. 10, 1968, RWEP, LC.

449 **"If the continent couldn't hold"**: *Charlotte Observer*, Oct. 24, 1968.

450 **"Bill's personal problem"**: Ralph Ellison, William Styron, Robert Penn Warren, and C. Vann Woodward, "The Uses of History in Fiction," *Southern Literary Journal* 1 (Spring 1969): 74.

450 **"Naturally, I was disappointed"**: William Styron to author, interview, Nov. 24, 2003.

450 **"We are enormously happy"**: Fanny Ellison to Rose Styron, Oct. 17, 1967, RWEP, LC.

451 **"I called our own agent"**: Rose Styron to author, interview, Nov. 24, 2003.

451 **"Ralph was furious"**: William Styron to author, interview.

451 **"True, Roxbury had never had"**: Rose Styron to author, interview.

451 **"Faulkner was truly an aristocrat"**: RWE, "Dictated by R.E. for Faulkner Essay," ms., June 4, 1968, RWEP, LC.

452 **"somewhat dry but well-organized talk"**: *Tougaloo Occasional Ripple*, Nov. 12, 1968.

452 **"a profound piece of writing"**: Larry Neal, "An Afterword," in *Black Fire: An Anthology of Afro-American Writing*, ed. Larry Neal and LeRoi Jones (New York: William Morrow, 1968), pp. 651–53.

452 **"a noisy writer"**: Eldridge Cleaver, *Soul on Ice* (New York: McGraw-Hill, 1968), p. 98.

452 **"vast incomprehension"**: RWE to University of Massachusetts–Boston (Irving Stock), Jan. 24, 1968, RWEP, LC.

452 **"catching the same kind"**: Nathan Scott to author, interview, June 20, 2000.

452 **"I would have thought"**: R. W. B. Lewis to author, interview, May 12, 2000.

453 **"the long neglected black masses"**: Walter Moore to RWE, June 28, 1968, RWEP, LC.

453 **"Dear Brother Ellison"**: Omojo to RWE, n.d. [1968], RWEP, LC.

453 **"a valuable, if fiery"**: *American Scholar* (Hiram Hayden) to RWE, Nov. 15, 1968, RWEP, LC.

453 **"commandeered the entire discussion"**: Jerry Watts, *Heroism and the Black Intellectual: Ralph Ellison, Politics, and Afro-American Intellectual Life* (Chapel Hill: U of North Carolina P, 1994), p. 63.

454 **"Ralph had a great thing"**: Shirley Hazzard to author, interview, Feb. 17, 2001.

454 **"everybody got quite drunk"**: Richard and Charlotte Wilbur to author, interview.

454 **"A kind of Visiting Writer's role"**: Richard and Charlotte Wilbur to author, interview.

454 **"spoke with unfaltering fluency"**: Nathan Scott to author, interview.

454 **"Ellison should have said something"**: Charles Harris to author, interview, Feb. 11, 2000.

455 **"I think he's gotten a bit pompous"**: John A. Williams, "My Man Himes: An Interview with Chester Himes," in *Amistad 1*, ed. Charles F. Harris and John A. Williams (New York: Vintage, 1970), p. 72.

455 **"Do you know what riffing is?"**: Charles Harris to author, interview.

455 **"and also potentially violent"**: Albert Murray to author, interview, June 4, 2001.

455 **"Horace, it never happened"**: Horace Porter to author, interview, Feb. 25, 2006.

455 **"out of the fear"**: RWE to the Art Gallery, State University of New York at Albany, ms., n.d. [1968], RWEP, LC.

455 **"that imbalance in American society"**: RWE, "Introduction," *Romare Bearden: Paintings and Projections,* exhibition catalogue, Art Gallery, State University of New York at Albany, 1968.

456 **"from a novel-in-progress"**: See RWE, "Night-Talk," *Quarterly Review of Literature* 16 (1969): 317.

457 *"And how do they feel"*: Ibid., p. 321.

458 **"Ralph Ellison is a writer"**: Citation, Presidential Medal of Freedom, Jan. 19, 1969, RWEP, LC.

458 **"his goals and options"**: RWE, "A Tribute to Lyndon Baines Johnson, Hero in the Struggle for Civil Rights," ms., n.d., RWEP, LC.

458 **"a beautiful moment"**: Helen Frankenthaler to RWE, March 2, 1969, RWEP, LC.

458 **"to believe more fervently"**: RWE to the French Embassy (Edouard Morot-Sir), Dec. 30, 1968, RWEP, LC.

459 **"That just proves"**: RWE and James Alan McPherson, "Indivisible Man," *The Atlantic Monthly* 226 (Dec. 1970): 47.

459 **"I am totally involved"**: RWE to Purdue University (W. J. Stuckey), Feb. 17, 1969, RWEP, LC.

459 **"So-called black studies"**: RWE to University of Pittsburgh Press, Jan. 22, 1969, RWEP, LC.

459 **"The rush is on"**: Peter Schrag, "The New Black Myths," *Harper's* (May 1969): 37.

459 **"Those people were so rude"**: RWE to Michael S. Harper and Robert B. Stepto, ms., draft of interview, March 7, 1976, RWEP, LC. Revised as "Study and Experience: An Interview with Ralph Ellison," in *Chant of Saints: A Gathering of Afro-American Literature, Art, and Scholarship,* ed. Michael S. Harper and Robert B. Stepto (Urbana: U of Illinois P, 1979), pp. 451–69.

460 **"I peppered Ellison"**: Emory Elliott to author, interview, Dec. 29, 2003.

460 **"Mr. Ellison, sir"**: Ibid.

461 **"I believe that Muhammad Ali"**: *Esquire* (Nov. 1969): 124–25.

461 "The encircled statement": Irwin Shaw to *Esquire* (Harold Hayes), July 21, 1969, RWEP, LC.

462 "We don't carry it": *New Republic* (March 14, 1994): 36.

462 "Race is a factor": *Amherst Student*, May 15, 1969.

463 "He is about to complete": Fanny Ellison to John Warren, Nov. 7, 1969, RWEP, LC.

463 "years ago, Duke's father": RWE, "Homage to Duke Ellington on His Birthday," *Washington Star*, April 27, 1969.

464 "to pinpoint the Black Man's achievements": University of Delaware Black Students Union (Mary Ruth Warner) to RWE, Dec. 30, 1968, RWEP, LC.

465 "so fast that while I could hear": RWE, "A Song of Innocence," *Iowa Review* 1 (Spring 1970): 30–40.

466 "Ralph could never understand": Stanley Crouch to author, interview, Jan. 17, 2005.

466 "they do not say much": James Alan McPherson, "Indivisible Man," *The Atlantic Monthly* 226 (Dec. 1970): 52.

466 "whether to the formal audience": *Iowa State Daily*, March 26, 1970.

466 "bone weary and disgusted": RWE to *Time* (Henry Grunwald), March 17, 1970, RWEP, LC.

467 "the time may have come": Daniel Patrick Moynihan, *The Negro Family: The Case for National Action* (Washington, D.C.: Office of Policy Planning and Research, U.S. Department of Labor, 1970).

467 "There can be no doubt": Stanley Edgar Hyman, "Richard Wright Reappraised," *The Atlantic Monthly* (March 1970): 127.

467 "Negro artists": RWE to Stanley Edgar Hyman, May 29, 1970, in John F. Callahan, ed., "Ralph Ellison Rediscovered," *New Republic* (March 1, 1999): 40–42.

467 "the fantasy of an America": RWE, "What America Would Be Like Without Blacks," *Time* (April 6, 1970): 54.

468 "Materially, psychologically": Ibid.

468 "Said a young white professor": RWE to Stanley Edgar Hyman, May 29, 1970. See also John F. Callahan, ed., "Ralph Ellison Rediscovered," p. 42.

468 "History has a way": Clifford Mason, "*Native Son* Strikes Home," *Life* (May 8, 1970): 12.

468 "editorial shoddiness": RWE to *Life* (Thomas Griffith), May 20, 1970, RWEP, LC.

18   *Professor in the Humanities*

470 "a dowdy unimpressive place": Ken Silverman to author, interview, May 1, 2002.

471 "I made the mistake": John Maynard to author, interview, May 1, 2002.

471 "We will be exploring": News release, New York University, Oct. 11, 1970.

472 "asking if I cared": RWE to Kristin and John Lattany, Jan. 21, 1971, RWEP, LC.

472 "as a whole": RWE to Alicia L. Johnson, Sept. 11, 1971, RWEP, LC.

472 "young black militants": *Black Scholar* (Nathan Hare) to RWE, Dec. 3, 1970, RWEP, LC.

472 "He says that this kid": John A. Williams, "My Man Himes: An Interview with Chester Himes," in *Amistad 1*, ed. Charles F. Harris and John A. Williams (New York: Vintage, 1970), pp. 71–72.

472 "Some of the interpretations": RWE to *College Language Association Journal* (Therman B. O'Daniel), Oct. 1, 1970, RWEP, LC.

473 "Ellison was a literary radical": Clyde Taylor to Avon Kirkland, interview, May 10, 1999, for the documentary film *Ralph Ellison: An American Journey* © 2004 New Images Productions Inc. Produced, written, and directed by Avon Kirkland.

473 "I always felt": John Hope Franklin to author, interview, June 16, 2001.

473 "I told them that Ellison": James Alan McPherson to author, interview, June 1, 2003.

473 "All kinds of people": Fanny Ellison to James Alan McPherson, Dec. 21, 1970.

474 "I never wanted": Nikki Giovanni, *Gemini: An Extended Autobiographical Statement on My First Twenty-five Years of Being a Black Poet* (New York: Bobbs-Merrill, 1971), pp. 142–43.

474 "He can put us down": *Time* (Jan. 17, 1972): 65.

474 "the fastest deteriorating area": Ms., n.d., RWEP, LC.

475 "One reason I live here": Hollie West, "Travels with Ralph Ellison Through Time and Thought," *Washington Post*, Aug. 20, 1973.

475 "Don't ever live in New York": Fanny Ellison to Peter "Tex" Schiwetz, April 3, 1970, RWEP, LC.

475 "We have an awful lot of fun": Ibid.

475 "a full and harmonious life": Fanny Ellison to John Warren, Nov. 7, 1969, RWEP, LC.

475 "Ralph, on the other hand": Fanny Ellison to Deborah Thayer, Aug. 23, 1970, RWEP, LC.

476 "There were very few": Amritjit Singh to author, interview, Dec. 28, 2003.

476 "a banal book": *New York Times*, Jan. 22, 1971.

478 "And there we all were": Fanny Ellison to John F. Callahan, Nov. 30, 1984, RWEP, LC.

478 "because in its quiet way": RWE to University of Virginia (Robert Kellogg), Jan. 25, 1978, RWEP, LC.

479 "the yearly Academy riot": RWE to Robert Penn Warren, April 28, 1971, RWEP, LC.

479 "you are still very much wanted": The White House (Lyndon Baines Johnson) to RWE, April 20, 1971, RWEP, LC.

481 "the grubbiness of the neighborhood": Fanny Ellison to Frances [Curry], Sept. 10, 1971, RWEP, LC.

481 "I was in awe": Ken Silverman to author, interview.

481 "omnibus course": John Maynard to author, interview.

482 "very few students": Robert Raymo to author, interview, May 1, 2002.

482 "Albert [Murray] and Anatole's objections": RWE, "Notes," in Ralph Ellison, *Juneteenth*, ed. John F. Callahan (New York: Vintage, 2000), p. 363.

482 "Behind a door": Amritjit Singh to author, interview, Dec. 27, 2003.

483 "My grandmother and grandfather": Jervis Anderson, "Profiles: Going to the Territory," *New Yorker* (Nov. 22, 1976): 81.

483 "Not only does it take time": RWE to James T. McFarland, May 10, 1971, RWEP, LC.

483 "It has been my plan": RWE to Stuart Omans, Sept. 14, 1971, RWEP, LC.

484 "deadline from my publishers": RWE to Harry Middleton, Nov. 27, 1972, RWEP, LC.

484 "hungry but nice": Fanny Ellison, ms. note, Nov. 10, 1972, RWEP, LC.

486 **"Leon adored Ralph"**: Toni Morrison to author, n.d. [July 9, 2004].

487 **"At Random House"**: Ibid.

488 **"My suspicion was that"**: Ibid.

488 **"Why shouldn't he be"**: Marian Bouché to RWE, Jan. 2, 1973, RWEP, LC.

488 **"the Great Big Black One"**: RWE to Harold Calicutt, Feb. 3, 1971, RWEP, LC.

488 **"Well, let's face it"**: Ibid.

489 **"because both my agent and my publisher"**: RWE to Angela Greene (National Public Radio), June 1, 1973, RWEP, LC.

489 **"and has thus produced"**: RWE to Herbert Ellison, Aug. 26, 1973, RWEP, LC.

489 **"Turnip greens!"**: Ibid.

490 **"it's fun and we feel lucky"**: Ibid.

490 **"How do you feel"**: Hollie West, "Ellison: Exploring the Life of a Not So Invisible Man," *Washington Post,* Aug. 19, 1973.

490 **"are going back South"**: Ibid.

491 **"It's another instance"**: Ibid.

19   *The Monkey on His Back*

493 **"When you lose 365 pages"**: *New York Times,* Feb. 18, 1974.

493 **"honorary members"**: RWE to New School of Social Research (John R. Everett), Feb. 21, 1974, RWEP, LC.

494 **"some black students arrived"**: Nicholas Lemann, "Issues of Perception, Issues of Substance," *Harvard Crimson* (Commencement 1975): 1.

494 **"a patronized, colonized slave"**: *Harvard Crimson,* commencement number, June 13, 1974.

494 **"the only serious intellectual endeavor"**: Martin Kilson to RWE, May 28, 1974, RWEP, LC.

494 **"He was a hero to me"**: Cornel West to author, interview, April 22, 2006.

494 **"Although I am overwhelmed"**: RWE to Harvard University (Derek Bok), Feb. 9, 1974, RWEP, LC.

495 **"the lack of students"**: New York University (R. Bayly Winder) to RWE, Feb. 14, 1974, RWEP, LC.

495 **"People came out in droves"**: Amritjit Singh to author, interview, Dec. 28, 2003.

495 **"very flexible about the terms"**: Harvard University (Henry Rosovsky) to RWE, April 12, 1974, RWEP, LC.

495 **"The dark underside"**: Baltimore *Sun,* May 17, 1974.

496 **"entering an Ivy League college"**: "Text of Address given by Ralph Ellison . . . at the annual meeting of the Associated Harvard Alumni on June 12, 1974," n.p., n.d., News Office, Harvard University, reprinted as RWE, "Address to the Harvard College Alumni, Class of 1949," in *The Collected Essays of Ralph Ellison,* ed. John F. Callahan (New York: Modern Library, 1995), p. 418.

496 **"A discontinuity had been imposed"**: Ibid., p. 420.

497 **"Out of experience proudly inherited"**: Citation, "Ralph Ellison: Doctor of Letters," June 13, 1974, RWEP, LC.

497 **"it was a time of harsh words"**: Henry Rosovsky to author, interview, Oct. 1, 2004.

497 **"in which he puts down"**: Ishmael Reed, "Ishmael Reed on Ishmael Reed: The Writer as Seer," *Black World* (June 1974): 28.

498 **"He saw the enormous jealousy"**: Stanley Crouch to author, interview, Jan. 17, 2005.

498 **"those who seem inclined"**: RWE to Marchette Chute, Sept. 27, 1974, RWEP, LC.

499 **"more intersexual and interracial"**: "Report of the Nominating Committee, Board of Trustees, Colonial Williamsburg Foundation," May 1975, RWEP, LC.

499 **"It's a traumatic thing"**: Fanny Ellison to Jacqueline Covo, n.d. [Dec. 1974], RWEP, LC.

499 **"I am not a Pan-Africanist"**: Ishmael Reed, Quincy Troupe, and Steve Cannon, "The Essential Ellison (Interview)," *Y'bird* 1 (Autumn 1977): 152.

500 **"A large and expanding middle-income group"**: *Los Angeles Times*, Jan. 29, 1975.

500 **"introducing what I hope"**: RWE to Eric Swenson, April 4, 1976, RWEP, LC.

500 **"economic class struggle"**: *New York Times*, April 28, 1975.

500 **"As a Negro American"**: RWE to Albany Public Library (Edgar Tompkins), Feb. 10, 1975, RWEP, LC.

501 **"You must *always* play"**: RWE, "The Little Man at Chehaw Station," *Collected Essays of Ralph Ellison,* p. 490.

501 **"So exhilarating was its effect"**: RWE to Lee B. Brawner, Feb. 24, 1974, RWEP, LC.

502 **"I dream constantly"**: Jervis Anderson, "Profiles: Going to the Territory," *New Yorker* (Nov. 22, 1976): 55.

502 **"His classmates monopolized him"**: Ibid.

503 **"I dare not try"**: RWE, "Ellison's Library Speech," ms., n.d. [June 1975], RWEP, LC.

503 **"Ralph made a decision"**: Dr. Melvin Todd to author, interview, July 12, 2001.

503 **"We were taking chances"**: Jervis Anderson, "Profiles," p. 91.

503 **"We love the garden"**: Fanny Ellison to Walter Gray and Dan Blanchard, July 28, 1975, RWEP, LC.

504 **"a massive fiction"**: American Academy of Arts and Letters archives, Feb. 1, 1975.

504 **"a word too long delayed"**: Robert Penn Warren to RWE, Dec. 18, 1975, RWEP, LC.

504 **"must be in"**: Michael S. Harper to RWE, Dec. 8, 1975, RWEP, LC.

504 **"the mystery of the symbols"**: Fanny Ellison to James Fanning, Dec. 5, 1977, RWEP, LC.

505 **"Ralph showed up"**: Richard and Charlotte Wilbur to author, interview, May 11, 2000.

505 **"Just the amount"**: RWE to Robert B. Stepto, March 7, 1976, RWEP, LC.

506 **"It was a great course"**: Ron Welburn to author, Jan. 6, 2004.

507 **"Ishmael Reed!"**: Ishmael Reed to author, interview, Nov. 2, 2004.

507 **"I was there"**: Quincy Troupe to author, interview, May 24, 2006.

507 **"Where on earth"**: Ishmael Reed et al., "The Essential Ellison," p. 135.

507 **"gave many kids the notion"**: Ibid., p. 150.

507 **"When did Baraka"**: Ibid., p. 154.

508 **"We are really about"**: In Michael S. Harper and Robert B. Stepto, "Ralph Ellison Interview," ms., transcript, March 7, 1976, RWEP, LC. Revised as "Study and Experience: An Interview with Ralph Ellison," in *Chant of Saints: A Gathering of Afro-American Literature, Art, and Scholarship,* ed. Michael S. Harper and Robert B. Stepto (Urbana: U of Illinois P, 1979), pp. 451–69.

508 "the ravages and taunts": Robert B. Stepto to RWE, Feb. 27, 1976, RWEP, LC.

508 "Ha, ha, ha": Michael S. Harper and Robert B. Stepto, "Ralph Ellison Interview."

508 "had changed the way": Horace Porter, ms., n.d., draft of personal essay on Ellison.

509 "looked youthful and relaxed": Horace Porter to author, interview, April 20, 2002.

509 "The discussion was extremely profitable": Robert G. O'Meally to RWE, May 17, 1976, RWEP, LC.

510 "going back to 1954": RWE, "Perspective of Literature," in Bernard Schwartz, ed., *American Law: The Third Century: The Law Bicentennial Volume* (New York: New York University Law School, 1976), p. 397.

512 "When you put a detail": Ishmael Reed et al., "The Essential Ellison," p. 156.

513 "Here is what he is doing": RWE, "Backpacking, A Plea to the Senator," ms., Nov. 22, 1976, RWEP, LC. See also Michael S. Harper and Robert B. Stepto, eds., *Chant of Saints,* pp. 445–50.

513 "He took a sort": William Grimes, "Did Ralph Ellison Leave a Second Classic?," *New York Times,* April 20, 1994.

514 "doubts about your project": RWE to *The New Yorker* (Jervis Anderson), Dec. 12, 1976, RWEP, LC.

514 "He was always meticulous": Robert B. Stepto to author, interview, Dec. 13, 2000.

514 "I saw that many of my answers": RWE to Ishmael Reed, Jan. 29, 1977, RWEP, LC.

515 "Wish I hadn't come": Fanny Ellison, ms., July 31, 1977, RWEP, LC.

515 "I was told that they saw": Ulrich Baer to author, interview, July 22, 2004.

515 "We stay well and occupied": Fanny Ellison to "Linda and Ritchie," March 14, 1978, RWEP, LC.

515 "plain-spoken, irreverent": Ibid.

515 "This takes a lot of doing": Ibid.

516 "because too many novelists": Fanny Ellison to Kristin Hunter, Sept. 10, 1978, RWEP, LC.

516 "I do not think": RWE to Lucy Golson, Sept. 25, 1978, RWEP, LC.

517 "the very complex . . . nature": James Alan McPherson to RWE, May 14, 1978, RWEP, LC.

518 "but, as with most annoyances": Fanny Ellison to Stewart Lillard, April 25, 1978, RWEP, LC.

518 "I fully appreciate": Marvin Sadik to RWE, May 23, 1978, RWEP, LC.

519 "Ralph is bearing down": Fanny Ellison to Edward Wilson, June 24, 1978, RWEP, LC.

519 "we close ourselves into": Fanny Ellison to Edward Wilson, draft, July 17, 1978, RWEP, LC.

20   *The Uncanny Penetration of the Past*

520 "If the cabin doesn't collapse": Fanny Ellison to Marisa Erskine, July 6, 1979, RWEP, LC.

520 "We don't move around much": Fanny Ellison to Jessan Dun De Credico, Aug. 15, 1983, RWEP, LC.

520 "a publisher's deadline": RWE to Macalester College, June 25, 1979, RWEP, LC.

521 "**Simply put, the 1960s**": Robert Bone, "Black Writing in the 1970s," *Nation* (Dec. 16, 1978): 677.

521 "**the most eloquent opponent**": Ibid.

522 "**tends to resist certain revisions**": *New York Times Book Review*, Jan. 17, 1982, RWEP, LC.

522 "**over-committed**": Note on Phelps-Stokes Fund (Franklin H. Williams) to RWE, Dec. 17, 1980, RWEP, LC.

523 "**serious, exhilarating**": RWE to James W. Tuttleton, [c. Sept. 30, 1979,] Archives of New York University.

523 "**It is as though**": RWE, [Address at Brown University, Sept. 19, 1979,] ms., RWEP, LC. For a revised version, see RWE, "Portrait of Inman Page: A Dedication Speech," in *The Collected Essays of Ralph Ellison*, ed. John F. Callahan (New York: Modern Library, 1995), pp. 585–90.

524 "**Thank God for that**": Revised as "Going to the Territory," *Collected Essays of Ralph Ellison*, pp. 591–692.

524 "**challenged opinions**": Kimberly Coleman, "Brown Celebrates Ellison," *Uwezo 17* (Oct. 1979): 1–2.

524 "**one of my most esteemed friends**": RWE to Century Association (Frank Streeter), Sept. 8, 1980, RWEP, LC.

525 "**Ralph was always**": Arthur M. Schlesinger, Jr., to author, interview, March 25, 2004.

525 "**who did not dance**": *New York Times Book Review*, Jan. 17, 1982.

526 "**too driven or deprived or depraved**": Robert G. O'Meally, *The Craft of Ralph Ellison* (Cambridge: Harvard UP, 1980), p. 48.

526 "**too driven or deprived or inexperienced**": RWE, "The World and the Jug," in *Shadow and Act* (New York: Random House, 1964), p. 140.

526 "**imposes upon me**": RWE, ms., n.d., RWEP, LC.

526 "**to put it mildly**": Ibid.

526 "**I think you should know**": RWE to Robert G. O'Meally, Sept. 25, 1982, RWEP, LC.

526 "**the blunders of a young scholar**": Robert G. O'Meally to RWE, Sept. 28, 1982, RWEP, LC.

527 "**the mind-blasting noise**": RWE to Kimberly W. Benston, June 15, 1984, RWEP, LC.

527 "**the headier competitions**": Kimberly W. Benston to author, interview, April 26, 2005.

528 "**contemporary trends and issues**": RWE to Ford Foundation (Richard S. Sharpe), July 10, 1980, RWEP, LC.

528 "**Ralph Ellison was a wonderfully complex**": John F. Callahan to author, interview, June 24, 2003.

528 "**Because they will link up**": Fanny Ellison to Jessan Dun De Credico, Aug. 15, 1983.

529 "**a brilliant study**": RWE to John D. and Catherine T. MacArthur Foundation (Gerald Freund), March 7, 1981, RWEP, LC.

529 "**Ralph was also impressed**": John Wright to author, interview, Dec. 28, 2003.

530 "**not only talented**": RWE to John D. and Catherine T. MacArthur Foundation (Gerald Freund), Feb. 15, 1981, RWEP, LC.

530 "**I by no means intend**": Ibid.

531 "**Keep This Nigger-Boy**": RWE, *Invisible Man* (New York: Modern Library, 1952), p. 26.

531 "a series of ideological metamorphoses": Ibid.

531 "considerable success at boring": RWE to State University of New York, Stony Brook (John Russell Brown), Dec. 26, 1984, RWEP, LC.

531 "Somehow Ellison got into his head": Henry Louis Gates, Jr., to author, interview, Nov. 10, 2001.

532 "The grounds which we share": RWE to Mrs. Charles Etta Tucker, n.d. [1985], RWEP, LC.

532 "I'm trying to make it": John Hersey, interview with RWE, ms., n.d. [1982], RWEP, LC.

532 "From large elements": Norman Podhoretz, "What Happened to Ralph Ellison?" *Commentary* (July–Aug. 1999): 56.

532 "it looks long enough": *New York Times*, March 1, 1982.

533 "The fiction writer abstracts": John Hersey, interview with RWE, ms., n.d. [1982], RWEP, LC.

533 "Part of what's taken so long": Walter Lowe, Jr., "Book Essay," *Playboy* (Oct. 1982): 42.

533 "the Reagan administration's attack": Andrew Young to RWE, May 5, 1982, RWEP, LC.

533 "is dismantling many of the processes": Walter Lowe, Jr., "Book Essay," p. 42.

534 "the philosophy of 'let it all hang out' ": Ibid.

534 "What with that hubbub": Fanny Ellison to Beryl Kouwenhoven, July 27, 1982, RWEP, LC.

534 "By now we've become accustomed": RWE to James L. Randolph, May 2, 1982, in "Ralph Ellison Rediscovered," John F. Callahan, ed., *New Republic* (March 1, 1999): 45–46.

535 "provides men and women": RWE to Charles L. Brown, April 10, 1985, RWEP, LC.

535 "I don't know how it all fits": RWE to Camille Randolph Rhone, Dec. 2, 1985, RWEP, LC.

535 "What strikes me as most curious": Cary Carson to author, Oct. 26, 2006.

535 "I was terribly, terribly fond": Louis Auchincloss to author, interview, March 24, 2004.

536 "garbled telephone message": RWE to Louis Auchincloss, May 26, 1989, RWEP, LC.

536 "I am not much of a lion": RWE to Andrew Heiskell, July 8, 1982, RWEP, LC.

536 "Someone on the board": Jonathan Fanton to author, interview, Feb. 3, 2000.

537 "the energy of the audience's excitement": *Baruch College Ticker*, April 12, 1983.

537 "You would have thought": *Washington Post*, March 29, 1983.

538 "never made much progress": Ibid.

538 "I knew for a fact": R. W. B. Lewis to author, interview, May 12, 2000.

538 "The trouble was that Ralph": Albert Murray to author, interview, May 15, 2000.

538 "I thought Stanley Hyman": Ted Weiss to author, interview, Dec. 14, 2000.

539 "at least once": Tobias Wolff to author, interview, Nov. 8, 2004.

539 "which I hoped would allow": RWE to American Academy and National Institute of Arts and Letters (Margaret M. Mills), June 20, 1983, RWEP, LC.

539 "I make a personal plea": John Kenneth Galbraith to RWE, June 4, 1984, RWEP, LC.

539 "I see Francis Steegmuller": Shirley Hazzard to author, interview, Feb. 17, 2001.

540 "Something is lost": RWE to Michel Fabre, June 7, 1983, RWEP, LC.

540 "for by giving artistic sanction": RWE to Erskine Caldwell, Sept. 20, 1983, RWEP, LC.

541 "Ralphie is getting real baldheaded": *Arna Bontemps–Langston Hughes Letters, 1925–1967,* ed. Charles H. Nichols (New York: Dodd, Mead, 1980), p. 374.

541 "Yes, yes": RWE to author, interview, April 30, 1983.

541 "Ray discussed with us": Marvina White to author, interview, Feb. 3, 2001.

542 "Learning the details": RWE to author, Oct. 13, 1988.

542 "Here we are": RWE to John [Roche], n.d. [1989], RWEP, LC.

543 "it's the 'getting place' ": RWE to Camille Randolph, Oct. 22, 1985, RWEP, LC.

543 "We live here *not* because": RWE to Levites Realty Management Corporation (Barry H. Levites), Feb. 8, 1986, RWEP, LC.

544 "This has nothing to do": Mary Battiata, "Saluting the Arts Medalists," *Washington Post,* April 24, 1985.

544 "Ralph Waldo Ellison is said to be": Ibid.

544 "I can visualize the house": RWE to Camille Randolph, Oct. 22, 1985.

544 "a rather tame spring season": RWE to Louis S. Auchincloss, May 8, 1986, RWEP, LC.

545 "reaffirms one's respect": *Publishers Weekly* (June 6, 1986): 62.

545 "judicious": *Kirkus* (June 1, 1986): 836–37.

545 "who has long tried": RWE to Center for the Study of Southern Culture (William Ferris), April 28, 1986, RWEP, LC.

21   *Flying Home*

546 "watched and took photographs": RWE to C. E. Tucker, Sept. 7, 1986, RWEP, LC.

546 "It's a good place": Fanny Ellison to Vance Bourjaily, Oct. 17, 1986, RWEP, LC.

546 "there is little in this volume": *New York Times Book Review,* Aug. 3, 1986.

547 "never fail to be elegantly written": *Los Angeles Times,* Aug. 8, 1986.

547 "the articulation of": Louis Menand, "Literature and Liberation," *New Republic* (Aug. 4, 1986): 40.

547 "In only three books": *Washington Post,* July 23, 1986.

548 "I thought *[Shadow and Act]* not only the best": Ernest Gaines to author, interview, May 18, 2006.

548 "When Civil Rights": Houston A. Baker, Jr., "Failed Prophet and Falling Stock: Why Ralph Ellison Was Never Avant-Garde," *Stanford Humanities Review* 7 (Spring 1999): 55.

548 "Ralph said, 'I didn't know' ": John F. Callahan to author, interview, Feb. 4, 2006.

549 "the most penetrating essays": Shelby Steele, "The Content of His Character," *The New Republic* (March 1, 1991): 28.

549 "Ellison became such": Cornel West to author, interview, April 3, 2006. See also T. S. Eliot, *The Use of Poetry and the Use of Criticism* [1933] (Cambridge: Harvard UP, 1964), p. 112.

549 "spectacular novel": Toni Morrison to author, n.d. [July 9, 2004].

550 "The length and form": Horace Porter, ms., n.d.

550 **"an unintended pretentiousness"**: RWE to John Simon Guggenheim Foundation, Jan. 7, 1987, RWEP, LC.

550 **"with his trademark southern charm"**: David Yaffe, *Fascinating Rhythm: Reading Jazz in American Writing* (Princeton: Princeton UP, 2005), p. 79.

550 **"worked tirelessly"**: Ted Panken, quoted in David Yaffe, *Fascinating Rhythm*, p. 78.

551 **"Bellow told me once"**: Stanley Crouch to author, interview, Aug. 16, 2005.

551 **"The Library of Congress"**: John F. Callahan to author, interview.

551 **"the mysterious processes of time"**: RWE to Tuskegee University, n.d. [1988], RWEP, LC.

552 **"I can't forget Emerson's powerful force"**: RWE to Alfred Kazin, Nov. 4, 1987, RWEP, LC.

552 **"We're still reliving our exciting experiences"**: RWE to Walter Grey, Nov. 28, 1986, RWEP, LC.

553 **"Time is cutting such a swath"**: RWE to David Diamond, March 3, 1987, RWEP, LC.

553 **"He seemed almost annoyed"**: Toni Morrison to author, July 9, 2004.

553 **"This was the closest I had ever come"**: Ibid.

554 **"When I was inducted"**: Ibid.

554 **"with some of the stuff"**: *New York Times*, April 1, 1988.

554 **"it would be disgraceful"**: American Academy and National Institute of Arts and Letters (Margaret Mills) to RWE, Aug. 3, 1988, Academy archives.

554 **"He made sport"**: *New York Times*, Oct. 26, 1988.

555 **"this crowded old nest"**: RWE to Leon Edel, Feb. 9, 1987, RWEP, LC.

555 **"Fanny would have traveled more"**: John F. Callahan to author, interview.

555 **"If you forget"**: Roderick Townley, "Television Makes Us See One Another," in *Conversations with Ralph Ellison,* ed. Maryemma Graham and Amritjit Singh (Jackson: UP of Mississippi, 1995), p. 389.

555 **"Now they smile"**: RWE to Roderick Townley, Aug. 5, 1989, RWEP, LC.

556 **"I'll be damn"**: *New York Times*, April 18, 1989.

556 **"When that car comes"**: RWE, "On Being the Target of Discrimination," in *The Collected Essays of Ralph Ellison,* ed. John F. Callahan (New York: Modern Library, 1995), p. 824.

556 **"The man is far too composed"**: David Remnick, "Visible Man," *New Yorker* (March 14, 1994): 34.

557 **"I couldn't have anticipated"**: RWE to Harold Bloom, Jan. 29, 1987, RWEP, LC.

557 **"I think that you've produced"**: RWE to Alan Nadel, Jan. 27, 1984, courtesy of Professor Alan Nadel.

557 **"Perhaps after reading"**: RWE to Robert G. O'Meally, April 17, 1989, RWEP, LC.

557 **"I was very glad"**: Robert G. O'Meally to author, Oct. 19, 2004.

558 **"The story keeps writing itself"**: RWE to Random House (Bert Krantz), Jan. 23, 1990, RWEP, LC.

558 **"fifteen years younger"**: David Remnick, "Visible Man," p. 35.

558 **"color became space"**: RWE, "Bearden," *Collected Essays of Ralph Ellison,* p. 833.

558 **"Just about the last thing"**: Rosanna Warren to author, interview, Aug. 8, 2006.

558 **"Red is indeed"**: RWE, ["Tribute to Robert Penn Warren,"] ms., n.d., RWEP, LC.

559 **"There was a mix-up"**: John F. Callahan to author, interview.

559 "dirtied by Frank Taylor": Richard and Charlotte Wilbur to author, interview, May 11, 2000.

559 "Neither Fanny nor I": RWE to Richard Wilbur, Feb. 24, 1987, RWEP, LC.

560 "the fun we had together": Charlotte Wilbur to Fanny Ellison and RWE, Feb. 15, 1987, RWEP, LC.

560 "pathologically isolated": Richard and Charlotte Wilbur to author, interview.

560 "his disinclination in the last years": Nathan and Charlotte Scott to author, interview, June 20, 2000.

560 "I'm not sure I can write": Horace Porter to author, interview, April 20, 2002.

560 "thousands of books": *Chicago Tribune*, June 18, 1992.

561 "a dark age coming": *Newark Star-Ledger*, April 10, 1992.

561 "it was the tenacity": RWE, ms., untitled, n.d. [1992], RWEP, LC.

561 "Cashew-brown, with long limbs": *Chicago Tribune*, June 21, 1992.

561 "We have a tremendous way to go": *Chicago Tribune*, June 22, 1992.

562 "don't mean a thing": RWE, ms., n.d. [April 1993], RWEP, LC.

562 "a modest apartment": David Remnick, "Visible Man," p. 34.

563 "polite in the high style": Ibid.

564 "not a little wine": Ibid.

564 "There are a lot of subtleties": Ibid., p. 38.

564 "kept calling, calling": John F. Callahan to author, interview.

566 "I had with me": Nathan Scott to author, interview, June 20, 2000.

ACKNOWLEDGMENTS

When two different editors approached me after Ralph Ellison's death in 1994 about writing his biography, I said no. I was at work on other projects. When one of the editors asked me again some years later, I again said no. I also told him that I was certain that someone else was at work on the project, but that I would get the facts for him.

I then contacted Professor John F. Callahan of Lewis and Clark College, who had edited and published much material from the Ralph Ellison Papers at the Library of Congress, including *Flying Home*, a collection of short stories, and *The Collected Essays of Ralph Ellison*. (Later would come the novel *Juneteenth*.) As I understood it, either officially or unofficially Callahan was Mrs. Fanny Ellison's main advisor in literary matters having to do with her late husband. John Callahan said that *he* had no intention of writing such a book. Also, no one else had Mrs. Ellison's support, or had been given unrestricted access to the papers at the Library of Congress. Would *I* be interested in taking on the project? After some reflection, I said yes. I had always admired Ellison's work. I had interviewed him at length in his apartment for a biography of Langston Hughes. He and his wife had collected his papers assiduously, so I would not have to rely on conjecture and hearsay. I then signed an agreement with Mrs. Ellison and her lawyer, John Silberman of John Silberman Associates of Manhattan, which gave me full access to the papers. Mrs. Ellison retained the right to read and comment on the manuscript before publication, but ceded the right to approve its final version. For his guidance as I prepared the book for printing, I thank Donn Zaretsky of John Silberman Associates, as well as Mr. Silberman. Through the late Fifi Oscard of the Fifi Oscard Agency—whose passing I regret—I signed a contract to publish the book with Alfred A. Knopf. This step allowed me to work once again with Jonathan Segal, my editor on *Days of Grace: A Memoir* (written with Arthur Ashe) and *Jackie Robinson: A Biography*. For his considerable patience and expert guidance, I am grateful.

Illness prevented Mrs. Ellison (who died in 2005) from giving me any direct help whatsoever in working on this book, but John Callahan was a strong critical voice that doubtless improved its quality. He was at all times a fair-minded defender of the legacy of Ralph Ellison and the best standards of biography. I was close to finishing the book in 2003 when Sharon Long, the dean of the School of Humanities and Sciences at Stanford University, where I was a professor, asked me to become the senior associate dean for the humanities for a term of three years. The rigors of the job hampered progress on finishing the book, but Dean Long was always sympathetic and accommodating as I pushed on.

Although the single biggest task in writing this life was reading the Ellison papers at the Library of Congress, the project led me to many other institutions and to many individuals who had known Ellison in one capacity or another. Several people were outstanding in their generosity. Avon Kirkland, for example, the founder of New Images, Inc., and the producer of the documentary film *Ralph Ellison: An American Journey*, gave me access to his large archive of interviews and visual material. I also thank his associate Carla Healey-London. Both Saul Bellow and Toni Morrison generously consented to interviews, as did William and Rose Styron, and Richard and Charlotte Wilbur. Sanora Babb, then in her nineties, spoke freely with me about her key friendship with Ellison in the late 1940s and gave me written permission to quote from her letters to him. The critic and novelist Stanley Crouch and James Alan McPherson of the University of Iowa Writers' Workshop, among others, were always ready to share with me their knowledge of Ellison.

The American Council of Learned Societies awarded me a fellowship that allowed me to spend a year at the Stanford Humanities Center, assisted by sabbatical support from the university.

At the American Academy of Arts and Letters (formerly the American Academy and National Institute of Arts and Letters), I was helped by Kathleen Keinholtz, archivist, and Vivian Dajani, executive director. At the American Academy in Rome, I thank Adele Chatfield-Taylor, the late John D'Arms, and Lester K. Little, as well as Roberta Carfagnini, Karen Rose Gonon, Christine Heumer, Pina Pasquantonio, Christina Pugliese, Milena Sales, and Alessandra Vinciguerra. At Bard College, I was aided by Helene Tieger of the library and Jessica Kemm of the alumni office, who put me in touch with former students, including Vera Gordon, Ivan Levison, George Lynes, and Eric Werthman. At Bennington College, where Ellison had been a trustee, I thank Oceana Wilson of the Crossett Library. The literary appraiser Bart Auerbach of Bartbooks guided me through photographic material left behind by Mrs. Ellison in her apartment when she died in November 2005. At Brown University, I thank the poet and professor Michael S. Harper, who knew Ellison well.

At the Century Association or club, several members and officials helped me, including Louis Auchincloss, Albert Murray, Sidney Offit, Arthur M. Schlesinger, Jr., and its able archivist, Russell A. Flinchum. At the University of Chicago, I thank the writer Richard Stern and Andrew Carroll of the university library. At the Colonial Williamsburg Foundation, I was aided by Cary Carson, to whom I was directed by Arthur Knight of the College of William and Mary. I thank Randall Birkett, head of special collections at Emory University, and also there my friend Rudolph Byrd; and Lawrence Jackson, with whom I had enjoyed several pleasant discussions while he, too, was reading in the Ellison papers at the Library of Congress.

At Harvard University, I learned much from Daniel Aaron, professor emeritus in American Civilization; Henry Louis Gates, Jr.; Martin Kilson, professor emeritus of Government; and Henry Rosovsky, former dean of Arts and Sciences. I thank Jim Hatch and Camille Billops of the Hatch-Billops Collection in Manhattan, and officials at the Lilly Library at the University of Indiana. At the University of Iowa, I thank, in addition to James Alan McPherson, Horace Porter in English, and the librarian Joyce K. Wiles. At Alfred A. Knopf, in addition to Jonathan Segal, I thank his assistants Robert Grover and Kyle McCarthy, and, for her many courtesies over the years, Ida Giragossian. The librarian of Congress, James H. Billington, made me feel welcome at LC; I also interviewed his predecessor, the late Daniel Boorstin. I was ably advised in my research there by Dr. Alice Lotvin Birney, curator in American literature in the Manuscript Division, and Adrienne Canon, specialist in African-American material. I thank the several skilled, courteous librarians and assistants in the reading room of the Manuscript Division. In the Division of Prints and Photographs, Maricia Battle and Bonnie Coles helped me with the collection of Ellison photographs. For access to Ellison material housed in the Jefferson Building of the Library of Congress, I thank Evan Larks, Clark Evans, and Jerry Wager.

At the William Morris Agency, Owen Laster and Daniel Strone shared with me their memories of Ralph Ellison. At the U.S. National Archives and Records, Susan Abbott, Gregory Plunges, and Horace H. Waters provided valuable information. At New York University, I thank John Maynard, Robert Raymo, Ken Silverman, Roger Deakins, Jonathan Lipman, and also Leslie Berlowitz, now of the American Academy of Arts and Sciences. Researching Ellison's native Oklahoma City, I am indebted to Hannah Atkins; Anita Arnold; Daniel Blanchard; Zethel Chamberlain; Dr. Gravelly Finley; Walter L. Gray; Denyvetta Davis of the Ralph Ellison Branch Library; Juanita Vivette Harris; Clara Luper; Burvis McBride; Helen Sutton; Ernest Sutton; Dr. Melvin Todd; Dr. Melvin B. Tolson, Jr.; and William A. Vivette. At the Oklahoma Historical Society: Bruce Fisher, David Draper Clark, and William D. Welge; at the University of Oklahoma, in Norman: Professor Robert Griswold and John Lovett; and at Langston University, Oklahoma: the archivist Dr. Kirby Ballard.

At Princeton University, in addition to Toni Morrison, who granted me two interviews and also wrote to me about Ellison, I thank Rene Boatman, her assistant. Also in Princeton: Ted and Renée Weiss; A. Walton Litz, professor emeritus; and Professor Cornel West. At the Queens Borough Branch Library in New York, John Hyslop. At the University of Paris, Michel Fabre and Genevieve Fabre. At Random House, I thank Robert Loomis and also Scott Moyers, who encouraged me to write this book. At the Schomburg Center for Research in Black Culture at the New York Public Library in Harlem: Dr. Howard Dodson, the head of the center, and Diana Lachatenere of Special Collections. As Stanford University too many people, in addition to Dean Sharon Long, helped me for me to list all of them here. They include the ever supportive top administrators in the Department of English Dagmar Logie and Alyce Boster, as well as Jay Fleigelman and Nicholas Jenkins, both of whom read portions of my manuscript; Shelley Fisher Fishkin; and Joseph Frank, the Dostoyevsky scholar who was once Ellison's colleague. Diane Middlebrook kindly lent me material on Oklahoma City she had gathered for her biography of Billy Tipton. I also thank the undergraduate assistants Sarah Griswold, Helen C. Hsu, and Jennie Park, as well as MaryAnn Coyne Wijtman for help with my photographs. I hired Mary Petrusewicz mainly to help me cut my overgrown manuscript one year while I was in the dean's office. At the Stanford in Washington Program, its director, Dr. Adrienne Jamieson, always welcomed me on my research trips to LC. I also thank my friend Bliss Carnochan, professor emeritus, as well as Brigitte Carnochan, who not only met the challenge of providing Knopf with an acceptable photograph of the author but provided professional assistance in organizing the photographic sections of this book.

At Tuskegee University (formerly Tuskegee Institute): Professor Xavier Nicholas helped me unselfishly; also, Deborah Haile of the university library; the archivist Cynthia Wilson; Edrice D. Leftwich, Office of the Registrar; Louis "Mike" Rabb; James Toland; Carolyn W. Ford; and Laly C. Washington. I also thank Michael Ellison Lewis of the Ellison family for his aid and courtesy. At Wellesley College, Professor William E. Cain for his keen scholarship and generosity; and at the University of Western Kentucky, for help with the Robert Penn Warren Papers: Professor Mary Ellen Miller and, in the library, Connie Mills. At Williams College: Sylvia Kennick-Brown; Professor David Lionel Smith; and Ebony Chatman, then at Stanford.

At Yale University, I interviewed before his death R. W. B. Lewis, for me the model of the ideal biographer, as well as his wife, Nancy Lewis. Also, Robert B. Stepto, who also knew Ellison. At the Beinecke Library at Yale, I thank Dr. Patricia C. Willis for access to the James Weldon Johnson Collection.

In addition to the above, I also either interviewed or was helped in other substantial ways by individuals such as Amiri Baraka; Saul Bellow's assistant at the time, Chris Walsh; Kimberly Benston of Haverford College; Martha Bernard; Houston A. Baker, Jr., and Charlotte Pierce-Baker; David Bradley; and Bliss Broyard. Also: Steve Cannon; Austin Curtis; Anne Margaret Daniel; Roger Deakins; Trey Ellis; Robert and Priscilla Ferguson; Barbara Foley; Marianne Forrest; John Hope Franklin; Diane Gaines; Ernest Gaines; Katherine A. Geffcken; Gene Goodheart; Donald Gibson, professor emeritus at Rutgers University; Maryemma Graham; Carlos Greaves, M.D.; Leo Hamalian; Charles Harris; Shirley Hazzard; George Henderson; McKay Jenkins; the novelist Charles Johnson; Susan Kiko; Richard Kostelanetz; the late Stanley Kunitz; the late Jacob Lawrence; Miriam Raccah Lewis; Jonathan Lipman; the late A. B. Magil; Ann Freeman Meyvaert; James Michael; Ralph Ellison's close friend and intellectual partner of many years Albert Murray, as well as Mozelle Murray and Michele Murray; Alan Nadel; Kenneth Neilson; Peter T. Nesbett; Dr. Doris Oliveira; Robert G. O'Meally; Richard Poirier; Ross Posnock; David and Kit Reed; Ishmael Reed; David and Pamela Roessel; Hazel Rowley; David Sarser; Nathan and Charlotte Scott; Bob Silver; Amritjit Singh; Alan Skvirsky; Shelby Steele; Milton Stern; Leslie Stifelson; Curtice Taylor; Quincy Troupe; Alan Wald; Cheryl Wall; the poet Rosanna Warren; Jerry G. Watts; Sidney Wolfe, M.D.; Ellen Wright of Paris; Jay Wright and Lois Wright; John Wright of the University of Minnesota; David Yaffe; and, as always, Richard Yarborough.

I'm sure that I have forgotten for the moment various individuals who helped me as I was researching and writing this book. To these persons I offer my sincere apologies. My wife, Marvina White, and my son, Luke Rampersad, know better than anyone else the steep personal cost of writing this book. Sorry, but it had to be done.

INDEX

Aaron, Daniel, 391, 402, 408, 409, 509, 518
Abel, Lionel, 537
Abrams, M. H., 410
Absalom, Absalom! (Faulkner), 359
Acheson, Dean, 438
A. C. Horn Paint Company, 89, 91–2, 236
Adams, George, 301, 304
Adams, Mabel, 301
Adams, Richard P., 296
Adventures of Augie March, The (Bellow), 269, 290, 314–15, 349, 352
Adventures of Huckleberry Finn (Mark Twain), 30, 197, 210, 358, 397, 506, 534
Advertisements for Myself (Mailer), 368–9
African American Review, 527
African-Americans, 11–12, 70, 135
    Communist Party and, 117, 152, 255
    Hollywood portrayal of, 247–8
    in *Invisible Man*, 241
    Jews and, 125
    in middle class, 499–500
    in migration to Oklahoma Territory, 5, 10
    Paris expatriate, 305–7
    radicalism in history of, 115–16
    RE's perception of, 77–8, 97–8, 133–4, 144–5, 146, 163, 174, 245–6, 384, 427–8, 460, 500–1, 510
    RE's views on culture of, 151, 188–9, 395–6, 420–1, 433–4, 547–9
    Wright's attitude toward, 97–8
    see also civil rights movement; race, racism
African independence movement, 300, 349, 366

African Patriotic League, 87
"Afternoon" (Ellison), 136–7, 142, 146
Against the Grain (Huysman), 62
Albee, Edward, 447, 507
Aldridge, Ira, 26
Aldridge, John, 322–3
Aldridge, Leslie, 322–3
Ali, Muhammad, 461
Allan, Lewis, 99
All Brave Sailors: The Story of the S.S. Booker T. Washington (Beecher), 203
Allen, Frederick Lewis, 270
All the King's Men (Warren), 250–1, 450
Alston, Charles "Spinky," 175
Amen Corner, The (Baldwin), 389
American, The (James), 557
American Academy in Rome, 309, 316–46
    fellows at, 317, 320–1
    Italy tour and, 318–19
    life at, 317, 321–3
    RE's extramarital affair at, 337–46
    RE's quarters at, 316–17, 329
    RE's unhappiness at, 321–3, 325
    U.S.I.S. lecture tour and, 339
    visiting artists and writers at, 325–6
    work on novel-in-progress at, 320, 325, 333, 336
American Academy of Arts and Letters, 3, 207, 309, 311, 326, 327, 371, 404, 405, 417–18, 424, 463–4, 476–7, 479, 498, 504, 507, 511, 514, 516, 525, 538–9, 542–3, 552–3, 558, 562
    see also National Institute of Arts and Letters
American Adam, The (Lewis), 238, 360
American Civil Liberties Union, 172, 330

American Committee for Cultural
Freedom, 333
American Council for African Culture, 423
American Council of Learned Societies, 395
American Daughter (Thompson), 208
*American Dilemma, An: The Negro
Problem and Modern Democracy*
(Myrdal), 181–2, 187, 200, 438, 496
American Dream, An (Mailer), 424
American Federation of Labor (AFL), 92,
129, 133
American Jewish Committee, 424
American Medical Center for Burma, 372
"American Negro, The: Three Views"
(Holmes), 159
"American Negro Writing—A Problem of
Identity" (Ellison), 201
"American Pluralism from the Negroes'
Side of the Line" (Ellison), 423
American Quarterly, 233
American Review, 487
American Revolution Bicentennial
Commission, 431, 432, 476, 477, 486,
489, 498, 510
American Scholar, The, 313, 315, 352, 424,
453, 501, 516
"American Scholar, The" (Emerson), 496, 551
American Writing, 136
Amistad, 454–5, 472
Ammons, James, 23, 107
Amsden, Arthur, 213–14
Amsden, Mabel, 213–14
Anderson, Ivy, 29
Anderson, Jervis, 502, 503, 513–14, 523
Anderson, M. Margaret, 162, 240
Anderson, Regina, 112
Anderson, Sherwood, 117, 142
"And Hickman Arrives" (Ellison), 372,
374–5, 456
Angell, Roger, 525
Angelou, Maya, 521, 547
Anna Livia Plurabelle (Joyce), 138
Annie Allen (Brooks), 249
Another Country (Baldwin), 388–9, 401
Antioch College, 291–2
Antioch Review, 160, 181, 187, 191, 199, 279
anti-Semitism, 39, 92, 231
black, 125
of RE, 39–40
antiwar movement, 400, 418

Aptheker, Herbert, 93, 152–3, 423
Arendt, Hannah, 404, 421
*Armed Vision, The: A Study in the Methods
of Modern Literary Criticism*
(Hyman), 237–8
Armstrong, Louis, 14, 29, 77, 197–8, 257,
355, 356, 366, 387, 565
Arrowsmith, William, 334
Arrowsmith (Lewis), 74
Arter, Alma, 406
"Artist and the City, The: The New York
Experience," 474
As I Lay Dying (Faulkner), 359
Ask the Professor, 69
Associated Council of the Arts, 427, 445
Associated Negro Press, 202
Association for the Study of Negro Life
and History, 445
"As the Spirit Moves Mahalia" (Ellison), 354
Astor, Brooke, 536
Astor, John Jacob, 566
Atkins, Hannah, 503
Atlantic Monthly, The, 178–9, 273, 288,
467, 541
RE portrait in, 473–4
Attaway, William, 141–2, 151, 180
Auchincloss, Louis, 535–6, 544–5
Auden, W. H., 113, 125, 216, 394, 464
Audubon, John James, 566
Author Meets the Critics, The, 276
Authors Guild Foundation, 445, 489
Awoonor, Kofi, 480

Babb, Sanora, 147–51, 165, 168, 171, 178,
230–1, 339
Babel, Isaac, 122
Bacall, Lauren, 515
"Background of American Negro
Expression, The—Folklore, Writing
and Music" (Ellison), 302
"Backwacking: A Plea to the Senator"
(Ellison), 513
Baer, Ulrich, 515
Baker, Carlos, 510
Baker, Ella, 407
Baker, Houston A., Jr., 548
Baldwin, James, 263, 281, 306–7, 325, 328,
398, 401, 402, 404, 405, 409, 410, 424,
453, 455, 468, 521, 554
literary success of, 388–90

Baldwin, Roger, 330, 331, 353

Baltimore Afro-American, 94

Bambara, Toni Cade, 404, 487, 521

Baraka, Amiri (LeRoi Jones), 379–80, 403–4, 414–15, 434, 452, 466, 500, 507, 527

Barber, Samuel, 479

Bard College, 350, 359–62, 364, 372, 380, 396, 518

Barnes, Djuna, 307

Barrow, Errol, 463

Barth, John, 487

Barthé, Richmond, 83–6, 88, 89–90, 236

Barthelme, Donald, 516

Basie, Count, 28–9, 171, 302, 321

Bassett, Theodore, 131

Bates, Add, 164, 167, 250

Bates, Amelie, 164, 191

Bates, John, 164, 191

"Battle Royal" (Ellison), 217, 224, 231, 234, 238–9

Beach, Joseph Warren, 105

"Bear, The" (Faulkner), 274, 352

Bearden, Romare, 397, 454, 455–6, 507, 517, 558

"Beating That Boy" (Ellison), 200

Beauvoir, Simone de, 190, 212, 493

bebop, 137, 197, 355, 387, 419

Becker, Stephen, 313

Beckett, Samuel, 454, 493

Beckham, Barry, 523

Beecher, John, 203–4

Beer Can by the Highway, The: Essays on What's American about America (Kouwenhoven), 476, 506, 555

Behrman, S. N., 410

Bell, John, 23, 55, 56, 70, 72, 80, 86, 95

Bellow, Saul, 252, 260–1, 269, 280, 290, 302, 312, 314–15, 320, 325, 328, 329, 331, 332, 335, 349, 352–4, 361, 362, 368, 372, 373, 376–7, 398, 409, 416–17, 418, 422, 447, 461, 481, 510, 534, 554, 560–1
   major works of, 349–50
   Nobel Prize awarded to, 511–12
   on RE, 359, 377–8, 513, 551
   RE contrasted with, 376, 512
   RE's friendship with, 349–50, 380, 384–5, 399
   RE's Tivoli stay and, 359–60, 362–4, 370, 376

Bellow, Sondra, 332, 335, 349, 364, 370, 376

Beloved (Morrison), 553, 554

Bennett, Hal, 453

Bennington College, 201–2, 211, 216, 239, 458, 485, 539

Benston, Kimberly, 526–7, 557

Berger, Monroe, 239

Bernard, Martha, 245

Bernstein, Leonard, 317, 367, 414

Berry, Abner, 131, 158, 262

Berryman, John, 209, 216

Bessie, Alvah, 147

Bessie, Simon Michael, 313

Best of Simple, The (Hughes), 511

Best Short Stories by Negro Writers, The (Hughes), 433

Bethune, Mary McLeod, 280, 296

"Between the World and Me" (Wright), 97

Beyond the Melting Pot (Glazer), 429–30

"Bibliography of Ralph Ellison's Published Writings, A" (Fabre and Benoit), 480

Big Sea, The (Hughes), 138–9

Big White Fog (Ward), 124, 139–40

Binswanger, Clara, 172, 216, 232, 405

Binswanger, Isadore, 172, 216

Bird: The Legend of Charlie Parker (Reisner), 386

"Birthmark, The" (Ellison), 136–7

Birth of a Nation, The (film), 24, 247–8, 449, 463

Bishop, Elizabeth, 516

Bixler, Paul, 181, 187, 188, 279

Black Academy of Arts and Letters, 449, 472

Black American Literature Forum, 527

"Black Ball, The" (Ellison), 105–6

Black Boy (Wright), 97–8, 187–90, 191, 194, 201, 208, 246, 510
   RE's review of, 178, 188, 199

"Black Boys and Native Sons" (Howe), 401

Black Culture and Black Consciousness (Levine), 529

Black Dispatch, 14, 24–5, 29, 31, 37, 39, 44, 45, 48, 158, 284

Black Fiction (Rosenblatt), 495

Black Film Foundation, 472

Black Fire: An Anthology of Afro-American Writing (Neal and Baraka), 452

"Black Hope" (Wright), 119, 131

Blacking Up (Toll), 506

Black Jacobins, The (James), 135
Black Lines: A Journal of Black Studies, 472
Black Metropolis (Cayton and Drake), 465
Blackmur, R. P., 105, 209, 238, 280, 291, 335
Black Odyssey (Ottley), 239, 245
Black Panther Party, 466, 479–80, 511
Black Power, 78, 385–6, 400, 413, 429, 434, 437, 438, 449, 460, 479, 485, 490, 500, 541
Black Power (Wright), 281, 300, 306
Black Rage (Grier and Cobbs), 412
Black Reconstruction in America (Du Bois), 561
Black Scholar, 472
Blackwell, Jean, 112
Black World, 472, 497
    see also *Negro Digest*
Bland, Edward, 366
Blaustein, Alfred, 317, 349
Bloodline (Gaines), 453
Blood on the Forge (Attaway), 151–2, 153
Bloodworth Orphans, The (Forrest), 521
Bloom, Harold, 556–7
Bloom, John Morton, 522
Bloomgarden, Alina, 551
"Blueprint for Negro Writing" (Wright), 99, 111–12, 117, 118, 130–1, 139, 141
blues, 27–8, 97, 120, 160, 188–9, 222, 302
    in *Invisible Man,* 197–8
    RE on, 12, 188, 403–4
Blues People (Baraka), 403
Bluest Eye, The (Morrison), 521, 553
Bly, Robert, 444
Bodkin, Maud, 238
Bok, Derek, 494–5
Bond, Julian, 485
Bond, Nina, 319–20, 332
Bone, Robert, 520–2
Bontemps, Arna, 141–2, 158, 279, 452–3, 541
Book Find Club, 168
Book-of-the-Month Club, 128, 130, 178, 180, 263, 468, 544
Book Week, 422–3
Boorstin, Daniel, 471, 477
Boren, David L., 502, 552
Borgerhoff, E. B. O., 291
Borges, Jorge Luis, 493
Boss Man (Cochran), 129

Botsford, Keith, 353–4
Botstein, Leon, 518
Bottegha Oscura, 335–6
Bourjaily, Vance, 372, 546
Bowen, Elizabeth, 271
Bowen, Hillard, 29
Bowles, Chester, 423
Bowles, Jane, 174
"Boy on a Train" (Ellison), 20, 100
Bradford, Roark, 58
Bradley, David, 547
Braithwaite, E. R., 433
Branam, Virgil Dodge, 31–2, 231, 250, 310, 431, 488–9
Brandeis University, 326–7
Brandel, Elsa, 254
Branson, Herman, 395
Brazelton, James H. A., 38
Bread and Stone (Bessie), 147
Bread Loaf Writers' Conference, 367
Breaux, Zelia N. Page, 26, 27–8, 32, 34, 41, 42, 43, 55, 73, 285, 291
Breit, Harvey, 264, 332
Brewster, Kingman, 480
"Bright and Morning Star" (Wright), 124, 145
Brodsky, Joseph, 560
Brooks, Cleanth, 464
Brooks, Gwendolyn, 249, 275, 281, 398, 423, 465, 507, 511, 521
Brooks, Harry, 64
Brooks, Lucille D., 293
Brooks, Van Wyck, 317, 394
Browder, Earl, 123, 189
Brown, Cecil, 473
Brown, Charles, 536
Brown, Claude, 427–8
Brown, Earl, 207
Brown, Francis, 7
Brown, H. Rap, 437
Brown, Lloyd, 262
Brown, Lucretia Ellison, *see* Ellison, Lucretia
Brown, May Belle, 7
Brown, Othello, 21, 283
Brown, Sterling, 111, 126
Brown, Tom, 7, 14, 21, 22, 283, 475, 544
Brown Girl (Marshall), 409
Brownstones (Marshall), 409
Brown University, 523–4, 526

Brown v. Board of Education, 298–9, 307, 309, 355, 369, 496, 509
Broyard, Anatole, 482, 522, 525
Brumm, Ursula, 314
Bryson, Lyman, 274
Buck, Pearl, 182, 327, 512
Buckley, William F., Jr., 390, 446
Buckmaster, Henrietta, 152, 168
Buford, Fanny, *see* Ellison, Fanny McConnell Buford
Buford, Ligon, 175, 177–8
Bunche, Ralph, 181, 296, 415
Burgess, Ernest W., 77
Burke, Kenneth, 96–7, 119, 156, 160–1, 163–4, 180, 189, 201, 207, 209, 218, 238, 257, 272, 291, 300, 312, 417, 425, 471, 476, 483, 506, 512, 527, 551
    RE influenced by, 159, 205–6
Burke, Libby, 209, 417
Burnett, Will, 124
Burns, Ben, 117, 131
Burns, James MacGregor, 444, 447–8
Butcher, Philip, 279
Buying Time, 543

"Cadillac Flambé" (Ellison), 374, 487
Caetani, Principessa, 335–6
Cain, William E., 121
"Calamus" (Whitman), 552
Caldwell, Erskine, 88, 146–7, 540
Calicutt, Harold, 29, 32, 261
Callahan, John F., 115, 523, 527–8, 529, 548, 555, 559, 563–6
Call It Sleep (Roth), 493
Cambridge School, 116, 164
Campanella, Roy, Jr., 534
Campbell, Carver, 59
Campbell, Joseph, 394
"Camp Lost Colony" (Ellison), 130
Camus, Albert, 161, 190, 454
Candida (Shaw), 75
Cannon, Steve, 433, 506, 512, 514
Capote, Truman, 233, 404, 430–1
Capps, Jack, 460–1
Carmichael, Stokely, 413, 490
Carnegie Commission on Educational Television, 424, 426, 429, 431–2, 444
Carson, Cary, 535
Carson, Rachel, 271
Carter, Benny, 128

Cartwright, Margaret, 273
Carver, George Washington, 53–4, 168, 295
"Case of Richard Wright, The: A Disservice to the Negro People" (Ford), 180
Catcher in the Rye, The (Salinger), 422
Cater, Douglas, 447
Catholic Interracial Council, 424
Catton, Bruce, 298
Cayton, Horace, 144, 161, 177, 259, 328, 330, 398, 464–5
CBS, 272, 274, 426, 439, 510
Census Bureau, U.S., 499–500
Center for Cross-Cultural Communication, 399
Century Association, 3, 371, 432, 445, 453–4, 465–6, 476–7, 484, 488, 505, 514, 516–17, 524–6, 540, 552, 558, 559
    RE admitted to, 393–4, 410–11
Cerf, Bennett, 147, 211, 264, 269, 272
"Cesspool" (Wright), 97
Challenge, 98
Chamberlain, Zethel, 38
Chaney, James, 406
Chaneysville Incident, The (Bradley), 547
"Change the Joke and Slip the Yoke" (Ellison), 351, 379, 547
"Chaos, Complexity and Possibility: The Historical Frequencies of Ralph Waldo Ellison" (Callahan), 527–8
Chapman, Chanler A., 363
Charles, Ray, 355
"Charlie Christian Story, The" (Ellison), 354
Charm: The Magazine for the Business Girl, 252
Chase, Lucia, 425
Cheever, John, 335, 338, 340, 365, 373, 377, 394, 416–17, 424, 426, 534
    RE's relationship with, 370–1
Cheever, Mary, 335, 340, 370, 417
Chester, Alfred, 307
Cheuse, Alan, 392
Chicago, University of, 373–4, 380, 381, 383–4
Chicago Defender, 177, 184, 208, 222, 244, 262, 266, 280
Chicago Public Library Harold Washington Literary Award, 561–2
Chicago Sun Book Week, 184

Chicago Tribune, 174, 561
China, 9, 386
Chisholm, Shirley, 480
Chomsky, Noam, 511
Christian, Charlie, 28, 137, 153–4, 302, 354,
    379–80, 430
Christian, Edward, 28
Christian Gauss Seminars in Criticism,
    266, 269, 275, 291
Christian Science Monitor, 261, 273
Chute, Marchette, 498
Ciardi, John, 325–6, 334, 336, 367, 391,
    444, 504, 545
Citizens Committee for Peace with
    Freedom in Vietnam, 438–9, 461
City in Crisis, The (Gans, Young, and
    Ellison), 455
Civil Rights Act of 1957, 348
civil rights movement, 38, 297, 323–4, 331,
    355, 375, 378–9, 406–8, 426, 430, 435,
    479–80, 485, 500
    increasing violence of, 396–8, 412–13,
        418–19, 425, 437, 446, 479, 490–1
    King assassination and, 446
    Malcolm X assassination and, 412–13
    RE's attitude toward, 348, 379, 385–7,
        490–1
    in RE's Senate testimony, 428–9
    Watts riots and, 418–19
    white backlash and, 466–7
    see also African-Americans; race, racism
Civil War, U.S., 116, 192, 428, 449
    RE's epiphany and, 286–7, 496–7
Clark, Carrie Langston, 122
Clark, Eleanor, 320, 335, 350, 390, 417
Clark, Kenneth, 250, 276, 299, 331, 421, 541
Clark, Mamie, 250, 299, 331
Clark, Ramsey, 445
Clarke, John Henrik, 234, 403, 423, 472
Clayton, Buck, 335
Clayton, Frederick, 154
Cleague, Albert, 438
Cleaver, Eldridge, 410, 452, 507
Clemens, Samuel, *see* Twain, Mark
Clifton, Lucille, 587, 547
*Clipper, The: A Monthly Literary
    Magazine,* 147
Coalition for a Democratic Majority, 486
Coalition for the Defense of the Black
    Panthers, 480

Cochran, Louis, 129
Cohen, Hettie, 380
Coleman, Bessie, 30
Coleman, Kimberly, 521
Coleman, Lonnie, 182
Coleman, Ornette, 419
College Language Association, 279, 472
Colonial Williamsburg Foundation, 476–8,
    495, 498–9, 534, 535
Color Curtain, The (Wright), 312
Color Purple, The (Walker), 521, 548
Coltrane, John, 355, 420
Comintern, 123–4
Commentary, 260, 353, 408, 435
Commission on Civil Rights, U.S., 394
Commission on Educational Television,
    424
Commission on Negro History and
    Culture, 445
Commission on Public Broadcasting, 486
Committee for Industrial Organization
    (CIO), 92, 103, 132–3
Committee of 100, 297, 397
Committee on Social Thought, 384
Common Ground, 162, 184, 240
Communist, The, 131, 140
Communist Party, U.S., 90, 92–3, 96, 98,
    108, 110, 123–4, 131, 172, 189
    African-American policy of, 117, 152,
        255
    antiwar policy of, 129–30, 132–5, 140
    Nazi-Soviet nonaggression pact and,
        127–8
    NNC and, 132–4
    RE's withdrawal from, 162
    Wright's break with, 161
Communist Workers Alliance, 111
Compromise, The (Richardson), 63
Conant, James, 448
Condition of Man, The (Mumford), 193
Confessions of Nat Turner, The (Styron),
    449–50
Confidence-Man, The (Melville), 253
Confluence: An International Forum, 288
Congress, U.S., 54, 135, 190, 244, 416, 432,
    528
Congress for Cultural Freedom, 330–1,
    336, 353
"Congress Jim Crow Didn't Attend, A"
    (Ellison), 134

Congress of Racial Equality (CORE), 375, 379, 437
Connelly, Marc, 58, 278
Connolly, Cyril, 211
Connor, Eugene "Bull," 396
Conrad, Joseph, 62, 105, 117
Cooney, Joan Ganz, 525–6
Cooper, James Fenimore, 30, 358
Copland, Aaron, 479
Cosby Show, The, 555
Costain, Thomas, 263
Cotton Candy on a Rainy Day (Giovanni), 508
Counter-Statement (Burke), 161, 205
Cousins, Norman, 278
Covici, Pascal, 199
Cowley, Malcolm, 119, 156, 352–3, 394, 498, 504, 553
Cox, Archibald, 497
Craft of Ralph Ellison, The (O'Meally), 526
Crane, Stephen, 300, 467
Crawford, Anthony, 8
Crime and Punishment (Dostoyevsky), 76, 121
Crisis, 130, 138, 151, 154, 515
Crisis of the Negro Intellectual, The (Cruse), 494
Cronkite, Walter, 522
Cross Section: A Collection of New American Writing (Seaver), 169, 173
Crouch, Stanley, 414, 466, 498, 504, 507, 527, 550–1, 563
Cruse, Harold, 494
Cry of Jazz, The (film), 366
Cullen, Countee, 30, 68, 79, 169
Cullman, Joseph F., III, 534
"Cultural Freedom in the Western Hemisphere," 330
cummings, e. e., 216
Curry, Frances, 265

Daedelus, 417
Dahmer, Vernon, 425
Daiches, David, 156, 352
Daily Oklahoman, 34, 102, 158, 284
Daily Worker, 93, 94–6, 98, 100, 103, 131, 156, 158, 167, 180, 244, 262
Dangling Man (Bellow), 260
Daniel, Clifton, 410
Dante Alighieri, 250, 334

"Daring Young Man on the Flying Trapeze, The" (Saroyan), 75–6
Darker Brother, The (Moon), 165, 169
Dartmouth College, 446
Davidson, Charlie, 448
Davidson, Donald, 375
Davidson, Harriet, 232
Davidson, Terry, 448
Davis, Allison, 395
Davis, Ben, Jr., 93, 131, 180, 190, 244
Davis, Charles T., 480, 483, 517, 532
Davis, Franklin, 33
Davis, Frank Marshall, 147
Davis, Henry Bowman, 33
Davis, John P., 132–3
Davis, Miles, 355–6, 387
Davis, Ossie, 412, 511
Davis, Robert Gorham, 308, 352
Dawson, William Levi, 41, 44–5, 53, 57, 60, 63, 70, 229, 283, 294–5, 558
Days of Wrath (Malraux), 83, 119
Dayton Youth Movement, 103–4
Death in Venice (Mann), 62
Debs, Eugene, 18
Delta, 540
Democratic Party, 8, 243, 332, 414, 486
Denby, William, 521
Dent, Thomas C., 433–4
DeVoto, Bernard, 270
Diamond, David, 553
Dickey, James, 434, 469
"Did You Ever Dream Lucky?" (Ellison), 297
Dies, Martin, 111, 116
Dillon, Douglas, 522
Diop, Alioune, 234
Direction, 107, 128, 141, 146
Dissent, 130, 401, 421
"Divided South Searches for Its Soul" (Warren), 326
Divine Comedy, The (Dante), 226, 334
Djilas, Milovan, 386
Doctor Zhivago (Pasternak), 365
Dodson, Howard, 551
Don't Cry, Scream (Madhubuti), 500
Don't You Want to Be Free? (Hughes), 108, 110, 122, 177
Dos Passos, John, 119, 330, 331
Dostoyevsky, Fyodor, 76, 119, 121, 122, 130, 161, 209, 322, 392, 421, 493

Doubleday, 356, 398
Douglas, Aaron, 92, 279
Douglas, William O., 271
Douglass, Frederick, 393
Down Beat, 355
Draft Riot of 1863, 116
Drake, St. Clair, 465, 472
Dreiser, Theodore, 75, 97, 119, 130, 146–7,
    152
Drye, Frank L., 54, 56, 57, 73–4, 79
Du Bois, W. E. B., 53, 77, 120, 130, 187,
    279, 371, 410, 446, 507, 510–11, 561
Duclos, Jacques, 189
Dumas, Henry, 392, 487
Dunbar, Paul Laurence, 29
Duncan, Hugh Dalziel, 506
Dunjee, Roscoe, 24–5, 37, 39, 158, 284,
    430, 503
Dupee, Fred, 363, 370
Dusk of Dawn (Du Bois), 510–11
Dutchman (Baraka), 403
"Dynamic in American Letters, The"
    (Mailer), 424–5

East of Eden (Steinbeck), 268
Ebony, 117
Eckman, Fern Marja, 389
Edel, Leon, 365, 404, 471
Editions Denoël, 305–6
Edwards, Harry, 486
Einstein, Albert, 203, 217
Eisenhower, Dwight D., 174, 332, 348, 427,
    439
Elbow Room (McPherson), 517
Eliot, T. S., 62, 76–7, 85, 97, 106, 116,
    117–19, 164, 225, 247, 249, 255, 262,
    266, 300, 381, 383, 407, 473, 511–12,
    523–4, 549
    RE's encounter with, 329
Ellington, Duke, 14, 29, 72, 87, 302, 321,
    355, 356, 463–4, 517
Elliott, Emory, 460–1
Ellis, Trey, 534
Ellison, Ada, 405, 514
Ellison, Alfred (brother), 5
Ellison, Alfred (grandfather), 7, 8–9
Ellison, Fanny McConnell Buford
    Babb affair and, 230–1
    background of, 175–8
    in European lecture tour, 294–5, 305–8

in Fisk University visit, 278–9
in Georgia vacation, 478–9
illness of, 334–7
infertility of, 229, 338–9, 381
Key West condo purchase and, 504–5,
    531–2, 559–60
marriage of, 209, 215–16, 229–30,
    288–90, 338–48, 367, 381, 385, 398,
    475–6, 519, 555
in New England sojourn, 288–91
in Oklahoma City visit, 429–30
Plainfield house and, 433, 435–6,
    440–4, 475, 489–90, 492, 520
RE's correspondence with, 182, 185,
    214–15, 294, 295, 296, 331, 341–6, 381, 383
RE's death and, 565–6
RE's first meeting with, 175, 178
RE's Rome affair and, 338–41, 345–8,
    381
in Rome, 316–22, 325, 326, 334–5
in Salzburg visit, 300–5
Styron-Roxbury incident and, 450–1
in Vermont, 191–2
white friendships of, 215–16, 231–4
Ellison, Harriet Walker, 7, 8, 9
Ellison, Herbert Maurice, 7, 13, 14–15, 19,
    20–2, 28, 33, 39, 46, 75, 80, 86, 95, 101,
    145, 229, 259, 279, 283, 354, 385, 426,
    478, 502–3
    personality of, 20, 72–3
    in Plainfield visit, 514–15
    RE's correspondence with, 103–4, 130,
        284, 300, 447–8, 489–90
    RE's relationship with, 102–4, 107–8,
        144, 266, 405, 514–15
    in World War II, 140
Ellison, Ida Milsap "Brownie," 7, 10–11, 13,
    14, 18, 20–1, 33, 43, 46, 48, 49, 50, 54,
    57, 66, 80, 95, 104, 108, 145, 266, 279,
    283–4, 430, 465
    death of, 101–2
    poverty of, 18–20
    RE's correspondence with, 55–6, 58,
        60, 61, 63–4, 65, 66, 70–1, 72, 75, 79,
        84, 86, 91, 101–2
Ellison, Jim, 7
Ellison, Lewis, 5–11, 19, 21, 23, 266
    gravesite of, 430
Ellison, Lucretia, 7, 14, 17, 66, 277–8
Ellison, Mamie, 277

Ellison, Ralph Waldo
acting debut of, 63
adolescence of, 26, 31–2
African art interest of, 397–8, 399, 486, 499, 522
ambition of, 20, 32, 58, 90, 114, 174, 178, 205, 225
anticommunism of, 141–2, 244–5, 333–4, 365, 386
anti-Semitism of, 39–40
on approach to fiction, 276–7
archives hoarded by, 528–9, 556–7
arts studies of, 68–70, 117–21
in Asian lecture tour, 343–5
awards and honors of, 3, 309, 458–9, 501–2, 541–4, 551–2, 561–2
birth of, 5–6, 11
black students and, 385–6, 459–60, 462, 482, 490, 506, 524
black writers and, 404, 452–5, 473, 486–7, 497–8, 507–10, 547–8
boyhood friendships of, 25–6, 29, 31–4
as celebrity, 264, 266, 274, 290–2, 425–6
chaos theme of, 162, 309–11, 313–14
child desired by, 229–30, 337–41
childhood of, 13–17, 19–21
college friends of, 55–6, 58–9
college novel project of, 124–5
Communist dogma of, 121–4, 127–30, 135, 137, 140
as Communist Party member, 93
contemporary black fiction and, 520–2
creative writing fellowship of, 187, 191–2, 200, 206–7, 209, 211
daily routine of, 499, 562
death and funeral of, 564–6
deaths of friends and contemporaries of, 544–5, 558–9
depression of, 179, 383–4
draft status of, 140, 143, 163, 172
dress style of, 74–5, 361, 372, 373–4, 376, 448, 473, 481, 502, 505, 564
drinking of, 232, 239, 250, 362, 382–3, 385, 454, 484, 507, 516, 525, 533, 538–9
early reviews and articles of, 112–13, 127, 129–30, 134–5, 139–40, 141, 151, 153, 156, 165, 181
editorial experience of, 154–8
education issues and, 394–5, 424, 426, 428, 432, 443–4, 518, 536

at eightieth birthday dinner, 563–4
elementary education of, 14, 18, 22–3
in European lecture tour, 304–9
extramarital affairs of, 147–51, 337–41
fiction writing studied by, 104–6
first college lecture of, 201
first professional writing of, 99–100
first published fiction of, 128
first writing venture of, 43
fortieth birthday of, 295
Harvard epiphany of, 286–7, 496–7
high school graduation of, 35
hoboing experience of, 49–51
homosexual advances rejected by, 61–3, 85–6, 236
honorary degrees awarded to, 397, 438, 469, 484, 494, 495–6, 518, 526, 562
Ida Ellison's death and, 101–2
illnesses of, 94, 126, 137, 150, 153, 179, 184, 186, 278, 305, 311, 322
janitor job of, 143, 159
Jewish friendships of, 231–2, 250, 391
Key West condominium purchase and, 504–5, 531–2, 559–60
lecture fees of, 446, 464, 551, 553
lecture style of, 201, 281–2, 445–6, 476, 506
leftist radicalization of, 82–3, 85, 90–3, 100–1
leftist writings of, 156–7, 161–2
Lewis Ellison's death and, 6–7, 12, 17–18, 20
literary influences on, 105–6, 171
literary reputation of, 409
marriages of, *see* Ellison, Fanny McConnell Buford; Ellison, Rose Poindexter
merchant marine voyages of, 169, 170–2, 185–6
musical studies and performance ambitions of, 25–8, 31, 41–2, 47, 109
music essays of, 354–5
myth and symbols studies of, 163–4
naming of, 7, 11–12
Nazi prison camp novel project of, 180–1, 187, 194, 204
new jazz criticized by, 354–6, 366, 372–3, 386–8, 419–20
New York Jews as seen by, 124–5
pen name of, 156

Ellison, Ralph Waldo (*cont'd*)
　photographic interest of, 214, 221,
　　241–2, 251, 325, 479
　poetry of, 69, 91
　prosperity of, 397, 464, 481, 485, 499,
　　513–14
　race riot witnessed by, 167–8
　rise of conservatism and, 533–4
　scholarship and critical essays on,
　　526–7
　sculpture interest of, 72–3, 79, 109
　self-identity of, 17, 34–5, 107–8
　Senate testimony of, 427–8
　seventy-fifth birthday of, 557
　sex and, 32–3, 62, 64–5, 89, 110, 114–15
　sexism of, 114–15
　short-story form and, 136–7, 252–3
　shyness of, 18, 147
　song copyrighted by, 122–3
　in Southern seminar and lecture tour,
　　293–7
　stammer of, 201, 270, 361, 385, 526
　Steveson's romance with, 40–1
　stomach ailments of, 55, 60, 66, 71, 137,
　　144, 172, 175, 179, 185, 311
　teaching style of, 360–1, 445–6, 471,
　　481–3, 505–6
　technology and electronics interest of,
　　23, 33–4, 251–2, 308
　"Uncle Tom" confrontation and,
　　439–40
　unfinished second novel of, *see* novel-
　　in-progress
　unpublished memoir of, 18
　Vermont sojourns of, 164–5, 191–5,
　　212–16
　white friends of, 33–4, 42, 141–2, 146–7,
　　231–4, 349, 391
　White House visits of, 417–18, 424, 431,
　　463, 543–4
　white women and, 147–51
　writer's worldview of, 67–8
　writing process of, 109, 165, 204–5
　writing "touch" breakthrough of, 182–3
　Yiddish language proficiency of, 232
　zoo episode and, 19
Ellison, Rose Poindexter, 109–10, 113, 115,
　　122, 126–7, 128, 130, 135–6, 137, 138,
　　143, 156, 159, 164, 178, 558
　extramarital affair of, 165, 168

　RE's divorce from, 187, 196
　RE's infidelity to, 149–51
Ellison, William, 528
"Ellison and *Communitas*," 523
Emergency Black Survival Fund, 533
Emergency Campaign for Social Justice,
　485
Emerson, Ralph Waldo, 7, 11–12, 192, 193,
　　197, 200, 210, 257, 286, 287, 403, 442,
　　496–7, 500, 552
Emmons, Brooks, 317
Emperor Jones, The (O'Neill), 58
Empson, William, 238
Encounter, 324, 468
Encyclopaedia Britannica, 463
Engle, Paul, 174, 369–70, 372, 559
Epstein, Jason, 356
Epstein, Joseph, 501, 516
Eros, 415
Erskine, Albert, 211, 233, 242, 250, 253, 254,
　　255, 256, 268, 271, 272, 311, 313, 315,
　　331, 398–9, 417, 433, 487, 498–9, 529,
　　532, 540, 559, 563
Erskine, Marisa, 250, 417, 563
Erskine, Silvia, 563
Escape from Freedom (Fromm), 201
Escudero, Vicente, 306
Esquire, 74, 75, 103, 355–6, 363, 379, 420,
　　461, 484, 513, 545
Evans, Harry, 563
Even the Dead Arise (Ward), 177
existentialism, 245–6
"Extravagance of Laughter, An" (Ellison),
　540–1

Fabre, Michel, 126, 161, 465, 480, 523, 540
Faith and the Good Thing (Johnson), 521
"Fallacies of Legislative Criticism"
　(Brumm), 314
Fanton, Jonathan, 536–7
Farmer, James, 511
Farrell, James T., 97
Faubus, Orval, 348
Faulkner, William, 109, 119, 209, 215, 240,
　　248, 252–3, 255, 261, 266, 274,
　　299–300, 314, 333, 352, 358, 360, 450,
　　451, 467, 500, 511–12, 517–18, 545, 551
　RE influenced by, 359, 456–7, 532
　RE on, 210, 248–9, 324
　RE's encounter with, 271–2

Fauset, Arthur Huff, 112–13, 152
"February" (Ellison), 308
Federal Bureau of Investigation (FBI), 243, 280, 511
Federal Theatre Project, 124
Federal Writers' Project, 114, 126, 143–4, 154, 169, 239, 537
Feiffer, Jules, 399
Fellowship of Southern Writers, 555
Fergusson, Francis, 332
Ferris, Bill, 545
Festival of the Arts and Humanities, 417
Fiedler, Leslie, 363
Fight for Freedom (Hughes), 312–13
Fight for Freedom campaign, 297
Finley, Gravelly, 73, 341
Finley, Saretta, *see* Slaughter, Saretta
Finley, Tuffy, 341
Finnegans Wake (Joyce), 138, 202
"Fire and Cloud" (Wright), 108
Fire Next Time, The (Baldwin), 398, 401, 409
Fischer, Brigitte, 325
Fischer, L. B., 169
Fisk University, 278–9
Fitzgerald, F. Scott, 315, 383, 523, 527
Fitzpatrick, Frank N., 29, 503
Flaubert and Madame Bovary: A Double Portrait (Steegmuller), 212
Flight to Canada (Reed), 508
Flying Home (Ellison), 169, 173–4, 253, 311–12, 336, 483–4
Foley, Martha, 269
Foote, Shelby, 469
Ford, Harry, 326
Ford, James W., 93, 95, 110, 131
Ford, Nick Aaron, 480
Ford, Robert, 180
Ford Foundation, 395, 528, 541
Forrest, Leon, 486–7, 508, 521, 523, 529, 563, 566
Four Quartets (Eliot), 247, 255, 407
'47: *The Magazine of the Year*, 216
'48: *The Magazine of the Year*, 217, 219, 221–2, 224
Foster, Luther, 282, 293
Fowler, Gene, 129
Fox, Joe, 563, 566
Foxes of Harrow, The (Yerby), 218
France, 3, 94, 120, 128, 135, 305–7, 353

RE honored by, 458
Wright's emigration to, 207, 211–12
Franco, Francisco, 93, 125, 305, 353
Frank, Joseph, 392, 493, 527
Frank, Waldo, 123
Frankenthaler, Helen, 334, 391, 417, 458
Franklin, John Hope, 472, 473, 494
Franklin Library, 510–11, 522
Franks, Frederick, 460–1
Frazer, J. G., 164
Frazier, E. Franklin, 157
Freedom House Bookshelf Committee, 386
Freedom Riders, 379
Freedom to the Free, 394
Free-Lance Pallbearers, The (Reed), 433, 521
Freeman, Ann, 334
Freud, Goethe, Wagner (Mann), 102
Freud, Sigmund, 156, 249
Friends of the Johnson Library, 485–6
Friends of the Lincoln Brigade, 94
Friends of the Soviet Union, 90
Fromm, Erich, 201
From Ritual to Romance (Weston), 164
Frost, Robert, 367, 377
Fruttero, Carlo, 325
Frye, Northrop, 351
Fuller, Charles, 534
Fuller, Hoyt, 472
"Function of the Novel in American Democracy, The" (Ellison), 437, 446–7

Gaines, Ernest, 453, 455, 487, 548
Galbraith, John Kenneth, 539
Gandhi, Mohandas K. (Mahatma), 541
Gannett, Lewis, 260
Gans, Herbert, 455
Garvey, Marcus, 139, 254
Gates, Henry Louis, Jr., 531, 557, 563
Geertz, Clifford, 497
Geismar, Maxwell, 184, 203, 263
Geller, Allan, 399
Gemini (Giovanni), 474
Genovese, Eugene, 450
Germany, Nazi, 125, 134, 140
    in Nazi-Soviet nonaggression pact, 127–8, 131
Gertrude Clarke Whittall Poetry and Literature Fund, 403
Gettysburg Address, 53, 287, 496

Ghana, 312, 349, 365, 366, 480
Gibson, Donald, 480
Gill, Brendan, 174, 271
Gillespie, Dizzy, 384, 387, 419
Ginsberg, Allen, 269, 368, 462
Ginzburg, Ralph, 415
Giordano, Alberto, 337, 340
Giovanni, Nikki, 474, 507–8, 547
Giovanni's Room (Baldwin), 389, 401
Gish, Lillian, 463
Glazer, Nathan, 393, 428–9, 435
God Bless the Child (Hunter), 404
Going to the Territory (Ellison), 540–1, 545–7, 555, 563
Gold, Herbert, 354
Gold, Mike, 95, 117, 131, 167
Goldberg, Arthur, 444
Goldberg, Bertrand, 384
Goldberger, Paul, 525
"Golden Age, Time Past, The" (Ellison), 137–8, 356
Golden Apples, The (Welty), 210
Golden Bough, The (Frazer), 164
Golden Day, The (Mumford), 405
"Golden Day" culture, 193, 258, 358
Golden Slippers (Bontemps), 158
Goldin, Leon, 317, 334, 337
Golding, William, 389
Goldwater, Barry, 406, 407
Gollancz, Victor, 268
"Good Life, The" (Ellison), 130
Goodman, Andrew, 406
Goodman, Benny, 128, 137, 355
"Good Morning Revolution" (Hughes), 82
"Goodnight Irene" (Ellison), 105
Gordon, Caroline, 320
Gordon, Vera, 362
Gore, Albert, Jr., 522
Gorilla, My Love (Cade), 404, 521
Go Tell It On the Mountain (Baldwin), 281, 389, 401
Gottlieb, Saul, 295–6
Gottschalk, Louis, 41
Graham, Katharine, 431
Graham, Martha, 544
Graham, Shirley, 180
Grammar of Motives, A (Burke), 205
Granger, Lester, 177, 348
Grapes of Wrath, The (Steinbeck), 130, 147–8

Great Britain, 94, 128, 135, 140, 349
Great Depression, 37–8, 42, 43, 49, 65, 73, 80, 82, 141, 428, 533
Greek Tragedy (Murray), 164
Greenberg, Jack, 297, 415
Greene, Graham, 328–9
Gregorian, Vartan, 536
Gregory, Horace, 404
Griffith, D. W., 247, 449
Grunwald, Henry, 467
Guggenheimer, Ida Espen, 172–3, 178, 179, 187, 189–92, 193, 199, 209, 214, 215–16, 232, 240, 241, 242, 245, 250, 258–9, 369
Guinier, Ewart, 494
Guion, David, 88
Gulf Stream, The (Homer), 106

Haas, Robert K., 300
Hahn, Maud, 337, 349
Hahn, Walter, 317, 334, 337, 349
Hall, Donald, 307, 333
Halpern, Daniel, 504
Halverson, Marvin, 393–4
Hamid, Sufi Abdul, 92
Hamilton, Hamish, 256
Hamlin, Eva, 72, 82–3
Hammon, Jupiter, 116
Hammond, John, 432, 525
Hampton, Lionel, 128
Hanes, R. Philip, Jr., 445
Hansberry, Lorraine, 404
Harcourt Brace, 173, 179
Harding, Vincent, 449
"Hard Time Keeping Up, A" (Ellison), 106
Hardwick, Elizabeth, 447
Hare, Nathan, 472
Harlem, 92–3, 212, 229, 366, 427
    Lafargue Clinic of, 207–8, 219–21
    1943 race riot in, 166–7, 255, 428
    RE's arrival in, 81–2
    RE's exploration of, 86–8
Harlem Citizens League, 92
Harlem Cultural Council, 423
"Harlem Is Nowhere" (Ellison), 219–22, 420–1
Harlem Labor Union, 92
Harlem Merchants Association, 92
Harlem Quarterly, 234
Harlem Renaissance, 30, 79, 82, 92, 98, 111, 279, 434, 520

Harlem Suitcase Theater, 108, 122
Harlem Writers Guild, 423
Harold Oram Associates, 292, 319, 345, 372
Harper, Emerson, 94–5, 98, 122
Harper, Michael S., 202–3, 504, 508, 514, 523, 527, 529, 557, 563, 566
Harper, Toy, 94–5, 98, 122, 262
Harper's, 173, 178, 222, 361, 433, 434–5, 444, 453, 455, 459
Harper's Bazaar, 168, 216
Harris, Abram, 374
Harris, Charles, 391, 454–5
Harris, Joel Chandler, 310
Harris, Marguerite Tjader, 128, 146
Harris, Mark, 371
Harris, Roy, 430
Harrison, Hazel Lucille, 61, 71–2, 75, 80, 85, 91, 501
Harrison, Jane, 164
Harvard University, 3, 285–7, 397, 399, 428, 448, 495–7, 552
Hastie, William, 297
Hawkes, John, 378
Hawkins, Coleman, 29, 387
Hawthorne, Nathaniel, 98, 136, 192, 200, 359, 383
Hayakawa, S. I., 439
Hayden, Hiram, 313, 453
Hayden, Robert, 279, 464, 473, 521
Hayes, George, 171
Hayes, Harold, 484
Haynes, Leroy, 306
Haywood, Harry, 127, 134–5
Hazzard, Shirley, 405, 454, 539
Hebald, Cecile, 325
Hebestreit, Ludwig W., 41–2, 73
Hecht, Anthony, 317, 538
Hegel, Friedrich, 131, 134
Heinemann, Larry, 554
Heiskell, Andrew, 536
Heller, Joseph, 406, 446
Hellman, Lillian, 146–7, 207, 367, 424, 516
Hemingway, Ernest, 3, 75, 89, 96, 102, 103, 109, 117, 119, 124, 128, 134, 142, 146–7, 200, 210, 225, 240, 252–3, 268, 273, 300, 314, 335, 410, 430, 454, 467, 504–5, 511–12, 551, 559, 560
 RE influenced by, 99–100, 105–6, 118, 171, 358

Hemingway, Mary, 410, 417, 430, 436, 440, 473, 515
Henderson, Fletcher, 29
Henderson the Rain King (Bellow), 315, 349–50, 363, 368, 512
Hentoff, Nat, 402, 418
Herald Tribune Book Review, 260, 275
"Heritage" (Cullen), 68
Herndon, Angelo, 152–4, 158–9, 162–3
Herndon, Milton, 152
Hero, The (Raglan), 164, 194
Hersey, John, 216, 309, 327, 400, 417, 418, 504, 532, 559
Herzog (Bellow), 409, 416
Hickman, Louis, 176
Hicks, Granville, 113, 118, 127, 131, 329–30, 336, 352, 377, 408, 446
"Hidden Name and Complex Fate" (Ellison), 403, 408
Higginbotham, A. Leon, Jr., 423
Higgins, Rodney G., 176–7
High Fidelity, 308, 318
Hill, Annie, 80, 86
Himes, Chester, 202, 218–19, 259, 281, 328, 455, 465, 472
Hitchcock, Curtice, 211
Hitchcock, Margaret Unwin, 211
Hitler, Adolf, 96, 110, 125, 127, 128, 135, 184
Holiday, 274, 398
Holiday, Billie, 356, 484
Hollander, John, 474
Hollingsworth, Stanley, 334, 337
Holmes, Eugene, 157, 159, 190
"Homage to Duke Ellington on His Birthday" (Ellison), 463
Home of the Brave (film), 247
Home to Harlem (McKay), 92
Hook, Sidney, 353, 402, 471
Hope for Poetry, A (Lewis), 83
Horizon, 211, 216–17, 224, 238–9
Horne, Lena, 348
House Committee on Un-American Activities (HUAC), 111, 243
House Made of Dawn (Momaday), 487
Hoving, Thomas, 444
Howard, Vilma, 307
Howe, Irving, 130, 260–1, 269, 274, 311, 391, 409, 434, 453, 461, 468, 473, 559
 RE's controversy with, 400–3
Howe, James Wong, 148–9, 230

Hudson Review, 260, 334, 356, 377
Huggins, Nathan I., 494
Hughes, Langston, 30, 43–4, 75, 79, 87, 88,
    93–4, 95, 96, 98, 108, 110, 111, 120, 122,
    123, 126, 132, 142, 148, 158, 162, 167,
    169, 174, 177, 184, 189, 202–3, 207,
    222, 233, 244, 259, 262, 271, 279, 296,
    312–13, 330, 365–6, 392, 404, 453, 507,
    511, 540, 541, 542
  anti-Communist movement and, 244
  Communist Party affiliation of, 92
  death of, 433
  RE's friendship with, 82–3, 85, 90–1,
    123
  RE's rebuke of, 138–9
"Humanities and Their Place in Today's
    World, The" (Ellison), 296–7
Human Stain, The (Roth), 482
Humelsine, Carlisle H., 432, 476
Humphrey, Hubert, 425, 447, 449, 463, 511
Hunter, Kristin, 404, 516
Hunter College, 281–2
Hurok, Sol, 447
Hurry Home (Wideman), 521
Hurston, Zora Neale, 90, 120, 141–2, 189,
    296, 452
Huxley, Julian, 381
Hyman, Stanley Edgar, 156, 163–4, 165,
    191, 194, 198, 200, 201, 205, 211, 216,
    229, 232, 235, 241, 242, 246, 250, 252,
    258, 259, 265, 272, 285, 286, 288,
    311–12, 369, 389, 402, 417, 467, 468,
    469, 471, 485, 538
  background of, 159–60
  RE's correspondence with, 237–8, 253,
    296, 300, 370, 380
  RE's friendship with, 160–1, 166
  RE's literary skirmish with, 351
"Hymie's Bull" (Ellison), 99–100, 107, 128

"I Did Not Learn Their Names" (Ellison),
    100
Idiot, The (Dostoyevsky), 209, 322
"I Do Not Apologize" (Ellison), 435
If He Hollers Let Him Go (Himes), 202–3
Ignatow, David, 537
"I Have Seen Black Hands" (Wright), 97
I Know Why the Caged Bird Sings
    (Angelou), 521
Illusion in Java (Fowler), 129

Imes, William Lloyd, 92, 129
"Imprisoned in Words" (Ellison), 210
"In a Strange Country" (Ellison), 171, 173,
    178, 184
"Indivisible Man" (McPherson and
    Ellison), 473
*In Love and Trouble: Stories of Black
    Women* (Walker), 521
Innis, Roy, 437, 485
Institute for Afro-American Culture, 480
Institute for the Study of the Holocaust,
    461
Institute of Jazz Studies, 266
International Congress on Races and Anti-
    Semitism, 95
International Rescue Committee, 203
International Workers Order (IWO), 90,
    108, 112
Interpretation of Dreams, The (Freud), 30
In the Castle of My Skin (Lamming), 281
"In the Fascist Styx" (Slochower), 159
"Introduction to Flamenco" (Ellison), 308
Introduction to the Science of Sociology
    (Park and Burgess), 77
Intruder in the Dust (film), 247–8
*Invisible Criticism: Ralph Ellison and the
    American Canon* (Nadel), 557
Invisible Man (Ellison), 31, 182–3, 261, 263,
    292, 294, 307, 351, 356–7, 388, 389,
    392, 405, 434, 452, 462, 469, 491, 495,
    506, 508, 509, 510, 512, 520, 528,
    530–1, 533, 538, 546, 547, 548, 551,
    552, 556, 563
  as allegory, 218, 235–6
  American history in, 225–6
  autobiographical foundation of, 217,
    225–6, 236
  bicentennial edition of, 511
  "black studies" movement and, 459
  British edition of, 268
  Burke's influence on, 205–6
  chaos theme in, 253, 255–6, 313–14, 315
  civil rights movement prophesied in,
    406–7
  contract for, 210–11
  critical success of, 263–4
  dedication of, 258–9, 266
  ending of, 257–8
  epic form of, 227
  epilogue of, 254–8

European sales of, 268
European translations of, 325
first paragraph of, 194–5
form of, 197
French edition of, 305, 306
"Harlem Is Nowhere" project and,
    220–1
incest theme of, 227–8, 364
Italian edition of, 325
jazz and blues and, 197–8
last line of, 255, 557
Moby-Dick and, 195–6, 197, 205, 228
number symbols in, 226
paperback edition of, 282
plot of, 224–5, 226
prologue of, 259
proposed movie treatment of, 534
publication party for, 260
Quogue writing venue and, 207–9
as required college text, 403, 459–61
RE's commitment to, 204–5
RE's "Uncle Tom" confrontation and,
    439–40
reviews and criticisms of, 259–63, 273,
    420, 422, 473–4
rituals in, 217–18
screen rights of, 450
second main section of, 235
spine of, 200, 204
Steegmuller's office writing venue and,
    236–7
surrealism in, 197, 218
symbolism in, 226–7
third major section of, 240–1
thirtieth-anniversary edition of, 534
title of, 254, 255–6
Tuskegee Institute in, 224–5, 226,
    228–9
Unamuno allusions in, 121
Vermont writing venue and, 212–16
world events in, 235, 242–3
Wright's reaction to, 263
writing process of, 204–5, 210–11
"Invisible Man" (Ellison), 217–18
"Invisible Man: Prologue to a Novel"
    (*Partisan Review*), 259
Invitation to Learning, 274
Iowa Review, 465
Irish Times, 216
Isherwood, Christopher, 113, 125, 216

Isom, Charles T., 103
"It Always Breaks Out" (Ellison), 393, 398
"I Tried to Be a Communist" (Wright),
    179–80
Ives, Charles, 207
I Wonder as I Wander (Hughes), 330

Jackson, Jesse, 543
Jackson, Mahalia, 354–5, 356
Jackson, Shirley, 159, 174, 201, 211, 233,
    237–8, 239, 241, 252, 258, 286, 369,
    417
James, C. L. R., 135, 275–6
James, Henry, 98, 105, 122, 197, 205, 270–1,
    313–15, 410, 452, 470, 557
Janeway, Elizabeth, 378
Janeway, Michael, 473
Japan, 147, 191, 343–4, 365
Javits, Jacob, 414, 425, 427–8
jazz, 14, 27–8, 77, 97, 128, 137, 153, 160,
    197, 200, 222, 257, 302, 321, 363, 383,
    403, 551
    in *Invisible Man*, 197–8
    RE's criticisms of, 354–6, 366, 372–3,
    386–8, 419–20
"Jazz: The Experimenters," 419
"Jazz Goes Intellectual: Bop!," 419
JB (MacLeish), 335
Jeffers, Robinson, 207, 564
Jefferson, Thomas, 378, 451, 477
Jerome, V. J., 131, 140
Jet, 163, 262
Jewish Frontier, 297
Jewish Labor Committee, 461
Jewish People's Voice, 124
Jews, 39–40, 77, 237, 269, 365, 391, 399,
    461, 507
    African-Americans and, 125
    among New York intellectuals, 353
    RE's friendships with, 231–2, 250
    RE's perception of, 124–5
Jews Without Money (Gold), 95
John D. and Catherine T. MacArthur
    Foundation, 529–30, 542
John Reed Club, 96, 122, 142
John Simon Guggenheim Memorial
    Foundation, 180, 187, 274, 309, 528
Johnson, Charles S., 176, 278–9, 462, 508,
    521, 529–30, 548, 563
Johnson, James P., 122–3

Johnson, James Weldon, 82, 176
Johnson, Lyndon B., 3, 400, 413, 414, 415,
    416, 417–18, 424, 431, 432, 434, 437,
    438, 439, 444–5, 447, 451, 458, 479,
    485, 486
Johnson, Michael P., 528
Johnson, Philip C., 447
Johnston, DeWitt, 283
Johnston, May Bell DeWitt, 278, 283–5,
    286, 291
Jones, Alice, 116
Jones, David D., 277
Jones, Gayl, 487, 508
Jones, Howard Mumford, 269, 476
Jones, James, 515
Jones, James Earl, 472
Jones, LeRoi, *see* Baraka, Amiri
Jones, Quincy, 534
Jordan, June, 487, 521, 547
Jordan, Vernon, 485
Josephs, Devereux C., 444
Joyce, James, 64, 97, 99, 109, 117, 138, 142,
    185, 196, 201–2, 233, 310, 351, 359, 473
    RE influenced by, 171, 456–7
Jubilee (Walker), 487
"Judge Lynch in New York" (Ellison), 127
Julius Rosenwald Fund, 180, 187, 200,
    206–7, 209, 211, 221
"Juneteenth" (Ellison), 422–3
Jung, Carl, 249

Kafka, Franz, 245
Kahn, Louis, 394
Karachi University, 344
Katz, Donald, 529
Kazin, Alfred, 127, 216, 233, 250, 269, 300,
    328, 352, 353, 364, 391, 402, 418, 422,
    424, 447, 450, 480
Keating, Kenneth B., 407
Kelley, William Melvin, 453
Kellogg, Paul, 209–10
Kempton, Murray, 332, 447
Kennedy, Jacqueline, 400, 431, 515
Kennedy, John F., 376, 394–5, 397, 400,
    413, 447
Kennedy, Mark, 366
Kennedy, Robert F., 379, 390, 400, 407,
    414, 427, 447, 513
Kent, Rockwell, 152
Kerner Commission, 446

Kerouac, Jack, 368
Kgositsile, Keorapetse, 435
Killens, John Oliver, 262, 297, 423
Killers of the Dream (Smith), 276
Kilson, Martin, 472, 494
King, Martin Luther, Jr., 323–4, 348, 396,
    397, 400, 407, 412, 420, 439, 446, 491,
    513, 533, 543
"King of the Bingo Game" (Ellison), 182–3,
    197
Kirkpatrick, Jeane, 486
Kissinger, Henry, 288, 394, 397, 407, 419,
    461, 536
Kittredge, George Lyman, 35
Klopfer, Donald, 272
Knock on Any Door (Motley), 218
Koch, Ed, 543, 555
Koestler, Arthur, 233
Kolatch, Myron, 401, 428
Kostelanetz, Richard, 398, 424, 443, 444,
    448
Kotelawala, John, 308
Kouwenhoven, John A., 476, 483, 503, 506,
    555
Kraft, Joseph, 410
Kreymborg, Alfred, 147
Kristol, Irving, 324
Ku Klux Klan, 24, 39, 44, 103, 247–8, 280,
    449
Kunitz, Elise, 417
Kunitz, Stanley, 201, 417, 418, 504

Lafargue Psychiatric Clinic, 207–8, 219–21
Lamming, George, 281
Langston, John Mercer, 43
Langston University, 16, 35–6, 37, 43–4
Larsen, Nella, 30
Laster, Owen, 450, 534, 563
"Last Day" (Ellison), 105
Last of the Mohicans, The (Cooper), 30
Law, Oliver, 94
Lawd Today! (Wright), 97
Lawrence, Jacob, 488, 507, 517
Lazenberry, Joe, 59, 73, 123–4
League of American Writers, 107, 123, 125,
    129, 136, 140, 141, 146–7, 153, 154
League of Struggle for Negro Rights, 131–2
Leaves of Grass (Whitman), 552
Lee, Don L., 500, 507
Lee, Harper, 406, 434

Leonard, Bill, 272
Lerner, Edna, 312
Lerner, Max, 301, 313, 326–7, 331, 348
"Let America Be America Again"
    (Hughes), 82
Let Me Live (Herndon), 152
Let My People Go (Buckmaster), 152
"Letter from Birmingham City Jail" (King),
    401
Let the People Sing (Priestley), 130
Levi, Edward, 384
Levine, Harry, 153
Levine, Lawrence, 529, 531
Levison, Ivan, 360–1
Levison, Stanley, 348
Lewis, Cecil Day, 83
Lewis, John, 412
Lewis, John L., 132–3
Lewis, Nancy, 238, 291, 332, 390, 408
Lewis, R. W. B. "Dick," 238, 260–1, 280,
    291, 332, 360, 378, 390–1, 408, 452,
    459, 471, 523, 538, 566
Lewis, Sinclair, 74–5, 119, 512
Lewisohn family, 38–40, 47, 73, 461
Liberal Imagination, The (Trilling), 313
Liberator, 435
Library of Congress, 403, 408, 437–8, 551
Lie Down in Darkness (Styron), 313
Life, 207, 221, 244, 264, 289, 324, 332, 431,
    468–9
Life Among the Savages (Jackson), 286
Life and Loves of Mr. Jiveass Nigger, The
    (Brown), 473
Light in August (Faulkner), 261, 324
Lillard, Stewart, 518, 528
Lincoln, Abraham, 53, 287, 358, 394, 467,
    496, 500
Lincoln, C. Eric, 472
Lindsay, John V., 425
Lish, Gordon, 513
Literature and Dialectical Materialism
    (Strachey), 90, 117–18
"Literature and the Crisis of Negro
    Sensibility" (Ellison), 294
"Little Man at Chehaw Station, The"
    (Ellison), 501, 516, 540–1
"Little Man Behind the Stove, The"
    (Ellison), 500, 510
Litz, A. Walton, 517
Living Novel, The (symposium), 352

"Living with Music" (Ellison), 318
Locke, Alain, 79–80, 82, 126, 152
Lolita (Nabokov), 363–4, 416, 422
Lonely Crowd, The (Reisman), 353
Lonely Crusade (Himes), 218–19
Long Way from Home, A (McKay), 111
Los Angeles Times, 499, 547
"Lottery, The" (Jackson), 237–8
Louis, Joe, 133, 177, 327, 471
Love Story (Segal), 476
Lowell, Ralph, 444
Lowell, Robert, 417–18, 464
Ludwig, Jack, 353–4, 370, 372
Lurie, Alison, 505
Lynchers, The (Wideman), 521
Lynd, Staughton, 438
Lynes, George, 361, 503
Lynes, Russell, 361, 503, 559

Macdonald, Dwight, 371, 418, 447
MacDonald, William, 317
MacDowell Colony, 274
MacLeish, Archibald, 118, 270, 311, 326,
    334, 335, 336, 338, 371, 394, 516
Macmillan, Harold, 349
MacNeice, Louis, 125
Magic Barrel, The (Malamud), 364
Magic Mountain, The (Mann), 62
Magil, A. B., 157, 222
Mailer, Norman, 174, 269, 371, 415, 422,
    424–5, 431, 444, 446, 513, 543
    RE's literary conflict with, 367–9
Malamud, Bernard, 269, 364, 402, 404,
    418, 422, 536, 539, 545
Malcolm X, 400, 406, 412, 413, 414, 415,
    466, 507
Malraux, André, 3, 83, 106, 109, 112,
    119–20, 122, 128, 134, 178, 190, 383,
    458, 483, 500
"Man Become Invisible, A" (*Life*), 264
Manchester, William, 469
Manchild in the Promised Land (Brown), 427
Mann, Augusta, 237
Mann, Klaus, 154–5
Mann, Samuel, 237
Mann, Thomas, 62, 91, 102, 126, 128, 154
Manning, Robert, 473
Man's Fate (Malraux), 83, 106, 119–20
"Man Who Lived Underground, The"
    (Wright), 161, 246

Mariners, Renegades and Castaways
    (James), 276
Mark Twain, 20, 30, 192, 200, 210, 240,
    299–300, 302, 315, 352, 358, 397, 467,
    500, 534, 537, 557
Marsalis, Wynton, 550–1, 564
Marshall, Paule, 409–10
Marshall, Thurgood, 297
Marx, Karl, 107, 122, 131, 156, 163, 249
Marx, Leo, 476
Mason, Charlotte Osgood, 90
Mason, Clifford, 468, 469
Massachusetts Review, 504, 508, 513
Masses & Mainstream, 262
Masters, Edgar Lee, 75
Matthiessen, Peter, 307
Maud Martha (Brooks), 281
Maurois, André, 74, 328–9
Maynard, John, 471, 481
McBride, Mary Margaret, 272
McCabe, Edward P., 5
McCarthy, Cormac, 433, 529, 531
McCarthy, Eugene, 447, 528
McCarthy, Mary, 242
McConnell, Ulysses, 175
McConnell, Willie Mae, 175–6
McFarland, Lamonia, 30
McGovern, George, 486
McGrory, Mary, 270
McKay, Claude, 30, 92–3, 110–12, 123
McKinley, William, 9
McLuhan, Marshall, 439
McMillan, James, 136
McPherson, James Alan, 425, 453, 472,
    473, 478, 508, 517, 523, 527, 529–31,
    542, 563, 566
Mead, Frank, 25, 29, 35, 283
Mead, Joe, 25, 283
Mead, Margaret, 462
Meadman, Dhimah Rose, 126–7, 128, 131,
    135–6, 143
Mehta, G. L., 278, 290
Mehta, Ved, 410
Melville, Herman, 11, 170, 192, 193, 195–6,
    200, 210, 240, 253, 257, 276, 299–300,
    302, 322, 383, 442, 551
Menand, Louis, 547
Mendelssohn, Peter, 155
Menen, Aubrey, 323
Menninger, Karl, 218

Meredith, James, 437
Merkin, June, 252
Metronome, 356
Metropolitan Museum of Art, 499, 522
Miller, Arthur, 174, 327, 354, 377, 395, 447
Miller, Charlie, 48–51
Miller, Kelly, 77–8
Miller, Loren, 148
Mills, Margaret, 554
Milosz, Czeslaw, 560
Milsap, Georgia, 20
Milsap, Minnie, 57
Milsap, Polk, 20, 102
Milsap, Will, 57
Minerva Awards, 536
Minor, Robert, 180
Minow, Newton, 424, 432, 444
Minty Alley (James), 135
Minus, Marian, 98, 103
Mr. Sammler's Planet (Bellow), 512
"Mister Toussan" (Ellison), 146, 157, 222–3
Mitchell, Clarence, 348
Mitchell, Joseph, 563
Mitgang, Herbert, 532
Moby-Dick (Melville), 205, 228, 253, 276,
    311, 322
    Invisible Man and, 195–6, 197, 205, 228
Modern Jazz Quartet, 355, 419
Modern Language Association, 279, 424,
    474, 493, 527, 540, 548
Modern Negro Art (Porter), 181
Momaday, N. Scott, 487
Monk, Thelonious, 550
Montage of a Dream Deferred (Hughes), 541
Moon, Bucklin, 165, 169, 182, 200
Moore, A. Elese, 42, 47
Moore, Julia "Chubby," 55–6, 66, 295
Moore, Marianne, 216, 431, 444
Morison, Samuel Eliot, 498
Morot-Sir, Edouard, 458
Morris, Willie, 423, 434–5, 439–40, 451,
    455, 466
Morris, Wright, 260, 363, 377, 446
Morrison, Toni, 359, 486–7, 488, 508, 521,
    529–30, 536, 549–50
    RE's relationship with, 553–4
Moten, Benny, 29, 302
Motherwell, Robert, 391, 397, 417
Motley, Constance Baker, 407
Moton, Catherine, 57, 78–9

Moton, Robert, Jr., 59
Moton, Robert Russa, 54, 56, 74
Moynihan, Daniel Patrick, 428–9, 435, 467
Muhammad, Elijah, 406
Muhlhauser, Fred, 311
Muhlhauser, Lucille, 311
Mulatto (Hughes), 82
Mule Bone (Hughes and Hurston), 90
Mumbo Jumbo (Reed), 506, 521, 548
Mumford, Lewis, 3, 193, 228, 233, 404–5, 418
Mumford, L. Quincy, 425
Murray, Albert, 61, 74–6, 222, 229, 231, 234, 241, 259, 275, 282–3, 293, 294, 295, 300, 319, 320, 321–2, 323, 336, 350, 351, 355, 356, 362, 363, 365, 366, 371, 377, 382, 390, 406, 417, 429, 435, 436–7, 448, 455, 482, 494, 508, 521, 538, 550, 563, 566
    RE's friendship with, 327–8, 454, 498–9, 564
Murray, Gilbert, 164
Murray, Michele, 222, 282, 327, 382, 563
Murray, Mozelle, 222, 231, 241, 259, 282, 294, 327, 382, 390, 406, 436–7, 563
Murray, William H. "Alfalfa Bill," 10, 37–8
Museum of African Art, 489
Museum of the City of New York, 518, 536
Myrdal, Gunnar, 181, 200, 438, 496
"Myth of the Flawed Southerner, The" (Ellison), 447

Nabokov, Nicholas, 330–1
Nabokov, Vladimir, 363, 416
Nadel, Alan, 557
Nagayo, Yoshiro, 278
Naguid, Jack, 108, 109
Naguid, Nina, 108, 109
Naked and the Dead, The (Mailer), 174, 367–8
Narrows, The (Petry), 281
Nash, Howard M., 77
Nashville Tennessean, 242, 261
Nation, 43, 260, 350, 353, 422, 520
National Association for the Advancement of Colored People (NAACP), 49, 103, 151, 297, 299, 312–13, 327, 348, 366, 375, 397, 407, 423, 437, 455, 464, 480
    Legal Defense Fund of, 265, 297, 349, 397, 415, 463, 485, 515

National Association of Colored Women, 296
National Association of Intergroup Relations Officials, 423–4
National Book Award, 3, 269, 284, 286, 305, 309, 363–4, 367, 401, 444, 447, 476, 506, 530, 548, 554, 559
National Book Award of 1953, 268–81
    committee vote on, 269–70
    post-award lecture appearances and, 276–82
    radio interviews and, 272, 274
    reactions and criticisms of, 273–4
    RE's acceptance speech for, 270–1
National Citizens' Committee for Public Television, 432, 443–4
National Committee for Support of the Public Schools, 426
National Council of the Arts, Sciences and Professions, 244, 414, 415, 426–7, 431
National Educational Television (NET), 419, 424, 425, 426
National Endowment for the Arts (NEA), 414, 416, 515, 543
National Endowment for the Humanities (NEH), 414, 416, 515, 536, 543
National Institute of Arts and Letters, 207, 311, 371, 416, 425, 463–4, 479, 504, 511, 516, 538–9, 542–3, 552–3, 562
    RE elected to, 404–6
    see also American Academy of Arts and Letters
National Maritime Union, 93, 168
National Medal of the Arts, 543–4
National Negro Congress (NNC), 132–4, 136, 140, 141
National Portrait Gallery, 486, 518
National Urban League, 177, 182, 423–4, 455, 485
Nation of Islam, 406, 486
Native Son (Wright), 114–15, 136, 155, 178, 181, 203, 219, 223, 260, 263, 273, 306, 461, 481
    commercial success of, 128, 130–1
    Communist dogma in, 130–1
    RE–*Life* controversy and, 468–9
    RE's defense of, 131–2
    RE's reaction to, 118–19
Naval Academy, U.S., 243

Naylor, Gloria, 529, 547
Nazi-Soviet nonaggression pact, 127–8
NBC, 270, 272, 347, 348, 349, 562
Neal, Larry, 452, 472
Neely, Alvin, 47, 54, 61–3, 66–7, 69, 74, 224, 229, 283
"Negro Artist and the Racial Mountain, The" (Hughes), 43
"Negro Community in the United States, The," 393
Negro Digest, 184, 234, 472
  see also Black World
"Negro in America, The," 417
"Negro in American History, The" (Ellison), 449
Negro Industrial Clerical Alliance, 92
"Negro in New York, The," 111
Negro Labor Committee, 92
Negro People's Theatre, 177
Negro Playwrights Company, 138–9, 141
Negro Publication Society, 152
Negro Quarterly, The: A Review of Negro Life and Culture, 152–3, 154, 155–6, 157–8, 159–60, 162–4, 165, 167, 190, 234
Negro Story, 203
Nehru, Jawaharlal, 235
Nemerov, Howard, 238, 241–2
New American Library, 282, 290, 304, 326
"New Black Myths, The" (*Harper's*), 459
New Challenge, 98, 100
New Deal, 533, 537
New Essays on Invisible Man (O'Meally), 557
New Faces, 109
New Leader, 398, 401–2, 428, 468
Newman, Arnold, 289
New Masses, 95–7, 103, 118, 122, 141, 147, 148, 152, 153, 160, 165–6, 174, 178, 222–3, 262, 329, 399
  RE's work published in, 112–13, 114, 127, 129–30, 134–7, 140, 146, 151
  "Way It Is" essay in, 156–7, 161
New Negro, The (Locke, ed.), 79
New Negro Poets: U.S.A. (Hughes), 404
Newport Jazz Festival, 297, 355, 448
New Republic, 119, 139, 156, 199, 209, 353, 389, 404
  RE's review for, 200–1, 203–4
New School for Social Research, 96, 309, 423, 445, 536

Newsday, 412, 438
New Song, A (Hughes), 90, 110
Newsweek, 371, 408, 426, 479
Newton, Herbert, 108, 110
New World A-Coming (Ottley), 116, 165, 169
New World Writing, 297
New York Amsterdam News, 125, 207, 273, 448
New Yorker, The, 159–60, 168, 173, 199, 237, 252, 281, 398, 448, 502, 503, 513–14, 525, 562, 563, 564
New York Herald Tribune, 174, 260, 422
New York Post, 166–7, 207, 255, 313
New York Public Library, 112, 123
New York Review of Books, 391, 403
New York Star, 239–40
New York Times, 70, 102, 126, 260, 264, 348, 352, 407, 418, 482, 485, 493, 499, 500, 522, 525, 532, 536, 554, 555, 562
New York Times Book Review, 174, 239, 249, 260, 263, 281, 308, 408, 473, 508, 546
New York Times Magazine, 429
New York University, 182, 469, 515
  RE's professorship at, 469, 470–1, 476, 484–5, 493, 494–5, 497, 498, 505–6, 514, 519
New York Writers Project, 96, 108, 109, 125, 126, 129, 239
  RE at, 110–11, 114, 115–17
Nigger of the Narcissus, The (Conrad), 105
"Night-Talk" (Ellison), 456–8
Nightwood (Barnes), 307
Nin, Anaïs, 212, 504
Nixon, Richard, 376, 449, 461, 463, 467, 486, 487, 497
Nkrumah, Kwame, 300, 349
Nobel Prize, 296, 329, 365, 511–12, 529, 530
Noble Savage, 354, 456
  first issue of, 364, 374
Nobody Knows My Name (Baldwin), 389
No Day of Triumph (Redding), 159
Noguchi, Isamu, 332
Norman, Dorothy, 207, 233, 235, 278, 290, 312, 332
Norman, Edward, 233, 235
Norstad, Lauris, 431–2
North, Alex, 109
North, Joseph, 151–2, 156–7

North Toward Home (Morris), 435

Norton, Charles Eliot, 228

Nostromo (Conrad), 62

"Note on Commercial Theater" (Hughes), 138–9

Notes from Underground (Dostoyevsky), 121, 161, 209

Notes of a Hanging Judge (Crouch), 550

Notes of a Native Son (Baldwin), 325, 389

novel-in-progress (Ellison), 358–9, 380, 386, 431, 482, 499, 532, 557–8
    central characters of, 356–8
    chaos in, 310–11
    Cliofus in, 310, 393, 465, 538
    comic tone of, 532
    Faulkner's influence on, 359, 456–7
    Joyce's influence on, 456–7
    opening section of, 522
    pages lost in fire, 443, 493, 538
    and Plainfield writing venue, 432–3, 435–7, 511, 520
    as prophecy, 413
    published excerpts from, 372, 374–5, 393, 398, 422–3, 456–8, 465, 487, 513, 521
    RE's readings from, 392, 393, 399, 537–8, 542
    Tivoli writing venue and, 359, 362–4, 365, 371–2, 376

Nugent, Richard Bruce, 111–12

Oasis, The (McCarthy), 242

Oates, Joyce Carol, 504, 516

O'Connor, Frank, 288

O'Daniel, Therman B., 472

Oklahoma City, Okla., 32, 354
    black community of, 13–14
    Deep Deuce section of, 14, 284, 430
    Jim Crow in, 13–14, 16, 24–5, 29, 38
    library branch named for RE in, 501–3
    RE's return visits to, 283–6, 429–30, 552

"Old Man" (Faulkner), 215

Old Man and the Sea, The (Hemingway), 3, 268–9, 273

O'Meally, Robert G., 509, 518, 526, 557

Omni-Americans, The (Murray), 498

"On Becoming a Writer" (Ellison), 408, 537

"On Being the Target of Discrimination" (Ellison), 555–6

"On Bird, Bird-Watching, and Jazz" (Ellison), 386

O'Neal, Frederick, 423

O'Neill, Eugene, 58, 68, 109, 511–12, 531

On Native Grounds (Kazin), 269, 328

On the Road (Kerouac), 368

Operation Breadbasket, 543

Oppenheimer, Dorothea, 453

Oppenheimer, Judy, 258

Opportunity, 278

Oregon Trail, The (Parkman), 360

Organizer, The, 122–3

Oswald, Lee Harvey, 400

Ottley, Roi, 111–12, 116, 165, 169, 239–40, 245

Our Town (Wilder), 371

"Out of the Hospital and Under the Bar" (Ellison), 393

Outsider, The (Wright), 263, 275

Oxherding Tale (Johnson), 548

Paco's Story (Heinemann), 554

Page, Inman E., 26–7, 32, 523–4

Page, Oran "Hot Lips," 28

Page, Sarah, 22

Panel on Educational Research and Development, 394, 395

Paris Review, 307–8, 336, 435

Park, Robert E., 77

Parker, Charlie "Yardbird," 355, 386–8, 409, 419, 550

Parker, Dorothy, 363

Parks, Gordon, 221, 231, 241, 264, 332, 454, 473, 483

Parks, Rosa, 323, 348

Partisan Review, 96, 122, 259, 275, 333, 351, 353, 363, 386, 393, 398, 407, 560–1

Pasternak, Boris, 365

Patriotic Gore (Wilson), 266, 398

Patterson, Frederick Douglass, 74, 79, 80, 282

Patterson, Orlando, 494

Patterson, Raymond, 541

Payne, W. Henri, 61

PEN (Poets, Essayists, and Novelists), 268, 311, 327–8, 366, 415, 424, 543
    RE elected to, 290

Pen America, 397, 543

Pen Centre for Writers in Exile, 328–9

Pen International, 327–9, 343, 365

People's Voice, 162, 243
Percy, Walker, 434
Perkins, Dexter, 280
"Perspectives on the American
     Experience," 398
Peters, Brock, 472
Petry, Ann, 281, 521
Phelps Stokes Fund, 522
Phillips, William, 122, 333, 351, 386
Philosophy of Literary Form, The (Burke),
     156, 205
Phylon, 154, 366
Picture of Dorian Gray, The (Wilde), 62
Pinky (film), 247
Pious, Robert Savion, 81, 83
Pittman, Portia Washington, 70
Pittsburgh Courier, 125, 144, 273
Pius XII, Pope, 322
Plainfield house, 436, 444, 492, 503, 511,
     518–19, 520, 546, 556
     fire and rebuilding of, 440–3, 448–9,
     481
     Herbert Ellison's visit to, 514–15
     RE's return to, 489–90
Playboy, 533, 534
Plessy v. Ferguson, 16, 297
Plimpton, Calvin H., 436, 462, 463
Plimpton, George, 307–8, 394
Plimpton, Ruth, 463
PMLA, 540
Podhoretz, Norman, 408, 409, 435, 486,
     532
Poe, Edgar Allan, 121
Poindexter, Rose, *see* Ellison, Rose
     Poindexter
Poirier, Richard, 370
Poitier, Sidney, 433, 534
Polish Writers' Association, 333
Polite, Carlene, 453
Polite, Margie, 166
Pollack, Jackson, 388
Poplowitz, Ellen, *see* Wright, Ellen
     Poplowitz
Popular Front, 92, 189
Porter, Arabel, 326
Porter, Carla, 550
Porter, Horace, 455, 508–9, 550, 560
Porter, James A., 181
Porter, Katherine Anne, 285, 311
Porter, Zachary Ellison, 550

Portrait of the Artist as a Young Man
     (Joyce), 201–2, 228
Poston, Ted, 111
Pound, Ezra, 97, 249, 333–4, 361, 434
Powell, Adam Clayton, Jr., 92, 129, 138,
     190, 354, 413
Powell, Lewis F., 496
Prashker, Betty A., 526
Prescott, Orville, 260, 352
Présence Africaine, 234, 330, 449
"President and the Negro, The"
     (Moynihan), 435
Price, Reynolds, 434, 504
Priestley, J. B., 130, 328–9
Primer for White Folks (Moon), 200
Princeton University, 266, 269, 279–80,
     291, 332, 391, 393, 415, 493
Pritchard, N. H., 433
Pritchett, V. S., 291, 328–9
Proust, Marcel, 117, 118
Pryor, Richard, 534
Psychology of Art, The (Malraux), 119
Publishers Weekly, 545
Pudd'nhead Wilson (Mark Twain), 506
Pulitzer Prize, 249, 273, 275, 325, 367, 449,
     487, 511, 517, 521, 530, 554
Pushcart Press, 503–4

Quarles, Benjamin, 393
Quarterly Review of Literature, 362, 374–5,
     422, 456
Queen Mary, 95

Rabb, Louis "Mike," 54, 59, 80, 226, 282, 294
race, racism, 53, 88–9, 247–8, 386, 390,
     394–7, 466–7, 471, 496, 503
     Brown decision and, 298–9
     Moynihan report on, 428–9, 435
     in Oklahoma City, 13–14, 16, 24–5
     postwar desegregation and, 243, 278,
     280
     in RE-black students exchanges,
     385–6, 459–60, 462, 482, 490, 506, 524
     in RE-black writers exchanges, 404,
     452–5, 473, 486–7, 497–8, 507–10,
     547–8
     RE's attitude toward, 4, 16–17, 24–5,
     34, 77–8, 97–8, 298–9, 386, 390–1,
     406, 427–8, 449, 462, 466–8, 500–1
     school desegregation and, 293, 298–9

Tulsa riot and, 21–2, 24
see also African-Americans; civil rights
   movement
Raglan, Lord, 164, 194
Rahv, Philip, 122, 333
Raisin in the Sun, A (Hansberry), 404
"Ralph Ellison: Shadow or Act?"
   (Kgositsile), 435
Ralph Ellison on Work-in-Progress, 425
Ramparts, 449
Ramsey, Eugene, 265, 370, 405–6, 474
Randolph, A. Philip, 129, 133–4, 140–1, 463
Randolph, Camille, 13, 14–15, 544
Randolph, Iphigenia, 13
Randolph, James L., 13, 15, 24, 167–8, 430,
   534, 544
Randolph, Jefferson Davis, 11, 13–17, 43,
   47, 430
Randolph, Taylor, 15
Randolph, Thomas Jefferson, 11, 13, 15,
   23–4
Randolph, Uretta, 13, 14, 15, 16, 23
Randolph, Wade, 15
Random House, 152, 211, 216, 217, 230,
   242, 246, 253, 255–6, 259, 260, 263,
   264, 270, 272, 398, 407, 423, 454, 481,
   486–7, 534, 540, 546, 563, 566
Raphael, Lennox, 433
Rauschenberg, Robert, 439, 516
Raymo, Robert, 481–2
Razaf, Andy, 197
Reagan, Ronald, 3, 533–4, 543–4, 554, 555
"Recent Negro Fiction" (Ellison), 141, 142
Red Badge of Courage, The (Crane), 300
*Red Badge of Courage and Four Great
   Stories of Stephen Crane, The,* 376
Reddick, L. D., 112, 158
Redding, J. Saunders, 159, 249, 262
Reed, Ishmael, 433, 453, 497–8, 506–7,
   508, 512, 514, 521, 529–30, 548
Reich, William, 368
Reid, John, 305
Reinhardt, Max, 301
Reisner, Robert George, 386
Remarque, Erich Maria, 155
"Remembering Jimmy" (Ellison), 354
"Remembering Richard Wright" (Ellison),
   481, 483, 540
"Remembering Shooting-Flying"
   (Hemingway), 103

Remnick, David, 562–3
Renascent, 453
Reporter, 247, 352
Republican Party, 8, 243, 406
Rexroth, Kenneth, 263
Reynal & Hitchcock, 173, 179, 182, 187,
   204, 206–7, 211, 559
"Rhetoric of Hitler's Battle, The" (Burke),
   96–7, 205
Rhinelander, Leonard "Kip," 116
Ribicoff, Abraham, 427
Rice, Alfred, 440, 469
Rice, Elmer, 327, 365
Richards, I. A., 238
Richardson, Elliot, 497
Richardson, Willis, 63
"Richard Wright and Negro Fiction"
   (Ellison), 141
"Richard Wright's Blues" (Ellison), 188–9,
   195
Riegger, Wallingford, 91
Riesman, David, 353
Rivers, Larry, 424
Roach, Max, 387
*Road to Liberation for the Negro People,
   The,* 95
Roark, James L., 528
Robbins, Warren M., 399
Roberts, Isabel, 316, 318
Roberts, Laurance, 316, 318
Robert S. Abbott Memorial Awards, 280
Robeson, Paul, 58, 92, 138, 139, 244
Robinson, Jackie, 243, 247, 480
Robinson, Sugar Ray, 327
Rochester, Sterling, 94
Rockefeller, Abby Aldrich, 477
Rockefeller, John D., Jr., 44, 432, 477
Rockefeller, Nelson, 406
Rockefeller, Rodman C., 445, 464
Rockefeller, Winthrop, 477
Rockefeller Foundation, 301, 408, 427
Roethke, Theodore, 201, 273, 326, 417
Rogers, J. A., 111
"Role of the Novel in Creating the
   American Experience" (Ellison), 302
Rollins, Howard E., 534
Romains, Jules, 311
"Roof, The Steeple and the People, The"
   (Ellison), 375
Roosevelt, Eleanor, 269, 278, 296, 349

Roosevelt, Franklin D., 93, 130, 141, 147, 187, 189, 400, 533
"Rosalie" (Redding), 159
Rosenberg, Harold, 474, 483
Rosenblatt, Roger, 495
Rosenthal, M. L., 471
Rosovsky, Henry, 494–5, 497
Rosskam, Edwin, 144
Rostropovich, Mstislav, 497
Roth, Henry, 406, 493
Roth, Philip, 391, 393, 464, 482
Rourke, Constance, 300, 476
Rowan, Carl, 394
Rowland, Dick, 22
Rubin, Louis D., Jr., 375, 555
Rukeyser, Muriel, 123
Rushing, Jimmy, 28, 302, 321, 354, 356, 430
Russell & Volkening, 173, 274
Russwurm Award, 280–1
Rustin, Bayard, 348, 407, 461–2, 486, 543
Rutgers University, 373, 386, 391–3, 397, 399, 407, 560–1

Sachar, Abram L., 326
Sadik, Marvin, 518
Salinger, J. D., 422
Salt Eaters, The (Cade), 404
Salzburg Seminar, 294, 300–4, 505
Sanchez, Sonia, 507, 547
Sancton, Thomas, 200, 209–10
Sands, Diana, 472
Saroyan, William, 75–6
Sarser, David, 251–2, 308, 331
Sartre, Jean-Paul, 190–1, 212, 245
Saturday Night in Harlem, 130
Saturday Review of Literature, 208, 260, 264, 278, 306, 352, 354, 377, 379, 386, 388, 398, 408
Savage, Augusta, 83, 85–6, 92
Savage Holiday (Wright), 306
Schaap, Dick, 406
Scheuer, James H., 445
Schiwetz, Tex, 475, 478–9
Schlesinger, Arthur M., Jr., 353, 394, 525, 537–8, 554
Schomburg Collection, 88, 112, 116, 445
Schuyler, George, 277
Schwartz, Delmore, 260, 269, 311
Schwerner, Michael, 406
Scott, Charlotte, 382, 517, 566

Scott, Emmett Jay, 79
Scott, Hazel, 138
Scott, Leslie, 382
Scott, Nathan A., Jr., 374, 381–2, 383, 393, 398, 443, 452, 453, 473, 517, 523, 524, 558, 560, 566
Scott, Nathan A., III, 382
Scottsboro Boys, 49, 152
Seagrave, Gordon, 372
Seaver, Edwin, 169, 173
Secker & Warburg, 431
Second American Writers' Congress, 96, 123
Second International Writers Congress, 94
Segal, Erich, 476
Segregation: The Inner Conflict in the South (Warren), 324
Seize the Day (Bellow), 332, 349
Senghor, Léopold Sédar, 427
Sengstacke, John, 177, 280
Sessions, Roger, 507
Seyersted, Per, 505
Seymour, Whitney North, 432, 489
S. Fischer Verlag, 304
Shadow and Act (Ellison), 181, 194, 210, 222, 419, 431, 434, 435, 481, 509, 520, 526, 540, 541, 546, 559, 563
   assessment of, 409–10
   black American culture and, 547–9
   contract for, 398–9
   dedication of, 62, 408
   reviews and criticisms of, 408–10
   sales of, 409–10
   title of, 407
"Shadow and the Act, The" (Ellison), 247
"Shadowing Ellison" (Wright), 529
Shahn, Ben, 325
Shakespeare in Harlem (Hughes), 158
Shannon, Edgar, 477, 517–18
Shapiro, Karl, 269, 408
Shaw, George Bernard, 29, 30, 38, 75
Shawn, William, 159, 168, 199, 398
Shils, Edward, 384
"Short Happy Life of Francis Macomber, The" (Hemingway), 165
Show Boat (musical), 138
Sillen, Samuel, 129, 146, 151, 156–7, 160
Silone, Ignazio, 281, 326
Silver, Horace, 355
Silver Chalice, The (Costain), 263

Silverman, Kenneth, 470, 481, 519
Simenon, Georges, 285, 291
Simpson, Alan, 374
Sinatra, Frank, 431
Singer, Isaac Bashevis, 516, 536
Singh, Amritjit, 476, 482–3, 495, 505
Sipuel v. Board of Regents, 243
Sjomar, Vilgot, 303–4
Slaughter, Edna Randolph, 13, 19, 47–8,
    341, 430, 464
Slaughter, Saretta, 13, 47, 55, 73, 341
Slaughter, Wyatt H., 11, 13, 19, 22, 47–8,
    341, 430
Slave, The (Baraka), 415
"Slick" (Ellison), 23, 105–7, 109, 112, 128
"Slick Gonna Learn" (Ellison), 128
Sloane, William, 391, 397
Slochower, Harry, 154–6, 159, 160, 161, 163,
    172
Smith, Bessie, 26, 471
Smith, Lillian, 182, 250, 276
Snodgrass, W. D., 399
Snowden, Frank, 321
"Society, Morality, and the Novel"
    (Ellison), 336, 352
Society for the Arts, Religion, and
    Contemporary Culture, 393–4
Society for the Libraries in New York, 510
Sojourner Truth: God's Faithful Pilgrim
    (Fauset), 112–13
Sokolow, Anna, 109
Soledad Brothers, 479
Sollors, Werner, 526–7
Solotaroff, Ted, 487
"Song of Innocence, A" (Ellison), 465
Song of Solomon (Morrison), 521, 553
"Song of Spain" (Hughes), 93
Soon, One Morning, 393
Sophie's Choice (Styron), 451
Soul on Ice (Cleaver), 410, 452
Souls of Black Folk, The (Du Bois), 120, 410
"Sound and the Mainstream" (Ellison), 409
Southern Christian Leadership Conference
    (SCLS), 348, 375, 407, 415
Sovern, Michael, 525
Soviet Union, 82, 90, 100, 111, 123, 130, 133,
    134, 140, 147, 242, 244, 280, 461, 473,
    561
    in Nazi-Soviet nonaggression pact,
    127–8, 131

Spain, 9, 93–4, 304
    RE's lecture tour in, 304–5
Spanish Civil War, 93–6, 125
Speaking for You (Benston), 557
Spender, Stephen, 217, 233, 268
Spingarn Medal, 397
Spock, Benjamin, 511
Sprague, Morteza Drexel, 61–2, 75–7, 259,
    282, 294, 298, 299–300, 408, 431
Stafford, Jean, 313
Stalin, Joseph, 123, 127, 189
Stanton, Frank, 426
State Department, U.S., 94, 312, 353, 366
Stearns, Marshall, 266, 281
Steegmuller, Beatrice Stein, 172, 212–13,
    215, 216, 232, 233, 236, 242, 250, 253,
    259, 331, 332, 405
Steegmuller, Francis, 172, 212–13, 215, 216,
    232, 233, 236–7, 240, 241, 242, 250,
    259, 331, 332, 405
Steele, Shelby, 548, 563
Stegner, Wallace, 408, 487
Stein, Edward, 213, 215, 232
Stein, Gerda, 240
Stein, Gertrude, 68, 97, 99, 109, 117, 142,
    212, 360
Stein, Gretchen, 213, 215, 232
Steinbeck, John, 130, 146–8, 160, 268, 327,
    333, 371, 511
"Stepchild Fantasy" (Ellison), 208
Stephen Hero (Joyce), 185
"Steps of the Pentagon" (Mailer), 444
Stepto, Robert B., 505–6, 508, 514, 523,
    527, 529, 531, 566
Stern, Isaac, 414, 447
Stern, Richard, 373–4, 380, 381–5
Stevens, Roger L., 414, 415–16, 427, 474,
    516
Stevens, Wallace, 207, 216
Steveson, Vivian, 40–1, 55, 73, 558–9
Stewart, Jimmie, 430, 501–2, 552
Stewart, Rex, 29
Stillness at Appamattox, A (Catton), 298
Stokes, Marie, 103
Stokes, W. O., 103, 104
Stokowski, Leopold, 45, 70
"Storm of Blizzard Proportions, A"
    (Ellison), 171
Story, 108, 124
Story of English, The, 555

Stout, Rex, 147

Stowe, Harriet Beecher, 130, 203, 467

Strachey, John, 90, 117–18

Strange, John, 102, 104

Strange, Ollie, 102, 104

Strange Fruit (Smith), 182, 250

Stranger and Alone (Redding), 249

Strauss, Helen, 398

Street, The (Petry), 281

Student Nonviolent Coordinating
    Committee (SNCC), 407, 412, 413, 437

Studies in Black Literature, 480

Styron, Rose, 417, 426, 439, 450–1

Styron, William, 313, 317, 320, 417, 418,
    423, 439, 444, 445, 447, 450–1, 476,
    566

Sula (Morrison), 521, 553

Sullivan, Harry Stack, 84–6, 89, 236

Sun Also Rises, The (Hemingway), 100,
    197, 300, 360

Supreme Court, U.S., 25, 49, 152, 276, 327,
    422
    Brown decision of, 298–9, 307
    Plessy decision of, 16, 297
    Sipuel decision of, 243

surrealism, 164
    in *Invisible Man,* 197, 218
    in novel-in-progress, 357, 456

Survey Graphic, 79, 209

Sutton, Frank, 103

Sutton, Percy, 485

Symbols in Society (Duncan), 506

"TAC Negro Show" (Ellison), 130

Taggard, Genevieve, 90, 147

Tamarack Review, 399

"Tape, Disks and Coexistence" (Sarser),
    308

Tap Roots (Street), 159

Tar Baby (Morrison), 553

Tarry, Ellen, 111–12, 277, 537

Tate, Allen, 317, 320, 375, 421, 434, 451, 504

Taylor, Cecil, 419

Taylor, Clyde, 473

Taylor, Frank, 173, 187, 211, 216, 224, 233,
    259, 272, 393, 559

Taylor, Nan, 233, 272

"Tell It Like It Is, Baby" (Ellison), 422

"Ten Young Novelists in Search of Pity"
    (Kazin), 352

"That I Had the Wings" (Ellison), 162

Themis (Harrison), 164

There Is a Tree More Ancient Than Eden
    (Forrest), 486–7, 521

These Low Grounds (Turpin), 99

Things of This World (Wilbur), 367

Things That I Do in the Dark (Jordan), 521

Third American Writers' Congress, 125–6

Third Generation, The (Himes), 281

Third Life of Grange Copeland, The
    (Walker), 521

"30 Years on the 'Raft of Hope'" (Yardley),
    534

Thomas, Norman, 330, 331

Thompson, James, 433

Thompson, Louise, 90, 93–4, 95, 108, 122

Thoreau, Henry David, 11, 192, 197, 200,
    210, 277

Thornton, Charles, 432

Three Lives (Stein), 360

Thurman, Wallace, 30

Thurmond, Strom, 243

Till, Emmet, 348

Tillich, Paul, 394

"Tillman and Tackhead" (Ellison), 105–6

Time, 119, 260, 275, 280, 307, 331, 354, 390,
    408, 467–8, 474, 525

Time Capsule, 274

Tobacco Road (Caldwell), 88, 540

Today, 270, 556, 562

Todd, Melvin, 503

To Have and Have Not (Hemingway), 102

*To Heal and to Build: The Programs of
    Lyndon B. Johnson* (Burns), 447

Toilet, The (Baraka), 415

Toll, Robert, 506

Toller, Ernst, 155

Tomorrow: The Magazine of the Future,
    165, 169, 173, 178, 181, 182–3, 184

Toomer, Jean, 123, 183

Toscanini, Arturo, 251

To Sir, With Love (Braithwaite), 433

Tourgée, Albion, 30

"Tracking the Fox" (Crouch), 504

"Tradition and the Individual Talent"
    (Eliot), 225

*Tragic Sense of Life in Men and Nations,
    The* (Unamuno), 120, 121

Train Whistle Guitar (Murray), 498

transcendentalism, 11, 258

"Transcontinental" (Wright), 97
Transformation of American Society, The,
    510
Tree, Marietta Peabody, 400, 463
Trend, 156
Tricolor: A New American Newsfront, 184
Trilling, Diana, 333, 353, 480
Trilling, Lionel, 249, 313–14, 333, 336,
    352–3, 363, 461
Trinity Church Cemetery, 566
Troupe, Quincy, 499, 504, 507, 512, 514
Truman, Harry, 243, 439
Tulsa Riot, 21–2, 24, 226
Tulsa Tribune, 22
Turner, Nat, 449–50
Turpin, Waters, 99
Tuskegee Institute, 44–80, 398
    faculty of, 53–4
    in *Invisible Man,* 224–5, 226, 228–9, 282
    no-travel crisis at, 66–7
    RE honored by, 397, 551–2
    RE's arts interest at, 68–70
    RE's departure from, 79–80, 84–5
    RE's financial struggle at, 54–8, 59–60,
        63–5, 67, 75, 78–9
    RE's girlfriends at, 55–6, 62, 64–5
    RE's journey to, 48–51
    RE's literary studies at, 75–7
    RE's literary vision and, 67–8
    RE's music studies at, 59–60
    RE's sociology studies at, 77–8
    RE's studies and school life at, 57–9, 61
    RE's visits to, 282–3, 293–5, 299–300
    RE-Williams friendship at, 60–1, 63,
        65–6
Tuskegee Messenger, 57
Tuttleton, James W., 505, 514
12 Million Black Voices (Wright), 97,
    144–5, 157, 162, 169
"Twentieth-Century Fiction and the Black
    Mask of Humanity" (Ellison), 210,
    288
Twentieth Century Novel, The (Beach), 105
Twin City Sentinel, 277
Tyson, Cicely, 511

Ullian, Lewis, 304, 305, 306
Ulysses (Joyce), 64, 351
Umbra, 433–4
Unamuno, Miguel de, 120–1

"Uncle Remus" (Harris), 310
Uncle Tom's Children: Four Novellas
    (Wright), 108–9, 118, 306
United Federation of Teachers (UFT), 462
United Nations, 353, 444
United States Information Service, 339
Universal Negro Improvement
    Association, 87
"University as Villain, The" (Bellow), 350
University of Iowa Writers' Workshop,
    369–70, 372, 559
Updike, John, 404
Up from Slavery (Washington), 52, 386, 510
"Urban Culture and the Negro," 439
USA: The Novel, 424, 425
"Uses of History in Fiction, The," 449

Vanity Fair, 29
Vauthier, Simone, 302–3
Veblen, Thorstein, 249
Venturi, Robert, 317
Verve, 119
"Very Stern Discipline, A: An Interview
    with Ralph Ellison" (*Harper's*), 433–5
Victim, The (Bellow), 260
Vidal, Gore, 370
Vietnam War, 400, 415, 417–18, 424, 428,
    434, 438, 444, 447, 459, 461, 491, 533
Viking Press, 199, 307, 336
Virginia, University of, 478, 493, 517–18
Virginia Kirkus Review, 259
Vivette, Pauline Brown, 38, 40
Vogue, 241, 450
Volkening, Henry, 169, 173, 204, 210, 256
Vonnegut, Kurt, 446, 480

Walcott, Bess Bolden, 59, 294–5
Walcott, Carolyn, 58–9, 61
Walker, Alice, 521, 529–30, 547, 548
Walker, Margaret, 126, 487
Walk Hard—Talk Loud (Zinberg), 140
Walking to Sleep (Wilbur), 462–3
Wallace, George, 394–5, 406
Wallace, Henry, 243
Waller, Fats, 197
Walters, Barbara, 536
Wapshot Scandal, The (Cheever), 416
Ward, John William, 280, 517
Ward, Ted, 124, 126, 138, 139–40, 177, 208
Warren, Earl, 298

Warren, Robert Penn, 250, 260, 274, 300, 309, 317, 320, 324, 326, 334, 335, 336, 390, 391, 394, 417, 418, 420, 421, 422, 433, 444, 449, 450, 451, 473, 488, 498, 504, 507, 529, 560
  death of, 558
  RE's first meeting with, 272
  RE's friendship with, 350, 558
  RE's Yale position and, 407–8
Warren, Rosanna, 320, 335, 558
Washington, Booker T., 52–3, 56, 61, 79, 386, 540, 552
Washington, Harold, 561
Washington, Laly Charlton, 58–9, 75, 294–5
Washington Post, 261, 414, 427, 431, 490, 537–8
Washington Post Book World, 534
Washington Star, 270, 463
Waste Land, The (Eliot), 62, 76–7, 85, 116, 164, 300
Watergate scandal, 497
Waters, Ethel, 29
Watkins, Maston, 10
Watts, Jerry, 453
Watts riots of 1965, 418–19
Way Down South (film), 123
"Way It Is, The" (Ellison), 156–7, 161
Weaver, Edith, 288, 289, 290
Weaver, Richard, 288, 290
Weaver, Robert C., 394
Webb, Constance, 100, 276
Webster, Harvey Curtiss, 260
Weeks, Edward, 273, 473
Wein, George, 355
Weiskopf, Franz Carl, 154
Weiss, Renée, 362, 370, 374–5
Weiss, Ted, 362, 364, 370, 374–5, 538
Weixlmann, Joe, 527
Welburn, Ron, 506
Well of Loneliness (Hall), 64
Welty, Eudora, 209–10, 271, 451
Wertham, Frederic, 184, 207–8, 220–1, 276
Werthman, Eric, 360, 361, 362
Wescott, Glenway, 553
West, Anthony, 286
West, Cornel, 494, 549
West, Dorothy, 98
West, Hollie, 475, 490–1
Western Review, 314

Weston, Jessie, 116, 164
West Point, 459–60
WEVD, 168, 263
"What America Would Be Like Without Blacks" (Ellison), 467–8
"What Happened to Ralph Ellison" (Podhoretz), 409
"What's Wrong with the American Novel?," 313
Whistle (Jones), 515
Whitby, A. Baxter, 29
Whitby, Lloyd, 29
Whitby, Malcolm, 29, 44, 45, 47, 73
White, Clarence Cameron, 41
White, Walter, 312
"White Negro, The" (Mailer), 368
Whitman, Walt, 11, 197, 200, 210, 354, 552
Who Speaks for the Negro? (Warren), 407, 420, 473
Wideman, John Edgar, 521, 529–30, 546–7, 563
Wien, George, 448
Wiesel, Elie, 461
Wilbur, Charlotte, 229, 367, 390, 432, 436, 442, 449, 454, 503, 504–5, 559–60
Wilbur, Richard, 229, 317, 367, 390, 413, 416, 432, 436, 442, 449, 454, 462–3, 469, 498–9, 503, 504–5, 559–60
Wilde, Oscar, 62
Wilder, Douglas, 535
Wilder, Thornton, 371
Wilkerson, Doxey, 243
Wilkins, Roy, 437, 480, 485, 510, 511, 515
William Morris Agency, 169, 274, 398–9, 450, 563
Williams, Franklin, 482
Williams, John A., 453, 454–5, 472
Williams, Martin, 409, 419–20
Williams, Seelie, 64
Williams, Walter Bowie, 52, 60–1, 63, 65–9, 71, 74–7, 85, 259
William Styron's Nat Turner: Ten Black Writers Respond, 450
Wilson, Charles, 168
Wilson, David (RE's pen name), 156
Wilson, Eddie Hugh, 8
Wilson, Edmund, 266, 269, 389, 398
Wilson, Teddy, 128
Winchell, Walter, 361
Winder, R. Bayly, 469

Wingate, Henry, 440
Winters, Yvor, 238
Wirth, Nicholas, 116
WNYC, 263, 277, 278
Wolff, Tobias, 539
Women's Conference of the Society for
    Ethical Culture, 240
Women's Trade Union League, 172
Woods, Katherine, 165
Woodward, C. Vann, 407, 426, 447, 449,
    450, 451, 464
Works Progress Administration (WPA), 83,
    93, 111, 177, 537
"World and the Jug, The" (Ellison), 401–3,
    547
World Revolution (James), 276
Wright, Ellen Poplowitz, 126, 136, 161, 207,
    209, 211–12, 256, 266–7, 305, 308, 328,
    378
Wright, Jay, 392
Wright, John, 527, 529
Wright, Julia, 161, 207, 211–12
Wright, Rachel, 229
Wright, Richard, 96, 102, 104, 108, 110,
    111–12, 113, 114, 117, 118–20, 121, 122,
    123, 124, 126, 128, 129, 133, 135, 138,
    141, 142, 144–7, 151, 155, 159, 164, 169,
    174, 178, 179, 181, 183, 184, 187, 188,
    190, 191, 194, 195, 196, 218, 225, 229,
    246, 259, 260, 276, 281, 300, 312, 314,
    328, 330, 331, 455, 465, 467, 468, 472,
    483, 510, 511, 523, 526, 553
    alienation theme and, 201–2
    commercial success of, 128, 130–1
    death of, 378

Invisible Man as seen by, 263
literary success of, 108–9, 129
marriages of, 135–6
in move to France, 207, 211–12
in RE-Howe literary controversy, 401–2
RE influenced by, 97–100, 105, 106–7,
    110
RE's correspondence with, 208, 217,
    219, 221, 222, 234, 262, 263–4, 269, 275
RE's friendship with, 97–8, 100,
    179–80, 480–1
RE's Paris visit to, 305–6
Wright, Sarah, 453
Writer's Experience, The, 408
Writers' Literary Agency, 169

Yaffe, David, 550
Yale University, 407–8, 423, 459, 558
Yardley, Jonathan, 534, 547
Yellow Black Radio Broke-Down (Reed), 521
Yerby, Frank, 218
Yergan, Max, 133, 243
Young, Andrew, 533
Young, C. J., 37
Young, Lester, 28
Young, Whitney, Jr., 455
Youngblood (Killens), 297
Younge, Sammy, Jr., 425
Yourcenar, Marguerite, 319
"Youth" (Hughes), 43
Yugen, 380

Zinberg, Len, 129–30, 140
Zuckerman, Morton, 541
Zweig, Stefan, 155

A NOTE ON THE TYPE

This book was set in Fairfield, a typeface designed by the distinguished American artist and engraver Rudolph Ruzicka (1883–1978). In its structure Fairfield displays the sober and sane qualities of the master craftsman whose talents were dedicated to clarity. Ruzicka was born in Bohemia and came to America in 1894. He designed and illustrated many books, and was the creator of a considerable list of individual prints in a variety of techniques.

Composed by Creative Graphics, Allentown, Pennsylvania
Printed and bound by Berryville Graphics, Berryville, Virginia
Designed by Wesley Gott